DATE DUE			

the
human

arena

AN INTRODUCTION TO
THE SOCIAL SCIENCES

edited by
GILBERT ABCARIAN
MONTE PALMER
FLORIDA STATE UNIVERSITY

HOLT, RINEHART AND WINSTON, INC.
new york   chicago   san francisco
atlanta   dallas   montreal   toronto

To Our Mothers

ANNIE ABCARIAN
ESTHER I. PALMER

Photograph Credits
  Parts I and II: Charles Gatewood
  Part III: © Burk UZZLE, Magnum
  Part IV: Diana Davies
  Part V: Dennis Stock © 1970 Magnum Photos

The Human Arena: An Introduction to the Social Sciences
by Gilbert Abcarian and Monte Palmer
Copyright © 1971 by Holt, Rinehart and Winston, Inc.
All rights reserved
Library of Congress Catalog Card Number: 76–156395
SBN: 03–081314–X
Printed in the United States of America
1 2 3 4   0 9 0   9 8 7 6 5 4 3 2 1

preface

Academic life for both student and teacher is often a grim and losing race
between the good intentions of textbook authors and the complex realities
of social life. A harsh judgment? Of course. But it is not one to be rejected
out of hand at a time when cries for "relevance" and experimentation in
social science are heard from many quarters.

We do not claim to have won that race with this book. But we do
hope that we may have lowered the odds against failure through our selection and organization of readings, together with the choice of problems on
which these readings focus. We hope this assumption is borne out in the
experiences of students and teachers with *The Human Arena*. As important, we hope that the readings will encourage the sort of classroom interchange that promotes student-teacher understanding and tolerance, even as
they generate differences of perspective and evaluation.

Numerous teachers and students around the country have called our
attention to a series of pitfalls found in currently available social science
texts. Among these many criticisms the following were most recurrent.

Some texts are characterized by endless pages of boring generalizations
or, at the other extreme, technical details whose significance is lost on students. A few texts chop social life into neat but artificial categories of Culture, Economics, Politics, and so on, as though human affairs and personal
experience can be neatly compartmentalized. Still others are too complex,
or lacking in contemporary materials that engage the interest of and are
useful to the student. Above all, many texts lack a conceptual framework or
general orientation that helps integrate the readings and give them a sense
of intellectual relevance for and realistic focus on current social life. Every
effort has been made to avoid these pitfalls in *The Human Arena*.

Our purpose is to present material that will perform several basic functions: stir student interest in the various social sciences, provide analytical
tools for the understanding of social processes and institutions, and precipi-
tate the kind of thought and discussion that leads the student to critical
examination of his most basic social attitudes and values.

The Human Arena has several feaures that will commend themselves to
both instructor and student. The readings are highly interdisciplinary, reflecting the major concerns of contemporary social and behavioral science. The
reader should be pleased by the contemporary flavor and broad range of
the material chosen. In this connection the editors have indicated to the

student the significance of each selection and the manner in which each relates to earlier and later ones. Finally, we have sought to present material that will undermine apathy and stimulate intellectual involvement of the student.

Part One, "Science and Society," provides the student with a general introduction to the context and functions of the social sciences. As clearly as possible, it explores such questions as these: What is social science and how do social scientists go about their work? How scientific is social science? What contribution, if any, do social scientists make to society?

Part Two, "Self and Society," stresses the individual, his development, and his role in society. Here, we examine several vital questions. What does he expect from society? How does his own behavior change as he adjusts to those around him?

Part Three, "Equilibrium and Social Control," examines the various means employed by societies to shape the development of the individual and to control his behavior. Such inquiry helps us understand how the individual is inducted into his culture, how he is taught to conform, and how his attitudes and behavior are affected by his social milieu. In brief, this part asks: What makes society hang together?

Part Four, "Disequilibrium and Social Conflict," comes to grips with the fact that the social control mechanisms available to all societies may be ineffective to their regulatory task. As candidly as possible the selections in this part ponder questions and dilemmas of social disorganization: What are the roots of human conflict? What are the major sources of change and stress in American society? Is it true that the social control mechanisms of American society are collapsing? If so, what happens to individuals subjected to an environment of constant change and stress?

Finally, Part Five, "Conflict Resolution and Social Reintegration," analyzes the dilemmas and prospects for social progress in the perspective of the reformer and the critic. The reformer challenges us with the perennial question: "What must be done?" The critic responds: "Act honestly and rationally before the habit of muddling through and botching up human problems leads to disaster."

Each part, as well as each reading, is introduced by an essay or introduction that serves as a bridge from earlier to later material.

For valuable suggestions and counsel at various stages of manuscript development, we are indebted to Harrison V. Chase of Florida State University, Keith P. Fabian, Donald C. Glenn, G. W. Markert, Joseph Olson, Thelma Peters, Donald D. Schaffer, and Lawerence M. Winebrenner, of Miami-Dade Junior College, and James F. Coovelis of Chabot College. We are also indebted to Nancy Sullivan for valuable assistance in the preparation of the index.

G. A.
M. P.

contents

x   Contents

INTRODUCTION

MAN AND SOCIETY

> . . . in the nature of man, we find three principall causes of quarrell. First, competition; secondly, diffidence; thirdly, glory . . . during the time men live without a common power to keep them all in awe, they are in that condition which is called Warre; and such a warre, as is of every man, against every man . . . and the life of man, solitary, poore, nasty, brutish, and short.

So wrote Thomas Hobbes during the middle of the sixteenth century. Writing in the middle of the next century, Jean Jacques Rousseau found man's natural state to be quite different:

> . . . man has hardly any evils other than those he has given himself. . . . it is not without difficulty that we have succeeded in making ourselves so unhappy.

> Savage man, when he has eaten, is at peace with all nature, and the friend of all his fellow-men. It is sometimes a question of disputing his meal, he never comes to blows without first having compared the difficulty of winning with that of finding his subsistence elsewhere; and as pride is not involved in the fight, it is ended by a few blows; the victor eats, the vanquished goes off to seek his fortune, all is pacified.

Which view of man is correct? Are men born to avarice and greed, or is man naturally cooperative and just? Is conflict man's natural state or an unnatural perversion? If Rousseau is correct, the prospects for mankind are unlimited. Human conflict for Rousseau is but a social malady, the cure for which lies within the grasp of human intelligence. But if Hobbes is correct, the outlook for mankind is bleak indeed. If conflict is man's "natural" state, peace must be a perversion and a fantasy. If Hobbes has described reality with accuracy, the natural urge to avarice can be stemmed by nothing less than dictatorship.

1

The exercise of human intelligence by the masses poses the constant threat of expanded conflict and must, for the security of society, give way to subservience or conformity.

Hobbes and Rousseau have come to symbolize the conflict and the cooperative models of society, respectively. For Hobbesians, man is basically evil and must be rigidly controlled. For Rousseauans, man is basically good and needs only to be liberated from artificial restraints. For the contemporary social scientist, man is neither good nor bad. Rather, the modern social scientist sees man as possessing various needs and drives which, depending upon circumstances, can lead either to conflict or to cooperation. The challenge of the social scientist is not to prove the inherent virtue or wickedness of man, but, through better understanding of human behavior, to improve his potential for cooperation and a better way of life.

HUMAN NEEDS AND HUMAN COOPERATION

Every society, whether a primitive tribe or modern nation, faces certain recurrent problems upon whose satisfactory resolution the existence and improvement of social life depend. Basically, these problems revolve around the satisfaction of fundamental human needs.

Man's most basic needs, of course, are sustenance, security, and sex. They are basic because they are essential to the biologic survival of man. In addition to these purely biologic drives, however, psychologists have noted a number of social needs: the need for affection, the desire for recognition, the search for self-actualization, the wish to possess, and, perhaps, the passion for domination and power. Man, in short, appears to possess a need to go beyond mere survival as a biological entity. As one noted psychologist has discussed the need for self-actualization:

> As I follow the experience of many clients in the therapeutic relationship which we endeavor to create for them, it seems to me that each one has the same problem. Below the level of the problem situation about which the individual is complaining—behind the trouble with studies, or wife, or employer, or with his own uncontrollable or bizarre behavior, or with his frightening feelings lies one central search. It seems to me that at bottom each person is asking: "Who am I, really? How can I get in touch with this real self, underlying all my surface behavior? How can I become myself?"
>
> . . . it appears that the goal the individual most wishes to achieve, the end which he knowingly or unknowingly pursues, is to become himself.[1]

Human needs require cooperation for their fulfillment. The drives for power, recognition, affection, self-actualization, and procreation cannot, by their very nature, be achieved without the cooperation of other individuals. Further, the need for security and sustenance, to be met at a level beyond

[1] Carl R. Rodgers, *Becoming a Person*. Austin, Texas: The Hogg Foundation for Mental Hygiene, the University of Texas Press, 1968, pp. 9–10.

a worldwide nuclear conflagration involving the sorts of speculations found in the following quotation?

> Here I have tried to make the point that if we have a posture which might result in 40 million dead in a general war, and as a result of poor planning, apathy, or other causes, our posture deteriorates and a war occurs with 80 million dead, we have suffered an additional disaster, an *unnecessary* additional disaster that is almost as bad as the original disaster. If on the contrary, by spending a few billion dollars, or by being more competent or lucky, we can cut the number of dead from 40 to 20 million, we have done something vastly worth doing! The survivors will not dance in the streets or congratulate each other if there have been 20 million men, women, and children killed; yet it would have been a worthwhile achievement to limit casualties to this number.

> Perhaps the most important item is not the numbers of dead or the number of years it takes for economic recuperation; rather, it is the question "Will the survivors envy the dead?" It is in some sense true that one may never recuperate from a thermonuclear war. The world may be permanently (i.e., for perhaps 10,000 years) more hostile to human life as a result of such a war. Therefore, if the question, "Can we restore the prewar conditions of life?" is asked, the answer must be "NO!" But there are other relevant questions to be asked. For example, "How much more hostile will the environment be? Will it be so hostile that we or our descendants would prefer being dead than alive? Perhaps even more pertinent is the question, "How happy or normal a life can the survivors and their descendants hope to have?" *Despite a widespread belief to the contrary, objective studies indicate that even though the amount of human tragedy would be greatly increased in the postwar world, the increase would not preclude normal and happy lives for the majority of survivors and their descendants.*[2]

CONSENSUS AND DISSENSUS

Everything that maximizes social cooperation and stability, unfortunately, is not necessarily consistent with the freedom of the individual. Indeed, the price of cooperation has frequently been so high as to render the individual a helpless cog in a vast, impersonal machine. Does the urgency of cooperation and control in the modern world permit the luxury of "becoming a person?" Has the need for security overwhelmed the need for self-actualization, if indeed the need to become a person truly does exist? Must human values, to use the language of the protestor and the humanist, be sacrificed for the sake of survival? Is there room any longer for dissent and the dissenter?

Dissensus implies disagreement and conflict within a society. It suggests that social values and institutions are not passively accepted by every segment

[2] Herman Kahn, *On Thermonuclear War*. Princeton, N.J.: Princeton University Press, 1960, pp. 20–21.

of society. From a purely scientific standpoint, the term dissensus does not necessarily convey a negative meaning; rather, it signifies the objective fact that consensus is lacking. Of course, one may take an evaluative position and conclude that dissensus is either bad or good. Whether dissensus contributes to or detracts from such values as self-actualization is a question of the type of behavior involved and a moral evaluation of its social consequences by individuals who may have quite different perspectives.

The readings that follow refer to dissensus in two different but inter-related ways. First, they explore examples of normative dissensus, that is, differences in ideas about proper types of behavior. Second, they discuss examples of behavioral dissensus, that is, conflicts over different patterns of actual behavior. It is important to bear in mind that these two forms of dissensus may function, separately or simultaneously, on three distinct levels: that of the individual, that of small groups or associations, and, finally, at the level of the total national or international society.

Whichever level occupies one's attention, it is well to bear in mind that dissensus is characteristic both of social stability and social conflict. Actually, change on any of these levels is inconceivable without dissensus for the simple reason that change and conflict are inseparable. At any given point in the life of the individual, group, or larger society, it is often a matter of intense disagreement whether a greater degree of consensus or dissensus is needed. Rigid consensus can lead to stagnation, while unrestrained dissensus may lead to social chaos. Furthermore, too much of one may lead to the intensification of the other, as when a dictatorship generates violent reactions, or when wholesale protest against prevailing standards and institutions is met by a clamor for "law and order." The desire to punish "deviants" or "rebels" through some social control mechanism serves as an example of the latter.

Let us suppose that Mr. X displays inclinations toward deviance in the form of radical political activity. What sorts of social control responses might be anticipated? Assuming that his radical politics are regarded, rightly or wrongly, as a source of strain or danger to the community or the larger society, a number of reactions might be anticipated.

Society's first line of defense against radicalism might be preventive, that is, to forestall the strain itself by certain steps that prevent his inclina-tions toward political radicalism from becoming overt. Failing in this, another response is that of draining or canalizing his radicalism into forms and channels that are not regarded as socially disruptive. If they appear to be disruptive, however, a further and more serious reaction would be that of making such activity either difficult to express or very costly in which to engage. Up to this point, the emergence of strain has not been prevented, but in fact has taken the form of overt behavior; society has responded largely in terms of deterring or "managing" behavior in order to protect itself. All this failing, two final techniques of social control might be employed. The deviant could be removed from the social system through such techniques as confinement and execution, or attempts could be made to resocialize him through such measures as psychotherapy.

Political radicalism is only one of a vast array of behavior patterns that are regarded as a challenge to the prevailing social control system. The question of whether deviant behavior is or is not subversive and whether the individual at all times and in all circumstances should subordinate himself to the demands of social control is a matter over which men often disagree.

The extent to which individual behavior is constrained varies widely from society to society. In the United States, where we find a complex set of interacting subcultures and value systems, there are a relatively small number of dominant national values. Hence cultural pluralism rather than homogeneity is characteristic and provides wide latitude for a variety of individual behavior patterns. This environment of pluralism itself lends to conflict over values but also to a good deal of toleration of differences. Why and when society intervenes in the behavior of individuals is a fascinating topic but not one explained by simple answers.

THE MANAGEMENT OF CONFLICT

The crucial problem facing societies is not to eliminate conflict, an impossible task in any case, but to keep it within manageable and productive limits. In terms of economic or technological development, the ideal blend of cooperation and conflict is one that promotes sufficient conflict to generate a healthy spirit of competition but not so much as to threaten social foundations.

Conflict management is a continuous process. Yesterday's solutions seldom fit today's problems. Patterns of cooperation and adjustment must be revised constantly to cope with the demands of a changing environment. Ability to adapt to past environmental changes offers no guarantee of future success. The sources of current domestic and foreign conflict with which the United States must deal are probably more complex than those of any previous point in its history. It is doubtful whether Americans can cope with problems of nuclear war, race riots, and poverty without radical restructuring of established modes of cooperation and conflict management.

The paradox posed by the simultaneous growth of American prosperity and conflict results from the fact that social technology has not kept pace with physical technology. The tensions and conflicts resulting from advanced physical technology—nuclear weapons, mass urbanization, automation, economic imbalance—are severely straining and perhaps overwhelming patterns of cooperation and conflict management currently employed in the United States and elsewhere. If men are not to become the victims of their own development, the governments of the world will be well advised to pursue social technology with a vigor equal to their pursuit of physical technology.

THE SOCIAL SCIENCES

Social technology is the realm of the social sciences, namely, psychology, sociology, anthropology, economics, political science, and history.

Psychologists study the mind of the individual. They ask: How do people think? How do they learn? What are the basic human needs? What factors influence the way the individual sees his world? What happens when certain needs are frustrated? To what extent is the thought process shaped by the physical environment? The social environment? How much pressure can individuals take before they crack? How can anxiety levels be manipulated? How are individuals best manipulated? How can frustration be reduced? Is cooperation learned or instinctual? Can the cooperative or social tendencies be strengthened? The psychologist, and particularly the social psychologist, views society from the perspective of the individual. He seeks to understand what the individual brings to society, what impact society has on the individual, how individuals cope with the demands of society, and what defense mechanisms are available to him.

Sociologists think less in terms of individuals and more in terms of collective units. They explore the circumstances under which societies remain stable and under which they change or collapse. Sociologists ask: What impact does industrialization and urbanization have upon family solidarity? Which form of family structure is best suited to an industrialized society? What are the mechanisms of social control and how can they be improved? Why have they broken down in the urban ghettos? How can social change be stimulated, controlled, or stopped?

While he poses questions similar to those of the sociologist, the anthropologist is more concerned with primitive societies than with the complexities of modern life. He treats primitive societies as a laboratory in which we can study human behavior in a relatively simple and uncomplicated form. Does understanding human behavior in the South Sea islands help one understand human behavior in New York City? Why? Why not? How similar are primitive religions to modern religions? Do they serve the same function? Why have primitive societies remained primitive? Under what conditions do they change? These are typical anthropological questions.

Rather than studying whole societies, the economist focuses on the ways in which societies perform certain specialized functions. He inquires how societies provide for material wants and why some societies produce more than others. He may wish to know how economic development can be fostered in the less developed states of Asia, Africa, and Latin America, or how capitalist and socialist economics differ.

Political scientists are also interested in a specialized aspect of society. In the words of one scholar, political scientists basically are concerned with "who gets what, when, and how." Who rules whom? Why are some populations docile while others rebel? How do people influence government and, conversely, how do governments manipulate the people? Are the political control mechanisms in democracies radically different from control methods in the Soviet Union? Does communism work the same in China as it does in Russia? Why do people vote? Who votes the most? Do all votes count the same? Which form of government provides the greatest potential for resolving conflict?

Historians record the past. Where the past is obscure, they attempt to provide plausible explanations of what might have been. The task of the historian is both easier and more difficult than that of his fellow social scientist. On the one hand, he is spared the turmoil of the present. He possesses a sense of perspective that comes from studying events at their conclusion rather than at their inception. On the other hand, he labors under severe handicaps. Accurate information about the past is difficult to come by. Memories become embellished with time. Crucial documents are frequently missing. When interpretations of the past are made, he must learn how to test their validity. How do we really know what happened one hundred or one thousand years ago? Can history be recreated? If the past can be portrayed accurately, what does that tell us about the future? Does history repeat itself or is history a long series of unique events?

Each of the social science disciplines studies a different facet of man's social behavior for reasons of scientific precision and specialization. It would be a mistake to assume that any one aspect of man's social behavior can be studied in total isolation from the others. Would the American economy be the same if American society were organized along tribal lines? Are voting habits influenced by economic factors? Does an individual's outlook on life influence his political and economic behavior? If social technology is to keep pace with physical technology all facets of human behavior and their interrelationships must be better understood. The appropriate tool for such an understanding is social science.

SCIENCE AND SOCIETY

In developing their views of human nature Hobbes and Rousseau utilized a priori reasoning. Without prior research and with little intention of verifying their propositions, each man categorically declared rather than *validated* the position he held to be true.

If social scientists are to make meaningful contributions to the "human" problems of the twentieth century, they cannot proceed in the manner of Hobbes or Rousseau. Instead of a priori assertions, social scientists must rigorously attempt to apply the scientific method to all theories. Rather than engaging in declarative statements of truth, social scientists must state their ideas and intuitions in the form of testable propositions. If testing and empirical observation prove the propositions to be in error, they must be rejected or modified. Only in this manner can a reliable body of information and theory be created sufficient enough to enable scientists to do their share in helping to understand and solve contemporary social problems.

The sections which follow are divided into five basic parts. The first discusses the present state and characteristics of scientific knowledge in the social sciences. Part Two explores human nature and its impact on society. Part Three examines the manner in which society molds the individual to conform and cooperate. Part Four identifies some sources of conflict that exist within society. Part Five, finally, provides a critique of the inadequate efforts currently being made to control the sources of conflict and the resultant social disorganization and escalated conflict in the present period.

part

one

SCIENCE
AND SOCIETY

Social science is the study of human behavior: it explores the way men develop psychologically, how they think, the way they organize their society, the manner in which they provide for their sustenance, and how they resolve their conflicts.

In the study of human behavior the social scientist has an obligation to be scientific. He must leave no stone unturned in his pursuit of knowledge. He must rigorously test his propositions and discard or modify his interpretations or assertions in the light of contrary evidence.

Application of the scientific method to the social sciences has not been easy. Human behavior is elusive and often defies accurate measures. The tools of the social scientist are primitive and poorly suited to their task. Standards of accuracy and the admissibility of knowledge vary markedly both within and among the social science disciplines. What is fact to one researcher may be opinion to another. Furthermore, the social scientist deals constantly with issues of great emotion and controversies such as race, sex, war, crime, poverty, insanity, religion, economic depression, and social conflict, to mention but a few. It is debatable whether a researcher can be truly scientific about questions involving his own personal emotions and values.

Despite substantial difficulties, each of the social sciences has built impressive structures of scientific theory. In the opening selection, "An Outline of Intellectual Rubbish," Bertrand Russell, mathematician, philosopher, and one of the great wits of the twentieth century, undertakes a searching look at the scientific endeavors and pretensions of the social scientist. In the two articles that follow, sociologist Daniel Lerner traces the growth of the social sciences in the United States, while philosopher of science Alfred North Whitehead discusses the delicate boundary between religion and science. Both writers ask disturbing questions. Is the only truth admissible as scientific that which can be measured empirically, or are there other forms of truths and knowledge beyond the immediate grasp of man which he must grudgingly accept on faith?

The three articles comprising Part One examine the assumptions and purposes underlying the social sciences and the foundations upon which the various structures of scientific social theory have been built. The intellectual precautions they offer should be kept in mind throughout the reading of this book.

1. AN OUTLINE OF INTELLECTUAL RUBBISH

bertrand russell

To what extent is man governed by false or misleading opinions perpetrated by governments, philosophers, demagogues, and other promoters of "rational" truth? Since all men are prone to foolish opinions,
how can one protect himself from at least some errors, misconceptions,
and follies, and engage in relatively sound thinking?

   In order to avoid foolish but common opinions, the individual is
well-advised to observe the facts of a case for himself, avoid emotional
involvement in beliefs, observe foreign ideas and customs that widen
one's horizons, be wary of flattery, recognize how fear contaminates
logical thinking, and generally perceive that every age possesses a
great deal of both wisdom and foolishness.

Man is a rational animal—so at least I have been told. Throughout a long
life, I have looked diligently for evidence in favor of this statement, but so
far I have not had the good fortune to come across it, though I have searched
in many countries spread over three continents. On the contrary, I have seen
the world plunging continually further into madness. I have seen great nations, formerly leaders of civilization, led astray by preachers of bombastic
nonsense. I have seen cruelty, persecution, and superstition increasing by
leaps and bounds, until we have almost reached the point where praise of
rationality is held to mark a man as an old fogey regrettably surviving from a
bygone age. All this is depressing, but gloom is a useless emotion. In order to
escape from it, I have been driven to study the past with more attention than

I had formerly given to it, and have found, as Erasmus found, that folly is perennial and yet the human race has survived. The follies of our own times are easier to bear when they are seen against the background of past follies. In what follows I shall mix the sillinesses of our day with those of former centuries. Perhaps the result may help in seeing our own times in perspective, and as not much worse than other ages that our ancestors lived through without ultimate disaster. . . .

Politics is largely governed by sententious platitudes which are devoid of truth.

One of the most widespread popular maxims is, "Human nature cannot be changed." No one can say whether this is true or not without first defining "human nature." But as used it is certainly false. When Mr. A utters the maxim, with an air of portentous and conclusive wisdom, what he means is that all men everywhere will always continue to behave as they do in his own home town. A little anthropology will dispel this belief. Among the Tibetans, one wife has many husbands, because men are too poor to support a whole wife; yet family life, according to travelers, is no more unhappy than elsewhere. The practice of lending one's wife to a guest is very common among uncivilized tribes. The Australian aborigines, at puberty, undergo a very painful operation which, throughout the rest of their lives, greatly diminishes sexual potency. Infanticide, which might seem contrary to human nature, was almost universal before the rise of Christianity, and is recommended by Plato to prevent over-population. Private property is not recognized among some savage tribes. Even among highly civilized people, economic considerations will override what is called "human nature." In Moscow, where there is an acute housing shortage, when an unmarried woman is pregnant, it often happens that a number of men contend for the legal right to be considered the father of the prospective child, because whoever is judged to be the father acquires the right to share the woman's room, and half a room is better than no roof.

In fact, adult "human nature" is extremely variable, according to the circumstances of education. Food and sex are very general requirements, but the hermits of the Thebaid eschewed sex altogether and reduced food to the lowest point compatible with survival. By diet and training, people can be made ferocious or meek, masterful or slavish, as may suit the educator. There is no nonsense so arrant that it cannot be made the creed of the vast majority by adequate governmental action. Plato intended his Republic to be founded on a myth which he admitted to be absurd, but he was rightly confident that the populace could be induced to believe it. Hobbes, who thought it important that people should reverence the government however unworthy it might be, meets the argument that it might be difficult to obtain general assent to anything so irrational by pointing out that people have been brought to believe in the Christian religion, and, in particular, in the dogma of transubstantiation. If he had been alive in 1940, he would have found ample confirmation of his contention in the devotion of German youth to the Nazis.

The power of governments over men's beliefs has been very great ever since the rise of large states. The great majority of Romans became Christian after the Roman Emperors had been converted. In the parts of the Roman Empire that were conquered by the Arabs, most people abandoned Christianity for Islam. The division of Western Europe into Protestant and Catholic regions was determined by the attitude of governments in the sixteenth century. But the power of governments over belief in the present day is vastly greater than at any earlier time. A belief, however untrue, is important when it dominates the actions of large masses of men. In this sense, the beliefs inculcated before the last war by the Japanese, Russian, and German governments were important. Since they were completely divergent, they could not all be true, though they could well all be false. Unfortunately, they were such as to inspire men with an ardent desire to kill one another, even to the point of almost completely inhibiting the impulse of self-preservation. No one can deny, in face of the evidence, that it is easy, given military power, to produce a population of fanatical lunatics. It would be equally easy to produce a population of sane and reasonable people, but many governments do not wish to do so, since such people would fail to admire the politicians who are at the head of these governments.

There is one peculiarly pernicious application of the doctrine that human nature cannot be changed. This is the dogmatic assertion that there will always be wars, because we are so constituted that we feel a need of them. What is true is that a man who has had the kind of diet and education that most men have will wish to fight when provoked. But he will not actually fight unless he has a chance of victory. It is very annoying to be stopped by a policeman, but we do not fight him because we know that he has the overwhelming forces of the state at his back. People who have no occasion for war do not make any impression of being psychologically thwarted. Sweden has had no war since 1814, but the Swedes are one of the happiest and most contented nations in the world. The only cloud upon their national happiness is fear of being involved in the next war. If political organization were such as to make war obviously unprofitable, there is nothing in human nature that would compel its occurrence, or make average people unhappy because of its not occurring. Exactly the same arguments that are now used about the impossibility of preventing war were formerly used in defense of dueling, yet few of us feel thwarted because we are not allowed to fight duels.

I am persuaded that there is absolutely no limit to the absurdities that can, by government action, come to be generally believed. Give me an adequate army, with power to provide it with more pay and better food than falls to the lot of the average man, and I will undertake, within 30 years, to make the majority of the population believe that two and two are three, that water freezes when it gets hot and boils when it gets cold, or any other nonsense that might seem to serve the interest of the state. Of course, even when these beliefs had been generated, people would not put the kettle in the refrigerator when they wanted it to boil. That cold makes water boil would be a Sunday truth, sacred and mystical, to be professed in awed tones, but not to be acted on in daily life. What would happen would be that any verbal denial of the mystic doctrine would be made illegal, and obstinate heretics would be "frozen" at the stake. No person who did not enthusiastically accept the official doctrine would be allowed to teach or to have any position of power. Only the very highest officials, in their cups, would whisper to each other what rubbish it all is; then they would laugh and drink again. This is hardly a caricature of what happens under some modern governments.

The discovery that man can be scientifically manipulated, and that governments can turn large masses this way or that as they choose, is one of the causes of our misfortunes. There is as much difference between a collection of mentally free citizens and a community molded by modern methods of propaganda as there is between a heap of raw materials and a battleship. Education, which was at first made universal in order that all might be able to read and write, has been found capable of serving quite other purposes. By instilling nonsense it unifies populations and generates collective enthusiasm. If all governments taught the same nonsense, the harm would not be so great. Unfortunately each has its own brand, and the diversity serves to produce hostility between the devotees of different creeds. If there is ever to be peace in the world, governments will have to agree either to inculcate no dogmas, or all to inculcate the same. The former, I fear, is a Utopian ideal, but perhaps they could agree to teach collectively that all public men, everywhere, are completely virtuous and perfectly wise. Perhaps, after the next war, the surviving politicians may find it prudent to combine on some such program.

But if conformity has its dangers, so has nonconformity.

Some "advanced thinkers" are of opinion that anyone who differs from the conventional opinion must be in the right. This is a delusion; if it were not, truth would be easier to come by than it is. There are infinite possibilities of error, and more cranks take up unfashionable errors than unfashionable truths. I met once an electrical engineer whose first words to men were: "How do you do. There are two methods of faith-healing: the one practiced by Christ and the one practiced by most Christian Scientists. I practice the method practiced by Christ." Shortly afterwards, he was sent to prison for making out fraudulent balance sheets. The law does not look kindly on the intrusion of faith into this region. I knew also an eminent lunacy doctor who took to philosophy, and taught a new logic which, as he frankly confessed, he had learned from his lunatics. When he died he left a will founding a professorship for the teaching of his new scientific methods, but unfortunately he left no assets. Arithmetic proved recalcitrant to lunatic logic. On one occasion a man came to ask me to recommend some of my books, as he was interested in philosophy. I did so, but he returned next day saying that he had been reading one of them, and had found only one statement he could understand, and that one seemed to him false. I asked him what it was, and he said it was the statement that Julius Caesar is dead. When I asked him why he did not agree, he drew himself up and said: "Because I am Julius Caesar." These examples may suffice to show that you cannot make sure of being right by being eccentric.

Science, which has always had to fight its way against popular beliefs, now has one of its most difficult battles in the sphere of psychology.

People who think they know all about human nature are always hopelessly at sea when they have to do with any abnormality. Some boys never learn to be what, in animals, is called "house-trained." The sort of person who won't stand any nonsense deals with such cases by punishment; the boy is beaten, and when he repeats the offense he is beaten worse. All medical men who have studied the matter know that punishment only aggravates the trouble. Sometimes the cause is physical, but usually it is psychological, and only curable by removing some deep-seated and probably unconscious grievance. But most people enjoy punishing anyone who irritates them, and so the medical view is rejected as fancy nonsense. The same sort of thing applies to men who are exhibitionists; they are sent to prison over and over again, but as soon as they come out they repeat the offense. A medical man who specialized in such ailments assured me that the exhibitionist can be cured by the simple device of having trousers that button up the back instead of the front. But this method is not tried because it does not satisfy people's vindictive impulses.

Broadly speaking, punishment is likely to prevent crimes that are sane in origin, but not those that spring from some psychological abnormality. This is now partially recognized; we distinguish between plain theft, which springs from what may be called rational self-interest, and kleptomania, which is a mark of something queer. And homicidal maniacs are not treated like ordinary murderers. But sexual aberrations rouse so much disgust that it is still impossible to have them treated medically rather than punitively. Indignation, though on the whole a useful social force, becomes harmful when it is directed against the victims of maladies that only medical skill can cure.

The same sort of thing happens as regards whole nations. During the 1914 – 18 war, very naturally, people's vindictive feelings were aroused against the Germans, who were severely punished after their defeat. During the second war it was argued that the Versailles Treaty was ridiculously mild, since it failed to teach a lesson; this time, we were told, there must be *real* severity. To my mind, we should have been more likely to prevent a repetition of German aggression if we had regarded the rank and file of the Nazis as we regard lunatics than by thinking of them as merely and simply criminals. Lunatics, of course, have to be restrained. But lunatics are restrained from prudence, not as a punishment, and so far as prudence permits we try to make them happy. Everybody recognizes that a homicidal maniac will only become more homicidal if he is made miserable. There were, of course, many men among the Nazis who were plain criminals, but there must also have been many who were more or less mad. If Germany is to be successfully incorporated in Western Europe, there must be a complete abandonment of all attempt to instill a feeling of special guilt. Those who are being punished seldom learn to feel kindly towards the men who punish them. And so long as the Germans hate the rest of mankind peace will be precarious.

When one reads of the beliefs of savages, or of the ancient Babylonians and Egyptians, they seem surprising by their capricious absurdity. But beliefs that are just as absurd are still entertained by the uneducated even in the most modern and civilized societies. I have been gravely assured, in America, that people born in March are unlucky and people born in May are peculiarly liable to corns. I do not know the history of these superstitions, but probably they are derived from Babylonian or Egyptian priestly lore. Beliefs begin in the higher social strata, and then, like mud in a river, sink gradually downwards in the educational scale; they may take 3,000 or 4,000 years to sink all the way. In America you may find your colored maid making some remark that comes straight out of Plato—not the parts of Plato that scholars quote, but the parts where he utters obvious nonsense, such as that men who do not pursue wisdom in this life will be born again as women. Commentators on great philosophers always politely ignore their silly remarks. . . .

To avoid the various foolish opinions to which mankind are prone, no superhuman genius is required. A few simple rules will keep you, not from *all* error, but from silly error.

If the matter is one that can be settled by observation, make the observation yourself. Aristotle could have avoided the mistake of thinking that women have fewer teeth than men, by the simple device of asking Mrs. Aristotle to keep her mouth open while he counted. He did not do so because he thought he knew. Thinking that you know when in fact you don't is a fatal mistake, to which we are all prone. I believe myself that hedgehogs eat black beetles, because I have been told that they do; but if I were writing a book on the habits of hedgehogs, I should not commit myself until I had seen one enjoying this unappetizing diet. Aristotle, however, was less cautious. Ancient and medieval authors knew all about unicorns and salamanders; not one of them thought it necessary to avoid dogmatic statements about them because he had never seen one of them.

Many matters, however, are less easily brought to the test of experience. If, like most of mankind, you have passionate convictions on many such matters, there are ways in which you can make yourself aware of your own bias. If an opinion contrary to your own makes you angry, that is a sign that you are subconsciously aware of having no good reason for thinking as you do. If someone maintains that two and two are five, or that Iceland is on the equator, you feel pity rather than anger, unless you know so little of arithmetic or geography that his opinion shakes your own contrary conviction. The most savage controversies are those about matters as to which there is no good evidence either way. Persecution is used in theology, not in arithmetic, because in arithmetic there is knowledge, but in theology there is only opinion. So whenever you find yourself getting angry about a difference of opinion, be on your guard; you will probably find, on examination, that your belief is going beyond what the evidence warrants.

A good way of ridding yourself of certain kinds of dogmatism is to become aware of opinions held in social circles different from your own. When I was young, I lived much outside my own country—in France, Germany, Italy, and the United States. I found this very profitable in diminishing the intensity of insular prejudice. If you cannot travel, seek out people with whom you disagree, and read a newspaper belonging to a party that is not yours. If the people and the newspaper seem mad, perverse, and wicked, remind yourself that you seem so to them. In this opinion both parties may be right, but they cannot both be wrong. This reflection should generate a certain caution.

Becoming aware of foreign customs, however, does not always have a beneficial effect. In the seventeenth century, when the Manchus conquered China, it was the custom among the Chinese for the women to have small feet, and among the Manchus for the men to wear pigtails. Instead of each dropping their own foolish custom, they each adopted the foolish custom of the other, and the Chinese continued to wear pigtails until they shook off the dominion of the Manchus in the revolution of 1911.

For those who have enough psychological imagination, it is a good plan to imagine an argument with a person having a different bias. This has one advantage, and only one, as compared with actual conversation with opponents; this one advantage is that the method is not subject to the same limitations of time and space. Mahatma Gandhi deplored railways and steamboats and machinery; he would have liked to undo the whole of the industrial revolution. You may never have an opportunity of actually meeting anyone who holds this opinion, because in Western countries most people take the advantage of modern technique for granted. But if you want to make sure that you are right in agreeing with the prevailing opinion, you will find it a good plan to test the arguments that occur to you by considering what Gandhi might have said in refutation of them. I have sometimes been led actually to change my mind as a result of this kind of imaginary dialogue, and, short of this, I have frequently found myself growing less dogmatic and cocksure through realizing the possible reasonableness of a hypothetical opponent.

Be very wary of opinions that flatter your self-esteem. Both men and women, nine times out of ten, are firmly convinced of the superior excellence of their own sex. There is abundant evidence on both sides. If you are a man, you can point out that most poets and men of science are male; if you are a woman, you can retort that so are most criminals. The question is inherently insoluble, but self-esteem conceals this from most people. We are all, whatever part of the world we come from, persuaded that our own nation is superior to all others. Seeing that each nation has its characteristic merits and demerits, we adjust our standard of values so as to make out that the merits possessed by our nation are the really important ones, while its demerits are comparatively trivial. Here, again, the rational man will admit that the question is one to which there is no demonstrably right answer. It is more difficult to deal with the self-esteem of man as man, because we cannot argue out the matter with some nonhuman mind. The only way I know of dealing with this general human conceit is to remind ourselves that man is a brief episode in the life of a small planet in a little corner of the universe, and that, for aught we know, other parts of the cosmos may contain beings as superior to ourselves as we are to jelly-fish.

Other passions besides self-esteem are common sources of error; of these perhaps the most important is fear. Fear sometimes operates directly, by inventing rumors of disaster in wartime, or by imagining objects of terror, such as ghosts; sometimes it operates indirectly, by creating belief in something comforting, such as the elixir of life, or heaven for ourselves and hell for our enemies. Fear has many forms—fear of death, fear of the dark, fear of the unknown, fear of the herd, and that vague generalized fear that comes to those who conceal from themselves their more specific terrors. Until you have admitted your own fears to yourself, and have guarded yourself by a difficult effort of will against their myth-making power, you cannot hope to think truly about many matters of great importance, especially those with which religious beliefs are concerned. Fear is the main source of superstition, and one of the main sources of cruelty. To conquer fear is the beginning of wisdom, in the pursuit of truth as in the endeavor after a worthy manner of life.

There are two ways of avoiding fear: one is by persuading ourselves that we are immune from disaster, and the other is by the practice of sheer courage. The latter is difficult, and to everybody becomes impossible at a certain point. The former has therefore always been more popular. Primitive magic has the purpose of securing safety, either by injuring enemies, or by protecting oneself by talismans, spells, or incantations. Without any essential change, belief in such ways of avoiding danger survived throughout the many centuries of Babylonian civilization, spread from Babylon throughout the Empire of Alexander, and was acquired by the Romans in the course of their absorption of Hellenistic culture. From the Romans it descended to medieval Christendom and Islam. Science has now lessened the belief in magic, but many people place more faith in mascots than they are willing to avow, and sorcery, while condemned by the Church, is still officially a *possible* sin.

Magic, however, was a crude way of avoiding terrors, and, moreover, not a very effective way, for wicked magicians might always prove stronger than good ones. In the fifteenth, sixteenth, and seventeenth centuries, dread of witches and sorcerers led to the burning of hundreds of thousands convicted of these crimes. But newer beliefs, particularly as to the future life, sought more effective ways of combating fear. Socrates on the day of his death (if Plato is to be believed) expressed the conviction that in the next world he would live in the company of the gods and heroes, and surrounded by just spirits who would never object to his endless argumentation. Plato, in his *Republic,* laid it down that cheerful views of the next world must be enforced by the state, not because they were true, but to make soldiers more willing to die in battle. He would have none of the traditional myths about Hades, because they represented the spirits of the dead as unhappy.

Orthodox Christianity, in the Ages of Faith, laid down very definite rules for salvation. First, you must be baptized; then, you must avoid all theological error; last, you must, before dying, repent of your sins and receive absolution. All this would not save you from purgatory, but it would insure your ultimate arrival in heaven. It was not necessary to *know* theology. An eminent Cardinal stated authoritatively that the requirements of orthodoxy would be satisfied if you murmured on your deathbed: "I believe all that the Church believes; the Church believes all that I believe." These very definite directions ought to have made Catholics sure of finding the way to heaven. Nevertheless, the dread of hell persisted, and has caused, in recent times, a great softening of the dogmas as to who will be damned. The doctrine, professed by many modern Christians, that everybody will go to heaven, ought to do away with the fear of death, but in fact this fear is too instinctive to be easily vanquished. F. W. H. Myers, whom spiritualism had converted to belief in a future life, questioned a woman who had lately lost her daughter as to what she supposed had become of her soul. The mother replied: "Oh well, I suppose she is enjoying eternal bliss, but I wish you wouldn't talk about such unpleasant subjects." In spite of all that theology can do, heaven remains, to most people, an "unpleasant subject."

The most refined religions, such as those of Marcus Aurelius and Spinoza, are still concerned with the conquest of fear. The Stoic doctrine was simple: it maintained that the only true good is virtue, of which no enemy can deprive me; consequently, there is no need to fear enemies. The difficulty was that no one could really believe virtue to be the only good, not even Marcus Aurelius, who, as Emperor, sought not only to make his subjects virtuous, but to protect them against barbarians, pestilences, and famines. Spinoza taught a somewhat similar doctrine. According to him, our true good consists in indifference to our mundane fortunes. Both these men sought to escape from fear by pretending that such things as physical suffering are not really evil. This is a noble way of escaping from fear, but is still based upon false belief. And if genuinely accepted, it would have the bad effect of making men indifferent, not only to their own sufferings, but also to those of others.

Under the influence of great fear, almost everybody becomes superstitious. The sailors who threw Jonah overboard imagined his presence to be the cause of the storm which threatened to wreck their ship. In a similar spirit the Japanese, at the time of the Tokyo earthquake, took to massacring Koreans and Liberals. When the Romans won victories in the Punic wars, the Carthaginians became persuaded that their misfortunes were due to a certain laxity which had crept into the worship of Moloch. Moloch liked having children sacrificed to him, and preferred them aristocratic; but the noble families of Carthage had adopted the practice of surreptitiously substituting plebeian children for their own offspring. This, it was thought, had displeased the god, and at the worst moments even the most aristocratic children were duly consumed in the fire. Strange to say, the Romans were victorious in spite of this democratic reform on the part of their enemies.

Collective fear stimulates herd instinct, and tends to produce ferocity towards those who are not regarded as members of the herd. So it was in the French Revolution, when dread of foreign armies produced the reign of terror. The Soviet government would have been less fierce if it had met with less hostility in its first years. Fear generates impulses of cruelty, and therefore promotes such superstitious beliefs as seem to justify cruelty. Neither a man nor a crowd nor a nation can be trusted to act humanely or to think sanely under the influence of a great fear. And for this reason poltroons are more prone to cruelty than brave men, and are also more prone to superstition. When I say this, I am thinking of men who are brave in all respects, not only in facing death. Many a man will have the courage to die gallantly, but will not have the courage to say, or even to think, that the cause for which he is asked to die is an unworthy one. Obloquy is, to most men, more painful than death; that is one reason why, in times of collective excitement, so few men venture to dissent from the prevailing opinion. No Carthaginian denied Moloch, because to do so would have required more courage than was required to face death in battle.

But we have been getting too solemn. Superstitions are not always dark and cruel; often they add to the gaiety of life. I received once a communication from the god Osiris, giving me his telephone number; he lived, at that time, in a suburb of Boston. Although I did not enroll myself among his worshipers, his letter gave me pleasure. I have frequently received letters from men announcing themselves as the Messiah, and urging me not to omit to mention this important fact in my lectures. During prohibition in America, there was a sect which maintained that the communion service ought to be celebrated in whisky, not in wine; this tenet gave them a legal right to a supply of hard liquor, and the sect grew rapidly. There is in England a sect which maintains that the English are the lost ten tribes; there is a stricter sect, which maintains that they are the only tribes of Ephraim and Manasseh. Whenever I encounter a member of either of these sects, I profess myself an adherent of the other, and much pleasant argumentation results. I like also the men who study the Great Pyramid, with a view to deciphering its mystical lore. Many great books have been written on this subject, some of which have been presented to me by their authors. It is a singular fact that the Great Pyramid always predicts the history of the world accurately up to the date of publication of the book in question, but after that date it becomes less reliable. Generally the author expects, very soon, wars in Egypt, followed by Armageddon and the coming of Antichrist, but by this time so many people have been recognized as Antichrist that the reader is reluctantly driven to skepticism.

I admire especially a certain prophetess who lived beside a lake in northern New York State about the year 1820. She announced to her numerous followers that she possessed the power of walking on water, and that she proposed to do so at 11 o'clock on a certain morning. At the stated time, the faithful assembled in their thousands beside the lake. She spoke to them saying: "Are you all entirely persuaded that I can walk on water?" With one voice they replied: "We are." "In that case," she announced, "there is no need for me to do so." And they all went home much edified.

Perhaps the world would lose some of its interest and variety if such beliefs were wholly replaced by cold science. Perhaps we may allow ourselves to be glad of the Abecedarians, who were so called because, having rejected all profane learning, they thought it wicked to learn the ABC. And we may enjoy the perplexity of the South American Jesuit who wondered how the sloth could have traveled, since the Flood, all the way from Mount Ararat to Peru—a journey which its extreme tardiness of locomotion rendered almost incredible. A wise man will enjoy the goods of which there is a plentiful supply, and of intellectual rubbish he will find an abundant diet, in our own age as in every other.

2. THE GROWTH OF SOCIAL SCIENCE IN AMERICA

daniel lerner

Every society engages in self-observation and evaluation by gathering and acting on information about itself. As Western societies gradually changed from a basically agricultural to an urban life style, social science developed in response to the need for understanding and solving the practical problems of social life, as opposed to older intellectual traditions of philosophizing and speculating in the abstract.

Beginning in the late nineteenth century and intensifying in the 1930s, social scientists became deeply involved in the analysis and formulation of remedial public policies. Today, social researchers explore virtually every facet of American life, a normal and indeed necessary development for any society that is committed to progress.

As the mode of self-observation evolved by dealing with the new human problems raised by the endlessly changing lifeways of modern society, social science developed primarily as an empirical, quantitative, policy-related *method of inquiry* (not as a system of beliefs). These three traits have grown together, from nineteenth-century Europe to contemporary America, in the continuing study of modern lifeways.

The great problems of the age issued from the newly uprooted and displaced class of industrial urban workers and their families. Removed from the subsistence relationships of agricultural life, and newly dependent upon their cash wages for livelihood, *how much* did these workers need to earn in order to maintain themselves? Employers wanted to determine this quantum. *How much* did they have to earn before there was a surplus left that could be taxed? Governments wanted to determine this quantum. *How much* did they have to save out of their wages every week to pay an unpredictable doctor's bill, to accumulate a daughter's dowry, to send a son through school? Workers wanted to determine these quanta. As modern society moved steadily onto a cash basis, the determination of such quanta became a critical need of private and public policy. The roots of social science lie in its responsiveness to these needs of modern society for empirical, quantitative, policy-related information about itself.

This explains the historic importance of Frederic Le Play in nineteenth-century France. Instead of writing philosophic treatises on the "New Society," Le Play devoted much of his life to the painstaking collection, classification, and analysis of first-hand data on over three hundred working class families in every European and several Asian countries. He produced comprehensive *monographies sociales* on these families, representing different industries and locales, of which the thirty-six most complete reports were subsequently published in his majestic *Les Oeuvriers Européens* (6 volumes, 1855). No ostrich empiricist, grubbing for facts in the desert sand, Le Play kept his eye constantly fixed on the larger issues of his time. By competent marshaling of weighted empirical evidence, Le Play confronted the great policy problems and the ideologies then being propagated concerning them. It was for this research that he was to win his great place in the history of social science.

The example of Le Play was vigorously recommended, by the *Saturday Review* in London, to "those who have charge of the welfare of England." One who responded was Charles Booth, a shipowner of Liverpool, who paid scant attention to the high intellectual claims of the newly-coined Sociology, but devoted much of his own time and money to the careful collection and statistical analysis of facts bearing on the critical problems of the new working class in Britain. His studies, modestly designed to show "the numerical relation which poverty, misery, and depravity bear to regular earnings and comparative comfort," were published in the monumental *Life and Labour of the People in London* (1891–1903). Their appearance undermined the moralizing ideologies which, in Victorian England, debated poverty as Good or Evil (and insanity as diabolical) but ignored the facts of the matter. There was no arguing Booth's precise statement of the "numerical relation"; nor could mere ideology withstand his striking maps which represented, in shades of color, the exact distribution and degrees of poverty in London. Booth was named to the Royal Commission on the Poor Law. Subsequently, his volume of statistics on the aged poor (1894) led to revision of old-age pensions (1899). By wedding research to policy more directly than Le Play had done— thus exhibiting what the French love to call *l'empirisme anglosaxonne*—Booth gave empirical, quantitative, policy-related research a great push forward.

This line of social inquiry appealed to the temper of Americans and the needs of their rapidly-changing society. The social service pioneers especially provided a vibrant reception for empirical research in America, as in the *Hull-House Maps and Papers* (1895). Booth's method of direct systematic observation was adopted also by a new school of sociological journalists— who came to be called by the epithet of Theodore Roosevelt, "the muck-rakers." While muckraking later declined into routine journalism, its early practitioners were serious and competent students of current realities. The work of Ida Tarbell and Lincoln Steffens stimulated the growth of American social research in the first decades of this century.

The academic fraternity systematized reformist journalism and bolstered social-service activism, their concerted efforts often showing the way to new laws and new institutions for observation and correction of social ills. Studies of labor exploitation led, through minimum wage and social security legisla-tion, to the modern methods of "industrial relations." Reports on urban misery led, through slum clearance and public housing, to urban redevelopment and city planning. Exposure of consumer exploitation led, through pure food and drug legislation, to regulation of fair trade practices. The New Deal, which appeared to be a government of social scientists in its early years, codified these conceptions and institutionalized them in an array of "alphabetical agencies." Some of these passed with the depression crisis (NRA, WPA, PWA). Others became a permanent part of the machinery of American government (SEC, FHA, SSA). These agencies conduct continuous research in key sectors of American society and take (or recommend) appropriate action where violations or malfunctions appear. The New Deal codified a relationship between social research and social policy which had developed through preceding decades under the regime of both major parties. The role of social scientists in the Democratic administration of Woodrow Wilson, par-ticularly during the wartime period, is well known. Less widely noted is the fact that the two major surveys, *Recent Economic Trends* and *Recent Social Trends*, were commissioned by the Republican administration of Herbert Hoover.

Social research has become an indispensable instrument of public policy, regardless of party, in the complex urban industrial society of modern America. The problems defined by Le Play have preoccupied American sociologists since the pioneer generations from L. F. Ward to R. E. Park. Among the leaders of the current generation, Talcott Parsons has systematized data on family roles and Robert Angell has codified our knowledge of cities; S. A.

Stouffer and P. F. Lazarsfeld collaborated in a monographic report on the family in the depression; R. K. Merton has made empirical studies of urban housing and occupations. These matters are under continuous study also by public and private agencies, to which the universities annually supply a corps of researchers. Oriented in the perspectives and trained in the methods of social science, these students occupy posts in education, in government, in business, and in the multitudinous array of civic and social-service agencies which guide a substantial portion of the nation's private and public affairs. Such organizations as the League for Industrial Democracy, League of Women Voters, Planned Parenthood League, Civil Liberties Union, World Affairs Council, Better Business Bureau—to name a random half-dozen of the several thousand voluntary associations that function in American society today— are usually directed and staffed by persons who were exposed to the social sciences through their higher education.

The growing corps of social researchers has extended the tradition of candid and comprehensive observation into virtually every important phase of contemporary American life. Sexuality and piety, work and wealth, leisure and health—all these varieties of human behavior are brought under informed scrutiny and often systematic study. These developments have been possible only in a society that placed a high value upon continuous self-improvement through self-study. Otherwise the prying into personal lives which such studies require would not be tolerated. Nor, in a society committed to an absolute myth, which laid down The Truth once and for all, would empirical inquiry into the way things really are serve any useful purpose. Social science flourishes only in a society which seeks to improve itself by learning where it needs improving.

3. RELIGION AND SCIENCE
alfred n. whitehead

Why the perennial clash between religion and science? What are the unique orientations of each, and how might religion, in particular, set about regaining some of the confidence and relevance it once commanded.

While religion and science have always been in some degree of conflict, each has changed constantly through new information and interpretation. Neither one is a closed conception of life unwilling to modify its viewpoints. Their clash reveals different yet basic preoccupations about life. To regain its former prestige, religion should cease to seek influence by appealing to fear and perform its one valuable mission: to give men an adventurous vision of love and understanding that will provide an ideal through which harmony and goodness will become the dominant facts of human existence.

The difficulty in approaching the question of the relations between Religion and Science is, that its elucidation requires that we have in our minds some clear idea of what we mean by either of the terms, "religion" and "science." Also I wish to speak in the most general way possible, and to keep in the background any comparison of particular creeds, scientific or religious. We have got to understand the type of connection which exists between the two spheres, and then to draw some definite conclusions respecting the existing situation which at present confronts the world.

The *conflict* between religion and science is what naturally occurs to our minds when we think of this subject. It seems as though, during the last half-century, the results of science and the beliefs of religion had come into a position of frank disagreement, from which there can be no escape, except by abandoning either the clear teaching of science, on the clear teaching of religion. This conclusion has been urged by controversialists on either side. Not by all controversialists, of course, but by those trenchant intellects which every controversy calls out into the open.

The distress of sensitive minds, and the zeal for truth, and the sense of the importance of the issues, must command our sincerest sympathy. When we consider what religion is for mankind, and what science is, it is no exaggeration to say that the future course of history depends upon the decision of this generation as to the relations between them. We have here the two strongest general forces (apart from the mere impulse of the various senses) which influence men, and they seem to be set one against the other—the force of our religious intuitions, and the force of our impulse to accurate observation and logical deduction.

A great English statesman once advised his countrymen to use large-scale maps, as a preservative against alarms, panics, and general misunderstanding of the true relations between nations. In the same way in dealing with the clash between permanent elements of human nature, it is well to map our history on a large scale, and to disengage ourselves from our immediate absorption in the present conflicts. When we do this, we immediately discover two great facts. In the first place, there has always been a conflict between religion and science; and in the second place, both religion and science have always been in a state of continual development. In the early days of Christianity, there was a general belief among Christians that the world was coming to an end in the lifetime of people then living. We can make only indirect inferences as to how far this belief was authoritatively proclaimed; but it is certain that it was widely held, and that it formed an impressive part of the popular religious doctrine. The belief proved itself to be mistaken, and Christian doctrine adjusted itself to the change. Again in the early Church individual theologians very confidently deduced from the Bible opinions concerning the nature of the physical universe. In the year A. D. 535, a monk named Cosmas wrote a book which he entitled, *Christian Topography*. He was a travelled man who had visited India and Ethiopia; and finally he lived in a monastery at Alexandria, which was then a great center of culture. In this book, basing himself upon the direct meaning of Biblical texts as construed by him in a literal fashion, he denied the existence of the antipodes, and asserted that the world is a flat parallelogram whose length is double its breadth.

In the seventeenth century the doctrine of the motion of the earth was condemned by a Catholic tribunal. A hundred years ago the extension of time demanded by geological science distressed religious people, Protestant and Catholic. And today the doctrine of evolution is an equal stumbling-block. These are only a few instances illustrating a general fact.

But all our ideas will be in a wrong perspective if we think that this recurring perplexity was confined to contradictions between religion and science; and that in these controversies religion was always wrong, and that science was always right. The true facts of the case are very much more complex, and refuse to be summarized in these simple terms. . . .

Science is even more changeable than theology. No man of science could subscribe without qualification to Galileo's beliefs, or to Newton's beliefs, or to all his own scientific beliefs of ten years ago.

In both regions of thought, additions, distinctions, and modifications have been introduced. So that now, even when the same assertion is made today as was made a thousand, or fifteen hundred years ago, it is made subject to limitations or expansions of meaning, which were not contemplated at the earlier epoch. We are told by logicians that a proposition must be either true or false, and that there is no middle term. But in practice, we may know that a proposition expresses an important truth, but that it is subject to limitations and qualifications which at present remain undiscovered. It is a general feature of our knowledge, that we are insistently aware of important truth; and yet that the only formulations of these truths which we are able to make presuppose a general standpoint of conceptions which may have to be modified. I will give you two illustrations, both from science: Galileo said that the earth moves and that the sun is fixed; the Inquisition said that the earth is fixed and the sun moves; and Newtonian astronomers, adopting an absolute theory of space, said that both the sun and the earth move. But now we say that any one of these three statements is equally true, provided that you have fixed your sense of "rest" and "motion" in the way required by the statement adopted. At the date of Galileo's controversy with the Inquisition, Galileo's way of stating the facts was, beyond question, the fruitful procedure for the sake of scientific research. But in itself it was not more true than the formulation of the Inquisition. But at that time the modern concepts of relative motion were in nobody's mind; so that the statements were made in ignorance of the qualifications required for their more perfect truth. Yet this question of the motions of the earth and the sun expresses a real fact in the universe; and all sides had got hold of important truths concerning it. But with the knowledge of those times, the truths appeared to be inconsistent. . . .

We should apply these same principles to the questions in which there is a variance between science and religion. We would believe nothing in either sphere of thought which does not appear to us to be certified by solid reasons based upon the critical research either of ourselves or of competent authorities. But granting that we have honestly taken this precaution, a clash between the two on points of detail where they overlap should not lead us hastily to abandon doctrines for which we have solid evidence. It may be that we are more interested in one set of doctrines than in the other. But, if we have any sense of perspective and of the history of thought, we shall wait and refrain from mutual anathemas.

We should wait: but we should not wait passively, or in despair. The clash is a sign that there are wider truths and finer perspectives within which a reconciliation of a deeper religion and a more subtle science will be found.

In one sense, therefore, the conflict between science and religion is a slight matter which has been unduly emphasized. A mere logical contradiction cannot in itself point to more than the necessity of some readjustments, possibly of a very minor character on both sides. Remember the widely different aspects of events which are dealt with in science and in religion respectively. Science is concerned with the general conditions which are observed to regulate physical phenomena; whereas religion is wholly wrapped up in the contemplation of moral and aesthetic values. On the one side there is the law of gravitation, and on the other the contemplation of the beauty of holiness. What one side sees, the other misses; and vice versa.

Consider, for example, the lives of John Wesley and of Saint Francis of Assisi. For physical science you have in these lives merely ordinary examples of the operation of the principles of physiological chemistry, and of the dynamics of nervous reactions: for religion you have lives of the most profound significance in the history of the world. Can you be surprised that, in the absence of a perfect and complete phrasing of the principles of science and of the principles of religion which apply to these specific cases, the accounts of these lives from these divergent standpoints should involve discrepancies? It would be a miracle if it were not so. . . .

Religion will not regain its old power until it can face change in the same spirit as does science. Its principles may be eternal, but the expression of those principles requires continual development. This evolution of religion is in the main a disengagement of its own proper ideas from the adventitious notions which have crept into it by reason of the expression of its own ideas in terms of the imaginative picture of the world entertained in previous ages. Such a release of religion from the bonds of imperfect science is all to the good. It stresses its own genuine message. The great point to be kept in mind is that normally an advance in science will show that statements of various religious beliefs require some sort of modification. It may be that they have to be expanded or explained, or indeed entirely restated. If the religion is a sound expression of truth, this modification will only exhibit more adequately the exact point which is of importance. This process is a gain. In so far, therefore, as any religion has any contact with physical facts, it is to be expected that the point of view of those facts must be continually modified as scientific knowledge advances. In this way, the exact relevance of these facts for religious thought will grow more and more clear. The progress of science must result in the unceasing codification of religious thought, to the great advantage of religion. . . .

So far, my point has been this: that religion is the expression of one type of fundamental experiences of mankind: that religious thought develops into an increasing accuracy of expression, disengaged from adventitious imagery: that the interaction between religion and science is one great factor in promoting this development.

I now come to my second reason for the modern fading of interest in religion. This involves the ultimate question which I stated in my opening sentences. We have to know what we mean by religion. The churches, in their presentation of their answers to this query, have put forward aspects of religion which are expressed in terms either suited to the emotional reactions of bygone times or directed to excite modern emotional interests of nonreligious character. What I mean under the first heading is that religious appeal is directed partly to excite that instinctive fear of the wrath of a tyrant which was inbred in the unhappy populations of the arbitrary empires of the ancient world, and in particular to excite that fear of an all-powerful arbitrary tyrant behind the unknown forces of nature. This appeal to the ready instinct of brute fear is losing its force. It lacks any directness of response, because modern science and modern conditions of life have taught us to meet occasions of apprehension by a critical analysis of their causes and conditions. Religion is the reaction of human nature to its search for God. The presentation of God under the aspect of power awakens every modern instinct of critical reaction. This is fatal; for religion collapses unless its main positions command immediacy of assent. In this respect the old phraseology is at variance with the psychology of modern civilizations. This change in psychology is largely due to science, and is one of the chief ways in which the advance of science has weakened the hold of the old religious forms of expression. The nonreligious motive which has entered into modern religious thought is the desire for a comfortable organization of modern society. Religion has been presented as valuable for the ordering of life. Its claims have been rested upon its function as a sanction to right conduct. Also the purpose of right conduct quickly degenerates into the formation of pleasing social relations. We have here a subtle degradation of religious ideas, following upon their gradual purification under the influence of keener ethical intuitions. Conduct is a by-product of religion —an inevitable by-product, but not the main point. Every great religious teacher has revolted against the presentation of religion as a mere sanction of rules of conduct. Saint Paul denounced the Law, and Puritan divines spoke of the filthy rags of righteousness. The insistence upon rules of conduct marks the ebb of religious fervour. Above and beyond all things, the religious life is not a research after comfort. I must now state, in all diffidence, what I conceive to be the essential character of the religious spirit.

Religion is the vision of something which stands beyond, behind, and within, the passing flux of immediate things; something which is real, and yet waiting to be realized; something which is a remote possibility, and yet the greatest of present facts; something that gives meaning to all that passes, and yet eludes apprehension; something whose possession is the final good, and yet is beyond all reach; something which is the ultimate ideal, and the hopeless quest.

The immediate reaction of human nature to the religious vision is worship. Religion has emerged into human experience mixed with the crudest fancies of barbaric imagination. Gradually, slowly, steadily the vision recurs in history under nobler form and with clearer expression. It is the one element in human experience which persistently shows an upward trend. It fades and then recurs. But when it renews its force, it recurs with an added richness and purity of content. The fact of the religious vision, and its history of persistent expansion, is our one ground for optimism. Apart from it, human life is a flash of occasional enjoyments lighting up a mass of pain and misery, a bagatelle of transient experience.

The vision claims nothing but worship; and worship is a surrender to the claim for assimilation, urged with the motive force of mutual love. The vision never overrules. It is always there, and it has the power of love presenting the one purpose whose fulfillment is eternal harmony. Such order as we find in nature is never force—it presents itself as the one harmonious adjustment of complex detail. Evil is the brute motive force of fragmentary purpose, disregarding the eternal vision. Evil is overruling, retarding, hurting. The power of God is the worship He inspires. That religion is strong which in its ritual and its modes of thought evokes an apprehension of the commanding vision. The worship of God is not a rule of safety—it is an adventure of the spirit, a flight after the unattainable. The death of religion comes with the repression of the high hope of adventure.

part

two

SELF AND SOCIETY
the components
of social analysis

The central concerns of the social sciences are the individual and the societies he has created. Supported by physiologists and biologists, psychologists have devoted much of their effort toward studying the individual as a natural rather than social entity. What are the basic human needs and drives? How does man behave when free of social constraints? In short, the psychologist explores the sort of behavior the individual brings to society. The sociologist, economist, historian, anthropologist, and political scientist, on the other hand, have focused their efforts primarily on the manner in which the individual is shaped and molded by forces in the society about him. Many environmental determinists regard the individual as human putty, readily twisted to fit whatever societal expectations the accident of birth has imposed upon him.

The readings in Part Two are divided into two sections, "The Individual as Raw Material" and "Culture and Society as a Mold." The three selections which comprise "The Individual as Raw Material" illustrate diverse types of social behavior that have their origins in the biologic drives of the individual. In "On Aggression," the ethologist, Konrad Lorenz, suggests that much of man's aggressive behavior is biologic in nature, differs little from aggressive behavior in other animal species, and finds outlets regardless of social forms. In the second selection, "Human Nature in Politics," James C. Davies argues cogently that man's political behavior, while outwardly affected by social forces, changes radically when his basic psychological needs are not fulfilled. Davies argues that social drives are secondary to biologic needs. Finally, in the selection entitled "The Biologic Need for Social Behavior," Eric Berne suggests that society itself is based on the instinctual urges of man and that biological necessity, not reason, binds men together.

41

The next group of selections ("Culture and Society as a Mold"), on the other hand, convincingly illustrate the profound role of social environment in the shaping of human behavior. In "Cultural Relativism and Premarital Sex Norms," sociologist Harold T. Christensen illustrates how codes of sexual behavior differ markedly from society to society depending upon prevailing societal norms rather than upon natural urges. While the sexual urge is clearly biologic, it is the structure of society that determines how and under what conditions the biologic urge may or may not be fulfilled. Cultural relativity, the notion that behavior and ethical standards are not universal but are determined by the particular social environment, is also the theme of the second selection by Mirza M. Hussain, "Islam and Socialism." "A Theory of Social Integration" by Peter M. Blau traces the process by which individuals attempt to conform with and gain the acceptance of others, a process central to the molding of individuals who are able to adapt to the norms of their society. In the fourth article, "The Development of Political Attitudes in Children," Robert D. Hess and Judith V. Torney describe how children learn and express political attitudes. In the final article, "Inner- and Other-Directed Societies," David Riesman suggests that many persons are becoming less individualistic and increasingly more dependent upon the norms of society as guides to behavior.

The question of whether biologic or societal forces play the dominant role in shaping human behavior is unlikely to be resolved in the near future. Understanding the impact of both, however, is clearly crucial to study of the social sciences.

THE INDIVIDUAL
AS RAW MATERIAL

4. ON AGGRESSION
konrad lorenz

In this selection, Professor Lorenz examines and compares the aggressive behavior of a variety of animal species ranging from tropical fish to human beings. The inescapable conclusion of this truly fascinating study is that the aggressive behavior of man may well have its roots in the instinctive urges of those lower species from which he evolved.

In the following passages Professor Lorenz suggests that aggression not only is an inherent part of all animal behavior but that aggression, like sexual reproduction, is essential to the survival of the species. In the interest of comparison, the student should draw as many parallels as possible between the instinctive or biologically determined behavior of lower animals, and similar behavior among human beings. Are the antisocial aspects of human behavior learned or intuitive? Can learned behavior overcome biologically determined urges?

What is the value of all this fighting? In nature, fighting is such an ever-present process, its behavior mechanisms and weapons are so highly developed and have so obviously arisen under the selection pressure of a species-preserving function, that it is our duty to ask this Darwinian question.

The layman, misguided by sensationalism in press and film, imagines the relationship between the various "wild beasts of the jungle" to be a bloodthirsty struggle, all against all. In a widely shown film, a Bengal tiger was seen fighting with a python, and immediately afterward the python with a crocodile. With a clear conscience I can assert that such things never occur under natural conditions. What advantage would one of these animals gain from exterminating the other? Neither of them interferes with the other's vital interests.

Darwin's expression, "the struggle for existence," is sometimes errone-ously interpreted as the struggle between different species. In reality, the struggle Darwin was thinking of and which drives evolution forward is the competition between near relations. What causes a species to disappear or become transformed into a different species is the profitable "invention" that falls by chance to one or a few of its members in the everlasting gamble of hereditary change. The descendants of these lucky ones gradually outstrip all others until the particular species consists only of individuals who possess the new "invention."

There are, however, fightlike contests between members of different species: at night an owl kills and eats even well-armed birds of prey, in spite of their vigorous defense, and when these birds meet the owl by day they attack it ferociously. Almost every animal capable of self-defense, from the smallest rodent upward, fights furiously when it is cornered and has no means of escape. Besides these three particular types of inter-specific fighting, there are other, less typical cases; for instance, two cave-nesting birds of different species may fight for a nesting cavity. Something must be said here about these three types of inter-specific fighting in order to explain their peculiarity and to dis-tinguish them from the *intra*-specific aggression which is really the subject of this book.

The survival value of inter-specific fights is much more evident than that of intra-specific contests. The way in which a predatory animal and its prey influence each other's evolution is a classical example of how the selection pressure of a certain function causes corresponding adaptations. The swiftness of the hunted ungulate forces its feline pursuers to evolve enormous leaping power and sharply armed toes. Paleontological discoveries have shown im-pressive examples of such evolutionary competition between weapons of attack and those of defense. The teeth of grazing animals have achieved better and better grinding power, while, in their parallel evolution, nutritional plants have devised means of protecting themselves against being eaten, as by the storage of silicates and the development of hard, wooden thorns. This kind of "fight" between the eater and the eaten never goes so far that the predator causes extinction of the prey: a state of equilibrium is always established be-tween them, endurable by both species. The last lions would have died of hunger long before they had killed the last pair of antelopes or zebras; or, in terms of human commercialism, the whaling industry would go bankrupt before the last whales became extinct. What directly threatens the existence of an animal species is never the "eating enemy" but the competitor. In pre-historic times man took the Dingo, a primitive domestic dog, to Australia. It ran wild there, but it did not exterminate a single species of its quarry; instead, it destroyed the large marsupial beasts of prey which ate the same animals as it did itself. The large marsupial predators, the Tasmanian Devil and the Marsupial Wolf, were far superior to the Dingo in strength, but the hunting methods of these "old-fashioned," relatively stupid and slow creatures were inferior to those of the "modern" mammal. The Dingo reduced the marsupial population to such a degree that their methods no longer "paid," and today they exist only in Tasmania, where the Dingo has never penetrated.

In yet another respect the fight between predator and prey is not a fight in the real sense of the word: the stroke of the paw with which a lion kills his prey may resemble the movements that he makes when he strikes his rival, just as a shotgun and a rifle resemble each other outwardly; but the inner motives of the hunter are basically different from those of the fighter. The buffalo which the lion fells provokes his aggression as little as the appetizing turkey which I have just seen hanging in the larder provokes mine. The differences in these inner drives can clearly be seen in the expression movements of the animal: a dog about to catch a hunted rabbit has the same kind of excitedly happy expression as he has when he greets his master or awaits some longed-for treat. From many excellent photographs it can be seen that the lion, in the dramatic moment before he springs, is in no way angry. Growling, laying the ears back, and other well-known expression movements of fighting behavior are seen in predatory animals only when they are very afraid of a wildly resisting prey, and even then the expressions are only suggested.

The opposite process, the "counteroffensive" of the prey against the predator, is more nearly related to genuine aggression. Social animals in particular take every possible chance to attack the "eating enemy" that threatens their safety. This process is called "mobbing." Crows or other birds "mob" a cat or any other nocturnal predator, if they catch sight of it by day.

The survival value of this attack on the eating enemy is self-evident. Even if the attacker is small and defenseless, he may do his enemy considerable harm. All animals which hunt singly have a chance of success only if they take their prey by surprise. If a fox is followed through the wood by a loudly screaming jay, or a sparrow hawk is pursued by a flock of warning wagtails, his hunting is spoiled for the time being. Many birds will mob an owl, if they find one in the daytime, and drive it so far away that it will hunt somewhere else the next night. In some social animals such as jackdaws and many kinds of geese, the function of mobbing is particularly interesting. In jackdaws, its most important survival value is to teach the young, inexperienced birds what a dangerous eating enemy looks like, which they do not know instinctively. Among birds, this is a unique case of traditionally acquired knowledge. . . .

Among the larger, more defense-minded herbivores which, en masse, are a match for even the biggest predators, mobbing is particularly effective; according to reliable reports, zebras will molest even a leopard if they catch him on a veldt where cover is sparse. The reaction of social attack against the wolf is still so ingrained in domestic cattle and pigs that one can sometimes land oneself in danger by going through a field of cows with a nervous dog which, instead of barking at them or at least fleeing independently, seeks refuge between the legs of its owner. Once, when I was out with my bitch Stasi, I was obliged to jump into a lake and swim for safety when a herd of young cattle half encircled us and advanced threateningly; and when he was in southern Hungary during the First World War my brother spent a pleasant afternoon up a tree with his Scotch terrier under his arm, because a herd of half-wild Hungarian swine, disturbed while grazing in the wood, encircled them, and with bared tusks and unmistakable intentions began to close in on them.

Much more could be said about these effective attacks on the real or supposed enemy. In some birds and fishes, to serve this special purpose brightly colored "aposematic" or warning colors have evolved, which predators notice and associate with unpleasant experiences with the particular species. Poisonous, evil-tasting, or otherwise specially protected animals have, in many cases, "chosen" for these warning signals the combination of red, white, and black; and it is remarkable that the Common Sheldrake and the Sumatra Barb, two creatures which have nothing in common either with each other or the above-named groups, should have done the same thing. It has long been known that Common Sheldrake mob predatory animals and that they so disgust the fox with the sight of their brightly colored plumage that they can nest safely in inhabited foxholes. I bought some Sumatra Barbs because I had asked myself why these fishes looked so poisonous; in a large communal aquarium, they immediately answered my question by mobbing big Cichlids so persistently that I had to save the giant predators from the only apparently harmless dwarfs.

There is a third form of fighting behavior, and its survival value is as easily demonstrated as that of the predator's attack on its prey or the mobbing by the prey of the eating enemy. With H. Hediger, we call this third behavior pattern the *critical reaction*. The expression "fighting like a cornered rat" has become symbolic of the desperate struggle in which the fighter stakes his all, because he cannot escape and can expect no mercy. This most violent form of fighting behavior is motivated by fear, by the most intense flight impulses whose natural outlet is prevented by the fact that the danger is too near; so the animal, not daring to turn its back on it, fights with the proverbial courage of desperation. Such a contingency may also occur when, as with the cornered rat, flight is prevented by lack of space, or by strong social ties, like those which forbid an animal to desert its brood or family. The attack which a hen or goose makes on everything that goes too near her chicks or goslings can also be classified as a critical reaction. Many animals will attack desperately when surprised by an enemy at less than a certain critical distance, whereas they would have fled if they had noticed his coming from farther away. As Hediger has described, lion tamers maneuver their great beasts of prey into their positions in the arena by playing a dangerous game with the margin between flight distance and critical distance; and thousands of big game hunting stories testify to the dangerousness of large beasts of prey in dense cover. The reason is that in such circumstances the flight distance is particularly small, because the animal feels safe, imagining that it will not be noticed by a man even if he should penetrate the cover and get quite close; but if in so doing the man oversteps the animal's critical distance, a so-called hunting accident happens quickly and disastrously.

All the cases described above, in which animals of different species fight against each other, have one thing in common: every one of the fighters gains an obvious advantage by its behavior or, at least, in the interests of preserving the species it "ought to" gain one. But intra-specific aggression, aggression in the proper and narrower sense of the word, also fulfills a species-preserving function. Here, too, the Darwinian question "What for?" may and must be asked. Many people will not see the obvious justification for this question, and those accustomed to the classical psychoanalytical way of thinking will probably regard it as a frivolous attempt to vindicate the life-destroying principle or, purely and simply, evil. The average normal civilized human being witnesses aggression only when two of his fellow citizens or two of his domestic animals fight, and therefore sees only its evil effects. In addition there is the alarming progression of aggressive actions ranging from cocks fighting in the barnyard to dogs biting each other, boys thrashing each other, young men throwing beer mugs at each other's heads, and so on to bar-room brawls about politics, and finally to wars and atom bombs.

With humanity in its present cultural and technological situation, we have good reason to consider intra-specific aggression the greatest of all dangers. We shall not improve our chances of counteracting it if we accept it as something metaphysical and inevitable, but on the other hand, we shall perhaps succeed in finding remedies if we investigate the chain of its natural causation. Wherever man has achieved the power of voluntarily guiding a natural phenomenon in a certain direction, he has owed it to his understanding of the chain of causes which formed it. Physiology, the science concerned with the normal life processes and how they fulfill their species-preserving function, forms the essential foundation for pathology, the science investigating their disturbances. Let us forget for a moment that the aggression drive has become derailed under conditions of civilization, and let us inquire impartially into its natural causes. For the reasons already given, as good Darwinians we must inquire into the species-preserving function which, under natural—or rather precultural—conditions, is fulfilled by fights within the species, and which by the process of selection has caused the advanced development of intra-specific fighting behavior in so many higher animals. It is not only fishes that fight their own species: the majority of vertebrates do so too, man included.

5. HUMAN NATURE IN POLITICS
james c. davies

In the introduction to this section it was suggested that man's behavior is conditioned both by the pursuit of biologic urges (e.g., food, sex) and by social learning (e.g., how to cooperate in a work group or sewing circle).

From James C. Davies, *Human Nature in Politics*. New York: John Wiley & Sons, Inc., 1963, pp. 11–17.

In the following selection, Professor Davies argues persuasively that when confronted with situations of severe deprivation or strain, an individual's social learning will give way to the pursuit of basic biologic necessities. Implicit in this argument is the suggestion that fulfillment of man's biologic needs is prior to and essential for the effective functioning of his social relationships. Do you agree? Can you think of situations in which this is not the case? Is mind dominant over matter?

In 1944–1945 at the University of Minnesota a number of conscientious objectors to military service subjected themselves to a series of starvation experiments. For the first twelve weeks (the control period) they were given an ample, well-balanced, but regulated diet averaging 3870 calories per day. For the next twenty-four weeks (the experimental period) they were given a semi-starvation diet averaging 1470 calories per day. This period of nearly six months was followed by twelve weeks of rehabilitation, during which the average daily food intake was gradually increased to 1780 and then 2840 calories, after which the subjects' food intake was unrestricted and climbed to an over-normal average of 4740 calories per day. The experimenters made a variety of observations, mainly of medical significance, but the psychological ones are of basic political relevance. Let us consider a "typical" case from this group of 32 whose experiences were observed throughout the year-long study.

"Don" was twenty-five years old, an architect, unmarried but with a girl friend to whom he wrote a letter almost every day. He was an active participant in the educational program these conscientious objectors had established to prepare themselves for post-war relief work outside the United States. During the control period his weight was 142 pounds (64.7 kg); during the experimental period it dropped finally to 115 pounds (52.1 kg); at the end of twelve weeks' rehabilitation it rose to 120 pounds (54.2 kg), and twenty-one weeks later to 163 pounds (74.1 kg), some 21 pounds (9.5 kg) more than he had weighed before the experiments began.

During the third experimental week his morale was high, and he maintained his interest and work in architecture. Although he had less desire to move about and tired easily when he did, his mental energy, along with his acumen, remained unimpaired. Unlike some of the other subjects, he was not preoccupied with thoughts of food, even during the fourth week. By the eighth week he reported having dreams about food. By the twelfth week not only his dreams but his conscious thoughts revolved around food as steadily as the earth around the sun. He got aches, pains, and cramps whether he exercised or not. He became more restless, irritable, and—in one of the ominous and universal symptoms of starvation—increasingly apathetic. He had difficulty concentrating on any activity for very long. He lost self-confidence to the point where he sought more control by the experimenters, saying, "I think it is a good idea to put strong checks on us." Writing in his diary during the twelfth week, he observed that he enjoyed being alone, that his thoughts and moods had turned inwards, that his interest in other individuals and in post-war relief work overseas had declined, and that what he now dreamed of was being an architect and leading "a personal home life" in a small-town or rural environment.

By the sixteenth week he suffered severe hunger pangs and headaches. When his girl came several hundred miles to visit him two weeks later, he found the visit a strain and "felt that it had been impossible for him to achieve rapport with her." As Brozek further reported, "the egocentric effects of the semi-starvation, added to a new realization of the importance of personal security, led to a dropping of all relief study and training." He began to spend most of his time "just sitting." By the end of the starvation period he had virtually stopped his studies and letter writing. In the final starvation interview he repeatedly expressed the hope that he would be placed in the one out of the four groups that was to get the most abundant rehabilitation diet.

At the start of the rehabilitation period he immediately felt better and wanted to do things. But during the third week he became obsessed with the belief he was not getting his allotted quota of food. He spent his time going over his personal effects, read devotional religious literature, and had no wish to take part in group activities. Later he became interested in relief and rehabilitation work again, as his religious interest diminished, but he wanted to do this work in the United States. Five months after the end of the starvation period, in Brozek's words, "the importance of attaining physical security had been sharply focussed by his semi-starvation experience," and "Don" had decided not to do relief work but go back to his architectural training and "get started on his own." This was his mental condition despite his expressed greater awareness of the need to provide food for starving people everywhere.

As the major study reports, withdrawal and apathy symptoms among the subjects during the starvation period were accompanied by strong feelings of group identity, as starved ones against the well-fed world outside. But during rehabilitation, the discontents and suspicions that arose tended to have a nongroup flavor quite different from the strong group feeling before and during the experimental period.

Reports of historical instances of widespread and chronic starvation lend color to the scientifically gray Minnesota findings.

On the Russian famine, 1918–1922: In the interest of obtaining better rations, children denounced their parents or other members of the family to the Cheka as anti-Communists.

On starvation in the Nazi concentration camp at Belsen, 1944–1945: Loss of normal moral standards and sense of responsibility for the welfare of others was widespread; in severe cases interest in others did not extend beyond child or parent; eventually the insinct to survive alone remained, even to the extent of eating human flesh.

On French PWs, including some who were active in the anti-Nazi Resistance: These individuals . . . lost in the detention camps their interest in political questions and became concerned only with the immediate problems of the internment life and the possibility of escape. In the last stages the men were overcome with apathy and resignation.

In large societies (including nations or parts of nations), when food becomes scarce there is thus a breakdown of social ties, of property rights, the devaluation of treasured objects and of virtue (including sexual) in the omnipotent physical desire for food. A momentary worsening of the food supply may produce local food riots, which may broaden and deepen into rebellion. But extreme hunger, as starvation approaches, produces apathy and manipulability. People become too weak and too busy staying alive to take either strong or concerted action against government.

There are two reasons for introducing a discussion of the political relevance of the physical needs by considering chronic hunger. The first is to describe a condition with which modern men in industrial society, notably including readers and writers of books, are rarely if ever familiar (except following either economic breakdown or deliberate action of government), and one with which contemporary men in many nonindustrial societies have occasionally or often been only too well acquainted. People who have always eaten regularly find it hard to comprehend the catastrophic consequences of hunger on thought and action, just as it is hard for virtually all people to experience vicariously and understand the consequences of a deprivation of air or water. But it is necessary to appreciate what starvation does to people in order to understand its political impact. This brings us to the second and significant reason: the depoliticization that follows deprivation.

We have noted several consequences of starvation: constant preoccupation with food, apathy, loss of self-confidence, a turning away from other individuals and society and a turning toward oneself, and a breakdown of social ties and moral standards. What in short we see is very much like what Thomas Hobbes, writing in cold bitterness in France about his reaction to the Puritan Revolution in England, described as the state of nature. There is the war of all against all and the solitary, brutish, short life of man. Only in a very primitive sense, except as in such instances as the Netherlands in 1944–1945, can there be anything like what we call society, let alone political society. To assume that ordinary or extraordinary persons in such a hungry condition can in any way concern themselves with matters of public policy is to assume a kind of madness that prefers order, justice, and individual responsibility therefor to survival itself—prefers means when ends cannot be met. The organism will not permit this. Politics cannot exist for people who are in such circumstances. The man with food to dispense can rule without protest. We have noted the desire of "Don," the Minnesota experimental subject, to have the experimenters "put strong checks on us."

Putting the problem of physical needs in broader context, we may state the proposition that the needs for food, clothing, shelter, health, and safety (i.e., freedom from bodily harm) do not ordinarily find *direct* political expression. With the exception of physical safety, the search for satisfaction of these needs is ordinarily carried on by social but nonpolitical means. Physical safety, in the form of protection against violence, is characteristically sought from government, but training for safety is often done privately in the family, when parents teach their children to be careful in crossing streets, walking alone in the dark, etc. Satisfaction of them is more a precondition of political participation than a cause of it, in the sense that good physical health is more a precondition than a cause of intellectual activity. When the means to satisfy physical needs are readily available through private channels, individuals do not look to government to provide the means. And when the means are so nearly unavailable that people are constantly preoccupied with eating, staying warm, dry, healthy, and alive, they have no time to consider public policy. Extreme physical need destroys politics for the needful. By this I mean that they can take no effective voluntary part in making any basic decisions of the sort that affect the whole community.

There is available some more lifelike and more systematic evidence on these phenomena. In their research on unemployment during the Great Depression that started in the late 1920s, Zawadzki and Lazarsfeld studied unemployed individuals in Warsaw and in the Austrian village of Marienthal. They found a general desocialization and widespread resignation and apathy. In Marienthal more than four out of five persons were either resigned to unemployment or broken by it. No political activity was reported among any of the people. In summarizing their Warsaw findings they explained:

> The masses cease to exist as such when the social bond—the consciousness of belonging together—does not bind any longer. There remain only scattered, loose, perplexed, and hopeless individuals. The unemployed are a mass only numerically, not socially.

Without enough to eat there is not a society. Without a society, the adjective "political" has no noun to modify.

6. THE BIOLOGIC NEED FOR SOCIAL BEHAVIOR

eric berne

The preceding selections have suggested that much of man's social behavior is biologically determined.

In the present selection the author argues that regardless of its origins, man is dependent on social behavior for his biologic survival. Without affection and social stimulation, says the author, "your spinal cord will shrivel up."

From *Games People Play*. Reprinted by permission of Grove Press, Inc. Copyright © 1964 by Eric Berne.

Spitz has found that infants deprived of handling over a long period will tend at length to sink into an irreversible decline and are prone to succumb eventually to intercurrent disease. In effect, this means that what he calls emotional deprivation can have a fatal outcome. These observations give rise to the idea of *stimulus-hunger,* and indicate that the most favored forms of stimuli are those provided by physical intimacy, a conclusion not hard to accept on the basis of everyday experience.

An allied phenomenon is seen in grown-ups subjected to sensory deprivation. Experimentally, such deprivation may call forth a transient psychosis, or at least give rise to temporary mental disturbances. In the past, social and sensory deprivation is noted to have had similar effects in individuals condemned to long periods of solitary imprisonment. Indeed, solitary confinement is one of the punishments most dreaded even by prisoners hardened to physical brutality, and is now a notorious procedure for inducing political compliance. (Conversely, the best of the known weapons against political compliance is social organization.)

On the biological side, it is probable that emotional and sensory deprivation tends to bring about or encourage organic changes. If the reticular activating system of the brain stem is not sufficiently stimulated, degenerative changes in the nerve cells may follow, at least indirectly. This may be a secondary effect due to poor nutrition, but the poor nutrition itself may be a product of apathy, as in infants suffering from marasmus. Hence a biological chain may be postulated leading from emotional and sensory deprivation through apathy to degenerative changes and death. In this sense, stimulus-hunger has the same relationship to survival of the human organism as food-hunger.

Indeed, not only biologically but also psychologically and socially, stimulus-hunger in many ways parallels the hunger for food. Such terms as malnutrition, satiation, gourmet, gourmand, faddist, ascetic, culinary arts, and good cook are easily transferred from the field of nutrition to the field of sensation. Overstuffing has its parallel in overstimulation. In both spheres under ordinary conditions where ample supplies are available and a diversified menu is possible, choices will be heavily influenced by an individual's idiosyncrasies. It is possible that some or many of these idiosyncrasies are constitutionally determined, but this is irrelevant to the problems at issue here.

The social psychiatrist's concern in the matter is with what happens after the infant is separated from his mother in the normal course of growth. What has been said so far may be summarized by the "colloquialism": "If you are not stroked, your spinal cord will shrivel up." Hence, after the period of close intimacy with the mother is over, the individual for the rest of his life is confronted with a dilemma upon whose horns his destiny and survival are continually being tossed. One horn is the social, psychological and biological forces which stand in the way of continued physical intimacy in the infant style; the other is his perpetual striving for its attainment. Under most conditions he will compromise. He learns to do with more subtle, even symbolic, forms of handling, until the merest nod of recognition may serve the purpose to some extent, although his original craving for physical contact may remain unabated.

This process of compromise may be called by various terms, such as sublimation; but whatever it is called, the result is a partial transformation of the infantile stimulus-hunger into something which may be termed *recognition-hunger*. As the complexities of compromise increase, each person becomes more and more individual in his quest for recognition, and it is these differentia which lend variety to social intercourse and which determine the individual's destiny. A movie actor may require hundreds of strokes each week from anonymous and undifferentiated admirers to keep his spinal cord from shriveling, while a scientist may keep physically and mentally healthy on one stroke a year from a respected master.

"Stroking" may be used as a general term for intimate physical contact; in practice it may take various forms. Some people literally stroke an infant; others hug or pat it, while some people pinch it playfully or flip it with a fingertip. These all have their analogues in conversation, so that it seems one might predict how an individual would handle a baby by listening to him talk. By an extension of meaning, "stroking" may be employed colloquially to denote any act implying recognition of another's presence. Hence a *stroke* may be used as the fundamental unit of social action. An exchange of strokes constitutes a *transaction*, which is the unit of social intercourse.

As far as the theory of games is concerned, the principle which emerges here is that any social intercourse whatever has a biological advantage over no intercourse at all. This has been experimentally demonstrated in the case of rats through some remarkable experiments by S. Levine in which not only physical, mental and emotional development but also the biochemistry of the brain and even resistance to leukemia were favorably affected by handling. The significant feature of these experiments was that gentle handling and painful electric shocks were equally effective in promoting the health of the animals.

This validation of what has been said above encourages us to proceed with increased confidence to the next section.

Granted that handling of infants, and its symbolic equivalent in grown-ups, recognition, have a survival value. The question is, What next? In everyday terms, what can people do after they have exchanged greetings, whether the greeting consists of a collegiate "Hi!" or an Oriental ritual lasting several hours? After stimulus-hunger and recognition-hunger comes *structure-hunger*. The perennial problem of adolescents is: "What do you say to her (him) then?" And to many people besides adolescents, nothing is more uncomfortable than a social hiatus, a period of silent, unstructured time when no one present can think of anything more interesting to say than: "Don't you think the walls are perpendicular tonight?" The eternal problem of the human being is how to structure his waking hours. In this existential sense, the function of all social living is to lend mutual assistance for this project.

The operational aspect of time-structuring may be called programing.

It has three aspects: material, social and individual. The most common, convenient, comfortable, and utilitarian method of structuring time is by a project designed to deal with the material of external reality: what is commonly known as work. Such a project is technically called an *activity;* the term "work" is unsuitable because a general theory of social psychiatry must recognize that social intercourse is also a form of work.

Material programing arises from the vicissitudes encountered in dealing with external reality; it is of interest here only insofar as activities offer a matrix for "stroking," recognition, and other more complex forms of social intercourse. Material programing is not primarily a social problem; in essence it is based on data processing. The activity of building a boat relies on a long series of measurements and probability estimates, and any social exchange which occurs must be subordinated to these in order for the building to proceed.

Social programing results in traditional ritualistic or semi-ritualistic interchanges. The chief criterion for it is local acceptability, popularly called "good manners." Parents in all parts of the world teach their children manners, which means that they know the proper greeting, eating, emunctory, courting and mourning rituals, and also how to carry on topical conversations with appropriate strictures and reinforcements. The strictures and reinforcements constitute tact or diplomacy, some of which is universal and some local. Belching at meals or asking after another man's wife are each encouraged or forbidden by local ancestral tradition, and indeed there is a high degree of inverse correlation between these particular transactions. Usually in localities where people belch at meals, it is unwise to ask after the womenfolk; and in localities where people are asking after the womenfolk, it is unwise to belch at meals. Usually formal rituals precede semi-ritualistic topical conversations, and the latter may be distinguished by calling them *pastimes.*

As people become better acquainted, more and more *individual programing* creeps in, so that "incidents" begin to occur. These incidents superficially appear to be adventitious, and may be so described by the parties concerned, but careful scrutiny reveals that they tend to follow definite patterns which are amenable to sorting and classification, and that the sequence is circumscribed by unspoken rules and regulations. These regulations remain latent as long as the amities or hostilities proceed according to Hoyle, but they become manifest if an illegal move is made, giving rise to a symbolic, verbal or legal cry of "Foul!" Such sequences, which in contrast to pastimes are based more on individual than on social programing, may be called *games.* Family life and married life, as well as life in organizations of various kinds, may year after year be based on variations of the same game.

To say that the bulk of social activity consists of playing games does not necessarily mean that it is mostly "fun" or that the parties are not seriously engaged in the relationship. On the one hand, "playing" football and other athletic "games" may not be fun at all, and the players may be intensely grim;

and such games share with gambling and other forms of "play" the potentiality for being very serious indeed, sometimes fatal. On the other hand, some authors, for instance Huizinga, include under "play" such serious things as cannibal feasts. Hence calling such tragic behavior as suicide, alcohol and drug addiction, criminality or schizophrenia "playing games" is not irresponsible, facetious or barbaric. The essential characteristic of human play is not that the emotions are spurious, but that they are regulated. This is revealed when sanctions are imposed on an illegitimate emotional display. Play may be grimly serious, or even fatally serious, but the social sanctions are serious only if the rules are broken.

Pastimes and games are substitutes for the real living of real intimacy. Because of this they may be regarded as preliminary engagements rather than as unions, which is why they are characterized as poignant forms of play. Intimacy begins when individual (usually instinctual) programing becomes more intense, and both social patterning and ulterior restrictions and motives begin to give way. It is the only completely satisfying answer to stimulus-hunger, recognition-hunger and structure-hunger. Its prototype is the act of loving impregnation.

Structure-hunger has the same survival value as stimulus-hunger. Stimulus-hunger and recognition-hunger express the need to avoid sensory and emotional starvation, both of which lead to biological deterioration. Structure-hunger expresses the need to avoid boredom, and Kierkegaard has pointed out the evils which result from unstructured time. If it persists for any length of time, boredom becomes synonymous with emotional starvation and can have the same consequences.

The solitary individual can structure time in two ways: activity and fantasy. An individual can remain solitary even in the presence of others, as every schoolteacher knows. When one is a member of a social aggregation of two or more people, there are several options for structuring time. In order of complexity, these are: (1) Rituals (2) Pastimes (3) Games (4) Intimacy and (5) Activity, which may form a matrix for any of the others. The goal of each member of the aggregation is to obtain as many satisfactions as possible from his transactions with other members. The more accessible he is, the more satisfactions he can obtain. Most of the programing of his social operations is automatic. Since some of the "satisfactions" obtained under this programing, such as self-destructive ones, are difficult to recognize in the usual sense of the word "satisfactions," it would be better to substitute some more non-committal term, such as "gains" or "advantages."

The advantages of social contact revolve around somatic and psychic equilibrium. They are related to the following factors: (1) the relief of tension (2) the avoidance of noxious situations (3) the procurement of stroking and (4) the maintenance of an established equilibrium. All these items have been investigated and discussed in great detail by physiologists, psychologists, and psychoanalysts. Translated into terms of social psychiatry, they may be stated as (1) the primary internal advantages (2) the primary external advantages (3) the secondary advantages and (4) the existential advantages. The first three parallel the "gains from illness" described by Freud: the internal paranosic gain, the external paranosic gain, and the epinosic gain, respectively. Experience has shown that it is more useful and enlightening to investigate social transactions from the point of view of the advantages gained than to treat them as defensive operations. In the first place, the best defense is to engage in no transactions at all; in the second place, the concept of "defenses" covers only part of the first two classes of advantages, and the rest of them, together with the third and fourth classes, are lost to this point of view.

The most gratifying forms of social contact, whether or not they are embedded in a matrix of activity, are games and intimacy. Prolonged intimacy is rare, and even then it is primarily a private matter; significant social intercourse most commonly takes the form of games. . . .

CULTURE AND SOCIETY
AS A MOLD

7. CULTURAL RELATIVISM
AND PREMARITAL SEX NORMS
harold t. christensen

The central theme of the next selection is that an individual's behavior is largely molded by the society in which he lives.

In the following selection, Professor Christensen clearly illustrates this point by demonstrating the marked difference in premarital sex norms (behavior standards) among Mormon, rural American, and Danish cultures. Specifically, the author suggests that attitudes toward sex are not universal, but vary from place to place and time to time. Implicit in this selection, moreover, is the further suggestion that the more "advanced" the culture, the more liberal its attitudes toward sex. Do you agree? If matters as important as sex vary markedly from culture to culture, can there be any absolute "goods" that don't vary from culture to culture?

In noting that behavioral standards vary over time and from society to society, William Graham Sumner made the now classic statement: "The mores can make anything right." By this he meant that moral problems are interpreted differently by different societies—that questions of right and wrong are relative to the particular culture in which the behavior occurs. This theory has been labeled *cultural relativism*. It challenges the notion of absolute standards of judgment to be applied uniformly regardless of time or place.

But there has been little quantitative research to test the theory of cultural relativism, especially as applied to modern Western societies. Furthermore, the tendency has been to stop with a simple noting of attitudinal and behavioral differences, without pinning down the relativism of the *consequences* of these differences. For example, it is well known that some societies

From Harold T. Christensen, "Cultural Relativism and Premarital Sex Norms," *American Sociological Review*, XXV, No. 1, February 1960, pp. 31–39. By permission of the author and the American Sociological Association.

are rather restrictive and others very permissive regarding premarital sexual behavior;[1] but there is almost no information as to whether this behavior has the same or different *effects* (in terms of mental health, subsequent social behavior, or both) across these contrasting types of societies.

This paper is an attempt to illuminate further the notion of cultural relativism by applying it to differing sets of premarital sex norms. Since premarital pregnancy can be reliably measured by use of a method known as "record linkage," [2] whereas most other levels of sexual behavior are more elusive, the focus here is upon this phenomenon. We are interested in both regularities and variations among the cultures studied, with special reference to the consequences of premarital pregnancy.

Specifically, it is hypothesized that the more permissive the culture regarding sexual matters, the greatest will be the incidence of premarital pregnancy, *but the lesser will be the effects of such pregnancy as pressure either for hasty marriage or for subsequent divorce.* It is further hypothesized that certain aspects of premarital pregnancy *are not culturally relevant.*

In order to treat culture as a variable, we have made identical observations in three widely divergent areas. The first is the state of Utah, where the Mormon Church is dominant and premarital sex norms tend to be extremely conservative, almost to the point of being puritanical. Here, religion is a motivating force in the lives of most people, and the religious interpretation of premarital sexual intercourse is that it is an extremely grievous sin. Waiting until marriage for sexual intercourse—"keeping the law of chastity"—is regarded as one of the highest of virtues.[3]

The second is the state of Indiana, which in many ways is typical of the United States as a whole. It is centrally located and heterogeneous in culture. It is approximately an average state in size, in rural-urban distribution, in population numbers and composition, and in various social indices such as median income, school attendance, and marriage, birth, and divorce rates. The "chastity norm" is a part of the prevailing culture in Indiana as in most of the United States—in prescription even if less so in practice. And there are religious incentives, promoted by a variety of denominations, which give support to the sexual mores.

The third location is Denmark, which, like all of Scandinavia, has a long tradition of sexual intercourse during the engagement. This goes back three or four centuries at least, in spite of efforts by the State Lutheran Church to

---

[1] See e.g., George Peter Murdock, *Social Structure,* New York: Macmillan, pp. 260–283.
[2] For descriptions of this method, see Christensen, *loc. cit.;* and Harold T. Christensen, "The Method of Record Linkage Applied to Family Data," *Marriage and Family Living,* 20 (February, 1958), pp. 38–43.
[3] In this connection, it is interesting to recall Kinsey's finding to the effect that religiously devout men and women participate less in all socially disapproved forms of sexual behavior. He regarded religion as being the "most important factor in restricting premarital activity in the United States." See Alfred C. Kinsey *et al., Sexual Behavior in the Human Female,* Philadelphia: Saunders, 1953, pp. 324, 686–687, and *passim.*

establish a chastity code. In this connection, it is important to point out that, although most Danes have their names on the church records, they seldom attend church services. Except for a few, religion in Denmark is not a strong motivating force in the lives of the people. Croog notes the importance of understanding the *ring engagement*—which has almost the status of a formal marriage, including rights to sexual intercourse, and obligations to marry if pregnancy results—as background for interpreting sexual behavior in Denmark. He also explains how this pattern of sexual freedom is spreading to include the more informal "going steady" relationships; and how these practices are encouraged by a liberal clergy, by welfare laws which make abortion and unmarried motherhood relatively easy, and by the facility with which premarital sexual behavior can be rationalized since "everyone is doing it." [4] Svalastoga cites five recent empirical studies to support his claim that: "Coitus before marriage may now safely be considered the rule and chastity the exception in Scandinavia." [5]

Thus these three areas have widely different norms regarding premarital sexual behavior. At the one extreme is Utah, dominated by a homogeneous culture and conservative religious tradition. There, the moral condemnation of premarital sexual intercourse under all circumstances has the support of strong supernatural sanctions. At the other extreme is Denmark, with a liberal tradition in sexual matters, and a religious membership, which, though homogeneous, is only nominal. There, premarital sexual intercourse, if accompanied by love and the intent to marry, tends to be an accepted practice. Somewhere in between these two extremes lies Indiana, with norms more moderate, more variable, and yet somewhat typical of the country of which it is a part.

INCIDENCES OF PREMARITAL CONCEPTION

For any accurate measure of premarital conception, one needs to know three quantities: abortion among the unmarried, both spontaneous and induced; illegitimacy, that is, birth outside of marriage; and the number of weddings that are preceded by pregnancy.[6]

[4] Sydney H. Croog, "Aspects of the Cultural Background of Premarital Pregnancy in Denmark," *Social Forces,* 30 (December, 1951), pp. 215–219.
[5] Kaare Svalastoga, "The Family in Scandinavia," *Marriage and Family Living,* 16 (November, 1954), pp. 374–380; quotation from p. 337.
[6] Strickly speaking, early birth within marriage provides the only available accurate measure of premarital conception. Some unmarried women have abortions and illegitimate births; the term "premarital" hardly describes them. Yet, since it is likely that the majority of such women later get married, no great violence is done in using the concepts in this way. In Denmark, for example, one study has shown that by age six well over half of all children born out of wedlock are then living with their mother who has since been married—in most cases to the child's father. See "Den Familiemaessige Placering af Børn Født For Uden For Aegteskab," *Statistisk Maanedsskrift,* 30 (No. 9, 1954), pp. 193–195.

Unfortunately, there are no available statistics to enable us to make comparisons on the relative numbers of abortions.

With regard to illegitimacy, official statistics for 1955, which are typical of recent years, show the per cent of all births occurring outside of wedlock to be .9 for Utah, 2.9 for Indiana, and 6.6 for Denmark. Thus, in these societies, illegitimacy increases with each advance in the sexual permissiveness of the culture.

Although illegitimacy rates can be obtained from published statistics for whole populations, it has been necessary to conduct sample studies for measures of the premarital conceptions which end in postmarital births.[7] As a consequence, the following analysis relies heavily upon the writer's earlier record linkage studies of Utah County, Utah, and Tippecanoe County, Indiana, and his more recent parallel investigation of Copenhagen, Denmark. The Utah County data were derived by comparing marriages occurring during the years 1905–7, 1913–15, 1921–23, and 1929–31 with birth records for four years following each wedding, in order to find the date of the first birth. This process yielded 1,670 cases. The Tippecanoe County data were derived by taking marriages which occurred during the years 1919–21, 1929–31, and 1939–41, matching them with the birth records searched for five years following the wedding, and finally checking against the divorce records to discover which marriages ended in failure. The result consisted of 1,531 cases involving a first child, with 137 of these cases terminating in divorce. The Copenhagen data were derived by taking every third marriage which occurred during a single year, 1938, eliminating cases involving remarriage and those in which the wife was thirty or more years of age, and then checking both birth and divorce recordings for sixteen years following the wedding. These steps provided a sample of 1,029 cases involving a first child, with 215 ending in divorce.

These samples from three cultures are not, of course, strictly comparable. They were drawn in slightly different ways and have somewhat different compositions. Nevertheless, the contrasts reported below are of sufficient magnitude to suggest at least tentative answers to the problem posed.

From Table 1, it may be observed that the same general pattern holds for this phenomenon as was previously noted for illegitimacy. The six months index, which is a sure minimum measure of premarital conception, makes the clearest comparison. It shows the lowest incidence of premarital pregnancy in Utah, a somewhat higher incidence in Indiana, but a considerably higher incidence in Denmark. The nine months index is less valuable since it includes unknown numbers of postmarital conceptions.[8] The higher rate for Utah than

---

[7] Denmark has published nation-wide statistics on this phenomenon, but the United States has not.

[8] The normal period of uterogestation in human beings is 266 days, or slightly less than nine calendar months. Furthermore, premature births would cause a number of early postmarital conception cases to be included in this index.

TABLE 1. SELECTED INDICES OF PREMARITAL CONCEPTION

	United States		Denmark	
Indices	Utah County, Utah	Tippecanoe County, Indiana	City of Copenhagen	Entire Country
I. Illegitimacy Rate	.9	2.9	11.2	6.6
II. Premarital Conception Rates A. Child Born Within First 6 Months of Marriage	9.0	9.7 (10.0)	24.2 (31.1)	32.9 (34.9)
B. Child Born Within First 9 Months of Marriage	30.9	23.9 (26.1)	30.5 (39.3)	44.3 (48.5)

for Indiana may simply reflect the tendency to earlier postmarital conceptions in Utah.

These findings may be viewed as validation for our earlier labelings. In these cross-cultural comparisons, behavior has been found to be consistent with attitudes; and attitudes *plus behavior* have differentiated Utah and Denmark at opposite ends of a continuum describing premarital sex norms with Indiana in between. An interesting contrast between Copenhagen and the whole of Denmark can be seen by comparing the last two columns of Table 1. Copenhagen shows higher illegitimacy rates than the national figures, but relatively low rates of premarital conception.

ASSOCIATED FACTORS

Not only does the incidence of premarital pregnancy differ from culture to culture, as demonstrated above, but it varies among certain sub-groups within each culture. As shown in Table 2, there are strong and consistent tendencies for premarital conception to be higher with young age at marriage in contrast to the older ages, with a civil wedding in contrast to the religious ceremony, and with a laboring occupation in contrast to the more skilled and professional ways of earning a living. Each of these differences was found to be in the same direction and to be statistically significant for each of the three cultures studied, which is evidence of certain cross-cultural regularities.

Perhaps youth gets into difficulties of this kind because of its lack of sophistication. Furthermore, since premarital pregnancy encourages earlier marriages than couples otherwise would undertake, marriages of this sort are certain to involve more of the younger-aged persons. The disproportionately high premarital pregnancy percentages for persons in the laboring occupations may largely be due to the greater sexual permissiveness found in the lower social classes, plus their relative lack of education. But, whatever the complete

TABLE 2. FACTORS ASSOCIATED WITH PREMARITAL CONCEPTION

| | Per Cent of First Births Premaritally Conceived | | |
| | --- | --- | --- |
Factors	Utah County, Utah	Tippecanoe County, Indiana	Copenhagen, Denmark
Wife's Age at Marriage			
Young Group	14.4	13.2	29.0
Older Group	7.7	5.7	15.1
Type of Ceremony			
Civil	16.6	21.0	37.0
Religious	1.1	9.9	13.5
Husband's Occupation			
Laborer	17.9	16.0	30.0
All Other	8.6	7.2	18.2

explanation, there is the strong suggestion here that broad cultural norms may be to some extent overruled by the operation of other factors.[9]

Effect upon Timing of the Wedding

The tendency to be philosophical about a premarital pregnancy when it happens, so as not to be stampeded into a marriage, seems to be much more characteristic of Denmark than of Indiana or Utah. It is suggested, perhaps, by the higher Danish illegitimacy rates. But even stronger evidence is presented in Figure 1, which has been constructed from estimated dates of conception calculated by counting back 266 days from each date of birth.

Apparently, in Denmark there is little pressure to hurry marriage merely because of pregnancy.[10] In Indiana the tendency is to marry immediately after the pregnancy is definitely known so as to hide the fact from the public. Couples who have premarital sexual intercourse in Utah, on the other hand, seem to hurry marriage because of that fact alone, without waiting for pregnancy to force them into it (religious guilt is a sufficient sanction once the "law of chastity" has been broken).[11]

[9] Of course, these factors also have cultural content, but they—and possibly many others—seem not to be confined by the limits of an area or a society; hence the suggestion of cross-cultural regularities.

[10] In attempting to explain this situation to the writer, several Danish scholars have pointed to the current great housing shortage in Copenhagen—which means waiting for a place to live, thereby discouraging any rush into marriage. When reminded that the figures used here are for 1938 marriages, however, these observers were quick to admit that the argument doesn't apply, since there was little housing shortage then.

[11] Although this latter explanation is speculative, it is plausible. Chastity is so stressed in Mormon culture that the religiously oriented offender may panic and try to ease his conscience by getting married.

As Kinsey has pointed out, "The psychologic significance of any type of sexual activity very largely depends upon what the individual and his social group choose to make of it." [12] Since in Danish culture there is less stigma placed on premarital conception and on illegitimacy than in Indiana, and especially in Utah, the differences in timing pattern for the wedding once pregnancy has occurred may be explained in cultural terms.

Effects upon the Divorce Rate

This type of explanation may also apply to possible variations in divorce rate differentials of premarital pregnancy *versus* postmarital pregnancy cases. We would hypothesize that the more liberal the culture the *less* likely is premarital pregnancy to be followed by divorce. This hypothesis is tested with data from the Indiana and Danish samples.

For Tippecanoe County, it has been reported earlier that the divorce rate is significantly higher for premarital than postmarital pregnancy couples. For marriages occurring in Copenhagen during 1948, Holm has shown that, with age controlled, the divorce rate is not significantly different for couples bearing a child within the first nine months of marriage than for all other cases. At first glance, this seems to bear out our hypothesis.

TABLE 3. DIVORCE RATE COMPARISONS BY INTERVAL TO FIRST BIRTH
(for births occurring within 5 years of the wedding)

Classification	Copenhagen, Denmark			Tippecanoe County, Indiana		
	Number of Cases	Number Divorced	Per Cent Divorced	Number of Cases	Number Divorced	Per Cent Divorced
Interval Between Marriage and First Birth						
(1) 0–139 days (premarital pregnancy, marriage delayed)	176	60	34.1	71	14	19.7
(2) 140–265 days (premarital pregnancy, marriage hurried)	129	31	24.0	276	39	14.1
(3) 266 days–4.99 years (postmarital pregnancy)	572	111	19.4	1184	84	7.1
Percentage Difference Between Divorce Rates						
(4) Between lines 2 and 1			42.1			39.7
(5) Between lines 3 and 2			23.7			98.6

---

[12] Kinsey, *op. cit.*, p. 320.

It is to be noted, however, that Holm did not compare premarital pregnancy cases with postmarital pregnancy cases, as was done for Tippecanoe County, but rather with all non-premarital pregnancy cases, including childless couples. Since those who become divorced are less likely to have children than those who do not,[13] the inclusion of childless cases in the non-premarital pregnancy category would raise the divorce rate for that category and, in this way, would obscure the true comparison. What is needed is a comparison between divorce rates of premarital and postmarital pregnancy cases; for unless non-conceivers are excluded, it is impossible to determine the effects of conception timing.

Table 3 is designed to compare the Copenhagen and Tippecanoe County samples concerning possible effects of premarital and postmarital pregnancy upon the divorce rate. As noted above, these two samples are not strictly comparable, but they are approximately so.[14] It seems probable that the following generalizations are at least tentatively justified:

(1) In both populations there is the clear tendency for the divorce rate to fall as the length of interval between marriage and first birth increases. This means that premarital pregnancy cases are more likely to end in divorce than are postmarital pregnancy cases,[15] and that those premarital pregnancy couples who delay marriage for a considerable time after the knowledge of pregnancy have the highest divorce rate of all—in Denmark as well as Indiana.

(2) The *relative* difference in divorce rate between premarital pregnancy couples who hurried marriage and those who delayed it is essentially the same

[13] In the writer's Copenhagen sample of 1938 marriages, for example, 57.0 per cent of the childless marriages ended in divorce or separation as compared with 20.9 per cent of the fertile marriages. A primary explanation for this differential is that many of the divorces occur relatively soon after the wedding, before the couple has decided to start a family.

[14] See descriptions of the two samples, above. Calculations for Table 3 are based uniformly on cases having a first child born within five years of the wedding. Although absolute divorce rates cannot be compared across the two samples—since they would be influenced in distinctive ways by differential emigration and differential lengths of time of exposure to the divorce possibility—there seems to be no good reason why the *relative* rates by pregnancy timing cannot be compared.

[15] There is an interesting parallel finding from the Copenhagen data: marriages in which the wife had borne an illegitimate child previously showed a divorce rate of 45.7, as compared with 20.9 for childbearing marriages where she had not. A partial explanation, of course, may be that a selective factor is operating, which may mean that the least stable personalities are the ones most likely to become pregnant before marriage and also to be divorced later. But another possibility is that, through such things as resentment about the necessity to marry, guilt feelings, and poor preparation and unsuitable personality matching because of a hasty or pressured marriage, the premarital pregnancy may itself help to bring about divorce. In the Tippecanoe County study, the writer controlled other divorce-producing factors, through matching, and still found premarital pregnancy to be significantly associated with high divorce; see Christensen and Meissner, *loc. cit.*

for both populations. Thus, Copenhagen figures show a 42.1 per cent difference between these two rates as compared with a difference of 39.7 per cent in Tippecanoe County, an intersample difference that is not significant.

The facts that both samples show substantially higher divorce rates for couples who delay marriage after knowledge of pregnancy and that the differentials in this respect are about the same in the two cultures suggest universal tendencies for certain pregnant couples to marry under the pressure of social responsibility (for example, sympathy for the lover, consideration for the future child, or parental influence). The data also suggest that, statistically speaking, such "shot gun" marriages do not turn out well.

(3) The *relative* difference in divorce rate between postmarital pregnancy couples and the premarital couples who married soon after the discovery of pregnancy is four times greater in the Indiana sample (98.6 per cent compared with 23.7 per cent), an intersample difference that by some tests is statistically significant.

The fact that the postmarital pregnancy divorce rate is lower in both cultures is evidence that premarital pregnancy—even when associated with an early wedding—tends generally to make marriage's survival chances less than even. This may be because some marriages take place under pressure from others and are therefore accompanied by resentment, or because in their haste to escape public scorn the couple marries without adequate preparation, or in the absence of love, or in the face of ill-matched personalities. But the fact that the postmarital-premarital pregnancy divorce rate differential is substantially less in Denmark, gives strong support to our hypothesis. It seems probable that in Denmark, where sexual relations outside of marriage are more or less accepted, premarital pregnancy will have less negative effect upon marriage than in Indiana, where it is expected that sexual intercourse and pregnancy be confined to marriage.

SUMMARY AND THEORY

Premarital sex norms in Utah, Indiana, and Denmark stand in sharp contrast—with Utah being very conservative or restrictive, and Denmark being extremely liberal or permissive. As might be expected, therefore, premarital pregnancy rates were found to be lowest in the Utah sample and highest in the Danish sample, with the difference being considerable. Furthermore, certain consequences of premarital pregnancy were found to vary from culture to culture. Thus permissive Denmark, at the time of the study, showed the longest delay between premarital conception and the wedding, and the smallest divorce rate differential between premarital pregnancy and postmarital pregnancy cases.[16] In all three cultures the same factors were associated with premarital pregnancy: namely, young age at marriage, a civil wedding, and a laboring occupation.

In some respects our data give support to the idea of cultural relativism. It has been shown that both the rates and effects of premarital pregnancy are to a considerable extent relative to the cultures involved. The most liberal culture was found to have the most premarital pregnancy, but also the least negative effects therefrom; in Denmark there is less pressure than in the American cases either to speed up the wedding or to resort to divorce when premarital pregnancy occurs. Thus, the relationship is not simply a matter of how premarital pregnancy affects subsequent behavior, considered in a vacuum, but rather how it affects this behavior in the light of particular norms. Cultural norms represent an intervening variable.

But there are also *regularities* among the cultures studied. In all of them, pregnancy usually takes place within marriage. In all of them also, premarital pregnancy is found to be associated with young age, a civil wedding, and a laboring occupation. Finally, the Indiana-Denmark comparisons reveal a parallel phenomenon of higher divorce rates for premarital pregnancy than for postmarital pregnancy cases. These rates are especially high, and in similar magnitude within both cultures, for couples who delay marriage until just before the child is born. Forced marriage, in other words, seems to work against marital success regardless of the culture. All of this suggests the existence of certain universals which are to some extent independent of the cultural variable.

The present analysis is concerned with *inter*cultural comparisons. The next step is to see if the theory applies to the *intra*cultural level, that is, when interpersonal differences are taken into account. We hypothesize both regularity and variability at that level also, with personal values having very much the same effects as cultural norms are found to have in this report.

[16] As noted above, divorce rate comparison does not include the Utah sample since data were not available. It is believed, however, that the Utah divorce rate differential (between premarital and postmarital pregnancy cases) probably is the greatest of the three areas—because premarital sexual intimacy is most strongly condemned there.

This unestablished assumption can be argued by an analogy. The drinking of alcoholic beverage is also strongly condemned in Utah (and in the rest of Mormon culture). Research shows that Mormon college students have the lowest incidence of drinking among religious groups, but that, of the drinkers, Mormon students have a very high rate of alcoholism. This suggests that cultural restrictions can lower the incidence of the condemned practice, but that for those who indulge, the negative effects are apt to be extreme. Cf. Robert Strauss and Selden D. Bacon, *Drinking in College,* New Haven: Yale University Press, 1953, *passim*.

8. ISLAM AND SOCIALISM
mirza m. hussain

The author of the following piece is a most articulate Moslem theologian. In line with our discussion of cultural relativism, he argues convincingly that Islamic sexual norms are not only different from those of the West, but also that they are more practical both in terms of health and morals. Do you agree? Can you justify your answer in scientific terms? Moral terms?

It is the most conspicuous characteristic of the European writers that they throw mud at any and every social scheme superior to their own, thinking that some of it would stick. Many a broad joke is cracked against Islam. Many venomous shafts are hurled at its Holy Founder. Puny pens are dipped in gall to portray Islamic society in dark and sombre colors. With what effect? Every dispassionate student of Islam knows. All charges fall off as water off the duck's back. Time and again, those who volunteer to defend Islam, have to deplore the critics' inconvenient habit of pointing to a mote in another's eye, but complacently forgetting a beam in their own. When anyone even of their own flesh and blood stands forth and says that the only man to appraise sex truly and honestly and equipoise men and women in the social framework and anticipate and provide for all pre-marital and post-marital problems, and thus stave off all sexual catastrophes by a superb code of law was Muhammad (peace and blessings of God be upon him), the self-obsessed Westerners stand aghast and feel frustrated at this challenge to their ill-imagined primacy. Failing to stand up to it they even go into paroxysm of pain at this unstinted testimony to the excellence of Islam as a perfect social polity. . . .

But Islam delved deep into the core of the problem. It did not shirk any hostile reaction. Mutual relations between males and females were properly adjusted. It did not pursue a lop-sided policy of unduly favoring one sex at the cost of the other. It is the crowning glory of Islam that it came to grips with the sex problem, and made humanity safe against moral chaos. One institution responsible for the health of Muslim society in the heyday of its glory was *purdah*. There were no moral lapses, no scandals, no misbehaviors, because the two sexes were kept apart in a wholesome isolation. Even in the one and the same family, the members of both the sexes unless they were husband and wife were expected to avoid indecent intimacy and immodest promiscuity. . . .

From Mirza M. Hussain, *Islam and Socialism*, Lahore, Pakistan: Muhammad Ashraf, 1947. By permission of the publisher.

It is an unabashed lie that a Muslim woman is consigned to the gloom of the four walls of her house and that an open air is a forbidden fruit, which she cannot taste without defying the Islamic injunction of *purdah*. Muslim women can leave their homes when an occasion for it arises. They can avail themselves of all the opportunities of physical and intellectual growth which the outside world holds for them. They can go for a walk. They can accompany their own male guardians in their pleasure jaunts. They can even travel alone. They can go to mosques. They can attend and convene meetings; hold debates and discuss questions of the day. They can accompany their husbands to the battle-fronts. But all their movements in the out-of-doors life must not infringe the spirit of the Islamic injunctions which abhor indecent behavior and disallow the type of freedom which has wrecked social life in the Western countries. These restraints have for their object "the promotion of decency among women, the improvement of their dress and demeanor and their protection from insult." In its scrupulous attention to female modesty and its supreme care to avoid every act which tends to injure it, the Holy Quran says:

> And stay quietly in your houses and make not a dazzling display like that of the former times of Ignorance.   (33:33)

> And that they should not strike their feet in order to draw attention to their hidden ornaments.   (24:31)

> Be not too complaisant of speech, lest one in whose heart is a disease should be moved with desire.   (33:32)

In the first instance, women are exhorted to keep indoors with dignity. If at all they come out, they should remain self-contained and self-restrained, solemn and serious and avoid stilted swinging gait which characterized women in the pre-Islamic period. The dress should be plain and simple, otherwise it will invite hungry gazes from every quarter. There should also be no tinkling ornaments because the prescribed veil can at best conceal sight only and not sound. Jingling ornaments are a taboo, because they betray the woman and defeat the ends of the *purdah* injunctions. Even in her conversation with a stranger a Muslim woman must be very modest and speak in a lower key. The depravity of morals which has undermined the foundations of the modern society calls for immediate correction. What correction can be quicker in effect and more adequate in scope than the Quranic injunction of the privacy of women and their dignified aloofness from the hurly-burly of political life. . . .

The foregoing discussion amply proves that *purdah* is neither very stringent nor lax. It is moderate. It imposes healthy restraints on contacts between men and women. It is both of sight and sound and, in short, of all those parts and motions which provoke low passions. Those "progressives" who are loth to go to this length betray their ignorance of the psychological implications of *purdah* as an effective remedy against the insidious virus of sex-immorality. Mr. A. A. Brill in his illuminating essay on *Sexuality and Its Role in the Neurosis* writes that touching, looking, tasting, smelling and exhibiting yield symbolic sexual gratification. There are individuals who can get an outlet by these means. They are designated in the literature as toucheurs, voyeurs (peepers) and pinchers (sadists). In the course of his essay, Mr. Brill says he could report a number of cases whose fixed outlets could only be attained through kissing, and to whom genital approximation was not only not desirable, but even abhorrent.

Sympathy, shame, modesty, disgust and morality are the cultural dams which not only hold in check the flood of sexual impulses, but also enable the individual to sublimate them for aims other than sexual. The wire-drawn, subtle interpretations of the *purdah* regulations of some Westernized "radicals" to exclude the face from the prescribed veil crumble before the astounding discoveries of the psychoanalysts, who have proved that the sense of smell is still active in the sexual life of the modern man. In 1890 Fliess discovered *"sexualstellen"*—sexual spots in the nose, which he proved to have a direct connection with sexual functioning in painful menstruation. Fliess would cocainize those spots in the nose and the pain would cease. There is ample literature on the subject. May it be said to the credit of the American investigators that they have made valuable contributions. Whether we realize it or not, all the senses play a part in the sex instinct. The face which starts most impulses and is also highly sensitive to external objects cannot be left out of *purdah* without leaving a dangerous loophole in the whole institution. Mr. A. A. Brill quite aptly remarks, "Behind the surface, the sexual emotions are in full blast, a fact which is readily seen by any observer." The only way to prevent their volcanic eruptions is to minimize contacts between men and women and put their respective behavior in the strait jacket of chastity. Islam has accomplished this social reform through the institution of *purdah* which is designed mainly to ensure sexual purity in society.

Left to itself, sex is like Mazepa's horse, untamed and untamable. It must needs be bridled and blinkered by moral restraints and saddled with social responsibilities to harness its vast energy to the welfare of society. *Purdah* is some such scheme to accomplish this task. Its traducers travesty it to make it look inhuman and barbarous. The classical charges invariably levelled against it are:

1. It injures the health of women by consigning and confining them to the four walls of the home.

2. It induces morbid introversion in *purdah*-observing women who for sheer want of healthy diversions are constantly lost in prurient thoughts.

3. It prevents a right choice of a life-partner and thus paves the way for domestic distress and dislocation, as the ill-matched pair must always be at loggerheads.

These stock charges cannot stand a moment's scrutiny. They envisage some evils, which must vitiate the Muslim homes and, as a necessary corollary, they must be conspicuous by their absence in the homes of peoples who abhor *purdah* and impose no limitations on their women-folk. But even a tyro knows that it is not so.

I deal with these charges categorically to expose their obvious fallacy. Under the first charge of ill-health as the concomitant evil of *purdah,* the onus of proving that the Muslim women have comparatively weaker physiques lies on the critics. But they have never been able and will never be able to support their contention by a reference to the vital statistics of the Muslim and non-Muslim countries. Who can say that a Muslim woman is weaker than a Hindu or Christian woman! The matter does end here. Weak mothers mean weak children. This chain of cause and effect should inevitably lead to the devitalization of the whole nation which swears by *purdah* as a great social institution. If the isolation of women from the throngs of men and their consequent abstention from the taxing tasks of the outside world must undermine their health, the Muslim people should, in the course of fourteen centuries, have been extinct or should have been near about vanishing point. But the truth is the other way round. Muslims all the world over are known for their warlike qualities, heroic demeanor and physical prowess which can never be found in a race set on the road to physical decay. The Muslims can give point to sturdier races in physique and bravery. How could they be stout and sturdy, brave and gallant, if their mothers had been victims of ill-health born of *purdah?* It is an open secret that an average Muslim home is blessed with radiant motherhood. Here in India, no one can gainsay the fact that Muslims are stronger and healthier than their compatriots who do not observe *purdah* in their homes. It, therefore, stands to reason that infant mortality is less among Muslims than in others. Or at least the detractors of *purdah* should produce data to prove that it is not so and also link up the alleged higher morality with the so-called pernicious practice of *purdah.* Mortality in India is terrific. But it is due to economic poverty. As such it afflicts every other section of population besides Muslims.

Those who labor the charge of poor health as the outcome of *purdah,* miss the basic fact of the biological tragedy of a woman. They conveniently forget that a normal woman's physique is delicate and is best preserved in the congenial atmosphere of happy domesticity. Nature wants her to be tender and soft and not tough and rough. The crown and climax of womanhood lies in being wife and mother. She does not gain in health if she tears herself from the hearth-stone and cradle and exposes herself to the heat and burden of the market-place. This busybodying with the male functions destroys her muliebrity and reduces her fitness for the discharge of the sacred tasks of a wife and a mother. A virile woman is a contradiction in terms. A women who does not observe "splendid isolation" from the rugged and toughening tasks of the outdoor life will eventually undermine her mental and bodily aptitude for bearing and rearing children. The conception of a woman's health is diagonally opposite from that of man's health. This difference arises from the dissimilarity of the tasks assigned to them by Nature. A stout and sturdy woman whom we often meet in the street and stadium, is a mannish woman, and not a healthy woman. Muscular toughness impairs and not improves her maternal efficiency. Thus *purdah* is a helpful device to save a woman from the deleterious effects of the toil and tumult which attend a man's life. It preserves her natural delicacy, tenderness and geniality and thus conduces to her wifely and motherly virtues. It demarcates her sphere of work from that of a man and avoids mutual rivalry which has wrecked social life in the West. It is a false notion of equality to bracket man and woman in every walk of life regardless of their natural differences. The West has paid heavily for ignoring this in the form of ruined homes and the pestilential growth of sexual vices.

The second charge that a *purdah*-observing woman is prurient-minded is baseless. Lost in her domestic duties from daylight to candle-light and from candle-light to dawn, a woman in *purdah* is more immune against sex-obsession than the one who rambles on the road-side. There is no distracting atmosphere at home. The all-absorbing thought of the domestic well-being leaves her little time to indulge in sensual reveries. On the other hand, a woman who gads about on the road is exposed to irresistible temptations and is incapable of maintaining her mental poise and serenity. The possibility of her going off the rails is much greater than the one who reigns over her domestic domain and is constantly engaged in the performance of her household duties. Those who indict *purdah* on this second count lay themselves open to the charge of barking up the wrong tree. The horrible state of moral depravity prevalent in the West is a clear and convincing rebuttal of the charge against sex-segregation as a menace to a woman's chastity. Some insight into what has overtaken the West as a result of the indiscriminate intermingling of sexes may be gained by a reference to the report on the moral welfare work presented to the Diocesan Conference of the Church of England. The authors of the report, 1946, say, "At least one in every eight children born in England and Wales is conceived outside wedlock. One hundred thousand women in England and Wales are becoming pregnant outside of marriage every year and of all the children born, at least one in eight is conceived outside marriage. Of all girls who marry under 20 years of age, no less than 40 per cent are already pregnant on their wedding day." These grisly figures betray the delirious display of lust and passion. They indicate that the *homo-sapien* in the West lives on no higher plane than that of the anthropoid apes. Divorced from the primrose path of domestic duties and female functions, young women are being tossed like a derelict bark on the turbulent waters of sex-impulse. Even the vast use of contraceptives and other sundry birth-control contrivances have totally failed to camouflage the havoc wrought by the uncontrolled dragon of sex. All the scientific researches and the ameliorative devices have gone down the laboratory sink. The Western mind is at the end of its tether. It has failed to find a way out of the impasse of its own creation. The world of science and art, which it created for itself, is not only being liquidated, but is going clean out of existence leaving not a wrack behind. Sex-ridden and sex-driven as the West is, it is like a car with a defective brake running down-hill. Uncontrolled and uncurbed sex is like a violent fever which keeps the sufferer tossing and tumbling in his bed. The figures of unmarried mothers given above give one an idea of the terrible shape of things to come. The only antidote for this excessive sexuality is to segregate sexes to their respective spheres. *Purdah* is designed to achieve this ideal state.

The third count in the indictment of *purdah* is the absence of a reasonable facility for the choice of a suitable spouse. This again is based on a serious misapprehension and is belied by the experience of the West itself. There men and women meet freely and enter the "holy" state of matrimony at their own sweet will. Their liberty to choose their life-partners is not "marred" by sex-segregation of any kind. This should have enabled the West to present a gladdening spectacle of happy homes. There should have been no divorces or their number should have been negligible. But it is an open secret that in the Western countries domestic failures culminating in scandalous separations are much greater than are to be met with in the Muslim countries, where promiscuous intermingling of sexes is regarded with extreme disfavor. A passing glance at the divorce figures of some Western countries will substantiate my contention. In 1905, 68,000 couples were involved in divorce in the United States. In 1924, the number rose to 170,867. In the U. S. A. in 1924, every seventh marriage was dissolved by divorce. The ratio in France was 21 to 1; in Germany 24 to 1; in Switzerland 10 to 3; in Norway 30 to 1; in Great Britain 96 to 1; and in Canada 161 to 1. No doubt these figures relate to the "twenties." But as they relate to a normal period, they have not been falsified by the later developments. The moral decay which still continues unabated, has only augmented these figures. It is thus clear that the freedom of the choice of a spouse is no sure guarantee for happy wedlocks. It is foolish to put premium on juvenile sanity and to credit the "hot-bloods" with the capacity for cool thinking and dispassionate appraisement of their spouses' merits. When young people come into contact, they may scan the facial charms in a minute's stare, but they cannot size up the mind and heart and soul behind a handsome face. Hence the passion which is inflamed by a fair complexion or almond and gazelle eyes or a shapely nose or dark curly hair is often like a fire of straw. It is soon kindled, but it also soon dies out. Thus a marriage based on love at first sight is false and fickle, futile and frivolous. Left to themselves, the young folk cannot do better than this. Hence these love or companionate marriages drive the infatuated, maddened couple to commit dreadful crimes. The existence of *purdah* leaves no occasion for romantic contacts. The marital ties are arranged through the parents. Sobered with their own experiences, the parents' choice is certainly more sagacious and the resultant marriages are happier because more secure and stable than those contracted independently by the young couples. This is why the divorce figures in the Muslim countries are smaller. Thus the third count against the Islamic institution of *purdah* also does not rest on any reliable data.

The hostility against *purdah* springs from the nauseating notion of equality in every sphere of life. Equality in the enjoyment of human rights is not prejudiced by confining a woman to the tasks which her sex determines for her. It is sheer mercy that *purdah* lets her have her being as a "feminine woman" and enables her to grow to the full height of her real personality. Women celebrated for valiant performances, political acumen and vast erudition neglect and forget the functions of their own sex and invade the sphere of a man's privileges. A woman endeavoring to wield the club of Hercules outrages her sex and is no more pardonable than a man for endeavoring to twirl her distaff. They both ridicule their sex by this most unnatural nonsense. Rousseau spoke the truth when he observed, "The dignity of woman consists in being unknown to the world. Her glory is the esteem of her husband; her pleasure the happiness of her family." It is often said that *purdah* means solitary imprisonment and deprives a woman of recreation in the open air. It is a fabricated fable. *Purdah* does not signify anything of the kind. It does not deny sunshine and open air to woman. It permits every such diversion which conduces to her health. But it certainly forbids every such entertainment or recreation which crucifies her sex and robs her of her modesty and gentleness. Men naturally like in women what is opposite their own characters. When a woman develops manly qualities, she only works herself out of her husband's favors. This ruins the family life which is the pivot of civilization. Colton quite correctly observes:

> Recreation or pleasure is to a woman what the sun is to the flower; if moderately enjoyed, it beautifies, it refreshes and improves; if immoderately, it withers, deteriorates and destroys. But the duties of domestic life, exercized as they must be, in retirement, and calling forth all the sensibilities of the female, are, perhaps, as necessary to the full development of her charms, as the shades and shadows are to the rose; confirming its beauty, and increasing its fragrance.

Thus *purdah* is a device to delimit the respective spheres of both the sexes and avoid their collision. It is an errant nonsense to regard it as a negation of human equality. Islam grants woman a right to inheritance and divorce as it does to man. If her legal share in the inheritance is not equal to that of man, it argues no male superiority. . . .

9. A THEORY OF SOCIAL
INTEGRATION

peter m. blau

The preceding selections have introduced the concept of cultural relativism. With the present selection we begin an examination of the
processes by which a society molds or socializes individuals into its
image.

In the following selection, Professor Blau describes the manner in
which the behavior of individuals is shaped by their desire to appeal to
and win acceptance by other members of society.

Essential Vocabulary

ego: The individual.
alter: The person that the ego is seeking to win.
alter ego (s):   Other individual (s) in competition with ego for the favors
of alter.

. . . There are a number of factors that make a person attractive to others.
If he has high social status in the society at large, they are likely to find him
more attractive than if his social status is low. If his values and theirs are
similar, they are more likely to enjoy association with him and to be interested in having him as a companion. If the personality needs he expresses in
social interaction are complementary to their needs, they may derive some
special gratification from him that draws them to him. In general, if a person's
qualities are valued by the other members of the group, he will tend to be
attractive to them. However, every individual has a large repertory of qualities,
and which of these find expression in his conduct in a given group is, of course,
not a matter of chance.

A person who is motivated to attain an integrated position in a group has
strong incentives not simply to wait until the others discover his good qualities
but to exert effort to prove himself an attractive associate. He will try to
impress them. This involves, essentially, revealing characteristics that he
assumes to be positively valued by the others and concealing those he expects
to be negatively valued. Goffman's perceptive discussion of this strategy of
"impression management," as he calls it, shows in detail how people seek to
control the image they present in social situations and thus the impressions

they make. Creating an impressive image of one's self is a complicated process. When one enters a group, he must infer from the few immediately available clues what the values of the others are, predict on the basis of this inference which of his qualities would make a favorable impression, and adapt his conduct accordingly. Moreover, his very concern with making a good impression is likely to interfere with his ability to do so, unless it remains below the threshold of his full awareness as well as theirs. If they suspect him of deliberately putting up a front, they will not consider his behavior a reliable indication of his actual qualities but will instead discount it, and he will have made an unfavorable impression. And if he becomes too self-conscious about putting his best foot forward, he is likely to trip over his own feet and thus make a poor impression. Creating a good first impression is a subtle form of bragging, but its success depends on its being so subtle that it does not appear to be bragging at all.

Despite these pitfalls and difficulties, many people do manage to create a good impression. Even the fact that one does so, however, is not sufficient for him to become integrated with the other members of the group. It is important in this connection to distinguish between feeling attracted to a person and acting upon the feeling by seeking to associate with him. If a person has impressed others with his outstanding qualities, they will feel attracted to him. But in a group situation other feelings and expectations will arise that prevent them from giving expression to their feeling of attraction in social interaction.

REACTIONS TO BEING IMPRESSED

Paradoxically, the more attractive a person's impressive qualities make him appear to the others in a group, the more reluctant will they be, at least initially, to approach him freely and to draw him into friendly social intercourse. There are several reasons for this. Attraction to an individual makes us vulnerable and creates a need for defenses. If we are not interested in associating with somebody and do so only as the occasion demands it, he cannot hurt us by rejecting us; but, if we find him attractive, his possible rejection poses a threat against which we shall try to protect ourselves by resisting the temptation to make overtures to him. Indeed, this fear of being rejected by one who has demonstrated his impressive qualities is quite realistic. We are most impressed by qualities that are superior to our own and to those we usually encounter. Given this comparative frame of reference, a person whose qualities impress us is unlikely to find ours impressive. In a social situation, moreover, where many of us have been impressed by him and feel attracted to him, he is in a position to choose among a large pool of available companions, and this increases the chances that any one of us will be rejected. Hence the first reaction to being impressed is a defensive reluctance to initiate social contacts for fear of rejection.

It now becomes necessary to dispense with the fiction that there is *one* person who tries to impress the other members of the group. Actually, of course, every member wants to make a favorable impression on the others, particularly (but not only) in new groups. Indeed, every member has three formal roles in this interaction: first, each member is ego, the person who seeks to impress others; second, each member is alter, one of the others to whom ego wants to become attractive; third, each member is also alter ego, one of the individuals with whom ego competes for the attraction of alters.

Since it can be assumed that everybody likes to be popular among his peers, the members of a group compete *with* one another for being highly attractive *to* one another. The more successful ego is in impressing others in their role as alter with his outstanding qualities, the more will he antagonize them in their role as alter ego, because his impressive qualities threaten their popularity in the group. In contrast to economic markets, where a firm's competitors are distinct from its customers (other firms which sell the same product are generally not its customers), a group member's competitors are identical with the "customers" whose output of attraction is the object of the competition for popularity. Every member has an interest in withholding evidence of his attraction to others, since manifestations of it would give them a competitive advantage over him by contributing to their popularity. The reluctance freely to express attraction to others in the group is not merely a psychological defense mechanism but a strategic weapon in the competition for popularity.

The structural constraints of the competitive context reinforce the defensive tendencies toward which fear of rejection predisposes the members of groups. Each individual is interested not only in suppressing his attraction to another but also in defending his standing in the group by preventing the others from becoming too attracted to that person. Once we have convinced ourselves that a person is not so attractive as he appears, we will convey this opinion to others, for example, by ostentatiously turning away while he tells a story, thereby raising doubts in their minds about his attractiveness. Since the best defense is an offense, defensive tactics merge with the strategy of creating a good impression. An individual may shift the conversation from a topic on which another person has an opportunity to be impressive to one on which he has. He may even take advantage of the fact that the others, too, are threatened by a person who appears to be very impressive and try to make him look ridiculous. This, if successful, is a most effective strategy; it means impressing others by doing what they wanted to have done but did not quite dare to do themselves. It is often possible to deflate the image a person has presented of himself because the competitive situation encourages group members to present inflated images.

Why do people feel attracted to a person who has impressed them with his superior qualities? The answer is probably that his qualities raise in them the expectation that they will benefit from associating with him. In a work group they may look forward to being advised by such a competent colleague; at a party, to being entertained by such an amusing companion; and, in any situation, to being seen in such distinguished company. By creating a favorable impression, therefore, a person implicitly promises others that they will benefit from associating with him. To be sure, he can live on credit for a while, because it would be a breach of etiquette to make demands on him too quickly. But, as long as the impressions he has created is all the others have to go by, he does live on credit. An impostor is an individual who is skilled in extending his credit far beyond his resources. Deliberate deception, however, is merely the extreme case of a much more common phenomenon, namely, the misrepresentations typically made by those who are anxious to make a good impression.

When we make inferences from the impression a person creates, we are not so much interested in simple facts as in evaluations, for example, not in how many years he has played the piano but whether he plays it well. Thus we expect a person to present an evaluation rather than a mere factual description of himself in social interaction. Of course, an individual can hardly be completely objective in evaluating his own qualities. If he must compete with others to prove his attractiveness, he is under particularly strong pressures to present too high an evaluation of himself, creating an impression that raises expectations which he will not be able to live up to. In sum, competition for popularity constrains members of a group to present an inflated image of themselves which exposes them to ridicule and embarrassment, on the one hand, and to take advantage of one another's weaknesses rather than express feelings of attraction and support, on the other.

If such competitive processes were to prevail, the group would undoubtedly disintegrate. The crucial theoretical point is that, although a person's integration in a group depends on his being attractive to the others, the social processes generated by pervasive concern with making a good impression create an impasse that makes social integration impossible. What prevents disintegration and promotes cohesiveness is the tendency of group members *not* to remain preoccupied with appearing impressive but to redirect their efforts to cope with the problems posed by the impending impasse.

The very characteristics of a group member that impress others also make him appear unapproachable to them. His superior qualities, which make associating with him inviting, also raise doubts in the minds of others as to whether he will find them attractive associates and threaten their own standing in the group; and these doubts and threats give rise to defensive tactics. Unless he can break through these defenses, he will not be able to achieve an integrated position in the group.

An important method for penetrating the defense of other group members (but not the only method, as will be seen presently) is for a person to demonstrate that, even though he has attractive qualities, as he has already shown, he is quite easily approachable. Completely reversing his earlier strategy of presenting only the most impressive parts of his self, he now flaunts his weaknesses. Having first impressed us with his Harvard accent and Beacon Hill friends, he may tell a story that reveals his immigrant background. After having talked only of the successes he has enjoyed in his career, he may let us in on the defeats he has suffered. Having earlier carefully protected himself against ridicule or even made jokes at the expense of others, he may relate an incident that makes us laugh at, as well as with, him. Whatever the content of his remarks, they show him as a person willing to admit his shortcomings. (Situations where a modicum of social integration must be achieved quickly, such as parties, furnish good illustrations of such changes in strategy from creating an impression to demonstrating approachability.)

Such self-deprecating modesty is disarming—literally so, since it obviates the need for defenses. As the listeners sympathize with a person's troubles or smile at his blunders, they will feel drawn to him, because he ceases to be a threat against which they have to protect themselves. By calling attention to his weaknesses and demonstrating his approachability, a person gives public notice that he withdraws from the competition for superior standing in the group and that all he wants to accomplish with his attractive qualities is to win full acceptance as a peer. Self-deprecation thus removes the threat his attractiveness has posed for the other members and induces them to act upon their feeling of attraction to him by engaging him in social intercourse. It serves, consequently, the function of contributing to social integration.

When a member surrenders his claim to superior standing in the group, he invites others to follow his example; and, the more members who do so, the easier it becomes for the rest to do likewise. The first person at a gathering who relates how he once committed a terrible *faux pas* makes a self-deprecating statement. His admission may well encourage others to talk about social blunders they have made. Once most members of the group have reported such incidents, for still another to tell about his *faux pas* is not so much self-deprecation as an attempt to establish a link with the rest. If members of a group are characterized by similar experiences or attributes, particularly if these set them apart from the majority in the community, this is a common bond. After one has discovered the characteristics of most of the others, he can link himself to them by indicating that he shares some of these characteristics, for example, that his ethnic background is the same as theirs. Establishing such links is a substitute for self-deprecation, for it also serves to show that an individual does not seek superior standing but only acceptance as a peer. Each member's demonstration that he considers himself no better than the rest and merely seeks acceptance as an equal makes it easier for the others to let their hair down, too, and these social processes promote mutual attraction and group cohesiveness.

The question arises whether self-deprecation may not have social consequences which are the very opposite of those here ascribed to it. Do we not often react to ostentatious modesty with embarrassment rather than with warmth and acceptance? Indeed, we do, but only under certain conditions. If a person whose qualities we admire modestly admits to some shortcomings, this will increase our liking for him and not cause us discomfort. But if a person whom we do not find attractive insists on revealing his shortcomings, the chances are that we shall be embarrassed; for his exhibition of modesty is a claim for acceptance which our failure to be attracted to him prevents us from honoring, and, when the expectations of one person are not fulfilled by others, embarrassment arises, as Goffman points out. Self-deprecating modesty does not make one attractive, it merely activates already existing feelings of attraction by reducing the reluctance to express them. Therefore, unless the weaknesses a person admits are less salient qualities than those with which he has impressed others, he will not have demonstrated that he is approachable as well as attractive but, instead, will have provided evidence that he is, all things considered, really unattractive.

The main thesis advanced here is that, for a person to become fully accepted and integrated in a group, he must prove himself not only attractive but also approachable. Impressive qualities that make a person attractive simultaneously discourage others from freely approaching and accepting him. Concern with winning acceptance in a peer group, therefore, puts an individual under pressure to shift his strategy from impressing others to demonstrating his approachability. These strategies are beautifully illustrated in *Brideshead Revisited,* where the speaker describes his wife as adept in "first impressing the impressionable with her chic and my celebrity and, superiority once firmly established, changing quickly to a pose of almost flirtatious affability."

It is, of course, not possible to present empirical tests of all the hypotheses implied by the above theory. Even quite limited empirical checks, however, serve to curb fruitless speculation and clarify conflicting assumptions. A theory according to which a given variable may have contradictory consequences may be suspected of making unscientific assumptions that are inherently untestable. Thus the conception that a mother's unconscious rejection of her child may find expression either in overt rejection or, through reaction-formation, in strong attachment is, without further qualification, intrinsically untestable. The same is true of the notion that the socioeconomic position of a class manifests itself either in class-consciousness or in the very opposite—false consciousness. The statement that outstanding qualities make a person more attractive to others (thus increasing his chances of integration) and less approachable (thus decreasing these chances) is equally meaningless without further specification, since it predicts both a direct and an inverse correlation between superior qualities and social integration.

It is possible, however, to derive a more precise inference from the theory. If group members are classified on the basis of two attributes, common sense would lead us to expect that those with two positive qualities have the greatest chance of being accepted by their peers, and those with two negative qualities, the least chance. In contrast, the theory implies that the members who are positive on the more salient attribute (and hence attractive) and negative on the less salient one (and hence also approachable) are most likely to win the acceptance of their peers. And the members who are negative on the more salient but positive on the less salient attribute are expected to be least likely to be integrated. In short, the theory predicts that the greatest contrast in integration is not between the plus-plus and the minus-minus category but between the plus-minus and the minus-plus category.

A study of twelve work groups in a public assistance agency furnishes data that can be used to test this prediction. Each work group consisted of five or six caseworkers under a supervisor. (Responses from supervisors are not included in the analysis here.) The use of first names among peers, since it was not standard practice in this agency, was indicative of friendly acceptance. Whether a caseworker was or was not called by his first name by some of the other members of his own work group, as reported by the others, is the measure of integration employed.

Respondents are classified on the basis of both sociometric status and background characteristics. Thus popularity—the number of "friendship" choices received from outsiders as well as from the in-group—is presumably indicative of attractive qualities, whatever the specific attributes that attract others to any given individual. Background characteristics also make a person more or less attractive, but their residual effect that is not already reflected in the sociometric choices is undoubtedly a less salient force than that manifested in these choices. Experienced oldtimers, for example, are generally more attractive associates but, partly for this very reason, less approachable ones than newcomers—workers who had been with the agency less than one year. (Although oldtimers are not necessarily more attractive than newcomers, they were so in this agency; that is, there was a direct relationship between seniority and popularity.) If popularity is held constant, the implications of seniority for attractiveness have been largely removed, so to speak, and the remaining influences of seniority are probably due primarily to its unapproachability component.

The naïve assumption would be that newcomers are less integrated in their work group than equally attractive oldtimers. The expectation derived from the theory, on the other hand, is that popular newcomers, as individuals who are easily approachable as well as attractive, are most likely to be integrated among peers—more so than popular oldtimers—and that unpopular oldtimers are least likely to be integrated—less so than unpopular newcomers. The distinctive significance of being not only attractive but also approachable becomes particularly evident if one singles out the highly integrated workers (those called by the majority of the in-group rather than simply by some by their first name). Only 35 per cent of the twenty-six popular oldtimers were highly integrated despite their attractiveness, in contrast to all four of the popular newcomers, whose attractiveness was complemented by greater approachability (and, among the unpopular workers, 8 per cent of the thirteen oldtimers and 18 per cent of the seventeen newcomers were highly integrated). This pattern of findings differs sharply from the cumulative effects the same two factors had on other aspects of the caseworker's position in his work group, such as his status as a regular consultant to colleagues. Both popularity and seniority, independently, increased the chances of being named often by colleagues as a consultant, so that their effects were cumulative. Popular oldtimers were the most prone to be consulted, and unpopular newcomers the least.

The prestige and manners of people with a middle-class background are likely to make them less easily approachable than those who originated in the working class, particularly for others who themselves have a working-class background, as did most caseworkers in the agency. When father's occupation is substituted for seniority, the impact of popularity and socioeconomic origin on integration again confirms the theoretical expectation. A worker's attractiveness, as indicated by his popularity, significantly enhanced his chances of integration in his peer group only if it was combined with a working-class origin, which made him readily approachable. (Whether the same results would be obtained in an organization the majority of whose members have a middle-class background is, of course, a question that cannot be answered on the basis of the available data.) Four other background factors may have the same implications for approachability as seniority and socioeconomic origin— whether a caseworker is white or Negro, Protestant or not, male or female, and old or young. (Except for a relationship between age and seniority, there were no significant relationships between any two of the six background variables.) Five of the six tables that indicate the influence of both popularity and one of these characteristics reveal the predicted pattern; that is, the plus-minus category contained the highest proportion of integrated workers, and the minus-plus category, the lowest.

While any one of these findings could also be interpreted differently, the theory advanced provides a single explanation for all of them. Moreover, the same results are obtained if sociometric measures other than popularity are used as indications of attractive qualities. When the effects of respect (being named by peers as one of the best caseworkers in the group) and the same background characteristics are determined, all six findings are in agreement with the specific prediction. The respected workers with a "low" background were most often integrated among peers, and the workers who were not respected with a "high" background were integrated least often, regardless of which of the six background factors is under consideration. Finally, when the frequency of being consulted by colleagues is substituted as the sociometric measure in these tables, four of six show the expected contrast in integration between the plus-minus and the minus-plus category. Although not all these tests are independent, the fact that fifteen of eighteen confirm the prediction is suggestive. These findings do not prove the theory, of course, but they seem to support one inference derived from it, namely, that individuals who have characteristics that make them approachable as well as some that make them attractive have the best chance of winning acceptance in their peer group.

An attempt to analyze processes of social integration in abstraction from other group processes is likely to be misleading, since it leaves out of consideration the influence the latter forces have upon the former. Thus people are not exclusively concerned with the position they occupy in the group in which they presently find themselves, as the previous discussion may wrongly have implied, but they have various other interests—such as obtaining satisfaction in their work, to name only one—and these also influence their interaction. Moreover, a group member's attractiveness to others depends not so much on his clever strategies in impressing them as on his actual qualities and performance, because social reality is not a mirage. Indeed, a basic difference between group life and more transient, isolated social relations—say, that between salesman and customer—is that members of a group have an opportunity to check the reliability of first impression, in subsequent interaction with a person and in comparing one another's impression of him. Finally, social acceptance as an equal is not the only form social attraction to a person may take, and other forms appear not to be contingent on approachability. . . . Oldtimers are presumed to be less approachable than newcomers, and this had the expected effect on their chances of being accepted on a first-name basis. Despite their greater unapproachability, however, oldtimers were more attractive consultants than newcomers, even when popularity (or respect, as a matter of fact) is held constant. These considerations raise some questions concerning the earlier conceptualization.

Unapproachability has indirect as well as direct social consequences, just as does impressive behavior and for the same reasons. If a person appears to have outstanding qualities, others will be attracted to him but will also infer that he may well not be attracted to them, because past experience tells them that people with superior qualities are generally not easily approachable. On the basis of the same past experience, however, people will also infer that an aloof and unapproachable person probably has outstanding qualities, otherwise he would not be so self-assured. And since people do make these inferences, self-assured and even arrogant conduct can serve as a strategy to impress others (hence people cultivate poise). But whether one employs this strategy or another to impress the members of a group, he still must cope with the defenses his implicit claim of superiority arouses in them. Sooner or later, he must prove his approachability or face the consequences.

This, however, is an alternative that has not yet been considered. A person may be willing to face the consequences of having impressed others and, instead of appeasing their defensive reactions, live up to the expectations his outstanding qualities have raised. Others expect some benefit from associating with a person who apparently has superior qualities, and, if he provides those benefits, he furnishes them incentives for associating with him. For example, a worker's superior competence motivates his colleagues to associate with him to obtain his advice. Or a person's sparkling wit at social gatherings induces his acquaintances to invite him to make their parties a success. An individual's ability to live up to the expectations of others depends not only on his capacity to supply desired services but also on his having the sagacity to refrain from presenting too impressive a front at first. The diffident person is one who anticipates this and carefully manages to raise only expectations that he can easily meet or even surpass.

There are, then, two different methods of dealing with the problem posed by the defensive reactions that occur in groups as each member tries to prove his attractiveness to the others. The situation at this stage may be described figuratively as an attractive force behind a defensive barrier that prevents its activation. The person who demonstrates his approachability lessens the attractive force somewhat but lowers the barrier enough to make it easy for others to associate with him. The person who provides services does not lower the barrier but increases the attractive force so much that the others are constrained by self-interest to relinquish their defenses and associate with him.

A member of a group who utilizes his superior qualities for the benefit of others not only makes himself an attractive associate but also earns respect and deference. By rendering significant services, he establishes social obligations. If he helps the rest of the group to attain important objectives, collectively or individually, they will be under obligation to him. The respect his demonstrated ability commands and the obligations his services create will induce others to follow his suggestions and defer to his wishes. Their deference is his reward for past contributions and his incentive for continuing to contribute in the future. These social processes, then, in which some members come to command the respect and deference of others, give rise to social differentiation in the group.

The theory can now be reformulated briefly: A group is cohesive if bonds of social attraction unite its members. For social integration to prevail in a group and a cohesive unit to develop, its members must be concerned with attracting one another. To prove himself an attractive associate, each member will seek to impress the others with his good qualities. But the resulting competition for popularity and defensive reactions against letting one's self be impressed by others threaten to lead to an impasse in which social integration would be impossible. If groups do not distintegrate, and many obviously do not, it is because other social processes forestall it.

In the course of the competition that motivates group members to reveal their best qualities to one another, it becomes evident that some have abilities that permit them to make important contributions to the achievement of common or individual goals. These contributions are a source of social attraction. Their significance forces other members to override their own defenses and seek to draw the person who makes them into the group and associate with him. At the same time the obligations incurred by the rest of the group to a member who contributes to the achievement of their goals constrains them to repay him with respect and deference. In short, the very processes required for social integration in a group give rise to other processes that lead to social differentiation. Hence social differentiation seems inevitable. (To state that some form of social differentiation is inevitable in face-to-face groups does *not*, of course, imply that all existing forms of social inequality are necessary prerequisites of collective life.)

The attraction and deference of other members to one who furnishes valued services intensify their need for integrative bonds simultaneously with relieving his. Since the benefits he has to offer make the others eager to associate with him, and since his abilities command their respect, he attains and sustains a secure position in the group without having to demonstrate his approachability. The others, however, are anxious to prove themselves attractive associates without having as yet been successful in overcoming one another's resistance to expressing feelings of attraction. Besides, paying respect and deference to him undermines their self-confidence, and it threatens the impressive image they have tried to present to one another, thus increasing their need for social support. Under these conditions a group member will be under pressure to dispel the defenses of others and induce them to accept him as a peer by demonstrating his approachability. In doing so, he turns to his advantage the fact that by his deference he has already given the rest some evidence of his willingness to surrender any claim to a superordinate position. These tendencies give rise to bonds of mutual attraction. Thus it appears that processes of social integration also promote differentiation and that processes of social differentiation, in turn, help to strengthen the group's integrative forces.

Following Homans' suggestive conceptualization, these patterns of social interaction may be looked upon as exchange processes. A person with superior qualities which enable him to provide services that are in demand receives the respect and deference of others in a group, which bestows superordinate status upon him, in exchange for rendering these services. A person who is not able to offer services that are in demand must settle for a lower position in the group. He can exchange his ready acceptance of others like him and his conformity to group norms for their acceptance of him. To put it into a somewhat different perspective, he wins social acceptance in exchange for ceasing to compete for superior standing in the group and for the contribution to social integration he thereby makes.

In conclusion, two important tasks required to improve the theory here suggested should be mentioned. The first is to derive operational hypotheses from the theory and test them in empirical research. One such hypothesis and preliminary tests of it have been presented. Many others have been implicit. To illustrate by making another hypothesis explicit: a person's tendency to demonstrate his approachability in a group to which he is attracted is expected to vary inversely with his ability to render valued services to its other members.

The second task is to extend the theory and systematically analyze the dynamics of the exchange processes discussed. A few brief examples of these further dynamic processes must suffice at this point. Since deference is a high price, group members will search for ways to obtain needed services at less cost. They will be motivated to improve their own qualifications for furnishing those services. A person who succeeds in doing so not only can dispense with services for which he had to pay with deference but also earns the respect of others who up to then had merely accepted or liked him. Those unable to make any contributions that win them at least limited respect may leave the group, and new members with greater potentials may be recruited in their place. Group members may also exchange services with one another, instead of receiving them from one with superior abilities in exchange for deference. Such practices threaten the position of the informal leader or leaders of the group. To avert this threat, informal leaders often seek to fortify their position by winning the loyalty or even affection of the others. Such positive sentiments toward the leader make deferring to his wishes and complying with his requests less onerous for others—not as much of a burden from which they will try to escape. These tendencies also reflect the dilemma posed at the beginning of this paper. Group members who are liked by associates experience pressures to become concerned with earning their respect, and those who command the respect of others are constrained to devote efforts to courting their affection.

10. THE DEVELOPMENT OF POLITICAL ATTITUDES IN CHILDREN

robert d. hess and judith v. torney

Only quite recently have social scientists turned to systematic, empirical study of the political attitudes of children in an attempt to account for the principal sources, agents, and characteristics of such attitudes.

In reading the following, note the complex ways in which general attitudes gradually become politicized through the socialization process, the specific kinds of political attitudes held by children of various age and grade groups, and the nature of change in such attitudes over various time spans. In particular, consider the significance of the total socialization process as a gigantic mold that tends to produce socially desirable political orientations among children.

Reprinted from Robert D. Hess and Judith V. Torney, *The Development of Political Attitudes in Children,* Chicago: Aldine Publishing Company, 1967; copyright © 1967 by Robert D. Hess and Judith V. Torney.

The purpose of this study was to examine the socialization of children into the political system of the United States. The initial thrust of the study was descriptive—an attempt to chart and document the growth of political behavior. This is one of a growing number of studies of the development of citizenship and political behavior in children and adolescents, representing a relatively recent interest of political scientists, sociologists, and child psychologists. As a result of this and other similar studies, future investigations will be more focused and more precise. It will be important to examine from different perspectives some of the issues raised in this volume.

Political socialization has been studied in this project as a special case of socialization into institutions, examining the ways that individuals learn to interact with these large segments of the social system. The assumption is that social learning in the political area bears certain similarities to socialization into other institutions. This process is viewed not as one which involves the acquisition of traits or opinions, but rather the development of relationships between the individual and the institutions. In this complex process, the individual acquires images of institutions and persons and complementary attitudes about himself and how he should behave (what the institutions and their representatives expect of him).

For the purposes of analysis and presentation of data, we have distinguished among several types of behavior: relationships to the nation, to authority figures and institutions representing the national government, to laws and authority figures who enforce them, to processes of influence on public policy, and to elections and political parties.

The focus of the study is not limited to children's beliefs but attempts also to delineate the procedures through which they acquire political behavior. These processes of acquisition include the accumulation of specific knowledge and attitudes taught by other individuals—teachers, parents, and other authority figures; the acquisition of beliefs, attitudes, and orientations by transfer of feelings held toward other authority figures in the preceptual environment; accepting ideas, beliefs, and behavior by imitation or identification; and modification by the mediating effects of level of conceptual development and ability that the child possesses.

The data summarized here are taken from hour-long questionnaires administered to approximately 12,000 children in elementary grades two through eight. The data were collected in one large city and one small city of each major region of the United States (West, South, North Central, Northeast) during the period from December 1961 through May 1962. In each city, two schools from working-class areas and two schools from middle-class areas were tested.

In this summary, the findings are grouped to respond to three questions: First, what is the content of attitudes which children develop during the elementary-school years—what are their beliefs about political figures and organizations and their ideas about how citizens should behave? Second, from which sources or agents are political attitudes and behavior acquired and what experiences influence this process? Third, what is the pattern (rate and sequence) of change and growth in attitudes, and through what processes are they acquired?

POLITICAL ATTITUDES ACQUIRED
DURING ELEMENTARY SCHOOL

The young child's involvement with the political system begins with a strong positive attachment to the country; the United States is seen an ideal and as superior to other countries. This attachment to the country is stable and shows almost no change through elementary-school years. This bond is possibly the most basic and essential aspect of socialization into involvement with the political life of the nation. Essentially an emotional tie, it apparently grows from complex psychological and social needs and is exceedingly resistant to change or argument. It is a powerful emotional bond that is particularly important in time of national emergency.

The young child perceives figures and institutions of government as powerful, competent, benign, and infallible and trusts them to offer him protection and help. This early faith in political authority figures seems to be general among young children in this country. There is also reason to believe that it is characteristic of other countries. The age trends in the data give little support to the notion that all these attitudes are learned as primarily political orientations. The child also draws from previous experience with family figures and may endow figures whom he sees as powerful and authoritative with benign and helpful qualities. This response appears to be *compensatory;* it develops as a result of the child's inferior and vulnerable place in the system and serves to reassure the child that powerful authority is not dangerous.

The child's initial relationship with governmental authority is with the President, whom he sees in highly positive terms, indicating his basic trust in the benevolence of government. Indeed, interviews of first- and second-grade children indicated that the President is the major figure in the child's emerging political world. The small child often believes the President is available to the individual citizen, either by visits to the White House or by telephone. The President's concern is personal and nurturant. He is the tie to the governmental system through which other objects—institutions, processes—become familiar and understood. The Vice President, for example, is described in interviews as the President's helper, and the Congress frequently is seen as working for the President. The President is the critical point of contact for the child in the political socialization process.

The early image of the President centers around personal qualities. With increasing age of a child, the President's qualities directly related to his office become more prominent than his personal attractiveness, and the child develops a concept of the *Presidency* as separate from the President. This distinction appears when one compares children's attitudes toward President Eisenhower with those toward President Kennedy. Despite his narrow victory, and lacking the popular image that was characteristic of Eisenhower, Kennedy within weeks of his inauguration was rated as positively as Eisenhower had been in his second term. Emerging along with attitudes toward the President are attitudes toward other positions in the system which endow their incumbents with status and prestige in the eyes of the child. The expectations that are developed with regard to these roles (judge, senator) will later allow the child to criticize the occupant of a role without expressing disloyalty to the system.

The policeman is also among the political figures which are salient to the young child. Children believe that the policeman is nurturant and that his job is to help persons in trouble and to prevent crime, rather than to exercise the more punitive functions of catching and punishing criminals. Despite his importance as an authority figure, however, children do not see him as a representative of national government. They express a strong personal liking for the policeman; this attraction declines steadily throughout the elementary-school years to a level which is positive but considerably lower than their regard for the President.

On most attributes, policemen were rated at approximately the same level as senators and consistently lower than the President. They were somewhat lower than "father" on personal items ("I like him") but superior to "father" on role performance items ("Knows more," "Is a leader," "Makes important decisions"). The child holds the policeman in awe. Most young children have high regard for law and for law-enforcement authorities. The elementary-school child, especially at early grade-levels, sees laws as just and unchangeable and believes that punishment is an inevitable consequence of wrongdoing. The young child believes that laws are made by persons in administrative positions, especially by the President; this view is later modified to recognize the legislative process. There are some changes with age in this general picture, as will be noted later, but norms about the justice of law and necessity for conformity are established firmly at an early age. Deviations from these norms do not result from ignorance or from a failure to accept the norms themselves. The reasons for noncompliance must be sought in other areas of personality and socialization. As with orientations toward authority figures, the attitudes toward law appear to be transferred from attitudes toward rules in other systems, especially the school and the family. If this transfer model is valid in these basic areas of orientation toward authority and law, the child's experiences with rules in other groups (family and school) are very influential in the political socialization process.

The young child's trust in the political system is expressed not only by a view of figures and institutions as benign, but through a view of the obligation of the citizen primarily to be a good person. This image of the citizen persists, but the obligations to vote and express interest in governmental affairs become more dominant elements of the norms of adult citizenship as the child grows older. The belief that the citizen should be interested in political matters is apparent in the behavior reported by elementary-school children; by the end of the eighth grade most children have acquired some interest in governmental activities and have participated in discussions about political issues and problems.

Children begin engaging in political activities (such as wearing campaign buttons) at an early age, occasionally as early as the third grade; there is a gradual increase through the eighth grade in the number of children who report such activities. The elementary-school child's view of the election process and of the mechanisms of influence on governmental action is dominated by an image of the citizen as powerful and the individual vote as the most effective force in the political process. The sense of efficacy in influencing political processes increases with age. Children in elementary school, even in the eighth grade, have a very limited knowledge of the techniques and effectiveness of pressure groups in elections and in determining governmental policy.

The child's image of political parties develops late, and the nature of the differences between the two major parties is not clearly defined. Parties are apparently first associated with candidates who are identified as Republican or Democrat; interest in an election and a candidate may be the most instrumental mechanism for developing party affiliation. Although taking sides in an election is a prominent aspect of children's political behavior, a meaningful party commitment is usually not acquired until the upper grades of elementary school. Even at this age, a large proportion of children report that, if they could vote, they would vote independently of party affiliation; in general they believe that partisan commitment may be desirable for adults, but that it should be deferred until adulthood.

In viewing politics, particularly the relationship between the two parties and the conduct of elections, children wish to minimize conflict. They see disagreement as undesirable and prefer to believe that politicians never say unkind things about one another during an election campaign. They also have a firm conviction that following an election campaign the conflict that may have arisen should be forgotten; the loser should join in support of the winning candidate and he, in return, should be gracious and forgiving. Thus by the end of the eighth grade, children have developed a sense of the need for consensus and majority rule in democratic processes. Typically, they have not recognized the role of debate, disagreement, and conflict in the operation of a democratic political system.

These are the dominant themes in the responses obtained to our questions. There is a great deal of agreement about certain basic points, especially loyalty to the country and respect for the office of the President. Regard for law and recognition of the need for law enforcement and obedience on the part of the citizen are equally important. The obligation of the citizen to vote is also prominent. Of particular note is the strong emphasis children place upon independence from party affiliation and upon voting for the most qualified candidate rather than supporting the party of one's choice. This may be an idealistic but temporary view of the operation of the political system which is supported by belief in the power of the individual vote and ignorance about the importance of pressure groups.

Children are socialized toward an ideal norm; this norm provides a standard against which the behavior of candidates and of individual citizens, as well as of persons who occupy positions in government, may be judged, The importance of early faith in government, attachment to the system, and belief in the power of the individual citizen as necessary bases for further political socialization should be considered in discussing possible curricular changes in civic education. It seems likely that before the child is informed about conflict and disagreement he should have sufficient time to internalize and become attached to the ideal norms of the system. Building on this firm attachment and acceptance of the basic worth of the country and the individual citizen, it may then be possible to explain the usefulness of disagreement and debate and to show the function of consensus in uniting a nation after the conflict of a political campaign. Recognition of the need for disagreement, its resolution, and subsequent consensus can probably be introduced at a relatively early age, perhaps as early as the fourth or fifth grade. The unpleasant aspects of political life (corruption) should perhaps be left until a later time, when they can be viewed as deviations, rather than being mistaken for normal or usual behavior.

AGENTS FOR POLITICAL SOCIALIZATION

What are the agents (institutions, persons) from which political attitudes and behavior are acquired? What experiences are related to the acquisition of political attitudes?

From the viewpoint of the totality of socialization into the political system, these results indicate that the effectiveness of the family in transmitting attitudes has been overestimated in previous research. The family transmits preference for a political party, but in most other areas its most effective role is to support other institutions in teaching political information and orientations. Clearcut similarities among children in the same family are confined to partisanship and related attitudes, such as feelings of distress or pleasure over the outcome of an election campaign. Aside from party preference, the influence of the family seems to be primarily indirect and to influence attitudes toward authority, rules, and compliance.

There is some relationship between family structure and the child's interest in the political system. Children who see their fathers as powerful tend to be more informed and interested in political matters; children who see their mothers as the dominant authority in the family tend to be less interested in politics and to acquire attitudes at a later period than do children who see the father as the dominant parent or see both parents as equal in authority.

The school apparently plays the largest part in teaching attitudes, conceptions, and beliefs about the operation of the political system. While it may be argued that the family contributes much to the socialization that goes into basic loyalty to the country, the school gives content, information, and concepts which expand and elaborate these early feelings of attachment.

The young child's attitude toward authority or institutions, however, seems not to correspond directly to the amount of emphasis on these topics reported by the teachers. Compliance to rules and authorities is a major focus of civic education in elementary school. Teachers' ratings of the importance of various topics clearly indicate that the strongest emphasis is placed upon compliance to law, authority, and school regulations. Indeed, it seems likely that much of what is called citizenship training in the public schools does not teach the child about the city, state, or national government, but it is an attempt to teach regard for the rules and standards of conduct of the school.

In contrast to its emphasis on compliance, the school curriculum underemphasizes the rights and obligations of a citizen to participate in government. The school focuses on the obligation and right to vote but does not offer the child sufficient understanding of procedures open to individuals for legitimately influencing the government. Nor does it adequately explain and emphasize the importance of group action to achieve desirable ends.

Teachers tend not to deal with partisanship or to discuss the role and importance of conflict in the operation of the system, perhaps because of the position of the school in the community. They apparently stress the virtue of independent political action oriented toward assessment of candidates' worth rather than an alignment with a group or political party. This preference may follow from explicit or implicit prohibitions against teaching controversial topics; or perhaps it reflects the desire of the school to present political life and information without bias. In either case, it leaves the elementary school child with inadequate information at a time when he is becoming oriented toward the importance of political participation.

The school stresses ideal norms and ignores the tougher, less pleasant facts of political life in the United States. While it would probably be unwise to discuss political corruption in early grades, the process of socialization should include a somewhat more realistic view of the operation of the political system. For example, achieving political goals and influencing elected officials are facilitated by participation in organized groups, particularly political parties. Yet the school appears to spend relatively little time dealing with the functions of political parties, community action, and pressure groups in achieving community goals. It may be argued that by teaching a myth of governmental responsiveness to the average voter, the school produces an unjustified sense of confidence. The "average" voter may be ineffective because he has been socialized to believe that the citizen has more power than is actually the case.

The school is particularly important for children who come from working-class or low socioeconomic areas. Much of what working-class children learn at school is not reinforced by home and community. It may be for these reasons that the school seems to have somewhat less effect upon children from these areas of the city than it does on the children from more prosperous sections.

Participation in peer group organizations within the school or outside it does not have a significant effect upon the political socialization process. Group membership and activity seem to be related to political activity, but apparently only because the child who is active tends to be active in several areas of endeavor. Our data give no evidence that participation in group activities or membership in any one of several youth organizations leads to a greater or earlier acceptance of the basic elements of citizenship and democratic process.

Religious affiliation has a strong but limited effect on political socialization in the elementary-school years. The most marked relationship between religious affiliation and involvement is the socialization of party affiliation and candidate preference. The data were gathered in the year and a half following the election of President Kennedy, and the relationship between religious affiliation and reaction to the selection of a President who was of the Catholic faith was particularly strong. This preference cut across the influence of social class and outweighted, in many cases, the importance of party affiliation.

It is our conclusion from these data that the school stands out as the central, salient, and dominant force in the political socialization of the young child. Since this study began at the second-grade level, where a firm attachment to the country had already been established, it is difficult to specify the effectiveness of the school in transmitting this early loyalty to the nation. The recital of the pledge of allegiance and singing "The Star Spangled Banner" are rituals supporting this attachment.

The influence of the family is, of course, considerable, but in our opinion, much less than has been assumed by many other researchers. The influence of the family upon party choice is well-known and important; this aspect of the process of political socialization seems to be similar to the selection of a particular church denomination as a result of family loyalty and identification. Choices of this type obviously are influential in adult life, but they are independent of the much larger process of socialization into a network of behavior that relates a citizen to the government, and citizens to one another.

The role played by the school in this process suggests a need for greater attention and more systematic evaluation of the methods, curriculum, and timing of political socialization. In the school curriculum, the topics that deal with civic education and the concepts that are part of our democratic heritage are usually taught unsystematically. There has been relatively little attempt to state which concepts are basic to the operation of the democratic system and to teach these in an early age in an effective manner. It seems likely that many children who can recite the articles of the Bill of Rights would not be able to explain why these sections are important or what the consequences would be if they were not upheld. Underlying the political behavior and attitudes which can be observed are basic concepts which provide the logic for a democratic system—such as a view of conflicts as a dimension of behavior, a regard for the rights of minorities, and compliance to majority rule. These elements can be taught and should result in more informed and rational political attitudes and action. In our opinion, there has been little attempt to seek out and define the basic concepts on which our system is based and to construct a curriculum in the early grades to transmit these concepts and an understanding of their importance. Perhaps what is needed is a revising of the curriculum in ways comparable to the new advances in the teaching of mathematics and the sciences. Such an effort would examine the conceptual bases of civic education and teaching, then order them in a sequence that would lead the child to an emerging sense of how the system should operate, the principles on which it depends, and his own effectiveness and role within it.

PROCESSES AND MEDIATIONS OF POLITICAL SOCIALIZATION

The process of political socialization can be considered within two major categories. The first has to do with the rate and sequence with which attitudes are acquired by children; it is concerned with developmental changes and patterns of acquisition related to chronological age or grade in school. The second has to do with the factors which influence the transmission of political orientations; it deals with the circumstances which retard or facilitate children's acquisition of attitudes.

Developmental Patterns: The Rate and Sequence of Political Socialization

The most striking feature of political socialization in the elementary school is the extent to which basic orientations have been acquired by children by the end of the eighth grade.[1] Many attitudes, concepts, and types of involvement approximate toward the end of the eighth grade the attitudes and orientations of the teachers. Although there are exceptions (noted below), political socialization is well advanced by the end of elementary school.

This conclusion seems not to apply in the areas of partisanship and in the understanding of the role of pressure groups in forming governmental policy. The tendency of many children to see themselves as independent of

[1] Our data underestimate the true extent of socialization since testing was spread over a period of time beginning in the fall and ending in late winter, not toward the end of the school term.

party affiliation appears to reflect the socialization within the school. It seems likely that some subsequent re-socialization will stimulate greater affiliation with one of the major parties and a loyalty to the candidates of that party.

The acquisition of political orientations and information proceeds rapidly but not evenly during the elementary-school years. In some areas, such as attachment to the nation, attitudes are acquired early. In others, particularly voting and partisan behavior, the emphasis seems to occur relatively late in the elementary-school years. The period between grades three and five seems to be especially important in the acquisition of political information. Before this time, concepts such as government and political party may evoke some recognition in the child, but few children understand more than their most elementary aspects.

The child's early conception of the nation is vague, and national symbols such as the flag are crucial points of focus. Evaluative judgments of political objects in all areas are acquired first. These are supplemented later by acquisition of more complex information and attitudes which are usually consistent with these evaluations.

The process of induction into the governmental system seems to occur initially through a feeling of high regard for political authority figures. The point of contact and initial affiliation is *persons;* the governmental image later includes institutions and less personal aspects of the system. The early attachment of the child to political authority figures seems not to derive from teaching in the home or the school but to reflect the child's need to see authority figures as benign because they are powerful. The tendency to attribute benevolence to authority appears to be a way of dealing with feelings of vulnerability in the face of superior power.

Despite the decline in the personal respect for authority figures, a basic regard for the roles of authority in the system and for the competence necessary to perform these roles seems not to diminish. Apparently the feelings of liking for political authority figures are transformed into feelings of confidence in and esteem for the roles which these figures occupy and for institutions.

The young child's conceptions of law and the rules of the school and home are not greatly differentiated. His early regard for law is an extension of his feeling that it is important to obey adults. Thus the induction into compliance with authority and law appears to be mediated through visible authority figures, initially through the parents, possibly through the classroom teacher, and in the political arena through the policeman and the President.

Individual Characteristics Which Affect the Acquisition of Political Attitudes and Behavior

In this study, the major mediating influences investigated were sex, social class, and intelligence (estimated by IQ scores). Though many of the sex differences in political attitudes and activities were not large, they were consistent across grades. There was also considerable consistency among the items on which sex differences appeared. Among the most prominent differences is that the boys acquire attitudes more rapidly than girls and they are more interested in political matters. In addition, boys report more political activity than do girls.

Compared with boys, girls tend to be more attached to personal figures of the system. They relate to the political system more through trust and reliance on figures and the inherent goodness of the system than do their male peers. There are no differences between males and females in basic attachment, loyalty, and support of the country. In general, the differences between males and females are consistent with sex differences reported by other investigators. Girls tend to be more oriented toward persons, more expressive and trustful in their attitudes toward the system, its representatives, and institutions. Boys tend to be more task-oriented and are more willing to accept and see benefit in conflict and disagreement.

Party affiliation in itself has relatively little effect upon the acquisition of basic attitudes and political orientation. For example, it has no relationship to attachment to the nation or compliance to the system of law. Children who favor the Republican party show no difference whatsoever in basic loyalty to the country when compared with the children who express preference for the Democratic party. Although there are no differences between children who identify with the two major parties, children who do not identify with any political party—that is, who are uncommitted—are less active and less interested in political affairs. It may be that the first sign of political apathy in the socialization process is a lack of concern about elections, campaigns, and party affiliation. At the elementary-school level, children who see themselves as politically independent are the most active of all in political affairs, exceeding the involvement of children who identify themselves as Democrats or Republicans. This tendency toward independence seems to reflect the ideal independent voter as he is sometimes portrayed in adult political situations—intelligent, evaluating the merits of the campaign or issue, interested in political affairs and election outcomes, active in political matters, and deeply involved in the operation of the political system.

The intelligence of the child is one of the most important mediating influences in the acquisition of political behavior. In general, the effect of high IQ is to accelerate the process of political socialization for children of all social status levels. For example, children of high intelligence at a given age are more likely to see the government represented by institutions rather than by a powerful leader. Although the acquisition of political attitudes and of the concept of institutional aspects of government is accelerated in children of higher IQ, there is no difference between children of high and of low intelligence in their basic attachment to the nation. These fundamental allegiances are apparently taught so thoroughly that virtually all children within normal IQ range have been socialized in these critical areas.

Children of high intelligence tend to regard the system in less absolute terms. They are less likely to see laws as unquestionably fair, or to view punishment as an inevitable consequence of lawbreaking. This is not to suggest that they are casual about the importance of law; the obligation of the citizen to comply is accepted equally by children of high and low intelligence. However, brighter children seem to be more critically aware of the possibility that lawbreakers may not always be apprehended by the police and brought to justice in the courts, and more aware of the possibility that some laws may be unjust.

Children of high IQ also have more reservations about the competence and intentions of governmental figures and institutions. They are less idealistic about the system and expect less from it. Brighter children are somewhat more realistic about the operation of the system, without sacrificing the ideal norms which they have been taught. This interpretation is supported by the finding that these children are more interested in governmental matters and tend to emphasize the importance of interest in political affairs more than do other children. They are also more likely to participate in political discussions and to express concern about questions that are of contemporary interest to adults.

Feelings of efficacy in relation to government are very strongly related to level of intelligence. Some of the largest differences among the IQ groups appear in the sense of efficacy. Voting is also more salient as an aspect of government to children of high intelligence. They are more inclined to see voting as an obligation of the good citizen than are children who are less gifted. Children of high intelligence seem less bound to the status quo and more willing to accept change in government. They are particularly likely to be independent of party affiliation and to accept the idea that the citizen should vote for the candidate rather than conform with party allegiance.

In summary, children of high intelligence are more active, more likely to discuss political matters, more interested in current events; they have a greater sense of efficacy and a greater sense of the importance of voting and citizen participation. Intelligence is associated with greater involvement in political affairs.

The influence of social status seems to be less marked than the impact of IQ. When intelligence is held constant, social status differences are greatly reduced in most political orientations and attitudes studied in this research. Basic affiliation and loyalty to the nation do not vary by social status. It seems to be a consistent finding that socialization into national loyalty occurs early within all social groups. Differences in political involvement and behavior which are observed within the population are apparently built upon this basic feeling of loyalty to the country.

Differences by IQ increase with age; this is less true of differences by social status. Some very distinctive social class differences remain, however. There is a difference between social status groups in their attachment to certain governmental figures. Children from working-class homes tend to have a higher regard for policemen and for the President than do children from high-er-status homes. However, the perception of responsiveness and willingness to help exhibited by governmental figures shows no social class variation. Like high-IQ children, children from high-status families see laws as less rigid, but they accept on a par with working-class children the citizen's obligation to comply to law.

The expression of interest in political matters is not related to social status. However, the child's report of his parent's or his family's interest in government is strongly related to social class, with children from higher-status homes reporting more parental interest in government and national affairs than other children. Children from high social status also report more frequent participation in political discussions and a greater concern for contemporary national issues. These children are similar to those of high intelligence. How-ever, this relationship with social status is maintained when IQ is held con-stant. Although there are differences in these types of participation and con-cern, no social class differences appear in the acceptance of voting as a duty of the citizen. This obligation is accepted equally by children of high and low status.

Perhaps the most marked social class difference in these data is the tendency for low-status children to feel less efficacious in dealing with the political system than do children from high-status homes. The combination of intelligence and social status in their effect upon feelings of efficacy make for dramatic differences between the high-status/high-IQ children and low-status/low-IQ children. Although there are no social status differences in expressed interest in political affairs, there are differences among the status groups in the amount of political activity reported. This may reflect, as indi-cated earlier, a greater tendency for middle-class communities and families to support and reinforce the teaching of the schools with regard to obligations of political participation and involvement.

Choice of political party is related to social status similarly for children and adults. The tendency for working-class children to favor the Democratic party does not appear until grade five, however, suggesting that party affiliation is not salient to younger children and that the effect of family and social class in this area becomes stronger during the late elementary-school and high-school years.

There are a number of parallels between the effects of social status and the effects of IQ in the socialization of political orientations and involvement. Our data lead to the conclusion that children in working-class areas of the city are less completely socialized (in the sense of being prepared for political participation) than children for middle-class homes. The same general con-clusion may be made about children of low intelligence. These effects are com-pounded by the fact that schools in working-class areas have a disproportion-ate number of children with relatively low IQ's. An evaluation of the curriculum and of the role of the school in political socialization must take into account this relative disadvantage of children who come from working-class homes and those of every social class level who are not intellectually gifted. For these children, it may be necessary to devise more effective teaching methods or to spend a greater amount of time in teaching the basic concepts of government and political behavior. Low-status children perceive their teacher as relatively much more effective than their own parents in teaching citizenship. This is probably an indication of a general lack of community and family support in working-class areas for the attitudes and concepts taught by the school. Perhaps the school should exert particular effort to transmit to these children an understanding of the operation of the political system and the importance of the democratic principles on which our system operates.

11. INNER- AND OTHER-DIRECTED SOCIETIES

david riesman, nathan glazer, and reuel denny

In the book from which the following selection is taken, the author outlines three distinct personality types: the tradition-directed individual, the inner-directed individual, and the other-directed individual.

The tradition-directed individual lives in the unchanging world of the tribe or isolated village, a world in which the rules of behavior are so clear and so unchanging that to survive requires only mechanical conformity.

The selection begins with a discussion of "inner-directed" individuals, individuals who have been socialized to internalize (feel deeply or make a matter of conscience) the values of their society. Inner-directed individuals know good from bad and right from wrong regardless of how varied the circumstances and regardless of the behavior of others. He is the individual who keeps his head when all about him have lost theirs.

Just as the preceding selection argued that changes in American socialization patterns have altered innovative behavior, the author of the present article argues that changing socialization patterns are making us less "inner-directed" and more "other-directed," that is, prone to

Reprinted by permission of Yale University Press from *The Lonely Crowd,* by David Riesman, Nathan Glazer, Reuel Denny, Doubleday & Company abridged edition, pp. 29–38. Copyright © 1950, 1953 by Yale University Press.

spend considerably less time listening to the inner voice of conscience and considerably more time listening to the voice of others. Is this good or bad? If this trend continues, what are the consequences for society?

A definition of inner-direction.   In western history the society that emerged with the Renaissance and Reformation and that is only now vanishing serves to illustrate the type of society in which inner-direction is the principal mode of securing conformity. Such a society is characterized by increased personal mobility, by a rapid accumulation of capital (teamed with devastating technological shifts), and by an almost constant *expansion:* intensive expansion in the production of goods and people, and extensive expansion in exploration, colonization, and imperialism. The greater choices this society gives—and the greater initiatives it demands in order to cope with its novel problems—are handled by character types who can manage to live socially without strict and self-evident tradition-direction. These are the inner-directed types.

The concept of inner-direction is intended to cover a very wide range of types. Thus, while it is essential for the study of certain problems to differentiate between Protestant and Catholic countries and their character types, between the effects of the Reformation and the effects of the Renaissance, between the puritan ethic of the European north and west and the somewhat more hedonistic ethic of the European east and south, while all these are valid and, for certain purposes, important distinctions, the concentration of this study on the development of modes of conformity permits their neglect. It allows the grouping together of these otherwise distinct developments because they have one thing in common: *the source of direction for the individual is "inner" in the sense that it is implanted early in life by the elders and directed toward generalized but nonetheless inescapably destined goals.*

We can see what this means when we realize that, in societies in which tradition-direction is the dominant mode of insuring conformity, attention is focused on securing external *behavioral* conformity. While behavior is minutely prescribed, individuality of character need not be highly developed to meet prescriptions that are objectified in ritual and etiquette—though to be sure, a social character *capable* of such behavioral attention and obedience is requisite. By contrast, societies in which inner-direction becomes important, though they also are concerned with behavioral conformity, cannot be satisfied with behavioral conformity alone. Too many novel situations are presented, situations which a code cannot encompass in advance. Consequently the problem of personal choice, solved in the earlier period of high growth potential by channeling choice through rigid social organization, in the period of transitional growth is solved by channeling choice through a rigid though highly individualized character.

This rigidity is a complex matter. While any society dependent on inner-direction seems to present people with a wide choice of aims—such as money, possessions, power, knowledge, fame, goodness—these aims are ideologically interrelated, and the selection made by any one individual remains relatively unalterable throughout his life. Moreover, the means to those ends, though not fitted into as tight a social frame of reference as in the society dependent on tradition-direction, are nevertheless limited by the new voluntary associations—for instance, the Quakers, the Masons, the Mechanics' Associations— to which people tie themselves. Indeed, the term "tradition-direction" could be misleading if the reader were to conclude that the force of tradition has no weight for the inner-directed character. On the contrary, he is very considerably bound by traditions: they limit his ends and inhibit his choice of means. The point is rather that a splintering of tradition takes place, connected in part with the increasing division of labor and stratification of society. Even if the individual's choice of tradition is largely determined for him by his family, as it is in most cases, he cannot help becoming aware of the existence of competing traditions—hence of tradition as such. As a result he possesses a somewhat greater degree of flexibility in adapting himself to ever changing requirements and in return requires more from his environment.

As the control of the primary group is loosened—the group that both socializes the young and controls the adult in the earlier era—a new psychological mechanism appropriate to the more open society is "invented": it is what I like to describe as a psychological gyroscope. This instrument, once it is set by the parents and other authorities, keeps the inner-directed person, as we shall see, "on course" even when tradition, as responded to by his character, no longer dictates his moves. The inner-directed person becomes capable of maintaining a delicate balance between the demands upon him of his life goal and the buffetings of his external environment.

This metaphor of the gyroscope, like any other, must not be taken literally. It would be a mistake to see the inner-directed man as incapable of learning from experience or as insensitive to public opinion in matters of external conformity. He can receive and utilize certain signals from outside, provided that they can be reconciled with the limited maneuverability that his gyroscope permits him. His pilot is not quite automatic.

Huizinga's *The Waning of the Middle Ages* gives a picture of the anguish and turmoil, the conflict of values, out of which the new forms slowly emerged. Already by the late Middle Ages people were forced to live under new conditions of awareness. As their self-consciousness and their individuality developed, they had to make themselves at home in the world in novel ways. They still have to.

The problem facing the societies in the stage of transitional growth is that of reaching a point at which resources become plentiful enough or are utilized effectively enough to permit a rapid accumulation of capital. This rapid accumulation has to be achieved even while the social product is being drawn on at an accelerated rate to maintain the rising population and satisfy the consumer demands that go with the way of life that has already been adopted. For most countries, unless capital and techniques can be imported from other countries in still later phases of the population curve, every effort to increase national resources at a rapid rate must actually be at the expense of current standards of living. We have seen this occur in the U.S.S.R., now in the stage of transitional growth. For western Europe this transition was long-drawn-out and painful. For America, Canada, and Australia—at once beneficiaries of European techniques and native resources—the transition was rapid and relatively easy.

The tradition-directed person, as has been said, hardly thinks of himself as an individual. Still less does it occur to him that he might shape his own destiny in terms of personal, lifelong goals or that the destiny of his children might be separate from that of the family group. He is not sufficiently separated psychologically from himself (or, therefore, sufficiently close to himself), his family, or group to think in these terms. In the phase of transitional growth, however, people of inner-directed character do gain a feeling of control over their own lives and see their children also as individuals with careers to make. At the same time, with the shift out of agriculture and, later, with the end of child labor, children no longer become an unequivocal economic asset. And with the growth of habits of scientific thought, religious and magical views of human fertility—views that in an earlier phase of the population curve made sense for the culture if it was to reproduce itself—give way to "rational," individualistic attitudes. Indeed, just as the rapid accumulation of productive capital requires that people be imbued with the "Protestant ethic" (as Max Weber characterized one manifestation of what is here termed inner-direction), so also the decreased number of progeny requires a profound change in values—a change so deep that, in all probability, it has to be rooted in character structure.

As the birth rate begins to follow the death rate downward, societies move toward the epoch of incipient decline of population. Fewer and fewer people work on the land or in the extractive industries or even in manufacturing. Hours are short. People may have material abundance and leisure besides. They pay for these changes however—here, as always, the solution of old problems gives rise to new ones—by finding themselves in a centralized and bureaucratized society and a world shrunken and agitated by the contact —accelerated by industrialization—of races, nations, and cultures.

The hard enduringness and enterprise of the inner-directed types are somewhat less necessary under these new conditions. Increasingly, *other people* are the problem, not the material environment. And as people mix more widely and become more sensitive to each other, the surviving traditions from the stage of high growth potential—much disrupted, in any case, during the violent spurt of industrialization—become still further attenuated. Gyroscopic control is no longer sufficiently flexible, and a new psychological mechanism is called for.

Furthermore, the "scarcity psychology" of many inner-directed people, which was socially adaptive during the period of heavy capital accumulation that accompanied transitional growth of population, needs to give way to an "abundance psychology" capable of "wasteful" luxury consumption of leisure and of the surplus product. Unless people want to destroy the surplus product in war, which still does require heavy capital equipment, they must learn to enjoy and engage in those services that are expensive in terms of man power but not of capital—poetry and philosophy, for instance. Indeed, in the period of incipient decline, nonproductive consumers, both the increasing number of old people and the diminishing number of as yet untrained young, form a high proportion of the population, and these need both the economic opportunity to be prodigal and the character structure to allow it.

Has this need for still another slate of character types actually been acknowledged to any degree? My observations lead me to believe that in America it has.

A definition of other-direction.   The type of character I shall describe as other-directed seems to be emerging in very recent years in the upper middle class of our larger cities: more prominently in New York than in Boston, in Los Angeles than in Spokane, in Cincinnati than in Chillicothe. Yet in some respects this type is strikingly similar to the American, whom Tocqueville and other curious and astonished visitors from Europe, even before the Revolution, thought to be a new kind of man. Indeed, travelers' reports on America impress us with their unanimity. The American is said to be shallower, freer with his money, friendlier, more uncertain of himself and his values, more demanding of approval than the European. It all adds up to a pattern which, without stretching matters too far, resembles the kind of character that a number of social scientists have seen as developing in contemporary, highly industrialized, and bureaucratic America: Fromm's "marketer," Mill's "fixer," Arnold Green's "middle class male child."

It is my impression that the middle-class American of today is decisively different from those Americans of Tocqueville's writings who nevertheless strike us as so contemporary, and much of this book will be devoted to discussing these differences. It is also my impression that the conditions I believe to be responsible for other-direction are affecting increasing numbers of people in the metropolitan centers of the advanced industrial countries. My analysis of the other-directed character is thus at once an analysis of the American and of contemporary man. Much of the time I find it hard or impossible to say where one ends and the other begins. Tentatively, I am inclined to think that the other-directed type does find itself most at home in America, due to certain unique elements in American society, such as its recruitment from Europe and its lack of any feudal past. As against this, I am also inclined to put more weight on capitalism, industrialism, and urbanization—these being international tendencies—than on any character-forming peculiarities of the American scene.

Bearing these qualifications in mind, it seems appropriate to treat contemporary metropolitan America as our illustration of a society—so far, perhaps, the only illustration—in which other-direction is the dominant mode of insuring conformity. It would be premature, however, to say that it is already the dominant mode in America as a whole. But since the other-directed types are to be found among the young, in the larger cities, and among the upper income groups, we may assume that, unless present trends are reversed, the hegemony of other-direction lies not far off.

If we wanted to cast our social character types into social class molds, we could say that inner-direction is the typical character of the "old" middle class—the banker, the tradesman, the small entrepreneur, the technically oriented engineer, etc.—while other-direction is becoming the typical character of the "new" middle class—the bureaucrat, the salaried employee in business, etc. Many of the economic factors associated with the recent growth of the "new" middle class are well known. They have been discussed by James Burnham, Colin Clark, Peter Drucker, and others. There is a decline in the numbers and in the proportion of the working population engaged in production and extraction—agriculture, heavy industry, heavy transport—and an increase in the numbers and the proportion engaged in white-collar work and the service trades. People who are literate, educated, and provided with the necessities of life by an ever more efficient machine industry and agriculture, turn increasingly to the "tertiary" economic realm. The service industries prosper among the people as a whole and no longer only in court circles.

Education, leisure, services, these go together with an increased consumption of words and images from the new mass media of communications. While societies in the phase of transitional growth begin the process of distributing words from urban centers, the flow becomes a torrent in the societies of incipient population decline. This process, while modulated by profound national and class differences, connected with differences in literacy and loquacity, takes place everywhere in the industrialized lands. Increasingly, relations with the outer world and with oneself are mediated by the flow of mass communication. For the other-directed types political events are likewise experienced through a screen of words by which the events are habitually atomized and personalized—or pseudo-personalized. For the inner-directed person who remains still extant in this period the tendency is rather to systematize and moralize this flow of words.

These developments lead, for large numbers of people, to changes in paths to success and to the requirement of more "socialized" behavior both for success and for marital and personal adaptation. Connected with such changes are changes in the family and in child-rearing practices. In the smaller families of urban life, and with the spread of "permissive" child care to ever wider strata of the population, there is a relaxation of older patterns of discipline. Under these newer patterns the peer-group (the group of one's associates of the same age and class) becomes much more important to the child, while the parents make him feel guilty not so much about violation of inner standards as about failure to be popular or otherwise to manage his relations with these other children. Moreover, the pressures of the school and the peer-group are reinforced and continued—in a manner whose inner paradoxes I shall discuss later—by the mass media: movies, radio, comics, and popular culture media generally. Under these conditions types of character emerge that we shall here term other-directed. To them much of the discussion in the ensuing chapters is devoted. *What is common to all the other-directed people is that their contemporaries are the source of direction for the individual—either those known to him or those with whom he is indirectly acquainted, through friends and through the mass media. This source is of course "internalized" in the sense that dependence on it for guidance in life is implanted early. The goals toward which the other-directed person strives shift with that guidance: it is only the process of striving itself and the process of paying close attention to the signals from others that remain unaltered throughout life.* This mode of keeping in touch with others permits a close behavioral conformity, not through drill in behavior itself, as in the tradition-directed character, but rather through an exceptional sensitivity to the actions and wishes of others.

Of course, it matters very much who these "others" are: whether they are the individual's immediate circle or a "higher" circle or the anonymous voices of the mass media; whether the individual fears the hostility of chance acquaintances or only of those who "count." But his need for approval and direction from others—and contemporary others rather than ancestors—goes beyond the reasons that lead most people in any era to care very much what others think of them. While all people want and need to be liked by some of the people some of the time, it is only the modern other-directed types who make this their chief source of direction and chief area of sensitivity.

It is perhaps the insatiable force of this psychological need for approval that differentiates people of the metropolitan, American upper middle class, whom we regard as other-directed, from very similar types that have appeared in capital cities and among other classes in previous historical periods, whether in Imperial Canton, in eighteenth- and nineteenth-century Europe, or in ancient Athens, Alexandria, or Rome. In all these groups fashion not only ruled as a substitute for morals and customs, but it was a rapidly changing fashion that held sway. It could do so because, although the mass media were in their infancy, the group corresponding to the American upper middle class was comparably small and the elite structure was extremely reverberant. It can be argued, for example, that a copy of *The Spectator* covered its potential readership more thoroughly in the late eighteenth century than *The New Yorker* covers its readership today. . . .

part

three

EQUILIBRIUM AND SOCIAL CONTROL
the manipulation
of human behavior

As we have seen, social institutions exist to serve man's biologic and social needs. To the extent that they accomplish this end, there is little reason to expect change or social instability. Yet change and conflict appear to be recurrent features of human existence.

Because they threaten the continuing satisfaction of human needs, the forces of change customarily have been resisted as subversive. Rather than seeking the greater individual freedom made possible by change, man frequently has devoted his greatest efforts toward strengthening the rigidities that limit his freedom. In times of stress, democracy and liberty repeatedly have bowed to the urge for security and control.

The selections in Part Three examine man's fear of instability and change. They describe the mechanisms he has devised to insure conformity, including his utopian dreams for perfectly controlled societies.

In Section I, T. W. Adorno and his associates examine the "authoritarian personality," that individual whose personality traits lead him to favor security and order over personal freedom. This discussion is followed by a selection from Erich Fromm's *Escape from Freedom*. Fromm argues that the uncertainties and ambiguities associated with pure freedom are more than the average man can tolerate.

Section II examines various forms of social control devised by man to insure the stability of his societies. Max Gluckman, an anthropologist, discusses superstition as a control mechanism in primitive tribes, and sociologists Wilbert E. Moore and Melvin Tumin discuss the advantages of keeping the masses ignorant. Dostoevsky's famous attack on the use of organized religion to beguile the masses follows.

In the next two selections, sociologists Joost A. M. Meerloo and Vance Packard discuss the brainwashing of prisoners by the Communist Chinese and the brainwashing of the American public by Madison Avenue, respectively. Remaining readings in this section include John K. Galbraith's warning of the dehumanizing impact of industrial society, Niccolo Machiavelli's yet to be contradicted advice to the Prince on how best to keep the masses obedient, C. Wright Mills' thesis that all significant forms of American power are actually concentrated in the hands of a small "power elite," and finally Stokely Carmichael's and Charles V. Hamilton's analysis of racism as a means of controlling and perpetually exploiting the black community.

Section III shifts the discussion from control techniques to man's perennial visions of the perfectly ordered society, a society in which everyone lives in ordered harmony without fear and with perfect peace of mind. The Utopias reviewed range from anthropologist Robert Redfield's idealized description of life in primitive societies to Aldous Huxley's *Brave New World*.

FREEDOM AS A BURDEN

12. THE AUTHORITARIAN PERSONALITY

t. w. adorno, e. frenkel-brunswik, d. j. levinson, and r. n. sanford

Stimulated by the horrors of the Second World War, a group of California psychologists conducted an extensive array of personality tests designed to discover the personality profile of individuals most likely to support fascist leaders of the Hitlerian variety.

Among the characteristics of "fascist prone" or "authoritarian" personalities were such traits as intolerance of ambiguity, the tendency to see all issues in rigid terms of good or bad, and marked tendencies toward ethnic, racial, and religious prejudice. In particular, fascist-prone individuals manifested a strong desire for rigid, highly structured laws and regulations. Freedom for such individuals was clearly a source of anxiety.

The following passage contains both the portrait of a typical fascist-prone individual, as well as the now famous "F" or "Fascist" scale. Fascist-prone individuals answered "yes" to most of the questions on the scale.

CAST: Mack, an authoritarian personality
Larry, a non-authoritarian personality

MACK: A MAN HIGH ON ETHNOCENTRISM

This subject is a twenty-four year old college freshman who intends to study law and hopes eventually to become a corporation lawyer or a criminal lawyer.

His grades are B— on the average. After graduating from high school and

From T. W. Adorno, Else Frenkel-Brunswik, Daniel J. Levinson, R. Nevitt Sanford, *The Authoritarian Personality*, New York: John Wiley & Sons, Inc., 1964, pp. 7, 32–55, 226.

attending business school for a year, he worked in the Civil Service in Washington, D. C. His brief sojourn in the Army was terminated by a medical discharge—because of a stomach condition—when he was attending Officer Candidate School.

He is a Methodist, as was his mother, but he does not attend services and he thinks religion is not important to him. His political party affiliation is, like his father's, Democratic. He "agrees" with the political trends expressed by the Anti-New Deal Democrats and "disagrees" with the New Deal Democrats; he "disagrees" with the traditional Republicans but "agrees" with the Willkie-type Republicans.

The subject is of "Irish" extraction and was born in San Francisco. Both of his parents were born in the United States. He states in his questionnaire that his father is a retired lumberman who owns his own home and has a retired income of $1,000. It is learned in the interview that the father was a worker in the woods and in the mills and it is to be inferred that his income derives mainly from a pension. The mother died when the subject was six. He has a sister four years his senior.

The protocol of his interview follows:

Vocation. This student has decided to make law his vocation. He says he has been out of school three years and is now a freshman at the University. However, he went for two years to business school and in addition has attended night school; but he has to start at the beginning here. He had a Civil Service job in Washington, being for a time principal clerk in one of the sections of the War Department. (What made you decide to be a lawyer?) "I decided when I was in Washington. Of course, I was half decided when I was at business school, where business law was emphasized. When I was in high school, my financial means were such that I figured I had better get a general business education and then go to work. (In what ways does law appeal to you?) Well, it seems to me to unlock an awful lot of doors. In any profession, you go so far and then you bump up against it. It is the fundamental basis of our government. It is really the foundation of our enterprise. Sometime I have hopes of making it available to people without funds, so that they can have equal sittings in the court. I want to go in for a general practice at the start and then maybe corporate law and then maybe criminal law. Law will be more important in the future than ever before. There is a trend toward more stringent laws, more regimentation. This will be true whether the form of government alters or not. Economists have determined that for the good of everybody there has to be central control. (What does your father think of the law?) My father is quite interested in it. Of course, he wanted business for me. He has business ability but he is a very retiring fellow. He wouldn't meet people. He owned some lumber land, but mostly he preferred working for other people. He is very unassuming; he worked in the woods and in the mills. His $1,000 income now is from investments, stocks and bonds. He hasn't worked for thirty years. At the time he worked, the wage was around

$75 a month. He had stomach trouble. Yes, he owns his own home in a little town. We have our own cistern and an electric pump that I helped install. He built the old house himself and he has all the modern conveniences. He can get by all right on $1,000 a year."

Income.   (You want to earn $5,000 per year?) "Well, $5,000 sounds like a lot of money right now. It depends on where you live and how. In ordinary circumstances you could live comfortably on it. The opportunities for a lawyer in a small town are limited, but I do like the small town. Especially those that are adjacent to the mountains. I enjoy hunting, fishing, and camping. But I like the conveniences of the city. In the city you have finer houses and the theaters. I haven't found any place I like better than California, and I have traveled quite a lot. I'm going to travel to Alaska. My father's brother died there in the Yukon. There are great possibilities there in the future. If a person studies it carefully and locates properly, he goes up with a town. I worked with some men lumbering last summer who worked on the Alaska highway. They found it pretty tough going. But these difficulties can be overcome if big capitalists get interested. There is a huge pool of oil up there, you know, and that ought to be developed."

Politics.   "I voted for Dewey. In previous times I would have voted for FDR, but I worked there in Washington and saw things I would put a stop to. There is a concentration of power in the bureaus. People who work there have different attitudes. In the Civil Service you are paid according to how many people are under you, so they want people to come in. They think of themselves only. I'm not mercenary enough to understand it. I would simplify things by a competent administration. There is too much overlapping and bungling. I was the right-hand man of the General there when the OWI was introduced. They put up this building for $600,000 with little purpose in mind. They did the same thing that the Army monitoring service was already doing. The OWI wanted to take it over. Even after the OWI took it over, the War Department still helped prepare the communiques; but the OWI wanted credit. All that duplication at a tremendous outlay of money for no purpose. And all the time our department was crying for personnel. I worked many hours overtime for no pay because I was in the Civil Service. I was there from September, 1940, to September, 1942. I was there when war was declared. I worked then for thirty-seven hours straight. It was quite a day in Washington. I liked living in Washington very much. I like being close to the center of things. You can learn a lot about how the government functions. There are daily events at your fingertips that by the time it gets here have changed somehow. It was fun knowing about the background, knowing about the secret committees. My salary was $2,000 a year. Living conditions, of course, were terrible. (What did you like about Dewey especially?) I liked Dewey's background, his frankness, honesty, his clear-cut way of presenting his case. I think that at heart he is a very honest man, interested in maintaining the old government traditions. (How do you see things shaping up for the future?) If we maintain our present system of government, and I think we will for a time, some things will have to be altered. The system in Washington has outgrown the limits of one man to control. We have got to eliminate confusion. The man who runs it must pick his lieutenants carefully. The way it is now, there is no clear authority. You have to consult a half a dozen agencies to get anywhere. This will recede very little after the war. Eventually the President will have to appoint a strong Cabinet to run things for him. There is no doubt that the system is becoming more centralized. I doubt that President Roosevelt will be reelected. It depends on the way the war goes. From his speeches, one seems to see that he feels he is necessary to the United States. He has control of the Party and will run as long as he is physically able. The popular vote in the last election was very close. It was skillful politics that enabled the old guard to win. Considering his obstacles, Dewey did very well. In ordinary times, he would have had a landslide. People who had sons in the war effort felt that taking the President out might prolong the war. That was wrong. The Army and the Navy were prepared for the war ten years in advance. General Marshall would have had a lot to say, whoever was elected. I have sat beside him and heard him talk. Nobody could alter his position. A change of presidents might have altered our relations to England, but not to Russia. Recently there has been a lot of opposition to Churchill. He has been OK in war, but how he will be in peace is a question. There is, of course, close feeling between Roosevelt and Churchill. But Roosevelt would come out second-best in a contest with Winnie. Of course, a lot of Roosevelt's ideas came from Hoover. (Would there be a difference in our relations with Russia?) No, there would be no difference in our relations with Russia. I think Joe Stalin would play pretty fair with us. And Dewey is honest to the death. He has a good background, though not of the wealthy class, and he would think of the average people. His honesty and straightforwardness appeal to me greatly. But a man has to use some underhandedness to get across the highest ideals."

Religion. "On my father's side, my folks were Catholic. My father and his brothers and sisters were Catholic. Father was never deeply religious, but he was a good man. He drank but little, and he never smoked. He was very honest and strict in his dealings. He followed the church rules without going to church. It stems back to his not wanting to meet people. He was very retiring, and I can't understand it. The other members of his family were not that way. His sisters are very average. My mother was a Methodist and quite strict up until her death. I was sick much of the time. She brought us up very strictly under this guidance. Her aunt took us in hand when Mother died and saw that we attended Sunday School with her children. That was up until I was twelve or thirteen. Then I got out of the habit. I like church OK, though I disagree with some of its doctrines. I like the music and singing in church. I was so busy since high school that I stopped going. I have gone in for social things in spite of a great dread of them. But I looked at my father and saw that I had to do differently. Yes, the teachings of Sunday School did mean something. But the arbitrary beliefs were too much. I grew up quickly. My father has allowed me to do as I pleased, although he forced some decisions upon me. About smoking, he said I must do it in front of him, if I must. He also provided wines and liquors in the ice chest. I soon tired of smoking and never took much to drinking. I have a stubborn nature, and if he had tried to stop me, I probably would have taken it up. (Under what conditions might you turn to religion?) Yes, under some conditions I might. I have had a lot of sickness, stomach trouble ever since I was twelve. I was in the hospital once for three months. During those periods, I like to turn to the Bible. I like the history and sayings of Christ, principally. I like to consider them and analyze them and figure out how they affect me. I'm not so interested in the apostles' sayings—that's not first-hand, so I don't accept it entirely. I have to be assured of it factually. I have always tried to live according to His Ten Commandments. I like to receive just treatment and to give it to others. (What about your conception of God?) Well, I have none especially. The closest conception I got was when I was in the service, that is, God as strictly man, greater than any on this earth, one that would treat us as a father would his son. I don't think God is terrible in His justice. If one lives justly, his laxness will be overlooked. The thing is to make things happier and juster on the earth."

Minorities.   "My mother comes from an Irish-English-German background. I think of myself as Irish—perhaps because my father is definitely so, and proud of it. He likes the thought of St. Patrick's Day. I have a quick temper like the Irish. If there is a lot of Irish in people, they are very enjoyable. They are easy spenders, even though they never have much. They have the ability to make other people happy. They are often witty. I wish I were more like that. But there is too much of the lackadaisical and laziness in some classes of Irish. (Which groups would you contrast with the Irish?) The Irish are most different from the Germans or Dutch or maybe the Scandinavians— perhaps Polish or White Russians, where you find a more stolid person in thought and action. The types that I have encountered have a solid build and are not very excitable. (Question about Irish assimilating.) I like to think of an Irish strain; it is enjoyable. Yet in some people the Irish seems to predominate. It depends on the individual. I don't have any desire to be Irish, but I like people who are. I never met an Irishman I didn't like. My brother-in-law is very definitely Irish. (What about groups of people you dislike?) Principally those I don't understand very well. Austrians, the Japanese I never cared for; Filipinos—I don't know—I'd just as soon leave them as have them. Up home there were Austrians and Poles, though I find the Polish people interesting. I have a little dislike for Jewish people. I don't think they are as courteous or as interested in humanity as they ought to be. And I resent that, though I have had few dealings with them. They accent the clannish and the material. It may be my imagination, but it seems to me you can see their eyes light up when you hand them a coin. I avoid the Jewish clothiers because they have second-rate stuff. I have to be careful about how I dress. I mean, I buy things so seldom I have to be careful I get good things. (Can you tell that a person is a Jew?) Sometimes; usually only after I get their ideas. Like one of the girls in Public Speaking. She had all the characteristics, but she left a favorable impression on me, even though her ideas I disagree with. (You mean there are certain ideas which characterize the Jews?) Yes, to stick together, no matter what; to always be in a group; to have Jewish sororities and Jewish organizations. If a Jew fails in his business, he's helped to get started again. Their attention is directed very greatly toward wealth. Girls at the Jewish sorority house all have fur coats, expensive but no taste. Almost a superiority idea. I resent any show of superiority in people, and I try to keep it down myself. I like to talk with working people. (Do you think the dislike of Jews is increasing?) No, I think this war has made people closer together in this country. I've come across Jewish soldiers and sailors; they would be liked and accepted if they would be willing to mix, but they would rather be alone, though I would have accepted them the same as anybody. I think they have interesting ideas, but they have to have something in return. (Do you think the Jews have done their part in the war effort?) Perhaps they have, but they are businessmen, and they have been fully repaid. (Do you think the Jews are a political force in this country?) Yes, in New York there is an organization for Jewish immigration and comfort of Jews. They are very well organized. This should not be allowed. (What do you think is the danger?) I don't believe it is a danger except in a concentration of wealth in a certain class. I hate to see people in this country take on the burdens of people who have been misfits in other countries. We have enough problems at home without helping the oppressed of other countries. The Jews won't intermingle. So they are not a great contribution to our country—though Jewish scientists and doctors have contributed a great deal. I checked on the immigration. Three-quarters of those leaving Europe arrive here. They are very thorough in it. They are businessmen and they will bring pressure to bear on Congress. We ought to prevent further immigration and concentrate on trying to get them to mingle and become a part of our people. (Do you think they would mingle more if they felt there was no prejudice against them?) If they would mingle more, there would be more willingness to break down the barriers on the part of other people. Of course, they have always been downtrodden, but that's no reason for resentment. (I notice you stated you wouldn't marry a Jew.) I certainly wouldn't. I would date that girl in Public Speaking, but she doesn't emphasize her Jewishness. She was accepted by the whole class. I would marry her if she had thrown off her Jewishness, but I wouldn't be able to associate with her class." . . .

General Ethnocentrism

It was noted in Mack's discussion of Jews that he tends to think in ingroup-outgroup terms: he seems to think of the Jews as constituting a relatively homogeneous group that is categorically different from the group to which he feels that he belongs. A logical next step was to explore further his conception of his own group, and to inquire into his opinions and attitudes concerning various other groups.

In the interview with this man the general topic of imagery and attitudes concerning minority groups was introduced by inviting him to discuss his own ingroup belongingness. Most striking in this discussion is the *stereotyped* way in which he speaks of the Irish and of the groups with which they are contrasted. Each ethnic group is regarded as a homogeneous entity, and little mention is made of exceptions. There is no attempt to explain how the groups came to be as they are, beyond the assumption of different "blood strains." What a person is like depends on how much "Irish" or other "strain" he has in him. The Irish have certain *approved traits*—quick temper, easy spending, ability to make people laugh and be happy—and certain traits which he regards as *faults*—lackadaisicalness and laziness.

It is interesting to compare this ingroup appraisal with his appraisal of the Jews, who are described in the same terms but who are conceived of as lacking the good traits of the Irish. Also noteworthy is the contradiction in his attitude toward ambition and power: whereas he criticizes it in the outgroup, he regrets its lack in the ingroup. The problem for him is not how to eliminate an unequal distribution of power, but how to make sure that the bulk of power is in the right (ingroup) hands. Whereas a major fault of the Jews as noted above is their "clannishness" and their failure to assimilate, the existence of an unassimilated Irish strain is "enjoyable." Once again, something for which Jews are blamed is seen as a virtue in the ingroup. Both ingroups and outgroups are thought of in the same general terms; the same evaluative criteria are applied to groups generally, and a given characteristic, such as clannishness or power, is good or bad depending on what group has it.

Unfortunately, there was not time to explore the subject's ideas concerning the other groups which he mentions among his dislikes—Austrians, Japanese, Filipinos—nor to inquire how far this list might have been expanded. Even by itself, however, the fact that the subject rejects other groups just as he rejects the Jews is important.

Larry's first remark calls attention to the fact that views about people and groups may be distorted or at least influenced by personal factors. Mack, on the other hand, shows little such self-orientation or self-awareness; he does not suggest that his confident generalization might have any of the possible inaccuracies of personal opinions, nor does he feel obliged to account for them on the basis of real experience. One might ask whether such differences in the degree of *intraception,* i.e., the inclination to adopt a subjective, psychological, human approach to personal and social problems, do not as a general rule distinguish nonethnocentric from ethnocentric individuals.

Characteristics notable in Mack's ideology concerning minorities but relatively lacking in that of Larry might be described as follows: (a) *Stereotypy*—the tendency mechanically to subsume things under rigid categories. (b) The idea that groups are *homogeneous* units which more or less totally determine the nature of their numbers. This places the responsibility for intergroup tensions entirely on outgroups as independent entries. The only question asked is how outgroups can change in order to make themselves acceptable to the ingroup; there is no suggestion that the ingroup might need to modify its behavior and attitudes. Larry, in contrast, places the responsibilities primarily on the ingroup and urges understanding and education within the ingroup as the basis for solving the problem. (c) The tendency to explain group differences in terms of "blood strain"—how quick a temper a man has depends on how much Irish he has in him. This is in contrast to Larry's attempt at explanation in social, psychological, and historical terms. (d) Mack favors total assimilation by outgroups, as well as total *segregation* of those outgroup members who refuse to assimilate. Larry, for his part, seems neither to threaten segregation nor demand assimilation. He says he wants full "social equality" and interaction, rather than dominance by the ingroup and submission by outgroups. (e) Since he is relatively free of the stereotypes about ingroups and outgroups, and since groups are not his units of social description, Larry stands in opposition to Mack's tendency to think of groups in terms of their coherence and in terms of a *hierarchical arrangement* with powerful ingroups at the top and weak outgroups at the bottom.

The question, raised earlier, of whether an individual who is against Jews tends to be hostile to other minority groups as well is answered in the case of one man at least. Mack rejects a variety of ethnic groups. And Larry, for his part, is opposed to all such "prejudice." The first question for research, then, would be: Is it generally true that a person who rejects one minority group tends to reject all or most of them? Or, is it to be found more frequently that there is a tendency to have a special group against which most of the individual's hostility is directed? How broad is the ethnocentric rejection, that is to say, how many different groups are brought within the conception of outgroup? Are they extranational as well as intranational? What are the main objective characteristics of these groups? What traits are most commonly assigned to them by ethnocentric individuals? What imagery, if any, applies to all outgroups, and what is reserved for particular outgroups? Is the tendency, found in Mack but not in Larry, to make a rigid distinction between the ingroup and the outgroup, common in the population at large? Are Mack's ways of thinking about groups—rigid categories, always placing blame on the outgroup, and so forth—typical of ethnocentric individuals?

If ethnocentrism is conceived of as the tendency to express opinions and attitudes that are hostile toward a variety of ethnic groups and uncritically favorable to the group with which the individual is identified, then is it possible to rank individuals according to the degree of their ethnocentrism, as was proposed in the case of anti-Semitism? This would make it possible to determine the quantitative relations of ethnocentrism to numerous other factors— in the contemporary social situation of the individual, in his history, and in his personality. But, to pursue the general approach outlined above, it seems best first to explore further the outlook of the ethnocentric individual before raising fundamental questions of determination. What of his opinions and attitudes concerning other groups than ethnic or national ones? How does he approach social problems generally?

Politics

In his discussion of politics Mack deals at considerable length with the attributes of what for him is the outgroup. The structure and dynamics of the outgroup are conceived as follows. It is closely cohesive and power-seeking. Power is sought as an end in itself, and to attain it any means may be employed, no matter how wasteful or harmful to others. Selfishness and money-mindedness are important aspects of this power drive. At the same time, however, he ascribes to the outgroup characteristics which are the opposite of powerful: it is inefficient (shows bungling and confusion), wasteful and poorly organized; this inadequacy is attributed to the "fact" that the power arrangements within it are inadequate, with no clear authority and with lieutenants who are both too few and too carelessly selected. In addition to organizational weakness there is also physical weakness. (The reference to Roosevelt's physical ability brings to mind the argument of his political opposition that he was physically too weak to carry the burdens of a wartime president.) A further attribution of weakness to the New Deal is the idea of Roosevelt's submissiveness toward more powerful leaders—"he would come out second-best in a contest with Winnie," his ideas came from Hoover, and it is implied that he would lose out with Stalin if the latter did not play fair with us.

Parenthetically, it may be noted that there is an apparent inconsistency between Mack's general ethnocentrism and his acceptance of Stalin. This apparent discrepancy may possibly be explained in terms of our subject's attitude toward power: his admiration for power is great enough so that he can accept and momentarily ally himself with a distant outgroup when that group is not seen as a direct threat to himself. It is probably a safe guess that like many who supported cooperation with Russia during the war, this man's attitude has now changed, and Russia is regarded as a threat to the ingroup.

Mack's conception of the relations between the outgroup and the ingroup is simple: the outgroup with its selfish, materialistic, power-seeking drives, on the one hand, and its inefficiency and weakness on the other, is out to control and exploit the ingroup—to take power from it, to take over its functions, to grab all the credit, to seduce people into its fold by skillful manipulation, in short, to weaken the ingroup and run everything itself, for its own narrow, selfish ends.

When he comes to the political ingroup, Mack speaks only of admired characteristics, and the only political agencies discussed are the man, Dewey, and the army. The ingroup characteristics fall in exactly the same dimensions as do those ascribed to the outgroup, sometimes being identical and sometimes the exact opposite. Whether there is identity or reversal seems to follow a simple rule: those outgroup characteristics which have an aspect of *power* are kept intact in the ingroup, only now they are regarded as good, whereas for each outgroup characteristic signifying *weakness* or *immorality* there is an ingroup characteristic signifying the opposite.

To consider the reversals first, the inefficiency of the New Deal is in direct contrast to Dewey's clear-cut, straightforward approach. Roosevelt's "skillful politics" is the opposite of Dewey's frankness and honesty-to-the-death. Roosevelt's submission to stronger leaders is in contrast to Dewey's determined overcoming of obstacles and to General Marshall's indomitable firmness. The organizational confusion of the outgroup is to be corrected by the concentration of power in a small, closely knit organization having clearly defined levels of authority with a strong leader at the top and a cabinet of carefully chosen lieutenants.

It becomes clear, then, that the only real difference between the ingroup and the outgroup is the greater weakness of the latter. Leaving aside the weaknesses of the outgroup, we find that in all respects the conceptions of outgroup and ingroup are identical: both seek to concentrate power in a small, cohesive organization the only purpose of which is to maintain itself. While the outgroup is accused of selfishness and materialism, the only virtues of the ingroup are the honesty and efficiency of its methods; there is no reference to its ends.

Whatever the ingroup aims might be, however, they will presumably benefit the ingroup, for Mack tells us that one of the reasons for supporting Dewey is that "he would think of the *average* people," with whom the subject seems to be identified. We know from Mack's discussion of ethnic groups that "average" is not an all-inclusive conception, but rather an ingroup from which he excludes a large proportion of the population. We see also that wealthy people are excluded from his concept of average. That this latter is not typical equalitarianism, however, is shown by his desire to become a corporation lawyer, and by has favoring a form of stratified social organization which in the economic sphere would—far from averaging things out—perpetuate the present distribution of wealth. This would seem to place the subject on the conservative side. Certainly, he quotes with approval many of the slogans of contemporary American conservatism, and he tells us that

Dewey is to be supported because he is "interested in maintaining the old government traditions." Yet there is reason to believe that his conservatism is not of the traditional kind. The type of centralized control which he favors is certainly out of keeping with traditional conservative principles of free competition and restriction of government's functions. Indeed, there is a suggestion that his apparent conservatism is in reality a kind of anticonservatism. We may note his remark "if we maintain our present system of government, and I think we will for a time, some things will have to be altered." Why should he suggest that our system of government might *not* be maintained, and why does he think that at best it will be maintained only *for a time?* He seems to give us the answer himself, for the changes which he suggests as a means of maintaining the conservative tradition are actually changes which would overthrow it entirely.

The main points considered so far are Mack's attribution of both power and weakness to the outgroup and of only power to the ingroup. It must be noted, however, that weakness, too, is thought of as existing in the ingroup, though in a different form. Thus, when Mack describes the OWI as a power-seeking behemoth, the War Department is pictured in a situation of distress: "And all the time our department was crying for personnel." Again, Dewey's campaign is seen as a sort of struggle between David and Goliath, in which the clean-cut, straightforward younger man loses only because of the overwhelming power and lack of scruple which opposes him: "It was skilful politics that enabled the old guard to win. Considering his obstacles, Dewey did very well. In ordinary times he would have had a landslide." This imagery of persecution is expressed not only in Mack's political thinking but also in his discussion of himself and his life in Washington. There is a clear note of self-pity in his remarks that he "worked many hours overtime for no pay," that when war was declared he "worked for thirty-seven hours straight," and that "living conditions were terrible."

It is important to note that weakness in Mack and his group is only implied in these statements. What he seems to be trying to tell us is that in so far as the ingroup might appear to be weak at any time, this is due only to persecution by an outgroup that is momentarily—and unfairly—stronger. It is important to note further that his feelings of being persecuted do not lead to sympathy for other persecuted people nor to any inclination to eliminate persecution generally, but only to the thought that justice would consist in his group becoming the powerful one. Here, as is typical of people with persecution fantasies, Mack believes that he (his group) is essentially strong but is at the same time in a weak position; he can solve this dilemma only by attributing evil (dishonesty, unfairness, and so on) and undeserved power to his opponent. His desire to be attached to the same kind of power which he decries in the outgroup is expressed in his wanting to be "close to the center of things," and "know about the background" of important daily events, to be in on "the secret committees." . . .

THE F SCALE

2.   Although many people may scoff, it may yet be shown that astrology can explain a lot of things.

3.   America is getting so far from the true American way of life that force may be necessary to restore it.

6.   It is only natural and right that women be restricted in certain ways in which men have more freedom.

9.   Too many people today are living in an unnatural, soft way; we should return to the fundamentals, to a more red-blooded, active way of life.

10.   It is more than a remarkable coincidence that Japan had an earthquake on Pearl Harbor Day, December 7, 1944.

12.   The modern church, with its many rules and hypocrisies, does not appeal to the deeply religious person; it appeals mainly to the childish, the insecure, and the uncritical.

14.   After we finish off the Germans and Japs, we ought to concentrate on other enemies of the human race such as rats, snakes, and germs.

17.   Familiarity breeds contempt.

19.   One should avoid doing things in public which appear wrong to others, even though one knows that these things are really all right.

20.   One of the main values of progressive education is that it gives the child great freedom in expressing those natural impulses and desires so often frowned upon by conventional middle-class society.

23.   He is, indeed, contemptible who does not feel an undying love, gratitude, and respect for his parents.

24.   Today everything is unstable; we should be prepared for a period of constant change, conflict, and upheaval.

28.   Novels or stories that tell about what people think and feel are more interesting than those which contain mainly action, romance, and adventure.

30.   Reports of atrocities in Europe have been greatly exaggerated for propaganda purposes.

31.   Homosexuality is a particularly rotten form of delinquency and ought to be severely punished.

32.   It is essential for learning or effective work that our teachers or bosses outline in detail what is to be done and exactly how to go about it.

35.   There are some activities so flagrantly un-American that, when responsible officials won't take the proper steps, the wide-awake citizen should take the law into his own hands.

38.   There is too much emphasis in college on intellectual and theoretical topics, not enough emphasis on practical matters and on the homely virtues of living.

39.   Every person should have a deep faith in some supernatural force higher than himself to which he gives total allegiance and whose decisions he does not question.

42.   No matter how they act on the surface, men are interested in women for only one reason.

43.   Sciences like chemistry, physics, and medicine have carried men very

far, but there are many important things that can never possibly be understood by the human mind.

46.   The sexual orgies of the old Greeks and Romans are nursery school stuff compared to some of the goings-on in this country today, even in circles where people might least expect it.

47.   No insult to our honor should ever go unpunished.

50.   Obedience and respect for authority are the most important virtues children should learn.

53.   There are some things too intimate or personal to talk about even with one's closest friends.

55.   Although leisure is a fine thing, it is good hard work that makes life interesting and worthwhile.

56.   After the war, we may expect a crime wave; the control of gangsters and ruffians will become a major social problem.

58.   *What* a man does is not so important so long as he does it well.

59.   Human nature being what it is, there will always be war and conflict.

60.   Which of the following are the most important for a person to have or to be? *Mark* X *the three most important.*

> artistic and sensuous
> popular, good personality
> drive, determination, will power
> broad, humanitarian social outlook
> neatness and good manners
> sensitivity and understanding
> efficiency, practicality, thrift
> intellectual and serious
> emotional expressiveness, warmth, intimacy
> kindness and charity

65.   It is entirely possible that this series of wars and conflicts will be ended once and for all by a world-destroying earthquake, flood, or other catastrophe.

66.   Books and movies ought not to deal so much with the sordid and seamy side of life; they ought to concentrate on themes that are entertaining or uplifting.

67.   When you come right down to it, it's human nature never to do anything without an eye to one's own profit.

70.   To a greater extent than most people realize, our lives are governed by plots hatched in secret by politicians.

73.   Nowadays when so many different kinds of people move around so much and mix together so freely, a person has to be especially careful to protect himself against infection and disease.

74.   What this country needs is fewer laws and agencies, and more courageous, tireless, devoted leaders whom the people can put their faith in.

75.   Sex crimes, such as rape and attacks on children, deserve more than mere imprisonment; such criminals ought to be publicly whipped.

77.   No sane, normal, decent person could ever think of hurting a close friend or relative.

13. ESCAPE FROM FREEDOM

erich fromm

In addition to basic physiological needs, the individual craves a relationship with the outside world in order to avoid loneliness and the sense of isolation. It is possible for personal freedom, however valued, to become oppressive and frightening when it comes into conflict with the need for social relationships and gratifications. Thus there are conditions under which freedom may become an intolerable burden rather than an unmitigated blessing.

Professor Fromm analyzes the mechanisms through which escape from freedom is sought, the impact of these mechanisms on certain personality types, and some dangers that are posed in an age when technology dominates the human spirit.

. . . When man is born, the stage is set for him. He has to eat and drink, and therefore he has to work; and this means he has to work under the particular conditions and in the ways that are determined for him by the kind of society into which he is born. Both factors, his need to live and the social system, in principle are unalterable by him as an individual, and they are the factors which determine the development of those other traits that show greater plasticity.

Thus the mode of life, as it is determined for the individual by the peculiarity of an economic system, becomes the primary factor in determining his whole character structure, because the imperative need for self-preservation forces him to accept the conditions under which he has to live. This does not mean that he cannot try, together with others, to effect certain economic and political changes; but primarily his personality is molded by the particular mode of life, as he has already been confronted with it as a child through the medium of the family, which represents all the features that are typical of a particular society or class.

The physiologically conditioned needs are not the only imperative part of man's nature. There is another part just as compelling, one which is not rooted in bodily processes but in the very essence of the human mode and practice of life: the need to be related to the world outside oneself, the need to avoid aloneness. To feel completely alone and isolated leads to mental disintegration just as physical starvation leads to death. This relatedness to others is not identical with physical contact. An individual may be alone in a physical sense for many years and yet he may be related to ideas, values, or at least social patterns that give him a feeling of communion and "belonging." On the other hand, he may live among people and yet be overcome with an utter feeling of isolation, the outcome of which, if it transcends a certain limit, is the state of insanity which schizophrenic disturbances represent. This lack of relatedness to values, symbols, patterns, we may call moral aloneness and state that moral aloneness is as intolerable as the physical aloneness, or rather that physical aloneness becomes unbearable only if it implies also moral aloneness. The spiritual relatedness to the world can assume many forms; the monk in his cell who believes in God and the political prisoner kept in isolation who feels one with his fellow fighters are not alone morally. Neither is the English gentleman who wears his dinner jacket in the most exotic surroundings nor the petty bourgeois who, though being deeply isolated from his fellow men, feels one with his nation or its symbols. The kind of relatedness to the world may be noble or trivial, but even being related to the basest kind of pattern is immensely preferable to being alone. Religion and nationalism, as well as any custom and any belief however absurd and degrading, if it only connects the individual with others, are refuges from what man most dreads: isolation.

The compelling need to avoid moral isolation has been described most forcefully by Balzac in this passage from *The Inventor's Suffering:*

"But learn one thing, impress it upon your mind which is still so malleable: man has a horror for aloneness. And of all kinds of aloneness, moral aloneness is the most terrible. The first hermits lived with God, they inhabited the world which is most populated, the world of the spirits. The first thought of man, be he a leper or a prisoner, a sinner or an invalid, is: to have a companion of his fate. In order to satisfy this drive which is life itself, he applies all his strength, all his power, the energy of his whole life. Would Satan have found companions without this overpowering craving? On this theme one could write a whole epic, which would be the prologue to *Paradise Lost* because *Paradise Lost* is nothing but the apology of rebellion."

Any attempt to answer the question why the fear of isolation is so powerful in man would lead us far away from the main road we are following in this book. However, in order not to give the reader the impression that the need to feel one with others has some mysterious quality, I should like to indicate in what direction I think the answer lies.

One important element is the fact that men cannot live without some sort of co-operation with others. In any conceivable kind of culture man needs to co-operate with others if he wants to survive, whether for the purpose of defending himself against enemies or dangers of nature, or in order that he may be able to work and produce. Even Robinson Crusoe was accompanied by his man Friday; without him he would probably not only have become insane but would actually have died. Each person experiences this need for the help of others very drastically as a child. On account of the factual inability of the human child to take care of itself with regard to all-important functions, communication with others is a matter of life and death for the child. The possibility of being left alone is necessarily the most serious threat to the child's whole existence.

There is another element, however, which makes the need to "belong" so compelling: the fact of subjective self-consciousness, of the faculty of thinking by which man is aware of himself as an individual entity, different from nature and other people. Although the degree of this awareness varies, as will be pointed out in the next chapter, its existence confronts man with a problem which is essentially human: by being aware of himself as distinct from nature and other people, by being aware—even very dimly—of death, sickness, aging, he necessarily feels his insignificance and smallness in comparison with the universe and all others who are not "he." Unless he belonged somewhere, unless his life had some meaning and direction, he would feel like a particle of dust and be overcome by his individual insignificance. He would not be able to relate himself to any system which would give meaning and direction to his life, he would be filled with doubt, and this doubt eventually would paralyze his ability to act—that is, to live.

Before we proceed, it may be helpful to sum up what has been pointed out with regard to our general approach to the problems of social psychology. Human nature is neither a biologically fixed and innate sum total of drives nor is it a lifeless shadow of cultural patterns to which it adapts itself smoothly; it is the product of human evolution, but it also has certain inherent mechanisms and laws. There are certain factors in man's nature which are fixed and unchangeable: the necessity to satisfy the physiologically conditioned drives and the necessity to avoid isolation and moral aloneness. We have seen that the individual has to accept the mode of life rooted in the system of production and distribution peculiar for any given society. In the process of dynamic adaptation to culture, a number of powerful drives develop which motivate the actions and feelings of the individual. The individual may or may not be conscious of these drives, but in any case they are forceful and demand satisfaction once they have developed. They become powerful forces which in their turn become effective in molding the social process. This discussion will always be centered around the main theme of this book: that man, the more he gains freedom in the sense of emerging from the original oneness with man and nature and the more he becomes an "individual," has no choice but to unite himself with the world in the spontaneity of love and productive work or else to seek a kind of security by such ties with the world as destroy his freedom and the integrity of his individual self. . . .

Once the primary bonds which gave security to the individual are severed, once the individual faces the world outside of himself as a completely separate entity, two courses are open to him since he has to overcome the unbearable state of powerlessness and aloneness. By one course he can progress to "positive freedom"; he can relate himself spontaneously to the world in love and work, in the genuine expression of his emotional, sensuous, and intellectual capacities; he can thus become one again with man, nature, and himself, without giving up the independence and integrity of his individual self. The other course open to him is to fall back, to give up his freedom, and to try to overcome his aloneness by eliminating the gap that has arisen between his individual self and the world. This second course never reunites him with the world in the way he was related to it before he merged as an "individual," for the fact of his separateness cannot be reversed; it is an escape from an unbearable situation which would make life impossible if it were prolonged. This course of escape, therefore, is characterized by its compulsive character, like every escape from threatening panic; it is also characterized by the more or less complete surrender of individuality and the integrity of the self. Thus it is not a solution which leads to happiness and positive freedom; it is, in principle, a solution which is to be found in all neurotic phenomena. It assuages an unbearable anxiety and makes life possible by avoiding panic; yet it does not *solve* the underlying problem and is paid for by a kind of life that often consists only of automatic or compulsive activities. . . .

The first mechanism of escape from freedom I am going to deal with is the tendency to give up the independence of one's own individual self and to fuse one's self with somebody or something outside of oneself in order to acquire the strength which the individual self is lacking. Or, to put it in different words, to seek for new, "secondary bonds" as a substitute for the primary bonds which have been lost.

The more distinct forms of this mechanism are to be found in the striving for submission and domination, or, as we would rather put it, in the masochistic and sadistic strivings as they exist in varying degrees in normal and neurotic persons respectively. We shall first describe these tendencies and then try to show that both of them are an escape from an unbearable aloneness.

The most frequent forms in which *masochistic* strivings appear are feelings of inferiority, powerlessness, individual insignificance. The analysis of persons who are obsessed by these feelings show that, while they consciously complain about these feelings and want to get rid of them, unconsciously some power within themselves drives them to feel inferior or insignificant. Their feelings are more than realizations of actual shortcomings and weaknesses (although they are usually rationalized as though they were); these persons show a tendency to belittle themselves, to make themselves weak, and not to master things. Quite regularly these people show a marked dependence on powers outside of themselves, on other people, or institutions, or nature. They tend not to assert themselves, not to do what they want, but to submit to the factual or alleged orders of these outside forces. Often they are quite incapable of experiencing the feeling "I want" or "I am." Life, as a whole, is felt by them as something overwhelmingly powerful, which they cannot master or control. . . .

Besides these masochistic trends, the very opposite of them, namely, *sadistic* tendencies, are regularly to be found in the same kind of characters. They vary in strength, are more or less conscious, yet they are never missing. We find three kinds of sadistic tendencies, more or less closely knit together. One is to make others dependent on oneself and to have absolute and unrestricted power over them, so as to make of them nothing but instruments, "clay in the potter's hand." Another consists of the impulse not only to rule over others in this absolute fashion, but to exploit them, to use them, to steal from them, to disembowel them, and, so to speak, to incorporate anything eatable in them. This desire can refer to material things as well as to immaterial ones, such as the emotional or intellectual qualities a person has to offer. A third kind of sadistic tendency is the wish to make others suffer or to see them suffer. This suffering can be physical, but more often it is mental suffering. Its aim is to hurt actively, to humiliate, embarrass others, or to see them in embarrassing and humiliating situations.

Sadistic tendencies for obvious reasons are usually less conscious and more rationalized than the socially more harmless masochistic trends. Often they are entirely covered up by reaction formations of overgoodness or overconcern for others. Some of the most frequent rationalizations are the following: "I rule over you because I know what is best for you, and in your own interest you should follow me without opposition." Or, "I am so wonderful and unique, that I have a right to expect that other people become dependent on me." Another rationalization which often covers the exploiting tendencies is: "I have done so much for you, and now I am entitled to take from you what I want." The more aggressive kind of sadistic impulse finds its most frequent rationalization in two forms: "I have been hurt by others and my wish to hurt them is nothing but retaliation," or, "By striking first I am defending myself or my friends against the danger of being hurt." . . .

Both the masochistic and sadistic strivings tend to help the individual to escape his unbearable feeling of aloneness and powerlessness. Psychoanalytic and other empirical observations of masochistic persons give ample evidence (which I cannot quote here without transcending the scope of this book) that they are filled with a terror of aloneness and insignificance. Frequently this feeling is not conscious; often it is covered by compensatory feelings of eminence and perfection. However, if one only penetrates deeply enough into the unconscious dynamics of such a person, one finds these feelings without fail. The individual finds himself "free" in the negative sense, that is, alone with his self and confronting an alienated, hostile world. In this situation, to quote a telling description of Dostoevski, in *The Brothers Karamazov,* he has "no more pressing need than the one to find somebody to whom he can surrender, as quickly as possible, that gift of freedom which he, the unfortunate creature, was born with." The frightened individual seeks for somebody or something to tie his self to; he cannot bear to be his own individual self any longer, and he tries frantically to get rid of it and to feel security again by the elimination of this burden: the self.

Masochism is one way toward this goal. The different forms which the masochistic strivings assume have one aim: *to get rid of the individual self, to lose oneself;* in other words, *to get rid of the burden of freedom.* This aim is obvious in those masochistic strivings in which the individual seeks to submit to a person or power which he feels as being overwhelmingly strong. (Incidentally, the conviction of superior strength of another person is always to be understood in relative terms. It can be based either upon the actual strength of the other person, or upon a conviction of one's own utter insignificance and powerlessness. In the latter event a mouse or a leaf can assume threatening features.) In other forms of masochistic strivings the essential aim is the same. In the masochistic feeling of smallness we find a tendency which serves to increase the original feeling of insignificance. How is this to be understood? Can we assume that by making a fear worse one is trying to remedy it? Indeed, this is what the masochistic person does. As long as I struggle between my desire to be independent and strong and my feeling of insignificance or powerlessness I am caught in a tormenting conflict. If I succeed in reducing my individual self to nothing, if I can overcome the awareness of my separateness as an individual, I may save myself from this conflict. To feel utterly small and helpless is one way toward this aim; to be overwhelmed by pain and agony another; to be overcome by the effects of intoxication still another. The phantasy of suicide is the last hope if all other means have not succeeded in bringing relief from the burden of aloneness. . . .

The implication of this for masochism is that the individual is driven by an unbearable feeling of aloneness and insignificance. He then attempts to overcome it by getting rid of his self (as a psychological, not as a physiological entity); his way to achieve this is to belittle himself, to suffer, to make himself utterly insignificant. But pain and suffering are not what he wants; pain and suffering are the price he pays for an aim which he compulsively tries to attain. The price is dear. He has to pay more and more and, like a peon, he only gets into greater debt without ever getting what he has paid for: inner peace and tranquillity. . . .

The annihilation of the individual self and the attempt to overcome thereby the unbearable feeling of powerlessness are only one side of the masochistic strivings. The other side is the attempt to become a part of a bigger and more powerful whole outside of oneself, to submerge and participate in it. This power can be a person, an institution, God, the nation, conscience, or a psychic compulsion. By becoming part of a power which is felt as unshakably strong, eternal, and glamorous, one participates in its strength and glory. One surrenders one's own self and renounces all strength and pride connected with it, one loses one's integrity as an individual and surrenders freedom; but one gains a new security and a new pride in the participation in the power in which one submerges. One gains also security against the torture of doubt. The masochistic person, whether his master is an authority outside of himself or whether he has internalized the master as conscience or a psychic compulsion, is saved from making decisions, saved from the final responsibility for the fate of his self, and thereby saved from the doubt of what decision to make. He is also saved from the doubt of what the meaning of his life is or who "he" is. These questions are answered by the relationship to the power to which he has attached himself. The meaning of his life and the identity of his self are determined by the greater whole into which the self has submerged. . . .

At this point a question will have arisen in the mind of many a reader: Is not sadism, as we have described it here, identical with the craving for power? The answer to this question is that although the more destructive forms of sadism, in which the aim is to hurt and torture another person, are not identical with the wish for power, the latter is the most significant expression of sadism. The problem has gained added significance in the present day. Since Hobbes, one has seen in power the basic motive of human behavior; the following centuries, however, gave increased weight to legal and moral factors which tended to curb power. With the rise of Fascism, the lust for power and the conviction of its right has reached new heights. Millions are impressed by the victories of power and take it for the sign of strength. To be sure, power over people is an expression of superior strength in a purely material sense. If I have the power over another person to kill him, I am "stronger" than he is. But in a psychological sense, *the lust for power is not rooted in strength but in weakness*. It is the expression of the inability of the individual self to stand alone and live. It is the desperate attempt to gain secondary strength where genuine strength is lacking. . . .

Although the character of persons in whom sado-masochistic drives are dominant can be characterized as sado-masochistic, such persons are not necessarily neurotic. It depends to a large extent on the particular tasks people have to fulfill in their social situation and what patterns of feelings and behavior are present in their culture whether or not a particular kind of character structure is "neurotic" or "normal." As a matter of fact, for great parts of the lower middle class in Germany and other European countries, the sado-masochistic character is typical, and, as will be shown later, it is this kind of character structure to which Nazi ideology had its strongest appeal. Since the term "sado-masochistic" is associated with ideas of perversion and neurosis, I prefer to speak instead of the sado-masochistic character, especially when not the neurotic but the normal person is meant, of the *"authoritarian character."* This terminology is justifiable because the sado-masochistic person is always characterized by his attitude toward authority. He admires authority and tends to submit to it, but at the same time he wants to be an authority himself and have others submit to him. There is an additional reason for choosing this term. The Fascist systems call themselves authoritarian because of the dominant role of authority in their social and political structure. By the term "authoritarian character," we imply that it represents the personality structure which is the human basis of Fascism. . . .

The attitude of the authoritarian character toward life, his whole philosophy, is determined by his emotional strivings. The authoritarian character loves those conditions that limit human freedom, he loves being submitted to fate. It depends on his social position what "fate" means to him. For a soldier it may mean the will or whim of his superior, to which he gladly submits. For the small businessman the economic laws are his fate. Crisis and prosperity to him are not social phenomena which might be changed by human activity, but the expression of a higher power to which one has to submit. For those on the top of the pyramid it is basically not different. The difference lies only in the size and generality of the power to which one submits, not in the feeling of dependence as such.

Not only the forces that determine one's own life directly but also those that seem to determine life in general are felt as unchangeable fate. It is fate that there are wars and that one part of mankind has to be ruled by another. It is fate that the amount of suffering can never be less than it always has been. Fate may be rationalized philosophically as "natural law" or as "destiny of man," religiously as the "will of the Lord," ethically as "duty"—for the authoritarian character it is always a higher power outside of the individual, toward which the individual can do nothing but submit. The authoritarian character worships the past. What has been, will eternally be. To wish or to work for something that has not yet been before is crime or madness. The miracle of creation—and creation is always a miracle—is outside of his range of emotional experience. . . .

AUTOMATON CONFORMITY

In the mechanisms we have been discussing, the individual overcomes the feeling of insignificance in comparison with the overwhelming power of the world outside of himself either by renouncing his individual integrity, or by destroying others so that the world ceases to be threatening.

Other mechanisms of escape are the withdrawal from the world so completely that it loses its threat (the picture we find in certain psychotic states), and the inflation of oneself psychologically to such an extent that the world outside becomes small in comparison. Although these mechanisms of escape are important for individual psychology, they are only of minor relevance culturally. I shall not, therefore, discuss them further here, but instead will turn to another mechanism of escape which is of the greatest social significance.

This particular mechanism is the solution that the majority of normal individuals find in modern society. To put it briefly, the individual ceases to be himself; he adopts entirely the kind of personality offered to him by cultural patterns; and he therefore becomes exactly as all others are and as they expect him to be. The discrepancy between "I" and the world disappears and with it the conscious fear of aloneness and powerlessness. This mechanism can be compared with the protective coloring some animals assume. They look so similar to their surroundings that they are hardly distinguishable from them.

The person who gives up his individual self and becomes an automaton, identical with millions of other automatons around him, need not feel alone and anxious any more. But the price he pays, however, is high; it is the loss of his self. . . .

It has been the thesis of this book that freedom has a twofold meaning for modern man: that he has been freed from traditional authorities and has become an "individual," but that at the same time he has become isolated, powerless, and an instrument of purposes outside of himself, alienated from himself and others; furthermore, that this state undermines his self, weakens and frightens him, and makes him ready for submission to new kinds of bondage. Positive freedom on the other hand is identical with the full realization of the individual's potentialities, together with his ability to live actively and spontaneously. Freedom has reached a critical point where, driven by the logic of its own dynamism, it threatens to change into its opposite. The future of democracy depends on the realization of the individualism that has been the ideological aim of modern thought since the Renaissance. The cultural and political crisis of our day is not due to the fact that there is too much individualism but that what we believe to be individualism has become an empty shell. The victory of freedom is possible only if democracy develops into a society in which the individual, his growth and happiness, is the aim and purpose of culture, in which life does not need any justification in success or anything else, and in which the individual is not subordinated to or manipulated by any power outside of himself, be it the State or the economic machine; finally, a society in which his conscience and ideals are not the internalization of external demands, but are really *his* and express the aims that result from the peculiarity of his self. . . .

Only if man masters society and subordinates the economic machine to the purposes of human happiness and only if he actively participates in the social process, can he overcome what now drives him into despair—his aloneness and his feeling of powerlessness. Man does not suffer so much from poverty today as he suffers from the fact that he has become a cog in a large machine, an automaton, that his life has become empty and lost its meaning. The victory over all kinds of authoritarian systems will be possible only if democracy does not retreat but takes the offensive and proceeds to realize what has been its aim in the minds of those who fought for freedom throughout the last centuries. It will triumph over the forces of nihilism only if it can imbue people with a faith that is the strongest the human mind is capable of, the faith in life and in truth, and in freedom as the active and spontaneous realization of the individual self.

MECHANISMS OF SOCIAL CONTROL

14. THE UTILITY OF SUPERSTITION
max gluckman

In the introduction to Part Three, it was suggested that belief systems are a crucial social control mechanism. The following selection illustrates how belief in witchcraft prevalent among most African tribes serves as an important social control mechanism. Note that in the reading by Dostoevsky the organized religions of the West may be used in identical fashion.

. . . It was early observed that the belief in witchcraft involved the idea that Africans thought it "singular that they alone should be sick while all the people around them were enjoying good health." In this observation lay an important clue to understanding the system of beliefs in witchcraft and magic. Another clue was the observation, made by many administrators and missionaries, that men accused their personal enemies of bewitching them: wherefore, said these observers, the charges of witchcraft were obviously fraudulent. . . .

Witchcraft as a theory of causation does not deny that men fall ill from eating certain foods, but it explains why some of them fall ill at some times and not at other times. . . .

Witchcraft as a theory of causation is concerned with the singularity of misfortune.

Other cultures give different kinds of answers to this metaphysical problem, why certain events happen to certain people at certain times and places. There are the will of God or of gods, Kismet, Karma, Fate, Providence, the action of ancestral spirits. African tribes also employ some of these other

From Max Gluckman, *Custom and Conflict in Africa*. New York: Barnes & Noble, Inc. By permission of Basil Blackwell, Publishers, London.

answers to varying degrees. The agnostic scientist may call it "chance," the intersection of two chains of events in space-time: a boy taking the cattle to water, trod on a snake sunning itself in the path. . . .

If the consultation is about an illness, the guilty witch has to be approached in certain customary ways to withdraw his witchcraft, and this he does with equal formality. If he reacts to the charge with anger, it is proof of his guilt and of his continued ill will. But if the witch is sought because he caused a death, the chief's oracle must confirm the verdict before he can be punished or required to pay compensation. In Central and South Africa he was required at the chief's orders to drink the oracle-poison himself. If he vomited it, he was declared innocent; if it stupefied him, he was guilty and might be killed. This ordeal had at least the merit that it was not death which proved innocence. . . .

The building up of community out of intensively interrelated groups of kinsfolk, with but few specialized relationships, is based on the stationary subsistence economies which are characteristic of Africa. All men, including even chiefs, live at approximately the same standard. They gain their living by simple tools and are heavily threatened by natural disasters. There is pressure on all men, and especially on the rich, to be generous in sharing: production is individualistic, but consumption is largely communal. What each man has to do is demarcated by his social position, and any failure to reach the standard is severely reprobated. But so is any unusual success beyond a man's appropriate due. Exceptional achievement is bought at the cost of one's fellows. The man who is too successful is suspected of being a witch and himself is suspicious of the witchcraft of his envious fellows. Among the Bemba of Northern Rhodesia to find one beehive in the woods is luck, to find two is very good luck, to find three is witchcraft. . . .

African life nowadays is changing rapidly, and witchcraft accusations now involve circumstances arising from Africa's absorption in Western economy and polity. Conflicts between old and new social principles produce new animosities, which are not controlled by custom, and these open the way to new forms of accusation. Charges, previously excluded, as by a Zulu against his father, are now made. The system of witchcraft beliefs, originally tied to certain social relations, can be adapted to new situations of conflict—to competition for jobs in towns, to the rising standard of living, made possible by new goods, which breaches the previous egalitarianism, and so forth. In response to this situation there have arisen in Africa movements designed to cleanse the country of witches, held responsible for social disintegration, for falling yields on over-cultivated lands, for new diseases. The philosophy of these movements against witchcraft is that if Africans would cease to hate one another and would love each other, misfortune would pass. These movements are short-lived, and they tend to be replaced by religious movements involving messianic elements.

15. SOME SOCIAL FUNCTIONS
OF IGNORANCE

wilbert e. moore
and melvin tumin

It is customary to assume that social stability and orderly progress depend solely upon increasing knowledge, education, and rationality of a nation's citizenry. Ignorance, on the other hand, has been regarded as the antithesis of social stability. Since knowledge is always imperfect, it is appropriate to ask whether its opposite, ignorance, sometimes may not serve as a positive rather than negative force in the operation and stabilization of social institutions and values.

In the essay that follows the authors identify five integrative functions of ignorance within society. Taken together they suggest that social scientists have begun to realize that ignorance may perform positive social functions that were once attributed exclusively to the exercise of "reason."

Ignorance is commonly viewed today as the natural enemy of stability and orderly progress in social life. It is equally commonly believed, as a corollary, that any increase in knowledge automatically brings with it an increase in benefits to mankind. As a result education, as the formal technique of imparting this knowledge to the uninformed, has become elevated in many lay and professional circles to the status of a panacea for all of man's ills.

This enthusiasm for education, and for the "rational" approach which is considered its handmaiden, is found throughout the social sciences. That sociologists share this enthusiasm is indicated by the readiness with which, as applied scientists, they advocate such things as enhanced knowledge on the part of prospective marriage partners; improved lines of communication in industry; increased awareness of community and national affairs; greater knowledge about the "real" meaning of such terms as race and nationality; increased sensitivity to personal differences and the nuances of interpersonal relations; and therapeutic treatment of neuroses through giving the patient a knowledge of the sources of his anxieties.

The rationalistic bias, which finds its way into many sociological writings of the last half century, may, however, be contrasted with several developments in social science that have served to diminish the importance ascribed

From Wilbert E. Moore and Melvin Tumin, "Some Social Functions of Ignorance," *American Sociological Review*, XIV, December 1949. By permission of the authors and the American Sociological Association.

to rational, scientific knowledge. Two of these may be singled out for special mention. The first has been the careful study and analysis of the functions of magic, ritual, and superstition in social organization. This culminates, perhaps, in the findings of Malinowski concerning the role of magic as a means for providing a subjective and socially sanctioned security with regard to anxiety-producing features of the physical and social environment.

The second development has been the distinction between irrational and nonrational orientations, and the recognition of the high importance in society of ultimate values and attitudes toward them. This development is exemplified especially in the works of Pareto and Parsons.

The first of these developments calls attention to a widespread type of social action that functions as a "satisfactory" alternative to complete knowledge and perfect control. And, since resort to magic is so generally distributed throughout human society, there is at least some doubt that it is likely to be eliminated by any predictable expansion of knowledge and technique.

The second development emphasizes the fact that empirical knowledge and ignorance do not in combination exhaust the socially significant orientations of the individual to his environment. It thus helps to distinguish clearly between ignorance, on the one hand, and ultimate, including superempirical, values, on the other.

Neither of these developments, however, has included an explicit examination of the role of ignorance as such. Both have served to narrow and redefine its relation to other types of orientations. But in both there is some implication that genuine ignorance, as distinct from knowledge on the one hand and nonrational beliefs and values on the other, is only a disturbing element in social action and relations, and is accordingly subject to successive constrictions in importance.

It is the central purpose of this paper to examine explicitly some of the contexts in which ignorance, rather than complete knowledge,[1] performs specifiable functions in social structure and action. Some of the observations that will be made have already been recognized in the literature. It is suggested, however, that their significance has ordinarily been missed, since they provide uncomfortable exceptions to the prevailing rationalistic emphasis in sociological writing.

The central theorem of this paper holds that, quite apart from the role of ultimate values and the attitudes relative to them, perfect knowledge is itself impossible, and an inherently impossible basis of social action and social relations. Put conversely, ignorance is both inescapable and an intrinsic

[1] Ignorance is to be taken here as simply referring to "not knowing," that is, the absence of empirically valid knowledge. "Perfect knowledge" is considered as the totality of all knowledge ideally available to man in general, and not simply that which is believed available within any context of social action. Ignorance may refer to past, present, or future conditions or events, as long as valid knowledge is conceivably available. For the purposes of this paper, ignorance is to be kept distinct from "error," whether of fact or of logic, and from the act of *ignoring* what is known.

element in social organization generally, although there are marked differences in the specific forms, degrees, and functions of ignorance in known social organizations.

The following attempt to classify the sociological functions of ignorance is necessarily rudimentary and primitive. There is unquestionably some, and perhaps considerable, overlapping among the various categories. It is to be hoped that the greatest portion of this overlapping is due to the fact that attention will be focussed on primary functions in specific action contexts, ignoring, for purposes of classification, the secondary and derivative functions. It is also possible that further investigation and analysis would reduce the variety of specific functions to more general principles.

1. As Preservative of Privileged Position

The function of ignorance that is most obvious, particularly to the cynical, is its role in preserving social differentials. However, a purely cynical view is likely to overlook the extent to which the continuity of any social structure depends upon differential access to knowledge in general, and, *a fortiori,* to specialized knowledge of various kinds. In many instances, of course, the counterpart of ignorance on the part of the outsider is *secrecy* on the part of the possessor of knowledge. Some of the outstanding examples of this general function of ignorance are summarized in the following paragraphs.

a. The specialist and the consumer.   Ignorance on the part of a consumer of specialized services (for example, medical or legal advice) helps to preserve the privileged position of a specialized dispenser of these services. This is in some measure a by-product of the division of labor, and theoretically the same persons may occupy super-ordinate or subordinate positions as one or another service or skill is demanded. However, there are both theoretical and empirical bases for concluding that some persons whose skills are both scarce and functionally important will occupy a generalized superior status. Although that status is not solely the product of the ignorance of others, in concrete instances it is partially maintained by such ignorance.

One evidence of the function of ignorance as a preservative of privileged position lies in the situation where the consumer acquires, through continuous exposure to the services of the specialist, a sense of his own ability to deal with his problems, and thus to dispense with the service of the specialist (e.g., where we learn how to treat common colds, simple fevers, and bruises, and where we learn how to send stern notes concerning contractual obligations). Thus the range of situations in which the special services are believed to be required is altered from the original position.

On the other hand, the specialist commonly develops devices to protect himself against this sort of attrition. A common device is that of specialized and possibly esoteric vocabulary, or the use of instruments and techniques not intrinsically required for the solution but seemingly so. However, the central point remains that real or presumed differential knowledge and skills are inherently necessary to maintain mutually satisfactory relationships between specialist and consumer.

b. The specialist and the potential competitor. Another facet to the preservation of the privileged position of the specialist is perhaps worthy of special mention. It was noted in the preceding paragraphs that the specialist's position may be endangered by "the patient becoming his own physician." A related danger is that the privileged position of the specialist will be so attractive that too many competitors will appear in the market. This is simply another, and more common, way of saying that ignorance operates to protect the specialist from potential competitors. Perhaps the commonest devices for guarding against this danger are "trade secrets" and their protection through the control by the specialists themselves of training and thus of access to the privileged positions. Examples in contemporary society are to be found in the limited access to certain professions and in the restriction of apprenticeship on the part of various craft unions. Although often justified as a means for protecting technical standards, these restrictions appear also to preserve a sharp distinction between the knowledge of specialists and the ignorance of aspirants. For the society as a whole the result may be a restriction in essential services, either directly through limitation of the number of specialists or indirectly through increasing costs so that other goods or services must be sacrificed by the consumer.

c. Role differentiation and the maintenance of power. In any society internal social order is in part maintained by allocating statuses and differentiating roles along lines of age, sex, and generation. These differentials serve as hooks on which differences in life-chances are hung, and the result is that differentials in knowledge also fall along these lines. In non-literate societies, this tends to result in a monopoly of skills on the part of the elders and the consequent monopoly of power in their hands. It also results in sexual division of special skills, providing females with sources of power that their physique would not otherwise give them, and providing males with a source of power that acts as a balance to the power inherent in the female's control of sexual access.

The universal diffusion of age-respect as an organizing principle of social relations in primitive societies is functionally dependent upon and compatible with differential distribution of skills and knowledge along age lines. Since most primitive societies surround these differentials with traditional sanctions, and since knowledge of alternatives is highly limited, the situation is essentially stable.

The contrasting case in Western civilization serves further to document these contentions. In Western society there is an observable attrition in parental control over children and an equalization of power as between the sexes, in part because of the accessibility of extra-familial sources of knowledge and skill. Where the young can learn skills independently of the instruction of their parents, and where females have an increasing access to economic independence, there tends to be a marked attenuation of the power based on the former parental and male monopolies of knowledge and skills. It should be noted, however, that the extra-familial access to knowledge and skills (and the power derived therefrom) is by no means unlimited. Censorship, whether by State or Church, is one obvious form of limiting access to knowledge as a means of preserving power structures.

d. Avoidance of jealousy over unequal rewards.   Ignorance operates to maintain smooth social relations by preventing jealousy and internal dissension where differential rewards to approximate status equals are not based on uniformly known and accepted criteria. It is a common administrative rule of formal organizations that salaries are confidential. The efficacy of this rule may rest upon the existence of special treatment and individual agreements, which if known, would give rise to intramural bickering. It may also rest upon the lack of absolutely objective criteria of performance, so that the person not equally rewarded may claim as bias what is in fact a difference of judgment. Whether the confidential differentials are based on favoritism, meeting outside offers, or some commonly acceptable criteria that are debatable in their application, ignorance of the differentials serves a positive function where either the public statement of the criteria or their open application to particular cases would create difficulties.

This principle also applies outside of formal organizations. Even invitations to dinner or other "social" events are commonly confidential if the criteria or inclusion and exclusion are not both self-evident and defensible. Within the family, younger children, who are likely to regard themselves as the equals of their older brothers and sisters, may be kept in ignorance of the privileges of the latter as a device less fraught with potential conflict than the principle of age differentials.

e. Secrecy and security.   As a general principle, ignorance serves to maintain the security of the individual or of the social system as a whole wherever knowledge would aid an actual or potential enemy. This principle is commonly understood, although in somewhat different terms, with reference to national security. However, the principle operates in other contexts also. The success of a military or law-enforcement undertaking, and the security of its participants, may depend upon the element of *surprise*. Indeed, any power structure may depend in part upon ignorance not only of its specific activities, but also of its basic intentions. Even the security of the individual may depend upon ignorance by others of personal attributes or past experiences that have no intrinsic bearing on his present status but which would be regarded unfavorably if known: for example, the technical Negro who is passing for white, the reformed ex-convict, the person below or above the required age for his position, the illegitimate child subsequently adopted.

2. As Reinforcement of Traditional Values

a. Isolation and traditionalism. Traditional behavior depends in part upon ignorance of alternatives. The classical case of ignorance reinforcing traditional behavior is the significance of isolation from new stimuli in the maintenance of the round of customary practices in primitive and peasant societies. It is likely, however, that isolation alone does not account for the failure to explore alternatives; having achieved some kind of working equilibrium, such a system is not likely to foster inquiry. There is no "good" reason why it should do so, and ample reason, in terms of continued stability, why it should not. However, no social system is without internal strains and dissident elements; it is here especially that ignorance of alternatives helps preserve the existing order of things. It is also possible that knowledge and acceptance of alternatives would result in a more stable set of relations.

The same generic phenomenon is found in any society in the isolation of the individual from new ideas. Where the individual's notions of right and wrong are rigidified, susceptibility to new knowledge and influences is minimized. The "conservative" is a short-hand term for this phenomenon. As this equilibrium may also have its weak points, ignorance may be necessary to preserve whatever balance has been achieved.

b. Ignorance of normative violations. Another way in which ignorance serves to protect the traditional normative structure is through reinforcing the assumption that deviation from the rules is statistically insignificant. This is especially crucial in those situations where there is a strong tendency to deviate which is repressed but which would be expressed if it were known that deviation was statistically popular rather than limited. This is perhaps particularly true of sexual conduct, but may occur with respect to any system of norms that is subject to considerable pressure or internal strain. In a sense, therefore, the normative system as such may suffer more from knowledge of violations than from the violations themselves.

A similar conclusion may derive from a somewhat different functional context. There is the possibility that various activities are contrary to particular normative prescriptions, yet perform a function in the maintenance of the approved structure as a whole. Ignorance of violations would thus serve to prevent outraged suppression of these functionally significant practices, of which perhaps the most common examples are prostitution and gambling.

c. Reinforcement of group mandates. Ignorance also serves to reinforce ultimate values and heighten the sense of community through induction of subservience of individual to group interests. This is made possible in part by active or passive barriers to knowledge of the consequences of following individual as against group mandates. All socialization processes in all human societies operate to reduce curiosity and knowledge about the presumed socially dysfunctional alternative of pursuing individual tendencies. These processes act so effectively in most cases that the matter rarely appears as a matter of choice, much less as a conflict. All social groups thus require some quotient of ignorance to preserve "esprit de corps."

3. As Preservative of Fair Competition

Most competitive systems, whether in economic production and exchange or in games of chance and skill, assume not only a uniform range of knowledge and rational skill but also an explicit or implicit ignorance. Thus the idea of the "free competitive market" assumes equal initial access on the part of all concerned, and an impersonal limitation on advantage of all participants. In such a situation, differential access to knowledge gives inequitable advantages and destroys the freedom and fairness of competition. Similarly, the rationale of an open-class system of stratification assumes equality of opportunity, which includes as a major element equal access to knowledge and technical training requisite for class mobility. The normative justification of the system is thus endangered by notable inequalities of access to knowledge, *unless there is an effective range of ignorance about this also.*

There is, however, in the impersonal market system a more fundamental role of ignorance, rather than of equally limited knowledge that might in principle be extended to equally perfect knowledge. To keep the system genuinely and impersonally competitive, each competitor must *not* know all the policies and decisions of his competitors. Such knowledge would unavoidably destroy the bases of competition either through the creation of overwhelming power combinations or, in other circumstances, making the outcome so certain that no further action would be required. Indeed, the inability to predict results, whether from simply inadequate or from structurally barred knowledge, is a prerequisite to many situations of competition and conflict. Illustrations of this principle range all the way from poker games and athletic events to armed warfare.

4. As Preservative of Stereotypes

Viewed from the standpoint of the individual actor, all social behavior is directed toward stereotypes of other social units, representing greater or lesser degrees of abstraction or misconception of the precise and complete characteristics of the other units. So-called primary and informal groups tend to reduce the role of stereotypes to a minimum by great emphasis on wide ranges of personal knowledge and involvement, whereas formally structured relations in their nature emphasize the stringently limited role of the actor. Even in the former case, however, ignorance of the *full* range of individual characteristics and motivations is not only factually present, but also intrinsically necessary. The most intimate of friends are happily ignorant of some of each other's habits and thoughts. In fact, an important element of socialization involves acquisition of the habit of appearing to conform to the expected stereotypes demanded in standard situations.

a. Bureaucratic organization. The general principles discussed in the preceding paragraph have a special relevance in formal bureaucratic structures, which by their nature depend upon narrowly and precisely defined roles and, therefore, personalities. The nature of the established relations among individuals in such organizations is such as to foster ignorance of "irrelevant" personal characteristics, and indeed to require such ignorance whenever knowledge would impair impersonal fulfillment of duties. The rules that define authority and function are such as to make possible the cooperative interdependence of actual or potential personal enemies, just as in the military services the subordinate is required to "salute the uniform and not the man." Similarly, in state-entertaining a strict protocol makes it unnecessary and probably inadvisable to inquire into the personal merits of attending officials.

It is also well known, of course, that in strictly bureaucratic organizations, where membership constitutes an occupation and frequent face-to-face contact is the rule, the expected ignorance is subject to attrition by greater familiarity and the establishment of "informal" procedures and relations. These are likely to be based upon characteristics and attitudes irrelevant and possibly inimical to the formal expectations, although they may be more effective components of the operating organization than are the official and limited expectations. The continuity of the organization thus depends upon an effective balance between the ignorance required for orderly procedure and the knowledge acquired by participants.

b. Ethnic and class stereotypes. Among the more commonly recognized stereotypes that at least partially thrive on ignorance, are those relating to ethnic groups and other minorities that may be the object of scapegoat reactions. It is true that "education in the facts" often does little to remove the prejudice that supports, and the discrimination that expresses, the stereotype. It may nevertheless be asserted that knowledge that the facts do not support one's stereotype may significantly affect the quantity and quality of intensity with which these stereotypes are held and acted upon. Maintenance of the stereotype in the face of superior knowledge then at least involves the cost and strain of additional rationalization.

The element of ignorance in stereotypical behavior is also illustrated in reference to class. It appears that the notion of "typical class behavior" is a most significant basis of social action precisely at those points where there is least knowledge of the actual heterogeneity internal to "classes." This may be stated in a more general way. The idea that there are characteristics and attributes common to a social class is likely to be most firmly believed precisely by those farthest removed, in the class structure, from the class in question.

In a highly complex open-class system, most relationships between status unequals take place not in the general context of inter-class relations, but in specific contexts of bureaucratic superior and inferior, landlord and tenant, professional and client. Many of these relationships may specifically rule out questions of general inequality (as in market relations), and in others the ranks of the actors may vary with the context of the action. It is only where the specific attributes of individuals and the specific contexts of action are unknown, ignored, or irrelevant that the more general category of class is likely to have any significance. Yet for certain limited purposes social action may be structured along class lines as long as the stereotype with its component of ignorance is maintained.

5. As Incentive Appropriate to the System

a. Anxiety and work.   There are a variety of situations in which ignorance of present rating or future chances is used as a device to create anxieties and spur activity in a competitive system. Thus, in a bureaucratic organization rules are ordinarily thought of as giving predictability. However, they may be so constructed and applied as they relate to persons in the lower strata that prediction is difficult and the worker is expected to be motivated by his insecurity.[2] With slight modifications, the principle would appear to fit the situation of students, but more especially of their teachers. Indeed, to the extent that risk, uncertainty, and insecurity have ignorance as a common component and anxiety as a common incentive, the principle is a general feature of the rationale of competition.

It is easy to see that the principle, so generalized, has a point of diminishing or negative returns, varying with the circumstances. There is unquestionably an attrition of motive when anxiety is prolonged, owing to the way anxiety typically produces personal disorganization and is thus disruptive of the organization required for efficient performance.[3]

b. The aleatory principle.   Ignorance also operates as an incentive in a quite different context from that just discussed. Here attention is directed to the role of "new experience" in human life, where the attractiveness of the new experience depends in part upon the uncertainty of the outcome. Certainly the attractiveness of many games of chance, as well as of those games and sports where chance may equalize or offset known differences in skill and performance, rests in large measure on their unpredictable outcome. In fact, there is some rough evidence that ignorance of the future in recreational activities

[2] See Alvin W. Gouldner, "Discussion" of Wilbert E. Moore, "Industrial Sociology: Status and Prospects," *American Sociological Review,* 13: 382–400, August, 1948, at p. 398.
[3] See Allison Davis, "The Motivation of the Underprivileged Worker," in William F. Whyte, ed., *Industry and Society* (New York: McGraw-Hill Book Co., 1946), pp. 84–106.

assumes an especially significant role where routine (read: perfect predictability) and boredom are characteristic of work assignments and where there is
a sharp break between working time and leisure time.

THE INTERPLAY OF IGNORANCE AND KNOWLEDGE

Knowledge and ignorance may for some purposes be viewed as polar
antipodes on a continuum. Seen this way, there is an objective relationship
between them that is at least analytically independent of any actor's definition
of the situation.[4] That relationship may be described in the following terms:
For every increase in what is known about a given phenomenon there is a
corresponding decrease in what is unknown. In any actual situation of social
action, however, this analytical relationship between the known and the unknown is conditioned by the fact that social actors always know at least
somewhat less than the totality of what is theoretically knowable. At least in
some contexts, therefore, recognition of ignorance by the actor is prerequisite
to the acquisition of knowledge, and may itself be regarded as a gain in
knowledge.

Where there is a felt need, by an individual or group, for a solution to
a problem, ignorance can operate as a factor dynamic to social change. There
is, of course, no intrinsic directionality in ignorance or its recognition which
determines that empirically valid rather than invalid solutions will result. But
each of these alternative possibilities has differential consequences for the
later interplay of ignorance and knowledge. For, by and large, those "solutions" which are psychologically reassuring but empirically invalid or superempirical may simply postpone the crisis or problem situation. And since in
doing so they may distract attention from and possibly hide the source of the
problem, it can also be said that they tend tacitly to institutionalize those crises
or problems where psychological reassurance is not by itself sufficient.

On the other hand, it may also be said that while empirically valid solutions do eliminate the specific problems to which they are relevant, they by no
means reduce the inherently problematic character of social life and are not
therefore more *generally* final in the reassurance they provide. For, there is
no exception to the rule that every time a culture works out an empirically
valid answer to a problem, it thereby generates a host of derivative problems,
if only in terms of the social reorganization required to incorporate the new
solution. In one sense, then, the difference reduces to one where the maintenance of ignorance institutionalizes old problems and the acquisition of knowledge makes continuous the introduction of new problems. The dynamic role

---

[4] This continuous distribution of knowledge and ignorance makes many of the observations in this paper reversibly viewable as functions of limited knowledge rather than of
ignorance.

of ignorance in social change is thus displayed in the recognition of its existence and the subsequent formulation of answers, whether empirically valid or not.

SUMMARY NOTE

Ignorance is not a simple analytical element, but rather a more or less hidden component of situations usually discussed in other terms. It follows that the categories of function treated here are not entirely homogeneous. Thus, in some instances such as market competition ignorance may be viewed as an element or condition within a circumscribed system. In other instances such as the maintenance of national security, ignorance may be a necessary condition for outsiders. In all these instances, however, the problem is one of shifting perspective, since maintenance of position or the existing relationships may be viewed within a narrower or broader frame of reference.

Functional analysis must distinguish elements necessary for *any* social structure and those necessary within particular, given configurations. If a single society is taken as the unit of reference, then it may be necessary to distinguish the whole and the part. Known societies are not so neatly intermeshed as to assure that a particular function of ignorance within a segment of society (for example, the privileged position of the specialist with regard to potential competitors) is favorable to other segments, or to the society as a whole.

If the foregoing observations are sound, it follows that ignorance must be viewed not simply as a passive or dysfunctional condition, but as an active and often positive element in operating structures and relations.

16. THE GRAND INQUISITOR
fyodor dostoevsky

One function of social control is to provide the masses with values and perspectives that will protect them from their own follies and antisocial dispositions. Men of power, whose responsibility it is to use their authority in such a way as to produce meaningful satisfactions and security for ordinary people, frequently must make difficult choices to that end. Sometimes they must do so in situations where benevolent misrepresentation may appear preferable to disruptive truth.

From Fyodor Dostoevsky, *The Brothers Karamazov.*

Taken from a famous novel by one of the modern world's great novelists, the following selection dramatically links Christianity with the problem of social control in a highly charged religious setting. Here, the masses look to one man who must interpret and control an unusual event having the gravest implications for established order and cherished beliefs.

". . . Do you know, Alyosha—don't laugh! I made a poem about a year ago. If you can waste another ten minutes on me, I'll tell it to you."

"You wrote a poem?"

"Oh, no, I didn't write it," laughed Ivan, "and I've never written two lines of poetry in my life. But I made up this poem in prose and I remembered it. I was carried away when I made it up. You will be my first reader—that is, listener. Why should an author forego even one listener?" smiled Ivan. "Shall I tell it to you?"

"I am all attention," said Alyosha.

"My poem is called 'The Grand Inquisitor'; it's a ridiculous thing, but I want to tell it to you." . . .

"My story is laid in Spain, in Seville, in the most terrible time of the Inquisition, when fires were lighted every day to the glory of God, and 'in the splendid *auto da fé* the wicked heretics were burnt.' . . .

"In His infinite mercy He came once more among men in that human shape in which He walked among men for three years fifteen centuries ago. He came down to the 'hot pavement' of the southern town in which on the day before almost a hundred heretics had, *ad majorem gloriam Dei,* been burnt by the cardinal, the Grand Inquisitor, in a magnificent *auto da fé,* in the presence of the king, the court, the knights, the cardinals, the most charming ladies of the court, and the whole population of Seville.

"He came softly, unobserved, and yet, strange to say, every one recognized Him. That might be one of the best passages in the poem. I mean, why they recognized Him. The people are irresistibly drawn to Him, they surround Him, they flock about Him, follow Him. He moves silently in their midst with a gentle smile of infinite compassion. The sun of love burns in His heart, light and power shine from His eyes, and their radiance, shed on the people, stirs their hearts with responsive love. He holds out His hands to them, blesses them, and a healing virtue comes from contact with Him, even with His garments. And old man in the crowd, blind from childhood, cries out, 'O Lord, heal me and I shall see Thee!' and, as it were, scales fall from his eyes and the blind man sees Him. The crowd weeps and kisses the earth under His feet. Children throw flowers before Him, sing, and cry hosannah. 'It is He—it is He!' all repeat. 'It must be He, it can be no one but Him!' He stops at the steps of the Seville cathedral at the moment when the weeping mourners are bringing in a little open white coffin. In it lies a child of seven, the only daughter of a prominent citizen. The dead child lies hidden in flowers. 'He will raise your child,' the crowd shouts to the weeping mother. The priest, coming to meet the coffin, looks perplexed, and frowns, but the mother of the dead child throws herself at His feet with a wail. 'If it is Thou, raise my child!' she cries, holding out her hands to Him. The procession halts, the coffin is laid on the steps at His feet. He looks with compassion, and His lips once more softly pronounce, 'Maiden, arise!' and the maiden arises. The little girl sits up in the coffin and looks round, smiling with wide-open wondering eyes, holding a bunch of white roses they had put in her hand.

"There are cries, sobs, confusion among the people, and at that moment the cardinal himself, the Grand Inquisitor, passes by the cathedral. He is an old man, almost ninety, tall and erect, with a withered face and sunken eyes, in which there is still a gleam of light. He is not dressed in his gorgeous cardinal's robes, as he was the day before, when he was burning the enemies of the Roman Church—at that moment he was wearing his coarse, old, monk's cassock. At a distance behind him come his gloomy assistants and slaves and the 'holy guard.' He stops at the sight of the crowd and watches it from a distance. He sees everything; he sees them set the coffin down at His feet, sees the child rise up, and his face darkens. He knits his thick grey brows and his eyes gleam with a sinister fire. He holds out his finger and bids the guards take Him. And such is his power, so completely are the people cowed into submission and trembling obedience to him, that the crowd immediately makes way for the guards, and in the midst of deathlike silence they lay hands on Him and lead Him away. The crowd instantly bows down to the earth, like one man, before the old inquisitor. He blesses the people in silence and passes on.

"The guards lead their prisoner to the close, gloomy vaulted prison in the ancient palace of the Holy Inquisition and shut Him in it. The day passes and is followed by the dark, burning 'breathless' night of Seville. The air is 'fragrant with laurel and lemon.' In the pitch darkness the iron door of the prison is suddenly opened and the Grand Inquisitor himself comes in with a light in his hand. He is alone; the door is closed at once behind him. He stands in the doorway and for a minute or two gazes in His face. At last he goes up slowly, sets the light on the table and speaks.

" 'Is it Thou? Thou?' but receiving no answer, he adds at once, 'Don't answer, be silent. What canst Thou say, indeed? I know too well what Thou wouldst say. And Thou hast no right to add anything to what Thou hadst said of old. Why, then, art Thou come to hinder us? For Thou hast come to hinder us, and Thou knowest that. But dost Thou know what will be tomorrow? I know not who Thou art and care not to know whether it is Thou or only a semblance of Him, but tomorrow I shall condemn Thee and burn Thee at the stake as the worst of heretics. And the very people who have today kissed Thy feet, tomorrow at the faintest sign from me will rush to heap up the embers of Thy fire. Knowest Thou that? Yes, maybe Thou knowest it,' he added with thoughtful penetration, never for a moment taking his eyes off the Prisoner."

"I don't quite understand, Ivan. What does it mean?" Alyosha, who had been listening in silence, said with a smile. "Is it simply a wild fantasy, or a mistake on the part of the old man—some impossible *qui pro quo?*"

"Take it as the last," said Ivan, laughing, "if you are so corrupted by modern realism and can't stand anything fantastic. If you like it to be a case of mistaken identity, let it be so. It is true," he went on, laughing, "the old man was ninety, and he might well be crazy over his set idea. He might have been struck by the appearance of the Prisoner. It might, in fact, be simply his ravings, the delusion of an old man of ninety, overexcited by the *auto da fé* of a hundred heretics the day before. But does it matter to us after all whether it was a mistake of identity or a wild fantasy? All that matters is that the old man should speak out, should speak openly of what he has thought in silence for ninety years."

"And the Prisoner too is silent? Does He look at him and not say a word?"

"That's inevitable in any case," Ivan laughed again. "The old man has told Him He hasn't the right to add anything to what He has said of old. One may say it is the most fundamental feature of Roman Catholicism, in my opinion at least. 'All has been given by Thee to the Pope,' they say, 'and all, therefore, is still in the Pope's hands, and there is no need for Thee to come at all. Thou must not meddle for the time, at least.' That's how they speak and write too—the Jesuits, at any rate. I have read it myself in the works of their theologians."

" 'Hast Thou the right to reveal to us one of the mysteries of that world from which Thou hast come?' my old man asks Him, and answers the question for Him. 'No, Thou hast not; that Thou mayest not add to what has been said of old, and mayest not take from men the freedom which Thou didst exalt when Thou wast on earth. Whatsoever Thou revealest anew will encroach on men's freedom of faith; for it will be manifest as a miracle, and the freedom of their faith was dearer to Thee than anything in those days fifteen hundred years ago. Didst Thou not often say then, "I will make you free"? But now Thou hast seen these "free" men,' the old man adds suddenly, with a pensive smile. 'Yes, we've paid dearly for it,' he goes on, looking sternly at Him, 'but at last we have completed that work in Thy name. For fifteen centuries we have been wrestling with Thy freedom, but now it is ended and over for good. Dost Thou not believe that it's over for good? Thou lookest meekly at me and deignest not even to be wroth with me. But let me tell Thee that now, today, people are more persuaded than ever that they have perfect freedom, yet they have brought their freedom to us and laid it humbly at our feet. But that has been our doing. Was this what Thou didst? Was this Thy freedom?' "

"I don't understand again," Alyosha broke in. "Is he ironical, is he jesting?"

"Not a bit of it! He claims it as a merit for himself and his Church that at last they have vanquished freedom and have done so to make men happy."

" 'For now' (he is speaking of the Inquisition, of course) 'for the first time it has become possible to think of the happiness of men. Man was created a rebel; and how can rebels be happy? Thou wast warned,' he says to Him. 'Thou hast had no lack of admonitions, and warnings, but Thou didst not listen to those warnings; Thou didst reject the only way by which men might be made happy. But, fortunately, departing Thou didst hand on the work to us. Thou hast promised, Thou hast established by Thy word, Thou hast given to us the right to bind and to unbind, and now, of course, Thou canst not think of taking it away. Why, then, hast Thou come to hinder us?' " . . .

" 'Listen, then. We are not working with Thee, but with *him*—that is our mystery. It's long—eight centuries—since we have been on *his* side and not on Thine. Just eight centuries ago, we took from him what Thou didst reject with scorn, that last gift he offered Thee, showing Thee all the kingdoms of the earth. We took from him Rome and the sword of Caesar, and proclaimed ourselves sole rulers of the earth, though hitherto we have not been able to complete our work. But whose fault is that? Oh, the work is only beginning, but it has begun. It has long to await completion and the earth has yet much to suffer, but we shall triumph and shall be Caesars, and then we shall plan the universal happiness of man. But Thou mightest have taken even the sword of Caesar.

" 'Why didst Thou reject that last gift?

" 'Hadst Thou accepted that last counsel of the mighty spirit, Thou wouldst have accomplished all that man seeks on earth—that is, some one to worship, some one to keep his conscience, and some means of uniting all in one unanimous and harmonious antheap, for the craving for universal unity is the third and last anguish of men. Mankind as a whole has always striven to organize a universal state. There have been many great nations with great histories, but the more highly they were developed the more unhappy they were, for they felt more acutely than other people the craving for worldwide union. The great conquerors, Timours and Ghenghis-Khans, whirled like hurricanes over the face of the earth striving to subdue its people, and they too were but the unconscious expression of the same craving for universal unity. Hadst Thou taken the world and Caesar's purple, Thou wouldst have founded the universal state and have given universal peace.

For who can rule men if not he who holds their conscience and their bread in his hands.

" 'We have taken the sword of Caesar, and in taking it, of course, have rejected Thee and followed *him*.

" 'Oh, ages are yet to come of the confusion of free thought, of their science and cannibalism. For having begun to build their tower of Babel without us, they will end, of course, with cannibalism. But then the beast will crawl to us and lick our feet and spatter them with tears of blood. And we shall sit upon the beast and raise the cup, and on it will be written, "Mystery." But then, and only then, the reign of peace and happiness will come for men.

" 'Thou art proud of Thine elect, but Thou hast only the elect, while we give rest to all. And besides, how many of those elect, those mighty ones who could become elect, have grown weary waiting for Thee, and have transferred and will transfer the powers of their spirit and the warmth of their heart to the other camp, and end by raising their *free* banner against Thee. Thou didst Thyself lift up that banner. But with us all will be happy and will no more rebel nor destroy one another as under Thy freedom.

" 'Oh, we shall persuade them that they will only become free when they renounce their freedom to us and submit to us. And shall we be right or shall we be lying? They will be convinced that we are right, for they will remember the horrors of slavery and confusion to which Thy freedom brought them. Freedom, free thought and science, will lead them into such straits and will bring them face to face with such marvels and insoluble mysteries, that some of them, the fierce and rebellious, will destroy themselves, others, rebellious but weak, will destroy one another, while the rest, weak and unhappy, will crawl fawning to our feet and whine to us: "Yes, you were right, you alone possess His mystery, and we come back to you, save us from ourselves!"

" 'Receiving bread from us, they will see clearly that we take the bread made by their hands from them, to give it to them, without any miracle. They will see that we do not change the stones to bread, but in truth they will be more thankful for taking it from our hands than for the bread itself! For they will remember only too well that in old days, without our help, even the bread they made turned to stones in their hands, while since they have come back to us, the very stones have turned to bread in their hands. Too, too well they know the value of complete submission! And until men know that, they will be unhappy. Who is most to blame for their not knowing it, speak? Who scattered the flock and sent it astray on unknown paths? But the flock will come together again and will submit once more, and then it will be once for all. Then we shall give them the quiet humble happiness of weak creatures such as they are by nature. Oh, we shall persuade them at last not to be proud, for Thou didst lift them up and thereby taught them to be proud. We shall show them that they are weak, that they are only pitiful children, but that childlike happiness is the sweetest of all. They will become timid and will look to us and huddle close to us in fear, as chicks to the hen. They will marvel at us and will be awe-stricken before us, and will be proud at our being so powerful and clever, that we have been able to subdue such a turbulent flock of thousands of millions. They will tremble impotently before our wrath, their minds will grow fearful, they will be quick to shed tears like women and children, but they will be just as ready at a sign from us to pass to laughter and rejoicing, to happy mirth and childish song. Yes, we shall set them to work, but in their leisure hours we shall make their life like a child's game, with children's songs and innocent dance. Oh, we shall allow them even sin, they are weak and helpless, and they will love us like children because we allow them to sin. We shall tell them that every sin will be expiated, if it is done with our permission, that we allow them to sin because we love them, and the punishment for these sins we take upon ourselves. And we shall take it upon ourselves, and they will adore us as their saviours who have taken on themselves their sins before God. And they will have no secrets from us. We shall allow or forbid them to live with their wives and mistresses, to have or not to have children—according to whether they have been obedient or disobedient—and they will submit to us gladly and cheerfully. The most painful secrets of their conscience, all, all they will bring to us, and we shall have an answer for all. And they will be glad to believe our answer, for it will save them from the great anxiety and terrible agony they endure at present in making a free decision for themselves. And all will be happy, all the millions of creatures except the hundred thousand who rule over them. For only we, we who guard the mystery, shall be unhappy.

" 'There will be thousands of millions of happy babes, and a hundred thousand sufferers who have taken upon themselves the curse of the knowledge of good and evil. Peacefully they will die, peacefully they will expire in Thy name, and beyond the grave they will find nothing but death. But we shall keep the secret, and for their happiness we shall allure them with the reward of heaven and eternity. Though if there were anything in the other world, it certainly would not be for such as they.

" 'It is prophesied that Thou wilt come again in victory, Thou wilt come with Thy chosen, the proud and strong, but we will say that they have only saved themselves, but we have saved all. We are told that the harlot who sits upon the beast, and holds in her hands the *mystery,* shall be put to shame, that the weak will rise up again, and will rend her royal purple and will strip naked her loathsome body. But then I will stand up and point out to Thee the thousand millions of happy children who have known no sin. And we who have taken their sins upon us for their happiness will stand up before Thee and say: "Judge us if Thou canst and darest." Know that I fear Thee not. Know that I too have been in the wilderness, I too have lived on roots and locusts, I too prized the freedom with which Thou hast blessed men, and I too was striving to stand among Thy elect, among the strong and powerful, thirsting "to make up the number." But I awakened and would not serve madness. I turned back and joined the ranks of those *who have corrected Thy work*. I left the proud and went back to the humble, for the happiness of the humble. What I say to Thee will come to pass, and our dominion will be built up. I repeat, tomorrow Thou shalt see that obedient flock who at a sign from me will hasten to heap up the hot cinders about the pile on which I shall burn Thee for coming to hinder us. For if any one has ever deserved our fires, it is Thou. Tomorrow I shall burn Thee. *Dixi.*' "

Ivan stopped. He was carried away as he talked and spoke with excitement; when he had finished, he suddenly smiled.

Alyosha had listened in silence; toward the end he was greatly moved and seemed several times on the point of interrupting, but restrained himself. Now his words came with a rush.

"But. . . that's absurd!" he cried, flushing. "Your poem is in praise of Jesus, not in blame of Him—as you meant it to be. And who will believe you about freedom? Is that the way to understand it? That's not the idea of it in the Orthodox Church. . . That's Rome, and not even the whole of Rome, it's false—those are the worst of the Catholics, the Inquisitors, the Jesuits! . . .And there could not be such a fantastic creature as your Inquisitor. What are these sins of mankind they take on themselves? Who are these keepers of the mystery who have taken some curse upon themselves for the happiness of mankind? When have they been seen? We know the Jesuits, they are spoken ill of, but surely they are not what you describe? They are not that at all, not at all . . . . They are simply the Romish army for the earthly sovereignty of the world in the future, with the Pontiff of Rome for Emperor. . . that's their ideal, but there's no sort of mystery or lofty melancholy about it. . . It's simple lust of power, of filthy earthly gain, of domination—something like a universal serfdom with them as masters—that's all they stand for. They don't even believe in God perhaps. Your suffering inquisitor is a mere fantasy."

"Stay, stay," laughed Ivan, "how hot you are! A fantasy you say, let it be so! Of course it's a fantasy. But allow me to say: do you really think that the Roman Catholic movement of the last centuries is actually nothing but the lust of power, of filthy earthly gain? Is that Father Païssy's teaching?"

"No, no, on the contrary, Father Païssy did once say something the same as you. . .but of course it's not the same, not a bit the same," Alyosha hastily corrected himself.

"A precious admission, in spite of your 'not a bit the same.' I ask you why your Jesuits and Inquisitors have united simply for vile material gain? Why can there not be among them one martyr oppressed by great sorrow and loving humanity? You see, only suppose that there was one such man among all those who desire nothing but filthy material gain—if there's only one like my old inquisitor, who had himself eaten roots in the desert and made frenzied efforts to subdue his flesh to make himself free and perfect. But yet all his

life he loved humanity, and suddenly his eyes were opened, and he saw that
it is no great moral blessedness to attain perfection and freedom, if at the same
time one gains the conviction that billions of God's creatures have been
created as a mockery, that they will never be capable of using their freedom,
that these poor rebels can never turn into giants to complete the tower, that
it was not for such geese that the great idealist dreamt his dream of harmony.
Seeing all that he turned back and joined—the clever people. Surely that
could have happened?"

"Joined whom, what clever people?" cried Alyosha, completely carried
away. "They have no such great cleverness and no mysteries and secrets. . .
Perhaps nothing but Atheism, that's all their secret. Your inquisitor does not
believe in God, that's his secret!"

"What if it is so! At last you have guessed it. It's perfectly true that
that's the whole secret, but isn't that suffering, at least for a man like that,
who has wasted his whole life in the desert and yet could not shake off his
incurable love of humanity? In his old age he reached the clear conviction
that nothing but the advice of the great dread spirit could build up any
tolerable sort of life for the feeble, unruly 'incomplete, empirical creatures
created in jest.' And so, convinced of this, he sees that he must follow the
council of the wise spirit, the dread spirit of death and destruction, and therefore accept lying and deception, and lead men consciously to death and
destruction, and yet deceive them all the way so that they may not notice
where they are being led, that the poor blind creatures may at least on the way
think themselves happy. And note, the deception is in the name of Him in
Whose ideal the old man had so fervently believed all his life long. Is not that
tragic? And if only one such stood at the head of the whole army 'filled with
the lust of power only for the sake of filthy gain'—would not one such be
enough to make a tragedy? More than that, one such standing at the head
is enough to create the actual leading idea of the Roman Church with all
its armies and Jesuits, its highest idea. I tell you frankly that I firmly believe
that there has always been such a man among those who stood at the head
of the movement. Who knows, there may have been some such even among
the Roman Popes. Who knows, perhaps the spirit of that accursed old man
who loves mankind so obstinately in his own way, is to be found even now
in a whole multitude of such old men, existing not by chance but by agreement, as a secret league formed long ago for the guarding of the mystery,
to guard it from the weak and the unhappy, so as to make them happy. No
doubt it is so, and so it must be indeed. I fancy that even among the Masons
there's something of the same mystery at the bottom, and that that's why the
Catholics so detest the Masons as their rivals breaking up the unity of the idea,
while it is so essential that there should be one flock and one shepherd. . . . .
But from the way I defend my idea I might be an author impatient of your
criticism. Enough of it."

"You are perhaps a Mason yourself!" broke suddenly from Alyosha.

"You don't believe in God," he added, speaking this time very sorrowfully. He fancied besides that his brother was looking at him ironically. "How does your poem end?" he asked, suddenly looking down. "Or was it the end?"

"I meant it to end like this:

"When the Inquisitor ceased speaking he waited some time for his Prisoner to answer him. His silence weighed down upon him. He saw the Prisoner had listened intently all the time, looking gently in his face and evidently not wishing to reply. The old man longed for Him to say something, however bitter and terrible. But He suddenly approached the old man in silence and softly kissed him on his bloodless aged lips. That was all His answer. The old man shuddered. His lips moved. He went to the door, opened it, and said to Him: 'Go, and come no more. . . Come not at all, never, never!' And he let Him out into the dark alleys of the town. The Prisoner went away."

"And the old man?"

"The kiss glows in his heart, but the old man adheres to his idea."

17. BRAINWASHING AND MENTICIDE
joost a. m. meerloo

Thought control is a widespread if imperfect technique of inducing political orthodoxy and regimentation in many nations. Most Americans learned about "brainwashing" by North Koreans and Chinese in the aftermath of the Korean War of the 1950s, when various reports indicated that some American prisoners of war had been subjected to severe politically oriented psychological pressures.

While there is presently little systematic evidence about the domestic aspects and consequences of brainwashing in contemporary totalitarian societies, some data involving foreign civilian and military prisoners have been gathered by researchers. Their findings, as in the following study, suggest some tentative insights into the techniques, purposes, and consequences of brainwashing and menticide as explicit control devices.

During the last thirty years several political agencies have tried to misuse psychological and psychiatric experience to further their private aims. Active psychological warfare and political mental torture are now accepted concepts in totalitarian countries. A prime result of the political pressure, both overt

From Joost A. M. Meerloo, "Brainwashing and Menticide: Some Implications of Conscious and Unconscious Thought Control," *Psychoanalysis and Psychoanalytic Review,* XLV, 1958, pp. 83–90, 98.

and unobtrusive, has been a cynical re-evaluation of human values. A new profession of specialists has emerged whose task it is not to cure, but to aggravate and manipulate the weaknesses of selected victims so that they might become more easily amenable to influence, and to prescribed political ideologies.

We may define such planned enforcement of ideas and mental coercion applied as a political tool as "thought control." The provocation of false confessions in the service of political propaganda can be defined as "brainwashing" or "menticide." The United Nations defined the systematic suppression, starvation and killing of minorities as the crime of *genocide,* the murder of a species. The new more subtle crime is *menticide,* the murder of the potentialities of the free creative mind.

I wish to say no more at this time concerning the obviously sensational impact of this problem of brainwashing. It is interesting to know, however, why people reacted so hysterically and dramatically to the first detailed news on brainwashing. Terrible fears were aroused in them: especially the fear of conformity and the fear of the evil eye that can see through the person and magically dig the truth out of him.

The psychiatric problem of thought control can be approached from different angles. One may ask "what is the political technique of mental and spiritual terror?" One may make a survey of the political variations in coercive strategy. Various psychiatric and psychological schools have given different explanations of psychodynamics involved in political thought control and brainwashing.

I am here concerned, above all, with the more general question: "What do we clinicians learn from this extensive political experiment on human guinea pigs?"

Enforced interrogation, inquisition, persuasion and mental coercion in the service of thought control and thought reform exist in many places. What lessons can be derived from the cynical political experiment with human beings? What are its implications?

There is overwhelming evidence that dictatorial regimes have improved their techniques of mental terror and mental coercion in the last quarter-century. I have followed this problem since 1933 when I along with a number of others suspected that one of the psychopathic patients in the Netherlands was used as a political tool and scapegoat in starting the Reichstag fire—the signal Hitler needed so badly in order to take dictatorial power into his own hands. At that time we had hardly any notion that a man could be changed into a servile robot with a built-in gramophone record, speaking his master's voice. When Marinus Van der Lubbe came before a German court and world forum in order to confess his crime in public, psychiatric observers thought that he had been treated with special narcotics and sedatives. At least they felt that he behaved very strangely—as if he were "punch-drunk." There was, of course, no possibility of further study after his conviction and hanging. It was not until the confesion at the Nüremberg trials that we heard how Van der

Lubbe had been used as a willing political tool and that the very men who had punished and killed him had been the ones who had urged him to start the fire.

True, we knew of the Pavlovian technique of conditioning animals as a kind of scientific training, but, in those days, it was impossible for us psychiatrists to believe that such a laboratory experiment could be used to transform a human's mind, even temporarily, into an imitative voice speaking only the thoughts of the master.

Yet, we must not forget that enforced persuasion and inquisition by means of subtle or not so subtle intimidation had existed as long as mankind itself. As a matter of fact, every time two people meet in exchange of thought, a subtle dialectic battle starts about who is the stronger one in his capacity to communicate and dominate and who is the weaker; who is the more persuasive one and who the more submissive. When, however, psychic arguments are not sufficient, often a different kind of talk with iron fists may start. Religious wars often occurred in the service of enforced persuasion and conversion. The more subtle techniques of coercive interrogation we learned, for example, from the Inquisition of the Middle Ages. Many witches were finally made to "confess" their sexual union with the devil Beelzebub.

What then is new about this question of coercive persuasion and brainwashing?

Two big developments made these old problems of enforced persuasion of decisive importance in our era:

In the first place, the modern strategy of totalitarian governments developed a systematic political thought control and thought reform as a strategy of absolute control over the minds of people. Without such control of man's mind, no dictatorship can remain in existence.

In the second place, the technical development of the means of communication made mankind much more susceptible and sensitive to the influence and mental manipulations by political ideologies and to strange absurd suggestions from the outside. We all live daily in a web of noises and suggestions.

Let us make a survey of the most prominent points that come to the fore in this new development. I prefer to treat the general implications of the problem because they bring the clinical aspects to the fore more clearly; namely: 1. The technique of individual mental coercion and brainwashing. 2. The technique of mass-coercion and mass-seduction. 3. The problem of unobtrusive and unconscious mental coercion and 4. Ways by which a free society can resist, neutralize, and counteract these strange mental intrusions.

THE TECHNIQUE OF INDIVIDUAL MENTAL COERCION

The totalitarian brainwashing technique involves a double task. First, the mind of the victim has to be broken down—made empty according to the brainwasher's terminology; then a clean gramophone record has to be filled with new grooves, a new ideology.

The methods used are simple enough. Soldiers and officers who were prisoners of war in Korea and China were submitted to a systematic regime of mental submission followed by political propaganda in which hunger and isolation played the most important part in breaking down the victim's mental resistance. If perceptual isolation and coercive persuasion are applied day in and day out, most people will lose their individual critical distinctions and gradually follow the suggestions of their inquisitors. This happens especially when a clever alternation of hunger and giving food is used as a system of Pavlovian conditioning and training. Then new ideas are hammered in with repetitious ideological catchwords, launched after enforced, long-lasting interrogation and sleeplessness.

Especially, however, when the interrogators are able to arouse a man's deep-seated feelings of guilt can they make him even more abject and dependent, more willing to confess any crime. This subtle manipulation of man's feelings of shame and guilt was also the old coercive tool of the inquisitor but is also one of the prominent modern instruments of brainwashing. The prisoners of war in Korea were invited in a seemingly innocent way to write down their autobiographies and to describe their own mistakes and failures in life. In doing so, they inadvertently surrendered to their inquisitors details concerning personal weakness and confusion, which were investigated and analyzed again and again and finally led to mental submission, confession, and conversion. We may also say it this way: The brainwasher blackmails man's inner need to communicate. The need to talk and to communicate in days of loneliness and great boredom gradually becomes a need to confess. Abject dependency arouses all man's masochistic traits.

In the new military regulations we have to guide the soldiers to adhere strictly to the rules and to give no information at all, and they must learn that willful silence affords better protection for their infantile need to talk and to communicate.

The official data indicate that nearly 70% of the prisoners of war in Korea, unprepared for such subtle psychic attacks on their integrity, communicated with the enemy in a way not permitted by military rules. This does not mean, however, that they may be regarded as real collaborators or traitors.

For psychiatry and social psychology a few facts came to the fore which were rather surprising:

How weak and submissive is the human mind under such abnormal, stressful circumstances! Hunger can break the mental dignity and integrity of most people. When man is alone, without sufficient food, without his daily work and without his usual human contacts, he easily breaks down. He unconsciously accepts the verdict of the inquisitor and accepts the self-image imposed on him by this new father image. In brainwashing, man's masochism is the victor. Psychiatrists could have gathered some of this from previous studies of prison-psychoses and contagious delusions in isolated communities but they had to learn it anew from this political experiment.

In the laboratory this inner breakdown of man can be provoked in a rather short time by the exclusion of sensory contact with the outside world. In many a student—serving as a human guinea pig—such extreme isolation, sensory deprivation and lack of verification of reality caused fearful dreams and actual hallucinations *within twelve hours.*

When the normal sensory stimulation from the outside world fails to enter the mind and the sense of time and space disappears, the inner world of primary unconscious processes begins to take over. These experiments revealed that most men need a continual verification of and confrontation with reality lest their infantile anxieties and fantasies begin to dominate them. We now have a more exact picture of why the lonely and isolated man breaks down so easily especially in the age of advertised togetherness. Isolation and living on one's own inner resources is a state for which one has to be carefully trained.

The methods of political thought-control have also directed our attention to the importance of the process of interrogation of patients. We are more convinced now that the ways and methods of interrogation and interviewing are able to influence patients and to bias the information we obtain.

Experiences with brainwashed soldiers have greatly improved our understanding. We are consequently able now to inform the courts of justice how easy it is to imprint subjective feelings on some of the accused. With the help of the third degree and even with the threat of so-called truth serum or lie detector one can coerce people into false confessions.

This poses many questions concerning our own communication with patients, our own ways of interrogation and subsequent treatment. Are we sufficiently aware of the fact that the rhythmic, repeated, intimate talks and therapeutic sessions inadvertently can have a subtle, coercive action on patients? Even our benevolent silent attitude can have this effect. What we ascribe as positive and negative transference towards our patients—and from the patients toward us—has a much greater persuasive and suggestive action than many therapists would want to admit.

Unobtrusively we can transplant our ideas to the patients. Current psychotherapy and psychoanalysis are well aware of these facts and try to prevent them by emphasizing the final analysis of the transference as one of the most basic processes in every therapeutic encounter. This awareness of subjectivity and prejudice cannot be granted, however, to other more physical, medical methods where patients are just as much submitted to psychic persuasion and conditioning with neither doctor nor patient being aware of it. Take, for instance, the habit of taking tranquillizers, sedatives and sleeping drugs. Not only mental and physical health can be affected by it, but, at the same time, the mild addict can gradually become a more submissive, masochistic personality, dependent on the physician and his chemical magic.

In the initial phases of brainwashing technique, narcotics were used as additional means of breaking down mental resistance. The old device *"in vino veritas"*—the truth is in the wine—was the first aphorism dedicated to such forms of coercive thought control. But the totalitarian inquisitor discovered rather soon that hunger, lack of sleep, cold, dirt and isolation brought about with greater rapidity the regression and mental breakdown they wanted. This is not completely true for the application of pain and physical torture so often used by the inquisition of the Middle Ages. Experience showed that pain more often aroused rebellion and resistance in the person while the "hunger-isolation" treatment led more easily to a submissive form of dependency.

THE TECHNIQUES OF MASS-COERCION AND MASS-SEDUCTION

The art of convincing other groups and nations of the subjective truth of the "chosen tribe or country" is as old as human history. Most religions have wanted to convert the non-believers, often forcefully and with the sword. Napoleon changed such persuasion into a military science in his "Bureau de l'Opinion Publique." In the meantime the science of advertising and propaganda discovered new methods by which to imprint onto the public favorable suggestions before actual selling of the product. Even when people are skeptical about ads, the repeated clichés and slogans have an impact. A gradual penetration into man's unconsciousness takes place no matter how much he may criticize the cheap suggestion. In the end he buys the commodity he did not first need or want.

As far as our subject of thought control is concerned it is not so important that one soap outsells another. Much day-to-day advertising and public-opinion engineering makes use of the psychological experience that a repeated suggestion, no matter how far-fetched, may gradually creep through the barriers of our critical defenses into the deeper layers of our psyche and leave some "memento" behind. The next time we hear the familiar slogan combined with the same musical jingle, our recognition acts automatically. Inwardly we say "Aha," and without critical awareness we buy the soap we will perhaps never use. The advertiser does not even need the trick of subliminal advertising to make some imprint on the minds, provided his product arouses some basic need.

The unobtrusive penetration and unconscious leakage through man's critical barriers that occurs even in a free democracy becomes, however, a thousandfold stronger persuasion when the suggestions are backed by political terror. Then, man's unconscious urge to surrender and merge with the stronger party easily takes over. The passive defense of identification with the aggressor takes hold of man.

The collective terror in a totalitarian state with the help of secret police and concentration camps makes people much more submissive and obedient to the partisans in power. Under such strain and stress the spirit may seem to be critical but the will yields.

Such are the two sides of our problem. On one side we see the engineers of mass opinion trying to use our best psychoanalytic knowledge in the service of propaganda and advertising. On the other side we discover political systems that not only use this unconscious penetration into the psyche to sell products but also to implant and imprint ideologies and slogans in the public mind.

The current Chinese program of thought reform and thought control is an example of how far this idea of mental mass submission may be executed. Hitler's idea of equalization and merging (*Gleichschaltung*) was based on the same coercive principle. In a totalitarian system the luxury of having an individual ego and an individual opinion is superfluous. All thinking and feeling belong to the monolithic party.

It is not my task here to describe the ways in which the conductor of enforced pessimism and despair relate to the psychological warfare and actual cold war now in progress. A few illustrations may be given of what happens, however, of special affects worked on the individual psyche by such continual mental attack.

Totalitarian strategy in its tactical description of the techniques of mass intimidation and collective control discovered that the arousing of simple panic, fear and terror do not suffice. Too great a mental pressure exerted over a long period of time loses its frightening impact and often stirs rebellion and critical resistance in the people, militating against the final aim of producing obedient automatic thought machines out of human beings.

In order to better reach its goal, the more scientific strategy makes use of *waves of terror* "with in-between periods of relative calm and freedom"—the so-called *"breaking spell,"* (*peredishka*). These intervals of relative freedom and lack of overt tensions can be used to much better advantage for political persuasion and mass-hypnosis provided some new wave of terror is anticipated. It is completely comparable with the patient in hypnotherapy who becomes easier to hypnotize at every session. The alternation of terror and breathing spell, for example, the alternation of a cold war of hatred with the opposite propaganda for harmonious, peaceful coexistence, can gradually cause confusion and increased anxious anticipation in people.

The Nazis had already been playing that psychological cat-and-mouse game very cleverly in the occupied countries. People ask themselves: "But what will happen tomorrow?" Gradually a silent panic saps their critical potentials and the passive expectation of renewed terror makes them easy marks for ideological slogans. According to totalitarian strategists, well-applied waves of terror are the best recipes for terrorizing people into cooperation and collaboration. It is the latent silent panic in people that makes them into more submissive and suggestible beings. On the other hand, overwhelming fear and acute fright may make rebels of them.

I make a special point of this strategy of *fractionalized panic* because its paralyzing influence is not enough known, and in actual politics we can easily be surprised by it.

When we are unable to live with unsolved riddles and the awe of mystery, we may unknowingly surrender to an easier theory.

We have learned that the mental pressure of brainwashing and thought control can cause an inner conflagration that can lead to an atrophy of ego and personality. Many people who had returned from concentration camps after brainwashing and torture needed months before they were restored to their previous personalities again.

There exist many ways in which to build up man's inner strength and help him become a free and strong self-confident being. Psychiatrists and psychologists have built up appropriate systems of psychotherapy. Yet, we must be aware of the fact that specific political and also cultural currents are in conflict with these psychotherapeutic ideals. The aim of these currents is adjustment, dependency and conformity; not freedom and self-realization and self-confidence. Our psychiatric battle for the integrity of the individual mind, however, goes far beyond accusing some enemy of brainwashing soldiers; we must see it as a general social phenomenon.

There exist everywhere subtle influences and powers which are able to creep unseen inside the psyche in order to make man more submissive. Take, for instance, the technological suggestion that inner peace and contentment can be found or bought through chemical sedation and the magic of pacifying tablets or through the mild hypnosis of machine-music or the frenzy of speedy, noisy motors.

Man has to battle inwardly for every insight. That is not only true in psychoanalysis and psychotherapy but more so to attain his political insights and certainties. His inner strength and mental backbone depend on a free, unlimited knowledge of himself and on man's simple self-confidence that he or his heirs eventually will reach that goal. It depends on his unfrustrated belief in human values and on his awareness of belonging to a group of other people, who like him and have esteem for him. It depends, too, on his education in both freedom and self-discipline.

The simple formulation for the cultivation of man's inner morale and strength is a variation of the old formulation the oracle of Delphi gave to mankind:

Know and Trust Thyself

18. THE CONSUMER
AS PACKAGED SOUL

vance packard

Persuasion techniques through saturation advertising are commonplace in the American economic system—and they work! Advertising agencies staffed with highly skilled psychologists and other behavioral experts in consumer "engineering" spend vast amounts of time and money to create a sense of immediate personal need for such widely different products as soap, automobiles, and houses.

Is it likely that in the next few decades we are headed toward an authoritarian society in which "biocontrol" will produce a controlled society in which mental, emotional, and sense processes will be determined largely by electronic signals? Do present trends suggest that American society will succumb to forces of manipulation, or is this expectation a mere fantasy of disgruntled critics?

The disturbing Orwellian configurations of the world toward which the persuaders seem to be nudging us—even if unwittingly—can be seen most clearly in some of their bolder, more imaginative efforts.

These ventures, which we will now examine, seem to the author to represent plausible projections into the future of some of the more insidious or ambitious persuasion techniques we've been exploring in this book.

In early 1956 a retired advertising man named John G. Schneider (formerly with Fuller, Smith and Ross, Kenyon and Eckhardt, and other ad agencies) wrote a satirical novel called *The Golden Kazoo,* which projected to the 1960 Presidential election the trends in political merchandising that had already become clear. By 1960 the ad men from Madison Avenue have taken over completely (just as Whitaker and Baxter started taking over in California). Schneider explained this was the culmination of the trend started in 1952 when ad men entered the very top policy-making councils of both parties, when "for the first time" candidates became "merchandise," political campaigns became "sales-promotion jobs," and the electorate was a "market."

By 1960 the Presidency is just another product to peddle through tried-and-true merchandising strategies. Speeches are banned as too dull for citizens accustomed to TV to take. (Even the five-minute quickies of 1956 had become unendurable.) Instead the candidate is given a walk-on or center-piece type of treatment in "spectaculars" carefully designed to drive home a big point. (Remember the election-eve pageant of 1956 where "little people" reported to President Eisenhower on why they liked him?)

From Vance Packard, *The Hidden Persuaders,* reprinted by permission of the David McKay Co., 1957.

The 1960 contest, as projected by Schneider, boiled down to a gigantic struggle between two giant ad agencies, one called Reade and Bratton for the Republicans and one simply called B.S.&J. for the Democrats. When one of the two candidates, Henry Clay Adams, timidly suggests he ought to make a foreign-policy speech on the crisis in the atomic age his account executive Blade Reade gives him a real lecture. "Look," he said, "if you want to impress the longhairs, intellectuals, and Columbia students, do it on your own time, not on my TV time. Consider your market, man! . . . Your market is forty, fifty million slobs sitting at home catching your stuff on TV and radio. Are those slobs worried about the atomic age! Nuts. They're worried about next Friday's grocery bill." Several of the merchandising journals gave Mr. Schneider's book a careful review, and none that I saw expressed shock or pain at his implications.

So much for fictional projections into the future. Some of the real-life situations that are being heralded as trends are perhaps more astonishing or disconcerting, as you choose.

A vast development of homes going up at Miramar, Florida, is being called the world's most perfect community by its backers. *Tide,* the merchandisers' journal, admonished America's merchandisers to pay attention to this trail-blazing development as it might be "tomorrow's marketing target." The journal said of Miramar: "Its immediate success . . . has a particular significance for marketers, for the trend to 'packaged' homes in 'packaged' communities may indicate where and how tomorrow's consumer will live. . . ." Its founder, youthful Robert W. Gordon, advises me Miramar has become "a bustling little community" and is well on its way to offering a "completely integrated community" for four thousand families.

What does it mean to buy a "packaged" home in a "packaged" community? For many (but apparently not all) of the Miramar families it means they simply had to bring their suitcases, nothing more. No fuss with moving vans, or shopping for food, or waiting for your new neighbors to make friendly overtures. The homes are completely furnished, even down to linens, china, silver, and a refrigerator full of food. And you pay for it all, even the refrigerator full of food, on the installment plan.

Perhaps the most novel and portentous service available at Miramar— and all for the one packaged price—is that it may also package your social life for you. As Mr. Gordon put it: "Anyone can move into one of the homes with nothing but their personal possessions, and start living as a part of the community five minutes later." Where else could you be playing bridge with your new neighbors the same night you move in! In short, friendship is being merchandized along with real estate, all in one glossy package. *Tide* described this aspect of its town of tomorrow in these words: "To make Miramar as homey and congenial as possible, the builders have established what might be called 'regimented recreation.' As soon as a family moves in the lady of the house will get an invitation to join any number of activities ranging from bridge games to literary teas. Her husband will be introduced, by Miramar, to local groups interested in anything from fish breeding to water skiing."

In the trends toward other-mindedness, group living, and consumption-mindedness as spelled out by Dr. Riesman, Miramar may represent something of an ultimate for modern man. . . .

Eventually—say by A.D. 2000—perhaps all this depth manipulation of the psychological variety will seem amusingly old-fashioned. By then perhaps the biophysicists will take over with "biocontrol," which is depth persuasion carried to its ultimate. Biocontrol is the new science of controlling mental processes, emotional reactions, and sense perceptions by bioelectrical signals.

The National Electronics Conference meeting in Chicago in 1956 heard electrical engineer Curtiss R. Schafer, of the Norden-Ketay Corporation, explore the startling possibilities of biocontrol. As he envisioned it, electronics could take over the control of unruly humans. This could save the indoctrinators and thought controllers a lot of fuss and bother. He made it sound relatively simple.

Planes, missiles, and machine tools already are guided by electronics, and the human brain—being essentially a digital computer—can be, too. Already, through biocontrol, scientists have changed people's sense of balance. And they have made animals with full bellies feel hunger, and made them feel fearful when they have nothing to fear. *Time* magazine quoted him as explaining:

> The ultimate achievement of biocontrol may be the control of man himself . . . . The controlled subjects would never be permitted to think as individuals. A few months after birth, a surgeon would equip each child with a socket mounted under the scalp and electrodes reaching selected areas of brain tissue. . . . The child's sensory perceptions and muscular activity could be either modified or completely controlled by bioelectric signals radiating from state-controlled transmitters.

He added the reassuring thought that the electrodes "cause no discomfort."

I am sure that the psycho-persuaders of today would be appalled at the prospect of such indignity being committed on man. They are mostly decent, likable people, products of our relentlessly progressive era. Most of them want to control us just a little bit, in order to sell us some product we may find useful or disseminate with us a viewpoint that may be entirely worthy.

But when you are manipulating, where do you stop? Who is to fix the point at which manipulative attempts become socially undesirable?

19. THE FUTURE OF THE INDUSTRIAL SYSTEM

john k. galbraith

What is the future of the American economy? Can the state control big business? Can American industry exist without centralized planning? Is "private industry" really private? Is socialism inevitable? How different are the American and Soviet industrial systems? Would greater congruency among the world's major industrial complexes bode good or ill for humanity? Would it bode good or ill for the individual?

In the following selection, Professor Galbraith offers some interesting comments on the above and related questions.

In the latter part of the last century and the early decades of this, no subject was more discussed than the future of capitalism. Economists, men of unspecific wisdom, Chautauqua lecturers, editorial writers, knowledgeable ecclesiastics and socialists contributed their personal revelation. It was taken for granted that the economic system was in a state of development and in time would transform itself into something hopefully better but certainly different. Socialists drew strength from the belief that theirs was the plausible next stage in a natural process of change.

The future of the industrial system, by contrast, is not discussed. The prospect for agriculture is subject to debate—it is assumed to be in course of change. So are the chances for survival for the small entrepreneur or the private medical practitioner. But General Motors, General Electric and U.S. Steel are viewed as an ultimate achievement. One does not wonder where one is going if one is already there.

Yet to suppose that the industrial system is a terminal phenomenon is, *per se,* implausible. It is itself the product, in the last sixty years, of a vast and autonomous transformation. During this time the scale of the individual corporation has grown enormously. The entrepreneurial corporation has declined. The technostructure has developed, removed itself from control by the stockholders and acquired its own internal sources of capital. There has been a large change in its relations with the workers and a yet larger one in its relations with the state. It would be strange were such a manifestation of social dynamics to be now at an end. So to suggest is to deny one of the philosophical tenets of the system itself, one that is solemnly articulated on all occasions of business ritual—conventions, stockholders' meetings, board meetings, executive committee meetings, management development con-

From *The New Industrial State.* Copyright © 1967 by J. K. Galbraith. Reprinted by permission of the Publisher, Houghton Mifflin Company, pp. 388–399.

ferences, budget conferences, product review meetings, senior officer retreats and dealer relations workshops. It is that change is the law of economic life.

The future of the industrial system is not discussed partly because of the power it exercises over belief. It has succeeded, tacitly, in excluding the notion that it is a transitory, which would be to say that it is a somehow imperfect, phenomenon. More important, perhaps, to consider the future would be to fix attention on where it has already arrived. Among the least enchanting words in the business lexicon are planning, government control, state support and socialism. To consider the likelihood of these in the future would be to bring home the appalling extent to which they are already a fact. And it would not be ignored that these grievous things have arrived, at a minimum with the acquiescence and, at a maximum, on the demand, of the system itself.

Such reflection of the future would also emphasize the convergent tendencies of industrial societies, however different their popular or ideological billing; the convergence being to a roughly similar design for organization and planning. A word in review may be worthwhile. Convergence begins with modern large-scale production, with heavy requirements of capital, sophisticated technology and, as a prime consequence, elaborate organization. These require control of prices and, so far as possible, of what is bought at those prices. This is to say that planning must replace the market. In the Soviet-type economies, the control of prices is a function of the state. The management of demand (eased by the knowledge that their people will mostly want what Americans and Western Europeans already have) is partly by according preference to the alert and early-rising who are first to the store; partly, as in the case of houseroom, by direct allocation to the recipient; and partly, as in the case of automobiles, by making patience (as well as political position or need) a test of eligibility. With us this management is accomplished less formally by the corporations, their advertising agencies, salesmen, dealers and retailers. But these, obviously, are differences in method rather than purpose. Large-scale industrialism requires, in both cases, that the market and consumer sovereignty be extensively superseded.

Large-scale organization also requires autonomy. The intrusion of an external and uninformed will is damaging. In the non-Soviet systems this means excluding the capitalist from effective power. But the same imperative operates in the socialist economy. There the business firm seeks to minimize or exclude control by the bureaucracy. To gain autonomy for the enterprise is what, in substantial measure, the modern Communist theoretician calls reform. Nothing in our time is more interesting than that the erstwhile capitalist corporation and the erstwhile Communist firm should, under the imperatives of organization, come together as oligarchies of their own members. Ideology is not the relevant force. Large and complex organizations can use diverse knowledge and talent and thus function effectively only if under their own authority. This, it must be stressed once more, is not autonomy that subordinates a firm to the market. It is autonomy that allows the firm authority over its planning.

The industrial system has no inherent capacity for regulating total demand—for insuring a supply of purchasing power sufficient to acquire what it produces. So it relies on the state for this. At full employment there is no mechanism for holding prices and wages stable. This stabilization too is a function of the state. The Soviet-type systems also make a careful calculation of the income that is being provided in relation to the value of the goods available for purchase. Stabilization of wages and prices in general is, of course, a natural consequence of fixing individual prices and wage rates.

Finally, the industrial system must rely on the state for trained and educated manpower, now the decisive factor of production. So it also is under socialist industrialism. A decade ago, following the flight of the first Sputnik, there was great and fashionable concern in the United States for scientific and technical education. Many argued that the Soviet system, with its higher priority for state functions, among which education is prominent, had a natural advantage in this regard.

Thus convergence between the two ostensibly different industrial systems occurs at all fundamental points. This is an exceedingly fortunate thing. In time, and perhaps in less time than may be imagined, it will dispose of the notion of inevitable conflict based on irreconcilable difference. This will not be soon agreed. Marx did not foresee the convergence and he is accorded, with suitable interpretation, the remarkable, even supernatural, power of foreseeing all. Those who speak for the unbridgeable gulf that divides the free world from the Communist world and free enterprise from Communism are protected by an equally ecclesiastical faith that whatever the evolution of free enterprise may be, it cannot conceivably come to resemble socialism. But these positions can survive the evidence only for a time. Only the most committed ideologist or the most fervent propagandist can stand firm against the feeling that an increasing number of people regard him as obsolete. Vanity is a great force for intellectual modernization.

To recognize that industrial systems are convergent in their development will, one imagines, help toward agreement on the common dangers in the weapons competition, on ending it or shifting it to more benign areas. Perhaps nothing casts more light on the future of the industrial system than this, for it implies, in contrast with the present images, that it could have a future.

Given the deep dependence of the industrial system on the state and the nature of its motivational relationship to the state, i.e., its identification with public goals and the adaptation of these to its needs, the industrial system will not long be regarded as something apart from government. Rather it will increasingly be seen as part of a much larger complex which embraces both the industrial system and the state. Private enterprise was anciently so characterized because it was subordinate to the market and those in command derived their power from ownership of private property. The modern corporation is no longer subordinate to the market; those who run it no longer depend on property ownership for their authority. They must have autonomy within a framework of goals. But this fully allows them to work in association with the bureaucracy and, indeed, to perform for the bureaucracy tasks that it cannot do, or cannot do as well, for itself. In consequence, so we have seen, for tasks of technical sophistication, there is a close fusion of the industrial system with the state. Members of the technostructure work closely with their public counterparts not only in the development and manufacture of products but in advising them of their needs. Were it not so celebrated in ideology, it would long since have been agreed that the line that now divides public from so-called private organization in military procurement, space exploration and atomic energy is so indistinct as to be nearly imperceptible. Men move easily across the line. On retirement, admirals and generals, as well as high civil servants, go more or less automatically to the more closely associated industries. One experienced observer has already called these firms the "semi-nationalized" branch of the economy. It has been noted, "the Market mechanism, [is replaced by] . . . the administrative mechanism. For the profit share of private entrepreneurs, it substitutes the fixed fee, a payment in lieu of profits foregone. And for the independent private business unit, it substitutes the integrated hierarchical structure of an organization composed of an agency . . . and its contractors." [1]

The foregoing refers to firms which sell most of their output to the government—to Boeing which (at this writing) sells 65 per cent of its output to the government; General Dynamics which sells a like percentage; Raytheon which sells 70 per cent; Lockheed which sells 81 per cent; and Republic Aviation which sells 100 per cent.[2] But firms which have a smaller proportion of sales to the government are more dependent on it for the regulation of again, a functional necessity of the industrial system. But the goals this aggregate demand and not much less so for the stabilization of wages and prices, the underwriting of especially expensive technology and the supply of trained and educated manpower.

So comprehensive a relationship cannot be denied or ignored indefinitely. Increasingly it will be recognized that the mature corporation, as it develops, becomes part of the larger administrative complex associated with the state. In time the line between the two will disappear. Men will look back in amusement at the pretense that once caused people to refer to General Dynamics and North American Aviation and A. T. & T. as *private* business.

Though this recognition will not be universally welcomed, it will be healthy. There is always a presumption in social matters in favor of reality as opposed to myth. The autonomy of the technostructure is, to repeat yet

---

[1] From a study by Richard Tybout, *Government Contracting in Atomic Energy* (Ann Arbor: University of Michigan Press, 1956), p. 175. Professor Tybout is referring especially to cost-plus-fixed-fee contracts.

[2] Data from Michael D. Reagan, *Politics, Economics and the General Welfare* (Chicago: Scott, Foresman and Company, 1965), p. 113.

again, a functional necessity of the industrial system. But the goals this autonomy serves allow some range of choice. If the mature corporation is recognized to be part of the penumbra of the state, it will be more strongly in the service of social goals. It cannot plead its inherently private character or its subordination to the market as cover for the pursuit of different goals of particular interest to itself. The public agency has an unquestioned tendency to pursue goals that reflect its own interest and convenience and to adapt social objective thereto. But it cannot plead this as a superior right. There may well be danger in this association of public and economic power. But it is less if it is recognized.

Other changes can be imagined. As the public character of the mature corporation comes to be recognized, attention will doubtless focus on the position of the stockholder in this corporation. This is anomalous. He is a passive and functionless figure, remarkable only in his capacity to share, without effort or even without appreciable risk, in the gains from the growth by which the technostructure measures its success. No grant of feudal privilege has ever equaled, for effortless return, that of the grandparent who bought and endowed his descendants with a thousand shares of General Motors or General Electric. The beneficiaries of this foresight have become and remain rich by no exercise of effort or intelligence beyond the decision to do nothing, embracing as it did the decision not to sell. But these matters need not be pursued here. Questions of equity and social justice as between the fortuitously rich have their own special expertise.

Most of the individual developments which are leading, if the harshest term may be employed, to the socialization of the mature corporation will be conceded, even by men of the most conservative disposition. The control by the mature corporation over its prices, its influence on consumer behavior, the euthanasia of stockholder power, the regulation by the state of aggregate demand, the effort to stabilize prices and wages, the role of publicly supported research and development, the role of military, space and related procurement, the influence of the firm on these government activities and the modern role of education are, more or less, accepted facts of life.

What is avoided is reflection on the consequences of putting them all together, of seeing them as a system. But it cannot be supposed that the principal beams and buttresses of the industrial system have all been changed and that the structure remains as before. If the parts have changed, so then has the whole. If this associates the mature corporation inextricably with the state, the fact cannot be exorcised by a simple refusal to add.

It will be urged, of course, that the industrial system is not the whole economy. Apart from the world of General Motors, Standard Oil, Ford, General Electric, U.S. Steel, Chrysler, Texaco, Gulf, Western Electric and Du Pont is that of the independent retailer, the farmer, the shoe repairman, the bookmaker, narcotics peddler, pizza merchant and that of the car and dog laundry. Here prices are not controlled. Here the consumer is sovereign. Here pecuniary motivation is unimpaired. Here technology is simple and there is no research or development to make it otherwise. Here there are no government contracts; independence from the state is a reality. None of these entrepreneurs patrol the precincts of the Massachusetts Institute of Technology in search of talent. The existence of all this I concede. And this part of the economic system is not insignificant. It is not, however, the part of the economy with which this book has been concerned. It has been concerned with the world of the large corporation. This too is important; and it is more deeply characteristic of the modern industrial scene than the dog laundry or the small manufacturer with a large idea. One should always cherish his critics and protect them where possible from foolish error. The tendency of the mature corporation in the industrial system to become part of the administrative complex of the state ought not to be refuted by appeal to contrary tendencies outside the industrial system.

Some who dislike the notion that the industrial system merges into the state in its development will be tempted to assault not the tendency but those who adumbrate it. This, it must be urged, is not in keeping with contemporary ethics and manners. Once the bearers of bad tidings were hanged, disemboweled or made subject to some other equally sanguinary mistreatment. Now such reaction is regarded as lacking in delicacy. A doctor can inform even the most petulant client that he has terminal cancer without fear of adverse physical consequences. The aide who must advise a politician that a new poll shows him to be held in all but universal distaste need exercise only decent tact. Those who find unappealing the present intelligence are urged to exercise similar restraint.

They should also be aware of the causes. It is part of the vanity of modern man that he can decide the character of his economic system. His area of decision is, in fact, exceedingly small. He could, conceivably, decide whether or not he wishes to have a high level of industrialization. Thereafter the imperatives of organization, technology and planning operate similarly, and we have seen to a broadly similar result, on all societies. Given the decision to have modern industry, much of what happens is inevitable and the same.

The two questions most asked about an economic system are whether it serves man's physical needs and whether it is consistent with his liberty. There is little doubt as to the ability of the industrial system to serve man's needs. As we have seen, it is able to manage them only because it serves them abundantly. It requires a mechanism for making men want what it provides. But this mechanism would not work—wants would not be subject to manipulation —had not these wants been dulled by sufficiency.

The prospects for liberty involve far more interesting questions. It has always been imagined, especially by conservatives, that to associate all, or a large part, of economic activity with the state is to endanger freedom. The individual and his preferences, in one way or another, will be sacrificed to the needs and conveniences of the apparatus created ostensibly to serve him. As the industrial system evolves into a penumbra of the state, the question of its relation to liberty thus arises in urgent form. In recent years, in the

Soviet-type economies, there has been an ill-concealed conflict between the state and the intellectuals. In essence, this has been a conflict between those for whom the needs of the government, including above all its needs as economic planner and producer of goods, are pre-eminent and those who assert the high but inconvenient claims of uninhibited intellectual and artistic expression. Is this a warning?

The instinct which warns of dangers in this association of economic and public power is sound. It comes close to being the subject of this book. But conservatives have looked in the wrong direction for the danger. They have feared that the state might reach out and destroy the vigorous, money-making entrepreneur. They have not noticed that, all the while, the successors to the entrepreneur were uniting themselves ever more closely with the state and rejoicing in the result. They were also, and with enthusiasm, accepting abridgement of their freedom. Part of this is implicit in the subordination of individual personality to the needs of organization. Some of it is in the exact pattern of the classical business expectation. The president of Republic Aviation is not much more likely in public to speak critically, or even candidly, of the Air Force than is the head of a Soviet *combinat* of the ministry to which he reports. No modern head of the Ford Motor Company will ever react with the same pristine vigor to the presumed foolishness of Washington as did its founder. No head of Montgomery Ward will ever again breathe defiance of a President as did Sewell Avery. Manners may be involved. But it would also be conceded that "too much is at stake."

The problem, however, is not the freedom of the businessman. Business orators have spoken much about freedom in the past. But it can be laid down as a rule that those who speak most of liberty are least inclined to use it. The high executive who speaks fulsomely of personal freedom carefully submits his speeches on the subject for review and elimination of controversial words, phrases and ideas, as befits a good organization man. The general who tells his troops, and the world, that they are in the forefront of the fight for freedom is a man who has always submitted happily to army discipline. The high State Department official, who adverts feelingly to the values of the free world extravagantly admires the orthodoxy of his own views.

The danger to liberty lies in the subordination of belief to the needs of the industrial system. In this the state and the industrial system will be partners. This threat has already been assessed, as also the means for minimizing it.

If we continue to believe that the goals of the industrial system—the expansion of output, the companion increase in consumption, technological advance, the public images that sustain it—are coordinate with life, then all of our lives will be in the service of these goals. What is consistent with these ends we shall have or be allowed; all else will be off limits. Our wants will be managed in accordance with the needs of the industrial system; the policies of the state will be subject to similar influence; education will be adapted to industrial need; the disciplines required by the industrial system will be the conventional morality of the community. All other goals will be made to seem precious, unimportant or antisocial. We will be bound to the ends of the industrial system. The state will add its moral, and perhaps some of its legal, power to their enforcement. What will eventuate, on the whole, will be the benign servitude of the household retainer who is taught to love her mistress and see her interests as her own, and not the compelled servitude of the field hand. But it will not be freedom.

If, on the other hand, the industrial system is only a part, and relatively a diminishing part, of life, there is much less occasion for concern. Aesthetic goals will have pride of place; those who serve them will not be subject to the goals of the industrial system; the industrial system itself will be subordinate to the claims of these dimensions of life. Intellectual preparation will be for its own sake and not for the better service to the industrial system. Men will not be entrapped by the belief that apart from the goals of the industrial system—apart from the production of goods and income by progressively more advanced technical methods—there is nothing important in life.

The foregoing being so, we may, over time, come to see the industrial system in fitting light as an essentially technical arrangement for providing convenient goods and services in adequate volume. Those who rise through its bureaucracy will so see themselves. And the public consequences will be in keeping, for if economic goals are the only goals of the society it is natural that the industrial system should dominate the state and the state should serve its ends. If other goals are strongly asserted, the industrial system will fall into its place as a detached and autonomous arm of the state, but responsive to the larger purposes of the society.

We have seen wherein the chance for salvation lies. The industrial system, in contrast with its economic antecedents, is intellectually demanding. It brings into existence, to serve its intellectual and scientific needs, the community that, hopefully, will reject its monopoly of social purpose.

20. THE LEADER AND THE MASSES
niccolo machiavelli

As we have seen, the manipulative use and goals of power are central themes in the study of social control mechanisms. Excerpts from one of the most famous political works of all time, written in the sixteenth century, are found below. Perennial aspects of power and its exercise by strong-willed leaders are probed—the relation of the masses to the leader, the impact of human nature on decision making, deception versus honesty, and the moral choice of means to achieve certain ends.

From Niccolo Machiavelli, *The Prince.*

In your view, do these passages accurately describe the behavior of power-seekers in the political arena regardless of time and place? Or do they represent atypical portraits of the process of political control inapplicable to our more enlightened world?

Now to continue with the list of characteristics. It should be the desire of every prince to be considered merciful and not cruel, yet he should take care not to make poor use of his clemency. Cesare Borgia was regarded as cruel, yet his cruelty reorganized Romagna and united it in peace and loyalty. Indeed, if we reflect, we shall see that this man was more merciful than the Florentines who, to avoid the charge of cruelty, allowed Pistoia to be destroyed.[1] A prince should care nothing for the accusation of cruelty so long as he keeps his subjects united and loyal; by making a very few examples he can be more truly merciful than those who through too much tender-heartedness allow disorders to arise whence come killings and rapine. For these offend an entire community, while the few executions ordered by the prince affect only a few individuals. . . .

Here the question arises; whether it is better to be loved than feared or feared than loved. The answer is that it would be desirable to be both but, since that is difficult, it is much safer to be feared than to be loved, if one must choose. For on men in general this observation may be made: they are ungrateful, fickle, and deceitful, eager to avoid dangers, and avid for gain, and while you are useful to them they are all with you, offering you their blood, their property, their lives, and their sons so long as danger is remote, as we noted above, but when it approaches they turn on you. Any prince, trusting only in their words and having no other preparations made, will fall to his ruin, for friendships that are bought at a price and not by greatness and nobility of soul are paid for indeed, but they are not owned and cannot be called upon in time of need. Men have less hesitation in offending a man who is loved than one who is feared, for love is held by a bond of obligation which, as men are wicked, is broken whenever personal advantage suggests it, but fear is accompanied by the dread of punishment which never relaxes.

Yet a prince should make himself feared in such a way that, if he does not thereby merit love, at least he may escape odium, for being feared and not hated may well go together. And indeed the prince may attain this end if he but respect the property and the women of his subjects and citizens. And if it should become necessary to seek the death of someone, he should find a proper justification and a public cause, and above all he should keep his hands off another's property, for men forget more readily the death of their father than the loss of their patrimony. Besides, pretexts for seizing property are never lacking, and when a prince begins to live by means of

[1] By unchecked rioting between opposing factions (1502).

rapine he will always find some excuse for plundering others, and conversely pretexts for execution are rare and are more quickly exhausted.

A prince at the head of his armies and with a vast number of soldiers under his command should give not the slightest heed if he is esteemed cruel, for without such a reputation he will not be able to keep his army united and ready for action. Among the marvelous things told of Hannibal is that, having a vast army under his command made up of all kinds and races of men and waging war far from his own country, he never allowed any dissension to arise either as between the troops and their leaders or among the troops themselves, and this both in times of good fortune and bad. This could only have come about through his most inhuman cruelty which, taken in conjunction with his great valor, kept him always an object of respect and terror in the eyes of his soldiers. And without the cruelty his other characteristics would not have achieved this effect. . . .

How laudable it is for a prince to keep his word and govern his actions by integrity rather than trickery will be understood by all. Nonetheless we have in our times seen great things accomplished by many princes who have thought little of keeping their promises and have known the art of mystifying the minds of men. Such princes have won out over those whose actions were based on fidelity to their word.

It must be understood that there are two ways of fighting, one with laws and the other with arms. The first is the way of men, the second is the style of beasts, but since very often the first does not suffice it is necessary to turn to the second. Therefore a prince must know how to play the beast as well as the man. This lesson was taught allegorically by the ancient writers who related that Achilles and many other princes were brought up by Chiron the Centaur, who took them under his discipline. The clear significance of this half-man and half-beast preceptorship is that a prince must know how to use either of these two natures and that one without the other has no enduring strength. Now since the prince must make use of the characteristics of beasts he should choose those of the fox and the lion, though the lion cannot defend himself against snares and the fox is helpless against wolves. One must be a fox in avoiding traps and a lion in frightening wolves. Such as choose simply the rôle of a lion do not rightly understand the matter. Hence a wise leader cannot and should not keep his word when keeping it is not to his advantage or when the reasons that made him give it are no longer valid. If men were good, this would not be a good precept, but since they are wicked and will not keep faith with you, you are not bound to keep faith with them. . . .

So a prince need not have all the aforementioned good qualities, but it is most essential that he appear to have them. Indeed, I should go so far as to say that having them and always practising them is harmful, while seeming to have them is useful. It is good to appear clement, trustworthy, humane, religious, and honest, and also to be so, but always with the mind so disposed that, when the occasion arises not to be so, you can become the opposite. It

must be understood that a prince and particularly a new prince cannot prac-
tise all the virtues for which men are accounted good, for the necessity of preserving the state often compels him to take actions which are opposed to
loyalty, charity, humanity, and religion. Hence he must have a spirit ready
to adapt itself as the varying winds of fortune command him. As I have
said, so far as he is able, a prince should stick to the path of good but, if the
necessity arises, he should know how to follow evil.

A prince must take great care that no word ever passes his lips that is not
full of the above mentioned five good qualities, and he must seem to all who
see and hear him a model of piety, loyalty, integrity, humanity, and religion.
Nothing is more necessary than to seem to possess this last quality, for men
in general judge more by the eye than the hand, as all can see but few can
feel. Everyone sees what you seem to be, few experience what you really are
and these few do not dare to set themselves up against the opinion of the
majority supported by the majesty of the state. In the actions of all men and
especially princes, where there is no court of appeal, the end is all that counts.
Let a prince then concern himself with the acquisition or the maintenance of a
state; the means employed will always be considered honorable and praised
by all, for the mass of mankind is always swayed by appearances and by the
outcome of an enterprise. And in the world there is only the mass, for the few
find their place only when the majority has no base of support. A certain
prince of our own times, whom it would not be well to name, preaches nothing
but peace and faith and yet is the enemy of both, and if he had observed either
he would already on numerous occasions have lost both his state and his
renown.

21. THE POWER ELITE

c. wright mills

While no one doubts that power in American society is distributed
unequally, there is widespread disagreement over whether a decisive
share of that power is held and jealously guarded by a distinct, relatively small and willful "elite."

The following passages are from a book that stirred a series of
acrimonious debates among social scientists and a good deal of criticism of the viewpoints expressed. An important point made by the
author—apart from the validity of his major thesis—is that power in
contemporary American society derives from institutional roles rather
than wealth in and of itself, and that "key decisions" made through
occupancy of such roles carries enormous consequences for millions
of people throughout the world.

Within American society, major national power now resides in the economic, the political, and the military domains. Other institutions seem off to the side of modern history, and, on occasion, duly subordinated to these. No family is as directly powerful in national affairs as any major corporation; no church is as directly powerful in the external biographies of young men in America today as the military establishment; no college is as powerful in the shaping of momentous events as the National Security Council. Religious, educational, and family institutions are not autonomous centers of national power; on the contrary, these decentralized areas are increasingly shaped by the big three, in which developments of decisive and immediate consequence now occur. . . .

At the pinnacle of each of the three enlarged and centralized domains, there have arisen those higher circles which make up the economic, the political, and the military elites. At the top of the economy, among the corporate rich, there are the chief executives; at the top of the political order, the members of the political directorate; at the top of the military establishment, the elite of soldier-statesmen clustered in and around the Joint Chiefs of Staff and the upper echelon. As each of these domains has coincided with the others, as decisions tend to become total in their consequence, the leading men in each of the three domains of power—the warlords, the corporation chieftains, the political directorate—tend to come together, to form the power elite of America. . . .

If we took the one hundred most powerful men in America, the one hundred wealthiest, and the one hundred most celebrated away from the institutional positions they now occupy, away from their resources of men and women and money, away from the media of mass communication that are now focused upon them—then they would be powerless and poor and uncelebrated. For power is not of a man. Wealth does not center in the person of the wealthy. Celebrity is not inherent in any personality. To be celebrated, to be wealthy, to have power requires access to major institutions, for the institutional positions men occupy determine in large part their chances to have and to hold these valued experiences. . . .

It is as fashionable, just now, to suppose that there is no power elite, as it was fashionable in the 'thirties to suppose a set of ruling-class villains to be the source of all social injustice and public malaise. I should be as far from supposing that some simple and unilateral ruling class could be firmly located as the prime mover of American society, as I should be from supposing that all historical change in America today is merely impersonal drift.

The view that all is blind drift is largely a fatalist projection of one's own feeling of impotence and perhaps, if one has ever been active politically in a principled way, a salve of one's guilt.

The view that all of history is due to the conspiracy of an easily located set of villains, or of heroes, is also a hurried projection from the difficult effort to understand how shifts in the structure of society open opportunities to various elites and how various elites take advantage or fail to take advantage of them. To accept either view—of all history as conspiracy or of all history as drift—is to relax the effort to understand the facts of power and the ways of the powerful. . . .

What I am asserting is that in this particular epoch a conjunction of historical circumstances has led to the rise of an elite of power; that the men of the circles composing this elite, severally and collectively, now make such key decisions as are made; and that, given the enlargement and the centralization of the means of power now available, the decisions that they make and fail to make carry more consequences for more people than has ever been the case in the world history of mankind.

I am also asserting that there has developed on the middle levels of power, a semi-organized stalemate, and that on the bottom level there has come into being a mass-like society which has little resemblence to the image of a society in which voluntary associations and classic publics hold the keys to power. The top of the American system of power is much more unified and much more powerful, the bottom is much more fragmented, and in truth, impotent, than is generally supposed by those who are distracted by the middling units of power which neither express such will as exists at the bottom nor determine the decisions at the top.

22. THE MENACE OF THE MILITARY-INDUSTRIAL COMPLEX

jack raymond

The author of the following selection believes that a strong military-industrial complex poses serious threats to the American way of life. While not alleging that a conspiracy exists, he does assert that collusion among military, industrial, and political leaders has produced a power phenomenon that relies on popular votes and vested interests to secure its objectives. These objectives may be used in the national interest—but not necessarily. A fundamental question that must be considered is the extent of the dangers against which Americans must guard.

Several months before he was due to leave office, President Dwight D. Eisenhower asked Dr. Malcolm Moos, his special assistant and speech writer (now President of the University of Minnesota), to put together some material that

From Jack Raymond, "Growing Threat of Our Military-Industrial Complex," *Harvard Business Review,* May-June 1968, pp. 53–64. Reprinted by permission of the *Harvard Business Review.* © 1968 by the President and Fellows of Harvard College; all rights reserved.

could be used in a farewell address to the nation. Eisenhower, who has a sense of history that too often has been overlooked by his detractors (with the exception of one writer, who speculated that the old soldier thought of himself as George Washington and therefore also wanted to be remembered for his farewell speech), told his assistant that he wanted something more than a platitudinous onward-and-upward Presidential sermon.

Dr. Moos, as was his custom for many major speeches, gathered excerpts of Eisenhower memoranda and some jottings based on extemporaneous remarks the President had made to small groups at the White House, and he added a few ideas of his own for the President's consideration. In their second or third discussion of the planned valedictory, Eisenhower suggested, "Let's bring Milton in, and we can meet regularly to put this in shape." Thereupon the President's brother, Dr. Milton Eisenhower, joined in a series of lengthy late-evening sessions at the White House that resulted in the now-famous parting warning against the dangers of the "military-industrial complex."

Whether or not he thought of matching Washington, President Eisenhower's farewell address, on January 17, 1961, may well be quoted long after the First President's parting admonition against permanent alliances with foreign nations. For while foreign alliances have become an accepted form of America's projection of power in modern times, a society based on war and the threat of war is so alien to the American self-image that even today, in time of war, the ingredients of military preparedness evoke stereotyped suspicions of unseen provocateurs and profiteers.

Hardly a day goes by that the phrase "military-industrial complex" is not cited and that the Eisenhower warning is not drawn on to drive home some point in a current controversy:

1. The National Committee for an Effective Congress recently stated: "The single most disturbing factor the committee found in the Administration's current policy is the alleged growing influence of the military-industrial complex—a factor former President Eisenhower warned against—and the stake of that complex in the war economy."

2. When the Administrtion decided in 1967 to construct a so-called "thin" antiballistic missile (ABM) defense network, Senator Wayne Morse of Oregon linked it to the war in Vietnam and rasped, "The American people desperately need to recognize, before it is too late, that we are being run in this country today by an industrial-military complex that makes its profits out of American blood, and jeopardizes all the future generations of American boys and girls."

3. At the annual meeting of the American Economic Association, Walter Adams of Michigan State University said the military-industrial complex was a "Frankenstein threatening to control the contract state which brought it into being"; and Seymour Melman of Columbia University said the complex points to "a complete transformation of society [toward] the Soviet type of State capitalism."

4. When several thousand women, led by former Congresswoman Jeanette Rankin, marched on the Capitol early in 1968 in protest against the war in Vietnam, their formal petition called for Congress to "listen to what the American people are saying and refuse the insatiable demands of the military-industrial complex."

In view of the current rhetorical vogue, let us go back to the original warning and examine exactly what Eisenhower said and what led him to say it, so that we may consider the nature of the "complex" and its significance for us today.

In his farewell address, Eisenhower reminded the American people that the United States, which until World War II had not had an armaments industry, was no longer able to risk emergency improvisations of national defense. It had been "compelled to create a permanent armaments industry of vast proportions" in support of a huge defense establishment costing more than the total net income of U.S. corporations. He pointed out:

"This conjunction of an immense military establishment and a large arms industry is now in the American experience. The total influence—economic, political, even spiritual—is felt in every city, every state house, every office of the Federal government. We recognize the imperative need for this development. Yet we must not fail to comprehend its grave implications. Our toil, resources and livelihood are involved; so is the very structure of our society.

"In the councils of government, we must guard against the acquisition of unwarranted influence, whether sought or unsought, by the military-industrial complex. The potential for the disastrous rise of misplaced power exists and will persist.

"We must never let the weight of this combination endanger our liberties or democratic processes. We should take nothing for granted." The foregoing is the passage that is most often quoted, but Eisenhower went on to sound the warning of a subtler, and perhaps more fundamental, alteration in the American system:

"Akin to, and largely responsible for the sweeping changes in our industrial-military posture, has been the technological revolution during recent decades.

"In this revolution, research has become central; it also becomes more formalized, complex, and costly. A steadily increasing share is conducted for, by, or at the direction of the Federal government.

"Today the solitary inventor, tinkering in his shop, has been overshadowed by task forces of scientists in laboratories and testing fields. In the same fashion, the free university, historically the fountainhead of free ideas and scientific discovery, has experienced a revolution in the conduct of research. Partly because of the huge costs involved, a government contract becomes virtually a substitute for intellectual curiosity. For every old blackboard there are now hundreds of electronic computers.

"The prospect of domination of the nation's scholars by Federal employment, project allocations, and the power of money is ever present—and is gravely to be regarded."

There, then, is the Eisenhower warning. Many found it surprising that a military man whose best friends were big businessmen should have uttered it. But it was consistent with his frequently expressed concern over the pressures that had assailed him in the White House. It was consistent also with the historical heritage of the country. For fear of, and aversion to, military influence are rooted deep in the American psyche. The English quartering of a standing army on colonial soil to fight the French and Indian Wars was one of the causes of the American revolution. The writers of the Declaration of Independence complained that King George had "affected to render the military independent of and superior to the Civil Power."

Moreover, there was cause enough in the American experience to question the motives behind defense buildups and arms purchases. Two American authors, H. C. Engelbrecht and F. C. Hanighen, contributed a lasting phrase with the title of their book, *Merchants of Death*. The book reports on a Congressional investigation in 1929 which disclosed that an "observer" for U.S. shipbuilders had tried to wreck the 1927 Geneva Naval Reductions Conference. The case came to light when the "observer" sued the shipbuilders for fees he claimed were due him for his work. It brought a public protest from President Herbert Hoover.

A Senate investigation conducted by Gerald P. Nye in the 1930's concentrated on the great profits made by defense manufacturers in World War I; it did much to arouse American suspicions that the arms makers were responsible for wars. President Franklin D. Roosevelt, pledging his cooperation with the Nye investigation, attributed the "mad race in armaments . . . in no small measure to the uncontrolled activities of the manufacturers and merchants of engines of destruction." Even in World War II there were many who blamed the "creeping involvement" of the U.S. economy in the war for America's ultimate participation in it.

Eisenhower's concern over the "complex" was based to a considerable extent on military spending pressures on his budget. At the height of a particularly aggravating dispute over the respective merits of Army and Air Force antiaircraft weapons, he declared that "obviously political and financial considerations" rather than "strict military needs" were influencing the weapons debate. And on another occasion, when asked whether he would be willing to allocate more money for defense if the nation could, as his critics insisted, afford it, he replied heatedly, "I would not." Anyone "with any sense," he said, knew that if military spending were not restrained, the country would become a "garrison state." . . .

It is evident, however, that in his farewell address Eisenhower was not warning of some nefarious conspiracy by military and industrial leaders (although he was more alert than most Americans to the political savvy of seemingly nonpolitical military men). He explained at his final news conference as President that he was not thinking so much of willful misuses of power as of "an almost insidious penetration of our own minds that the only thing the country is engaged in is weaponry and missiles—and I'll tell you we just can't afford that."

To understand and assess the military-industrial complex, we must identify it and consider its magnitude, its composition, and the interaction of its component parts.

The military-industrial complex includes all those elements of American society—economic, political, and professional—that have a material or philosophic stake in a large defense establishment. It includes not only the Armed Services and the companies that produce for them, but politicians in and out of government, workers and union leaders, ordinary citizens and local officials, teachers in schools, and academicians—in short, all who for reasons of "pork or patriotism" support the Armed Forces' requirements.

It may be simplistic to bundle diverse elements of the military-industrial complex into a single "it," but "it" is very real, as former Secretary of Defense Robert McNamara attested after seven years in his post. Characteristically, McNamara asserted he rarely lost to "it." He told an interviewer, "I'd say in this area we haven't lost more than 2% of the cases to the so-called military-industrial complex—and in those instances we failed to present our case properly." But what about the magnitude of the cases lost? Even a straight-across-the-board 2% of Pentagon expenditures in the nine budgets McNamara worked on in seven years, including estimates for fiscal year 1969, totals $10.3 billion—twice the estimated cost of the anti-China ABM defense system, which is considered by many to be the "complex's" latest prize.

The Pentagon's spending program supports not merely the tactics and strategy of the fighting fronts; it reaches into the lives of all of us on the domestic front. Allocations for military research spin off into jobs and products that can and do become important to the civilian economy. The decision to open a base or close one can affect grocery store owners and church fathers as well as night club operators and liquor dealers. The confluence of interests in the military budget thus results in unusual alliances as varying segments of society, motivated by monetary or social objectives, seek each other's support for shares of Pentagon expenditures. . . .

The benefactions of defense contracting appear more dramatic still when specific examples are considered. One good illustration is the city of Marietta, Georgia. Lockheed-Georgia Company, a division of Lockheed Aircraft Corporation, is located in Marietta and is the largest single industrial organization in the Southeast. About 90% of Lockheed-Georgia's business stems from defense contracts, the most important of which now are for the development and building of the C-5A military transport (worth about $1.4 billion) and for production of the C-141 Starlifter (worth another $600 million or more).

Lockheed-Georgia pays about $200 million a year in wages to 26,000 workers drawn from about 55 of Georgia's 159 counties—about one third of the state. Marietta's mayor, Howard Atherton, has said the impact of Lockheed-Georgia on his city's economy is "almost immeasurable." Robert Cox, a Machinists Union leader in Marietta, said defense spending "would almost have to be considered a major ingredient in the continuing low rate of unemployment in the metropolitan Atlanta area." Lockheed buys everything from soft drinks to metal parts from Georgia suppliers. Last year, the company spent $113 million with about 1,720 suppliers, many of them small businesses.

Lockheed-Georgia offers so good an example of spreading prosperity in a defense-oriented economy that the Pentagon cited it proudly in its *Defense Industry Bulletin,* as follows:

"Major subcontractors and subsystems contracts on the Starlifter are shared by 33 companies over the United States. Whatever the total of the employees of the subcontractors and vendors who draw their paychecks from funds derived from the C-141, it can be multiplied by five to give a truer estimate of the number whose livelihood is affected by this defense program. This is because in the communities involved there are grocers, clothiers, furniture dealers, appliance dealers, etc., who feed, clothe, house and, generally, care for the needs of those who are working specifically on a defense contract.

"After receiving the prime contract on the airframe of the C-141 from the Air Force Systems Command's Aeronautical Systems Division, Lockheed's plant in Georgia sublet the wing to Avco Corporation in Nashville, Tenn., in competitive bidding. The wing includes a fuel pump. The Tennessee subcontractor in Avco obtained the fuel pump from Pesco in Bedford, Ohio. To build the fuel pump, Pesco needed, among other things, a switch and a cannon plug. The Ohio firm bought the switch from the Micro Devices Company of Dayton, Ohio, and the cannon plug from a concern in Los Angeles, California.

"At this point, the defense dollar really begins to flow into communities over the United States. Micro of Ohio gathers components for the switch from the following areas: wire, from Westbury, N.Y.; glass, Shanton, Conn.; electrical material, Chicago and New York; disc, Cincinnati, Ohio; springs, Cincinnati; ceramics, Paramoit, Calif., and Sun Prairie, Wis.; epoxy, Canton, Mass.; and silver from New York City. The Los Angeles firm providing the cannon plug for Pesco's fuel pump follows a similar pattern in obtaining components from companies spread out over the nation. . . .

"A tracing of the path of the defense dollar through the subcontracting and vending program involving other parts of the Starlifter would find it in virtually every state going from prime contractor to major subcontractors into the third and fourth levels, to vendors and suppliers ad infinitum. For example, Rohr Corporation of Chula Vista, Calif., largest C-141 subcontractor, sublets 49% of its contract on engine nacelles. Companies receiving this 49% from Rohr, in turn sublet 40% of their part to other firms. Rohr's subcontractors at the time the study was made totaled $85.9 million; since then additional millions are being negotiated for follow-on C-141's."

No review of U.S. defense business would be complete without inclusion of the government's own mercantile interest in it, for the United States engages in the sale of arms as a source of revenue for the Treasury. In fact, the United States is the world's principal arms supplier. This is not surprising or novel. The United States was the arsenal of democracy in two world wars. And in the period immediately after World War II, it maintained its role as arms supplier in order to bolster Western Europe against threatened Communist aggression.

From 1949 to 1962 the U.S. Government alone (not counting private arms sales) sold $16.1 billion worth of military arms to other countries and gave away about $30.2 billion. Since 1962, when the current arms sales program began, Pentagon officials have been as aggressive as private arms merchants, with the result that the United States has sold over $11.1 billion worth of arms. In a speech in Los Angeles in the spring of 1966, the Pentagon official in charge of the sales program proudly estimated that it had yielded $1 billion in profits for American industry and 1.2 million man-years of employment for companies throughout the country.

So aggressive has been the Pentagon in selling abroad that for several years it managed to use the Export-Import Bank to provide easy credit for poorer, underdeveloped nations, much like the easy-credit terms that flourish between retailers and ghetto inhabitants.

Congress, angered by disclosures of so-called "Country X" accounts, ended the practice in 1967 and put ceilings on the grants and sales of arms to Latin America and Africa. However, the sale of arms abroad continues to be a big—very big—business. . . .

The military-industrial complex includes certain pressure groups. The most obvious of these are the organizations of the Army, Navy, and Air Force supporters, led by men with strong emotional and careerist ties to the services and virtually financed by the defense contractors.

The Association of the U.S. Army, the Air Force Association, and the Navy League—each with chapters throughout the country—are composed of active, reserve, and retired members of the Armed Forces, and of defense contractors, community leaders, and other supporters. These organizations are financed by membership fees, payments for contractors' exhibits at annual conventions, subscriptions to dinner meetings and rallies, and advertisements in official publications. They are regarded as the civilian "arm" or "spokesmen" of their respective services, and their officers maintain close contact with the active civilian and military leaders of the services. They unabashedly campaign in behalf of policies advocated by the active Army, Navy, and Air Force leaders. Occasionally they even choose sides between the military and the civilians in government, usually in favor of expanded military forces and bigger and better weapons, and in opposition to policies that suggest reduced "preparedness."

In its annual meeting of 1967 the Association of the U.S. Army welcomed the decision to produce and deploy the ABM system which the Army had so long advocated (more on this presently); in its annual meeting the Air

Force Association urged "contract definition" of an advanced manned strategic bomber, procurement and deployment of an improved manned interceptor, the F-12, and production of the SST supersonic transport; and in its annual meeting the Navy League called for additional ships—especially nuclear-powered carriers and submarines.

The Military Services, of course, carry on their own direct lobbying and public relations campaigns. They maintain legislative liaison staffs with officers stationed in the Capitol and concern themselves with legislation on the budget, broad military policies, pay, promotion, retirement, housing, medical care, and —not least—the military construction programs that provide most of the "pork barrel" projects. The Military Services thus keep members of Congress informed and solicit their interest in particular programs. In this way they have consistently created Congressional support for certain expanded arms programs, even when the White House has opposed them.

Of course, many members of Congress are active reservists, come from areas dependent on weapons manufacturing, or are dependent on other forms of military largess—a military base, for example. It is by now an old saw that if Georgia, the home state of the chairman of the Senate Armed Services Committee, received another military installation, it would sink.

The TFX story is probably the most outstanding example of the pressures that can be identified in the military-industrial complex—pressures that are still reverberating, in this case, more than five years after the initial Pentagon announcement of the award of a potential $7 billion contract to the General Dynamics Corporation.

The TFX (Tactical Fighter, Experimental), later named the F-111, a jet fighter-bomber, was the biggest contracting plum since World War II. The competition for the contract developed between Boeing, with headquarters in Seattle, and General Dynamics, with corporate headquarters in New York. Boeing planned to place the work in its Wichita, Kansas plant; General Dynamics planned to develop and build the plane in its Convair division at Forth Worth, Texas.

Inevitably, the politics of geography drew public notice. The then Vice President, Lyndon B. Johnson, was from Texas; the first Secretary of the Navy in the Kennedy Administration, John B. Connally, was Governor of Texas and a close friend and associate of Johnson; and the then Secretary of the Navy, Fred Korth, was one of the most prominent citizens of Texas. A Congressional committee brought out the fact that the bank of which Korth had been president held the General Dynamics checking account in Forth Worth.

Meanwhile, a number of members of Congress were also interested in the TFX award:

1. Several of them were in touch with Secretary of the Air Force Eugene Zuckert during the contract negotiations. One of them, Senator Mike Monroney of Oklahoma, said later he had visited Zuckert's office "to remind him of the vast government-owned plant in Tulsa, Oklahoma, which the Douglas

Aircraft Company operates, and its large unusued machinery and manpower capabilities."

2. Senator Stuart Symington of Missouri, a former Secretary of the Air Force, visited Zuckert to discuss the possibility of Missouri companies obtaining subcontracts from whichever manufacturer got the prime contract.

3. Senator Warren Magnuson of Washington inquired about the status of the competition. His fellow Washingtonian, Senator Henry M. Jackson, frequent butt of the jape that he is the "Senator from Boeing," openly said he had insisted on an investigation when Boeing did not win the contract.

4. Senators Frank Carlson and James B. Pearson, and Representative Garner E. Shriver, all of Kansas, where Boeing had an idle plant at Wichita, visited Zuckert as a group and told the Air Force Secretary that Boeing could do the job better than its competitor.

5. Representative Jim Wright of Fort Worth, Texas, made no bones about his interest and the reason for it:

> In the absence of a substantial contract of this type, the General Dynamics team at Fort Worth was faced with dismemberment. It meant the difference between employment or unemployment for thousands of my constituents. Let me be completely frank. I talked about this subject with everybody I could get to listen, both military and civilian officials. That does not in my judgment amount to undesirable political influence. The same sort of thing was being attempted by the other side. . . .

The list of the 100 largest prime contractors for the military in 1967 includes Massachusetts Institute of Technology, in sixty-second place with $94.9 million of contracts, and Johns Hopkins University, in seventy-third place with $71.1 million. The ranking of these universities among the leading defense contractors is hardly surprising. We have long been accustomed to the vital participation of the academic community in national defense, from the first nuclear chain reaction at the University of Chicago in World War II to the recent arrangements between many universities and the Central Intelligence Agency. And the Eisenhower farewell speech brought out, as no high government official before or since has done with equal candor, the "prospect of domination of the nation's scholars by Federal employment, project allocations and the power of money."

The Pentagon awards some $700 million a year in contracts to universities, colleges, and other nonprofit institutions. Without this kind of money, as noted in a report of the Carnegie Foundation for the Advancement of Teaching, "the whole character of many universities' research programs (and in consequence their instructional programs) would change. Faculties in many instances would shrink. Many research efforts would have to be abandoned completely. Others would be sharply curtailed." Thus, as Eisenhower warned, many universities have indeed become dependent on the government, not only for research activities, but also for faculties and instructional programs. Perhaps his own experience as President of Columbia University and his brother's as President of Johns Hopkins made Eisenhower specially conscious of this problem.

Recent incidents on campuses across the country have called attention to a general uneasiness, if not rebellion, against government research contracting on purely political grounds. At the University of Pennsylvania, two $1,000,000 research contracts for measuring the effectiveness of chemical-biological warfare were canceled after some professors threatened to wear gas masks at commencement. At Cornell University the faculty voted to cut ties with the Cornell Aeronautical Laboratory because the laboratory had received a $1,500,000 contract to plan counter-insurgency projects in Thailand.

Even such a relatively independent and well-enduring institution as Harvard University has encountered serious government pressure on "how things are to be done in laboratories and who may or may not appear in them," Dr. Nathan M. Pusey, President of Harvard, once complained. He referred specifically to the arrangement with the Atomic Energy Commission for maintenance of the $12 million electron accelerator on the university grounds. The government paid the cost of construction; Harvard and M.I.T. shared a $5 million-a-year contract to operate it. It was intended for "free and unfettered academic research of an unclassified nature," but the government insisted on federal security regulations that seemed more appropriate to a military site than a university campus. Harvard resisted and won many concessions, but finally signed the contract.

Having identified, described, and examined certain aspects of the military-industrial complex, we must consider its implications for us. Could the United States become a garrison state in which most of its energies are devoted to arms? Could the pressures of war and the frustrations of international affairs pave the way to a military coup such as that depicted in the novel *Seven Days in May?* Are the appeals for peace and disarmament being selfishly balked by the vested interests of the military-industrial complex? These are ancient forebodings in U.S. history, and the fact that they linger reveals a national awareness of our vulnerability. For it cannot be denied that the military-industrial complex flourishes in war and during the threat of war.

Yet this awareness of our vulnerability itself constitutes considerable protection for us. For example, we are often troubled by the intervention of the military in "civilian" affairs. But we can take encouragement from the very openness of that intervention. When General Earle G. Wheeler, the Chairman of the Joint Chiefs of Staff, boldly and publicly disagrees with the Secretary of Defense on policies for the war in Vietnam or on the desirability of constructing a full-scale antiballistic missile defense system; and when General Wallace M. Greene, the commandant of the Marine Corps, publicly demands a greater national devotion to the war in Vietnam than to the social revolution in the streets of America—these expressions by the military serve to identify them publicly with recognizable political attitudes. By joining the public debate in a manner that is authorized under our system, they also set themselves up as targets in that debate.

Moreover, as we have learned from experience, the military are not always unanimous in their professional view of the world and in their demands on the budget. Their rivalries for funds have sometimes exploded in fierce public lobbying and internecine bureaucratic warfare. This, too, mitigates against concerted action by the military to influence public policy. In addition, far from challenging civilian control, the military leaders in recent years have complained of civilians dominating the military in their professional competence. The complaint does honor to the principle of our democratic system.

Insofar as the economic threat of the military-industrial complex is concerned, it appears to reflect largely the familiar dangers of huge concentrations of economic power. And there is recurring evidence of the government's capacity to cope with the industrial giants. During the Kennedy Administration we saw the Secretary of Defense lead the charge against a sudden increase in the price of steel. In the Johnson Administration, in November 1965, the Defense Secretary also led in thwarting aluminum and copper price increases by threats to use the national stockpiles.

Another safety factor is that not all states and communities share equally in the defense business despite the fervent Administration efforts to spread the dollars. This inequality of benefits tends to create challenges to the activities of the military-industrial complex, even within its own constituencies. The result is high-pitched competition involving defense contractors and their political, military, legislative, and other allies. A single defense appropriations bill usually occupies several dozen members of Congress and several committee staffs for the better part of six months, and not all of these Congressmen have the same concerns and motives.

The competing demands of special interest groups that focus on major decisions often cancel each other out. A Congressman, for example, might be an Army reservist with a strong tendency toward its doctrine of national strategy which calls for certain types of military preparedness and weaponry; but he would vote for an Air Force appropriation if it meant a factory for his home city, a Navy appropriation if he were rallied by his political leaders on Capitol Hill, and an across-the-board economy cut if he needed to trade a vote with Wilbur Mills, Chairman of the House Ways and Means Committee.

The problem that confronts us is whether we can continue to depend on these countervailing pressures; or whether at some point in our future—nearer than we like to imagine, perhaps—the disparate impulses that go into the military-industrial complex, ranging from a crass desire for profits to honest fear for the safety of the country, may coalesce in such a powerful advocacy of more and better weapons and in such potent opposition to arms control that the entire country will be drawn to support this position.

I am not suggesting that the threat of our industrial-military complex is based in any way on a military-industrial conspiracy. There is no more of a conspiracy here than in numerous other matters where legitimate lobbies influence public policy makers, or where conflicts of interest affect decisions of the legislative and executive arms of government. The free enterprise system is frequently compromised, and political judgments influence every aspect of our national security—but not because of conspiracies. Rather, I am urging that we keep in mind the Eisenhower admonition: "We should take nothing for granted. . . . Only an alert and knowledgeable citizenry can compel the proper meshing of the huge industrial machinery of defense with our peaceful methods and goals, so that security and liberty may prosper together."

23. WHITE POWER AND BLACK POWER

stokely carmichael and charles v. hamilton

The character and consequences of social control as perceived by majority and minority groups differ greatly in most societies. In the United States, militant demands and actions by segments of the Black community have produced widely different perceptions of the relationship between racial conflict and social order.

Carmichael and Hamilton liken the plight of the Black American to that of former colonial subjects victimized by a paternalistic process of white supremacy. Their remarks suggest that even many liberal attitudes about race relations in America unwittingly sacrifice human welfare on the altar of social control. The authors portray a Black-White collision whose outcome may well be a fundamental change in traditional mechanisms of social control.

The black community perceives the "white power structure" in very concrete terms. The man in the ghetto sees his white landlord come only to collect exorbitant rents and fail to make necessary repairs, while both know that the white-dominated city building inspection department will wink at violations or impose only slight fines. The man in the ghetto sees the white policeman on the corner brutally manhandle a black drunkard in a doorway, and at the same time accept a pay-off from one of the agents of the white-controlled rackets. He sees the streets in the ghetto lined with uncollected garbage, and he knows that the powers which could send trucks in to collect that garbage

From *Black Power* by Stokely Carmichael and Charles V. Hamilton. Copyright © 1967 by Stokely Carmichael and Charles V. Hamilton. Reprinted by permission of Random House, Inc.

are white. When they don't, he knows the reason: the low political esteem in which the black community is held. He looks at the absence of a meaningful curriculum in the ghetto schools—for example, the history books that woefully overlook the historical achievements of black people—and he knows that the school board is controlled by whites. He is not about to listen to intellectual discourses on the pluralistic and fragmented nature of political power. He is faced with a "white power structure" as monolithic as Europe's colonial offices have been to African and Asian colonies.

There is another aspect of colonial politics frequently found in colonial Africa and in the United States: the process of indirect rule. Martin Kilson describes it in *Political Change in a West African State, A Study of the Modernization Process in Sierra Leone:* "Indirect rule is the method of local colonial administration through the agency of Chiefs who exercise executive authority. It was applied in one form or other throughout British colonial Africa and was, from the standpoint of the metropolitan power's budget, a form of colonialism-on-the-cheap" (p. 24). In other words, the white power structure rules the black community through local blacks who are responsive to the white leaders, the downtown, white machine, not to the black populace. These black politicians do not exercise effective power. They cannot be relied upon to make forceful demands in behalf of their black constituents, and they become no more than puppets. They put loyalty to a political party before loyalty to their constituents and thus nullify any bargaining power the black community might develop. Colonial politics causes the subject to muffle his voice while participating in the councils of the white power structure. The black man forfeits his opportunity to speak forcefully and clearly for his race, and he justifies this in terms of expediency. Thus, when one talks of a "Negro Establishment" in most places in this country, one is talking of an Establishment resting on a white power base; of hand-picked blacks whom that base projects as showpieces out front. These black "leaders" are, then, only as powerful as their white kingmakers will permit them to be. This is no less true of the North than the South.

Describing the political situation in Chicago, Wilson wrote in *Negro Politics:*

> Particularly annoying to the Negro politicians has been the partial loss of their ability to influence the appointment of Negroes to important or prestigious jobs on public boards and agencies. Negroes selected for membership on such bodies as the Board of Education, the Land Clearance Commission, the Community Conservation Board, the Chicago Plan Commission, and other groups are the "token leaders" . . . and control over their appointment has in part passed out of the Negro machine [p. 84].

Before Congressman William O. Dawson (black Congressman from the predominantly black First Congressional District of Southside Chicago) was co-opted by the white machine, he was an outspoken champion of the race.

Afterward, he became a tool of the downtown white Democratic power structure; the black community no longer had an effective representative who would articulate and fight to relieve their grievances. Mr. Dawson became assimilated. The white political bosses could rule the black community in the same fashion that Britain ruled the African colonies—by indirect rule. Note the result, as described in Silberman's *Crisis in Black and White:*

> Chicago provides an excellent example of how Negroes can be co-opted into inactivity. . . . Dawson surrendered far more than he has obtained for the Negro community. What Dawson obtained were the traditional benefits of the big-city political machine: low-paying jobs for a lot of followers; political intervention with the police and with bail bondsmen, social workers, housing officials, and other bureaucrats whose decisions can affect a poor constituent's life; and a slice of the "melon" in the form of public housing projects, welfare payments, and the like.
>
> What Dawson surrendered was the pride and dignity of his community; he threw away the opportunity to force Chicago's political and civic leaders to identify and deal with the fundamental problems of segregation and oppression [p. 206].

Dawson, and countless others like him, have an answer to this criticism: this is the proper way to operate; you must "play ball" with the party in order to exact maximum benefits. We reject this notion. It may well result in particular benefits—in terms of status or material gains—for individuals, but it does not speak to the alleviation of a multitude of social problems shared by the masses. They may also say: if I spoke up, I would no longer be permitted to take part in the party councils. I would be ousted, and then the black people would have neither voice nor access. Ultimately, this is, at best, a spurious argument, which does more to enhance the security of the individual person than it does to gain substantial benefits for the group.

In time, one notes that a gap develops between the leadership and the followers. The masses, correctly, no longer view the leaders as their legitimate representatives. They come to see them more for what they are, emissaries sent by the white society. Identity between the two is lost. This frequently occurred in Africa, and the analogy, again, is relevant. Former President of Ghana, Kwame Nkrumah, described the colonial situation in pre-independent Africa in his book *Africa Must Unite:*

> The principle of indirect rule adopted in West Africa, and also in other parts of the continent, allowed a certain amount of local self-government in that chiefs could rule their districts provided they did nothing contrary to the laws of the colonial power, and on condition they accepted certain orders from the colonial government. The system of indirect rule was notably successful for a time in Northern Nigeria, where the Emirs governed much as they had done before the colonial period. But the system had obvious dangers. In some cases, autocratic chiefs, propped up by the colonial government, became inefficient and unpopular, as the riots against the chiefs in Eastern Nigeria in 1929, and in Sierra Leone in 1936, showed.

In wide areas of East Africa, where there was no developed system of local government which could be used, headmen or "warrant" chiefs were appointed, usually from noble families. They were so closely tied up with the colonial power that many Africans thought chiefs were an invention of the British [p. 18].

This process of co-optation and a subsequent widening of the gap between the black elites and the masses is common under colonial rule. There has developed in this country an entire class of "captive leaders" in the black communities. These are black people with certain technical and administrative skills who could provide useful leadership roles in the black communities but do not because they have become beholden to the white power structure. These are black school teachers, county agents, junior executives in management positions with companies, etc. In a study of New Orleans contained in Professor Daniel C. Thompson's *The Negro Leadership Class,* public school teachers emerge as the largest professional group in the black community of that city: there were 1,600 of them in 1961. These people are college-trained, articulate, and in daily contact with the young minds of the black South. For the most part (fortunately there are a few exceptions), they are not sources of positive or aggressive community leadership. Thompson concluded:

> Depending as they do upon white officials, public school teachers have been greatly restricted in their leadership role . . . several laws passed by the Louisiana State Legislature, as well as rules and regulations adopted by the state and local school boards in recent years, have made it almost impossible for Negro teachers to identify with racial uplift organizations, or even to participate actively in the civil rights movement. This is definitely an important reason why some teachers have remained inactive and silent during heated controversies over civil rights [p. 46].

It is crystal clear that most of these people have accommodated themselves to the racist system. They have capitulated to colonial subjugation in exchange for the security of a few dollars and dubious status. They are effectively lost to the struggle for an improved black position which would fundamentally challenge that racist system. John A. Williams tells in *This is My Country Too* of how he went to Alabama State College (the state college for black people) in 1963 to interview a black professor, who brusquely told him: "Governor Wallace pays my salary; I have nothing to say to you. Excuse me, I have a class to get to" (p. 62).

When black people play colonial politics, they also mislead the white community into thinking that it has the sanction of the blacks. A professor of political science who made a study of black people in Detroit politics from 1956–1960 has concluded:

> The fact that the Negro participates in the system by voting and participating in the party politics in the North should not lead us to conclude that he has accepted the popular consensus of the society about the polity. His support and work for the Democratic party is more a strategic compromise in most

cases than a wholehearted endorsement of the party. My own work in Detroit led me to conclude that Negro party officers are not "loyal" to the Democratic party in the way that the ethnic groups or other organized groups such as labor have been. Although the Democratic Party-UAW coalition in Detroit has given the Negro a number of positions in the party hierarchy, it has not included him in the decision-making process.

. . . As in the colonial situation, the Negro has developed a submission-aggression syndrome. When he attends campaign strategy meetings he appears to be submissive, willingly accepting the strategies suggested by the white leaders. Despite their seeming acceptance of this condescending treatment, after these meetings the Negro precinct workers will tell you that they had to "go along with all that talk" in order to make sure that they were represented. They openly express their resentment of the party hierarchy and reveal themselves as much more militant about the Negro cause than was apparent during the meeting.[1]

This stance is not an uncommon one. More than a handful of black people will admit privately their contempt for insincere whites with whom they must work and deal. (In all likelihood, the contempt is mutual.) They feel secure in articulating their true feelings only when out of hearing range of "the man."

Those who would assume the responsibility of representing black people in this country must be able to throw off the notion that they can effectively do so and still maintain a maximum amount of security. Jobs will have to be sacrificed, positions of prestige and status given up, favors forfeited. It may well be—and we think it is—that leadership and security are basically incompatible. When one forcefully challenges the racist system, one cannot, at the same time, expect that system to reward him or even treat him comfortably. Political leadership which pacifies and stifles its voice and then rationalizes this on grounds of gaining "something for my people" is, at bottom, gaining only meaningless, token rewards that an affluent society is perfectly willing to give.

A final aspect of political colonialism is the manipulation of political boundaries and the devising of restrictive electoral systems. The point is frequently made that black people are only ten percent of the population—no less a personage than President Johnson has seen fit to remind us of this ratio. It is seldom pointed out that this minority is geographically located so as to create potential majority blocs—that strategic location being an ironic side-effect of segregation. But black people have never been able to utilize fully their numerical voting strength. Where we could vote, the white political machines have gerrymandered black neighborhoods so that the true voting strength is not reflected in political representation. Would anyone looking at the distribution of political power and representation in Manhattan ever think

[1] A. W. Singham, "The Political Socialization of Marginal Groups." Paper presented at the 1966 annual meeting of the American Political Science Association, New York City.

that black people represent sixty percent of the population? On the local level, election to City Councils by the at-large system, rather than by district, reduces the number of representatives coming out of the black community. In Detroit, which uses the at-large system, there was not a black man on the City Council until 1957 despite a vast black population, especially during World War II. Also, the larger the electoral district, the greater the likelihood of there not being a Negro elected because he has to appeal to whites for their votes too. Los Angeles, with very large City Council electoral districts, saw the first black Councilman only in 1963.

The decision-makers are most adept at devising ways or utilizing existing factors to maintain their monopoly of political power. . . .

Black people must redefine themselves, and only *they* can do that. Throughout this country, vast segments of the black communities are beginning to recognize the need to assert their own definitions, to reclaim their history, their culture; to create their own sense of community and togetherness. There is a growing resentment of the word "Negro," for example, because this term is the invention of our oppressor; it is *his* image of us that he describes. Many blacks are now calling themselves African-Americans, Afro-Americans or black people because that is *our* image of ourselves. When we begin to define our own image, the stereotypes—that is, lies—that our oppressor has developed will begin in the white community and end there. The black community will have a positive image of itself that *it* has created. This means we will no longer call ourselves lazy, apathetic, dumb, good-timers, shiftless, etc. Those are words used by white America to define us. If we accept these adjectives, as some of us have in the past, then we see ourselves only in a negative way, precisely the way white America wants us to see ourselves. Our incentive is broken and our will to fight is surrendered. From now on we shall view ourselves as African-Americans and as black people who are in fact energetic, determined, intelligent, beautiful and peace-loving. . . .

Only when black people fully develop this sense of community, of themselves, can they begin to deal effectively with the problems of racism in *this* country. This is what we mean by a new consciousness; this is the vital first step. . . .

The adoption of the concept of Black Power is one of the most legitimate and healthy developments in American politics and race relations in our time. The concept of Black Power speaks to all the needs mentioned in this chapter. It is a call for black people in this country to unite, to recognize their heritage, to build a sense of community. It is a call for black people to begin to define their own goals, to lead their own organizations and to support those organizations. It is a call to reject the racist institutions and values of this society.

The concept of Black Power rests on a fundamental premise: *Before a group can enter the open society, it must first close ranks.* By this we mean that group solidarity is necessary before a group can operate effectively from a bargaining position of strength in a pluralistic society. . . .

In the end, we cannot and shall not offer any guarantees that Black Power, if achieved, would be non-racist. No one can predict human behavior. Social change always has unanticipated consequences. If black racism is what the larger society fears, we cannot help them. We can only state what we hope will be the result, given the fact that the present situation is unacceptable and that we have no real alternative but to work for Black Power. The final truth is that the white society is not entitled to reassurances, even if it were possible to offer them.

UTOPIANISM
models of total integration

24. THE FOLK SOCIETY
robert redfield

For the radical, man's past is a series of blunders which serve only to inhibit his search for an ideal future. For the arch conservative, however, the past is a golden age which man has forsaken to his great detriment.

In the following selection Professor Redfield outlines the characteristics of a "folk society," the most elementary of human societal relationships.

Would you prefer life in a folk society to life in modern America? More important, is it possible to recreate the simple relationships of the past? Regardless of how appealing idealized versions of the past may seem, does constant preoccupation with lost utopias aid in the solution of modern problems?

It should be noted in passing that many anthropologists have found life in folk societies far less idealistic than the picture presented below.

The people who make up a folk society are much alike. Having lived in long intimacy with one another, and with no others, they have come to form a single biological type. The somatic homogeneity of local, inbred populations has been noted and studied. Since the people communicate with one another and with no others, one man's learned ways of doing and thinking are the same as another's. Another way of putting this is to say that in the ideal folk society, what one man knows and believes is the same as what all men know and believe. Habits are the same as customs. In real fact, of course, the differences among individuals in a primitive group and the different chances of experience prevent this ideal state of things from coming about. Nevertheless,

From Robert Redfield, "The Folk Society," *The American Journal of Sociology*, LII (January, 1947), 293–308. By permission of the University of Chicago Press. Copyright 1947 by the University of Chicago.

it is near enough to the truth for the student of a real folk society to report it fairly well by learning what goes on in the minds of a few of its members, and a primitive group has been presented, although sketchily, as learned about from a single member. The similarity among the members is found also as one generation is compared with its successor. Old people find young people doing, as they grow up, what the old people did at the same age, and what they have come to think right and proper. This is another way of saying that in such a society there is little change.

The members of the folk society have a strong sense of belonging together. The group which an outsider might recognize as composed of similar persons different from members of other groups is also the group of people who see their own resemblances and feel correspondingly united. Communicating intimately with each other, each has a strong claim on the sympathies of the others. Moreover, against such knowledge as they have of societies other than their own, they emphasize their own mutual likeness and value themselves as compared with others. They say of themselves "we" as against all others, who are "they."

Thus we may characterize the folk society as small, isolated, nonliterate, and homogeneous, with a strong sense of group solidarity. Are we not soon to acknowledge the simplicity of the technology of the ideal folk society? Something should certainly be said about the tools and tool-making of this generalized primitive group, but it is not easy to assign a meaning to "simple" in connection with technology which will do justice to the facts as known from the real folk societies. The preciseness with which each tool, in a large number of such tools, meets its needs in the case of the Eskimo, for example, makes one hesitate to use the word "simple." Some negative statements appear to be safe: secondary and tertiary tools—tools to make tools—are relatively few as compared with primary tools; there is no making of artifacts by multiple, rapid, machine manufacture; there is little or no use of natural power.

There is not much division of labor in the folk society: what one person does is what another does. In the ideal folk society all the tools and ways of production are shared by everybody. The "everybody" must mean "every adult man" or "every adult woman," for the obvious exception to the homogeneity of the folk society lies in the differences between what men do and know and what women do and know. These differences are clear and unexceptional (as compared with our modern urban society where they are less so). "Within the local group there is no such thing as a division of labor save as between the sexes," writes Radcliffe-Brown about the Andaman Islanders. ". . . . Every man is expected to be able to hunt pig, to harpoon turtle and to catch fish, and also to cut a canoe, to make bows and arrows and all the other objects that are made by men." So all men share the same interests and have, in general, the same experience of life.

We may conceive, also, of the ideal folk society as a group economically independent of all others: the people produce what they consume and consume what they produce. Few, if any, real societies are completely in this situation; some Eskimo groups perhaps most closely approach it. Although each little Andamanese band could get along without getting anything from any other, exchange of goods occurred between bands by a sort of periodic gift-giving.

The foregoing characterizations amount, roughly, to saying that the folk society is a little world off by itself, a world in which the recurrent problems of life are met by all its members in much the same way. This statement, while correct enough, fails to emphasize an important, perhaps the important, aspect of the folk society. The ways in which the members of the society meet the recurrent problems of life are conventionalized ways; they are the results of long intercommunication within the group in the face of these problems; and these conventionalized ways have become interrelated within one another so that they constitute a coherent and self-consistent system. Such a system is what we mean in saying that the folk society is characterized by "a culture." A culture is an organization or integration of conventional understandings. It is, as well, the acts and the objects, in so far as they represent the type characteristic of that society, which express and maintain these understandings. In the folk society this integrated whole, this system, provides for all the recurrent needs of the individual from birth to death and of the society through the seasons and the years. The society is to be described, and distinguished from others, largely by presenting this system.

This is not the same as saying, as was said early in this paper, that in the folk society what one man does is the same as what another man does. What one man does in a mob is the same as what another man does, but a mob is not a folk society. It is, so far as culture is concerned, its very antithesis. The members of a mob (which is a kind of "mass") each do the same thing, it is true, but it is a very immediate and particular thing, and it is done without much reference to tradition. It does not depend upon and express a great many conventional understandings related to one another. A mob has no culture. The folk society exhibits culture to the greatest conceivable degree. A mob is an aggregation of people doing the same simple things simultaneously. A folk society is an organization of people doing many different things successively as well as simultaneously. The members of a mob act with reference to the same object of attention. The members of a folk society are guided in acting by previously established comprehensive and interdependent conventional understandings; at any one time they do many different things, which are complexly related to one another to express collective sentiments and conceptions. When the turn comes for the boy to do what a man does, he does what a man does; thus, though in the end the experiences of all individuals of the same sex are alike, the activities of the society, seen at a moment of time, are diverse, while interdependent and consistent.

The Papago Indians, a few hundred of them, constituted a folk society in southern Arizona. Among these Indians a war party was not so simple a thing as a number of men going out together to kill the enemy. It was a complex activity involving everybody in the society both before, during, and after the expedition and dramatizing the religious and moral ideas fundamental to Papago life. Preparation for the expedition involved many practical or ritual acts on the part of the immediate participants, their wives and children, previously successful warriors, and many others. While the party was away, the various relatives of the warriors had many things to do or not to do—prayer, fasting, preparation of ritual paraphernalia, etc. These were specialized activities, each appropriate to just that kind of relative or other category of person. So the war was waged by everybody. These activities, different and special as they were, interlocked, so to speak, with each other to make a large whole, the society-during-a-war-expedition. And all these specialized activities obeyed fundamental principles, understood by all and expressed and reaffirmed in the very forms of the acts—the gestures of the rituals, the words of songs, the implied or expressed explanations and admonitions of the elders to the younger people. All understood that the end in view was the acquisition by the group of the supernatural power of the slain enemy. This power, potentially of great positive value, was dangerous, and the practices and rituals had as their purposes first the success of the war party and then the draining-off of the supernatural power acquired by the slaying into a safe and "usable" form.

We may say, then, that in the folk society conventional behavior is strongly patterned: it tends to conform to a type or a norm. These patterns are interrelated in thought and in action with one another, so that one tends to evoke others and to be consistent with the others. Every customary act among the Papago when the successful warriors return is consistent with and is a special form of the general conceptions held as to supernatural power. We may still further say that the patterns of what people think should be done are closely consistent with what they believe is done, and that there is one way, or a very few conventional ways, in which everybody has some understanding and some share, of meeting each need that arises. The culture of a folk society is, therefore, one of those wholes which is greater than its parts. Gaining a livelihood takes support from religion, and the relations of men to men are justified in the conceptions held of the supernatural world or in some other aspect of the culture. Life, for the member of the folk society, is not one activity and then another and different one; it is one large activity out of which one part may not be separated without affecting the rest.

A related characteristic of the folk society was implied when it was declared that the specialized activities incident to the Papago war party obeyed fundamental principles understood by all. These "principles" had to do with the ends of living, as conceived by the Papago. A near-ultimate good for the Papago was the acquisition of supernatural power. This end was not questioned; it was a sort of axiom in terms of which many lesser activities were understood. This suggests that we may say of the folk society that its ends are taken as given. The activities incident to the war party may be regarded as merely complementarily useful acts, aspects of the division of labor. They may also, and more significantly, be seen as expressions of unquestioned common ends. The folk society exists not so much in the exchange of useful functions as in common understandings as to the ends given. The ends are not stated as matters of doctrine, but are implied by the many acts which make up the living that goes on in the society. Therefore, the morale of a folk society—its power to act consistently over periods of time and to meet crises effectively is not dependent upon discipline exerted by force or upon devotion to some single principle of action but to the concurrence and consistency of many or all of the actions and conceptions which make up the whole round of life. In the trite phase, the folk society is a "design for living."

What is done in the ideal folk society is done not because somebody or some people decided, at once, that it should be done, but because it seems "necessarily" to flow from the very nature of things. There is, moreover, no disposition to reflect upon traditional acts and consider them objectively and critically. In short, behavior in the folk society is traditional, spontaneous, and uncritical. In any real folk society, of course, many things are done as a result of decision as to that particular action, but as to that class of actions tradition is the sufficient authority. The Indians decide now to go on a hunt; but it is not a matter of debate whether or not one should, from time to time, hunt.

The folkways are the ways that grow up out of long and intimate association of men with each other; in the society of our conception all the ways are folkways. Men act with reference to each other by understandings which are tacit and traditional. There are no formal contracts or other agreements. The rights and obligations of the individual come about not by special arrangement; they are, chiefly, aspects of the position of the individual as a person of one sex or the other, one age-group or another, one occupational group or another, and as one occupying just that position in a system of relationships which are traditional in the society. The individual's status is thus in large part fixed at birth; it changes as he lives, but it changes in ways which were "foreordained" by the nature of his particular society. The institutions of the folk society are of the sort which has been called "crescive"; they are not of the sort that is created deliberately for special purposes, as was the juvenile court. So, too, law is made up of the traditional conceptions of rights and obligations and the customary procedures whereby these rights and obligations are assured; legislation has no part in it.

If legislation has no part in the law of the ideal folk society, neither has codification, still less jurisprudence. Radin has collected material suggesting the limited extent to which real primitive people do question custom and do systematize their knowledge. In the known folk societies they do these things only to a limited extent. In the ideal folk society there is no objectivity and no systematization of knowledge as guided by what seems to be its "internal" order. The member of this mentally constructed society does not stand off from his customary conduct and subject it to scrutiny apart from its meaning for him as that meaning is defined in culture. Nor is there any habitual exercise of classification, experiment, and abstraction for its own sake, least of all for the sake of intellectual ends. There is common practical knowledge, but there is no science.

Behavior in the folk society is highly conventional, custom fixes the rights and duties of individuals, and knowledge is not critically examined or objectively and systematically formulated; but it must not be supposed that primitive man is a sort of automaton in which custom is the mainspring. It would be as mistaken to think of primitive man as strongly aware that he is constrained by custom. Within the limits set by custom there is invitation to excel in performance. There is lively competition, a sense of opportunity, and a feeling that what the culture moves one to do is well worth doing. "There is no drabness in such a life. It has about it all the allurements of personal experience, very much one's own, of competitive skill, of things well done." The interrelations and high degree of consistency among the elements of custom which are presented to the individual declare to him the importance of making his endeavors in the directions indicated by tradition. The culture sets goals which stimulate action by giving great meaning to it.

It has been said that the folk society is small and that its members have lived in long and intimate association with one another. It has also been said that in such societies there is little critical or abstract thinking. These characteristics are related to yet another characteristic of the folk society: behavior is personal, not impersonal. A "person" may be defined as that social object which I feel to respond to situations as I do, with all the sentiments and interests which I feel to be my own; a person is myself in another form, his qualities and values are inherent within him, and his significance for me is not merely one of utility. A "thing," on the other hand, is a social object which has no claim upon my sympathies, which responds to me, as I conceive it, mechanically; its value for me exists in so far as it serves my end. In the folk society all human beings admitted to the society are treated as persons; one does not deal impersonally ("thing-fashion") with any other participant in the little world of that society. Moreover, in the folk society much besides human beings is treated personally. The pattern of behavior which is first suggested by the inner experience of the individual—his wishes, fears, sensitivenesses, and interests of all sorts—is projected into all objects with which he comes into contact. Thus nature, too, is treated personally: the elements, the features of the landscape, the animals, and especially anything in the environment which by its appearance or behavior suggests that it has the attributes of mankind—to all these are attributed qualities of the human person.

In short, the personal and intimate life of the child in the family is extended, in the folk society, into the social world of the adult and even into inanimate objects. It is not merely that relations in such a society are personal; it is also that they are familial. The first contacts made as the infant becomes a person are with other persons; moreover, each of these first persons, he comes to learn, has a particular kind of relation to him which is associated with that one's genealogical position. The individual finds himself fixed within a constellation of familial relationships. The kinship connections provide a pattern in terms of which, in the ideal folk society, all personal relations are conventionalized and categorized. All relations are personal. But relations are not, in content of specific behavior, the same for everyone. As a mother is different from a father, and a grandson from a nephew, so are these classes of personal relationship, originating in genealogical connection, extended outward into all relationships whatever. In this sense, the folk society is a familial society. Lowie has demonstrated the qualification that is to be introduced into the statement of Maine that the primitive society is organized in terms of kinship rather than territory. It is true that the fact that men are neighbors contributes to their sense of belonging together. But the point to be emphasized in understanding the folk society is that whether mere contiguity or relationship as brother or as son is the circumstance uniting men into the society, the result is a group of people among whom prevail the personal and categorized relationships that characterize families as we know them, and in which the patterns of kinship tend to be extended outward from the group of genealogically connected individuals into the whole society. The kin are the type persons for all experience.

This general conception may be resolved into component or related conceptions. In the folk society family relationships are clearly distinguished from one another. Very special sorts of behavior may be expected by a mother's brother of his sister's son, and this behavior will be different from that expected by a father's brother of his brother's son. Among certain Australian tribes animals killed by a hunter must be divided so that nine or ten certain parts must be given to nine or ten corresponding relatives of the successful hunter—the right ribs to the father's brother, a piece of the flank to the mother's brother, and so on. The tendency to extend kinship outward takes many special forms. In many primitive societies kinship terms and kinship behavior (in reduced degree) are extended to persons not known to be genealogically related at all, but who are nevertheless regarded as kin. Among the central Australians, terms of relationship are extended "so as to embrace all persons who come into social contact with one another. . . . . In this way the whole society forms a body of relatives." In the folk society groupings which do not arise out of genealogical connection are few, and those that do exist tend to take on the attributes of kinship. Ritual kinship is common in primitive and peasant societies in the forms of blood brotherhood, godparental relationships, and other ceremonial sponsorships. These multiply kinship connections; in these cases the particular individuals to be united depend upon choice. Furthermore, there is frequently a recognizedly fictitious or metaphorical use of kinship terms to designate more casual relationships, as between host and guest or between worshipper and deity.

The real primitive and peasant societies differ very greatly as to the forms assumed by kinship. Nevertheless, it is possible to recognize two main types. In one of these the connection between husband and wife is emphasized, while neither one of the lineages, matrilineal or patrilineal, is singled out as contrasted with the other. In such a folk society the individual parental family is the social unit, and connections with relatives outside this family are of secondary importance. Such family organization is common where the population is small, the means of livelihood are by precarious collection of wild food, and larger units cannot permanently remain together because the natural resources will not allow it. But where a somewhat larger population remains together, either in a village or in a migratory band, there often, although by no means always, is found an emphasis upon one line of consanguine connection rather than the other with subordination of the conjugal connection. There results a segmentation of the society into equivalent kinship units. These may take the form of extended domestic groups or joint families (as in China) or may include many households of persons related in part through recognized genealogical connection and in part through the sharing of the same name or other symbolic designation, in the latter case we speak of the groups as clans. Even in societies where the individual parental family is an independent economic unit, as in the case of the eastern Eskimo, husband and wife never become a new social and economic unit with the completeness that is characteristic of our own society. When a marriage in primitive society comes to an end, the kinsmen of the dead spouse assert upon his property a claim they have never given up. On the whole, we may think of the family among folk peoples as made up of persons consanguinely connected. Marriage is, in comparison with what we in our society directly experience, an incident in the life of the individual who is born, brought up, and dies with his blood kinsmen. In such a society romantic love can hardly be elevated to a major principle.

In so far as the consanguine lines are well defined (and in some cases both lines may be of importance to the individual) the folk society may be thought of as composed of families rather than of individuals. It is the familial groups that act and are acted upon. There is strong solidarity within the kinship group, and the individual is responsible to all his kin as they are responsible to him. "The clan is a natural mutual aid society. . . . . A member belongs to the clan, he is not his own; if he is wrong, they will right him; if he does wrong, the responsibility is shared by them." Thus, in folk societies wherein the tendency to maintain consanguine connection has resulted in joint families or clans, it is usual to find that injuries done by an individual are regarded as injuries against his kinship group, and the group takes the steps to right the wrong. The step may be revenge regulated by custom or a property settlement. A considerable part of primitive law exists in the regulation of claims by one body of kin against another. The fact that the folk society is an organization of families rather than an aggregation of individuals is further expressed in many of those forms of marriage in which a certain kind of relative is the approved spouse. The customs by which in many primitive societies a man is expected to marry his deceased brother's widow or a woman to marry her deceased sister's husband express the view of marriage as an undertaking between kinship groups. One of the spouses having failed by death, the undertaking is to be carried on by some other representative of the family group. Indeed, in the arrangements for marriage—the selection of spouses by their relatives, in bride-price, dowry, and in many forms of familial negotiations leading to a marriage—the nature of marriage as a connubial form of social relations between kindreds finds expression.

It has been said in foregoing paragraphs that behavior in the folk society is traditional, spontaneous, and uncritical, that what one man does is much the same as what another man does, and that the patterns of conduct are clear and remain constant throughout the generations. It has also been suggested that the congruence of all parts of conventional behavior and social institutions with each other contributes to the sense of rightness which the member of the folk society feels to inhere in his traditional ways of action. In the well-known language of Sumner, the ways of life are folkways; furthermore, the folkways tend to be also mores—ways of doing or thinking to which attach notions of moral worth. The value of every traditional act or object or institution is, thus, something which the members of the society are not disposed to call into question; and should the value be called into question, the doing so is resented. This characteristic of the folk society may be briefly referred to by saying that it is a sacred society. In the folk society one may not, without calling into effect negative social sanctions, challenge as valueless what has come to be traditional in that society.

Presumably, the sacredness of social objects has its source, in part, at least, in the mere fact of habituation; probably the individual organism becomes early adjusted to certain habits, motor and mental, and to certain associations between one activity and another or between certain sense experiences and certain activities, and it is almost physiologically uncomfortable to change or even to entertain the idea of change. There arises "a feeling of impropriety of certain forms, of a particular social or religious value, or a superstitious fear of change." Probably the sacredness of social objects in the folk society is related also to the fact that in such well-organized cultures acts and objects suggest the traditions, beliefs, and conceptions which all share. There is reason to suppose that when what is traditionally done becomes less meaningful because people no longer know what the acts stand for, life becomes more secular. In the repetitious character of conventional action (aside from technical action) we have ritual; in its expressive character we have ceremony; in the folk society ritual tends also to be ceremonious, and ritual-ceremony tends to be sacred, not secular.

The sacredness of social objects is apparent in the ways in which, in the folk society, such an object is hedged around with restraints and protections that keep it away from the commonplace and the matter-of-fact. In the sacred there is alternatively, or in combination, holiness and dangerousness. When the Papago Indian returned from a successful war expedition, bringing the scalp of a slain Apache, the head-hairs of the enemy were treated as loaded with a tremendous "charge" of supernatural power; only old men, already successful warriors and purified through religious ritual, could touch the object and make it safe for incorporation into the home of the slayer. Made into the doll-like form of an Apache Indian, it was, at last, after much cere- monial preparation, held for an instant by the members of the slayer's family, addressed in respect and awe by kinship terms, and placed in the house, there to give off protective power. The Indians of San Pedro de la Laguna, Guatemala, recognize an officer, serving for life, whose function it is to keep custody of ten or a dozen Latin breviaries printed in the eighteenth century and to read prayers from one or another of these books on certain occasions. No one but this custodian may handle the books, save his assistants on ceremonial occasions, with his permission. Should anyone else touch a book he would go mad or be stricken with blindness. Incense and candles are burnt before the chest containing the books, yet the books are not gods— they are objects of sacredness.

In the folk society this disposition to regard objects as sacred extends, characteristically, even into the subsistence activities and into the foodstuffs of the people. Often the foodstuffs are personified as well as sacred. "'My granduncle used to say to me,' explained a Navajo Indian, "'If you are walk- ing along a trail and see a kernel of corn, pick it up. It is like a child lost and starving." According to the legends corn is just the same as a human being, only it is holier. . . . . When a man goes into a cornfield he feels that he is in a holy place, that he is walking among Holy People. . . . . Agriculture is a holy occupation. Even before you plant you sing songs. You continue this during the whole time your crops are growing. You cannot help but feel that you are in a holy place when you go through your fields and they are doing well.'" In the folk society, ideally conceived, nothing is solely a means to an immediate practical end. All activities, even the means of production, are ends in themselves, activities expressive of the ultimate values of the society.

This characterization of the ideal folk society could be greatly extended. Various of the elements that make up the conception could be differently combined with one another, and this point or that could be developed or further emphasized and its relations shown to other aspects of the conception. For example, it might be pointed out that where there is little or no systematic and reflective thinking the customary solutions to problems of practical action only imperfectly take the form of really effective and understood control of the means appropriate to accomplish the desired end, and that, instead, they tend to express the states of mind of the individuals who want the end brought about and fear that it may not be. We say this briefly in declaring that the folk society is characterized by much magic, for we may understand "magic" to refer to action with regard to an end—to instrumental action—but only to such instrumental action as does not effectively bring about that end, or is not really understood in so far as it does, and which is expressive of the way the doer thinks and feels rather than adapted to accomplishing the end. "Magic is based on specific experience of emotional states . . . ."

25. THE POVERTY OF UTOPIA
aldous huxley

In his hypothetical future society exhibiting perfect organization of each man's needs, abilities, and fantasies, Huxley portrays a confrontation between the ruling Controller—exemplifying technological, materialistic, authoritarian Man—and the Savage—symbolizing unreconstructed religious, idealistic, freedom-seeking Man. The former contemptuously dismisses personal nobility and heroism as "symptoms of political inefficiency," while the Savage, somehow having escaped totally successful conditioning, claims "the right to be unhappy."

Is a society purged of suffering and inefficiency capable of satisfying the individual, or does some deeply recessed need for protest against planned happiness lie buried in the human personality and render all efforts at drastic improvement of societies disruptive and immoral?

Art, science—you seem to have paid a fairly high price for your happiness," said the Savage, when they were alone. "Anything else?"

"Well, religion, of course," replied the Controller. "There used to be something called God—before the Nine Years' War. But I was forgetting; you know all about God, I suppose."

"Well . . ." The Savage hesitated. He would have liked to say something about solitude, about night, about the mesa lying pale under the moon, about the precipice, the plunge into shadowy darkness, about death. He would have liked to speak; but there were no words. Not even in Shakespeare.

The Controller, meanwhile, had crossed to the other side of the room and was unlocking a large safe set into the wall between the bookshelves. The heavy door swung open. Rummaging in the darkness within, "It's a subject," he said, "that has always had a great interest for me." He pulled out a thick black volume. "You've never read this, for example."

The Savage took it. *"The Holy Bible, containing the Old and New Testaments,"* he read aloud from the title-page.

"Nor this." It was a small book and had lost its cover.

"The Imitation of Christ."

"Nor this." He handed out another volume.

"The Varieties of Religious Experience. By William James."

"And I've got plenty more," Mustapha Mond continued, resuming his seat. "A whole collection of pornographic old books. God in the safe and Ford on the shelves." He pointed with a laugh to his avowed library—to the shelves of books, the rack full of reading-machine bobbins and sound-track rolls.

"But if you know about God, why don't you tell them?" asked the Savage indignantly. "Why don't you give them these books about God?"

"For the same reason as we don't give them *Othello:* they're old; they're about God hundreds of years ago. Not about God now."

"But God doesn't change."

"Men do, though."

"What difference does that make?"

"All the difference in the world," said Mustapha Mond. He got up again and walked to the safe. "There was a man called Cardinal Newman," he said. "A cardinal," he exclaimed parenthetically, "was a kind of Arch-Community-Songster."

" 'I Pandulph, of fair Milan, cardinal.' I've read about them in Shakespeare."

"Of course you have. Well, as I was saying, there was a man called Cardinal Newman. Ah, here's the book." He pulled it out. "And while I'm about it I'll take this one too. It's by a man called Maine de Biran. He was a philosopher, if you know what that was."

"A man who dreams of fewer things than there are in heaven and earth," said the Savage promptly.

"Quite so. I'll read you one of the things he *did* dream of in a moment. Meanwhile, listen to what this old Arch-Community-Songster said." He opened the book at the place marked by a slip of paper and began to read. " 'We are not our own any more than what we possess is our own. We did not make ourselves, we cannot be supreme over ourselves. We are not our own masters. We are God's property. Is it not our happiness thus to view the matter? Is it any happiness or any comfort, to consider that we *are* our own? It may be thought so by the young and prosperous. These may think it a great thing to have everything, as they suppose, their own way—to depend on no one—to have to think of nothing out of sight, to be without the irksomeness of continual acknowledgment, continual prayer, continual reference of what they do to the will of another. But as time goes on, they, as all men, will find that independence was not made for man—that it is an unnatural state—will do for a while, but will not carry us on safely to the end . . .' " Mustapha

Mond paused, put down the first book and, picking up the other, turned over the pages. "Take this, for example," he said, and in his deep voice once more began to read: " 'A man grows old; he feels in himself that radical sense of weakness, of listlessness, of discomfort, which accompanies the advance of age; and, feeling thus, imagines himself merely sick, lulling his fears with the notion that this distressing condition is due to some particular cause, from which, as from an illness, he hopes to recover. Vain imaginings! That sickness is old age; and a horrible disease it is. They say that it is the fear of death and of what comes after death that makes men turn to religion as they advance in years. But my own experience has given me the conviction that, quite apart from any such terrors or imaginings, the religious sentiment tends to develop as we grow older; to develop because, as the passions grow calm, as the fancy and sensibilities are less excited and less excitable, our reason becomes less troubled in its working, less obscured by the images, desires and distractions, in which it used to be absorbed; whereupon God emerges as from behind a cloud; our soul feels, sees, turns towards the source of all light; turns naturally and inevitably; for now that all that gave to the world of sensations its life and charms has begun to leak away from us, now that phenomenal existence is no more bolstered up by impressions from within or from without, we feel the need to lean on something that abides, something that will never play us false—a reality, an absolute and everlasting truth. Yes, we inevitably turn to God; for this religious sentiment is of its nature so pure, so delightful to the soul that experiences it, that it makes up to us for all our other losses.' " Mustapha Mond shut the book and leaned back in his chair. "One of the numerous things in heaven and earth that these philosophers didn't dream about was this" (he waved his hand), "us, the modern world. 'You can only be independent of God while you've got youth and prosperity; independence won't take you safely to the end.' Well, we've now got youth and prosperity right up to the end. What follows? Evidently, that we can be independent of God. 'The religious sentiment will compensate us for all our losses.' But there aren't any losses for us to compensate; religious sentiment is superfluous. And why should we go hunting for a substitute for youthful desires, when youthful desires never fail? A substitute for distractions, when we go on enjoying all the old fooleries to the very last? What need have we of repose when our minds and bodies continue to delight in activity? of consolation, when we have *soma?* of something immovable, when there is the social order?"

"Then you think there is no God?"

"No, I think there quite probably is one."

"Then why? . . ."

Mustapha Mond checked him. "But he manifests himself in different ways to different men. In premodern times he manifested himself as the being that's described in these books. Now . . ."

"How does he manifest himself now?" asked the Savage.

"Well, he manifests himself as an absence; as though he weren't there at all."

"That's your fault."

"Call it the fault of civilization. God isn't compatible with machinery and scientific medicine and universal happiness. You must make your choice. Our civilization has chosen machinery and medicine and happiness. That's why I have to keep these books locked up in the safe. They're smut. People would be shocked if . . ."

The Savage interrupted him. "But isn't it *natural* to feel there's a God?"

"You might as well ask if it's natural to do up one's trousers with zippers," said the Controller sarcastically. "You remind me of another of those old fellows called Bradley. He defined philosophy as the finding of bad reason for what one believes by instinct. As if one believed anything by instinct! One believes things because one has been conditioned to believe them. Finding bad reasons for what one believes for other bad reasons—that's philosophy. People believe in God because they've been conditioned to believe in God."

"But all the same," insisted the Savage, "it is natural to believe in God when you're alone—quite alone, in the night, thinking about death . . ."

"But people never are alone now," said Mustapha Mond. "We make them hate solitude; and we arrange their lives so that it's almost impossible for them ever to have it."

The Savage nodded gloomily. At Malpais he had suffered because they had shut him out from the communal activities of the pueblo, in civilized London he was suffering because he could never escape from those communal activities, never be quietly alone.

"Do you remember that bit in *King Lear?*" said the Savage at last. " 'The gods are just and of our pleasant vices make instruments to plague us; the dark and vicious place where thee he got cost him his eyes,' and Edmund answers—you remember, he's wounded, he's dying—'Thou hast spoken right; 'tis true. The wheel has come full circle; I am here.' What about that now? Doesn't there seem to be a God managing things, punishing, rewarding?"

"Well, does there?" questioned the Controller in his turn. "You can indulge in any number of pleasant vices with a freemartin and run no risks of having your eyes put out by your son's mistress. 'The wheel has come full circle; I am here.' But where would Edmund be nowadays? Sitting in a pneumatic chair, with his arm round a girl's waist, sucking away at his sex-hormone chewing-gum and looking at the feelies. The gods are just. No doubt. But their code of law is dictated, in the last resort, by the people who organize society; Providence takes its cue from men."

"Are you sure?" asked the Savage. "Are you quite sure that the Edmund in that pneumatic chair hasn't been just as heavily punished as the Edmund who's wounded and bleeding to death? The gods are just. Haven't they used his pleasant vices as an instrument to degrade him?"

"Degrade him from what position? As a happy, hard-working, goods-consuming citizen he's perfect. Of course, if you choose some other standard than ours, then perhaps you might say he was degraded. But you've got to stick to one set of postulates. You can't play Electro-magnetic Golf according to the rules of Centrifugal Bumble-puppy."

"But value dwells not in particular will," said the Savage. "It holds his estimate and dignity as well wherein 'tis precious of itself as in the prizer."

"Come, come," protested Mustapha Mond, "that's going rather far, isn't it?"

"If you allowed yourselves to think of God, you wouldn't allow yourselves to be degraded by pleasant vices. You'd have a reason for bearing things patiently, for doing things with courage. I've seen it with the Indians."

"I'm sure you have," said Mustapha Mond. "But then we aren't Indians. There isn't any need for a civilized man to bear anything that's seriously unpleasant. And as for doing things—Ford forbid that he should get the idea into his head. It would upset the whole social order if men started doing things on their own."

"What about self-denial, then? If you had a God, you'd have a reason for self-denial."

"But industrial civilization is only possible when there's no self-denial. Self-indulgence up to the very limits imposed by hygiene and economics. Otherwise the wheels stop turning."

"You'd have a reason for chastity!" said the Savage, blushing a little as he spoke the words.

"But chastity means passion, chastity means neurasthenia. And passion and neurasthenia mean instability. And instability means the end of civilization. You can't have a lasting civilization without plenty of pleasant vices."

"But God's the reason for everything noble and fine and heroic. If you had a God . . ."

"My dear young friend," said Mustapha Mond, "civilization has absolutely no need of nobility or heroism. These things are symptoms of political inefficiency. In a properly organized society like ours, nobody has any opportunities for being noble or heroic. Conditions have got to be thoroughly unstable before the occasion can arise. Where there are wars, where there are divided allegiances, where there are temptations to be resisted, objects of love to be fought for or defended—there, obviously, nobility and heroism have some sense. But there aren't any wars nowadays. The greatest care is taken to prevent you from loving any one too much. There's no such thing as a divided allegiance; you're so conditioned that you can't help doing what you ought to do. And what you ought to do is on the whole so pleasant, so many of the natural impulses are allowed free play, that there really aren't any temptations to resist. And if ever, by some unlucky chance, anything unpleasant should somehow happen, why, there's always *soma* to give you a holiday from the facts. And there's always *soma* to calm your anger, to reconcile you to your enemies, to make you patient and long-suffering. In the past you could only accomplish these things by making a great effort and after years of hard moral training. Now, you swallow two or three half-gramme tablets, and there you are. Anybody can be virtuous now. You can carry at least half your mortality about in a bottle. Christianity without tears—that's what *soma* is."

"But the tears are necessary. Don't you remember what Othello said? 'If after every tempest came such calms, may the winds blow till they have wakened death.' There's a story one of the old Indians used to tell us, about the Girl of Mátaski. The young men who wanted to marry her had to do a morning's hoeing in her garden. It seemed easy; but there were flies and mosquitoes, magic ones. Most of the young men simply couldn't stand the biting and stinging. But the one that could—he got the girl."

"Charming! But in civilized countries," said the Controller, "you can have girls without hoeing for them; and there aren't any flies or mosquitoes to sting you. We got rid of them all centuries ago."

The Savage nodded, frowning. "You got rid of them. Yes, that's just like you. Getting rid of everything unpleasant instead of learning to put up with it. Whether 'tis better in the mind to suffer the slings and arrows of outrageous fortune, or to take arms against a sea of troubles and by opposing end them . . . But you don't do either. Neither suffer nor oppose. You just abolish the slings and arrows. It's too easy."

He was suddenly silent, thinking of his mother. In her room on the thirty-seventh floor, Linda had floated in a sea of singing lights and perfumed caresses—floated away, out of space, out of time, out of the prison of her memories, her habits, her aged and bloated body. And Tomakin, ex-Director of Hatcheries and Conditioning, Tomakin was still on holiday—on holiday from humiliation and pain, in a world where he could not hear those words, that derisive laughter, could not see that hideous face, feel those moist and flabby arms round his neck, in a beautiful world . . .

"What you need," the Savage went on, "is something *with* tears for a change. Nothing costs enough here."

("Twelve and a half million dollars," Henry Foster had protested when the Savage told him that. "Twelve and a half million—that what the new Conditioning Centre cost. Not a cent less.")

"Exposing what is mortal and unsure to all that fortune, death and danger dare, even for an eggshell. Isn't there something in that?" he asked, looking up at Mustapha Mond. "Quite apart from God—though of course God would be a reason for it. Isn't there something in living dangerously?"

"There's a great deal in it," the Controller replied. "Men and women must have their adrenals stimulated from time to time."

"What?" questioned the Savage, uncomprehending.

"It's one of the conditions of perfect health. That's why we've made the V.P.S. treatments compulsory."

"V.P.S.?"

"Violent Passion Surrogate. Regularly once a month. We flood the whole system with adrenin. It's the complete physiological equivalent of fear and rage. All the tonic effects of murdering Desdemona and being murdered by Othello, without any of the inconveniences."

"But I like the inconveniences."

"We don't," said the Controller. "We prefer to do things comfortably."

"But I don't want comfort. I want God, I want poetry, I want real danger, I want freedom, I want goodness. I want sin."

"In fact," said Mustapha Mond, "you're claiming the right to be unhappy."

"All right then," said the Savage defiantly, "I'm claiming the right to be unhappy."

"Not to mention the right to grow old and ugly and impotent; the right to have syphilis and cancer; the right to have too little to eat; the right to be lousy; the right to live in constant apprehension of what may happen tomorrow; the right to catch typhoid; the right to be tortured by unspeakable pains of every kind." There was a long silence.

"I claim them all," said the Savage at last.

Mustapha Mond shrugged his shoulders. "You're welcome," he said.

26. POLITICS WITHOUT POWER

b. f. skinner

Huxley's *Brave New World* achieved "the good life" through the ultimate if somewhat unobtrusive use of coercion. In the following selection, a debate ensues between the founder of a small experimental colony and a visitor-skeptic. The latter charges that the unusual contentment of its inhabitants surely is artificially contrived by some set of skillful techniques that can only have despotic consequences.

Note the manner in which the debate between the founder and the skeptic symbolizes the latent conflict between politics and science, between traditional concepts of social organization and the far-reaching implications of contemporary behavioral science.

Castle got his chance to take up "general issues" that afternoon. A walk to the summit of Stone Hill had been planned for a large party, which included Mr. and Mrs. Meyerson and three or four children. It seemed unlikely that any serious discussion would be possible. But a storm had been threatening

Reprinted by permission of The Macmillan Company from B. F. Skinner, *Walden Two*. Copyright 1948 by B. F. Skinner.

all morning, and at lunch we heard it break. The afternoon was again open. I detected a certain activity in the dining room as plans were changed. As we were finishing dinner two young people approached our table and spoke to Rodge, Steve, and the girls.

"Do you play? Cornet, sax, trombone? We're getting up a concert. We even have a lonely tuba."

"You play, Steve," said Mary.

"Steve was the best little old trombone in the Philippines," said Rodge.

"Good! Anybody else? It's strictly amateur."

It appeared that Barbara could play popular tunes on the piano, mostly by ear, and it was thought that something might be arranged. They departed for the theater to look over the common stock of instruments, and Frazier, Castle, and I were left alone.

Castle immediately began to warm up his motors. He picked up an empty cigarette package which Barbara had left on the table, tore it in two, placed the halves together, and tore them again. Various husky noises issued from his throat. It was obvious that something was about to happen, and Frazier and I waited in silence.

"Mr. Frazier," Castle said at last, in a sudden roar, "I accuse you of one of the most diabolical machinations in the history of mankind!" He looked as steadily as possible at Frazier, but he was trembling, and his eyes were popping.

"Shall we go to my room?" Frazier said quietly.

It was a trick of Frazier's to adopt a contrasting tone of voice, and in this instance it was devastating. Castle came down to earth with a humiliating bump. He had prepared himself for a verbal battle of heroic dimensions, but he found himself humbly carrying his tray to the service window and trailing Frazier along the Walk.

I was not sure of the line Castle was going to take. Apparently he had done some thinking since morning, probably during the service, but I could not guess the result. Frazier's manner was also puzzling. His suggestion that we go to his room had sounded a little as if he were inviting a truculent companion to "step outside and say that again!" He had apparently expected the attack from Castle and had prepared the defenses to his satisfaction.

When we had settled ourselves in Frazier's room, with Frazier full-length on the bed, over which he had hastily pulled a cover, Castle began again in an unsuccessful attempt to duplicate the surprise and force of his first assault.

"A modern, mechanized, managerial Machiavelli—that is my final estimate of you, Mr. Frazier," he said, with the same challenging stare.

"It must be gratifying to know that one has reached a 'final estimate,' " said Frazier.

"An artist in power," Castle continued, "whose greatest art is to conceal art. The silent despot."

"Since we are dealing in 'M's,' why not sum it all up and say 'Mephistophelian'?" said Frazier, curiously reviving my fears of the preceding afternoon.

"I'm willing to do that!" said Castle. "And unless God is very sure of himself, I suspect He's by no means easy about this latest turn in the war of the angels. So far as I can see, you've blocked every path through which man was to struggle upward toward salvation. Intelligence, initiative—you have filled their places with a sort of degraded instinct, engineered compulsion. Walden Two is a marvel of efficient coordination—as efficient as an anthill!"

"Replacing intelligence with instinct—" muttered Frazier. "I had never thought of that. It's an interesting possibility. How's it done?" It was a crude maneuver. The question was a digression, intended to spoil Castle's timing and to direct our attention to practical affairs in which Frazier was more at home.

"The behavior of your members is carefully shaped in advance by a Plan," said Castle, not to be taken in, "and it's shaped to perpetuate that Plan. Intellectually Walden Two is quite as incapable of a spontaneous change of course as the life within a beehive."

"I see what you mean," said Frazier distantly. But he returned to his strategy. "And have you discovered the machinery of my power?"

"I have, indeed. We were looking in the wrong place. There's no *current* contact between you and the members of Walden Two. You threw us off the track very skillfully on that point last night. But you were behaving as a despot when you first laid your plans—when you designed the social structure and drew up the contract between community and member, when you worked out your educational practices and your guarantees against despotism —What a joke! Don't tell me you weren't in control *then!* Burris saw the point. What about your career as organizer? *There* was leadership! And the most damnable leadership in history, because you were setting the stage for the withdrawal of yourself as a personal force, knowing full well that everything that happened would still be your doing. Hundreds—you predicted millions—of unsuspecting souls were to fall within the scope of your ambitious scheme."

Castle was driving his argument home with great excitement, but Frazier was lying in exaggerated relaxation, staring at the ceiling, his hands cupped behind his head.

"Very good, Mr. Castle," he said softly. "I gave you the clue, of course, when we parted last night."

"You did, indeed. And I've wondered why. Were you led into that fatal error by your conceit? Perhaps that's the ultimate answer to your form of despotism. No one could enjoy the power you have seized without wishing to display it from time to time."

"I've admitted neither power nor despotism. But you're quite right in saying that I've exerted an influence and in one sense will continue to exert it forever. I believe you called me a *primum mobile*—not quite correctly, as I found upon looking the term up last night. But I did plan Walden Two— not as an architect plans a building, but as a scientist plans a long-term experiment, uncertain of the conditions he will meet but knowing how he will deal with them when they arise. In a sense, Walden Two is predetermined, but not as the behavior of a beehive is determined. Intelligence, no matter how much it may be shaped and extended by our educational system, will still function as intelligence. It will be used to puzzle out solutions to problems to which a beehive would quickly succumb. What the plan does is to keep intelligence on the right track, for the good of society rather than of the intelligent individual—or for the eventual rather than the immediate good of the individual. It does this by making sure that the individual will not forget his personal stake in the welfare of society."

"But you are forestalling many possibly useful acts of intelligence which aren't encompassed by your plan. You have ruled out points of view which may be more productive. You are implying that T. E. Frazier, looking at the world from the middle of the twentieth century, understands the best course for mankind forever."

"Yes, I suppose I do."

"But that's absurd!"

"Not at all. I don't say I foresee the course man will take a hundred years hence, let alone forever, but I know which he should take now."

"How can you be sure of it? It's certainly not a question you have answered experimentally."

"I think we're in the course of answering it," said Frazier. "But that's beside the point. There's no alternative. We must take that course."

"But that's fantastic. You who are taking it are in a small minority."

Frazier sat up.

"And the majority are in a big quandary," he said. "They're not on the road at all, or they're scrambling back toward their starting point, or sidling from one side of the road to the other like so many crabs. What do you think two world wars have been about? Something as simple as boundaries or trade? Nonsense. The world is trying to adjust to a new conception of man in relation to men."

"Perhaps it's merely trying to adjust to despots whose ideas are incompatible with the real nature of man."

"Mr. Castle," said Frazier very earnestly, "let me ask you a question. I warn you, it will be the most terrifying question of your life. *What would you do if you found yourself in possession of an effective science of behavior?* Suppose you suddenly found it possible to control the behavior of men as you wished. What would you do?"

"That's an assumption?"

"Take it as one if you like. *I* take it as a fact. And apparently you accept it as a fact too. I can hardly be as despotic as you claim unless I hold the key to an extensive practical control."

"What would I do?" said Castle thoughtfully. "I think I would dump your science of behavior in the ocean."

"And deny men all the help you could otherwise give them?"

"And give them the freedom they would otherwise lose forever!"

"How could you give them freedom?"

"By refusing to control them!"

"But you would only be leaving the control in other hands."

"Whose?"

"The charlatan, the demagogue, the salesman, the ward heeler, the bully, the cheat, the educator, the priest—all who are now in possession of the techniques of behavioral engineering."

"A pretty good share of the control would remain in the hands of the individual himself."

"That's an assumption, too, and it's your only hope. It's your only possible chance to avoid the implications of a science of behavior. If man is free, then a technology of behavior is impossible. But I'm asking you to consider the other case."

"Then my answer is that your assumption is contrary to fact and any further consideration idle."

"And your accusations—?"

"—were in terms of intention, not of possible achievement."

Frazier sighed dramatically.

"It's a little late to be proving that a behavioral technology is well advanced. How can you deny it? Many of its methods and techniques are really as old as the hills. Look at their frightful misuse in the hands of the Nazis! And what about the techniques of the psychological clinic? What about education? Or religion? Or practical politics? Or advertising and salesmanship? Bring them all together and you have a sort of rule-of-thumb technology of vast power. No, Mr. Castle, the science is there for the asking. But its techniques and methods are in the wrong hands—they are used for personal aggrandizement in a competitive world or, in the case of the psychologist and educator, for futilely corrective purposes. My question is, have you the courage to take up and wield the science of behavior for the good of mankind? You answer that you would dump it in the ocean!"

"I'd want to take it out of the hands of the politicians and advertisers and salesmen, too."

"And the psychologists and educators? You see, Mr. Castle, you can't have that kind of cake. The fact is, we not only *can* control human behavior, we *must*. But who's to do it, and what's to be done?"

"So long as a trace of personal freedom survives, I'll stick to my position," said Castle, very much out of countenance.

"Isn't it time we talked about freedom?" I said. "We parted a day or so ago on an agreement to let the question of freedom ring. It's time to answer, don't you think?"

"My answer is simple enough," said Frazier. "I deny that freedom exists at all. I must deny it—or my program would be absurd. You can't have a science about a subject matter which hops capriciously about. Perhaps we can never *prove* that man isn't free; it's an assumption. But the increasing success of a science of behavior makes it more and more plausible."

"On the contrary, a simple personal experience makes it untenable," said Castle. "The experience of freedom. I *know* that I'm free."

"It must be quite consoling," said Frazier.

"And what's more—you do, too," said Castle hotly. "When you deny your own freedom for the sake of playing with a science of behavior, you're acting in plain bad faith. That's the only way I can explain it." He tried to recover himself and shrugged his shoulders. "At least you'll grant that you *feel* free."

"The 'feeling of freedom' should deceive no one," said Frazier. "Give me a concrete case."

"Well, right now," Castle said. He picked up a book of matches. "I'm free to hold or drop these matches."

"You will, of course, do one or the other," said Frazier. "Linguistically or logically there seem to be two possibilities, but I submit that there's only one in fact. The determining forces may be subtle but they are inexorable. I suggest that as an orderly person you will probably hold—ah! you drop them! Well, you see, that's all part of your behavior with respect to me. You couldn't resist the temptation to prove me wrong. It was all lawful. You had no choice. The deciding factor entered rather late, and naturally you couldn't foresee the result when you first held them up. There was no strong likelihood that you would act in either direction, and so you said you were free."

"That's entirely too glib," said Castle. "It's easy to argue lawfulness after the fact. But let's see you predict what I will do in advance. Then I'll agree there's law."

"I didn't say that behavior is always predictable, any more than the weather is always predictable. There are often too many factors to be taken into account. We can't measure them all accurately, and we couldn't perform the mathematical operations needed to make a prediction if we had the measurements. The legality is usually an assumption—but none the less important in judging the issue at hand."

"Take a case where there's no choice, then," said Castle. "Certainly a man in jail isn't free in the sense in which I am free now."

"Good! That's an excellent start. Let us classify the kinds of determiners of human behavior. One class, as you suggest, is physical restraint—handcuffs, iron bars, forcible coercion. These are ways in which we shape human behavior according to our wishes. They're crude, and they sacrifice the affection of the controllee, but they often work. Now, what other ways are there of limiting freedom?"

Frazier had adopted a professorial tone and Castle refused to answer.

"The threat of force would be one," I said.

"Right. And here again we shan't encourage any loyalty on the part of the controllee. He has perhaps a shade more of the feeling of freedom, since he can always 'choose to act and accept the consequences,' but he doesn't feel exactly free. He knows his behavior is being coerced. Now what else?"

I had no answer.

"Force or the threat of force—I see no other possibility," said Castle after a moment.

"Precisely," said Frazier.

"But certainly a large part of my behavior has no connection with force at all. There's my freedom!" said Castle.

"I wasn't agreeing that there was no other possibility—merely that *you* could see no other. Not being a good behaviorist—or a good Christian, for that matter—you have no feeling for a tremendous power of a different sort."

"What's that?"

"I shall have to be technical," said Frazier. "But only for a moment. It's what the science of behavior calls 'reinforcement theory.'" The things that can happen to us fall into three classes. To some things we are indifferent. Other things we like—we want them to happen, and we take steps to make them happen again. Still other things we don't like—we don't want them to happen and we take steps to get rid of them or keep them from happening again.

"Now," Frazier continued earnestly, "if it's in our power to create any of the situations which a person likes or to remove any situation he doesn't like, we can control his behavior. When he behaves as we want him to behave, we simply create a situation he likes, or remove one he doesn't like. As a result, the probability that he will behave that way again goes up, which is what we want. Technically it's called 'positive reinforcement.'

"The old school made the amazing mistake of supposing that the reverse was true, that by removing a situation a person likes or setting up one he doesn't like—in other words by punishing him—it was possible to *reduce* the probability that he would behave in a given way again. That simple doesn't hold. It has been established beyond question. What is emerging at this critical stage in the evolution of society is a behavioral and cultural technology based on positive reinforcement alone. We are gradually discovering—at an untold cost in human suffering—that in the long run punishment doesn't reduce the probability that an act will occur. We have been so preoccupied with the contrary that we always take 'force' to mean punishment. We don't say we're using force when we send shiploads of food into a starving country, though we're displaying quite as much *power* as if we were sending troops and guns."

"I'm certainly not an advocate of force," said Castle. "But I can't agree that it's not effective."

"It's *temporarily* effective, that's the worst of it. That explains several thousand years of bloodshed. Even nature has been fooled. We 'instinctively' punish a person who doesn't behave as we like—we spank him if he's a child or strike him if he's a man. A nice distinction! The immediate effect of the blow teaches us to strike again. Retribution and revenge are the most natural things on earth. But in the long run the man we strike is no less likely to repeat his act."

"But he won't repeat it if we hit him hard enough," said Castle.

"He'll still *tend* to repeat it. He'll *want* to repeat it. We haven't really altered his potential behavior at all. That's the pity of it. If he doesn't repeat it in our presence, he will in the presence of someone else. Or it will be repeated in the disguise of a neurotic symptom. If we hit hard enough, we clear a little place for ourselves in the wilderness of civilization, but we make the rest of the wilderness still more terrible.

"Now, early forms of government are naturally based on punishment. It's the obvious technique when the physically strong control the weak. But we're in the throes of a great change to positive reinforcement—from a competitive society in which one man's reward is another man's punishment, to a cooperative society in which no one gains at the expense of anyone else.

"The change is slow and painful because the immediate, temporary effect of punishment overshadows the eventual advantage of positive reinforcement. We've all seen countless instances of the temporary effect of force, but clear evidence of the effect of not using force is rare. That's why I insist that Jesus, who was apparently the first to discover the power of refusing to punish, must have hit upon the principle by accident. He certainly had none of the experimental evidence which is available to us today, and I can't conceive that it was possible, no matter what the man's genius, to have discovered the principle from casual observation."

"A touch of revelation, perhaps?" said Castle.

"No, accident. Jesus discovered one principle because it had immediate consequences, and he got another thrown in for good measure."

I began to see light.

"You mean the principle of 'love your enemies'?" I said.

"Exactly! To 'do good to those who despitefully use you' has two unrelated consequences. You gain the peace of mind we talked about the other day. Let the stronger man push you around—at least you avoid the torture of your own rage. *That's* the immediate consequence. What an astonishing discovery it must have been to find that in the long run you could *control the stronger man* in the same way!"

"It's generous of you to give so much credit to your early colleague," said Castle, "but why are we still in the throes of so much misery? Twenty centuries should have been enough for one piece of behavioral engineering."

"The conditions which made the principle difficult to discover made it difficult to teach. The history of the Christian Church doesn't reveal many cases of doing good to one's enemies. To inoffensive heathens, perhaps, but not enemies. One must look outside the field of organized religion to find the principle in practice at all. Church governments are devotees of *power,* both temporal and bogus."

"But what has all this got to do with freedom?" I said hastily.

Frazier took time to reorganize his behavior. He looked steadily toward the window, against which the rain was beating heavily.

"Now that we *know* how positive reinforcement works and why negative doesn't," he said at last, "we can be more deliberate, and hence more success-ful, in our cultural design. We can achieve a sort of control under which the controlled, though they are following a code much more scrupulously than was ever the case under the old system, nevertheless *feel free*. They are doing what they want to do, not what they are forced to do. That's the source of the tremendous power of positive reinforcement—there's no restraint and no re-volt. By a careful cultural design, we control not the final behavior, but the *inclination* to behave—the motives, the desires, the wishes.

"The curious thing is that in that case *the question of freedom never arises*. Mr. Castle was free to drop the matchbook in the sense that nothing was preventing him. If it had been securely bound to his hand he wouldn't have been free. Nor would he have been quite free if I'd covered him with a gun and threatened to shoot him if he let it fall. The question of freedom arises when there is restraint—either physical or psychological.

"But restraint is only one sort of control, and absence of restraint isn't freedom. It's not control that's lacking when one feels 'free,' but the objec-tionable control of force. Mr. Castle felt free to hold or drop the matches in the sense that he felt no restraint—no threat of punishment in taking either course of action. He neglected to examine his positive reasons for holding or letting go, in spite of the fact that these were more compelling in this instance than any threat of force.

"We have no vocabulary of freedom in dealing with what we want to do," Frazier went on. "The question never arises. When men strike for free-dom, they strike against jails and the police, or the threat of them—against oppression. They never strike against forces which make them want to act the way they do. Yet, it seems to be understood that governments will operate only through force or the threat of force, and that all other principles of con-trol will be left to education, religion, and commerce. If this continues to be the case, we may as well give up. A government can never create a free people with the techniques now allotted to it.

"The question is: Can men live in freedom and peace? And the answer is: Yes, if we can build a social structure which will satisfy the needs of everyone and in which everyone will want to observe the supporting code. But so far this has been achieved only in Walden Two. Your ruthless accusations to the contrary, Mr. Castle, this is the freest place on earth. And it is free precisely because we make no use of force or the threat of force. Every bit of our research, from the nursery through the psychological management of our adult membership, is directed toward that end—to exploit every alternative to forc-ible control. By skillful planning, by a wise choice of techniques we *increase* the feeling of freedom.

"It's not planning which infringes upon freedom, but planning which uses force. A sense of freedom was practically unknown in the planned society of Nazi Germany, because the planners made a fantastic use of force and the threat of force.

"No, Mr. Castle, when a science of behavior has once been achieved, there's no alternative to a planned society. We can't leave mankind to an accidental or biased control. But by using the principle of positive reinforcement— carefully avoiding force or the threat of force—we can preserve a personal sense of freedom."

Frazier threw himself back upon the bed and stared at the ceiling.

"But you haven't denied that you are in complete control," said Castle. "You are still the long-range dictator."

"As you will," said Frazier, waving his hands loosely in the air and then cupping them behind his head. "In fact, I'm inclined to agree. When you have once grasped the principle of positive reinforcement, you can enjoy a sense of unlimited power. It's enough to satisfy the thirstiest tyrant."

"There you are, then," said Castle. "That's my case."

"But it's a limited sort of despotism," Frazier went on. "And I don't think anyone should worry about it. The despot must wield his power for the good of others. If he takes any step which reduces the sum total of human happiness, his power is reduced by a like amount. What better check against a malevolent despotism could you ask for?"

"The check I ask for," said Castle, "is nothing less than democracy. Let the people rule and power will not be misused. I can't see that the nature of the power matters. As a matter of fact, couldn't this principle of 'positive reinforcement,' as you call it, be used by a democratic government just as well as by your dictatorship?"

"No principle is consistently used by a democratic government. What do you mean by democracy, anyway?"

"Government by the people or according to the will of the people, naturally," said Castle.

"As exemplified by current practices in the United States?"

"I suppose so. Yes, I'll take my stand on that. It's not a perfect democracy, but it's the best there is at the moment."

"Then I say that democracy is a pious fraud," said Frazier. "In what sense is it 'government by the people'?"

"In an obvious sense, I should say."

"It isn't obvious at all. How is the people's will ascertained? In an election. But what a travesty! In a small committee meeting, or even a town hall, I can see some point in voting, especially on a yes-or-no question. But fifty million voters choosing a president—that's quite another thing."

"I can't see that the number of voters changes the principle," said Castle.

"The chance that one man's vote will decide the issue in a national election," said Frazier, speaking very deliberately, "is less than the chance that he will be killed on his way to the polls. We pay no attention whatsoever to chances of that magnitude in our daily affairs. We should call a man a fool who bought a sweepstakes ticket with similar odds against him."

"It must mean something or people wouldn't vote," said Castle.

"How many of them would go on voting if they were free of a lot of extraneous pressures? Do you think a man goes to the polls because of any effect which casting a vote has ever had? By no means. He goes to avoid being talked about by his neighbors, or to 'knife' a candidate whom he dislikes, marking his X as he might defile a campaign poster—and with the same irrational spite. No, a man has no logical reason to vote whatsoever. The chances of affecting the issue are too small to alter his behavior in any appreciable way."

"I believe the mathematicians have a name for that fallacy," said Castle. "It's true that your chances of deciding the issue get smaller as the number of voters increases, but the stakes get larger at the same rate."

"But do they? Is a national election really an important issue? Does it really matter very much who wins? The platforms of the two parties are carefully made as much alike as possible, and when the election is over we're all advised to accept the result like good sports. Only a few voters go on caring very much after a week or two. The rest know there's no real threat. Things will go on pretty much the same. Elections are sometimes turned by a few million voters who can't make up their minds until election day. It can't be much of an issue if that's the case."

"Even so, it's important that the people *feel* they've chosen the government they want," said Castle.

"On the contrary, that's the worst of it. Voting is a device for blaming conditions on the people. The people aren't rulers, they're scapegoats. And they file to the polls every so often to renew their right to the title."

"I daresay there are defects in the machinery of democracy," said Castle. "No one wholly approves of the average presidential campaign. The will of the people is likely to be unduly influenced, and perhaps incorrectly determined. But that's a matter of technique. I think we will eventually work out a better system for ascertaining what the people want done. Democracy isn't a method of polling opinion, it's the assignment of power to that opinion. Let's assume that the will of the people can be ascertained. What then?"

"I should ask you that. What then, indeed? Are the people skilled governors? No. And they become less and less skilled, relatively speaking, as the science of government advances. It's the same point I raised in our discussion of the group nursery: when we've once acquired a behavioral technology, we can't leave the control of behavior to the unskilled. Your answer is to deny that the technology exists—a very feeble answer, it seems to me.

"The one thing the people know," Frazier continued, "and the one thing about which they should be heard is how they like the existing state of affairs, and perhaps how they would like some other state of affairs. What they conspicuously don't know is how to get what they want. That's a matter for specialists."

"But the people have solved some pretty important problems," I said.

"Have they, in fact? The actual practice in a democracy is to vote, not for a given state of affairs, but for a man who claims to be able to achieve that state. I'm not a historian"—Frazier laughed explosively—"quite the contrary—but I suspect that that's always what is meant by the rule of the people—rule by a man chosen by the people."

"Isn't that a possible way out, though?" said Castle. "Suppose we need experts. Why not elect them?"

"For a very simple reason. The people are in no position to evaluate experts. And elected experts are never able to act as they think best. They can't experiment. The amateur doesn't appreciate the need for experimentation. He wants his expert to *know*. And he's utterly incapable of sustaining the period of doubt during which an experiment works itself out. The experts must either disguise their experiments and pretend to know the outcome in advance or stop experimenting altogether and struggle to maintain the *status quo.*"

" 'With all her faults, I love her still,' " said Castle. "I'll take democracy. We may have to muddle through. We may seem laughable to your streamlined Planners. But we have one thing on our side—freedom."

"I thought we had settled that," said Frazier.

"We had. But apparently not as you thought," said Castle. "I don't like despotism."

Frazier got up and went to the window. The rain had stopped, and the distant hills beyond the river had become visible. He stood with his back to us for perhaps a minute, which seemed very long against the energetic tempo of our conversation. Finally he turned.

"Can't I make you understand?" he said, holding out his hands in a gesture of appeal. *"I don't like despotism either!* I don't like the despotism of ignorance. I don't like the despotism of neglect, of irresponsibility, the despotism of accident, even. And I don't like the despotism of democracy!"

He turned back to the window.

"I don't think I follow you," said Castle, somewhat softened by Frazier's evident emotion.

"Democracy is the spawn of despotism," Frazier said, continuing to look out the window. "And like father, like son. Democracy is power and rule. It's not the will of the people, remember; it's the will of the majority." He turned and, in a husky voice which broke in flight like a tumbler pigeon on the word "out," he added, "My heart goes out to the everlasting minority." He seemed ready to cry, but I could not tell whether it was in sympathy for the oppressed or in rage at his failure to convince Castle.

"In a democracy," he went on, "there is *no* check against despotism, because the principle of democracy is supposed to be itself a check. But it guarantees only that the *majority* will not be despotically ruled."

"I don't agree that the minority has no say," said Castle. "But in any case it's better that at least half the people get what they want, instead of a small élite."

"There you are!" said Frazier, jumping up again just as he had started to sit down. "The majority are an élite. And they're despots. I want none of them! Let's have government for the benefit of all."

"But that isn't always possible," said Castle.

"It's possible much oftener than under a democracy. There are seldom any issues which have to be decided in an all-or-none fashion. A careful planner could work out a compromise which would be reasonably satisfying to everyone. But in a democracy, the majority solve the problem to their satisfaction, and the minority can be damned.

"The government of Walden Two," he continued, "has the virtues of democracy, but none of the defects. It's much closer to the theory or intent of democracy than the actual practice in America today. The will of the people is carefully ascertained. We have no election campaigns to falsify issues or obscure them with emotional appeals, but a careful study of the satisfaction of the membership is made. Every member has a direct channel through which he may protest to the Managers or even the Planners. And these protests are taken as seriously as the pilot of an airplane takes a sputtering engine. We don't need laws and a police force to compel a pilot to pay attention to a defective engine. Nor do we need laws to compel our Dairy Manager to pay attention to an epidemic among his cows. Similarly, our Behavioral and Cultural Managers need not be compelled to consider grievances. A grievance is a wheel to be oiled, or a broken pipe line to be repaired.

"Most of the people in Walden Two take no active part in running the government. And they don't want an active apart. The urge to have a say in how the country should be run is a recent thing. It was not part of early democracy. The original victory over tyranny was a constitutional guarantee of personal rights, including the right to protest if conditions were not satisfactory. But the business of ruling was left to somebody else. Nowadays, everybody fancies himself an expert in government and wants to have a say. Let's hope it's a temporary cultural pattern. I can remember when everyone could talk about the mechanical principles according to which his automobile ran or failed to run. Everyone was an automotive specialist and knew how to file the points of a magneto and take the shimmy out of front wheels. To suggest that these matters might be left to experts would have been called Fascism, if the term had been invented. But today no one knows how his car operates and I can't see that he's any the less happy.

"In Walden Two no one worries about the government except the few to whom that worry has been assigned. To suggest that everyone should take an interest would seem as fantastic as to suggest that everyone should become familiar with our Diesel engines. Even the constitutional rights of the members are seldom thought about, I'm sure. The only thing that matters is one's day-to-day happiness and a secure future. Any infringement there would undoubtedly 'arouse the electorate.' "

"I assume that your constitution at least can't be changed without a vote of the members," I said.

"Wrong again. It can be changed by a unanimous vote of the Planners and a two-thirds vote of the Managers. You're still thinking about government by the people. Get that out of your head. The people are in no better position to change the constitution than to decide upon current practices."

"Then what's to prevent your Planners from becoming despots?" I said. "Wouldn't it really be possible?"

"How?" said Frazier.

"Oh, in many ways, I imagine."

"Such as?"

"Well, if I were a Planner with a yen for despotism, I would begin by insinuating into the culture the notion that Planners were exceptional people. I would argue that they should be personally known to the members, and should therefore wear an identifying badge or uniform. This could be done under the guise of facilitating service to the members, but eventually the Planners would be set off as a separate caste. Then they'd be relieved from menial work on the ground that they were too busy with the affairs of the community. Then special quarters, perhaps quite luxurious, would be built for them. I'd bring the Managers around to this change in the constitution by giving them better quarters also. It would all be carefully propagandized, of course. Eventually more and more of the wealth of the community would be diverted to this élite, and I would come out with a true despotism. Isn't that possible?"

"If you mean, 'Isn't despotism possible?' the answer is yes," said Frazier. "Cultures which work for the advantage of a few last a long time. Look at India, where the oppressed aren't even aware that they are sick and miserable. But are the people strong, productive, progressive? If not, then the culture will eventually be replaced by competing cultures which work more efficiently. Our Planners know this. They know that any usurpation of power would weaken the community as a whole and eventually destroy the whole venture."

"A group of despotic planners might be willing to sacrifice the community," I said. "They wouldn't necessarily suffer if it failed. They could simply abscond with the funds."

"That would be a catastrophe. Like an earthquake, or a new and frightful epidemic, or a raid from another world. All we can do is take reasonable precautions. Your hypothetical case strikes me as implausible, that's all I can say."

"But isn't that just the weakness of your antidemocratic attitude?" Castle said. "Haven't you lost your guarantee against the usurpation of power?"

"There's no power to usurp," said Frazier. "There's no police, no military, no guns or bombs—tear-gas or atomic—to give strength to the few. In point of physical force the members are always clearly in power. Revolt is not only easy, it's inevitable if real dissatisfaction arises.

"And there's little real wealth to tempt anyone. It isn't true that the Planners could abscond with the funds. Our wealth is our happiness. The physical plant of the community would be practically worthless without the members.

"And then remember that the Planners are part of a noncompetitive culture in which a thirst for power is a curiosity. They have no reason to usurp. Their tradition is against it. Any gesture of personal domination would stand out as conspicuously as the theft of the bulletin board."

"But it's human to dominate," said Castle, "in any culture."

"That's an experimental question, Mr. Castle. You can't answer it from your armchair. But let's see what a usurpation of power would amount to. Insofar as the Planners rule at all, they do so through positive reinforcement. They don't use or threaten to use force. They have no machinery for that. In order to extend their power they would have to provide more and more satisfying conditions. A curious sort of despotism, Mr. Castle."

"But they might change to a different sort of power."

"That would require a unanimous vote. But the Planners are eventually demoted to simple citizenship. Their terms of office are staggered, and some of them are always so close to retirement that they wouldn't share in the selfish consequences. Why should they vote for the change?

"Usurpation of power is a threat only in a competitive culture," Frazier continued. "In Walden Two power is either destroyed or so diffused that usurpation is practically impossible. Personal ambition isn't essential in a good governor. As governmental technology advances, less and less is left to the decisions of governors, anyway. Eventually we shall have no use for Planners at all. The Managers will suffice."

Frazier turned to me in an open gesture of appeasement.

"Democracy is not a guarantee against despotism, Burris. Its virtues are of another sort. It has proved itself clearly superior to the despotic rule of a small élite. We have seen it survive in conflict with the despotic pattern in World War II. The democratic peoples proved themselves superior just because of their democracy. They could enlist the support of other peoples, who had less to fear from them than from an aggressive élite. They could marshal greater manpower in the long run because everyone had a stake in victory and few were suffering from the strain of forcible coercion. The despots couldn't convert the people they conquered while pretending to be a superior race. Every principle which seemed to strengthen the governmental structure of Fascism when the war began proved to be an eventual weakness.

"But the triumph of democracy doesn't mean it's the best government.

It was merely the better in a contest with a conspicuously bad one. Let's not stop with democracy. It isn't, and can't be, the best form of government, because it's based on a scientifically invalid conception of man. It fails to take account of the fact that in the long run *man is determined by the state. A laissez-faire* philosophy which trusts to the inherent goodness and wisdom of the common man is incompatible with the observed fact that men are made good or bad and wise or foolish by the environment in which they grow."

"But which comes first," I asked, "the hen or the egg? Men build society and society builds men. Where do we start?"

"It isn't a question of starting. The start has been made. It's a question of what's to be done from now on."

"Then it's to be revolution, is that it?" said Castle. "If democracy can't change itself into something better—"

"Revolution? You're not a very rewarding pupil, Mr. Castle. The change won't come about through power politics at all. It will take place at another level altogether."

"What level?"

Frazier waved his hand toward the window, through which we could see the drenched landscape of Walden Two.

"Well," said Castle, "you'd better hurry up. It's not a job to be done on four hours a day."

"Four hours a day is exactly what it needs," said Frazier with a smile. He lay back upon the bed, looking rather tired.

"I can think of a conspicuous case in which the change you're advocating is coming about at the level of power politics," I said.

Frazier sat up quickly, with obvious effort. He looked at me suspiciously.

"Russia," I said.

"Ah, Russia," he said with relief. He showed no inclination to go on.

"What about Russia, though?"

"What about it, indeed?"

"Isn't there a considerable resemblance between Russian communism and your own philosophy?"

"Russia, Russia," Frazier murmured evasively. "Our visitors always ask that. Russia is our rival. It's very flattering—if you consider the resources and the numbers of people involved."

"But you're dodging my question. Hasn't Russia done what you're trying to do, but at the level of power politics? I can imagine what a Communist would say of your program at Walden Two. Wouldn't he simply tell you to drop the experiment and go to work for the Party?"

"He would and he does."

"And what's your answer?"

"I can see only four things wrong with Russia," Frazier said, clearly enjoying the condescension. "As originally conceived, it was a good try. It sprang from humanitarian impulses which are a commonplace in Walden Two. But it quickly developed certain weaknesses. There are four of them, and they were inevitable. They were inevitable just because the attempt was made at the level of power politics." He waited for me to ask him what the weaknesses were.

"The first," he said, as soon as I had done so, "is a decline in the experimental spirit. Many promising experiments have simply been dropped. The group care of children, the altered structure of the family, the abandonment of religion, new kinds of personal incentives—all these problems were 'solved' by dropping back to practices which have prevailed in capitalistic societies for centuries. It was the old difficulty. A government in power can't experiment. It must know the answers or at least pretend to know them. Today the Russians contend that an optimal cultural pattern has been achieved, if not yet fully implemented. They dare not admit to any serious need for improvement. Revolutionary experimentation is dead.

"In the second place, Russia has overpropagandized, both to its own people and to the outside world. Their propaganda is much more extensive than any which ever enslaved a working class. That's a serious defect, for it has made it impossible to evaluate their success. We don't know how much of the current vigor of Russian communism is due to a strong, satisfying way of life, and how much to indoctrination. You may call it a temporary expedient, to counteract the propaganda embedded in an older culture. But that need has long since passed, yet the propaganda continues. So long as it goes on, no valid data on the effectiveness of Russian communism can be obtained. For all we know, the whole culture would fall apart if the supporting attitudes were taken away. And what is worse, it's hard to see how they can ever be taken away. Propaganda makes it impossible to progress toward a form of society in which it is unnecessary.

"The third weakness of the Russian government is its use of heroes. The first function of the hero, in Russia as elsewhere, is to piece out a defective governmental structure. Important decisions aren't made by appeal to a set of principles; they are personal acts. The process of governing is an art, not a science, and the government is only as good or as long-lasting as the artist. As to the second function of the hero—how long would communism last if all the pictures of Lenin and Satin were torn down? It's a question worth asking.

"But most important of all, the Russian experiment was based on power. You may argue that the seizure of power was also a temporary expedient, since the people who held it were intolerant and oppressive. But you can hardly defend the continued use of power in that way. The Russians are still a long way from a culture in which people behave as they *want* to behave, for their mutual good. In order to get its people to act as the communist pattern demands, the Russian government has had to use the techniques of capitalism. On the one hand it resorts to extravagant and uneven rewards. But an unequal distribution of wealth destroys more incentives than it creates. It obviously can't operate for the *common* good. On the other hand, the government also uses punishment or the threat of it. What kind of behavioral engineering do you call that?"

Frazier spat into the flowerpot in a gesture of disgust. Then he held out his hands with an exaggerated shrug and drew himself slowly to his feet. He had evidently had enough of Castle's "general issues."

27. BEYOND CLASS CONFLICT
karl marx and friedrich engels

Published in 1848 and the classic statement of the communist ideology and theory of history, the *Communist Manifesto* offers a deterministic theory of history in which the working class, through overthrow of the capitalist system, seizes national and international power preparatory to the establishment of a "classless" and eventually "utopian" human community. In the new society, which has abolished the state as an instrument of violence and degradation, the basic principle of social life is spontaneous association "in which the free development of each is the condition for the free development of all," a principle of natural individual morality presumably assuring order and happiness.

Can *social* control ever become a benign substitute for *political* coercion? Does man possess an ingrained sense of morality, or can he acquire one and thereby make government superfluous? Conversely, are present injustices and institutions somehow "natural" and therefore unchangeable, even through revolution and transformation?

The workingmen have no country. We cannot take from them what they have not got. Since the proletariat must first of all acquire political supremacy, must rise to be the leading class of the nation, must constitute itself *the* nation, it is, so far, itself national, though not in the bourgeois sense of the word.

National differences and antagonisms between peoples are vanishing gradually from day to day, owing to the development of the bourgeoisie, to freedom of commerce, to the world market, to uniformity in the mode of production and in the conditions of life corresponding thereto.

The supremacy of the proletariat will cause them to vanish still faster. United action, of the leading civilized countries at least, is one of the first conditions for the emancipation of the proletariat.

From Karl Marx and Friedrich Engels, *The Communist Manifesto.*

In proportion as the exploitation of one individual by another is put an end to, the exploitation of one nation by another will also be put an end to. In proportion as the antagonism between classes within the nation vanishes, the hostility of one nation to another will come to an end.

The charges against Communism made from a religious, a philosophical, and, generally, from an ideological standpoint, are not deserving of serious examination.

Does it require deep intuition to comprehend that man's ideas, views, and conceptions, in one word, man's consciousness, changes with every change in the conditions of his material existence, in his social relations and in his social life?

What else does the history of ideas prove, than that intellectual production changes its character in proportion as material production is changed? The ruling ideas of each age have ever been the ideas of its ruling class.

When people speak of ideas that revolutionize society, they do but express the fact that within the old society the elements of a new one have been created, and that the dissolution of the old ideas keeps even pace with the dissolution of the old conditions of existence.

When the ancient world was in its last throes, the ancient religions were overcome by Christianity. When Christian ideas succumbed in the 18th century to rationalist ideas, feudal society fought its death-battle with the then revolutionary bourgeoisie. The ideas of religious liberty and freedom of conscience, merely gave expression to the sway of free competition within the domain of knowledge.

"Undoubtedly," it will be said, "religion, moral, philosophical and juridical ideas have been modified in the course of historical development. But religion, morality, philosophy, political science, and law, constantly survived this change."

"There are, besides, eternal truths, such as Freedom, Justice, etc., that are common to all states of society. But Communism abolishes eternal truths, it abolishes all religion, and all morality, instead of constituting them on a new basis; it therefore acts in contradiction to all past historical experience."

What does this accusation reduce itself to? The history of all past society has consisted in the development of class antagonisms, antagonisms that assumed different forms at different epochs.

But whatever form they may have taken, one fact is common to all past ages, *viz.,* the exploitation of one part of society by the other. No wonder, then, that the social consciousness of past ages, despite all the multiplicity and variety it displays, moves within certain common forms, or general ideas, which cannot completely vanish except with the total disappearance of class antagonisms.

The Communist revolution is the most radical rupture with traditional property relations; no wonder that its development involves the most radical rupture with traditional ideas.

But let us have done with the bourgeois objections to Communism.

We have seen above, that the first step in the revolution by the working class, is to raise the proletariat to the position of ruling class, to establish democracy.

The proletariat will use its political supremacy to wrest, by degrees, all capital from the bourgeoisie, to centralize all instruments of production in the hands of the state, *i.e.,* of the proletariat organized as the ruling class; and to increase the total of productive forces as rapidly as possible.

Of course, in the beginning, this cannot be effected except by means of despotic inroads on the rights of property, and on the conditions of bourgeois production; by means of measures, therefore, which appear economically insufficient and untenable, but which, in the course of the movement, outstrip themselves, necessitate further inroads upon the old social order, and are unavoidable as a means of entirely revolutionizing the mode of production.

These measures will of course be different in different countries.

Nevertheless in the most advanced countries, the following will be pretty generally applicable.

1. Abolition of property in land and application of all rents of land to public purposes.
2. A heavy progressive or graduated income tax.
3. Abolition of all right of inheritance.
4. Confiscation of the property of all emigrants and rebels.
5. Centralization of credit in the hands of the state, by means of a national bank with state capital and an exclusive monopoly.
6. Centralization of the means of communication and transport in the hands of the state.
7. Extension of factories and instruments of production owned by the state: the bringing into cultivation of waste lands, and the improvement of the soil generally in accordance with a common plan.
8. Equal obligation of all to work. Establishment of industrial armies, especially for agriculture.
9. Combination of agriculture with manufacturing industries; gradual abolition of the distinction between town and country, by a more equable distribution of the population over the country.
10. Free education for all children in public schools. Abolition of child factory labor in its present form. Combination of education with industrial production, etc.

When, in the course of development, class distinctions have disappeared, and all production has been concentrated in the hands of a vast association of the whole nation, the public power will lose its political character. Political power, properly so called, is merely the organized power of one class for oppressing another. If the proletariat during its contest with the bourgeoisie is compelled, by the force of circumstances, to organise itself as a class; if, by means of a revolution, it makes itself the ruling class, and, as such sweeps away by force the old conditions of production, then it will, along with these conditions, have swept away the conditions for the existence of class antagonisms, and of classes generally, and will thereby have abolished its own supremacy as a class.

In place of the old bourgeois society, with its classes and class antagonisms, we shall have an association, in which the free development of each is the condition for the free development of all.

28. NO NEUROTICS IN CHINA
goffredo parise

Communist utopianism is generally associated with freedom from the burdens of material want. In the brief selection that follows, an Italian psychoanalyst argues that communism has solved China's psychological as well as its economic problems. Do you find his reasoning plausible?

I went to see Professor Suh Tsung-hwa, the most famous neurologist in China, in his psychiatric hospital. He is tall, elegant, old—an "old-fashioned Chinese." He speaks fluent French and English because he studied in London as a student of Freud's, in America, and also in Paris, where he was a close friend of Adler's. It was inevitable, therefore, that we should talk of psychoanalysis. He began with a deep bow.

"In China we do not use analysis because neuroses are almost unknown. They are an appanage of the bourgeoisie, not of a people who until just the other day were illiterate peasants. In my opinion, psychoanalysis was an interesting political and literary theory which developed with the crisis of the bourgeoisie. In any case, it is not a science. The libido, or sexual aggression, is everything to Freud. This is the same as saying that neither history nor ideology, but rather sex, is the basis of all human aspiration. It's easy to see that in a bourgeois society in the state of decline such a theory would have had success.

"This is true for two reasons: first, because it coincided with a time of conflict and crisis and therefore of neurosis within a part of European society. Second, because it also coincided with that society's political practices which produced the greatest of all possible neuroses—the two world wars. In other words, Freud's theory parallels the historical time in which it was

From Goffredo Parise, "No Neurotics in China." Reprinted from *Atlas* Magazine, translated from Corriere Della Sera, Milan.

born and developed, when capitalism was entering its most advanced stage—imperialism. One might say that Freud had created the theoretical and para-scientific bases of imperialism. . . .

"From 1940 on, Freud became to the capitalist world what Marx is to the Socialist world: the incontestable ideologist. Let us look at the relation between Freud, the capitalist masses and Western imperialism. In the West, religion has been reduced to the role of a purely administrative ritual, and, again thanks to Freud, it has lost its spiritual hegemony. In the minds and hearts of men, earning money has become an almost religious struggle and has been so magnified in daily life that it has assumed the character of a religious rite. Like money, sex too has increasingly assumed the role of a secret rite. On these two elements, then, sex and money, and on the Freudian theory which exalts them, is founded the new Western capitalist society and the new American imperialism. The first element, that is, money, is opposed to Marxism on the economic level; the second, sex and its related theories, is opposed to Marxism on the ideological level."

"If psychoanalysis is not used in China, what therapy do you use to treat neuroses?"

"I have already said that these neuroses and psychoses do not exist here, not even paranoia. At the bottom of these neuroses—a bourgeois sickness—is egoism. In the West, egoism is necessary for survival. Perennial competition, for example, is a neurotic way to live."

"There is no egoism in China, then?"

"Of course it exists, but we are fighting to destroy it. I will say, however, that in China even before the liberation it was the privilege of the few. But what about the rest of China, the other 80 percent or more, the Chinese peasants? The Chinese family has always been very large and very complex in its hierarchical structure. The single individual alone had little chance to express his private egoism. Already this collective condition, together with the teachings of Confucius, mitigated against an individualistic, egoistic concept of life. All the same, egoism is deeply rooted in the heart of man as a result of the struggle to survive. Now, this drive for survival, the struggle for life, ceased to exist in China when the Chinese began to work, live and be nourished in a Marxist society, free of the class system. The conclusion? Egoism equals neurosis equals class struggle."

"What are the mental illnesses most common in China?"

"Schizophrenia or dementia praecox, epilepsy and, in general, all the hereditary diseases."

"And how are they treated?"

"As in the West. In the most severe cases, we use electric-shock therapy and insulin. In the milder cases we still use some of the traditional cures of cauterization or needle application. And also work in the country, sports and conversation. Even slogans, like 'Never think about yourself.' "

With these words, the professor rose and guided me through the hospital. There were game rooms and workrooms where the patients were laboriously constructing ship models or small storks by braiding strands of nylon and beads. The rooms were clean and run by nurses wearing silent felt slippers. The dining room, the bathrooms and the courtyard reminded me of an orphanage or a summer camp for children, and the patients in their café-au-lait-colored clothes seemed indeed to be children. The expressions on their faces were tender and sad; their smiles were the automatic, uncomprehending smiles of the demented. I did not see any patients in a state of anger or agitation. Between one ward and another we took up the conversation again.

"If, as you say, neuroses do not exist here, what about depression?"

"There are some forms of depression which might be called remorse. Many workers, students and peasants feel a kind of guilt toward the Socialist society. They think that perhaps they have not dedicated enough faith and revolutionary energy to the Socialist construction of China. For example, they come to me and say, 'The Party does so much for me, and I do too little for the Party and my colleagues.' This idea sometimes becomes obsessive and even in some cases, a mania. At this point melancholia can result, which is still not a true neurosis."

Here I could no longer restrain myself. "The statements you have made seem paradoxical to a European. Quite honestly, it is difficult for me to believe them."

The professor bowed. "I understand perfectly. But first of all I will say to you that in spite of my scientific and cultural background in Europe, I am Chinese, a Marxist Chinese. I love the Chinese people much more than I do myself. These patients are my children and I am a father to them, for as you see I am old. I realize that to you, a European, what I have said may seem paradoxical. But the structure of relations among the Chinese would have seemed paradoxical to you even five centuries ago. It was very different from the West's. Five centures ago in Italy, humanism was at its apex while in China, to the contrary, not the individual but the Great Chinese Empire was at the zenith of its power. For the rest, I find myself unable to explain to you what seems a paradox, because, as I said, I am Chinese. I understand China; you do not. Perhaps staying here you could understand it too. We are able to understand you because European civilization is more explicit than implicit and, in general terms, much younger than that of China. Please don't take this phrase as an expression of nationalistic pride, which is quite strong in China but which would be very indelicate and probably vulgar to express to a foreign guest. I only want to say that you must not try to understand the mind of the Chinese, which is quite simple, sane and almost infantile, but rather the heart of the Chinese, which is very complicated, has suffered much pain and is old, ancient—so old that only the ear very well attuned to Chinese sounds can discover its beat."

29. THE ABSURD EFFORT TO MAKE THE WORLD OVER

william g. sumner

Several of the immediately preceding selections have stressed both the possibility and necessity of drastically reconstructing social life according to some moral or ideological master plan. Is this sort of planning, or "utopianism," helpful or harmful in building a humane future for man?

The author of the final selection in this section raises a series of strong objections to all such reformist efforts. How persuasive do you find his line of reasoning?

It will not probably be denied that the burden of proof is on those who affirm that our social condition is utterly diseased and in need of radical regeneration. My task at present, therefore, is entirely negative and critical: to examine the allegations of fact and the doctrines which are put forward to prove the correctness of the diagnosis and to warrant the use of the remedies proposed.

The propositions put forward by social reformers nowadays are chiefly of two kinds. There are assertions in historical form, chiefly in regard to the comparison of existing with earlier social states, which are plainly based on defective historical knowledge, or at most on current stock historical dicta which are uncritical and incorrect. Writers very often assert that something never existed before because they do not know that it ever existed before, or that something is worse than ever before because they are not possessed of detailed information about what has existed before. The other class of propositions consists of dogmatic statements which, whether true or not, are unverifiable. This class of propositions is the pest and bane of current economic and social discussion. Upon a more or less superficial view of some phenomenon a suggestion arises which is embodied in a philosophical proposition and promulgated as a truth. From the form and nature of such propositions they can always be brought under the head of "ethics." This word at least gives them an air of elevated sentiment and purpose, which is the only warrant they possess. It is impossible to test or verify them by any investigation or logical process whatsoever. It is therefore very difficult for anyone who feels a high responsibility for historical statements, and who absolutely rejects any statement which is unverifiable, to find a common

From A. G. Keller and Maurice R. Davie (eds.), *Essays of William Graham Sumner*. New Haven, Conn.: Yale University Press.

platform for discussion or to join issue satisfactorily in taking the negative.

When anyone asserts that the class of skilled and unskilled manual laborers of the United States is worse off now in respect to diet, clothing, lodgings, furniture, fuel, and lights; in respect to the age at which they can marry; the number of children they can provide for; the start in life which they can give to their children, and their chances of accumulating capital, than they ever have been at any former time, he makes a reckless assertion for which no facts have been offered in proof. Upon an appeal to facts, the contrary of this assertion would be clearly established. It suffices, therefore, to challenge those who are responsible for the assertion to make it good.

If it is said that the employed class are under much more stringent discipline than they were thirty years ago or earlier, it is true. It is not true that there has been any qualitative change in this respect within thirty years, but it is true that a movement which began at the first settlement of the country has been advancing with constant acceleration and has become a noticeable feature within our time. This movement is the advance in the industrial organization. The first settlement was made by agriculturists, and for a long time there was scarcely any organization. There were scattered farmers, each working for himself, and some small towns with only rudimentary commerce and handicrafts. As the country has filled up, the arts and professions have been differentiated and the industrial organization has been advancing. This fact and its significance has hardly been noticed at all; but the stage of the industrial organization existing at any time, and the rate of advance in its development, are the absolutely controlling social facts. Nine-tenths of the socialistic and semi-socialistic, and sentimental or ethical, suggestions by which we are overwhelmed come from failure to understand the phenomena of the industrial organization and its expansion. It controls us all because we are all in it. It creates the conditions of our existence, sets the limits of our social activity, regulates the bonds of our social relations, determines our conceptions of good and evil, suggests our life-philosophy, molds our inherited political institutions, and reforms the oldest and toughest customs, like marriage and property. I repeat that the turmoil of heterogeneous and antagonistic social whims and speculations in which we live is due to the failure to understand what the industrial organization is and its all-pervading control over human life, while the traditions of our school of philosophy lead us always to approach the industrial organization, not from the side of objective study, but from that of philosophical doctrine. Hence it is that we find that one method of measuring what we see happening by what are called ethical standards, and of proposing to attack the phenomena by methods thence deduced, is so popular.

The advance of a new country from the very simplest social coordination up to the highest organization is a most interesting and instructive chance to study the development of the organization. It has of course been attended all the way along by stricter subordination and higher discipline. All organization implies restriction of liberty. The gain of power is won by narrowing individual range. The methods of business in colonial days were loose and slack to an inconceivable degree. The movement of industry has been all the time toward promptitude, punctuality, and reliability. It has been attended all the way by lamentations about the good old times; about the decline of small industries; about the lost spirit of comradeship between employer and employee; about the narrowing of the interests of the workman; about his conversion into a machine or into a "ware," and about industrial war. These lamentations have all had reference to unquestionable phenomena attendant on advancing organization. In all occupations the same movement is discernible—in the learned professions, in schools, in trade, commerce, and transportation. It is to go on faster than ever, now that the continent is filled up by the first superficial layer of population over its whole extent and the intensification of industry has begun. The great inventions both make the intension of the organization possible and make it inevitable, with all its consequences, whatever they may be. I must expect to be told here, according to the current fashions of thinking, that we ought to control the development of the organization. The first instinct of the modern man is to get a law passed to forbid or prevent what, in his wisdom, he disapproves. A thing which is inevitable, however, is one which we cannot control. We have to make up our minds to it, adjust ourselves to it, and sit down to live with it. Its inevitableness may be disputed, in which case we must re-examine it; but if our analysis is correct, when we reach what is inevitable we reach the end, and our regulations must apply to ourselves, not to the social facts.

Now the intensification of the social organization is what gives us greater social power. It is to it that we owe our increased comfort and abundance. We are none of us ready to sacrifice this. On the contrary, we want more of it. We would not return to the colonial simplicity and the colonial exiguity if we could. If not, then we must pay the price. Our life is bounded on every side by conditions. We can have this if we will agree to submit to that. In the case of industrial power and product the great condition is combination of force under discipline and strict coordination. Hence the wild language about wage-slavery and capitalistic tyranny.

In any state of society no great achievements can be produced without great force. Formerly great force was attainable only by slavery aggregating the power of great numbers of men. Roman civilization was built on this. Ours has been built on steam. It is to be built on electricity. Then we are all forced into an organization around these natural forces and adapted to the methods or their application; and although we indulge in rhetoric about political liberty, nevertheless we find ourselves bound tight in a new set of conditions, which control the modes of our existence and determine the directions in which alone economic and social liberty can go.

If it is said that there are some persons in our time who have become rapidly and in a great degree rich, it is true; if it is said that large aggregations of wealth in the control of individuals is a social danger, it is not true.

The movement of the industrial organization which has just been described has brought out a great demand for men capable of managing great enterprises. Such have been called "captains of industry." The analogy with military leaders suggested by this name is not misleading. The great leaders in the development of the industrial organization need those talents of executive and administrative skill, power to command, courage, and fortitude, which were formerly called for in military affairs and scarcely anywhere else. The industrial army is also as dependent on its captains as a military body is on its generals. One of the worst features of the existing system is that the employees have a constant risk in their employer. If he is not competent to manage the business with success, they suffer with him. Capital also is dependent on the skill of the captain of industry for the certainty and magnitude of its profits. Under these circumstances there has been a great demand for men having the requisite ability for this function. As the organization has advanced, with more impersonal bonds of coherence and wider scope of operations, the value of this functionary has rapidly increased. The possession of the requisite ability is a natural monopoly. Consequently, all the conditions have concurred to give to those who possessed this monopoly excessive and constantly advancing rates of remuneration.

Another social function of the first importance in an intense organization is the solution of those crises in the operation of it which are called the conjuncture of the market. It is through the market that the lines of relation run which preserve the system in harmonious and rhythmical operation. The conjuncture is the momentary sharper misadjustment of supply and demand which indicates that a redistribution of productive effort is called for. The industrial organization needs to be insured against these conjunctures, which, if neglected, produce a crisis and catastrophe; and it needs that they shall be anticipated and guarded against as far as skill and foresight can do it. The rewards of this function for the bankers and capitalists who perform it are very great. The captains of industry and the capitalists who operate on the conjuncture, therefore, if they are successful, win, in these days, great fortunes in a short time. There are no earnings which are more legitimate or for which greater services are tendered to the whole industrial body. The popular notions about this matter really assume that all the wealth accumulated by these classes of persons would be here just the same if they had not existed. They are supposed to have appropriated it out of the common stock. This is so far from being true that, on the contrary, their own wealth would not be but for themselves; and besides that, millions more of wealth, many-fold greater than their own, scattered in the hands of thousands, would not exist but for them.

Within the last two years I have traveled from end to end of the German Empire several times on all kinds of trains. I reached the conviction, looking at the matter from the passenger's standpoint, that, if the Germans could find a Vanderbilt and put their railroads in his hands for twenty-five years, letting him reorganize the system and make twenty-five million dollars out of it for himself in that period, they would make an excellent bargain.

But it is repeated until it has become a commonplace which people are afraid to question, that there is some social danger in the possession of large amounts of wealth by individuals. I ask, Why? I heard a lecture two years ago by a man who holds perhaps the first chair of political economy in the world. He said, among other things, that there was great danger in our day from great accumulations; that this danger ought to be met by taxation, and he referred to the fortune of the Rothschilds and to the great fortunes made in America to prove his point. He omitted, however, to state in what the danger consisted or to specify what harm has ever been done by the Rothschild fortunes or by the great fortunes accumulated in America. It seemed to me that the assertions he was making, and the measures he was recommending, ex-cathedra, were very serious to be thrown out so recklessly. It is hardly to be expected that novelists, popular magazinists, amateur economists, and politicians will be more responsible. It would be easy, however, to show what good is done by accumulations of capital in a few hands—that is, under close and direct management, permitting prompt and accurate application; also to tell what harm is done by loose and unfounded denunciations of any social component or any social group. In the recent debates on the income tax the assumption that great accumulations of wealth are socially harmful and ought to be broken down by taxation was treated as an axiom, and we had direct proof how dangerous it is to fit out the average politician with such unverified and unverifiable dogmas as his warrant for his modes of handling the direful tool of taxation.

Great figures are set out as to the magnitude of certain fortunes and the proportionate amount of the national wealth held by a fraction of the population, and eloquent exclamation-points are set against them. If the figures were beyond criticism, what would they prove? Where is the rich man who is oppressing anybody? If there was one, the newspapers would ring with it. The facts about the accumulation of wealth do not constitute a plutocracy, as I will show below. Wealth, in itself considered, is only power, like steam, or electricity, or knowledge. The question of its good or ill turns on the question how it will be used. To prove any harm in aggregations of wealth it must be shown that great wealth is, as a rule, in the ordinary course of social affairs, put to a mischievous use. This cannot be shown beyond the very slightest degree, if at all.

Therefore, all the allegations of general mischief, social corruption, wrong, and evil in our society must be referred back to those who make them for particulars and specifications. As they are offered to us we cannot allow them to stand, because we discern in them faulty observation of facts, or incorrect interpretation of facts, or a construction of facts according to some philosophy, or misunderstanding of phenomena and their relations, or incorrect inferences, or crooked deductions.

Assuming, however, that the charges against the existing "capitalistic"— that is, industrial—order of things are established, it is proposed to remedy the ill by reconstructing the industrial system on the principles of democracy. Once more we must untangle the snarl of half ideas and muddled facts.

Democracy is, of course, a word to conjure with. We have a democratic-republican political system, and we like it so well that we are prone to take any new step which can be recommended as "democratic" or which will round out some "principle" of democracy to a fuller fulfillment. Everything connected with this domain of political thought is crusted over with false historical traditions, cheap philosophy, and undefined terms, but it is useless to try to criticize it. The whole drift of the world for five hundred years has been toward democracy. That drift, produced by great discoveries and inventions, and by the discovery of a new continent, has raised the middle class out of the servile class. In alliance with the crown they crushed the feudal classes. They made the crown absolute in order to do it. Then they turned against the crown and, with the aid of the handicraftsmen and peasants, conquered it. Now the next conflict which must inevitably come is that between the middle capitalist class and the proletariat, as the word has come to be used. If a certain construction is put on this conflict, it may be called that between democracy and plutocracy, for it seems that industrialism must be developed into plutocracy by the conflict itself. That is the conflict which stands before civilized society to-day. All the signs of the times indicate its commencement, and it is big with fate to mankind and to civilization.

Although we cannot criticize democracy profitably, it may be said of it, with reference to our present subject, that up to this time democracy never has done anything, either in politics, social affairs, or industry, to prove its power to bless mankind. If we confine our attention to the United States, there are three difficulties with regard to its alleged achievements, and they all have the most serious bearing on the proposed democratization of industry.

1. The time during which democracy has been tried in the United States is too short to warrant any inferences. A century or two is a very short time in the life of political institutions, and if the circumstances change rapidly during the period the experiment is vitiated.

2. The greatest question of all about American democracy is whether it is a cause or a consequence. It is popularly assumed to be a cause, and we ascribe to its beneficent action all the political vitality, all the easiness of social relations, all the industrial activity and enterprise which we experience and which we value and enjoy. I submit, however, that, on a more thorough examination of the matter, we shall find that democracy is a consequence. There are economic and sociological causes for our political vitality and

vigor, for the ease and elasticity of our social relations, and for our industrial power and success. Those causes have also produced democracy, given it success, and have made its faults and errors innocuous. Indeed, in any true philosophy, it must be held that in the economic forces which control the material prosperity of a population lie the real causes of its political institutions, its social class-adjustments, its industrial prosperity, its moral code, and its world-philosophy. If democracy and the industrial system are both products of the economic conditions which exist, it is plainly absurd to set democracy to defeat those conditions in the control of industry. If, however, it is not true that democracy is a consequence, and I am well aware that very few people believe it, then we must go back to the view that democracy is a cause. That being so, it is difficult to see how democracy, which has had a clear field here in America, is not responsible for the ills which Mr. Bellamy and his comrades in opinion see in our present social state, and it is difficult to see the grounds of asking us to intrust it also with industry. The first and chief proof of success of political measures and systems is that, under them, society advances in health and vigor and that industry develops without causing social disease. If this has not been the case in America, American democracy has not succeeded. Neither is it easy to see how the masses, if they have undertaken to rule, can escape the responsibilities of ruling, especially so far as the consequences affect themselves. If, then, they have brought all this distress upon themselves under the present system, what becomes of the argument for extending the system to a direct and complete control of industry?

3. It is by no means certain that democracy in the United States has not, up to this time, been living on a capital inherited from aristocracy and industrialism. We have no pure democracy. Our democracy is limited at every turn by institutions which were developed in England in connection with industrialism and aristocracy, and these institutions are of the essence of our system. While our people are passionately democratic in temper and will not tolerate a doctrine that one man is not as good as another, they have common sense enough to know that he is not; and it seems that they love and cling to the conservative institutions quite as strongly as they do to the democratic philosophy. They are, therefore, ruled by men who talk philosophy and govern by the institutions. Now it is open to Mr. Bellamy to say that the reason why democracy in America seems to be open to the charge made in the last paragraph, of responsibility for all the ill which he now finds in our society, is because it has been infected with industrialism (capitalism); but in that case he must widen the scope of his proposition and undertake to purify democracy before turning industry over to it. The socialists generally seem to think that they make their undertakings easier when they widen their scope, and make them easiest when they propose to remake everything; but in truth social tasks increase in difficulty in an enormous ratio as they are widened in scope.

The question, therefore, arises, if it is proposed to reorganize the social system on the principles of American democracy, whether the institutions of industrialism are to be retained. If so, all the virus of capitalism will be retained. It is forgotten, in many schemes of social reformation in which it is proposed to mix what we like with what we do not like, in order to extirpate the latter, that each must undergo a reaction from the other, and that what we like may be extirpated by what we do not like. We may find that instead of democratizing capitalism we have capitalized democracy—that is, have brought in plutocracy. Plutocracy is a political system in which the ruling force is wealth. The denunciation of capital which we hear from all the reformers is the most eloquent proof that the greatest power in the world to-day is capital. They know that it is, and confess it most when they deny it most strenuously. At present the power of capital is social and industrial, and only in a small degree political. So far as capital is political, it is on account of political abuses, such as tariffs and special legislation on the one hand and legislative strikes on the other. These conditions exist in the democracy to which it is proposed to transfer the industries. What does that mean except bringing all the power of capital once for all into the political arena and precipitating the conflict of democracy and plutocracy at once? Can anyone imagine that the masterfulness, the overbearing disposition, the greed of gain, and the ruthlessness in methods, which are the faults of the master of industry at his worst, would cease when he was a functionary of the State, which had relieved him of risk and endowed him with authority? Can anyone imagine that politicians would no longer be corruptly fond of money, intriguing, and crafty when they were charged, not only with patronage and government contracts, but also with factories, stores, ships, and railroads? Could we expect anything except that, when the politician and the master of industry were joined in one, we should have the vices of both unchecked by the restraints of either? In any socialistic state there will be one set of positions which will offer chances of wealth beyond the wildest dreams of avarice; *viz.,* on the governing committees. Then there will be rich men whose wealth will indeed be a menace to social interests, and instead of industrial peace there will be such war as no one has dreamed of yet: the war between the political ins and outs—that is, between those who are on the committee and those who want to get on it.

We must not drop the subject of democracy without one word more. The Greeks already had occasion to notice a most serious distinction between two principles of democracy which lie at its roots. Plutarch says that Solon got the archonship in part by promising equality, which some understood of esteem and dignity, others of measure and number. There is one democratic principle which means that each man should be esteemed for his merit and worth, for just what he is, without regard to birth, wealth, rank, or other adventitious circumstances. The other principle is that each one of us ought to be equal to all the others in what he gets and enjoys. The first principle is only partially realizable, but, so far as it goes, it is elevating and socially progressive and profitable. The second is not capable of an intelligible statement. The first is a principle of industrialism. It proceeds from and is intelligible only in a society built on the industrial virtues, free endeavor, security of property, and repression of the baser vices; that is, in a society whose industrial system is built on labor and exchange. The other is only a rule of division for robbers who have to divide plunder or monks who have to divide gifts. If, therefore, we want to democratize industry in the sense of the first principle, we need only perfect what we have now, especially on its political side. If we try to democratize it in the sense of the other principle, we corrupt politics at one stroke; we enter upon an industrial enterprise which will waste capital and bring us all to poverty, and we set loose greed and envy as ruling social passions.

If this poor old world is as bad as they say, one more reflection may check the zeal of the headlong reformer. It is at any rate a tough old world. It has taken its trend and curvature and all its twists and tangles from a long course of formation. All its wry and crooked gnarls and knobs are therefore stiff and stubborn. If we puny men by our arts can do anything at all to straighten them, it will only be by modifying the tendencies of some of the forces at work, so that, after a sufficient time, their action may be changed a little and slowly the lines of movement may be modified. This effort, however, can at most be only slight, and it will take a long time. In the meantime spontaneous forces will be at work, compared with which our efforts are like those of a man trying to deflect a river, and these forces will have changed the whole problem before our interferences have time to make themselves felt. The great stream of time and earthly things will sweep on just the same in spite of us. It bears with it now all the errors and follies of the past, the wreckage of all the philosophies, the fragments of all the civilizations, the wisdom of all the abandoned ethical systems, the debris of all the institutions, and the penalties of all the mistakes. It is only in imagination that we stand by and look at and criticize it and plan to change it. Everyone of us is a child of his age and cannot get out of it. He is in the stream and is swept along with it. All his sciences and philosophy come to him out of it. Therefore the tide will not be changed by us. It will shallow up both us and our experiments. It will absorb the efforts at change and take them into itself as new but trivial components, and the great movement of tradition and work will go on unchanged by our fads and schemes. The things which will change it are the great discoveries and inventions, the new reactions inside the social organism, and the changes in the earth itself on account of changes in the cosmical forces. These causes will make of it just what, in fidelity to them, it ought to be. The men will be carried along with it and be made by it. The utmost they can do by their cleverness will be to note and record their course as they are carried along, which is what we do now, and is that which leads us to the vain fancy that we can make or guide the movement. That is why it is the greatest folly of which a man can be capable, to sit down with a slate and pencil to plan out a new social world.

part

four

DISEQUILIBRIUM AND SOCIAL CONFLICT
protest and the crisis of values

Man's efforts to insure cooperation and control, while impressive, have yet to overcome his bent toward conflict and destruction. The present era of strife and conflict, rather than reflecting a humanistic refinement of centuries of social engineering, points to the frailty of his efforts toward harmony. Indeed, it could be argued that man's capacity for destruction has paralleled his success at cooperative social and technological development. Along with improvement in his capacity for cooperation and development, man has simultaneously expanded the magnitude of his problems. Part Four examines the sources, manifestations, and repercussions of conflict in modern society.

The selections in Section I explore the psychological sources of human conflict. The initial selection, taken from the *Leviathan* of Thomas Hobbes, represents the classic statement of man's inherent aggressiveness, greed, and amorality. In the two articles that follow, psychologists Gordon W. Allport and Elton B. McNeil offer clear scientific support for Hobbes' intuitive judgments.

Section II turns from the psychological to the institutional sources of human conflict in modern society. Supreme Court Justice William O. Douglas argues that the vigorous dissent and intellectual ferment once providing the life blood of the American political system is now enmeshed in official channels that are clogged and unresponsive. A little rebellion, Justice Douglas implies, might be a necessary thing. Nuclear physicist Herman Kahn outlines more than ten ways through which the United States could stumble into nuclear war. Kenneth Keniston examines violence and change among American youth, while Gilbert Abcarian discusses mounting alienation and right-wing extremism among ultraconservative Americans, and John B. Kirby explores connections between violence and conflict over values. The discussion next turns to a *Time* essay on changing sexual norms in the United States, then to a penetrating analysis of the crisis of modern women by feminist Ann Doubilet. In the final article of the section, conservationist Rene Dubos outlines in painful detail the ecological crisis facing the United States as well as the rest of the world.

Section III focuses on a special kind of crisis in American society—that of the American city. The initial selections, "Rioting, Insurrection, and Civil Disobedience" by Ralph W. Conant, and "Report on Civil Disorders" focus on the various sociological, psychological, economic, and political causes of urban decay and disorganization. These penetrating views are followed by Paul Jacobs' "Viewing America from the Bottom," a graphic account of how America looks, for example, from the eyes of the ghetto black or Puerto Rican.

Having examined the origins and manifestations of the various crises of modern civilization, Section IV examines various responses to the mounting pressures of social disorganization. Black Panther leader Eldridge Cleaver analyzes the dilemmas of the black man striving to survive in a white society. Sociologists Staughton Lynd and Robert Lindner analyze protest among youth in "The New Left" and "Prescription for Rebellion." Karl Menninger examines some absurdities of criminal punishment. Finally, Eric Hoffer vividly describes authoritarianism as a desperate attempt by many, especially members of the middle class, to escape an "unwanted self" by joining social movements.

SOCIAL STRESS
sources of conflict and disintegration

30. MAN IS A THREAT TO SOCIETY
thomas hobbes

The distinction between human passion and reason has fascinated social philosophers for centuries. Early social philosophers were fond of cataloging specific human passions, treating them as natural qualities of human personality. In his famous *Leviathan,* first published in 1651, Hobbes accepts the premise that man's nature is characterized by certain passions that threaten social order. But he suggests that one of these in particular—the fear of death—provides a rational solution to the "condition of war of one against the other," namely, common consent to entrust complete power to an absolute Sovereign in return for peace and security.

Is the individual antisocial "by nature"? Is he a friend or enemy of social unity and security? To what extent may social stress and crisis be traced to the individual as such?

So that in the nature of man, we find three principall causes of quarrell. First, Competition; Secondly, Diffidence; Thirdly, Glory.

The first, maketh men invade for Gain; the second, for Safety; and the third, for Reputation. The first use Violence, to make themselves Masters of other mens persons, wives, children, and cattell; the second, to defend them; the third, for trifles, as a word, a smile, a different opinion, and any other signe of undervalue, either direct in their Persons, or by reflexion in their Kindred, their Friends, their Nation, their Profession, or their Name.

Hereby it is manifest, that during the time men live without a common Power to keep them all in awe, they are in that condition which is called Warre; and such a warre, as is of every man, against every man. For Warre,

From Thomas Hobbes, *Leviathan.*

consisteth not in Battell onely, or the act of fighting; but in a tract of time, wherein the Will to contend by Battell is sufficiently known: and therefore the notion of *Time,* is to be considered in the nature of Warre; as it is in the nature of Weather. For as the nature of Foule weather, lyeth not in a showre or two of rain; but in an inclination thereto of many dayes together: So the nature of War, consisteth not in actuall fighting; but in the known disposition thereto, during all the time there is no assurance to the contrary. All other time is PEACE.

Whatsoever therefore is consequent to a time of Warre, where every man is Enemy to every man; the same is consequent to the time, wherein men live without other security, than what their own strength, and their own invention shall furnish them withall. In such condition, there is no place for Industry; because the fruit thereof is uncertain: and consequently no Culture of the Earth; no Navigation, nor use of the commodities that may be imported by Sea; no commodious Building; no Instruments of moving, and removing such things as require much force; no Knowledge of the face of the Earth; no account of Time; no Arts; no Letters; no Society; and which is worst of all, continuall feare, and danger of violent death; And the life of man, solitary, poore, nasty, brutish, and short.

It may seem strange to some man, that has not well weighed these things; that Nature should thus dissociate, and render men apt to invade, and destroy one another: and he may therefore, not trusting to this Inference, made from the Passions, desire perhaps to have the same confirmed by Experience. Let him therefore consider with himselfe, when taking a journey, he armes himselfe, and seeks to go well accompanied; when going to sleep, he locks his dores; when even in his house he locks his chests; and this when he knowes there bee Lawes, and publike Officers, armed, to revenge all injuries shall bee done him; what opinion he has of his fellow subjects, when he rides armed; of his fellow Citizens, when he locks his dores; and of his children, and servants, when he locks his chests. Does he not there as much accuse mankind by his actions, as I do by my words? But neither of us accuse mans nature in it. The Desires, and other Passions of man, are in themselves no Sin. No more are the Actions, that proceed from those Passions, till they know a Law that forbids them: which till Lawes be made they cannot know: nor can any Law be made, till they have agreed upon the Person that shall make it.

It may peradventure be thought, there was never such a time, nor condition of warre as this; and I believe it was never generally so, over all the world: but there are many places, where they live so now. For the savage people in many places of *America,* except the government of small Families, the concord whereof dependeth on naturall lust, have no government at all; and live at this day in that brutish manner, as I said before. Howsoever, it may be perceived what manner of life there would be, where there were no common Power to feare; by the manner of life, which men that have formerly lived under a peacefull government, use to degenerate into, in a civil Warre.

But though there had never been any time, wherein particular men were in a condition of warre one against another; yet in all times, Kings, and Persons of Soveraigne authority, because of their Independency, are in continuall jealousies, and in the state of posture of Gladiators; having their weapons pointing, and their eyes fixed on one another; that is, their Forts, Garrisons, and Guns upon the Frontiers of their Kingdomes; and continuall Spyes upon their neighbours; which is a posture of War. But because they uphold thereby, the Industry of their Subjects; there does not follow from it, that misery, which accompanies the Liberty of particular men.

To this warre of every man against every man, this also is consequent; that nothing can be Unjust. The notions of Right and Wrong, Justice and Injustice have there no place. Where there is no common Power, there is no Law: where no Law, no Injustice. Force, and Fraud, are in warre the two Cardinall vertues. Justice, and Injustice are none of the Faculties neither of the Body, nor Mind. If they were, they might be in a man that were alone in the world, as well as his Senses, and Passions. They are Qualities, that relate to men in Society, not in Solitude. It is consequent also to the same condition, that there be no Propriety, no Dominion, no *Mine* and *Thine* distinct; but onely that to be every mans, that he can get; and for so long, as he can keep it. And thus much for the ill condition, which man by meer Nature is actually placed in; though with a possibility to come out of it, consisting partly in the Passions, partly in his Reason.

The Passions that encline men to Peace, are Feare of Death; Desire of such things as are necessary to commodious living; and a Hope by their Industry to obtain them. And Reason suggesteth convenient Articles of Peace, upon which men may be drawn to agreement. These Articles, are they, which otherwise are called the Lawes of Nature.

31. ANXIETY, SEX, AND GUILT

gordon w. allport

The preceding selection examined human nature as a source of social conflict. Utilizing many of the same themes, the following selection, a classic in the literature of social psychology, illustrates graphically how sexual and economic anxieties result in individual and group conflict.

Based on your own experiences, are the sources of anxiety described in this selection increasing or decreasing? If the former, what can be done about it?

From Gordon W. Allport, *The Nature of Prejudice*, 1954, Addison-Wesley, Reading, Mass.

FEAR AND ANXIETY

Rational and adaptive fear entails the accurate perception of the source of danger. An illness, an approaching fire or flood, a highwayman are among the conditions that make for realistic fear. When we perceive the source of the threat accurately, we ordinarily strike back at it or withdraw to safety.

Sometimes the source of the fear is correctly perceived, but the person can do nothing to control it. A workman fearful of losing his job or citizens living in a vague apprehension of atomic warfare are swayed by fear, but they are powerless. Under such circumstances, the fear becomes chronic—and we speak of *anxiety.*

Chronic anxiety puts us on the alert and predisposes us to see all sorts of stimuli as menacing. A man who lives in constant dread of losing his job feels surrounded by danger. He is sensitized to perceive the Negro or the foreigner as trying to take his job away from him. Here is a displacement of a realistic fear.

Sometimes the source of the fear is not known, or has been forgotten or repressed. The fear may be merely a mounting residue of inner feelings of weakness in dealing with the hazards of the outer world. Time and again the sufferer may have failed to win in his encounters with life. He thus develops a generalized feeling of inadequacy. He is fearful of life itself. He is afraid of his own ineffectiveness and grows suspicious of other people whose greater competence he regards as a threat.

Anxiety then is a diffuse, irrational fear, not directed at an appropriate target and not controlled by self-insight. Like a grease spot, it has spread throughout the life and stains the individual's social relationships. Because he is far from satisfied in his affiliative needs, he may become compulsive— overpossessive toward some people (his own children, perhaps)—and over-rejective toward others. But these compulsive social relationships create further anxieties, and the vicious circle is intensified.

Existentialists tell us that anxiety is basic in every life. It is more prominent than aggression because the very conditions of human existence are mysterious and dreadful, though they are not always frustrating. It is for this reason that fear becomes even more readily diffused and character-conditioned than does aggression.

Anxiety, however, is like aggression in that people tend to be ashamed of it. Our ethical codes place a premium on courage and self-reliance. Pride and self-respect lead us to mask our anxiety. While we repress it in part, we also give it a displaced outlet—upon socially sanctioned sources of fear. Some people suffer an almost hysterical fear of "communists" in our midst. It is a socially allowable phobia. The same people would not be respected if they admitted the real source of much of their anxiety, which lies in personal inadequacy and dread of life.

There may, of course, be elements of realistic fear mingled with displaced fear. Communists in our midst do constitute a menace, though to a lesser degree than many demagogues and phobiacs would have us believe. A remarkable shift in public opinion came after Japan was defeated. Previously, the animosity knew no bounds. Not only was the nation considered sly and subhuman, but even loyal Japanese-Americans were herded into "relocation" camps. In 1943 the Russians were loved, the Japanese feared. Five years later the situation had more or less reversed itself. This shift demonstrates that a core of realism may be present even in conditions where much displacement is also taking place. Men are rational enough to *prefer* plausible targets for their fears if they are available.

So far as our knowledge now extends, it seems probable that the principal source of character-conditioned anxiety comes from a bad start in early life. In previous chapters we have several times noted the peculiarities of child training that may arouse lasting anxiety. The male child, in particular, strives against odds to achieve a masculine role, and may carry lasting anxiety with him concerning the degree of his success. The rejective parent creates a condition of profound apprehension that we know may underlie nervous disorders, delinquency, and hostility. The following case is by no means extreme, but serves to illustrate the subtlety of the process that may be involved.

When George was four years old his mother gave birth to his baby brother. George was fearful lest his baby brother displace him in his mother's affection. He worried and fretted, and came to hate his younger brother. The baby was ailing and the mother did, in fact, give more of her attention to him than to George. The four-year-old felt increasingly resentful and insecure. He tried at times to injure his young brother but was, of course, restrained and punished. Unfortunately, the mother died before she could restore the balance. George never recovered from the double deprivation.

When he entered school he was of a suspicious nature. He particularly resented strangers coming into the neighborhood, and had a fist fight with each newcomer. This method of testing strangers is common enough in boyhood circles. They must prove themselves to be regular guys in order to be accepted. Within a few weeks the distrust of the stranger is dissolved and the old boys and the new come to terms.

But there were certain types of strangers that George could not accept, even after the initial ritual of the fist fight. They were boys who seemed to him definitely alien to the community. They were so different that (like his baby brother) they seemed unassimilable intruders. They had odd homes, odd foods, odd coloring, and observed queer holidays. The strangeness would not wear off. The newcomer stood out sharply, was everywhere visible (like the baby brother of his earlier years). George's initial suspicion and hostility just didn't dissolve. He would accept boys who were like him (self-love), but he would reject boys who were alien to his self-image (symbols of his baby brother). Difference in ethnic membership came for George to have the same functional significance as the difference between him and his sibling rival.

In the community there are many Georges not necessarily working out their sibling rivalry but, for other reasons connected with early deprivations, suffering from nameless apprehension. Like George, they perceive differences between people as menacing. Feeling anxious for no consciously ascertainable reason, they seek to discover a cause for their anxiety. It lies, they decide, in some difference that can be rationalized as a source of their dread. When all the anxious Georges in a community put their fears together and agree on an imagined cause (the Negro, the Jew, the communist), a great deal of fear-produced hostility may result.

ECONOMIC INSECURITY

While much anxiety has its origin in childhood, the adult years are also potent sources, especially in connection with economic insufficiency. We have already cited considerable evidence to the effect that downward mobility, periods of unemployment and depression, and general economic dissatisfaction are all positively correlated with prejudice.

Sometimes, as we have likewise seen, there may be a realistic conflict involved, as when the upgrading of Negro workmen creates more competitors for certain jobs. It is not inconceivable, too, that members of one ethnic group may actually conspire to gain a monopoly of a business, a factory, or an occupation. But ordinarily, the "threat" that is felt is not geared to realities in that situation. The apprehensive and marginal man is vaguely terrified at any signs of ambition or progress on the part of any member of the out-group, whether or not it may constitute a realistic danger.

In most countries, people grow fiercely possessive of their property. It is a bastion of conservatism. Any threat, real or imagined, will invoke anxiety and anger (this blend is particularly suited to the growth of hatred). A grim reflection of this relationship is found in the experience of many Jews who were sent to concentration camps in central Europe during the Nazi control. These Jews often entrusted their property to some gentile friend. Most of the Jews were killed, and the property automatically became that of the friend. But occasionally a Jew returned, and found that he was cordially hated for claiming his property, which perhaps had been used up by the trustee, sometimes to buy food. One Jew, foreseeing this outcome, refused to ask gentile friends to guard his goods, saying, "Isn't it enough for my enemies to want me to die? I don't want my friends also to want me dead."

Outright greed is certainly a cause of prejudice. If we took a historical over-view of feelings against colonial people, Jews, and aborigines (including the American Indian), we should probably find that rationalization of greed is a principal source. The formula is simple enough: greed → grabbing → justifying.

The role of economic apprehension in anti-Semitism has often been commented on. In the United States it seems that the well-to-do are especially prone to anti-Semitism. The reason may be that the Jew is seen as a symbolic competitor. To keep him down is to avoid symbolically all potential threat. Hence he is excluded not only from occupations, but also from schools, clubs, neighborhoods. In this way a specious feeling of security and superiority results. McWilliams characterizes the total process as a "mask for privilege."

SELF-ESTEEM

Economic worries have their origins in hunger and the need to survive. But they continue to exist long after this rational function has been fulfilled. They ramify into the need for status, prestige, self-esteem. Food is no longer the issue, nor is money—excepting so far as it can buy that one thing in life that is always short in supply: *differential status.*

Not everyone can be "on top." Not everyone wants to be. But most people want to be higher on the status ladder than they are. "This hunger," writes Murphy, "operates like a vitamin deficiency." He regards it as the primary root of ethnic prejudice.

The hunger for status is matched by a haunting fear that one's status may not be secure. The effort to maintain a precarious position can bring with it an almost reflex disparagement of others. Asch gives one instance:

> We observe this in the racial pride of Southerners, in the preoccupation with face-saving and self-justification, which are probably born of deep, mostly not conscious but also not bearable, doubts of their position. Sectional pride in the face of the North, the pride of a decaying landed group in the face of a newly arising industrial order, the pride of the new industrialist in the face of the old aristocracy, of the wretched poor white in the face of the precariously inferior Negro—these are the reactions of a people unsure whether their failures are not their own fault.

The philosopher Hume once pointed out that envy seems to appear only when the distance between ourselves and those more fortunate than ourselves is small enough so that we can reasonably compare ourselves with them—the "narcissism of small differences." A schoolboy does not envy Aristotle, but he may envy his neighbor whose "A" in a course of study makes his own grades seem intolerably low. Slaves probably did not envy their rich masters—the gap was too great—but they may well have envied other slaves who had positions of favor. Whenever rigid class distinctions break down or mobility increases, there is much more occasion for envy. Americans are near enough to one another in education, opportunity, freedom, to feel envy for one another. That is why, paradoxically enough, augmented hatred may well accompany diminished class distance.

The easiest idea to sell anyone is that he is better than someone else. The appeal of the Ku Klux Klan and racist agitators rests on this type of salesmanship. Snobbery is a way of clutching at one's status, and it is as common, perhaps more common, among those who are low in the ladder. By turning their attention to unfavored out-groups, they are able to derive from the comparison a modicum of self-esteem. Out-groups, as status builders, have the special advantage of being near at hand, visible (or at least nameable), and occupying a lower position by common agreement, thus providing social support for one's own sense of status enhancement.

The theme of egoism (status) has run through many of our chapters. Perhaps Murphy is right in regarding it as the "primary root" of prejudice. Our purpose in the present discussion is to bring this theme into proper relation with the factors of fear and anxiety. High status, we feel, would abolish our basic apprehensions, and for this reason we struggle to achieve a secure position for ourselves—often at the expense of our fellows.

SEXUALITY

Sex, like anger or fear, may ramify throughout the life, and may affect social attitudes in devious ways. Like these other emotions, it is less diffuse when it is rationally and adaptively directed. But in sexual maladjustment, frustration, and conflict, a tenseness spreads outward from the erotic area of the life into many by-paths. Some maintain that it is impossible to understand group prejudice in the United States, particularly the prejudice of whites toward Negroes, without reference to sex maladjustment. Dingwall, a British anthropologist, writes:

> Sex dominates life in the United States in a manner and in a way which is found nowhere else in the world. Without a full appreciation of its influence and its results, no elucidation of the Negro problem is possible.

We may overlook the unproved assertion that Americans are more sex-ridden than people in other countries, while at the same time admitting that an important issue has been raised.

A housewife in a northern city was asked whether she would object to Negroes living on the same street. She replied,

> I wouldn't want to live with Negroes. They smell too much. They're of a different race. That's what creates racial hatreds. When I sleep with a Negro in the same bed, I'll live with them. But you know we can't.

Here the sexual barricade intrudes itself into a logically unrelated issue—the simple question of residence on the same street.

It is by no means only anti-Negro prejudice that reveals sex interest and sex accusations. An advertisement for an anti-Catholic pamphlet reads as follows:

See the nun bound hand and foot, gagged, lying in a dungeon because she refused to obey a priest. . . . Read about nun locked in a room stark naked with three drunken priests. . . . Poison, Murder, Rapine, Torturing and smothering babies. . . . If you want to know what goes on behind convent walls read this book *House of Death* or *Convent Brutality*.

The linking of lechery with the Roman Catholic Church (known also as "the mother of harlots") is an old and familiar trick of Catholic-haters. Dark tales of sexual debauchery were common a century ago, and were part of the whispering campaign of the Know-Nothing political party that flourished at that time.

The fierce persecution of the Mormons in the Nineteenth Century was related to their doctrine, and occasional practice, of polygamy. Granted that plural marriage, ended by law in 1896, was an unsound social policy, a prurience of interest and licentiousness of fantasies were revealed in the anti-Mormon tracts of the time. The opposition to the sect drew nourishment from the conflict that many people had within their own sex lives. Why should others be allowed a wider choice of sex partners than they? And during the 1920's perhaps the commonest accusation against communist Russia was that it "nationalized" its women.

In Europe it is common to accuse the Jews of gross sexual immorality. They are said to be given to overindulgence, rape, perversion. Hitler, whose own sex life was far from normal, contrived over and over again to accuse the Jews of perversion, of having syphilis, and of other disorders suspiciously akin to Hitler's own phobias. Streicher, the Number One Nazi Jew-baiter, at least in private conversation, mentioned circumcision about as often as he mentioned Jew. Some peculiar complex seemed to be haunting him (Could it be his castration-anxiety?), which he managed to project upon the Jews.

In America one seldom hears sex accusations against the Jews. Is it because there is less anti-Semitism? Is it that American Jews are more moral than European Jews? Neither explanation seems right. The reason, more probably is that in America we have in the Negro a preferred target for our sexual complexes.

There is a subtle psychological reason why Negroid characteristics favor an association of ideas with sex. The Negro seems dark, mysterious, distant— yet at the same time warm, human, and potentially accessible. These elements of mystery and forbiddenness are present in sex appeal in a Puritanical society. Sex is forbidden; colored people are forbidden; the ideas begin to fuse. It is no accident that prejudiced people call tolerant people "niggerlovers." The very choice of the word suggests that they are fighting the feeling of attraction in themselves.

The fact that interracial sex attraction exists is proved by the millions of mixed breeds in the country. Differences in color and social status seem to be sexually exciting rather than repelling. It has often been noted that liaisons with members of lower classes seem particularly attractive to people with higher status. The daughter of the patrician family who runs away with the coachman is almost as familiar a theme in literature as is the prodigal son who wastes his substance in riotous living with lower-class women. Both reveal the same truth.

We note that sun-bathing is for the purpose of darkening the skin—and is a pastime indulged in by male and female alike to enhance their attractiveness. There is intrigue in contrasting complexions. Moreno has reported that homosexual crushes between white and Negro adolescent girls were common in a reformatory, for difference in skin color in many instances seemed to serve as a functional substitute for difference in sex.

The attraction is further enhanced by the fact (or legend) that Negroes have an open and unashamed way of looking at life. Many people with suppressed sex lives would like the same freedom. They grow jealous and irritated at the openness and directness of sex life among others. They accuse the males of extreme sexual potency, and the females of shamelessness. Even the size of the genitalia becomes a subject of jealous exaggeration. Fantasies easily get mixed with fact.

This illicit fascination may become obsessional in some localities where life is otherwise intolerably dull. In her novel *Strange Fruit,* Lillian Smith has described the emotional aridness of a small southern town. Escape is sought in religious orgies, or in the excitement of race conflict. Or people may see in the Negro the lusty qualities they lack, and may alternately ridicule, desire, and persecute them. Forbidden fruit arouses contrasting emotional reactions. Helen McLean writes:

> In calling the Negro a child of nature, simple, lovable, without ambition, a person who gives way to his every impulse, white men have made a symbol which gives a secret gratification to those who are inhibited and crippled in their instinctual satisfactions. Indeed, white men are very loath to relinquish such a symbol.

Now this common cross-race sexual fascination seldom expresses itself normally. The mixed dating of adolescents is virtually a social impossibility. Legal intermarriage, where possible at all, is rare and is bedeviled by social complications that create grave problems even for the most devoted couples. Hence sexual liaisons are clandestine, illicit, and accompanied by feelings of guilt. Yet the fascination is so strong that this most rigid of taboos is frequently broken, more often by the white male, however, than by the white female.

The psychodynamic process that relates this sexual situation to prejudice may be described separately for the white female and white male. (It must, of course, be understood that not every individual is affected in the same way; but the process is probably common enough to be an important factor in the establishment and maintenance of prejudice.)

Suppose a white woman is fascinated by the taboo against the Negro male. She is unlikely to admit, even to herself, that she finds his color and lower status attractive. She may, however, "project" her feelings, and accordingly imagine that the desire exists on the *other* side—that Negro males have sexually aggressive tendencies toward her. What is an inner temptation is perceived as an outer threat. Overgeneralizing her conflict, she develops an anxiety and hostility respecting the whole Negro race.

In the case of the white male the process may be even more complex. Suppose he is anxious concerning his own sexual adequacy and attractiveness. One study of adult prisoners discovered a close relationship between this condition and high prejudice. Men who were antagonistic toward minority groups, on the whole, showed more fierce protest against their own sexual passivity, semi-impotence, or homosexual trends. The protest took the form of exaggerated toughness and hostility. These individuals committed more crimes of a sexual nature than did those who were sexually more secure. And the pseudo masculinity of the former group made them more hostile toward minorities.

Again, a male who is dissatisfied with his own marriage may grow envious when he hears rumors of Negro sexual prowess and license. He may also resent and fear the approach Negroes might make to white women who are potentially his. A state of rivalry may thus result, based on the same type of reasoning that says the supply of jobs is limited and if Negroes have them, whites will be deprived.

Or suppose the white male has taken his pleasure with Negro women. Such liaisons, being illicit, give rise to guilt. A wry sense of justice forces him to see that the Negro males, in principle, should have equal access to white women. Jealousy plus guilt create a disagreeable conflict. He, too, finds a way out by "projecting." It is the lecherous Negro male that is the real menace. He would deflower white womanhood. The deflowering of Negro womanhood is conveniently forgotten in the outburst of righteous indignation. The indignation is guilt-evading and restorative of self-respect.

For this reason the penalties visited upon male Negroes for sex transgressions (with white women) are disproportionately heavy. (Although in fact, of course, the bulk of transgression is on the white side.) During the years 1938–1948, in thirteen southern states, 15 whites and 187 Negroes were executed for rape. In these same states Negroes made up only 23.8 of the population. Unless we assume that Negroes commit rape fifty-three times as often as white men (in proportion to their numbers in the population), we are forced to conclude that bias is largely responsible for the unequal number of executions for this crime.

There is no doubt that lifting the sexual ban would reduce the glamor and the conflict. But the ban is a stubborn composite of several factors. It rests, in the first instance, upon a Puritanical view of sex activity of any sort. Sex itself is taboo. But since normal social intercourse and intermarriage are scarcely ever possible between Negroes and whites, any intimate relationships seem to take on an adulterous flavor.

The central question allegedly is intermarriage. Since this sounds like a legal, and therefore respectable, issue, it becomes the pivot of nearly all discussion. The fact that miscegenation between two healthy people has no weakening effect on the offspring is overlooked. Intermarriage cannot rationally be opposed on biological grounds. It can, however, be rationally opposed on the grounds of the handicap and conflict it would cause both parents and offspring in the present state of society. But the opposition is seldom stated in these mild terms, for to do so would imply that the present state of society should be improved so that miscegenation can safely take place.

For the most part the marriage issue is not rational. It comprises a fierce fusion of sex attraction, sex repression, guilt, status superiority, occupational advantage, and anxiety. It is because intermarriage would symbolize the abolition of prejudice that it is so strenuously fought.

Perhaps the most interesting feature of the whole situation is the way in which the issue of intermarriage has come to dominate discussion. When a Negro obtains a good pair of shoes and learns to write a literate letter, some whites think he wants to marry their sister. Perhaps most discussions of discrimination end with the fatal question, "But would *you* want a Negro to marry your sister?" The reasoning seems to be that unless all forms of discrimination are maintained, intermarriage will result. The same argument was used to defend slavery. Nearly a hundred years ago Abraham Lincoln was forced to protest against "that counterfeit logic which presumes that, if I do not want a Negro woman for a slave, I do necessarily want her for a wife."

Why the prejudiced person almost invariably hides behind the issue of marriage is itself a lesson in rationalization. He takes what is admittedly the argument most likely to confuse his opponent. Even the most tolerant person may not welcome intermarriage—because of the practical unwisdom in a prejudiced society. He may therefore say, "No, I wouldn't." The bigot then has the advantage, and replies in effect, "Now, see, there is ultimately an unbridgeable chasm, and I am therefore right in maintaining that we must look on Negroes as a different and undesirable group. All my strictures against them are justified. We had better not let down the barriers because it will raise their expectations and hopes of intermarriage." Thus, the intermarriage question (actually so irrelevant to most phases of the Negro question) is forcibly introduced to protest and justify prejudice.

GUILT

A non-Catholic boy had a broken romance with a Catholic girl, and this affair was preceded by a rather free infatuation with another Catholic girl. He wrote:

> Both girls begged me to come back and marry them. They promised anything if I would do so. Their groveling disgusted me. But I realized that the Catholic Church has only an ignorant, bigoted following to draw from.

Not he, but the Church, was somehow to blame for the unpleasant situation. A gentile businessman was guilty of unethical practices that forced a Jewish competitor into bankruptcy. He, too, consoled himself, saying:

> Well, they are always trying to run Christians out of business, and so I had to get him first.

The student was a cad; the gentile a cheat. But subjectively each evaded his sense of guilt by projection; others were guilty, not he.

Somewhat more subtle is the evidence that comes from clinical studies. We spoke previously of the child who through repressive training is made fearful of his own impulses, and comes therefore to fear the impulses of others. The California studies, to which we alluded, show among prejudiced people a marked tendency to regard others (but not oneself) as blameworthy. Interesting confirmation comes from comparable studies in India, where the psychologist, Mitra, discovered in Hindu boys having greatest prejudice against Muslims a high tendency to unconscious guilt reaction in the Rorschach test.

While nearly all people, to varying degrees, suffer from feelings of guilt, not all mix this emotional condition in with their ethnic attitudes. As in the case of anger, hatred, fear and sexuality, there are rational and adaptive responses to guilt. It is only certain personalities who allow these states to enter into the formation of character-conditioned bigotry.

Some of the ways in which people handle guilt feelings are benign and wholesome; some lead almost unavoidably to prejudice against out-groups. Let us list the principal modes of dealing with guilt.

1. Remorse and restitution.   This is the response that receives highest ethical approval. It is wholly intropunitive and avoids all temptation to shift blame to other shoulders. A person who is normally penitent and contrite for his own failings is not likely to find much in others, specifically in out-groups, to criticize.

Sometimes, though not often, we find among persecutors of out-groups converts who repent and devote themselves ever after to supporting the cause of those they at first hated. St. Paul's conversion represented such a shift. Somewhat more often we find a sensitive person who feels a *collective* guilt. It is likely that some white workers who devote themselves to the improvement of conditions for Negroes may have some such motivation. Being intropunitive to a high degree, they feel that their own group is at fault, and work hard to make amends.

2. Partial and sporadic restitution.   Some people who themselves hold firmly the doctrine of white supremacy will, up to a point, work for the betterment of the Negro. They feel that they can hold to a basic prejudice if only they act now and then as if it were nonexistent. "We frequently do good," wrote La Rochefoucault, "to enable us with impunity to do evil." In one community the woman who was most active in keeping Negroes out of the neighborhood and "in their place," was found at the same time to be the most active in devoting herself to Negro charities. Here is a case of "alternation" and "compromise."

3. Denial of guilt.   A common escape from feelings of guilt is to assert that there is no reason to have them. A familiar justification for discrimination against the Negroes is, "They are happier by themselves." A common Southern conceit is that Negroes prefer Southern to Northern employers because the former "understand" them better. During the Second World War, it was often said that Negroes, for this reason, preferred to serve under Southern rather than under Northern white officers. Also, it was maintained that they greatly preferred white to colored officers. The facts are entirely contradictory. When asked in a poll whether they would prefer to serve under white or Negro lieutenants, only four percent of the Northern and six percent of the Southern Negroes preferred white. Further, only one percent of the Northern Negroes preferred a white officer from the South, and only four percent of the Southern Negroes did so.

4. Discrediting the accuser.   No one likes another person to blame him for misconduct. A common defense against facing the justice of an accusation is to declare the accuser to be somehow off base. Hamlet confronted his mother with her faithlessness in marrying her husband's murderer. Rather than face her own guilt, his mother reproves Hamlet for "the coinage" of his brain, laying his charges to his madness. Hamlet tries to show her that she is but rationalizing to escape her own conscience:

> . . . Mother, for love of grace,
> Lay not that flattering unction to your soul,
> That not your trespass, but my madness speaks;
> It will but skin and film the ulcerous place,
> Whilst rank corruption, mining all within,
> Infect unseen. Confess yourself to heaven!
> Repent what's past; avoid what is to come;
> And do not spread the compost on the weeds,
> To make them ranker.

In the realm of ethnic relations those who would rouse the voice of conscience are called "agitators," "troublemakers," "communists."

5. Justification of conditions.   The simplest evasion of all is to say that the hated person is wholly to blame. Previously we saw that many people who are prejudiced take this path. This is prejudice without compunction. "Who could tolerate them? Look, they are dirty, lazy, sexually libertine." The fact that these qualities may be the very ones we have to fight in ourselves, makes it all the easier to see them in others. In any case, complete extropunitiveness, with recourse to the deserved reputation theory, avoids the necessity of guilt.

6. Projection.   The sense of guilt, by definition, means that I blame myself for some misdeed. But only Item 1 in this list (remorse and restitution) is strictly appropriate to this definition. It alone is a rationally adaptive mode of response. All others are devices for *guilt evasion.* Guilt-evading processes have one feature in common: the self-referred perception is repressed in favor of some external (extropunitive) perception. There is guilt somewhere, yes, but it is not *my* guilt.

Thus in all guilt evasion there is some projective mechanism at work. We have listed certain examples. But they do not cover all of the types of cases we find. For example, there is the device of pointing to greater sin in others in order to diminish the sense of sin in ourselves. The businessman quoted at the beginning of this section held that his cheating was excusable in view of the greater dishonesty of the Jewish group as a whole.

Whenever, and in whatever way, a correct appraisal of one's own emotional life fails and gives way to an incorrect judgment of other people, we are dealing with the psychodynamic process of *projection.*

32. PSYCHOLOGICAL SOURCES OF CONFLICT

elton b. mcneil

The previous article argued that anxiety and frustration lead to conflict. The present selection, using a similar theme, argues that frustration and anxiety are inescapable by-products of civilization. If frustration is inevitable and leads to aggression, can conflict ever be eliminated from society?

In man's attempt to apply the scientific method to human affairs, the study of aggression has commanded an inordinate amount of the energy of social scientists. Although recent events have expanded the scale on which human destructiveness can be expressed, and have multiplied the urgency of the need for a solution to the riddle of hostility, the primary source of anxiety about aggressive behavior is still highly personal and quite mundane. The parent

From Elton B. McNeil, "The Nature of Aggression," in *The Nature of Human Conflict,* Elton B. McNeil (ed.), © 1965. Reprinted by permission of Prentice-Hall, Inc., Englewood Cliffs, New Jersey.

whose belligerent child is rejected by playmates, the schoolteacher whose ire is provoked by negativism, the policeman whose dignity is outraged by the defiance of a delinquent, and the average citizen whose rights have been trampled on, all experience an anguish that they cannot summon up when they consider the possibility that man may one day be the instrument of his own mass extinction.

Personal frustration is woven tightly into the fabric of the life of each of us, making aggressive feelings an inevitable human experience. The paradox which aggression presents is that in all its abundance and despite the massive scrutiny it has endured since the beginning of time, it remains as enigmatic as if its presence had not yet been detected by man. An apt analogy might be to liken visible aggressive acts to a tree that resists man's efforts to uproot it because he is only dimly aware of the meaning of the concept "roots." In many respects the labors of the last forty years resemble such primitive efforts in our attempt to comprehend the notion of the roots of man's emotional life—roots which twist and turn in a seemingly incomprehensible fashion and plunge to depths to which man has seldom ventured. It is not surprising, then, that an account of this toil inevitably will contain murky observation, fanciful speculation, and valid as well as irrelevant and trivial fact. It is man's inability to distinguish between the momentous and the meaningless that constrains him from discarding what looks trivial but may, in fact, be vital. [Thus, any examination of the nature of human aggression will contain as much theory as fact.]

The bulk of human aggressiveness can be traced directly to frustration. The civilizing of the child cannot be accomplished without frustration of his needs, for the society insists that he must learn to satisfy his needs at specific times, in specified places, by specified techniques, and in relation only to specified objects. This systematic interference with the needs of its members seems to be a necessary condition of group living, for it makes the behavior of others a dependable and predictable event and allows planning for the common good. Although most well-socialized adults encounter many frustrations in the course of their daily lives, they use established patterns of reaction to overcome them and to prevent their recurrence. The seeming ease with which adults remove, or adjust to, obstacles in their paths is a sharp contrast to the child's fumbling attempt to apply his limited skill and primitive understanding to the management of frustration. Not only do the child's needs seem to him to be overpowering, but the few alternative ways he knows of satisfying them offer little hope of an easy restoration of his emotional equilibrium. The child's methods of meeting his many frustrations tend to be quite simple and direct and until he learns a variety of ways to solve his problems he is bound to feel like the helpless victim of the caprice of his environment. It is in this setting that some of the most fundamental personality characteristics of the individual are established and his success or failure in mastering frustration has the utmost relevance for the aggressiveness with which he will manage his life.

Frustration involves interference with the gratification of a motive, need, or drive. The source of frustration may be perceived by the individual as internal or external and it may take any of a number of forms. Frustration among children, for example, frequently appears as a physical obstruction since they live in a world built to an adult scale. Frustration can be due to sheer satiation with a task from which there is no escape or it can be caused by a discrepancy between an individual's desire to solve a problem and his ability to do so. Since so many of our working and social relationships are organized in terms of employers and employees and leaders and followers, frustration can issue directly from unsatisfactory leadership which thwarts gratification of the needs of others. The interpretation of what constitutes frustration is a highly personal and individual matter and depends almost completely on the perception one has that gratification is being, or will be, withheld. To an intensely ambitious person, for example, life may be the continuous pursuit of gratification which, when achieved, is at once replaced by the demands of a new set of goals. As long as gratification is possible, it is a challenge rather than a frustration.

DEFENSE MECHANISMS AND AGGRESSION

No attempt to understand the vicissitudes of human aggressive behavior is adequate without concepts similar to that of the defense mechanisms and the existence of an unconscious part of the self. The efforts, for centuries, to explain the motivation of human actions on a purely conscious and rational basis always produced embarrassing paradoxes or left a host of details unaccounted for. Emphasis on the intellectual rather than on the emotional aspects of man's nature suggested that man, when faced with conflict, ought to be able to draw up a balance sheet of pros and cons and then, examining the facts, make a rational decision. When psychoanalysis shifted the emphasis of psychiatric thinking to man's emotions, it became apparent that any attempt to add up the important facts could never strike a balance because essential facts were always missing. It was from these observations that a dynamic view of human functioning was formed and the notion of defense mechanisms evolved.

The ideal way of meeting frustrations or resolving conflicts would be to approach them as problems to solve and to effect the best compromise available. In many instances in our daily lives, exactly this procedure is followed. If society set no limits on the impulses and feelings the individual could express, no more than problem-solving skills would be needed to manage one's life. In a complex fashion, the members of a culture set up an interlocking system in which acceptance and reward are issued only to those who display certain kinds of behavior and become a specific kind of person. When one fails to fit these prescriptions, he is punished by being deprived of the very things a growing child most needs. Bad little boys and girls not only lose the love and acceptance of their parents, but, once a year, Santa Claus will not bring the presents that every good child receives. Through this process of systematically rewarding certain kinds of behavior and punishing others, the adults in the society manage to force the child to conform to the specifications it has set. If the process ended here, the management of prohibited impulses would be much simpler. There would be conformity as long as the prospect of being caught and punished was immediately apparent. Since a child cannot have all his experiences in life under the watchful supervision of the parent, he must learn to heed a broad set of standards of behavior which will be applicable even in unforeseen circumstances. The standards the child must learn define the kind of person he ought to become, and the failure to achieve these standards threatens to bring rejection from the parents, in particular, and other members of society, in general. Learned in childhood, these patterns of reaction and standards of behavior get stamped into the child's psychic structure and become so much a part of him that being less than the person he ought to be will produce an intense anxiety which is painful to endure.

Having accomplished this process of internalizing maxims of good and evil and success and failure, the developing child must now sort over his wishes, desires, feelings, and impulses to determine which are acceptable to him, and can be lived with without anxiety, and which must be eliminated for psychological comfort. The simplest and most pervasive example of this process is clearly demonstrable in the feelings of love and hate the child has toward his mother. Everyone is aware that children love their mothers because mothers care for them, minister to their needs, and provide gratification. The most casual observation would reveal that when the mother spanks the child, deprives him of things he desires, or interferes with his attempt at gratification of his needs, the child, at least at that moment, hates his mother and has powerful aggressive urges directed toward her. The society insists that such hostile feelings have no place in the mother-child relationship and that the child must be free of such emotions if he is to be accepted and loved by his mother and if he is to feel worthwhile as a person. It is at this point that the child faces a conflict he must resolve and he comes to learn that a number of avenues are oepn to him although each will be less satisfactory than being able to accept his impulses and feelings as a normal consequence of human existence. It is at this point that the child must learn to manipulate his feelings if he is to defend himself against the onslaught of unbearable anxiety.

What are the ways the child can use to avoid being caught, by himself or others, with contraband feelings? There are four elements or dimensions of the forbidden situation that he can alter to bring about a new situation more in keeping with society's dictates and his own anxieties. Momentarily, he feels that he hates his mother and wants to kill her. There is the *source* (himself) of the feeling, the *impulse* (hate), the *object* (mother) toward which it is directed, and the *aim* (kill) of the impulse. Alteration of any one of these aspects will produce a formula which is no longer threatening to his self-esteem or to the esteem others have for him. He can, for example, change the *source* in some fashion and not tamper with the other elements; now *he* doesn't hate his mother and want to kill her. Or he can alter the *impulse* so that he *loves* his mother, not hates her. The *object* can be transformed so that he hates *school* but not his mother. Another compromise that will solve his dilemma is to admit that he hates his mother but merely wishes to *reprimand* her rather than kill her. In each instance, a slight change in his perception of the reality of hating his mother cleans up the thought and makes it presentable. In extreme circumstances the whole thought must be changed leaving no element unaltered; in a less threatening situation it is necessary only to reduce the intensity of each element of the sequence. This means that the kind, quality, and degree of distortion will always be a function of the demands made by the environment and the internal psychic resources he has available to him. In one family a child must see, hear, speak, and think no evil while in another an aggressive outburst is a natural event which must be managed but is viewed as a reasonable consequence of the frustrations of living with other people.

At first, mechanisms for managing hostile feelings are practiced in a conscious form by the child. He will, for example, retain his feelings but suppress the overt attack on the mother to insure her continued acceptance of him. Such feelings must be hidden from the self as well as from others (after all, the best-adjusted adult could not be comfortably thinking murderous thoughts about others all day), and the act of altering a prohibited situation must be invisible to the self as well as to others. Through a process we can label, but not fully understand, the effort the child once made willfully and consciously becomes an event which occurs in so subtle a fashion that no one is the wiser.

This description of the perceptual maneuvering the child must go through to escape experiencing anxiety is particularly relevant to aggressive impulses because their potential destructiveness makes it necessary that they be highly regulated and controlled. The average person in our society is made quite uncomfortable by the sight of naked hostility in himself or in others since one of the hallmarks of maturity is control over aggression. The description of the need to defend oneself makes it appear that this is a consciously willed, mechanical process—something like a bag of tricks used when appropriate to the emergency. A more apt description would be that normal persons *cope* with frustrations and forbidden impulses and only *defend* against them when no other alternative remains. When defensive tactics relieve anxiety, this very relief will reinforce the defensive behavior and tend to solidify it into a habitual and characteristic pattern of reaction when faced with conflict in the future. When this occurs, they no longer act as emergency reactions but become predictable character traits that distinguish the individual for life. Since a variety of defense mechanisms is available to the individual he usually proceeds by trial-and-error to select those that are most effective in freeing him from guilt and anxiety. A mechanism that proves to be effective in one situation is tried in another and its use continued until it fails to accomplish its purpose. Highly flexible individuals may acquire a set of defenses which are adapted specifically to each situation; rigid or less resourceful persons may become general defenders who find one dramatic mechanism that works (such as thoroughgoing repression) and use it for a variety of situations and with all kinds of impulses.

Using hostility as the model of impulses to be dealt with, what are the ways in which it can be managed defensively? At a broad level, the choices of the individual are restricted to: *changing the situation* through the process of conscious problem-solving and working out a new relationship with the person toward whom he is hostile; *escaping from the situation* by running away or retreating into a fantasy life where the problems do not exist; *changing his perception of the hostile situation* through defense mechanisms which render it innocuous.

THE DEVELOPMENT OF AGGRESSION

Except in rare instances, the aggressive behavior of adults is much more sophisticated and polished than that of children. The adult not only has acquired an infinite variety of means for communicating his feelings, but he also has developed more than one kind of emotional response to frustration. These skills in managing aggression are gained during a lifetime of painful lessons at the hands of his parents, his teachers, and his peers. Only the most incorrigible of romantics would describe childhood as the golden years of carefree, happy play untroubled by the worries of the world. In retrospect it does seem that today's problems and responsibilities are more weighty and troublesome than those of youth, but this view is constructed of a combination of a hazy memory and the safe perspective of elapsed time. When we nostalgically recall a youth spent on a farm, we are likely to remember only the cool well water that slaked our thirst on a blistering summer's day. We selectively omit those memories that are painful or unpleasant in order not to disturb our idyllic image. This kind of recall has been labeled *old oaken bucket thinking,* and it is characteristic of the general conception each of us has of his own childhood. Even a casual observation of the emotional ups-and-downs of the daily life of an average child would immediately press home the truth that there is at least as much pain in childhood as there is pleasure.

It is not that a child weeps as much as he laughs—it is rather that conflicts cut deeper than comparable joys. A tally of the number of angers, resentments, jealousies, irritations, and rebellions that accumulate in just the child's first ten years is ample evidence for the pain of maturing. During development the child does not want for the opportunity to practice managing aggression.

Theorists are in general agreement that aggression is a fundamental characteristic of existence and begins as a reflection of the action and vitality of living. Through an aggressive or active relationship with his environment and the people in it, the child becomes an active participant in the development of his own personality. If he accepts the pressures of others passively, he acquires a psychic structure not of his own fashioning. In this sense, there are positive values of aggressiveness that are more than just derivatives of by-products of the more malignant qualities of aggression. Since children grow in a setting in which there are other children, aggression seems to be an inevitable consequence of living with others. Jealousy of other children, competition with them for a place in the family, and disputes over property are inescapable.

An important aim of the study of the development of aggression is to uncover the determinants of the form aggressive response will eventually take. It is clear that the overtness of the expression will depend on many factors, the most important of which will be the success the child achieves in reducing tension.

Since a child will learn whatever responses are rewarded by others or bring gratification of his needs, it is easy to see how he can grow in sophis-tication in the use of aggressive devices. When other individuals are blocking the child's way and frustrating him, he can, by accident, learn that an aggres-sive attack will remove them and free the path to gratification. This path, trod often enough, can become well-worn and evolve into the characteristic "style of life" of the mature individual. When the child discovers the benefits of hurt-ing others, and as he gains experience and learns more about the motivations of others, he will become more and more skilled in using this knowledge of their motivation as a means of controlling them and getting what he wants. Early in his life he may be stubborn and negativistic toward all adult requests, yet capable only of digging in his heels in defiance. As he becomes sensitive to the emotions of others, he begins to understand that he can outwit them or outwait them and that defiance of some adult demands will not bring down their wrath on him. Thus, strangers will cow a child and cause him to be more restrained simply because he cannot predict their response. With parents, the child knows exactly what to expect and how far he can go and he acts accordingly. With strangers, he is not safe until he tests their tolerance and probes for the weak spots in their relationships with children. This, of course, is distressing to the parent who takes it as a sign of personal failure in achieving control over the child. It is not that familiarity breeds contempt; it is rather that familiarity educates the child in predicting the parents' response. As the child progresses in his education in hostility, he acquires greater finesse and soon perceives that symbolic injury and psychological pain are much more excruciating than simple physical hurts. Once this insight is gained, he stands on the threshold of graduate study in the fine art of cruelty.

CULTURE AND AGGRESSION

Every culture must provide a solution to the hostility among its members which threatens constantly to disrupt the smooth flow of interpersonal relations so necessary to a well-functioning society. An examination of anthropological accounts of how aggression is managed in primitive or preliterate societies reveals a number of interesting variations but probably no single pattern that contains a universally acceptable answer.

Among the Pueblo Indians, the Hopi are a society based on a notable maladjustment of its people; maladjustment in the sense of a state in which continued friction predominates in personal relations and in which the worst is regularly and anxiously anticipated. Gossip, witchcraft, fear, discord, and mutual distrust pervade the daily interactions of the tribal members. In part, the antagonistic attitudes of the adults can be traced to the sharp and consistent restriction of the overt expression of aggression by the child after an earlier period in which his aggressiveness was a successful and rewarding way of behaving. At the same time, control over the child was gained by systematically grinding extensive fears into him from his first days. Among the Hopi, physical aggression is suppressed and competition with others is held to be in particularly bad taste so that it does not offer a culturally approved outlet for the dammed-up feelings. It is pointed out that only the verbal aggression in which he excels remains to the Hopi.

The Saulteaux are an offshoot of the Ojibwa-speaking peoples living near Lake Superior. To a casual observer the Saulteaux would appear to have interpersonal relations marked by cooperation, patience, and self-control; a tribe in which there were no official records of murder, suicide, war with whites, or other Indian tribes. Although there seemed to be no manifest expression of aggression, Saulteaux patterns of social behavior created a fundamental distrust in interpersonal relations, and the outwardly placid character traits were an effective façade for deep hostility and dislike of others. The chief culturally sanctioned means for disposing of this unexpressed aggression seemed to be malicious gossip, slanderous accusations behind the victim's back, and the use of sorcery and magic as a means of retaliation. These forms of covert aggression were widely used.

The ways of regulating aggression could be multiplied with the examination of each new culture. Hostility and aggressive behavior are the most powerful obstacles to the formation of a culture which can devote its energies to constructive efforts. Institutions to deal with such feelings are a cornerstone of the ultimate pattern a society will follow. Consideration of various cultures establishes a fundamental lesson about the management of anger. Starting with the premise that an average quantity of aggression is the inheritance of each individual, it becomes clear that a dependable relationship exists between the freedom for its overt expression and the degree to which covert forms of it will make their appearance. The quantity of aggression given in the beginning seems fixed and unalterable, and if it finds no overt channel for expression, it becomes covert; the proportion of open or hidden expression tolerated in public and private life comes to characterize both the individual as well as the society in which he lives. Further, it would appear that there are few adequate substitutes for the direct expression of aggression. The variety of substitutes needed seems to be a function of the number of frustrations the society imposes and, in general, how early they are forced on the child. In some social groups the rivalry and hatred expressed openly would seem to be beyond the bounds that group life could absorb, yet the social unit survives even if at some cost to its creativity. In other cultures the suppression of all form of overt hostility, and the guilt associated with angry thoughts, is so extensive that substitute forms of outlet must carry an unreasonable burden. It may be that a self-destructive cycle exists, one that comes to an equilibrium over a period of time. A culture that permits and encourages hostility and protects itself by directing the accumulated rage against enemies outside the society may, through destructive warfare and the inevitable reduction of tribal vigor or through the circumstances of encroachment by even stronger tribes, come to follow peaceful ways by necessity rather than by choice. Through a similar process of attrition, tribes which the environment once treated kindly may· find a more aggressive and warlike spirit is needed to wrest basic gratification from nature and they may gradually convert their institutions and child-rearing practices to the production and encouragement of a culturally useful aggression. Although evidence does not yet exist for this hypothesis, it seems reasonable to assume that a continual waxing and waning of cultural sanction of the proportion of overt and covert aggression is taking place in various cultures at all times. It may be reasonable, further, to assume that cultures at the extremes of both overt and covert permission of aggressive expression have within them the seeds of their own destruction. Just as the unsatisfactory results of corporal punishment drive parents to reason with their children and then dissatisfaction with this method leads to a return to spanking, it may be that at the extremes the cost of the methods of handling aggression may be so great as to force a reaction toward equilibrium and a median position. The relativism of cultural solutions to the problem of aggression are important to us because it sets a limit on human invention.

The cultural process channels aggression in directions that suit its purposes for the good of society. Once a pattern of expression is set for a society it may continue long past the time of its usefulness because it continues to be passed on to the next generation by parents who learned the lesson so well. Even within a society the relations between groups of different race, language, or religion may establish fixed patterns for the regulation of aggressive impulses. In the history of Negroes in our own society, for example, the roles they were required to take in their relations with the dominant white group allowed little variation in the expression of aggression. Before the Civil War, Negroes, as faithful slaves, were allowed to aggress only against members of their own group and were subject to an extreme penalty if open hostility toward the ruling whites were to become apparent. Since slaves depended on their masters for food, shelter, and protection, their situation was quite similar to that of the parent and child. Indeed, slaves were treated as though they were simple children in adult bodies. In this case the slave, as the child, obeyed a needed and feared master-parent toward whom aggressive feelings had to be suppressed and prevented from overt expression. Following emancipation, the Negro continued to live by the whim of the white master and was still required to suppress his hostility for fear of retaliation from his ex-masters. The overt behavior of the Negro became meek, humble, and unaggressive, concealing his true attitude from the whites and, sometimes, even from himself. In this way he assured his acceptance and continued reward for those who possessed the power to dispense the essential gratifications. Aggression became limited to fantasy life and even these feelings toward his oppressors took their toll in guilt. The masklike quality of the role of the deferential, obsequious Negro was most apparent when it is was sloughed off in the company of his companions who made no demands for suppression of angry feelings and toward whom less hostility existed. Today, as the compensations are made available by direct, aggressive action sanctioned by law and social sentiment, the pattern of inhibition of the expression of hostility is undergoing a steady alteration in the direction of freedom from restraint.

The sensitivity of the developing child to the limits he must maintain over his hostility and to the approved forms for its expression help him to establish a workable pattern of behavior in relations with others. Negroes, as a minority group in this culture, must learn one pattern to fit the demands of those close to them in their own group and must interchange this pattern with another when relating to members of the majority group.

A society can give informal sanction to the most extreme forms of aggressive expression. In A. Kardiner's evaluation (1945) of early Comanche Indian culture, for example, he described a society which developed strong and uninhibited individuals devoted almost exclusively to "criminal" ends. The society established an ideal of bravery and aggressive accomplishment and allowed no escape or form of passivity for its members. Status among the Comanche was determined by prowess, daring, strength, and skill, and a warrior's position among his fellow tribesmen diminished as these powers waned with advancing age. The culture avoided its own destruction by the simple device of directing all its warlike actions against outsiders in the neighboring tribes. When the Comanche were surrounded by white men, herded into a restricted territory, and kept from further marauding, it caused the decay of the culture, for the mainstay of its vigor had been swept away.

In line with Kardiner's analysis of the structure of this Indian culture, it is a reasonable statement that for any group, wars help to externalize aggression and to reduce animosity among its members. Hostility toward an outgroup may be the prime condition for internal peace. An excellent example of this hypothesis was furnished by reports on the Teton Dakota Indians. Prior to 1850, murder of one tribesman by another was frequent and the cause could usually be traced to the frustrations issuing from an unequal distribution of the tribal wealth. For thirty years following the arrival of the white man, there was a decrease of in-group homicide while the tribe presented a united front to this enemy from without. When peace with the white man was finally achieved, in-group murder made its reappearance.

Science-fiction writers are fond of imagining the earth beset by invaders from outer space and like to toy with the idea that the world would then respond to this threat by a peaceful unification for the common good. At best such a solution would be a temporary one and it would be a detour around the problem rather than a successful conquest of it.

II

SOCIETY IN CRISIS
alienation, violence, and change

33. AMERICA AT THE CROSSROADS
william o. douglas

Shortly following publication of the book from which the following passages are taken, demands were heard in Washington for the impeach-
ment of Associate Douglas. At issue was the question of whether or not
Douglas was "advocating" revolution in the United States. Several of the
passages arousing congressional ire are reproduced below. Do you
agree that Douglas condones revolution? Or is he merely engaging in
analysis and prediction?

The continuing episodes of protest and dissent in the United States have their
basis in the First Amendment to the Constitution, a great safety valve that is
lacking in most other nations of the world. The First Amendment creates a
sanctuary around the citizen's beliefs. His ideas, his conscience, his convictions are his own concern, not the government's.

After an American has been in a totalitarian country for several months,
he is greatly relieved when he reaches home. He feels that bonds have been
released and that he is free. He can speak above a whisper, and he walks
relaxed and unguarded as though he were no longer being followed. After a
recent trip I said to a neighbor, "It's wonderful to be back in a nation where
even a riot may be tolerated."

All dissenters are protected by the First Amendment. A "communist"
can be prosecuted for actions against society, but not for expressing his views
as to what the world order should be. Although television and radio time
as well as newspaper space is available to the affluent members of this society
to disseminate their views, most people cannot afford that space. Hence, the

means of protest, and the customary manner of dissent in America, from the days of the American Revolution, has been pamphleteering.

Other methods of expression, however, are also protected by the First Amendment—from picketing, to marching on the city streets, to walking to the State Capitol or to Congress, to assembling in parks and the like.

It was historically the practice of state police to use such labels as "breach of the peace" or "disorderly conduct" to break up groups of minorities who were protesting in these unorthodox ways. The real crime of the dissenters was that they were out of favor with the Establishment, and breach of the peace or disorderly conduct was used merely as a cloak to conceal the true nature of the prosecution.

In 1931 the Supreme Court, in an opinion by Chief Justice Charles Evans Hughes, held that the First Amendment was applicable to the States by reason of the Due Process Clause of the Fourteenth Amendment. That Clause provides that no State shall deny any person "liberty" without "due process." The Hughes Court held that the right to dissent, protest, and march for that purpose was within the purview of the First Amendment. Breach of the peace and disorderly conduct could, therefore, no longer be used as an excuse for the prosecution of minorities.

Parades, of course, can be regulated to avoid traffic problems and to allow for easy access to public offices by other people. Pickets may be regulated as to numbers and times and places. But the basic right of public protest may not be abridged.

While violence is not protected by the Constitution, lawful conduct, such as marching and picketing, often boils over into unlawful conduct because people are emotional, not rational, beings. So are the police; and very often they arrest the wrong people. For the police are an arm of the Establishment and view protesters with suspicion. Yet American protesters need not be submissive. A speaker who resists arrest is acting as a free man. The police do not have *carte blanche* to interfere with his freedom. They do not have the license to arrest at will or to silence people at will.

This is one of the many instances showing how the Constitution was designed to keep government off the backs of the people.

Our Constitutional right to protest allows us more freedom than most other people in the world enjoy. Yet the stresses and strains in our system have become so great and the dissents so violent and continuous that a great sense of insecurity has possessed much of the country.

This insecurity reflects international as well as local worries and concerns. At the international level we have become virtually paranoid. The world is filled with dangerous people. Every troublemaker across the globe is a communist. Our obsession is in part the product of a fear generated by Joseph McCarthy. Indeed a black silence of fear possesses the nation and is causing us to jettison some of our libertarian traditions. . . .

The dissent we witness is a reaffirmation of faith in man; it is protest against living under rules and prejudices and attitudes that produce the extremes of wealth and poverty and that make us dedicated to the destruction of people through arms, bombs, and gases, and that prepare us to think alike and be submissive objects for the regime of the computer.

One young man wrote me his dissent in a poem:

> Humans exist only to consume
> We the living have entered a tomb
> Machines are this world's best
> So humans are purchased to do the rest.

The dissent we witness is a protest against the belittling of man, against his debasement, against a society that makes "lawful" the exploitation of humans.

This period of dissent based on belief in man will indeed be our great renaissance. . . .

The truth is that a vast restructuring of our society is needed if remedies are to become available to the average person. Without that restructuring the good will that holds society together will be slowly dissipated.

It is that sense of futility which permeates the present series of protests and dissents. Where there is a persistent sense of futility, there is violence; and that is where we are today.

The use of violence is deep in our history.

Shay's Rebellion in 1786–1787 was sparked by a financial depression when land taxes were said to have become intolerable.

The Whiskey Rebellion of 1784 was a farmers' protest against a federal tax on distilled whiskeys.

Every subsequent decade showed fleeting examples of a similar kind.

In the 1930's we had "sit-down" strikes by which workers seized factories, an act which Chief Justice Hughes called "a high-handed proceeding without shadow of right."

The historic instances of violence have been episodic and have never become a constant feature of American life. Today that pattern has changed. Some demonstrations go on for months; and the protests at colleges have spread like a prairie grass fire.

We are witnessing, I think, a new American phenomenon. The two parties have become almost indistinguishable; and each is controlled by the Establishment. The modern day dissenters and protesters are functioning as the loyal opposition functions in England. They are the mounting voice of political opposition to the status quo, calling for revolutionary changes in our institutions.

Yet the powers-that-be faintly echo Adolf Hitler, who said in 1932:

> The streets of our country are in turmoil. The universities are filled with students rebelling and rioting.
>
> Communists are seeking to destroy our country. Russia is threatening

us with her might and the republic is in danger. Yes, danger from within and without.

We need law and order.

. . . Violence has no constitutional sanction; and every government from the beginning has moved against it.

But where grievances pile high and most of the elected spokesmen represent the Establishment, violence may be the only effective response. . . .

The search of the youth today is for ways and means to make the machine—and the vast bureaucracy of the corporation state and of government that runs that machine—the servant of man.

That is the revolution that is coming.

That revolution—now that the people hold the residual powers of government—need not be a repetition of 1776. It could be a revolution in the nature of an explosive political regeneration. It depends on how wise the Establishment is. If, with its stockpile of arms, it resolves to suppress the dissenters, America will face, I fear, an awful ordeal.

34. THINKING ABOUT
THE UNTHINKABLE
herman kahn

Of all the problems resulting from the technological revolution, none has been quite so terrifying as the development and proliferation of nuclear weapons. Professor Kahn outlines both the relative ease with which nuclear weapons can be obtained as well as some highly probable outcomes of this situation.

Can social scientists solve this problem? How can they contribute toward a solution?

I would like to discuss a "hypothetical" situation—what the world might look like in the year 2000,[1] if current technological trends continue without any drastic changes in the international political order. By this means I hope to

Reprinted by permission of the publisher, Horizon Press, from *Thinking about the Unthinkable* by Herman Kahn. Copyright 1962.

[1] I personally believe that technological progress, almost by itself, would make the situation critical much before the year 2000 unless compensating controls or other changes appear. However, by picking the year 2000 as a sort of outermost limit for the viability of the current system, I eliminate almost all of the objections of my more conservative colleagues.

make it clear that a continuation of the present international order is incompatible with probable technological developments. Once one is convinced that the strains on the system are large enough to bring about large changes, whether desired or not, one is intellectually and psychologically prepared to think hard about the next set of problems: When will these changes occur? How? What can we do to guide them?

We can gain a rough idea of one aspect of the possible military picture of the not-too-distant future by extrapolating from current expenditures for national defense and over-all growth rates. Today there are about twenty-five "small" nations which spend between a hundred million and a billion dollars a year on national defense. If present growth and defense trends continue, it is likely that before the end of the twentieth century there will be about twice as many nations in this bracket. And since continuing technological progress can be expected to reduce the cost of nuclear weapons and delivery systems to well within this budget,[2] there are likely to be fifty "small" nations capable of acquiring impressive nuclear weapons systems by the year 2000.

These systems will in all probability still not be anywhere near so destructive as those of the larger powers; nor will they be likely to contain a large invulnerable "second-strike" force. Nevertheless, by today's standards, small nations' forces are likely to be incredibly destructive.

In addition to the twenty-five nations which today spend between 100 million and a billion dollars there are about ten nations which now spend over a billion dollars a year on national defense. By the year 2000 there could be about twenty nations spending more than this amount, thus providing themselves with considerable strategic capability. These could include more than a few Polaris type submarines or space bombardment platforms in addition to the missile systems under development today. By amortizing the cost over ten years, any of these nations might even be able to build, within its

---

[2] While current ICBMs are expensive to procure and maintain, it is quite likely that future models will be much less expensive. This is obvious from looking at the technology of the very next generation of solid fueled or storable-propellant missiles. There is another reason why some models of ICBMs may reverse the normal trend of weapons systems to greater complexity and cost. Looking at the history of bombers, for example, one notes that the early bombers had inadequate performance, even for the minimum mission. Improvements in speed, range, and altitude were therefore of the greatest importance. This meant that technological improvements were applied to solving these problems with a consequent increase in cost. In the absence of active and passive defense (and possibly in their presence) even the Model T ICBM has a very impressive performance. This means that technological improvements may be used to reduce the procurement and operating costs rather than improve the performance. If one accepts this last remark, then one can almost confidently predict that in the next few decades it will be possible for advanced nations to maintain large forces of some models of ICBMs for systems costs of less than $1,000,000 a year per missile, and for less advanced nations to fabricate and maintain a force for systems' costs less than five times this figure.

regular defense budget, a nuclear doomsday machine or its near equivalent.[3] Although it is most unlikely that any nation would build such a device in the next ten to twenty years, there clearly are some circumstances in which a nation might wish it had built one. If the current international anarchy continues, it is likely that within the next thirty or forty years such circumstances would have occurred often enough to impel at least one and maybe more than one nation to build such a device. It is of some consolation that even if doomsday machines were to be built, their use would still remain unlikely. But, almost everyone agrees that the mere existence of a doomsday machine would be a vast and, in fact, unacceptable danger. Moreover, the serious possibility of such machines could greatly increase the pressures for preventive war beyond any yet felt.

If for no other reason, the technological possibilities that one or more doomsday machines could be built have made the continuation of international anarchy too dangerous for even the most optimistic prophets. It is likely, however, that the international order will change before any doomsday machines are built, partly because of the political impact of advancing military and non-military technology, and partly as a direct result of the actual or potential diffusion of "normal" weapons. It is difficult to believe the world will go unchanged if there are fifty independent, sovereign, small, and medium nations capable of acquiring seriously destructive modern weapons systems— not to mention the ten or twenty nations able to acquire fairly large systems. Even if many nations are not strongly motivated to acquire such systems, a weak motivation is likely to be sufficient, particularly in an unstable competitive situation.

The mere acquisition by many nations of nuclear weapons would not necessarily lead to cataclysmic instability. For example, the situation might turn out to be similar to the old dueling societies of the American West. In these societies many people were armed; when a quarrel broke out somebody was either wounded or killed. But life went on. The future development of the present world might be even more peaceful than the dueling analogy would suggest. Even before dueling became outlawed, there was a strong tendency in some of the dueling societies to restrict the role of duels. Individuals learned that force was no proper way of settling personal disputes. And it might indeed turn out that the war system will similarly "wither away" by itself.

However, both of the above possibilities, a viable dueling system or an evolutionary withering away of the war system without any "special controls," seem rather remote. The uncontrolled diffusion of nuclear weapons is more

---

[3] A near-doomsday machine can be defined as a device or a set of devices which when exploded in place will destroy all unprotected life on a continent and, in addition, have major worldwide effects. I have discussed the "strategic theory" of such machines in *OTW*, pp. 144–53.

likely to make things worse than better. One can draw up an impressive list of problems which would occur or be greatly aggravated as a result of such a diffusion.

SOME PROBLEMS IN THE NEAR FUTURE

1. Greater opportunities for blackmail, revenge, terrorism, and other mischief-making. In a world which is armed to its teeth with nuclear weapons, every quarrel or difference of opinion may lead to violence of a kind quite different from what is possible today. Today there are technical problems in rapidly escalating problems of mobilization, transportation, logistics, etc. This time and effort means that there are built-in safety features on the use or threat of violence. In the future these technical constraints may disappear. Even a relatively innocuous quarrel over fishing rights could involve the early use of a nuclear weapon or two as a demonstration (the literal modern equivalent of a shot across the bow). The other troublesome international problems, such as disputed frontiers or irredentist movements, can give rise to local "games of chicken." These games would build up pressures to threaten all-out war and violence on a scale previously unknown, in order to show resolve. It is not unreasonable to believe that every so often someone would miscalculate in this game of chicken and actually unleash a nuclear war.

2. More widespread capabilities for "local" Munichs, Pearl Harbors, and blitzkriegs. I have already mentioned an increased tendency to play the game of chicken and some of the increased risks to the players. An irresponsible, desperate, or determined decision maker might not waste time on the lower rungs of the escalation ladder. He might simply launch a disarming attack on his victim and present the world with a fait accompli. Even if the potential victim has a nuclear capability, it may not have enough second-strike capability to deter such an attack. While the other nations are likely to be indignant, they are not likely to start a nuclear war to avenge an accomplished fact. The attacker might even use the attacked nation as a hostage to prevent effective reprisals.

Sometimes an aggressor may not even need to launch his attack. He might merely launch an ultimatum. In many circumstances this will force the other side to choose between backing down or launching an attack itself. Both courses may be dangerous, but a competent aggressor should be able to make the second look worse; between accommodation and thermonuclear war most will choose accommodation. Therefore, it should not surprise us if such choices are manufactured. Where opportunities for gain are large in the event of extremely aggressive behavior, some nations will choose to indulge in such behavior. A world armed with nuclear weapons would provide a fertile field for paranoiacs, megalomaniacs, and indeed all kinds of fanatics.

3. Pressure to preempt because of points one and two.   To the extent that the aggressive behavior described above might actually occur, one could reasonably expect decision makers, at whom it might be directed, to note that they risk disaster by not acting, and therefore to note the importance of acting first. While few would wish to be either executioner or victim, most would prefer the first role to the second. A world in which "reciprocal fear of surprise attack" (or surprise ultimatum) is ever present is also a world in which there would be little stability. There would also be greater pressure toward psychological and political preemption. In any situation in which an important advantage can be gained by announcing, "One of us has to be responsible, and since it isn't going to be me, it has to be you," there is a tendency to use committal strategies, that is, to say it first and firmly.

4. Tendencies to neglect conventional military capabilities.   Because of an over-reliance on nuclear capabilities or fear of the other side's nuclear capabilities, it is likely to be difficult for most nations to remain committed to the notion of limited conventional war. Since nuclear weapons provide "more bang for the buck," they are unlikely to allocate money, manpower, thought, and other scarce commodities, to conventional or other limited-war situations. This is so notwithstanding what could well be their realization that they might be unwilling to use their nuclear capabilities in a crisis, and so must either wage an inadequate conventional war or issue rather weak threats in that direction. This tendency to neglect conventional military capabilities may well create many kinds of instabilities and opportunities for bluff, counter-bluff, or actual attacks that could result in defeat or escalation.

5. Greater danger of inadvertent war.   The possibility of inadvertent war would no doubt increase not only because there would be many more weapons and missiles available, but because there will be many more organizations in existence, each with different standards of training, organization, and degrees of responsibility. The possibility of unauthorized behavior, irresponsibility, misunderstanding of orders, or lax discipline inevitably increases. Mistakes can occur and the probability of most mistakes would increase if the military or political organization were weak or slipshod.

To be sure, a mistake need not set off a large-scale chain reaction. In fact, every small war or accident would bring pressures to reform the system, pressures that are likely to spur a relatively peaceful evolution out of the current system of virtual anarchy. Hopefully, nations will refuse to accept a situation in which nuclear accidents actually do occur, and, if at all possible, they will do something to correct a system which makes them likely.

6. Internal political problems (civil war, coup d'état, irresponsibility, etc.) and external factors (arms race, fear of fear, etc.).   Even in a world that is much less dangerous than the one I have been describing, there will be both responsible and irresponsible peace and accommodation movements. If every time a hard decision has to be made, a major portion of the country has to be risked; if every time a country's diplomat walks into a hostile conference room, every man, woman, and child feels threatened; if every time a nation stands firm against aggressive probes, panic seizes the hearts of many of its citizens, then many citizens will simply adopt an attitude of denial or apathetic fatalism. Others will call for "peace" at any price with such intensity that their governments will have to get out of their way. There may even be some who will say, "Better a fearful end than endless fear." Responsible political life is likely to suffer disastrously as a result of a combination of apathy, denial, and hysteria. The trouble with "negotiating" in this atmosphere is that, to put it mildly, it is not likely to produce thoughtful, considered suggestions or programs. It will instead invite blackmail and deception by the government which is in better control of its people, and irresponsible rigidity or destabilizing weakness by the government which cannot manipulate its people. The anxieties created by such a perilous world may increase the dangers even more should "peace" movements be accompanied by violence or even large-scale non-violence. Organized political life may be threatened even more gravely. Their threat might activate less pacific groups, which in turn might encourage governments to practice a rigid despotism in an attempt to prevent even small military or political groups from obtaining and using weapons either for protest or for revolutionary purposes. And, eventually, even the best of safeguards may fail.

7. Diffusion of nuclear weapons to irresponsible private organizations. To the extent that these advanced weapons or their components are treated as articles or commerce, perhaps for peaceful uses as in the Plowshare program, their cost would be well within the resources available to many large private organizations. In fact, if prices are lowered to $100,000 or so—and this is not all implausible—they are in some sense available to vast numbers of individuals. (Almost any dedicated or fanatic member of the middle class or any advanced nation could save up all or an appreciable fraction of this sum.) Exactly what this could mean is hard to grasp without detailed consideration of various "scenarios," but few will feel comfortable in a world in which Malayan guerrillas, Cuban rebels, Algerian terrorists, right-wing counterterrorists, the Puerto Rican Independence party, or even gangsters and atomic extortionists, might obtain access to nuclear weapons or other means of mass destruction. Even if nuclear weapons and their delivery systems do not become articles of commerce, almost all of their components will have peaceable "relatives" and therefore may become generally available. Only a few special parts or assemblies would have to be specially manufactured by organizations or individuals who wish to obtain actual nuclear weapons' capability.

8. More complicated future problems of control. Once weapons are allowed to become widely diffused, it becomes much more difficult to work out methods of arms control. Moreover, even if some serious crisis leads to a general agreement to prevent the use or threat of nuclear weapons in the future, it is likely to be harder to ratify and implement such an agreement once nuclear weapons have spread. The small powers would then have to be asked to accept a reduction in their current capability rather than simply to abstain from acquiring weapons. Of course, if the control measures were sufficiently complete, it might be that all nations could be treated equally. Even then it would be difficult if not impossible to get all of them to junk their nuclear weapons systems peacefully. As our experience with France has shown, it can even be quite difficult to induce a nation to acquiesce in controls that would prevent its acquisition of such systems and it will be even harder to find, or even estimate, the size of hidden stocks which would be a nucleus around which future arms control violators could base their conspiracy.

9. Intensified agent-provocateur problems. One thing which restrains the behavior of "respectable" large nations is that they do not wish to acquire a reputation for being blatantly aggressive. Therefore, when a nation wants to be aggressive it usually needs an excuse to make its aggression seem defensive or, at least, very special and limited. In the absence of a special situation, such as Berlin, it may become more difficult to bring about such "justifiable" aggression. It is, after all, almost impossible for a large power to make a small power look so provocative as to justify an attack. When the small nations have acquired nuclear weapons, however, not only does the danger of accidental incidents go up sharply but the dangers of "arranged accidents" also increase. Thus it becomes easier for the large power to arrange for, or to counterfeit, the firing of a nuclear missile by the small power. This incident then could be used to justify all kinds of ultimatums, or actual reprisals, up to and including the forceable disarming of the small power. If the arranged incident has been successfully and imaginatively staged, many will applaud the punishment of the small power which had shown itself to be so dangerously irresponsible.

10. Catalytic and anonymous war. The widespread diffusion of nuclear weapons would make many nations able, and in some cases also create the pressure, to aggravate an on-going crisis, or even touch off a war between two other powers for purposes of their own. Here again the situation is so complicated that one must construct and consider many scenarios to get a feeling for the many possibilities. However, even without systematic exploration one can list dangerous possibilities for anonymous mischief-making by third parties who control nuclear weapons. If a nation finds two of its cities destroyed by missiles from Polaris type submarines, how is it to react? Presumably it would be impossible to tell which of several nations was responsible. Moreover if any one nation was the obvious candidate, it might make it all the less dangerous for a third power to launch its attack. When the possible development of suitcase bombs is considered it becomes clear how private groups might foment a war between two nations.

Fortunately, although we may not have unlimited time before our system reaches the breaking point, we may have thirty or forty years. And we may have a gradual and peaceful change during that period, even without explicit agreements or the creation of a super-state. One reason why we may have so much time is obvious—nations like the United States, the Soviet Union, and the major European powers that have the greatest capability for making trouble are amazingly cautious about resorting to the use of modern arms, or even formal threats to use them. In addition to being cautious themselves, they restrain others. In others words deterrence is likely to work almost all of the time. The trouble is that one failure can be very destructive and possibly catastrophic. The unsatisfactory nature of a system of world order and security based upon present deterrence concepts with their ever-present possibility of failure, is not, of course, in itself a sufficient reason for us to weaken our deterrent. This could easily make matters worse, not only from a narrow national point of view, but also from the viewpoint of buying time within which to develop a more just and stable world order or, equally important, being in a position to influence the development of this order.

35. THE RADICAL COMMITMENT
kenneth keniston

In 1967 Professor Keniston, a Yale University psychologist, participated in a study of "Vietnam Summer," a program organized by the American New Left movement to protest American military involvement in Southeast Asia. A small number of highly active radical leaders took part in a series of seventeen intensive interviews. These interviews touched upon political development, childhood experiences, social values, and many other aspects of personal life. The average age of the interviewees was twenty-three; all came from comfortable backgrounds. In the book from which the following extracts are taken, the author seeks to emphasize "the recurrent themes in the past histories of the young men and women who led Vietnam Summer, constructing a schematized picture of the personal roots of the radical commitment."

Question: Do the personal testimonies of these interviewees articulate some of your own deepest feelings about the state of society and the world? Why?

Any interviewer who in effect asks a group of young men and women "How did you come to be what you are?" almost inevitably elicits answers that somewhat artificially integrate and sum up an ongoing process. Such answers must

From *Young Radicals: Notes on Committed Youth,* copyright © 1968 by Kenneth Keniston. Reprinted by permission of Harcourt, Brace & World, Inc.

be seen as provisional and preliminary, as progress (or non-progress) reports, as time slices across a moving flow. Yet such statements are useful, for in them the crucial themes of past and present life are often interwoven. . . .

One young woman, when I asked her if she had ever considered abandoning her work in the Movement, replied:

> No, I've really been very happy. This is one of the things I feel very positive about. . . . One of the things I've learned in the last two years is that you don't need very much to live on. . . . It gives me a completely different perspective on what it is that I decide to go into. I wouldn't mind having a car, but I would have to learn to drive first. I can think of ways to enjoy a nice way of life, but I don't feel obsessed with it. . . .
>
> I sort of feel myself to be open and I feel very happy. It is like I have built a whole new world. It has been a very good transition. I feel like I have a solid foundation. . . . I just saw a friend of mine from ten years ago the other day, and it was very difficult to talk to her. . . . You realize that the people you want to be your friends are people where you don't have to go through the whole process of justifying why you're doing what you're doing. . . . You end up eliminating a lot of your old friends. . . . The kind of people who get involved in the Movement are really people who have a strong need for friendship. . . . I don't feel as politically conscious as maybe I should. Maybe I'm approaching things much more pragmatically. How do you build something? How do you get things done? [1]

In this statement about herself, she introduces issues that will recur in these interviews: her relationship to middle-class monetary and success values, her feeling of openness to the future, her gradual entry into the Movement and her loss of her past friends, her need for friendship, her sense of ideological inadequacy, and finally—and perhaps most important—the questions with which she approaches her own future and the future of the Movement.

For this young woman, as for all of her fellow workers in Vietnam Summer, personality and politics are impossible to separate. Again and again, they stressed the personal origins of political beliefs, and the effects of political involvement in their personal lives. For many, political involvement had been a major catalyst for personal change:

> It was only when I first began to do my first political activity, which was—I can't remember, a boycott or peace work or something—but I really started to move personally. I started to put my mind to a project, an activity, a way of thinking. I really started to work hard in terms of learning how to do that

[1] All of the quotations in the text are from the young radicals I interviewed in Vietnam Summer. I have changed many personal, organizational, and place names. My own comments or amplifications are noted by brackets. I have used ellipses to indicate deletions from the original spoken narratives. Some quotations have been edited to eliminate unnecessary redundancy or to increase clarity. Apart from these minimal changes, they reflect accurately the spoken style of those I interviewed.

stuff. . . . I really put my personality into it. That's what I've been doing ever since. I obviously sublimate a lot of stuff into political activity.

Not only does this young radical underline the personal component of his political life, but he clearly indicates that a major part of the meaning of his radical commitment lies in its role in helping to start "to move personally." Another, summarizing his political development, said:

The politics came after the people. There was always a personal relationship first. And the most important thing of what you were going to do with a person was personal, not political. The political development came from that background, and from the reading I did.

Here again, the inseparability of the personal, especially the interpersonal, and the political is underlined.

As a rule, formal elaborated and dogmatic ideological considerations were seldom discussed in these interviews; they rarely formed a major part of the radical's presentation of himself to me. No doubt, had I had a political scientist inquiring about political philosophy, statements of formal ideology could have been obtained. But to give great emphasis to such statements would, I believe, falsify the personal position of these radicals, which rests on a set of time-honored principles rather than on any elaborately rationalized ideology. One interviewee, for example, volunteered:

One of the things that makes it difficult for me to trace where I came from is the fact that I don't have an ideology. If I did, if I knew precisely, I mean if I had clear political goals—well, I have something of an analysis of why certain things happen, and why certain things must happen. But it's not very tightly formulated and I'm very flexible about it. If I did have a rigid view, I would be better able to look back and say, "This is where this and that came from." . . . But I think it's better this way. It's more real, it ties in, it forces you to bring yourself together more as a unified thing rather than to say, "Here are my politics, Dr. Keniston, and this is where they came from. Now if you want to talk to me about a person, that is something else." But things really are together, and that's real. It's so— Things really *are* together.

And another noted in a similar vein:

I have never been an ideologue. I always have been a guy who winds up, in terms of ideology, taking it for the excitement of it and really examining it, but I have a lot of difficulty in putting together broad theories. I feel much more humble, I think, than other people do. I think I'm probably wrong about that, but it was always the organizing things that I felt the most at home with. . . .

Formal statements of rationalized philosophy, articulated interpretations of history and political life, and concrete visions of political objectives were almost completely absent in the interviews (and in this respect, as in many others, this is a typically American group). But what did emerge was a strong, if often largely implicit, belief in a set of basic moral principles: justice, decency, equality, responsibility, non-violence, and fairness. The issue of "tactics," too, was often discussed—the utility of demonstrations, community organizing, electoral politics, or "resistance" as instrumentalities for the New Left. But the primary orientation to basic principles, although one of the most important issues in their lives, was so taken for granted by them (and to a large extent at the time by me as well) that it was rarely emphasized in these young radicals' summaries of themselves. And questions about tactics seemed to them so much a pragmatic matter of effectiveness that they did not include them in their self-descriptions.

Convinced that the personal and the political were linked, and emphatically anti-ideological in their ideologies, these young men and women usually emphasized the personal satisfaction they derived from Movement activities. One individual, when asked why he planned to persist as a radical, said:

> Part of it is that it's something that I do well. I wouldn't like to have to get up at 9:00 o'clock every morning and finish work at 5:30 and be under somebody's authority. [Laughs] . . . and then one is contemporary with the mainstreams of society. One feels on top of things.

Another spoke in comparable terms about the "motion in the Movement":

> I've had a lot of help, because you know there's motion in the Movement. There are people doing things, there are things happening, there are all kinds of exciting people. That helps. That helps a lot.

Still another sustaining force for some of these young radicals is the conviction that they are part of a rising tide of radicalism that is increasingly required by modern American society. For example, one young man, after having discussed his own father's growing impatience with American society, said:

> It's happening now on a national basis, some of the people who are old liberals in the analysis of American society are increasingly radical. For example, Gunnar Myrdal, who back in the fifties had a kind of "growing pains" analysis—you know, America is young and is having growing pains—his analysis is different now: something has got to be done. And I found this also among people like my father, intellectual types, that they are getting the same type of response. A lot of people of your generation or my father's generation, and from your discipline, are getting drawn into political activities.

One prime source of satisfaction in the radical's commitment, then, derives from the feeling of contemporaneity, of being in motion with others, and of involvement with a changing, growing tide of radicalism.

For others, the satisfactions of Movement work come partly from a feeling of continuity with the values of the personal and collective past. One young man from a radical family summarized his recent development as follows:

It just seems to me that what happened was that I saw a different way of relating to people. When I started to look around at things, I felt that political activity was a vehicle for that. But it wasn't until last year that I really started feeling that I've come all the way back round full circle. Politics was no longer a vehicle, but this was *the thing*. And then I said to myself, "My God, it never *was* a vehicle. This is what you *were*. This is where you're *at*. This is where you've come from. This is how you're made up. And you aren't supposed to be doing anything else. You shouldn't feel badly about not doing this or not doing that. This is what you *are*."

It's just, you know, a nice feeling. It's very, very supportive, both that emotional and intellectual feeling. It helps you on. It's not something that happens once and there's beautiful flowing music. But once you get that feeling, it's there, and when the time comes and you start getting into the dumps, you can say, "Look, this is what you were made to do."

Another young man, this one not from a radical family, described a strong sense of continuity to the basic values of his family:

I had a good solid family, no parental trouble among themselves or with the kids. My old man is very straight with the kids. That's been very important, because it has kept in the back of my mind all the time concepts like responsibility, seriousness: "If you're going to work on this, you can't just do it on weekends." I have this whole complex of ideas about carrying through with what you start, being serious about it, being confident about it. I really never could have come close to just flipping out and becoming totally alienated. . . . It doesn't seem to me that simple. All capitalists don't beat their wives, all workers are not hopeless charlatans. . . . That kind of thing was in the back of my mind, nagging at me: "You're not involved, you're not doing anything." . . .

The values I got from my family, the ones that I've kept, are good. I've pared them and peeled them to fit my own style, but there is a good continuity here. I mean it's a new generation, but there's a lot from my old generation that can't be minimized. Otherwise, I might have flipped out or something like that, or just turned myself off altogether.

This young man, from a relatively apolitical background, links his involvement in the Movement and his escape from "just flipping out and becoming totally alienated" to his continuity with the values of his family.

No summary can characterize the satisfactions of Movement work: for each individual, they are numerous and complex. To return to a central theme in radical development, the crucial sustaining force in the radical commitment is probably an underlying sense of acting on one's basic principles. One individual, for example, who grew up in a religious family, argued that his "basic rhetoric" is a theological one, now translated into secular terms:

I don't get upset about sexual things, and I don't get upset about religious things. But I feel that honesty, among yourselves, is necessary. I feel that people should fulfill their commitments. I feel that one has to be serious, and able to work hard. . . . I feel those kinds of things. It's not that I'm against pot smoking or having great dances or wasting time or watching television—I love all those things. . . . But my vision had always been that all of a sudden a million people would march on Washington, singing "A Mighty Fortress Is Our God," and the government would come tumbling down. I would feel much more identified with that than if a million people marched on Washington singing "The Internationale." . . .

If I let down all of my defenses, I would wind up being Billy Graham or Elmer Gantry. That would be my first impulse, to say, "That's immoral." My basic rhetoric is a very theological one. . . . Maybe if I were born three or four hundred years earlier, I'd be a preacher. I'd say that the people should reform, that they should stop being sinners, that they should realize that the world has to be built on different foundations—"Tis the final conflict," "Let each man take his place." [Laughs] . . . My initial thing is to get up and preach to people and expect them to follow me. That's where my impulse is, to speak out to the world.

Here the underlying appeal to moral principle is clearly stated: the call to sinners to reform and repent. He went on to note, however, "My problem is that the basic rhetoric is one that's irrelevant. . . . [It] just doesn't work."

Still another, in the course of discussing whether he should buy a friend's Volkswagen microbus, indicated the importance of his underlying moral commitment:

It may cost me three hundred dollars, and I *had* been going to give that money to a political organization. I may buy it anyway—I think I probably will. It will be nice to have a microbus, and I will have a long life to give money away to political organizations.

[K. K.: But it's a conflict for you.] Right. [Pause] But right now, it looks like there aren't many more kinds of possessions I would like to have. I don't believe people should go crazy and work sixteen hours a day because the revolution isn't coming tomorrow. It's wrong not to live until then. But I feel very strongly that people with a lot of money should give it. That comes from the same kind of value—you absolutely must do what's good for everyone, not what's good for yourself. It would be impossible for me to do that. . . . I'm not uncommitted. I have meaning in my life, that's not the problem. I have other problems, but that's not one of them. . . . And that's something (it's certainly true that I got it from my parents) that was very valuable.

In asserting that "you absolutely must do what's good for everyone," and in connecting this value to his parents, this young man affirmed both his moral commitment and his link to his past.

Another aspect of the radical commitment involves a sense of having "grown up" through involvement in the Movement. Many noted how much they had changed, in ways they liked, since their involvement in the New Left:

I started off being very insecure in terms of what I was thinking and what I was saying. I usually felt I was wrong, and that I should follow other people's directions. But then, over the last years, I have realized that I am usually right. . . . It's not a matter of whether my predictions are right, whether Bobby Kennedy will run or not. . . . But I feel much more secure in myself, and I am much more willing at this point to project my alternatives onto people, and to push them very hard. I am more willing now to have people follow my direction and to take responsibility for it. That means the possibility of failure and getting people angry at you and all kinds of things. That was a very big struggle within myself. . . .

Finally, being committed to the Movement means being involved with other people, not being alone, being part of a meaningful group. The radical, as a member of a small political minority, must continually remind himself and be reminded that he is not alone. One individual, for example, said:

> You get these periodic shots in the arm that are very essential. Just like the parties around here. You'd think that in this place you wouldn't feel isolated. But after you get back to your apartment or to wherever you live, you see how few you are, and it gets to be very discouraging. There are billions of *them* out there, and we can't even move the students, we can't even get ten per cent of the students. But then, you have a party after the meeting on Thursday night, and you get sixty guys who you really like that are radical, and you say, "All right, sixty is enough." You feel reinspired and reinvigorated. It's the same thing with national meetings. You get people together and they give you a shot in the arm. You figure there are some other people around, and you're ready to go back to your own turf and do something yourself.

In raising the issue of helpless isolation ("There are billions of *them* out there"), and then dispelling it by discussing the importance of personal contact with others in the Movement, this young man pointed to a crucial theme in the political lives and personal histories of most of his fellows.

Yet whatever the sense of solidarity in the New Left, membership in a small, fragmented, struggling, and largely unsuccessful radical movement is clearly difficult to sustain. And sustaining most of those I interviewed was their basic feeling of self-respect or adequacy, a feeling they usually traced back to their families. One young woman, when I asked her how she managed to keep going when times were bad, said:

> I don't know. I always had the feeling in the family that I was better than [my siblings]. I was smarter than they were, I didn't have to study as hard, that my mother liked me best. . . . That's a terrible thing to think at times, and I felt guilty about it. And then my mother was very supportive. She was always very supportive, and even though I didn't always trust her, I always fell back to her. If I needed her, she was there. A lot of times I still do that now. . . . And I've been lucky because there has always been somebody there who had said the things that need to be said when I'm in a slump. Those have been my friends and my parents—my mother—even though she has all these bad things, when I'm down in the dumps, she is there, even now. I don't go to her any more, but when I was a kid I always did.

Another, describing himself in general, said:

> I'll tell you this much—I have . . . a funny kind of self-confidence. And what it did was probably to accentuate even more my need for what I'm

doing now. That is to say, "See, boob, you can really finish something; you can work on it and you can really see it through." And then you can say, "Well, that's good, let's look at what it was you finished, let's look at the part you played, what you did."

For all of their self-confidence and commitment to radicalism, these young men and women also have abundant self-doubts. Some of these are intimate and personal. One young man, discussing the undesirable aspects of his parents' relationship with each other, said:

> I find that I seem to be duplicating that relationship. I seem to be just moving irrationally into that, using my parents' relationship as a model for my relationship with Judy. In a sense, she puts more value—I do too, but I don't move naturally in that direction—on a *relationship* between people. And I put much more emphasis on the family being an arena from which you go out and do things . . . for instance, my father doesn't do any work around the house, and Judy gets angry at me because I don't take out the garbage or wash the dishes. It's not that I don't think I should, it's just that I've never seen it like that before. . . . That makes me very upset because I consider my father a failure.

This young man's most pressing self-doubts center on his fear of being like his father, a fear that is unusually intense in him, but that has echoes in others with whom he worked.

Others questioned their competence for the work they set out to do. One, discussing the aftereffects of a recent meeting that depressed him, said:

> I began to question a lot in terms of myself, about where I am in the Movement. Every so often that happens. The whole question came up of which tools I have at my disposal to do the job I want to do. Sometimes I feel that they are very very lacking. . . . I feel I should read more, but I feel I have worked so long and I'm so exhausted that I just can't. Or I read something that's non-political. I'm very very shoddy about it. It's very depressing to me, because I used to like to read like crazy when I was younger and I was in college. But now I don't. . . . I've never read a basic economics book. How about that?
>
> It may be very odd—I say odd because I can't find a better word—I really knew a hell of a lot for an eighteen- or nineteen-year-old kid. . . . . In terms of politics, I had been doing a lot of reading. I knew a pretty good deal. The problem is that (this may not be true) I haven't made three years' progress in three years' time in certain areas of knowledge. I have developed very well certain abilities, really pushed them almost to the limit of their development at this stage of my life. Yet there are other things which I need to have as a background. I need things that would give me more perspective to help me analyze what it is I've done and what it is I need to do. I need to know more about economics to know how that functions. I want to do more reading in history . . . for example, labor history. I don't know about that. I think if you have a radical perspective, you really should. I just don't have those things.

But for all of their personal and political self-doubts, and for all of the changes that have occurred in their lives in recent years, the most impressive feature of the radical commitment in these young men and women is the sense of continuity most of them feel with their pasts. One young man, discussing his parents' desire that he return to school, said:

> This summer they were talking about "Are you thinking about going back to school? We're proud of you and of what you're doing, and we don't want to push you, but let's sit down and talk about this." And I said, "Hey, great, let's *do* talk about it." I'm looking forward to really trying to explain to them the kinds of things I feel, that I am a very personal embodiment of what they are, what they created in a son, and what they brought me up to be. The thing I want to say to them is, "If you feel you've made a mistake, then tell me so. But *I* feel this is the way you brought me up. This is the way you and all the other influences that you put before me in life, that you provided for me—directly and indirectly—[that you] helped make me." I'd like to sit down and really talk with them.

Here again, two important issues are joined: the inner conflict between the Movement and the Academy, and the view of radicalism as an outgrowth of the core values of the past.

To these young men and women, then, being a radical means many things. It of course means a general commitment to the general goals and tactics of the New Left. But for all, this commitment is more personal and moral than dogmatic or formally ideological; and in telling me, a psychologist, who they were, they invariably underlined the connection between the private and the political in their lives. Being a radical means a commitment to others, to a Movement "in motion," and to some kind of effort to create a viable radicalism in America. The radical commitment rests on a set of basic moral principles and instincts more than on any formal and elaborated philosophy. And these principles were invariably felt to be continuous with the people and the principles of their personal past. Finally, being a radical meant being open to an indeterminate future.

36. RADICALISM ON THE RIGHT

gilbert abcarian

There are many approaches to the explanation of the resurgence of political radicalism in contemporary American society. Indeed, a basic element of crisis in our society is the conspicuous polarization of much political thinking and acting into "Left" and "Right" dimensions that began in the late 1950s and continues to the present.

From Gilbert Abcarian, "Alienation and the Radical Right," *Journal of Politics,* XXVII, November 1965.

The selection below analyzes the Radical Right movement, considering the basic ideological features that motivate it, and hypothesizing that alienation is a fundamental cause, or antecedent condition, that stimulates and sustains that ideology.

The ideology of the radical right consists of the first six of the nine features discussed below. Each element of that ideology will be illustrated briefly.

1. Individualism.   An imperative and unavoidable "choice" is posited by the Right between a "free" and a "collectivist" political destiny for Americans. Collectivism, in the words of Robert Welch, is a European "cancer" that has spawned governmental centralization that has resulted in massive bureaucracy, erosion of individual freedom and initiative, subversion of the federal system, and violation of the economic "laws of man and nature." Only a determined campaign of anticollectivism holds any promise of rediscovering traditional American individualism.

2. Republicanism.   "This is a Republic, not a democracy—Let's keep it that way!" says a mail sticker popular in Birch Society circles. This nation is not, cannot be, a democracy, for the central credo of democracy is equality, which is contrary to the laws of nature and which science demonstrates to be a false premise in the light of human experience. The philosophical presuppositions and functional processes of contemporary American democracy have proven bankrupt. In a "true republic," the will of the masses will be represented, but only through the consciences of representatives whose task it is to evaluate and interpret the intent of such will. Only republicanism, or government for the people by a qualified elite, can save us from the ravages of immoral mob-rule.

3. Fundamentalism.   Americans are implored to return to divine and eternal truths, both biblical and secular. On the religious side, the call is for a return to literal interpretation of the bible; on the political side, the call is for a return to "Americanism" and "Constitutionalism." Everywhere, we are tempted and seduced by ungodly forces. Our young must be protected against the siren calls of moral relativism and youthful idealism.

The nation is drifting aimlessly. National purpose has been lost. Worse than that, its very existence is threatened, for "we are at war, and we are losing that war simply because we don't or won't realize that we are in it." Opinion leaders have failed, or in some cases deliberately betrayed, us. Remedial action appears impossible owing to an inability to locate and exert effective influence upon those persons commanding the "real" centers of power—unless, that is, God-fearing, flag-respecting Americans return to the fundamentals. A small body of true believers can lead a return to the pristine fundamentals that once set this nation on a true course.

4. Purification. Conspiracy and betrayal—in the guise of social change—are felt to have reached ominous proportions. Monumental errors of judgment over the past several decades point to an alarming truth: "How can you explain the mistakes of our leaders for the last 30 years," the head of the Christian Crusade inquires, "if there aren't Communists giving them advice?" Destruction of the conspiracy cannot be separated from halting social and political change, for the primary threat to the nation is "treason right in our government."

The nation must be purified and redeemed. It is urgently necessary to expose the hydra-headed conspiracy that infests government, churches, educational institutions, and the mass media of communication. Purification is an urgent, patriotic duty.

5. Restoration. The U.S. is presumed to have attained a Golden or Heroic Age, usually, though not invariably, located somewhere in the century preceding "that man" F.D.R. The Golden Age constitutes a universally valid political model to which Americans must return, and one that the rest of the world must respect and emulate. But Americans have become careless with their sacred legacy. "In this land occurred the only true revolution in man's history. . . . It must be fought for, protected, and handed on . . . or one day we will spend our sunset years telling our children and our children's children what it was once like in the United States when men were free."

Domestically, the Golden Age is sometimes equated with the *status quo,* though more frequently located in the past. Internationally, the Golden Age is typically regarded as lost by the early twentieth century, owing to seduction into degrading and humiliating foreign entanglements. Despite the obstacles, the Golden Age can and must be restored by achieving victory over the domestic forces that block the return to authenticity by preaching and practicing compromise, coexistence and cooperation with national enemies.

6. Unilateralism. Because it has presumably failed to protect "vital" and "legitimate" interests and moral values, the complex of assumptions, policies and programs governing American foreign policy during the past several decades must be rejected. The prevailing policy consensus is a failure and has actually accelerated the communist plan for world enslavement. Public officials are guilty of "surrender" and "appeasement" and must be purged. Rep. Bruce Alger of Texas demands, characteristically, to know "If treason be defined as giving aid and comfort to the enemy, why isn't aid to Yugoslavia treason?"

The U.S. must invade Cuba, terminate diplomatic relations with communist states, withdraw from the U.N. and N.A.T.O., halt cultural exchange programs, encourage rebellion behind the iron curtain, etc. In short, the U.S. should act, rather than humbly react, and should do so in the spirit of justified unilateralism, unencumbered by false principles of diplomacy, expedience or multilateralism.

The political style of the radical right is reflected in the three remaining features to be discussed.

7. Telescoping.   Rightwing extremism expresses itself publicly in the form of telescoping—the process of compressing or coalescing levels and categories of political events and analyses which are ordinarily treated as distinct or unique. A characteristic example of telescoping is provided by Senator Thurmond's assertion that "communism is fundamentally socialism. When socialism, in turn, is understood, one cannot help but to realize that many of the domestic programs advocated in the U.S., and many of those adopted, fall clearly within the category of socialism."

In the same manner, former President Eisenhower has been portrayed as an instrument of the communist movement, while recent Supreme Court decisions on religion in the public schools, through compression of facts and reasoning, are regarded as facilitating various plots. Oversimplification is hence the central outcome of telescoping.

8. Reductionism.   In its belief that every major irritation in society has a simple cause, a simple explanation and a simple solution, the radical right reduces such irritations to communism. The list of problems and events treated reductionistically is enormous, ranging from urban renewal (a Marxist scheme to subvert state and local governments), to the cost of funerals (anti-capitalist subversion of the American way of life and death). International problems are similarly viewed in the reductionistic framework in terms of assessing those courses of action that will minimize or maximize the communist threat.

9. Protest through direct action.   Rightwing ideology is clarified and popularized through action programs, usually in the form of public protest. Welch speaks of the need to organize "all kinds of fronts." He insists that "for us to be too civilized is unquestionably to be defeated" and that the Birch Society "means business every step of the way." Direct action takes the form of censorship drives and demands, denunciation of public officials by private citizens, and a broad range of "seminars," "alerts," "schools" and "forums."

In order to develop certain relationships between radical rightist ideology and style, and the condition of alienation—the major burden of this study—it will be helpful to refer in passing to rightist literature for manifestations of specific forms of political alienation. As a prelude to such examination, let us be clear what alienation in general implies as the concept is employed by an increasing number of social and political scientists.

Alienation is experienced in varying forms and degrees of intensity when certain forces block the individual's quest for so-called authentic, or true, existence, when he feels unable to shake off a sense of cleavage, of an abyss, within himself, and between himself and other men. At bottom, the alienated man is convinced that he is unable to assume what he believes to be his rightful role in society. Or we may say, alternatively, that "The alienated man is acutely aware of the discrepancy between who he is and what he believes he should be."

Behind this bare hint at alienation is a large, impressive, but heterogeneous literature that traces alienation in its philosophical, political, religious, psychiatric, sociological and other aspects. One can hardly avoid encountering references these days to investigations of the "unattached," the "marginal," the "obsessed," the "normless" and the "isolated" man. Release from traditional ties and certitudes, the stresses created by large-scale industry and technology, the bureaucratization of the Western state—these and many other forces have been viewed as instrumentalizing and mechanizing the individual.

In summary, alienation analysis suggests that while the individual has achieved freedom of sorts from traditional restraints, that very freedom converts him into an instrument of purposes outside himself. His new-found freedom makes him apprehensive in the extreme. As Erich Fromm notes: "Freedom has reached a critical point where, driven by the logic of its own dynamism, it threatens to change into its opposite."

Resuming the main line of analysis, the general concept of alienation will be developed by employing four of its major variables—meaninglessness, normlessness, powerlessness and social isolation—as tools of analysis of radical rightist literature.

1. Meaninglessness. The experiences of the rightwing extremist leave him in great apprehension regarding the "absolutes" of truth, value and meaning. For he senses, often unconsciously, that traditional conceptions of such absolutes have atrophied or disappeared in the life of contemporary man. Robert Welch speaks of a "deep and basic anxiety" which he traces to a "loss of faith . . . in [the individual's] reasons for existence, in his purposes, and his hopes." Referring to the campus scene, William F. Buckley Jr. notes a student turn to the Right as the result of an awakening "to the great nothingness of liberalism" and the realization "that there is nothing in the liberal creed save an intricate methodological structure (Academic Freedom, Dissent, Democracy, the United Nations, Mrs. Roosevelt) on which you build and build and build, as tirelessly as Sisyphus, but which ends us up . . . helpless before the barbarians."

As a consequence of the tension brought on by apprehension about the efficacy of traditional absolutes and the compulsion to believe that some version of them is nevertheless operative, the rightwing extremist suffers from a sense of meaninglessness. He is troubled persistently by a realization that he is losing, or has already lost, his feeling of significance, worth, belonging and rootedness of thought and action. In the end, "things don't make sense anymore." Hence meaninglessness is simultaneously experienced and bitterly condemned.

2. Normlessness. The experienced loss of absolutes, of anchorage in necessary standards, rules and models results in the loss of a personal center of values and standards of certitude. The result is normlessness.

The fabric of morality provided through the centuries by Christianity is now "pierced and torn and weakened beyond needed dependability . . .," says

Mr. Welch. The outcome "is the rise of the amoral man" whose hallmark is "pragmatic opportunism with hedonistic aims."

Normlessness is evident in constant appeals of the Right for a "return" to the sacred "heritage" of traditional "Americanism." Return to purity and historical fidelity is presented as the overriding duty of patriots. "A great cleansing and uniting force for the nation" is urgently required, says Moral Re-Armament, Inc. For "Unfaithfulness in the home, perversion in high places and low, decadence in the arts, lawless youth, class war, race war, dishonesty—these are becoming the marks of American life. We are all responsible."

3. Powerlessness. The feeling that one has lost personal efficacy and the ability to act influentially and significantly within his social universe reflects alienation in the form of powerlessness.

In his remarks to a Senate subcommittee shortly after being relieved of his command in Germany, General Edwin Walker indicated loss of personal efficacy as follows: "We are at war, we are infiltrated. We are losing that war every day. Are our hands tied, yours and mine? We need a substitute for defeat. If it is not within the power of this Congress to provide it—then the people of these United States are not truly represented."

The powerless man feels unable to influence or control opinion and action within his environment. He may feel this way with such intensity that it becomes a serious, intrusive concern in the lives of others, as well as in his own. He does not understand or accept resignation and helplessness either in himself or in others. "America is at war, a war we are losing," says Moral Re-Armament. Republicans and Democrats—it is the same. We move heedless and headless without an ideology against an ideological enemy."

Perhaps nowhere is powerlessness expressed more forcefully or unmistakably than in the following statement by a Council member of the Birch Society: "The history and rise of the John Birch Society is the history of the revolted, misinformed, deceived, abused, angry American. . . . The basic fact which explains the creation and rise of the John Birch Society is that the American people are sick and tired of defeatism, humiliation, incompetence, surrender, and treason." The rightist is convinced that he is relatively powerless to exert levers against those who occupy local, state and national political commandposts.

4. Social isolation. Loneliness and solitariness, the hallmarks of social isolation, result from loss of a personal center of values and standards of certitude, and the feeling of functional insufficiency and ineffectiveness.

The head of the Christian Crusade, Rev. Billy James Hargis, has remarked sadly: "Everything is so impersonal now. The Government takes care of you with a check. . . . The government can't do anything about spiritual needs. It just hands out money."

Impersonality, emptiness and distrust come to characterize one's life.

"Let us all thank whatever God we severally worship," says Welch, "that there is so large a remnant of the really true believers still left." Welch goes on to note that precisely because the community of true believers is so small, "We desperately need their unshakable confidence in absolutes, in eternal principles and truths, in a world of increasing relativism, and transitoriness in all things."

Social isolation creates an obsessive interest in distinguishing between "friends" and "enemies," until preoccupation with that distinction frequently becomes the central concern of interpersonal relations.

37. VIOLENCE AND AMERICAN VALUES
john b. kirby

It is difficult for many Americans to concede that violent behavior is an inherent part of the American character, that it is a "normal" feature of the American political and historical experience. Even historians have tended to stress consensus and overlook conflict of a violent sort. This sanguine view is challenged through exploration of the connection between violence and values.

Very few social scientists have pictured violent behavior as an inherent part of the American character[1]. For the most part, they have seen violence as the product of individual abnormalities or of certain unique and unusual conditions which have occurred in the American past. Why this interpretation has found acceptance among historians can be understood, in part, as a result of what John Higham pointed out has been the concentration of American historiography on the unifying rather than the divisive forces in our society's develop-

From John B. Kirby, "Violence and the Conflict of American Values," *The Rocky Mountain Social Science Journal,* VI, October 1969, pp. 9–19.

[1] Sociologist Lewis A. Coser and psychiatrist Bruno Bettelheim provide interesting explanations for why this approach has not found wide acceptance in their own respective disciplines; see *The Annals of the American Academy of Political and Social Sciences,* 364 (March 1966), 9–10, 51–52. This entire issue of the *Annals* is devoted to the "Patterns of Violence" and contains many worthwhile interpretations, some of which have been noted in this paper. Evidence that some social scientists may be reevaluating their previous ideas is seen in a recent article in the *New York Times Magazine* (April 28, 1968), 24–25; 111–14, entitled, "Is America by Nature a Violent Society?"

ment.[2] Played down to a large extent has been the matter of social conflict, and although conflict and violence are not identical phenomena, the latter is often the product of the former. Moreover, the conflict which historians have acknowledged in their studies has generally been portrayed as lacking any deep-seated ideological or philosophical roots. Despite occasional outbursts of brutality and intolerance, historians have essentially accepted the notion that the American values formulated during the eighteenth century have been universally recognized (if not always adhered to) by the majority of the population; hence, the "homogeneous" quality of the "unchanging" American character.

The basic theme of this essay is that this "consensus" version of history, although valid in many respects, overlooks important considerations concerning the American system of values, which, if understood, may help more fully to explain both social conflict and violent behavior. "Value" is referred to here as what sociologist Robin Williams defines as the "criteria by which goals are chosen," rather than the concrete goals of action themselves.[3] In this sense, two values, which Alexis de Tocqueville discerned as essential to the American democratic ideal and to the concept of success, are of particular importance. One is the belief in equality of opportunity, meaning that all individuals theoretically have the right to compete on the same level with their fellow men in their quest for a determined goal—what David Potter has termed the right to "parity in competition." [4] Although certain minority groups, in particular the Negro, have historically been denied this right, one can argue that even these individuals have nevertheless subscribed to equality of opportunity as a *criterion* upon which their own ambitions could be achieved. The same qualification (in regard to minority groups) applies to Tocqueville's second doctrine of individual freedom, which expresses the faith that men should not only be given an equal chance to compete, but that they should be free from individual,

[2] John Higham, "The Cult of the 'American Consensus': Homogenizing Our History," *Commentary*, XXVII (February 1959), 93–100. In his criticism of the Boorstin, Hartz and Rossiter approach, Higham comments that "the conservative frame of reference . . . creates a paralyzing incapacity to deal with the elements of spontaneity, effervescence, and violence in American history" (*ibid.*, p. 100). In "Beyond Consensus: The Historian as Moral Critic," *The American Historical Review*, LXVII (April 1962), 609–25, Higham offers some suggestions regarding a new approach which includes both "causal history" and "moral history." For a somewhat different and more critical interpretation of recent American historiography, see Howard Zinn's "History as Private Enterprise," *Motive*, XXVIII (December 1967), 28–35.
[3] Robin M. Williams, Jr., *American Society: A Sociological Interpretation* (New York: Alfred A. Knopf, 1960), p. 400. Williams makes it clear that the individual does not have to be "aware" of the actual cultural factors that determine his values in order for the values to affect his sense of goal fulfillment (see p. 24).
[4] David M. Potter, *People of Plenty* (Chicago: University of Chicago Press, 1954), p. 92.

institutional, and, above all, state regulations that might impede their opportunities.[5]

Writers, such as sociologist Seymour Martin Lipset, who generally support the interpretation of the homogeneous American character have acknowledged that the desire for equality and the desire for individual achievement are, as Tocqueville described them in the 1830's, often contradictory. "The same equality," stated Tocqueville, "that renders him [the American] independent of each of his fellow citizens, taken severally, exposes him alone and unprotected to the influence of the greater number. . . ." [6] According to Lipset,

> complete commitment to equality involves rejecting some of the implications of valuing achievement; and the opposite is also true. Thus, when the equalitarianism of left or liberal politics is dominant, there is a reaction against achievement, and when the values of achievement prevail in a conservative political and economic atmosphere, men tend to depreciate some of the consequences of equality. . . .[7]

Lipset's point is that American culture reflects a cyclical development with respect to its ideological emphasis on equality and individual determination. Depending on the historical circumstances, one value may at any given time be considered more worthy of espousal by the population than the other. When individual self-assertiveness appears to go beyond reasonable bounds, there is a shift, either consciously or unconsciously, back to equal opportunity for all. For many historians, as Lipset implies, this cycle seems to account for the alternating periods of political reform and reaction that have occurred in much of American history.[8]

What Lipset describes, however, is a shifting of the goals rather than the actual values of equality and individualism. A people can alter its goals more

[5] Alexis de Tocqueville, *Democracy in America* (New York: Vintage Books, 1962), II, 9–13. In Chapters II and VIII, Book One, Volume II, Tocqueville most clearly expresses his concern about the contradictory nature of equality and individual freedom. Hans J. Morgenthau in *The Purpose of American Politics* (New York: Vintage Books, 1964), Ch. I, combines Tocqueville's two values into what he calls "equality in freedom," arguing that equality of opportunity has historically been realized through "freedom from restraints." Potter's *People of Plenty* provides a similar explanation in Ch. IV, "Abundance, Mobility and Status." To see how these ideas are related to the phenomenon, of "Social Darwinism," see Richard Hofstadter's *Social Darwinism in American Thought* (Boston: Beacon Press, 1944).

[6] Tocqueville, II, 11.

[7] Seymour Martin Lipset, *The First New Nation* (New York: Basic Books, 1963). Cited in *Individualism and Conformity in the American Character,* ed. Richard L. Rapson (Boston: D. C. Heath, 1967), p. 83.

[8] This view does not necessarily apply to simply the "consensus" school of historical analysis. In fact, an early "progressive" historian, Arthur M. Schlesinger, was one of the first writers to theorize on the "cyclical" approach to America's political development. See Arthur Schlesinger, Sr., "Tides of American Politics," *Yale Review,* XXIX (December 1939), pp. 217–30.

easily than it can alter the values upon which those goals are founded. Thus, they may redirect their goals if they find their ambitions frustrated, but they can seldom substitute different values on which the accepted criterion for success is dependent. Yet the American values of equality of opportunity and individual freedom not only often contradict each other, but if carried to their logical extreme, may very well render one another untenable. Tocqueville clearly recognized this difficulty in his own time, and it remains equally relevant today. When men engage in individual competition, it becomes evident that their freedom is, in effect, seriously limited by a number of factors that are largely beyond their control—other humans caught up in the same competitive race, environmental conditions that impede their struggle, and accidental circumstances that cannot be predicted. In the end, as Tocqueville noted, when the American "comes to survey the totality of his fellows and to place himself in contrast with so huge a body, he is instantly overwhelmed by the sense of his own insignificance and weakness." [9]

Americans, therefore, live constantly in a state of tension produced by two fundamental, but contradictory, abstract values. Hanging over the head of every American citizen is the fear of "his own insignificance and weakness." He will appear insignificant and weak both to himself and in the eyes of his fellow man by his failure to successfully achieve his stated goals; he has, within the theoretical definition of his accepted value structure, no one to blame but himself, although in reality there may be reasons for his apparent failures that transcend his own individual shortcomings. "The individual," states David Potter,

> driven by the belief that he should never rest content in his existing station and knowing that society demands advancement by him as proof of his merit, often feels stress and insecurity and is left with no sense of belonging either in the station to which he advances or in the one from which he set out. [10]

Yet in a society such as America's, where success is determined largely on the basis of individual accomplishment, men find it difficult to dismiss the values that shape their hopes and ambitions.

Although far from agreeing that they are the only causes, psychologists have accepted frustration and anxiety as being two important motivating forces which lead to aggressive and, in some instances, violent conduct. [11] Recent studies have also shown that the degree to which aggressive behavior is re-

[9] Tocqueville, II, 11.
[10] Potter, p. 105.
[11] Elton B. McNeil, "Violence and Human Development," *Annals,* vol. 364, pp. 151–56. See also in the same issue Bruno Bettelheim, "Violence: A Neglected Mode of Behavior," pp. 55–56. Two recent and opposing views on the origins of aggression and violence are found in Konrad Lorenz, *On Aggression* (New York: Harcourt, Brace and World, 1966) and Frederic Wertham, *A Sign for Cain: An Exploration in Human Violence* (New York: Macmillan, 1966). Lorenz argues that aggressive behavior is based on instinct, while Wertham maintains that it is derived from learned experience.

warded, either by individuals or by society as a whole, is important in explaining the intensity of the violence or its likelihood of being repeated.[12] In this context, because of its conflicting nature, the American value structure tends to intensify individual frustration and anxiety, while at the same time, since it holds out success as a tangible reward, it perpetuates and gives sanction to aggressive behavior.

It must be pointed out, however, that there is a positive side here, since both the past and present realization of the "American Dream," believed attained through the ideals of equality and individualism, has also served as a type of controlling factor in American life. Economic abundance (described by Potter in *People of Plenty*) has enabled many Americans to achieve some degree of material success; thus, middle and upper class citizens are generally nonviolent, since the contradiction in their system of values has not seriously impeded the fulfillment of their goals. That more violent criminal acts are committed by oppressed minorities is partially explained by the realization on their part that their similar ambitions stand little chance of ever being achieved. On the other hand, it might be argued that a continued acceptance of the American value system accounts for the infinite patience that Negroes have until recently shown in their three hundred-year struggle to find acceptance in America's mainstream.

Nevertheless, the latent disposition for violence remains inherent within the American system. Bruno Bettelheim has remarked that "violence exists . . . and each of us is born with his potential for it. But we are also born with opposite tendencies, and these must be carefully nurtured if they are to counterbalance the violence." [13] The fact is that the abstract values of equality of opportunity and individual freedom embody both tendencies mentioned by Bettelheim—one toward the control of violence by providing outlets for as well as the realization of natural, aggressive needs, the other toward encouraging violence through the intensification of frustration, anxiety, and conflict resulting from an inherent negation of the values themselves and the rewarding of aggression in the name of individual success or achievement. "Consensus" historians and their sociological allies have concentrated almost entirely on the former factor in their "character" studies in order to show the conciliatory and homogeneous quality of American life.[14] If one looks at the second tendency—

---

[12] Bettelheim, 54–55; Richard H. Walters, "Implications of Laboratory Studies of Aggression for the Control and Regulation of Violence," *Annals,* vol. 364, pp. 67–68.

[13] Bettelheim, 53.

[14] Potter may be considered an exception to this generalization, although he appears to see the basic conflict as arising from the transformation of equality as a "means to advancement" to an ideal "end" denoting "full equality in a classless society" (*People of Plenty,* pp. 92–99). The essential argument of this paper is that "equality of opportunity" as a *means* is, in itself, in direct conflict with "individual freedom" also considered as a criterion to "advancement." In other words, although the two values of equality and freedom may be viewed as both means and ends, they are used in this paper as "criteria by which goals are chosen," and in that context are considered to be contradictory.

the tendency toward social conflict—a different light is shed on the national image.

For the most part, the American novelist rather than the historian or the sociologist has given us an awareness of how human experience has been affected by a conflict in values. Novelists are not required to actually prove or disprove anything; they merely portray life as they see it. This means that complexity, ambivalence, and conflict are likely to be dominant features of their stories, since that is the way human beings often act. In other words, their characters may embody rational as well as irrational tendencies, and a good writer can often capture this ambivalent attitude more fully and authentically than can a social scientist. This may, of course, be achieved unconsciously by the author rather than as a specific purpose.

Nonetheless, from Charles Brockden Brown's *Wieland* to Negro novelist John A. Williams' *The Man Who Cried I Am,* there is an unqualified current of violence in our literature. Literary critic W. M. Frohock has postulated that there have been two distinct strains of violence reflected in the modern American novel.[15] One he calls the "novel of erosion," in which there is a combining of "violence of action with a feeling of time" as a destructive force. John Dos Passos' *Manhattan Transfer,* Thomas Wolfe's *You Can't Go Home Again,* and Ernest Hemingway's *The Sun Also Rises* are considered by Frohock to be outstanding examples. The mood in these novels and others like them is one of frustration and disillusionment with the social order; time is an "agent working upon a character" in such a way that, like the crowd that surrounds Jack Barnes of Hemingway's novel, there is a tendency to strike out at others through violent orgies or to disrupt the timeless activity of life by vicariously living the violence of bull fights. Frohock's second category is the "novel of destiny." Here violence "assumes a different aesthetic function"—time is not significant from the standpoint of what it does to the man, e.g., the gradual eroding of his values—but rather for "what the man does in the time allotted to him." Violence is assumed to be a way of life; aggression toward others and toward oneself is now accepted—this is man's fate. Robert Jordan in *For Whom the Bell Tolls* inflicts harm on other people, and, in the end, he himself faces a violent death. But if Jordan is finally defeated, he is neither impotent nor frustrated, as was Jake Barnes. According to Frohock, "his defeat possesses meaning; . . . a final note of acceptance replaces the old, too familiar note of despair." [16]

This acceptance of violence, constituting what historian David Brion Davis terms the "very quintessence of reality," has become a basic theme in much of American fiction produced since World War I. Davis sees the origins of this acceptance in the nineteenth century Romantic revolt against rationalism, with Herman Melville and Edgar Allen Poe as the earliest disciples. More

[15] W. M. Frohock, *The Novel of Violence in America* (Boston: Beacon Press, 1957), Ch. I.
[16] *Ibid.,* pp. 6–7.

recently, Davis believes, it has been related to an antirationalism created by an "international disenchantment with the view that life is essentially decent, rational, and peaceful." [17] Although the insights of Frohock and Davis are helpful here, they do not fully explain why the problem of "time" or "anti-rationalism" necessarily leads to the novelist's acceptance of violence as a way of life, which is, in effect, what both critics are saying.

In his *Studies in Classic American Literature,* D. H. Lawrence warned that "an artist is usually a damned liar, but his art, if it be art, will tell you the truth of his day." Trust the tale not the writer, he said, for it is the tale that carries the true moral.[18] Again, Tocqueville's observation concerning man's fear of his "own insignificance and weakness" provides a possible clue to the American tale: what this fear does to man, how it operates on him individually and through his relations with others, may be the underlying moral of much of our art. Ultimately, "disenchantment with the view that life is essentially decent, rational, and peaceful" becomes in the American context, "disenchantment" with the supposed rational and nonviolent values of equality of opportunity and individualism. In this regard, it is far less significant what the "style of life" is that a Hemingway attempted to create (if we accept Lawrence) than why he felt the necessity to create it in the first place. Neither is it important that Hemingway's heroes or the heroes of Hawthorne, Melville, and Faulkner do not necessarily fit the conceptualized definition of the American middle class. Frohock points out that Hemingway's characters "will probably not belong to the middle class, because the middle class resorts less often to violence than to due process." [19] Yet this appears only partially true, since both the novelist and his hero reflect the dominant value structure of American life; whether they ultimately accept it or not, or whether they attempt to understand it or merely escape from it, they remain tied to it. The need for the individualistic hero to prove himself through a violent act, as most brutally seen in a figure like Richard Wright's Bigger Thomas, is simply one aberration of the middle class belief in competitive struggle. The callous striking out at other human beings that characterizes so much of the fiction of Wright, Ralph Ellison, James Baldwin, and John Williams and which is also found in the nineteenth century short stories of the American Southwest, reflects again the agonizing and frustrating experience of men who are trying to rationalize the contradictory nature of their own identities.

[17] David Brion Davis, "Violence in American Literature," *Annals,* vol. 364, p. 35. In his analysis, Davis concludes that "the treatment of violence in our literature has grown increasingly ominous for a people who profess to believe in peace and brotherhood" (*ibid.,* 36).

[18] D. H. Lawrence, *Studies in Classic American Literature* (New York: Viking Press, 1966), p. 2. Lawrence was one of the earliest critics to perceive the importance of violence in the American novel.

[19] Frohock, *The Novel of Violence in America,* p. 9.

It may be argued, then, that throughout our literature there is a kind of human desperation—the need of the fictional hero to find meaningful outlets for his supposed abilities, to comprehend his acts in terms of the American system of values, and to guard against his own "insignificance and weakness." The savagery and brutality expressed through the writings of middle and upper class Southern writers in the nineteenth century, like Augustus Longstreet, Alexander McNutt, George Washington Harris, and even Mark Twain, is one unconscious manifestation of this desperation. Life in the Southwest as portrayed by a writer like Harris was often humorous, but the humor involved characters whose social relations and upward mobility were restricted by their particular environment and whose hope, therefore, of achieving "success" was tremendously limited. Harris' Sut Lovingood is funny, but he is often violently funny—people get hurt, some even killed, as a result of his practical jokes.[20] What explains Sut's cruelty towards other people? The answer is found, in part, in the person of Alexander McNutt's equally famous and brutal Chunkey, who exclaims in the course of a fierce struggle with a panther, "Id gin it to her—she fightin' for her supper, I fightin' for my life." [21]

"Fightin' " for one's life—either physically or psychologically—emerges as a central theme in not only the Southern stories of Harris and McNutt but in most of American literature, particularly that of the West. From Cooper's Natty Bumppo to Owen Wister's Virginian to Wallace Stegner's Bo Mason the heroic battle against the forces of nature or the striving to find individual expression through the values of equality and freedom as defined by the American ethic have been predominant concerns. Yet the often portrayed brutal confrontations of men against the Western environment has tended to cloud the real meaning of their conflicts: it is, in reality, not simply the frontier that the Western hero must overcome, but also other human beings. The Indians of Cooper's tales and the "bad guys" like Trampas in *The Virginian* do not hide the fact that these are also people and that the competitive struggle, so widely proclaimed in Western literature, demands that they be destroyed if the "good guys" are to achieve success.

In Wallace Stegner's *Big Rock Candy Mountain* the traditional Western theme is given a more modern orientation. Moreover, Stegner gives a good account of what happens to the individual who is unable or unwilling to reconcile the conflict of values. Bo Mason, the novel's central figure, is in constant

---

[20] See particularly Harris' stories of Sut Lovingood in "Parson John Bullen's Lizards," "Blown Up with Soda," and "Mrs. Yardley's Quilting." The opening paragraph in "Contempt of Court—Almost" is the clearest statement by Harris on violence and "human nater." All these stories can be found in Hennig Cohen and William B. Dillingham (eds.), *Humor of the Old Southwest* (Boston: Houghton Mifflin, 1964), pp. 156–202.

[21] Alexander G. McNutt, "Chunky's Fight with the Panther," *Humor of the Old Southwest*, p. 89.

search for the "American Dream": "There was somewhere, if you knew where to find it, some place where money could be made like drawing water from a well, some Big Rock Candy Mountain where life was effortless and rich and unrestricted and full of adventure and action, where something could be had for nothing." [22] Yet Bo never found his "Candy Mountain"—to the end he was in search of the magical means that would bring him his coveted "pile." Bo not only failed to reach his ultimate goal, but there was very little worthwhile gained from his struggles. His constant labors only brought devastation to himself, his wife, and his children. All of this takes place despite the fact that Bo Mason embodies those characteristics considered most important by Americans for the attainment of one's ambitions—he has desire, courage, and, at times, compassion, intelligence, and vision.

What tragically develops from Stegner's story is the futility of the means by which his hero attempts to realize his aims. The difficulties of the Bo Masons are that they are forced, no matter what the circumstances, to find some form of articulation for their very real individual hopes and desires. Yet they must do this not simply in association with other people, but in competition against them. This, in effect, places them in a state of isolation in relation to all other humans—their family, their friends, their enemies—the "totality of their fellows." In the mythology of the "American Dream," of course, this is what gives an individual like Bo his independence and freedom, but it is also, as Tocqueville saw, what "exposes him alone and unprotected to the influence of the greater number." To achieve, to "make a pile," Bo Mason, by the very nature of the American requirement of success itself, had to hurt or partially destroy other human beings, or they would very possibly destroy him. If he seemed to fail at times (as we all do), he would often take out his wrath on the only concrete source that for him explained his weakness and his lack of achievement—his wife, children, mistress, etc. How else could one comprehend the unfulfilled dream, when equality of opportunity supposedly existed, other than by believing that some other human had compromised one's chances for success?

Much of the violence that prevails in *Big Rock Candy Mountain,* in the tales of the Southwest of the nineteenth century, in the Western literature of writers like Owen Wister and more subtle commentators like Willa Cather and Mark Twain, and, finally, in the novels of the twentieth century can be at least partially explained on the basis of agonized frustration being directed toward other human beings who seem to provide the only justification for individual failure and weakness. It becomes the sole means of accounting for a condition which, in fact, has been caused by the inherent conflict of two abstract ideals that Alexis de Tocqueville perceived over 100 years ago. It is understandable, therefore, why many writers of the twentieth century have accepted violence as

[22] Wallace Stegner, *The Big Rock Candy Mountain* (New York: Hill and Wang, 1938), p. 38.

the true condition of man and the "very quintessence of reality." It is not abnormal for man to act aggressively toward his fellow men but, in reality, quite normal, for the American prerequisite for individual self-fulfillment ultimately determines that he must.

If this brief analysis is valid, then certain conclusions may tentatively be drawn. First, the American value structure, which is believed to be nonviolent, representative of the highest forms of due process, and a controlling factor (e.g., safety valve) for the lessening of frustration and anxiety, may also be responsible for the opposite tendencies when people consciously or unconsciously sense its contradictions. Second, the same value system that encourages competitive struggle between men often leads to outright aggression committed at the expense of other human beings, particularly those who may be closest personally to the aggressor. Moreover, since it is difficult—if not impossible—to alter the ideals that appear to provide the rationale for one's struggle, men often live in a continual state of tension, anxiety, and conflict with themselves and with others; if their ambitions are frustrated, they may turn aggressively on other human beings, who seemingly provide them with the only concrete explanations for their failure. Third, certain types of aggressive behavior (e.g., beating one's wife or children), although less dramatic than the violence committed by the more "criminal elements," may be potentially latent in all Americans who find themselves unable or unwilling to live with the inherent incongruity of their value system and the fear of personal anonymity. Lastly, despite the theory that an empirical adherence to equal opportunity and individualism may be responsible for what Daniel Boorstin has called the American "sense of givenness," that is, the nation's unchanging unity and homogeneity, it is also possible that these same values indicate the cause of social conflict and violence that has marked much of the American past and present. If men believe strongly in the worth of certain values, it makes little difference whether the values are derived from ideological dogma or, as Boorstin argues, from the direct experience of the "American landscape." [23] "Consensus" to a value system which is inherently contradictory may ultimately create intolerance or aggression when particular members of the "consensus" feel they have been excluded or unfairly treated by the value structure itself.

John F. Kennedy once remarked that America will not be healthy until the man of nonviolence is as much a hero as the man of war. This can occur only when American society formulates images and values that lead to peaceful cooperation rather than aggressive competition. America has yet to find what William James called a "moral equivalent" to war, conflict, and violence, because its basic value system often encourages just the opposite set of responses.

[23] Daniel J. Boorstin, *The Genius of American Politics* (Chicago: University of Chicago Press, 1953), Ch. I.

38. THE SECOND SEXUAL REVOLUTION

Moralists have long associated sexual license with the decline of civilizations and national power. While some historians have accepted this view, others have found that advanced civilizations and moral laxity walk hand in hand.

Assuming the accuracy of the following report by *Time* magazine, American sexual norms appear to have undergone a profound transformation. Should this transformation be viewed as an impending sign of doom? Or, conversely, is the loosening of sexual norms a means to greater intellectual freedom and cultural productivity?

The Orgone Box is a half-forgotten invention of the late Dr. Wilhelm Reich, one of Sigmund Freud's more brilliant disciples, who in his middle years turned into an almost classic specimen of the mad scientist. The device was supposed to gather, in physical form, that life force which Freud called libido and which Reich called orgone, a coinage derived from "orgasm." The narrow box, simply constructed of wood and lined with sheet metal, offered cures for almost all the ills of civilization and of the body; it was also widely believed to act, for the person sitting inside it, as a powerful sex stimulant. Hundreds of people hopefully bought it before the U.S. Government declared the device a fraud in 1954 and jailed its inventor. And yet, in a special sense, Dr. Reich may have been a prophet. For now it sometimes seems that all America is one big Orgone Box.

With today's model, it is no longer necessary to sit in cramped quarters for a specific time. Improved and enlarged to encompass the continent, the big machine works on its subjects continuously, day and night. From innumerable screens and stages, posters and pages, it flashes the larger-than-life-sized images of sex. From countless racks and shelves, it pushes the books which a few years ago were considered pornography. From myriad loudspeakers, it broadcasts the words and rhythms of pop-music erotica. And constantly, over the intellectual Muzak, comes the message that sex will save you and libido make you free.

The U.S. is still a long way from the rugged debaucheries of Restoration England or the perfumed corruption of the Gallant Century in France. But Greeks who have grown up with the memory of Aphrodite can only gape at the American goddesses, silken and seminude, in a million advertisements. Indians who have seen the temple sculptures of Konarak can only marvel at some of the illustrated matter sold in American drugstores; and Frenchmen who consider themselves the world's arbiters on the subject, can only smile at the urgency attached to it by Americans. The U.S. seems to be undergoing a revolution of mores and an erosion of morals that is turning it into what Reich called a "sex-affirming culture."

Two generations.   Men with memories ask, "What, again?" The first sexual revolution followed World War I, when flaming youth buried the Victorian era and anointed itself as the Jazz Age. In many ways it was an innocent revolution. In *This Side of Paradise,* F. Scott Fitzgerald alarmed mothers by telling them "how casually their daughters were accustomed to being kissed"; today mothers thank their stars if kissing is all their daughters are accustomed to. It was, nevertheless, a revolution that took nerve, and it was led by the daring few; today's is far more broadly based. In the 1920s, to praise sexual freedom was still outrageous; today sex is simply no longer shocking, in life or literature.

The difference between the '20s and '60s comes down, in part, to a difference between people. The rebels of the '20s had Victorian parents who laid down a Victorian law; it was something concrete and fairly well-defined to rise up against. The rebels of the '60s have parents with only the tattered remnants of a code, expressed for many of them in Ernest Hemingway's one-sentence manifesto: "What is moral is what you feel good after, and what is immoral is what you feel bad after." Adrift in a sea of permissiveness, they have little to rebel against. Parents, educators and the guardians of morality at large do pull themselves together to say "don't," but they usually sound halfhearted. Closed minds have not disappeared, but as a society, the U.S. seems to be dominated by what Congregationalist Minister and Educator Robert Elliot Fitch calls an "orgy of open-mindedness." Faith and principle are far from dead—but what stands out is an often desperate search for "new standards for a new age."

Wide-open atmosphere.   Thus everybody talks about the current sexual situation; but does everyone know what he's talking about? No new Kinsey report or Gallup poll can chart the most private—and most universal—of subjects. What people say does not necessarily reflect what they do, and what they do does not necessarily show how they feel about it. Yet out of an aggregate of words and actions, every society makes a statement about itself. Methodist Bishop Gerald Kennedy of Los Angeles sums it up: "The atmosphere is wide open. There is more promiscuity, and it is taken as a matter of course now by people. In my day they did it, but they knew it was wrong."

Publicly and dramatically, the change is evident in Spectator Sex—what may be seen and read. Thirty-five years ago, *Elmer Gantry* and *All Quiet on the Western Front* were banned in Boston: today Supreme Court decisions have had the net effect of allowing everything to be published except "hard-core pornography." It is hard to remember that as recently as 1948, in *The*

Naked and the Dead, Norman Mailer felt compelled to reduce his favorite four letters to three ("fug"), or that there was ever any fuss about poor old *Lady Chatterley's Lover* and his worshipful deification of sexual organs. John O'Hara, whose writing until recently was criticized as "sex-obsessed," appears positively Platonic alongside Calder Willingham and John Updike, who describe lyrically and in detail matters that used to be mentioned even in scientific works only in Latin.

Then there is Henry Miller with his scabrous *Tropics,* and William Burroughs' *Naked Lunch,* an incredible piece of hallucinatory homosexual depravity. And if these are classed as literature and are democratically available at the neighborhood drugstore, who is going to stop the cheap pornographer from putting out *Lust Hop, Lust Jungle, Lust Kicks, Lust Lover, Lust Lease, Lust Moll, Lust Team, Lust Girls,* and *Call Boy?* In girlie magazines, nudity stops only at the *mons Veneris—et quandoque ne ibi quidem.* Asks Dr. Paul Gebhard, the late Alfred Kinsey's successor at Indiana University's Institute for Sex Research: "What do you do after you show it all? I've talked to some of the publishers, and they are a little worried."

The next step.   The cult of pop hedonism and phony sexual sophistication grows apace. It produces such books as *Sex and the Single Man,* in which Dr. Albert Ellis, a supposedly reputable psychologist, offers crude but obvious instructions on how to seduce a girl, and the Playboy Clubs, which are designed to look wicked except that no one is supposed even to touch the "Bunnies" —creating the teasing impression of brothels without a second story. But by no means all of Spectator Sex is unpleasant. American clothes nowadays manage to be both free and attractive—necklines are down, skirts are up, ski pants are tight, girdles are out, and figures are better than ever, to which there can be very few objections.

Hollywood, of course, suggests more of morals and immorals to more people than any other single force. Gone with Marilyn Monroe is the last, and perhaps the greatest, of the sex symbols. Lesser girls in ever crasser if no more honest stories now symbolize very little except Hollywood's desire to outshock TV (easy because the living room still imposes some restraints) and outsex foreign movies (impossible). European films have the best-looking girls; they also have a natural, if sometimes amoral, attitude toward sex, somewhere between a shrug and a prayer, between desire and fatigue, which makes Hollywood eroticism seem coyly fraudulent.

As for Broadway, quite a few plays lately have opened with a couple in bed—to show right away, as Critic Walter Kerr says, that the male is not a homosexual. As another critic has seriously suggested, the next step in the theater will be to represent sexual intercourse onstage. . . .

The unique conflict.   It remains for each man and woman to walk through this sexual bombardment and determine for themselves what to them seems tasteless or objectionable, entertaining or merely dull. A healthy society must assume a certain degree of immunity on the part of its people. But no one can really calculate the effect this exposure is having on individual lives and minds. Above all, it is not an isolated phenomenon. It is part and symptom of an era in which morals are widely held to be both private and relative, in which pleasure is increasingly considered an almost constitutional right rather than a privilege, in which self-denial is increasingly seen as foolishness rather than virtue. While science has reduced fear of long-dreaded earthly dangers, such as pregnancy and VD, skepticism has diminished fear of divine punishment. In short, the Puritan ethic, so long the dominant moral force in the United States, is widely considered to be dying, if not dead, and there are few mourners.

The demise of Puritanism—whether permanent or not remains to be seen—is the latest phase in a conflict, as old as Christianity itself, between Eros and agape, between passionate love named for a pagan god and spiritual love through which man imitates God. It is a conflict unique to the Christian West. The religions of many other civilizations provide a clearly defined and positive place for sex. In the West, the tension between the two, and the general confusion about the many facets of love, leads to a kind of self-torment that, says Italian Author Leo Ferrero, "might well appear to a Chinese psychiatrist as symptomatic of insanity."

The decline of Puritanism. Yet that "insanity" is among the great mysteries and challenges of the Christian tradition—the belief that sex is not only the force by which man perpetuates himself on God's earth but also the symbol of his fall, and that it can be sanctified only in the sacrament of marriage.

The original American Puritans understood passion as well as human frailty: in Plymouth in the 1670s, while ordinary fornicators were fined £ 10, those who were engaged had to pay only half the fine. But a fatal fact about Puritanism, which led to its ever-increasing narrowness and decline, was its conviction that virtue could be legislated by the community, that human perfection could be organized on earth.

What the first sexual revolution in the U.S. attacked was not original Puritanism so much as its Victorian version—which had become a matter of prudery more than of purity, propriety more than of grace. The 19th century frantically insisted on propriety precisely because it felt its real faith and ethics disappearing. While it feared nudity like a plague, Victorian Puritanism had the effect of an all-covering gown that only inflames the imagination. By insisting on suppressing the sex instinct in everything, the age betrayed the fact that it really saw that instinct in everything. So, too, with Sigmund Freud, Victorianism's most perfect rebel.

Romantic revolt. Freudian psychology, or its popularized version, became one of the chief forces that combined against Puritanism. Gradually, the belief spread that repression, not license, was the great evil, and that sexual matters belonged in the realm of science, not morals. A second force was the New Woman, who swept aside the Victorian double standard, which was partly based on the almost universally held notion that women—or at any rate, ladies—did not enjoy sex. One eminent doctor said it was a "foul aspersion" on women to say they did. The celebrated 2nd century Physician Galen was (and is) often incompletely quoted to the effect that "every animal is sad after coitus." Actually, as Kinsey pointed out, he had added the qualification, "except the human female and the rooster." Siding with Galen, women claimed not only the right to work and to vote, but the even more important right to pleasure.

These two allies against Puritanism seemed to be joined by Eros in person. The cult of romantic passion, with its assertion that true love could exist only outside marriage, had first challenged Christianity in the 12th century; some consider it an uprising of the old paganism long ago driven underground by the church. From *Tristan* on, romance shaped the great literary myths of the West and became a kind of secular religion. Christianity learned to coexist with it.

But in the early 20th century, the religion of romance appeared in a new form, and its troubadour was D. H. Lawrence. Until then, it had been tinged by the polite and melancholy suggestion that desire, not fulfillment, was the best part of love. Lawrence countered vehemently that fulfillment is everything, that sex is the one great, true thing in life. More explicitly than anyone before him, he sentimentalized the orgasm, in whose "final massive and dark collision of the blood" he saw man's apotheosis and fusion with the divine.

Beyond prohibition. Christianity does not share this mystique of sex, insisting that the primary purpose of the sexual act as ordained by God is procreation. It never considered the flesh to be intrinsically evil. But for a thousand years, the Church was deeply influenced by the views of St. Augustine, a profligate in his youth and a moralist in middle age, who held that even within marriage, sex and its pleasures were dangerous—a necessary evil for the begetting of children. Gradually, partly under the influence of the Reformation, which denied the "higher value" of celibacy, Christianity began to move away from this austere Augustinian view, and toward an acceptance of pleasure in sex as a positive good.

In 1951, Pope Pius XII still warned against un-Christian hedonism, but reaffirmed it was right that "husband and wife shall find pleasure and happiness of mind and body." Today, says Father John Thomas, noted Roman Catholic sociologist, "what is needed is a whole new attitude by the church toward sexuality. There is in both Catholicism and Protestantism a relatively well-developed theology of sex on the negative side. Now more than prohibition is needed."

The Protestant churches have indeed gone far beyond prohibition through their wide approval of birth control not only as an aid in sensible family planning but, in the words of the Anglican bishops at the 1958 Lambeth conference, as a "gate to a new depth and joy in personal relationships between husband and wife." Ironically, it is Communism, having long ago silenced all its bold talk about "free love," which may be the most puritanical force in the world today. In *1984,* George Orwell attributed the old Victorian code to his fictional dictatorship: "goodsex" was marital intercourse without pleasure on the part of the woman, "sexcrime" was everything else.

Search for codes.   A great many Americans—probably the majority—live by the old religious morality. Or at least they try to; they may practice what Max Lerner describes as "patterned evasion," a heavy but charitable way of saying that to keep society going people must be free, up to a point, not to practice what they profess.

Many others now live by what State University of Iowa Sociologist Ira Reiss calls "permissiveness with affection." What this means to most people is that 1) morals are a private affair; 2) being in love justifies premarital sex, and by implication perhaps extramarital sex; 3) nothing really is wrong as long as nobody else "gets hurt."

This happens to be reminiscent of the moral code expressed in *Memoirs of a Woman of Pleasure,* otherwise known as *Fanny Hill,* the celebrated 18th century pornographic novel now freely available in the U.S. One of the principals "considered pleasure, of one sort or another, as the universal port of destination, and every wind that blew thither a good one, provided it blew nobody any harm."

No absolutes.   One trouble with this very humane-sounding principle is that it is extremely difficult, if not impossible, to know what, in the long run, will hurt others and what won't. Thus, in spite of what may often appear to be a sincere concern for others, it remains an essentially self-centered code. In his categorical imperative, Kant set down the opposite standard, a variation of the Golden Rule: Judge your every action as if it were to become a universal principle applicable to all.

Undoubtedly, that is a difficult code to live by, and few try to. But living by a lesser code can be difficult too, as is shown by the almost frantic attempt of sociologists and psychologists to give people something to hold on to without falling back on traditional rules. Typical of many is the effort of Lester A. Kirkendall of Oregon State University, in his recent book, *Premarital Intercourse and Interpersonal Relationships:* "The moral decision will be the one which works toward the creation of trust, confidence and integrity in relationships." What such well-intentioned but tautologous and empty advice may mean in practice is suggested by one earnest teacher who praises the Kirkendall code: "Now I have an answer. I just tell the girls and boys that they have to consider both sides of the question—will sexual intercourse strengthen or weaken their relationship?"

The "relationship" ethic is well expressed by Miami Psychologist Granville Fisher, who speaks for countless colleagues when he says: "Sex is not a moral question. For answers you don't turn to a body of absolutes. The criterion should not be, 'Is it morally right or wrong,' but, 'Is it socially feasible, is it personally healthy and rewarding, will it enrich human life?' " Dr. Fisher adds, correctly, that many Protestant churchmen are beginning to feel the same way. "They are no longer shaking their finger because the boys and girls give in to natural biological urges and experiment a bit. They don't say, 'Stop, you're wrong,' but, 'Is it meaningful?' "

Methodist Bishop Kennedy condemns premarital sex "in general" but adds, "I wouldn't stand in judgment. There would be exceptions." Recently, Wally Toevs, Presbyterian pastor at the University of Colorado, more or less condoned premarital sex when there is a "covenant of intimacy." A distinguished Protestant theologian privately recommends—he doesn't believe the U.S. is ready for him to say it publicly—the idea of a trial affair for some people, a "little marriage" in preparation for the "great marriage" which is to last.

Too much, too soon. From current reports on youth, "meaningful relationships" and "covenants of intimacy" are rampant. Teen-agers put great stock in staying cool. But even discounting the blasé talk, the notion is widely accepted today, on the basis of Kinsey and a few smaller, more recent studies, that the vast majority of American men and at least half the women now have sexual intercourse before marriage. Dr. Graham B. Blaine, Jr., psychiatrist to the Harvard and Radcliffe Health Service, estimates that within the past 15 years the number of college boys who had intercourse before graduation rose from 50% to 60%, the number of college girls from 25% to 40%. A Purdue sociologist estimates that one out of six brides is pregnant.

These figures may be flawed, and they certainly do not apply to all parts of the U.S. or to all schools. But there is almost universal agreement that youngsters are pushed toward adult behavior too soon, often by ambitious mothers who want them to be "well adjusted" and popular; hence champagne parties for teen-agers, padded brassières for twelve-year-olds, and "going steady" at ever younger ages. American youngsters tend to live as if adolescence were a last fling at life, rather than a preparation for it. Historian Arnold Toynbee, for one, considers this no laughing matter, for part of the modern West's creative energy, he believes, has sprung from the ability to postpone adolescents' "sexual awakening" to let them concentrate on the acquisition of knowledge.

Most significant of all, the age-old moral injunctions are less readily accepted by the young—partly because they sense that so many parents don't really believe in them either.

Crisis of virginity. "Nice girls don't" is undoubtedly still the majority view, but definitely weakening, as is "No nice boy will respect you if you go to bed with him." A generation ago, college boys strayed off campus to seek out professionals; today they are generally looked down on if they can't succeed with a coed.

In a way, the situation is the logical consequence of U.S. attitudes toward youth. In other societies, the young are chaperoned and restricted because it is assumed, human nature being what it is, that if they are exposed to temptation they will give in. The U.S., on the other hand, has set the young free, given them cars, given them prosperity—and yet still expects them to follow the rules. The compromise solution to this dilemma has long been petting, or "making out," as it is now known, which the U.S. did not invent but has carried to extreme lengths.

Now there are signs of resentment against a practice that overstimulates but blocks fulfillment. The resentment, however, is taking forms that alarm many parents. In a sweeping generalization, Dr. Blaine reports that "Radcliffe girls think petting is dirty because it is teasing. They feel if you are going to do that, it is better just to have intercourse." This may apply to some, but, as Harvard's President Pusey reported in a speech last week, 80% of Radcliffe girls get degrees with honors, "so they can't do all that running around they're supposed to."

Many girls are still sincere and even lyrical about saving themselves for marriage, but it is becoming a lot harder to hold the line. There is strong pressure not only from the boys but from other girls, many of whom consider a virgin downright square. The loss of virginity, even resulting in pregnancy, is simply no longer considered an American Tragedy. Says one student of the American vernacular: "The word virgin is taking on a slightly new meaning. It seems acceptable to consider a girl a virgin if she has had experience with only her husband before marriage, or with only one or two steadies." At a girls' college in Connecticut, one coed recently wrote a poem about the typical Yale man which concluded:

And so I yield myself completely to him.
Society says I should.
Damn society!

Talk of the pill. Some girls are bothered to the point of consulting analysts when they find that having an affair makes them uneasy; since everyone is telling them that sex is healthy, they feel guilty about feeling guilty. Some girls, says an Atlanta analyst, "are disturbed because they are no longer able to use fear of pregnancy as an excuse for chastity." In many parts of the country, physicians report the use of Saran Wrap as a male contraceptive, but such improvisation seems hardly necessary, since birth control devices of all kinds are sold freely, often at supermarkets. Parents have been known to buy diaphragms for their daughters (although in Cleveland recently, a woman was arrested for giving birth control information to her delinquent daughter).

The big new development is the oral contraceptive pill, widely used and even more widely discussed both at college and at home. A considerate boy asks a girl politely, "Are you on pills?" If not, he takes the precautions himself. Current joke definition of a good sport: A wife who keeps taking the Pill even when her husband is away.

In spite of all this, the number of illegitimate children born to teen-age mothers rose from 8.4 per thousand in 1940 to 16 in 1961, in the 20-to-25 age group from 11.2 per thousand to 41.2. Some girls neglect to use contraceptives, psychologists report, because they consciously or unconsciously want a child, others resent the planned, deliberate aspect; they think it "nicer" to get carried away on the spur of the moment. College girls have been known to take up collections for a classmate who needed an abortion, and some have had one without skipping a class.

Girls aren't things.   Still, by and large, campus sex is not casual. Boys look down on a "community chest," meaning a promiscuous girl. Sociologist David Riesman believes that, far more so than in the '20s, boys treat girls as persons rather than objects: "They sit down and really talk with them."

Not that talk is universally appreciated. When New York girls speak of a date as N.A.T.O., they mean contemptuously, "No Action, Talk Only." Some find the steady affair on the dull side. One Hunter girl told Writer Gael Greene: "Sex is so casual and taken for granted—I mean we go to dinner, we go home, get undressed like old married people, you know—and just go to bed. I mean I'm not saying I'd like to be raped on the living-room floor exactly. But I would love to just sit around on the sofa and neck."

The young seem to be earnestly trying to construct their own code, and are even rediscovering for themselves some of the older verities. "They are piecing together lives which are at least as whole as their parents," says Lutheran Minister Martin Marty. They marry early—probably too early—and they give the impression of escaping into marriage almost with a sense of relief. Often they are disappointed by what marriage brings.

Serial polygamy.   For the dominant fact about sexual mores in the U.S. remains the fragility of American marriage. The institution has never been easily sustained; "forsaking all others," in human terms, represents a belief that in an average life, loneliness is a greater threat than boredom. But the U.S. has a special concept of marriage, both Puritan and romantic. In most Eastern societies, marriages are arranged by families; the same is true in many parts of Europe, and there, even where young people are free to choose, they often choose for purely practical reasons. In arranged marriage, it is expected that love may or may not come later—and remarkably often it does. If not, it may be found outside marriage. The church, of course, does not sanction this system, but in European countries it has managed to live with it.

In the U.S., this notion is repugnant. St. Paul said that it is better to marry than to burn; except for Roman Catholics, Americans tend to believe that it is better to divorce than to burn. The European aim is to keep the family under one roof; the American aim is to provide personal happiness. Partly as a result, the U.S. has developed what sociologists call "serial polygamy," often consisting of little more than a succession of love affairs with slight legal trimmings. Cynics point out that serial polygamy was a fact even in Puritan times, when men had three or four wives because women were apt to die young: nowadays, divorce rather than death provides variety.

There is some sympathy for the European system. Says Psychiatrist Joseph Satten of the Menninger Foundation: "Fewer people feel now that infidelity demands a divorce. There is some value to this increased tolerance, because it may help keep our families together. But our society will suffer terribly if we equate freedom in sex with irresponsibility." Most Americans still feel that if the family is to be kept together, it cannot be through infidelity. There are, in fact, signs of stability in the divorce statistics, which have remained steady over the past four years.

Oh men, oh women.   Those marriages which do survive seem to be richer and more fun. Part of the reason may be that Americans are becoming more sophisticated and less inhibited in bed—as just about everyone is urging them to be. As respectable an authority as Robert C. Dodds, a minister in the United Church of Christ, and General Director of Planning for the National Council of Churches, appends a chapter on sex practices to a marriage handbook, in which a physician urges couples to explore and "conjure up various positions and actions of sexual intercourse." Old taboós are slowly beginning to disappear, and while the upper and educated classes were always more adventurous in their techniques, sexual class lines show signs of fading. Reportedly declining are such prudish practices as making love with one's clothes on or in total darkness.

The long-standing cold war between men and women in the U.S. may be heading for a *détente*. While American women often still seem too strong and American men too weak, the U.S. has learned that men have the kind of women they deserve. The image of the all-devouring, all-demanding but never-giving American Bitch is virtually gone, both in life and in literature (except possibly on Broadway, where so many plays are written by homosexuals). With the new legitimation of pleasure, the American woman increasingly tries to combine the roles of wife and mistress—with the same man, that is. It may be an unattainable goal, but the attempt is fascinating and often successful.

Perhaps American men have yet to discover that in her new and complicated role, woman must be wooed more than ever—and that wooing women is not a part-time occupation but a full-time attitude. But almost all American men have begun to accept the fact that women nowadays have to be competent and managing types—without giving up their femininity. As for the often-heard charge that American men really want mothers, Henry Miller, of all people, recently replied: "I have often wondered what is so objectionable about being mothered by the woman one loves."

Sexual democracy.   In extramarital sex, one of the chief trends is toward sexual democracy. Today's sexual adventuring seems to be among social equals, even if it means the best friend's wife or husband. The old double standard involved a reservoir of socially inferior women, some of them prostitutes, others "nice" girls but not really quite nice. The prostitutes' ranks are thinning more than ever. As for the little seamstress or shop-girl type, she hardly exists any longer; heaven and union wages protect the working girl.

Today's catalyst for sex, at least in urban communities, is the office girl, from head buyer to perky file clerk. To many men, the office remains a refuge from home, and to many girls a refuge from the eligible but sometimes dull young men they meet in the outside world. One of the difficulties of the office affair, except for those who relish intrigue for its own sake, is the problem of sheer logistics and security. Semipublic, semipermanent affairs are still not readily condoned—or perhaps even really enjoyed—in the U.S. American men seem to have decided that if there is love, only marriage will suffice in the long run, and if there is no love, only boredom can result; thus does life forever reinvent morality.

The new sin.   Some sociologists believe that the U.S. is moving toward a more Mediterranean attitude toward sex and life in general. But the U.S. still cannot relax about it the way Europe does, which accepts sex without much discussion, as it accepts bread and wine, earth and sin.

In contrast, the U.S. is forever trying to banish sin from the universe—and finding new sins to worry about. The new sex freedom in the U.S. does not necessarily set people free. Psychoanalyst Rollo May believes that it has minimized external social anxiety but increased internal tension. The great new sin today is no longer giving in to desire, he thinks, but not giving in to it fully or successfully enough. While enjoyment of sex has increased for many, the "competitive compulsion to prove oneself an acceptable sexual machine" makes many others feel neurotically guilty, hence impotent or frigid. As a fellow analyst puts it bluntly: "We are always anticipating the 21-gun salute, and worried if it doesn't happen." This preoccupation with the frequency and technique of orgasm, says May, leads to a new kind of inverted Puritanism.

If there is indeed a new Puritanism, it has its own Cotton Mather. Man, says Norman Mailer, "knows at the seed of his being that good orgasm opens his possibilities and bad orgasm imprisons him." Many people take this issue very seriously: next month, the American Association of Marriage Counselors will hold a three-day conference on the nature of orgasm.

There is also a tendency to see in sex not only personal but social salvation—the last area of freedom in an industrialized society, the last frontier. In one of the really "in" books of recent years, *Life Against Death,* Norman O. Brown has even suggested a kind of sexual utopia. In his vision, all repressions would be eliminated, along with civilization itself; the future would belong to sexuality, not just of the present "genital" variety, which Brown considers a form of tyranny, but the all-round, innocent sexuality a child enjoys.

Such notions mean burdening sex with too much deadly importance, suggesting an absurd vision of all those college kids making out, the clerks trying to learn the art of seduction from Dr. Albert Ellis, the young married couples in their hopeful conjugal beds—all only serving the great cause of some socio-sexual revolution.

The supreme act. Contemplating the situation from the vantage point of his 79 years, Historian Will Durant recently decided it was time to speak out, not only on sexual morality but on morals generally. Said he: "Most of our literature and social philosophy after 1850 was the voice of freedom against authority, of the child against the parent, of the pupil against the teacher. Through many years I shared in that individualistic revolt. I do not regret it; it is the function of youth to defend liberty and innovation, of the old to defend order and tradition, and of middle age to find a middle way. But now that I too am old, I wonder whether the battle I fought was not too completely won. Let us say humbly but publicly that we resent corruption in politics, dishonesty in business, faithlessness in marriage, pornography in literature, coarseness in language, chaos in music, meaninglessness in art."

Many Americans will share Durant's broad indignation, many will dissent from it. But one of the remarkable facts is that there is much less indignation in the churches today—at least as far as sexual morality goes. The watchword is to be positive, to stress the New Testament's values of faith, hope and charity rather than the prohibitions of the Commandments. Many sermons, if they deal with sexual transgressions at all, prefer to treat them simply as one kind of difficulty among many others. The meaning of sin in the U.S. today is no longer predominantly sexual.

Few will regret that. But many do feel the need for a reaffirmation of the spiritual meaning of sex. For the act of sex is above all the supreme act of communion between two people as sanctified by God and celebrated by poets. "Love's mysteries in souls do grow, but yet the body is his book," wrote John Donne. And out of this connection and commitment come children, who should be a responsibility—and a joy.

When sex is pursued only for pleasure, or only for gain, or even only to fill a void in society or in the soul, it becomes elusive, impersonal, ultimately disappointing. That is what Protestant Theologian Helmut Thielicke has in mind when he warns that "a dethroned god seems to be staging his comeback in a secularized world." Eros is accorded high rank today, "a rank that comes close to the deity it once had." The spiritual danger is that Eros may leave "no room for agape, which lives not by making claims but by giving."

The Victorians, who talked a great deal about love, knew little about sex. Perhaps it is time that modern Americans, who know a great deal about sex, once again start talking about love.

39. THE LIBERATION OF WOMEN

ann doubilet

What is the proper role of women in society? Are they more free or oppressed? In what does their happiness and security consist? These are several of the questions taken up below in an essay on one of the significant social movements of recent American history—the women's liberation movement. The author calls for drastic alterations in attitudes toward women and their social role.

Throughout the country young women like myself are coming together to fight for liberation. We are questioning our lack of self-fulfillment and are seeking to find the roots of our oppression. We have come to see that the basic problem lies in the roles we play—or are expected to play—as wives and mothers in the family system. It is not only the quality of the role that we question, but the fact that in spite of seemingly unlimited opportunities and new identities, the overwhelming majority of women are performing functional roles that have not changed in over 5,000 years.

Even in the most elite of women's colleges where we are supposedly preparing to fulfill our potential, the insidious sex-role ideology is ever-present. We have been socialized to feel that we are not and cannot be whole unless and until we are married and have children. It is not that we feel we are half without a man; we feel less than half.

Advanced industrialized society is making old contradictions even harder to reconcile. Many young women are now educated sufficiently to be economically self-sustaining. In addition, many have become relatively independent of the restrictive values of the families they came from. The possibility of assuming a full and equal role in society seems to be available to increasing numbers of women. But, as it has been well put by Myrna Wood and Cathy McAfee in

From Ann Doubilet, "A Woman's Place," *New Generation,* LI, Fall 1969, pp. 3–8.

Leviathan, precisely "because they have pushed the democratic myth to its limits, they know concretely how it limits them."

Because women like myself feel these contradictions very personally, we are not only exploring their psychological depths but are beginning to fight for concrete ways to overcome present constrictions in being wives and mothers. Many people in this country have gone far in questioning religious and cultural myths, but questioning the *family* system is still considered tremendously threatening to each of us and to the social order. That is not surprising, because the family plays a very specific economic role in a capitalist society, and questioning it *is* threatening.

First, it stabilizes the working force. In order to provide for his family, a man must "keep his nose to the grindstone." Since the wife is ostensibly denied the role of producer (although many married women work, it is generally considered to be supplementary, not "real" work), she must see to it that her husband stays on his job, no matter how alienating it is. Second, as part of the bargain, if he makes enough money, she can stay home and take good care of the house and serve as coordinator of the family unit's role as consumer. With its overproduction of goods and built-in obsolescence, our economy has a basic need to maintain a structural unit with a socialized need to consume. Third, the family is needed to socialize children to accept the harsh realities they will face in the competitive world, by teaching them to work hard, to "behave" and to conform.

Many young people are beginning to feel that the family doesn't meet their needs and that the historical conditions that gave rise to it no longer exist. The family, according to the classical definition, is a unit which fulfills reproductive, social, economic, emotional and sexual needs. But in an overpopulated world that no longer needs maximum reproduction of the species, where fewer and fewer people are needed to produce more and more goods, and where more and more men and women are breaking out of the family structure for satisfaction of their sexual and emotional needs, the old rationale becomes increasingly hard to justify. And so the "breakdown of the nuclear family" has become a commonplace subject in the mass media today.

And the evidence is quite compelling: One out of every three marriages today terminates in divorce. One out of every five American women, by the time they are 45, have had at least one abortion. With incredible rapidity, sexual relationships outside of marriage are becoming socially acceptable for younger men and women, who are insistent and outspoken about the need to change the existing hypocritical social mores. Older couples are not so outspoken, but the popularity of such dramas as *Peyton Place,* with their emphasis on clandestine adultery, wife-swapping, middle-aged swingers and frustrated, jealous spouses, attests to the universal nature of their discontent.

Single, independent, self-sustaining women do not, in the United States, have the status of the most dependent woman who is married and has children. There are exceptions to this, but they are just that—exceptions. When people involved in women's liberation try to explain the movement to cynics they are shown sudden respect if they mention that they themselves are married and thus are not frustrated bitches. But other women in the movement, even if they are full professors respected in their fields, are often looked at skeptically by outsiders who wonder just what is wrong with them that they haven't married and had children and therefore "resolved" their lives.

In exploring the problems of women, it is impossible to separate cultural and psychological oppression from economic and material oppression. For example, even though I grew up in relative affluence and went to so-called good schools, I was made to believe that my life would not "really start" until I found the "right guy" and got married. It never occurred to me that I would ever have to define my own life by myself.

There are women, of course, who *are* encouraged to define themselves and perhaps acquire skills, but usually they are urged to do so in order to have something to do before marriage, to supplement their husband's income during marriage, or to have something to fall back on in case of divorce or widowhood or when the children grow up. Although in certain professions women are increasingly being acknowledged as people, they are still the exception. And the sex-role ideology is generally in full control, with "motherhood" at the pinnacle.

As Vicki Pollard wrote in the first issue of *Women: A Journal of Liberation:*

> One of the worst things that happens to a woman when she announces that she is pregnant is that she is congratulated and praised as if she has accomplished the most difficult task in the world. People suddenly look at her in a totally new way. She is seen as being of great worth, possibly for the first time in her life. Women who have been leading active, working lives are made to feel as if only *now* are they finally getting down to the real business of life.

If new economic and social conditions are making us question the roles of wives and mothers as they are still constituted, they are also making it possible for us to explore new possibilities for meaningful lives. (I define meaningful as that which is relevant in a given period.) Thus we are searching for new answers on two levels, in terms of current realities and future possibilities.

For the foreseeable future most of us will continue to get married and have children. Therefore we need to find the means right now that will enable us to do so without the oppressive nature of the typical family structure.

Many people are exploring new forms of living together both within and outside of marriage. In reaction to the isolation of most young couples, communes have sprung up within many ranges of ideology and practice. Increasing numbers of young people see the need to rid themselves of the overindividualistic and privatized nature of American life. They believe that groups of people working together can perhaps unravel the locked-in binds couples often find themselves in.

One possible outcome of group living is the breakdown of the traditional sexual division of labor in regard to housework. And this is also happening among couples not living in communes. Why, many in the women's liberation movement are asking, should the division of labor be such that when the man and woman both work all day, he reads while she cooks, after having rushed to do the shopping on the way home? Then over dinner they discuss the problems of the world and the important jobs they may hold in the liberal establishment or the left movement, fighting discrimination in the world and fighting for social and economic equality. And then *she* does the dishes while he reads. Or, as is beginning to happen more and more, if he shares the chores, why should both he and she feel that he is helping *her* to do *her* work and thus he is deserving of praise and appreciation?

Many men try to laugh off our concern with housework, calling it a trivial concern. But we know it is a very basic one and that full equality for women will not come until all tasks around the house, including child care, are not considered "women's work" and are shared equally by both sexes. Other alternatives that a number of people have recently suggested include the "industrialization of housework," payment to women for their labor in the house, and free and good child-care services. While these are all fine ideas, they are not going to be accomplished for a long time and, furthermore, they still would not eliminate the sex-role division of housework as woman's work; it would just be less time-consuming.

For some reason men in a number of other countries don't seem to resist housework and child care as strenuously as American men. In Sweden, for example, there is a movement to help women take jobs by having men share in all the tasks around the home. Some couples have even gone so far as to entirely reverse the typical roles: she works at a job she loves; he, after quitting a job that bored him, takes care of the house and child in his new role of *hemmaman,* or house-husband.

We are not, however, asking for role reversal but for complete equality. And we are finding ways to attain it. For example, a number of couples have rearranged their lives so that outside work and housework for each are equally divided. One such couple has worked out the following arrangement: he goes to work in the morning, while she takes care of their newborn baby; at noon he comes home and they switch—he cares for the baby and she goes to work. They share equally in the housework, food shopping, etc.

They have not had many problems with this division, although he gets hostile stares from other men in the street when he is shopping in midafternoon with the baby on his back, and he can see that his strange role is very threatening to them. But he feels very strongly that men are generally deprived of being able to take care of children and that there is often tremendous competition between the parents for the love of the child. (A man may feel left out when his child can be quieted only by its mother. He may be jealous of the child and resentful that it is taking up so much of the energy and love of the wife that was previously directed at him.)

The particular couple I have referred to are both professionals, and they emphasize that their arrangement is definitely a class privilege, as it it not often that both parents are sufficiently trained to be able to hold down fairly elite part-time jobs. But they feel that many couples could make similar arrangements if they were willing to give up the financial status that comes with either one or two full-time jobs in the house. However, for themselves, they feel that they have found the best possible interim arrangement until they are able to go on to their next goal—successful communal lives with other families.

Communal life is a long-term goal of many of us in the women's liberation movement. In the meantime if we want children but do not want to be enslaved by the role of mother, we feel we must develop cooperative forms of child care. Many mothers have come into the women's movement out of the sad isolation they have been forced into while taking care of their small children. They are wary of even considering cooperative child care because they have been so inculcated with the romanticism of motherhood that to admit they don't want to take care of their children themselves fills them with guilt.

We are convinced that such facilities would also be in the interests of the children. Our own experience has shown us that children are limited both by their dependence on their parents for love and security and learning experiences and by their parents' dependence on them. Parents hang on to their children as private property because they are often so unfulfilled and frustrated by their own lives that they have to live through their children, and so children grow up feeling guilty about achieving their own independence. Although people understand this well (and many of us have gone and are still going through this struggle), it is crucial to understand how it limits new generations from exploring new possibilities for human growth and development.

Now that we know the lessons of such countries as Sweden and Israel, many of us are working to establish child-care facilities that would involve men as well as women. We too need cooperative child-care facilities run by both men and women because of the enormous divorce rate, which leaves young mothers to bring up their children alone. Children need to be around both male and female adult models, and if there are many different grownups around, it is even better.

One of the problems with the few day-care cooperatives now existing is that they are often limited to women who work part-time. We would like to find ways to help women who work full-time and have to spend half their salaries on baby sitters.

There are also women who would like to work but cannot afford to or, again, feel guilty about not taking care of their babies as they are "supposed" to. In this regard, we have been thinking of ways to put pressure on corporations and factories to provide day-care facilities for the mother or father who works there or for the people in the surrounding community. These centers would be funded by the corporation but controlled by the people whose children are using them and by the people interested in working in them. It is important to emphasize that we want these centers to free women so that choices are opened up for them; we do not want to emulate, for example, the Olivetti Corporation in Italy, where everything is provided for the workers, including day care, in order to make it impractical and almost impossible for them to leave the corporation.

Cooperative child-care facilities would also make it possible for women who do not wish to get married to have children. We must have the right to decide if and when we will have babies. Birth control and abortion are complex questions because, again, it is impossible to separate the economic oppression of having children with no help to take care of them from the psychological brainwashing that women's only real fulfillment is having children. Thus we find many unmarried white women aborting babies they would like to have but can't because they can't afford to raise them alone or bear the psychological stigma, and many married women having children they don't want because they feel they must.

Nevertheless, it is clear that women must have the right to control their own bodies, and that means making free, safe and effective birth control available for those women who want it. At the same time, it should not be used— as it is now—as a form of genocide for black, Puerto Rican and Third World women. Free birth control is now much more readily available for black and brown women in New York City than it is for poor white women.

Free, safe and effective abortions must also be made available to all women who want them. It is possible for rich women to have expensive, safe legal or illegal abortions, but obviously it is not for the poor. Safe abortions are almost entirely ruled out for most black women; very few abortions are performed in city hospitals, although sterilization and forced tube tying is becoming a common practice. Abortion must not be used for population control and genocide.

Across the country, women's liberation groups are concerning themselves with these questions. In Washington, D.C., an alliance of Women's Liberation and welfare mothers has been fighting the unequal treatment under the abortion law and the lack of concern about the problem on the part of the health hierarchy. The two groups became allied through an abortion-referral service started by Women's Liberation.

In New York a very large group of women has filed suit against the state to have the abortion law declared unconstitutional. We want this law repealed. We are fighting for our right as women to decide whether or not we will have children, and when. We know that this is our right and should not be decided by male legislators. (Indeed, almost all abortion laws on the books were made before women were given the vote!)

This is just a brief outline of some of the problems the women's movement is working on, but we have come to appreciate that they must be combined with a struggle to change our entire economic system to one which meets the needs of the majority of people, one in which the vast economic and technical resources available are allocated justly and where the control of the wealth of the country is not in the hands of a few.

When we begin to get rid of the superficial structures and mores that limit our lives, then the real problems of self-fulfillment and identity will be exposed. For example, marriage implies a certain ongoing commitment so that the partners don't continually have to ask for a reaffirmation of love. Many manners and structures of society exist so that we won't have to confront the deeper questions of identity. We should begin to explore the nature and content of our relationships and not hide behind the form. Although many of us see the limitations of marriage (formally contracted or not), we still persist in the myth that it will solve all our problems. It is not that marriage itself is necessarily unviable, but that the myth that it is one's salvation is wrong and stultifying. It is form without content. When we begin to look at the content of our relationships we come face to face with the ways in which society pushes us to form our identity.

Women are constantly being forced to please men and to be pleasant and charming and acquiescent. Our passivity is reinforced by men's need to be strong and have power over others in order to feel secure in their own masculinity. We believe that it is part of human nature to require love and that therefore we must discover new ways to give and receive love that let each of us develop our own potential and release our energies rather than being locked in by our needs. We must explore how these needs are developed; how society socializes us into crippling patterns that we then define as "feminine" or "masculine."

Many men, in turn, feel locked in by their masculine roles. They are socialized to keep up a strong front and to hide their feelings ("boys don't cry"), and in many ways they are prevented from exploring themselves and from reaching out to develop close relationships with each other for fear of exposing unallowed internal fears and doubts. Although they are not oppressed by the sex-role division in the same way as women are, and although they enjoy a certain sense of power from these divisions, they too are hampered by our distorted concepts of "masculine" and "feminine" and are not free. It will take strength and unity on the part of women to take away their monopoly on power, but we know that it will benefit both sexes.

Our involvement in the women's movement has given all of us great strength. As women, we hope to have a profound effect on the way in which people will be able to learn to work with each other in a world which is in great need of cooperative effort. In a nonoppressive way we are learning to work together and to help our sisters, and this strength has begun to change the nature of our needs for security and of our affirmation of ourselves as people. We have begun to be less dependent on our men to define us, and thus more able to begin to fight for equality; more able to challenge, confront and explore.

But individual relationships won't change overnight. And in that sense, the struggle is now becoming a political struggle to change the nature of society so that people can develop in a nonoppressive way. We cannot reach liberation in an oppressive society. We won't be able to break down the division of labor between man and woman until we achieve a society where all divisions between people—intellectual vs. laborer, professor vs. student, black vs. white, parent vs. child, farm vs. city, exploiter vs. exploited, those divisions which divide us all—are broken down.

We cannot predict at this point how relationships will look after this struggle, for we know that the history of mankind and womankind is the history of change. We do not imagine or project any ultimate static utopias; each new generation will have to decide for itself what is meaningful. The only constant we can project is permanent revolution.

40. THE HUMAN LANDSCAPE
rene dubos

In one of his last speeches, Adlai Stevenson referred to the Earth as "a little spaceship" on which we travel together "dependent on its vulnerable supplies of air and soil." With this as his theme, Dubos discusses man's relationship to his environment in the context of contemporary science and technology. All of us must become aware, he says, that we face grave problems as passengers on Spaceship Earth.

The expression "Spaceship Earth" is no mere catch phrase. Now that all habitable parts of the globe are occupied, the careful husbandry of its resources is a sine qua non of survival for the human species, more important than economic growth or political power. We are indeed travellers bound to the earth's

From Rene Dubos, "The Human Landscape," *Bulletin of the Atomic Scientists,* XXVI, March 1970, pp. 31–37. Reprinted by permission of Science and Public Affairs, the Bulletin of the Atomic Scientists. Copyright © 1970 by the Educational Foundation for Nuclear Science.

crust, drawing breath from its shallow envelope of air, using and reusing its limited supply of water. Yet we collectively behave as if we were not aware of the problems inherent in the limitations of the Spaceship Earth.

It would be easy, far too easy, to conclude from the present trend of events that mankind is on a course of self-destruction. I shall not discuss this real possibility but shall instead focus on the certainty that the values and amenities identified with humanness are rapidly deteriorating. All over the world, technological civilization is threatening the elements of nature that are essential to human life, and the values that make it worth living.

Some of the supplies on which man depends are rapidly being depleted. Even water will soon become scarce, not only in arid countries but also in the temperate zone. Most environments are being so grossly polluted that they may not long remain suitable for human existence. Smogs of various composition produced in urban and industrial areas are now hovering over the countryside and are beginning to spread over ocean masses. Sewage and chemical effluents are spoiling rivers, lakes and coast lines, and slowly but surely contaminating even the most carefully protected urban water supplies. Tin cans, plastic containers, discarded machines of all sorts, oil and other indegradable garbage are accumulating all over the landscape and in many cases ruining the land. Excessive sensory stimuli, and especially the mind-bewildering noise so ubiquitous as to be unavoidable, threaten to destroy the human quality of urban agglomerations.

MAN'S NEEDS

The ancient words soil, air, water, freedom are loaded with emotional content because they are associated with biological and mental needs that are woven in the fabric of man's nature. These needs are as vital today as they were in the distant past. Scientists and economists may learn a great deal about the intricacies of natural processes and of cost accounting. But scientific knowledge of environmental management will contribute little to health and happiness if it does not take into account the human values symbolized by phrases such as the good earth, a brilliant sky, sparkling waters, a place of one's own. Furthermore, the increase in population densities and in social complexity inevitably spells social regimentation, loss of privacy and other interferences with individual freedom which may eventually prove incompatible with the traditional ways of civilized life.

Man can, of course, invent devices and techniques to minimize the effects of environmental pollutants, but he cannot protect himself against everything all the time. He is so adaptable that he can learn to tolerate many shortages and environmental insults, but medical and social experience shows that such tolerances eventually have to be paid in the form of decreases in the quality of life.

We might take comfort from the fact that during his long biological history, man has become adapted to many different kinds of environment and has been able to survive under very difficult conditions. However, this adaptive process required thousands and thousands of years, whereas profound environmental changes now occur in the course of a few years—far too rapidly to allow for biological adaptation.

The fact that modern man is now moving into non-terrestrial environments might also be interpreted as evidence that he has escaped from the bondage of his evolutionary past and is becoming independent of his ancient biological attributes. But this is an erroneous interpretation. The human body and brain have not changed significantly during the past 100,000 years and there is no ground for the belief that they will change appreciably in the foreseeable future. The biological needs of modern man as well as his biological capabilities and limitations are essentially the same as those of the paleolithic hunter and the neolithic farmer. Civilization provides man with techniques that greatly enlarge the scope of his activities, but it does not change his fundamental nature.

Wherever he goes and whatever he does, in tropical deserts or arctic wastes, in outer space or ocean depths, man must maintain around himself a micro-environment similar to the one under which he evolved. He can survive outlandish areas only by functioning within enclosures that almost duplicate a Mediterranean atmosphere, as if he remained linked to the surface of the Earth by an umbilical cord. He may engage in casual flirtations with non-terrestrial worlds, but he is wedded to the Earth, his sole source of sustenance.

The strict dependence of the human organism on the narrow range of terrestrial conditions imposes inescapable constraints on civilized life. In practice, social and technological innovations are viable and humanly successful only to the extent that they are compatible with the unchangeable aspects of man's nature. Man can retain his biological and mental health only if his civilizations maintain a healthy environment.

MUCH MORE NEEDED

By "healthy environment" I imply much more than the maintenance of ecological equilibrium, the conservation of natural resources and the control of the forces that threaten biological and mental health. Man does not only survive and function in his environment; he is shaped by it, biologically, mentally, and socially. To be really "healthy" the environment must therefore provide conditions that favor the development of desirable human characteristics.

The very process of living involves a constant feedback between man and his environment with the result that both are constantly being modified in the course of this interplay. Individuals and their social groups acquire their distinctive characteristics as a consequence of the responses they make to the total environment. The exciting richness of the human landscape results not only from the genetic diversity of mankind but also and perhaps even more from the shaping influence that surroundings and ways of life exert on biological and social man.

Until a few decades ago, scientists and technologists took it for granted that all aspects of their work enriched human life and made it healthier and happier. Most enlightened persons also realized that scientific research generates wealth and power, as well as better understanding of man's nature and of the cosmos.

Confidence in the creative and predictive power of science is so great that several groups of scholars have now made it an academic profession to forecast the technological and medical advances that can be expected for the year 2000. Naturally enough, they predict spectacular breakthroughs in the production of nuclear energy, the development of electronic gadgets, the chemical synthesis of materials better than the natural ones, the discovery of drugs and surgical techniques that will keep men healthy or save them from death. From permament lunar installations to robot human slaves and to programmed dreams, many are the scientific miracles that can be anticipated for the year 2000. Individual scientists would differ as to what theoretical possibilities will be converted into reality during the forthcoming decades. But all of them would agree that scientific research is capable of providing very soon powerful new techniques for manipulating external nature and man's nature.

THE NEW PESSIMISM

In view of the miraculous achievements of modern science, and of the promise of many more to come, one might expect the general public to believe that life in the near future will be safe, abundant, comfortable and exhilarating. Yet, there prevails in modern societies—in particular, among educated groups —a feeling of uneasiness and even hostility toward science and its technological applications.

Most persons still trust that scientific research can increase the factual knowledge of man's nature and of the cosmos. Few are those who now believe, however, that such knowledge necessarily improves health and happiness. In fact, so many environmental values are being threatened by technological and social forces that the word "environment" has acquired almost a pejorative meaning which reflects public concern for the quality of man's relationship to the rest of creation.

Early in the twentieth century, the physiologist L. J. Henderson developed the view that the natural conditions peculiar to the planet Earth are uniquely suited for the emergence and maintenance of life. In his classical book, *The Fitness of the Environment,* he stated, "Darwinian fitness is compounded of a mutual relationship between the organism and the environment.

Of this, fitness of environment is quite as essential a component as the fitness which arises in the process of organic evolution."

Today, the word "environment" is no longer identified with fitness, but rather with the biological and social dangers arising from modern life, such as the degradation of nature, the exhaustion of resources, the effects of pollution, the behavioral disturbances caused by crowding and excessive stimuli, the thousand devils of the ecological crisis. For most laymen and not a few scientists, the word "environment" evokes not fitness but nightmares.

This atmosphere of anxiety, which has been called "the new pessimism" by James Reston in a *New York Times* editorial, has several different manifestations. One is the feeling that science has weakened or destroyed many of the traditional values by which men function, yet has failed to provide a new ethical system. Science, the saying goes, gives man everything to live with, but nothing to live for.

Experience has shown furthermore that the advantages derived from scientific discoveries and technological achievements usually have to be paid for in the form of new dangers and new threats to human welfare. The fact that nuclear science promises endless sources of energy, but also makes it possible to build ever more destructive weapons symbolizes the two faces of the scientific enterprise. All too often, there exists a painful discrepancy between what man aims for and what he gets. He sprays pesticides to get rid of insects and weeds, but thereby kills birds, fish, and flowering trees. He drives long distances to find unspoiled nature, but poisons the air and gets killed on the way. He builds machines to escape from physical work, but becomes their slave and experiences boredom. Every week the pages of magazines bear witness to the public's somber anticipation that the legend of the sorcerer's apprentice may soon be converted from `a literary symbol into a terrifying reality.

No one doubts the power of science, yet a characteristic aspect of the new pessimism is the feeling that the most distressing social problems generated by scientific technology are not amenable to scientific solutions. Many are those who believe indeed that an environmental catastrophe is inevitable. Fortunately, "catastrophe" can have two very different meanings, both applicable to the relationship between scientific technology and the future of the world community. In common usage, "catastrophe" denotes a disastrous event. In its etymological Greek sense, however, it means a change of course, an overturn not necessarily resulting in disaster. The disasters that threaten mankind are too obvious to need elaboration. But we can avoid them if we keep in mind the etymological meaning of the word and try to alter the present course of scientific technology.

In my judgment, scientists will contribute to the solution of the problems they create as soon as the scientific enterprise addresses itself in earnest to the present preoccupations of mankind. From this point of view, the technological breakthroughs predicted for the year 2000 are trivial and indeed irrelevant. They have no bearing on such problems as the rape of nature, environmental pollution, urban crowding, the feeling of alienation, racial and national conflicts and other threats to decent life. The man of flesh and bone will not be much impressed by the fact that a few of his contemporaries can explore the moon, program their dreams, or use robots as slaves, if the planet Earth has become unfit for his everyday life. He will not long continue to be interested in space acrobatics if he has to watch them with his feet deep in garbage and his eyes half-blinded by smog.

Science and the technologies derived from it obviously exert profound effects on all human enterprises in the modern world. But we have not yet seriously applied scientific thinking to the creation of a desirable human life in the here and now, let alone in the future.

When Rabindranath Tagore first arrived in Europe from India as a student on his way to England, he immediately sensed that the quality of the European landscape was a creation of human effort continued over many centuries. To him, the great adventure of European civilization had been what he called "the wooing of the earth." He saw in Europe a "great lesson in the perfect union of man and nature, not only through love, but through active communication."

Tagore's view of the human forces that have made the European land was rather sentimental and sounds antiquated. Yet the phrase "wooing of the earth" is ecologically more sound than the assertion that we must conquer nature. There cannot be "perfect union of man and nature" without some creative interplay between the two.

I shall illustrate with a few examples how the scientific enterprise can provide the kind of information that will help in maintaining the earth in a state suitable for human life, and in creating environments favorable for the more complete expression of human potentialities!

1. Physicists have shown that nuclear technologies could provide mankind with an endless source of energy. On the other hand, any perceptive person knows that energy improperly used contributes to the degradation of the environment. The so-called "conquest" of nature by the use of any form of energy is potentially dangerous if it is not carried out within the imperatives of certain ecological laws. Tagore's "wooing of the earth" means the achievement of a state in which man, other living things, and the physical environment can all survive and prosper.

The wise use of nuclear technologies requires that we develop the kind of ecological sciences that will enable us to foresee the consequences of environmental manipulations, measured not so much in terms of economics as in present and future human values. From this point of view, the creation and maintenance of sound ecological systems is more important than the "conquest" of nature.

2. Chemists and engineers will unquestionably produce more and more new materials and processes that will change many aspects of human life.

It is commonly assumed that man can and must adapt to these changes. But in fact human adaptability is not limitless.

We know little of the thresholds and ranges of human adaptability. It is certain in any case that the ready acceptance of social and technological changes does not mean that these are desirable. Past experience has shown for example that ionizing radiations and environmental pollution (of air, food and water) have deleterious effects that manifest themselves very slowly —they behave like the pestilence that stealth in the darkness. Similarly, social and technological innovations that appear to be readily tolerated may eventually ruin the quality of human life. The real limits of adaptability are not determined by what can be tolerated for a certain period of time, but by future consequences. These consequences are essential factors to be considered in deciding what technological and social innovations are safe and desirable.

3. Medical scientists will certainly develop new techniques and new drugs for the treatment of the degenerative and chronic diseases that now plague mankind. But such treatments will be increasingly expensive and, more importantly, will require highly specialized personnel. They cannot solve the massive health problems of the general public.

There is good reason to believe that most of the degenerative conditions that are becoming increasingly prevalent in the modern world need not have occurred in the first place. Greater knowledge of the environmental and social factors that cause disease would go much further toward improving human health than the discovery of drugs, surgical procedures, and other esoteric methods of treatment. Prevention is much less expensive than cure and always more effective.

4. Parochial man could theoretically be replaced by global man because technical procedures enable him to read, hear and see anything that goes on in the world. But in practice communication technology is only a small part of the communication.

We need more knowledge concerning the receptiveness of sense organs and of the brain to the information that technology can provide. We need to learn also how to make information become really formative, instead of being merely informative. Only those influences that are formative contribute to human development.

Pointing to some of the present inadequacies of science does not imply either a defeatist or anti-intellectual attitude. It directs attention rather to the need for scientific inquiry into new channels. The solution to our social and environmental problems is not in less science but in a kind of science which is subservient to the fundamental needs of man.

Our societies are slowly realizing that many social and technological practices are threatening human and environmental health. Rather grudgingly, they are developing palliative measures to control some of the most obvious dangers. This piecemeal social engineering will be helpful in many cases, but it will not solve the ecological crisis and its attendant threats to the quality of life. Technological fixes amount to little more than putting a finger in the dike, whereas what is needed is a comprehensive philosophy of man in his environment. Henderson's concept of the "fitness of the environment" provides a framework for such a philosophy.

Fitness implies that man has achieved some kind of adaptation to his environment. Many populations in the past have achieved a tolerable state of adaptation to their surroundings and ways of life, even when these were very primitive according to our standards. In any case, adaptive fitness lasts only as long as conditions are stable. Changes that upset the equilibrium between man and environment are likely to disturb physical and mental health and thereby to generate unhappiness.

Fitness also implies that all aspects of human development reflect the adaptive responses made by the organism to environmental stimuli. In the long run, most forms of adaptation involve evolutionary alterations of the genetic endowment. But in addition, the biological and mental characteristics of each individual are shaped by his responses to the environmental forces that impinge on him in the course of his development. Genes do not determine the traits by which we know a person; what they do is only to govern his biological responses to environmental influences. As a result each person is shaped by his environment as much as by his genetic endowment.

The environmental influences that are experienced very early during the formative phases of development (prenatal and early postnatal) have the most profound and lasting effects. From early nutrition to education, from technological forces to esthetic and ethical attitudes, countless are the early influences that make an irreversible imprint on the human body and mind. Most of the biological and mental characteristics that are assumed to be distinctive of the various ethnic groups—anywhere in the world—turn out to be the consequences of early environmental influences (biological and social) rather than of genetic constitution.

Human beings actualize only a small part of the potentialities they inherit in their genetic code, because these potentialities become reality only to the extent that circumstances favor phenotypic expression. In practice, mental development is greatly facilitated if the person—especially the child— is exposed at a critical time to the proper range of stimuli and acquires a wide awareness of the cosmos. Science and technology can play a crucial role in the shaping of mental attributes by making it possible to create environments more diversified and thereby more favorable for the expression of a wider range of human potentialities.

All men are migrants from a common origin. They have undergone biological and social changes that have enabled them to adapt to the different conditions they have encountered in the course of their migration. But as far as can be judged, all ethnic groups are similarly endowed with regard to biological and mental potentialities. This fact is of enormous practical importance because it justifies the belief that, given the proper opportunities, any population can shape its future and select the form it gives to its own culture, by focusing its attention on the biological, technological and social forces that affect human development.

Programs of social betterment should be based on the ability to predict the effects—both immediate and long-range—that social and technological manipulations will exert on the human organism and on ecological systems. Unfortunately, interest in scientific forecasting has been concerned almost exclusively with the technological and social developments themselves, rather than with their effects on human life and on ecological systems.

Needless to say, there exists some factual knowledge concerning man's interplay with his environment; but it is a highly episodic kind of knowledge, derived from attempts to solve a few special problems—for example, the training of combat forces for operation in the tropics or the Arctic, the preparation of men and vehicles for space travel, the planning of river basins for water and land management.

SOME EXAMPLES

Many scientific problems of relevance to human life in the urban and technological world cry out for investigation. Three examples will illustrate:

1. Everyone agrees that it is desirable to control environmental pollution. But what are the pollutants of air, water or food that are really significant? Sulfur dioxide, carbon monoxide, and the nitrogen oxides generated by automobile exhausts are the air pollutants most widely discussed. But the colloidal particles released from automobile tires and from the asbestos lining of brakes grossly contaminate the air of our cities and may well be more dangerous than some of the gases against which control efforts are now directed.

The acute effects of environmental pollution can be readily recognized, but what about the cumulative, delayed, and indirect effects? Does the young organism respond as does the adult? Does he develop forms of tolerance or hyper-susceptibility that affect his subsequent responses to the same or other pollutants?

Priorities with regard to the control of environmental pollution cannot be established rationally until such knowledge is available.

2. Everyone agrees that all cities of the world must be renovated or even rebuilt. Technologies are available for almost any kind of scheme imagined by city planners, architects, and sociologists. But hardly anything is known concerning the effects that the urban environments so created will have on human well-being and especially on the physical and mental development of children. We know how to create sanitary environments that permit the body to become large and vigorous. But what about the effect of the environmental factors on the mind? All too often housing developments are

designed as if they were to be used as disposable cubicles for dispensable people.

3. Everyone agrees that all citizens should be given the same educational opportunities. But what are the critical ages for receptivity to various kinds of stimuli and for the development of mental potentialities?

We must develop a science concerned with the effects that the environmental influences created by massive urbanization and by ubiquitous technology exert on physical, physiological and mental characteristics. We must learn how the effects of early deprivation or over-stimulation can be prevented and corrected.

These three examples have been selected to illustrate that the environment must be considered, not only from the point of view of technology, but even more with regard to the responses that the body and the mind make to the surroundings and ways of life. The same could be said, of course, for the responses of the total environment to technological interventions. The distant consequences of these responses, both for human welfare and for ecological systems, are the most important factors to be considered in social planning.

Few if any universities or research institutes, in this country or abroad, are equipped to deal effectively with the organization of existing knowledge, and with the acquisition of new knowledge, relevant to the interplay between environmental forces and the world community. In fact, the use of existing knowledge, and development of additional knowledge, will certainly require a cooperative approach between institutions either at an international or a regional level.

WORLD PROBLEMS

Certain problems obviously involve the whole world community. For example:

1. Weather modification: Who will be deprived of water if rain is made to fall on a given area?

2. Control of epidemics: How fast and along what routes do the various strains of influenza virus spread from one continent to another?

3. The protection of endangered species: Certain species of primates are used on enormous scale in American and European research laboratories. What should be done to prevent the populations of these primates from being destroyed in their countries of origin?

4. Brain drain and related problems pertaining to the education and utilization of scientists.

Other problems are more regional in character. For example:

1. The technical problems of agriculture and conservation are completely different in tropical, arid, and temperate areas. Soil management, plant rotations, animal husbandry must be designed to fit the geological, climatic, and

social conditions peculiar to each area. One cannot solve the problems of India by using knowledge and technologies developed for the conditions prevailing in Indiana.

2. Malnutrition may be due to shortage of calories in certain areas and to shortage of good quality protein elsewhere. The development of protein preparations that can serve as substitutes for animal and dairy products must be based on the kind of plant resources that can be economically produced. This in turn depends upon the geology and climate of the area under consideration.

3. A recent UNESCO conference urged the development of programs for monitoring pollutants in entire air sheds and water basins—but what pollutants? The chemical nature of air pollution on the United States' Pacific coast differs completely from what it is in Taiwan or in northern Europe. Water and food are chiefly polluted with microbes in certain parts of the world, with chemicals in industrialized countries.

4. Cosmic rays at high altitude, radio-nuclides absorption in areas of high radioactive background, marine chemistry and biology on different types of shore lines are but a few of the many examples that may have great potential important for different countries in the same region.

Global and regional problems, whether focused on man or on his environment, necessarily deal with complex systems in which several related factors interplay through feedback processes. The study of such multi-factorial systems demands conceptual approaches very different from those involving only one variable, which are the stock in trade of orthodox academic science. Furthermore, this kind of study requires research facilities that hardly exist at present, and that few institutions or countries can afford. Hence, the need for the development of a collective approach in the mission-oriented institutions, either on a global or a regional level. Fortunately, there is enough experience to feel confident that supra-national scientific centers can function and be effective!

The World Health Organization (WHO), with its multifarious control and study programs, and the World Meteorological Organization with its planned World Weather Watch are classic examples of scientific research and action on a global scale.

Even more promising, I believe, is the prospect for regional scientific centers. The Institute for Nutrition for Central America and Panama (INCAP) in Guatemala City, and the Satocholera Laboratory in East Pakistan can serve as examples of regional institutions devoted to problems of health. The Centre Européen pour la Recherche Nucléaire (CERN) in Geneva, and the International Center for Theoretical Physics at Trieste illustrate what can be done for theoretical science. The success of these very different types of scientific institutes should encourage the creation of other regional institutions throughout the world, in order to deal with the problems that are common to a group of nations.

DIVERSITY

Certain general principles are valid for all environmental problems, because they are based on unchangeable and universal aspects of ecological systems, and especially of man's nature.

The biological and mental constitution of *Homo sapiens* has changed only in minor details since the late Stone Age, and despite progress in theoretical genetics, there is no chance that it can be significantly or safely modified in the foreseeable future. This genetic stability defines the limits within which human life can be safely altered by social or technological innovation. Beyond these limits, any change is likely to have disastrous effects.

On the other hand, mankind has a large reserve of potentialities that have not yet been expressed. Science and technology can facilitate the actualization of these latent potentialities, and as more persons find it possible to express their innate endowments because they can select from a variety of conditions, society becomes richer and civilizations continue to unfold. In contrast, if the surroundings and ways of life are highly stereotyped—whether in prosperity or in poverty—the only components of man's nature that can flourish are those adapted to the narrow range of prevailing conditions. Creating diversified environments may result in some loss of efficiency, but diversity is vastly more important than efficiency, because it makes possible the germination of the seeds dormant in the human species. In the light of these facts, the continued existence of independent nations may be desirable even though it generates political problems, because the cultivation of national characteristics probably contributes to the cultural richness of mankind.

Diversity, however, does not imply complete permissiveness. Individual man must accept some form of discipline, because he can survive and indeed exist only when integrated in a social structure. For related ecological and social reasons, no group, large or small, can be entirely independent of the other groups within the confines of the Spaceship Earth. Total rejection of discipline is unbiologic because it would inevitably result in the disintegration of individual lives, of the social order, and of ecological systems.

In the final analysis, the interplay between man and his environment must be considered from three different points of view:

1. The frontiers of social and technological changes are determined, not by availability of power and technical prowess, but by unchangeable aspects of man's nature and of ecological systems.

2. The total environment must be sufficiently diversified to assure that each person can express as completely as possible his innate potentialities in accordance with his selected goals.

3. The expressions of individuality can be allowed only to the extent that they are compatible with the requirements of the social group and of the world community.

The universality of mankind, the uniqueness of each person, and the need for social integration are three determinants of human life that must be reconciled in order to achieve individual freedom, social health, and the diversity of civilizations.

URBAN CRISIS
challenge and response

41. RIOTING, INSURRECTION, AND CIVIL DISOBEDIENCE
ralph w. conant

Whether actual or imminent, violence is the most fundamental type of crisis that can confront any society, for the full array of social controls and values possessed by a society are put to an extreme test. In the following selection, one specific kind of violence, the riot, is subjected to careful analysis based on data gathered by members of the Lemburg Center for the Study of Violence at Brandeis University. The author concludes with a number of observations on the conditions under which civil protest with and without violence may be justified.

Rioting is a spontaneous outburst of group violence characterized by excitement mixed with rage. The outburst is usually directed against alleged perpetrators of injustice or gross misusers of political power. The typical rioter has no premeditated purpose, plan or direction, although systematic looting, arson and attack on persons may occur once the riot is underway. Also, criminals and conspirators may expand their routine activities in the wake of the riot chaos. While it is quite clear that riots are unpremeditated outbursts, they are not as a rule *senseless* outbursts. The rage behind riots is a shared rage growing out of specific rage-inducing experiences. In the United States, the rage felt by Negroes (increasingly manifested in ghetto riots) is based on centuries of oppression, and in latter times on discriminatory practices that frustrate equal opportunity to social, economic and political goals. While all riots stem from conflicts in society similar to those that inspire civil disobedience, they ordinarily do not develop directly from specific acts of civil dis-

Reprinted from *The American Scholar,* Vol. 37, No. 3, Summer 1968. Copyright © 1968 by the United Chapters of Phi Beta Kappa. By permission of the publishers.

obedience. Yet repeated failures of civil disobedience to achieve sought-after goals can and often do result in frustrations that provide fertile ground for the violent outbursts we call riots.

The factors universally associated with the occurrence and course of any riot are the following: (1) preconditions, (2) riot phases, and (3) social control. The discussion here is drawn from a review of the literature of collective behavior as well as on studies currently underway at the Lemberg Center for the Study of Violence at Brandeis University.

I. The Preconditions of Riot: Value Conflicts

All riots stem from intense conflicts within the value systems that stabilize the social and political processes of a nation. The ghetto riot is a concrete case of a group attempt to restructure value conflicts and clarify social relationships in a short time by deviant methods.

There are two classes of value conflicts, each of which gives rise to a different kind of struggle. The first calls for normative readjustment in which the dominant values of a society are being inequitably applied. In this case, the aggrieved groups protest, and if protest fails to attain readjustment, they riot.

The anti-draft rioter at the time of the Civil War was protesting the plight of the common man who could not, like his wealthier compatriots, buy his way out of the draft. American egalitarian values were not being applied across the board. The readjustment came only after the intensity of the riots stimulated public concern to force a change.

The contemporary ghetto riots grow out of the failure of the civil rights movement to achieve normative readjustment for black people through nonviolent protest. This failure has produced lines of cleavage which, if intensified, will result in the second type of value conflict, namely, value readjustment.

In this case, the dominant values of the society are brought under severe pressure for change. The social movement that organizes the activities of an aggrieved sector of the population, having given up hope for benefiting from the going value system, sets up a new configuration of values. The movement becomes revolutionary. When Americans gave up hope of benefiting from the English institutions of the monarchy and the colonial system, they set up their own egalitarian value system and staged a revolution.

Now, Black Power and Black Nationalist leaders are beginning to move in the direction of value readjustment. They are talking about organizing their people on the basis of separatist and collectivist values and they are moving away from the melting pot, individualistic values of our country, which are not working for them.

The hostile belief system. An aggrieved population erupts into violence on the basis of a preexisting hostile belief. During the anti-Catholic riots in the early part of the nineteenth century, the rioters really believed that the Pope, in Rome, was trying to take over the country. The anti-Negro rioters in Chicago and East St. Louis (and even in Detroit in 1943) really believed that Negroes were trying to appropriate their jobs and rape their women and kill their men.

Today, many rioters in black ghettos really believe in the malevolence of white society, its duplicity, and its basic commitment to oppressing Negroes. An important component of the hostile belief system is that the expected behavior of the identified adversary is seen as *extraordinary*—that is, beyond the pale of accepted norms. In the black ghettos, people are convinced, for example, that the police will behave toward them with extraordinary verbal incivility and physical brutality, far beyond any incivility and brutality displayed toward whites in similar circumstances. . . .

Relative deprivation. An important and almost universal causal factor in riots is a perception of real or imagined deprivation in relation to other groups in the society. As James R. Hundley has put it, the aggrieved see a gap between the conditions in which they find themselves and what could be achieved given a set of opportunities. Ghetto residents in the United States use middle-class white suburban living as a comparative point, and they feel acutely deprived. The areas of relative deprivation for the black American are pervasively economic, political and social.

Obstacles to change. Another universal causal factor behind riots is the lack of effective channels for bringing about change. Stanley Lieberson and Arnold Silverman, in their study of riots in United States cities between 1910 and 1961, note a correlation between cities in which riots have occurred and cities that elect officials at large rather than from wards. In this situation, Negroes are not likely to have adequate representation, if any. The result is that they feel deprived of a local political voice and are in fact deprived of a potential channel through which to air grievances. An aggrieved population with no access to grievance channels is bound to resort to rioting if one or more of their grievances become dramatized in a precipitating incident.

Hope of reward. While riot participants do not ordinarily think much in advance about the possible outcome of a riot, still those who participate harbor hopes, however vague, that extreme and violent behavior may bring about desired changes. Certainly the contagion effect had a significant role in the crescendo of ghetto riots in the United States during 1967. Part of the spirit was that things could not be made much worse by rioting, and riots might achieve unexpected concessions from influential whites. Any hard-pressed people are riot-prone and the more so if they see others like themselves making gains from rioting. What happens is spontaneous, but hope raises the combustion potential.

Communication. Ease of communication among potential rioters is less a *precondition* of riot than a necessary condition to the spread of riot, once started. Riots tend to occur in cities during warm weather when people are likely to be congregated in the streets and disengaged from normal daily activities.

II. The Phases of a Riot

A riot is a dynamic process which goes through different stages of development. If the preconditions described above exist, if a value conflict intensifies, hostile beliefs flourish, an incident that exemplifies the hostile beliefs occurs, communications are inadequate and rumor inflames feelings of resentment to a fever pitch, the process will get started. How far it will go depends upon a further process of interaction between the local authorities and an aroused community.

There are four stages within the riot process. Not all local civil disturbances go through all four stages; in fact, the majority do not reach stage three. It is still not certain at what point in the process it is appropriate to use the word "riot" to describe the event. In fact more information is needed about the process and better reporting of the phase structure itself.

Phase 1. The precipitating incident. All riots begin with a precipitating event, which is usually a gesture, act or event by the adversary that is seen by the aggrieved community as concrete evidence of the injustice or relative deprivation that is the substance of the hostility and rage felt by the aggrieved. The incident is inflammatory because it is typical of the adversary's behavior toward the aggrieved and responsible for the conditions suffered by the aggrieved. The incident is also taken as an excuse for striking back with "justified" violence in behavior akin to rage. The event may be distorted by rumor and made to seem more inflammatory than it actually is. In communities where the level of grievances is high, a seemingly minor incident may set off a riot; conversely, when the grievance level is low, a more dramatic event may be required to touch off the trouble. . . .

Phase 2. Confrontation. Following the instigating incident, the local population swarms to the scene. A process of "keynoting" begins to take place. Potential riot promoters begin to articulate the rage accumulating in the crowd and they vie with each other in suggesting violent courses of action. Others, frequently recognized ghetto leaders, suggest that the crowd disband to let tempers cool and to allow time for a more considered course of action. Law enforcement officers appear and try to disrupt the "keynoting" process by ordering and forcing the crowd to disperse. More often than not, their behavior, which will be discussed below, serves to elevate one or another hostile "keynoter" to a position of dominance, thus flipping the riot process into the next phase. . . .

Phase 3. Roman Holiday. If hostile "keynoting" reaches a sufficient crescendo in urban ghetto riots, a quantum jump in the riot process occurs and the threshold of phase 3 is crossed. Usually the crowd leaves the scene of the street confrontation and reassembles elsewhere. Older persons drop out for the time being and young people take over the action. They display an angry intoxication indistinguishable from glee. They hurl rocks and bricks and bottles at white-owned stores and at cars containing whites or police, wildly cheering every "hit." They taunt law-enforcement personnel, risk capture, and generally act out routine scenarios featuring the sortie, the ambush and the escape—the classic triad of violent action that they have seen whites go through endlessly on TV. They set the stage for looting, but are usually too involved in "the chase" and are too excited for systematic plunder. That action comes later in phase 3, when first younger, then older, adults, caught up on the Roman Holiday, and angered by tales of police brutality toward the kids, join in the spirit of righting ancient wrongs. . . .

Phase 4. Siege. If a city's value conflict continues to be expressed by admonishment from local authorities and violent suppression of the Roman Holiday behavior in the ghetto, the riot process will be kicked over into phase 4. The adversary relations between ghetto dwellers and local and City Hall whites reach such a degree of polarization that no direct communications of any kind can be established. Communications, such as they are, consist of symbolic, warlike acts. State and federal military assistance is summoned for even more violent repression. A curfew is declared. The ghetto is subjected to a state of siege. Citizens can no longer move freely into and out of their neighborhoods. Forces within the ghetto, now increasingly composed of adults, throw fire bombs at white-owned establishments, and disrupt fire fighting. Snipers attack invading paramilitary forces. The siege runs its course, like a Greek tragedy, until both sides tire of this fruitless and devastating way of solving a conflict.

III. Social Control

Studies of past and present riots show that the collective hostility of a community breaks out as a result of inattention to the value conflict (the long-range causes) and as a result of failures in social control (immediate causation). These failures are of two sorts: under-control and over-control. In the condition of under-control, law-enforcement personnel are insufficiently active. Although the condition may be brought about in various ways, the effect is always the same. The dissident group, noting the weakness of the authorities, seizes the opportunity to express its hostility. The inactivity of the police functions as an invitation to act out long-suppressed feelings, free of the social consequences of illegal behavior.

In some communities, as in the 1967 Detroit riot, under-control during early phase 3 produces an efflorescence of looting and is then suddenly replaced with over-control. In other communities, over-control is instituted early, during phase 2. Local and state police are rushed to the scene of the confrontation and begin to manhandle everyone in sight. Since the action is out of proportion to the event, it generates an intense reaction. If over-control is sufficiently repressive, as in the 1967 Milwaukee riot, where a 24-hour curfew was ordered early in phase 3 and the National Guard summoned, the disturbances are quieted. In Milwaukee, the ghetto was placed under a state of siege as the Roman Holiday was beginning to take hold in the community. No "catharsis" occurred and there was no improvement in ghetto-City Hall communications. The consequences of such premature repression cannot yet be discerned. Short of the use of overwhelming force, over-control usually leads to increased violence. The black people in the ghetto see the police as violent and strike back with increasing intensity. Studies being conducted currently at the Lemberg Center show that in the majority of instances, police violence toward ghetto residents precedes and supersedes ghetto violence.

An adequate law-enforcement response requires an effective police presence when illegal activities, such as looting, take place. Arrests can and should be made, without cruelty. It is not necessary that all offenders be caught and arrested to show that authorities intend to maintain order. Crowds can be broken up or contained through a variety of techniques not based on clubbing or shooting. The avoidance of both under- and over-control is a matter of police training for riot control. This was the deliberate pattern of police response in several cities (notably Pittsburgh) to the riots following the assassination of Martin Luther King in April. . . .

IV. Civil Insurrection

When community grievances go unresolved for long periods of time and efforts at communication and/or negotiation seem unproductive or hopeless, despair in the aggrieved community may impel established, aspiring or self-appointed leaders to organize acts of rebellion against civil authorities. Such acts constitute insurrection and differ from riots in that the latter are largely spontaneous and unpremeditated. The exceptions are riots that are instigated by insurrectionists.

Although insurrection is deliberate rebellion, the aim of the insurrectionist, unlike that of the revolutionary, is to put down persons in power, to force abandonment of obnoxious policies or adoption of desirable ones. The insurrectionist is not out to overthrow the system. (The organizers of the Boston Tea Party were insurrectionists, they were not yet revolutionaries.) Like the civil disobedient (or the rioter), the insurrectionist will settle for some specific adjustment in the system, such as a change in political leadership, increased representation in the system, repeal of an objectionable law, or abandonment of an inequitable policy. The revolutionary has lost hope for any effective participation in the existing system (as had the American revolutionaries by 1776) and presses for a total overthrow.[1]

Civil insurrection is in effect a stage of *civil protest* that develops from the same set of conditions that inspire acts of civil disobedience or riot. Riots do not turn into insurrection, although insurrectionists are often encouraged by riots to employ organized violence as a means to attain sought-after goals. The participants in acts of civil disobedience and riots are obviously seen by insurrectionists as potential participants in organized acts of violent protest. Indeed, the disobedients and the rioters may themselves be converted to insurrection tactics, not by existing insurrectionists, but by disillusionment and frustration in the other courses of action. . . .

V. The Justification of Civil Protest

There is substantial agreement among legal and political thinkers that nonviolent challenges to the policies and laws of civil authority are an indispensable mechanism of corrective change in a democratic society. Insofar as possible, procedures for challenge which may involve open and deliberate disobedience should be built into the laws and policies of the system, for such procedures give the system a quality of resilience and flexibility, the capacity to absorb constructive attack from within. . . .

Nonviolent civil disobedience is justified under the following circumstances:

1.   When an oppressed group is deprived of lawful channels for remedying its condition; conversely, a resort to civil disobedience is never politically legitimate where methods of due process in both the legal and political systems are available as remedies.
2.   As a means of resisting or refusing to participate in an obvious and intolerable evil perpetrated by civil authorities (for example, a policy of genocide or enslavement).
3.   When government takes or condones actions that are inconsistent with values on which the society and the political system are built, and thus violates the basic assumptions on which the regime's legitimacy rests.
4.   When it is certain that the law or policy in question violates the constitution of the regime and, therefore, would be ruled unconstitutional by proper authority if challenged.
5.   When a change in law or policy is demanded by social or economic need in the community and the normal procedures of law and politics are inadequate, obstructed or held captive by antilegal forces.

---

[1] In the dictionary, insurgency is a condition of revolt against recognized government that does not reach the proportions of an organized revolutionary government and is not recognized as belligerency. This definition squares with my own as outlined above. An important distinction between insurrection (which I am using synonymously with insurgency) and revolution is the existence of a revolutionary government which is installed when the existing government is brought down.

6. When the actions of government have become so obnoxious to one's own personal ethics (value system) that one would feel hypocritical in submitting to a law that enforces these actions: for example, the Fugitive Slave Law.

It seems to me that a citizen is justified in originating or participating in an act of civil disobedience under any of these circumstances, and, as Herbert Kelman has argued, that an act of civil disobedience in such circumstances should be generally regarded as *obligatory* in terms of the highest principles of citizenship. This does not mean that acts of civil disobedience should be ignored by civil authorities; on the contrary, aside from the damage such a policy would do to effectiveness of the act of civil disobedience, it must be considered the obligation of the regime to punish a law breaker *so long as the violated law is in force.* As William Buckley has argued, it is the individual's right to refuse to go along with his community, but the community, not the individual, must specify the consequences. For the regime to act otherwise would be to concede the right of personal veto over every act of government. At the same time, a conscientious challenge to civil authority (with full expectation of punishment) aimed at repairing a serious flaw in the system of justice is a step every citizen should know how *to decide* to take.

When is civil protest involving violence justified? Americans like to think of themselves as a peace-loving people, yet violence is and always has been an important and sometimes indispensable instrument of social, economic and political change in our national history. We do not need to be reminded of the role it has played in United States foreign policy and in domestic relations.

The fact is that Americans are *both* peace-loving and willing to resort to violence when other avenues of goal achievement seem closed or ineffective. In our national history violence was the ultimate instrument in our conquest of the lands on the North American continent that now comprise the nation. Violence freed the American colonists from British rule and later insured freedom of the seas (1812–1815). Violence abolished slavery, established the bargaining rights of labor, twice put down threatening tyrannies in Europe and once in the Asian Pacific. In the present day, violence is the unintended instrument of black citizens to break through oppressive discrimination in housing, employment, education and political rights.

Americans have always taken the position that violence could be justified *as an instrument of last resort* in the achievement of critical national goals or in the face of external threat.

While it is true that we have always felt most comfortable about government-sponsored violence and especially violence in response to an external threat, we have often rationalized *post factum* the use of violence by aggrieved segments of the population *when the cause was regarded as a just one in terms of our deeply held egalitarian values.* The anti-draft riots during the Civil War are one example; labor strife that finally led to legitimizing workers' bargaining rights is another. Two or three generations from now, the ghetto riots (and even the spasmodic insurrection that is bound to follow) will be seen as having contributed to the perfection of our system of egalitarian values. Thus, I conclude that violence in the cause of hewing to our most cherished goals of freedom, justice and equal opportunity for all our citizens is and will remain as indispensable a corrective ingredient in our system as peaceful acts of civil disobedience. The sole qualification is that all other avenues of legitimate and peaceful change first be substantially closed, exhausted or ineffective.

When an aggrieved segment of the population finds it necessary to resist, riot, or commit deliberate acts of insurrection, the government must respond firmly to enforce the law, to protect people and property from the consequences of violence, but it must, with equal energy and dedication, seek out the causes of the outbursts and move speedily to rectify any injustices that are found at the root of the trouble.

42. REPORT ON CIVIL DISORDERS

In the summer of 1967, President Lyndon B. Johnson appointed a Commission on Civil Disorders, charging it to investigate, analyze, and recommend solutions to the outburst of community conflict and violence in many parts of the United States. Attacked by both Right and Left for the (moderate) orientation of its membership, the Commission reported its findings the following year. It predicted that if Americans ignore "the historical patterns of Negro-white relations . . . we shall none of us escape the consequences." The Report identified the basic sources of conflict and disintegration and recommended an ameliorative list of "critical priorities" to cope with a continuing national crisis.

We have seen what happened. Why did it happen?

In addressing this question we shift our focus from the local to the national scene, from the particular events of the summer of 1967 to the factors within the society at large which have brought about the sudden violent mood of so many urban Negroes.

The record before this Commission reveals that the causes of recent racial disorders are imbedded in a massive tangle of issues and circumstances—social, economic, political, and psychological—which arise out of the historical pattern of Negro-white relations in America.

From *Report of the National Advisory Commission on Civil Disorders.* New York: Bantam Books, 1968.

These factors are both complex and interacting; they vary significantly in their effect from city to city and from year to year; and the consequences of one disorder, generating new grievances and new demands, become the causes of the next. It is this which creates the "thicket of tension, conflicting evidence and extreme opinions" cited by the President.

Despite these complexities, certain fundamental matters are clear. Of these, the most fundamental is the racial attitude and behavior of white Americans toward black Americans. Race prejudice has shaped our history decisively in the past; it now threatens to do so again. White racism is essentially responsible for the explosive mixture which has been accumulating in our cities since the end of World War II. At the base of this mixture are three of the most bitter fruits of white racial attitudes:

Pervasive discrimination and segregation.   The first is surely the continuing exclusion of great numbers of Negroes from the benefits of economic progress through discrimination in employment and education, and their enforced confinement in segregated housing and schools. The corrosive and degrading effects of this condition and the attitudes that underlie it are the source of the deepest bitterness and at the center of the problem of racial disorder.

Black migration and white exodus.   The second is the massive and growing concentration of impoverished Negroes in our major cities resulting from Negro migration from the rural South, rapid population growth and the continuing movement of the white middle-class to the suburbs. The consequence is a greatly increased burden on the already depleted resources of cities, creating a growing crisis of deteriorating facilities and services and unmet human needs.

Black ghettos.   Third, in the teeming racial ghettos, segregation and poverty have intersected to destroy opportunity and hope and to enforce failure. The ghettos too often mean men and women without jobs, families without men, and schools where children are processed instead of educated, until they return to the street—to crime, to narcotics, to dependency on welfare, and to bitterness and resentment against society in general and white society in particular.

These three forces have converged on the inner city in recent years and on the people who inhabit it. At the same time, most whites and many Negroes outside the ghetto have prospered to a degree unparalleled in the history of civilization. Through television—the universal appliance in the ghetto—and the other media of mass communications, this affluence has been endlessly flaunted before the eyes of the Negro poor and the jobless ghetto youth.

As Americans, most Negro citizens carry within themselves two basic aspirations of our society. They seek to share in both the material resources of our system and its intangible benefits—dignity, respect and acceptance. Outside the ghetto many have succeeded in achieving a decent standard of life, and in developing the inner resources which give life meaning and direction. Within the ghetto, however, it is rare that either aspiration is achieved.

Yet these facts alone—fundamental as they are—cannot be said to have caused the disorders. Other and more immediate factors help explain why these events happened now.

Recently, three powerful ingredients have begun to catalyze the mixture.

Frustrated hopes.   The expectations aroused by the great judicial and legislative victories of the civil rights movement have led to frustration, hostility and cynicism in the face of the persistent gap between promise and fulfillment. The dramatic struggle for equal rights in the South has sensitized Northern Negroes to the economic inequalities reflected in the deprivations of ghetto life.

Legitimation of violence.   A climate that tends toward the approval and encouragement of violence as a form of protest has been created by white terrorism directed against nonviolent protest, including instances of abuse and even murder of some civil rights workers in the South; by the open defiance of law and federal authority by state and local officials resisting desegregation; and by some protest groups engaging in civil disobedience who turn their backs on nonviolence, go beyond the Constitutionally protected rights of petition and free assembly, and resort to violence to attempt to compel alteration of laws and policies with which they disagree. This condition has been reinforced by a general erosion of respect for authority in American society and reduced effectiveness of social standards and community restraints on violence and crime. This in turn has largely resulted from rapid urbanization and the dramatic reduction in the average age of the total population.

Powerlessness.   Finally, many Negroes have come to believe that they are being exploited politically and economically by the white "power structure." Negroes, like people in poverty everywhere, in fact lack the channels of communication, influence and appeal that traditionally have been available to ethnic minorities within the city and which enabled them—unburdened by color—to scale the walls of the white ghettos in an earlier era. The frustrations of powerlessness have led some to the conviction that there is no effective alternative to violence as a means of expression and redress, as a way of "moving the system." More generally, the result is alienation and hostility toward the institutions of law and government and the white society which controls them. This is reflected in the reach toward racial consciousness and solidarity reflected in the slogan "Black Power."

These facts have combined to inspire a new mood among Negroes, particularly among the young. Self-esteem and enhanced racial pride are replacing apathy and submission to "the system." Moreover, Negro youth, who make up over half of the ghetto population, share the growing sense of alienation felt by many white youth in our country. Thus, their role in recent civil disorders reflects not only a shared sense of deprivation and victimization by white society but also the rising incidence of disruptive conduct by a segment of American youth throughout the society.

Incitement and encouragement of violence.   These conditions have created a volatile mixture of attitudes and beliefs which needs only a spark to ignite mass violence. Strident appeals to violence, first heard from white racists, were echoed and reinforced last summer in the inflammatory rhetoric of black racists and militants. Throughout the year, extremists crisscrossed the country preaching a doctrine of black power and violence. Their rhetoric was widely reported in the mass media; it was echoed by local "militants" and organizations; it became the ugly background noise of the violent summer.

We cannot measure with any precision the influence of these organizations and individuals in the ghetto, but we think it clear that the intolerable and unconscionable encouragement of violence heightened tensions, created a mood of acceptance and an expectation of violence, and thus contributed to the eruption of the disorders last summer.

The police.   It is the convergence of all these factors that makes the role of the police so difficult and so significant. Almost invariably the incident that ignites disorder arises from police action. Harlem, Watts, Newark and Detroit —all the major outbursts of recent years—were precipitated by routine arrests of Negroes for minor offenses by white police.

But the police are not merely the spark. In discharge of their obligation to maintain order and insure public safety in the disruptive conditions of ghetto life, they are inevitably involved in sharper and more frequent conflicts with ghetto residents than with the residents of other areas. Thus, to many Negroes police have come to symbolize white power, white racism and white repression. And the fact is that many police do reflect and express these white attitudes. The atmosphere of hostility and cynicism is reinforced by a widespread perception among Negroes of the existence of police brutality and corruption, and of a "double standard" of justice and protection—one for Negroes and one for whites. . . .

THE COMMISSION'S RECOMMENDATIONS

We do not claim competence to chart the details of programs within such complex and interrelated fields as employment, welfare, education and housing. We do believe it is essential to set forth goals and to recommend strategies to reach these goals.

That is the aim of the pages that follow. They contain our sense of the critical priorities. We discuss and recommend programs not to commit each of us to specific parts of such programs but to illustrate the type and dimension of action needed.

Much has been accomplished in recent years to formulate new directions for national policy and new channels for national emergency. Resources devoted to social programs have been greatly increased in many areas. Hence, few of our program suggestions are entirely novel. In some form, many are already in effect.

All this serves to underscore our basic conclusion: the need is not so much for the government to design new programs as it is for the nation to generate new will. Private enterprise, labor unions, the churches, the foundations, the universities—all our urban institutions—must deepen their involvement in the life of the city and their commitment to its revival and welfare.

OBJECTIVES FOR NATIONAL ACTION

Just as Lincoln, a century ago, put preservation of the Union above all else, so should we put creation of a true union—a single society and a single American identity—as our major goal. Toward that goal, we propose the following objectives for national action:

1. Opening up opportunities to those who are restricted by racial segregation and discrimination, and eliminating all barriers to their choice of jobs, education and housing.
2. Removing the frustration of powerlessness among disadvantaged by providing the means for them to deal with the problems that affect their own lives, and by increasing the capacity of our public and private institutions to respond to these problems.
3. Increasing communication across racial lines to destroy stereotypes, to halt polarization, to end distrust and hostility, and to create common ground for efforts toward common goals of public order and social justice.

There are those who oppose these aims as "rewarding the rioters." They are wrong. A great nation is not so easily intimidated. We propose these aims to fulfill our pledge of equality and to meet the fundamental needs of a democratic civilized society—domestic peace, social justice, and urban centers that are citadels of the human spirit.

There are others who say that violence is necessary—that fear alone can prod the nation to act decisively on behalf of racial minorities. They too are wrong. Violence and disorder compound injustice; they must be ended and they will be ended.

Our strategy is neither blind repression nor capitulation to lawlessness. Rather it is the affirmation of common possibilities, for all, within a single society.

43. VIEWING AMERICA
FROM THE BOTTOM
paul jacobs

A basic function of government is to provide all its citizens with security and a decent quality of life. But is it possible that the misery of some of the poorest Americans has been perpetuated in part by government itself? Jacobs believes this to be the case. He points out such environmental conditions as frustration, racism, and educational and economic deprivation as potential sources of social conflagration that the public ignores at great peril to all.

In America, the poor and especially the minority poor live inside a pen without an exit gate. And government, rather than helping weaken or break it down, has reinforced the fence that keeps them inside it. It is true that more of those caught inside escape now than before, but the undiminished masses within are all the angrier at not getting their chance to get out too. As the pressure from within increases, the frustrations and resentments build up to an exploding point, the people cooped up inside lash out and revolt.

Since the August 1965 revolt in Los Angeles, a few meaningful improvements have taken place. A few hundred residents of the barrios and the ghettos have had an opportunity to learn some things about organization and political action through the use of anti-poverty funds; a few dozen new organizations of the poor and the minority groups are beginning to make some demands upon the society.

Yet there has been no important fundamental change in Los Angeles or any other American city.

Mayor Yorty, who like so many other mayors is more interested in furthering his political career than in solving the city's real problems, spends weeks at a time in Asia and Europe as part of his campaign for higher office. And in the last gubernatorial elections, California's white voters accurately reflected the views of white America when it elected, by an overwhelming vote, a governor who had pledged himself to cut down on welfare payments, educational expenditures, and the social services.

He had carried out his pledges, too, for he takes himself seriously. His appointments are popular ones; characteristically, the real estate broker who led the fight against fair housing was made real estate commissioner, and a county supervisor who opposed welfare expenditures is now state welfare director. The Governor authorized an investigation of "welfare frauds" and

From *Prelude to Riot*, by Paul Jacobs. Copyright © 1966, 1967 by Paul Jacobs. Reprinted by permission of Random House, Inc.

denounced rioters as "mad dogs." His actions meet with such wide public approval that he has become a serious Presidential possibility.

Still, it's not only Republicans who give a low priority to the crisis of the cities; many Democrats also oppose any large-scale expenditure on behalf of the urban poor. The War on Poverty has been more rhetoric than combat— the amount of money spent thus far has been less than $100 per poor person in the country and a sizable percentage of that has gone to administrators. And even that niggardly sum has been slashed by Congress. The War on Poverty has not had Presidential leadership either, for his priorities and those of the Congress are twisted, too.

These twisted priorities, which prevent America from curing her cities' cancers, have their roots in old but ignoble traditions in American life, traditions which have developed alongside those of a higher order. And now, confronted as we are with wars in the cities, we must honestly recognize the existence of the traditions before we can deal honestly with them.

First, we must admit that we *are* a racist country. Deep down in their visceral being, millions of white Americans believe that race *does* matter. They believe that they have a higher status and are more intelligent than non-whites.

Without extraordinary effort no one can escape the pervasive sense of white superiority that dominates American life. Thus, although Lyndon Johnson makes a speech at Howard University, carefully shaping in his mind and mouth the word "Negro" in order not to offend his audience, he *thinks* about Negroes or Mexican-Americans or Puerto Ricans as a white man who grew up in a racist country.

Along with its tradition of racism, America has always had a tradition of contempt and dislike for the poor. That tradition is a strong strain in our Puritan heritage, brought here by the first settlers and reinforced over the years by the success the country achieved through work and efficiency. Americans as a people, are convinced that only those who don't want to work are poor, since otherwise they would not be in that condition. After all, everyone can get an education in America; there are plenty of jobs for skilled workers; and finally, they think, other poor people have made it.

Indeed, those who have made it, who have come out of poverty, out of ghettos, are often the worst offenders against the people who remain.

And because so many Americans combine racism with a sense of moral superiority toward the poor, they behave as masters, either ordering how the poor shall live or suggesting, firmly, what they must do. Southern conservative racists say they "take care of their niggers"; Northern liberals say they know what's best for their "clients," the welfare recipients. Both groups share a belief that the poor and especially the non-white poor are incapable of making their own decisions, whether these decisions involve how to look for a job or how long a hambone can be kept in the refrigerator of a public housing project apartment.

We are trapped, too, by the great size and regional diversity of the country. Ignorant of each other's ways, separated from each other by sectionalism and local prejudices, we are especially ignorant about the texture of life for those who are poor or of a different color.

Discovering that ignorance was a frightening lesson for me, for I found out quickly, when I began this book, how little I know. And while my ignorance came as a great personal shock, since I had always believed I was fairly knowledgeable about American society, such ignorance is nearly catastrophic in a more general sense: the fact is that before I began this book, I *was* fairly knowledgeable. I *was* better informed than the great majority of Americans, I did have many more Negro, Spanish-speaking Mexican-American, Oriental, and Indian friends than most Americans, and I was certainly far more aware of the existence of their problems than are most Americans. Yet I really knew very little.

Only a few months ago I was discussing this book at a meeting of liberals in New York City. One of them, a decent man who tries to behave decently, argued with me about my pessimism: "Look," he said, "it's not as bad as you say. Why, right now some of us have made it possible for eleven or twelve Negro families to live on Park Avenue."

I looked at him in shocked silence for a moment or two and then said, "Thousands of Negroes live on Park Avenue. But they're all above 96th Street. That's Park Avenue, too, you know."

But it isn't to him or to most other white New Yorkers: *their* Park Avenue ends at 96th Street.

I don't want to single out that decent man, though, for I too have had and still have my own foreshortened Park Avenues. For example, I was arrested twice during the year I was writing this book. Both times I went to jail, and it was not until then that I understood what life is like for those to whom an arrest is a more common experience, those who are not writers with bail funds and attorneys readily available.

Outside of jail I had to learn how to make my eyes and ears work better for me, too. For a whole year I looked at the walls of the housing projects in Boyle Heights on which the "chicano" gangs had spray-painted their names in huge letters and all I saw was vandalism. It was not until the year was nearly over that I saw something besides vandalism in the unique lettering style of the gangs' names. I finally learned to see that these teen-agers in Los Angeles are seeking an identity of their own, linked to their direct connection with Mexico and the Southwest. Anyone who wants to observe how an art form can develop inside a gang culture has only to go over to Boyle Heights and East Los Angeles and look at the gang graffiti.

But very few people will go. And of those who do, very few will stay to talk and listen.

Too few of the Negroes who have made it out go back, either. Middle- and upper-class Negroes are just as frightened of and alienated from the

Negro poor as are the whites, just as ignorant of the lives of the Negro poor as are the whites. So, too, the new middle class of Spanish descent, whose Spanish is minimal, have very little in common with those poor Mexican farmworkers living on the eastern edge of the serape belt in Los Angeles or the Puerto Ricans in Chicago and New York. The middle- and upper-class members of minority groups may be joined by color or ethnic background to the poor minority people, but they are much more widely separated from them by class.

And my own ignorance still appalls me even though I have managed to learn a few things. Never again will I read, without suspicion, what some social scientist writes about disorganization in *"The* Negro Family" for I have seen no such unit as *"the"* Negro family. This is not to suggest that life in fatherless Negro families doesn't have enormous difficulties; obviously, the absence of a male parent in the house is going to have consequences for the family unit. But very often I have seen that absence compensated for in other ways.

And in Mexican-American family life, where more often the father *is* present, I have seen a grievous distortion of the male role, a glorification of the male, of the quality called "machismo," which stunts and thwarts the women's lives. Yet I have also been in poor Mexican-American family homes where the parents are devoted to each other, where each child is treated like a tiny saint, where love makes poverty almost bearable. Almost.

One important characteristic of ghetto life is the transiency: you can have very close friends, but in a few months they're always gone, and a year later you can't even remember their names. Because rapid turnover and mobility are a matter of course in the ghetto, neither the school nor the neighborhood nor the church exists long enough in any person's life to provide the set of values those institutions intend. That is one reason why looting and stealing and vandalism are perceived differently inside the ghetto than outside.

Of course, I have seen disgusting things, too, inside the barrios and ghettos—hate and violence, bitter, uncontrolled anger, unbridled viciousness. I have seen little children out in the street all day, without any parental control, learning the worst habits of the slums. I have observed absolute indifference to the needs of others and have watched vandalism become a way of life. One afternoon, waiting for a traffic light to change in Watts, I saw a Negro teen-age boy knock an elderly Negro woman to the ground, grab her purse, and run frantically toward a car which screamed off down the street as soon as he got into it. The old woman stood there, sobbing as if her heart was going to break. Later that afternoon, as I was describing the incident to one of my Negro friends in Watts and explaining my own feeling of helplessness because I had been going in the opposite direction from the way in which the thieves had driven and couldn't turn my car around in time, he asked me if I would have chased the purse-snatchers if my car had been going the other way.

"Yes," I said, "wouldn't you have?"

"No, not in a million years. First of all, if you caught up with them, they probably would have killed you. And secondly, I wouldn't turn in anybody to the goddamn cops. That shit's okay for you white guys, but not for me any more. Maybe five years ago I might have chased after that guy and given the license plate to the cops, but not any more, not any more."

My friend is wrong, but after research for this book showed me what the police's relations are with the ghetto, and the ghetto's relation with the whole community, I see his point. I understand, too, why so many middle-class Negroes and Puerto Ricans are sympathetic to the rioters, even while they disapprove of their specific acts.

One night at the other side of the continent I saw a group of Puerto Rican kids go into a phone booth on 34th Street, in New York, rip off the dialing apparatus, and run down the street, laughing. As I continued to walk on 34th Street, I reached Seventh Avenue and saw a well-dressed middle-aged Negro couple emerge from Macy's, loaded down with parcels. The woman stood on the sidewalk, the man stepped out into the street, trying vainly to stop the taxicabs which passed him by, empty. A minute or two later he and the woman wordlessly exchanged roles and she went out into the street while he remained on the sidewalk, holding the packages. Finally, a cab stopped and he rushed into it after her.

Now, that family has a man in it and one who obviously works, for they were clearly not welfare recipients. If they have children, there is a male model in the house, a working father. Does it matter very much? Does the fact that he is working help his image or his self-image if he cannot get a cab to stop for him?

Yet that experience is perfectly ordinary and routine for almost all Negroes and Puerto Ricans in New York. Most white cab drivers and some minority ones, too, are afraid to pick up Negroes and Puerto Ricans. Their fear is understandable, for cab drivers do get knifed and shot. And so the endless circling around continues and grows worse, the fires of bitterness and hate are stoked higher for all of us caught in this trap. That is why putting larger amounts of money into the cities, although absolutely essential, will do very little good unless the expenditures are accompanied by radically new approaches to the problems.

These new approaches must be interconnected, too, for the problems are interdependent. We cannot work for a solution of the nation's educational crisis without simultaneous working for a solution of the welfare crisis; the medical needs of the people who live in Boyle Heights cannot be met without providing some form of adequate income for the residents of Watts. A global approach is required instead of the present fragmented one. But what is demanded most of all is a willingness to scrap traditional ways, to run risks, to innovate.

For example the entire welfare system, as it is now, must be abolished and a whole new view substituted, based on the principle that human beings have a basic *right* to a reasonable income even if they cannot work. To make such a change requires more than just changing the name of the welfare institution, as has just happened in Los Angeles and New York; it means changing its entire orientation. For too many years now social work and social welfare have focused on adjusting people to live within their environment instead of helping them in their own efforts to change that environment. And for too many years social workers, like teachers and those in other service occupations, have been obsessed with a phony "professionalism" based on the possession of a graduate degree as the sole important criterion of ability.

The educational system is in the same rotten condition. No amount of tinkering with it will repair its fundamental faults, although a few more children might be helped than are presently being helped. The character of the school curriculum must change radically, and the character of the teaching process along with it: no change will be of any consequence without a new breed of educators, willing to experiment, to junk what has been drilled into them by *their* teachers as the proper way to teach. Principals must be imbued with a willingness to resist administrators, teachers to resist principals, and administrators taxpayers. Above all, the priorities of the system must change, technology put into its proper place, and the citizen's education given more emphasis than the astronaut's.

The same broad general principles can be stated for *every* institution of the society with which the poor have contact. New hospitals will help, but unless the doctors stop being the kind of doctors American medicine produces today, the hospitals will be of only limited assistance.

The police system must change, too, and that means the police will need to do more than learn Spanish or send a police car to the elementary schools so that the little kids can ride around the schoolyard with the siren blowing. City government and state government and federal government all would need new perspectives, too, before any fundamental changes can take place in the lives of those caught in the double trap of racism and poverty. New tax structures are needed along with new forms of government that meet the needs of regions and cities.

These new forms might even require junking the private enterprise system in many key areas of American life. Technology is forcing us into new kinds of government, but we are not yet engaged in consciously creating these forms; instead, they come into existence in hasty and ill-conceived response to immediate pressures. Yet although I believe private enterprise may be replaced by some form of public enterprise society, I do not believe such a society would *necessarily* be free of racism. It is possible to have a racist socialist society, just as it is possible to have a poverty-free socialist society that is still destructive of human dignity.

I am not attempting here to provide an exact blueprint of what should be done in Los Angeles and America: none are available although hundreds of good ideas, some certainly worth trying, have been suggested as possible partial solutions to the problems. But these ideas will not be effective unless the country as a whole develops the will to change. It is that *will* which is missing now, and yet without it change will not take place and the country will continue toward complete disaster.

And it is horrifying to see the complete absence of leadership, at all levels of government, from the President down to the mayors. Nearly every official in government is convinced that the urban crisis is beyond any solution within the accepted capabilities of American society, as it is today. Yet instead of facing the crisis honestly, too many political leaders of both parties have shown a shameless lust to attach themselves to the inevitable counter-reaction to Negro and Puerto Rican wars on the whites. Thus, they have reinforced America's sickness, its disease of racial superiority, instead of attempting to understand government's responsibility in creating the bitterness and hatred that burst out, finally, in looting, burning and killing.

Tanks and armored cars, shotguns and rifles, billy clubs and riot helmets are the only answers that the leaders of America give to the oppressed. The President proclaims a day of prayer at the same time as he announces the beefing up of the National Guard. Cynical political expediency makes the short-term programs useless except for the professional anti-poverty bureaucrats; no long-term proposals going to the heart of the problems have been proposed. And in the midst of all the turmoil in the society are the frightened policemen, lashing out indiscriminately at hippies, peace marchers and the minorities. Chief Parker is dead but his spirit is still very much alive all through the land.

The police have reason to be frightened, too. In Plainfield, New Jersey, a white police officer was all but dismembered by an angry mob after he had killed a Negro child; in Los Angeles I heard a story of how two white officers were set upon by another mob in a housing project after the policemen had shot a kid who they said stole a car. And perhaps they were right, but it had made no difference to the Negroes who surrounded them, ripped out their car radio and threatened to stomp them to death. Fortunately for the officers, according to the story, they were saved from certain death by the arrival of two Negro project policemen who, armed only with moral authority, broke up the scene.

I do not know if this story is true or not, but it doesn't matter—if it hasn't happened yet, it might still happen. And then what will be the reaction of the LAPD to the killing of their officers? It will be much like that of the police and National Guardsmen who poured bullets into any house in Detroit or Newark where they even suspected snipers of hiding. Unless a radical change takes place, America *will* have its own Sharpeville.

Which city will be next? Which city will break the record for deaths and destruction just as Los Angeles did for the past and Detroit did for Los Angeles? Will it be your city? Yes, it will be unless the country, as a whole, comes to understand that government, as it is today in America, is still a government of, by and for the white. A Negro may be in the Cabinet and another on the Supreme Court, but the government is still white. The police departments may recruit Negroes, Mexicans and Puerto Ricans, but they will be defending a white society. And so inevitably, the non-whites in the country have started trying to build their own societies. America is polarizing at a fantastic rate of speed. And the next riot may be started by whites, burning down the Negro sections of the cities.

Only a few months ago, I sat talking with a Negro friend, who seemed very depressed.

"What's bugging you?" I asked.

"I had a nightmare last night," he said. "You know, the last time in Watts, I was out on the streets trying to cool it. Well, in my nightmare it happened again, but this time I wasn't cooling it, this time I was up on a roof with a rifle, sniping. And down below on the street, there was a white guy and I shot him, I killed him. And you know who he was? He was you. I killed you."

His nightmare is becoming our reality.

IV

MAN IN CRISIS
protest and
deviant behavior

44. BLACK MAN AND
WHITE SOCIETY
eldridge cleaver

How have white images of America affected the black man? In his much-discussed book, *Soul on Ice,* which he wrote in prison, Mr. Cleaver explores some of the consequences of the white man's civilization in the twentieth-century United States. In the selection below, the author traces two contradictory images of America and their consequences for black citizens when long-established myths are suddenly shattered.

From the beginning, America has been a schizophrenic nation. Its two conflicting images of itself were never reconciled, because never before has the survival of its most cherished myths made a reconciliation mandatory. Once before, during the bitter struggle between North and South climaxed by the Civil War, the two images of America came into conflict, although whites North and South scarcely understood it. The image of America held by its most alienated citizens was advanced neither by the North nor by the South; it was perhaps best expressed by Frederick Douglass, who was born into slavery in 1817, escaped to the North, and became the greatest leader-spokesman for the blacks of his era. In words that can still, years later, arouse an audience of black Americans, Frederick Douglass delivered, in 1852, a scorching indictment in his Fourth of July oration in Rochester:

> What to the American slave is your Fourth of July? I answer: a day that reveals to him, more than all other days in the year, the gross injustice and cruelty to which he is the constant victim. To him your celebration is a sham; your boasted liberty, an unholy licence; your national greatness, swelling

vanity; your sounds of rejoicing are empty and heartless; your denunciation of tyrants, brass-fronted impudence; your shouts of liberty and equality, hollow mockery; your prayers and hymns, your sermons and thanksgivings, with all your religious parade and solemnity, are, to him, more bombast, fraud, deception, impiety and hypocrisy—a thin veil to cover up crimes which would disgrace a nation of savages. . . .

You boast of your love of liberty, your superior civilization, and your pure Christianity, while the whole political power of the nation (as embodied in the two great political parties) is solemnly pledged to support and per- petuate the enslavement of three millions of your countrymen. You hurl your anathemas at the crown-headed tyrants of Russia and Austria and pride yourselves on your democratic institutions, while you yourselves consent to be the mere *tools* and *bodyguards* of the tyrants of Virginia and Carolina.

You invite to your shores fugitives of oppression from abroad, honor them with banquets, greet them with ovations, cheer them, toast them, salute them, protect them, and pour out your money to them like water; but the fugitive from your own land you advertise, hunt, arrest, shoot, and kill. You glory in your refinement and your universal education; yet you maintain a system as barbarous and dreadful as ever stained the character of a nation— a system begun in avarice, supported in pride, and perpetuated in cruelty.

You shed tears over fallen Hungary, and make the sad story of her wrongs the theme of your poets, statesmen and orators, till your gallant sons are ready to fly to arms to vindicate her cause against the oppressor; but, in regard to the ten thousand wrongs of the American slave, you would enforce the strictest silence, and would hail him as an enemy of the nation who dares to make these wrongs the subject of public discourse!

This most alienated view of America was preached by the Abolitionists, and by Harriet Beecher Stowe in her *Uncle Tom's Cabin*. But such a view of America was too distasteful to receive wide attention, and serious debate about America's image and her reality was engaged in only on the fringes of society. Even when confronted with overwhelming evidence to the contrary, most white Americans have found it possible, after steadying their rattled nerves, to settle comfortably back into their vaunted belief that America is dedicated to the proposition that all men are created equal and endowed by their Creator with certain inalienable rights—life, liberty and the pursuit of happiness. With the Constitution for a rudder and the Declaration of Inde- pendence as its guiding star, the ship of state is sailing always toward a brighter vision of freedom and justice for all.

Because there is no common ground between these two contradictory images of America, they had to be kept apart. But the moment the blacks were let into the white world—let out of the voiceless and faceless cages of their ghettos, singing, walking, talking, dancing, writing, and orating *their* image of America and of Americans—the white world was suddenly challenged to match its practice to its preachments. And this is why those whites who abandon the *white* image of America and adopt the *black* are greeted with such unmitigated hostility by their elders.

For all these years whites have been taught to believe in the myth they preached, while Negroes have had to face the bitter reality of what America practiced. But without the lies and distortions, white Americans would not have been able to do the things they have done. When whites are forced to look honestly upon the objective proof of their deeds, the cement of mendacity holding white society together swiftly disintegrates. On the other hand, the core of the black world's vision remains intact, and in fact begins to expand and spread into the psychological territory vacated by the non-viable white lies, i.e., into the minds of young whites. It is remarkable how the system worked for so many years, how the majority of whites remained effectively unaware of any contradiction between their view of the world and that world itself. The mechanism by which this was rendered possible requires examination at this point.

Let us recall that the white man, in order to justify slavery and, later on, to justify segregation, elaborated a complex, all-pervasive myth which at one time classified the black man as a subhuman beast of burden. The myth was progressively modified, gradually elevating the blacks on the scale of evolution, following their slowly changing status, until the plateau of separate-but-equal was reached at the close of the nineteenth century. During slavery, the black was seen as a mindless Supermasculine Menial. Forced to do the back-breaking work, he was conceived in terms of his ability to do such work— "field niggers," etc. The white man administered the plantation, doing all the thinking, exercising omnipotent power over the slaves. He had little difficulty dissociating himself from the black slaves, and he could not conceive of their positions being reversed or even reversible.

Blacks and whites being conceived as mutually exclusive types, those attributes imputed to the blacks could not also be imputed to the whites—at least not in equal degree—without blurring the line separating the races. These images were based upon the social function of the two races, the work they performed. The ideal white man was one who knew how to use his head, who knew how to manage and control things and get things done. Those whites who were not in a position to perform these functions nevertheless aspired to them. The ideal black man was one who did exactly as he was told, and did it efficiently and cheerfully. "Slaves," said Frederick Douglass, "are generally expected to sing as well as to work." As the black man's position and function became more varied, the images of white and black, having become stereotypes, lagged behind.

The separate-but-equal doctrine was promulgated by the Supreme Court in 1896. It had the same purpose domestically as the Open Door Policy toward China in the international arena: to stabilize a situation and subordinate a nonwhite population so that racist exploiters could manipulate those people according to their own selfish interests. These doctrines were foisted off as *the epitome of enlightened justice, the highest expression of morality.* Sanctified by religion, justified by philosophy and legalized by the Supreme Court, separate-but-equal was enforced by day by agencies of the law, and by the KKK & Co. under cover of night. Booker T. Washington, the Martin Luther King of his day, accepted separate-but-equal in the name of all Negroes. W. E. B. DuBois denounced it.

Separate-but-equal marked the last stage of the white man's flight into cultural neurosis, and the beginning of the black man's frantic striving to assert his humanity and equalize his position with the white. Blacks ventured into all fields of endeavor to which they could gain entrance. Their goal was to present in all fields a performance that would equal or surpass that of the whites. It was long axiomatic among blacks that a black had to be twice as competent as a white in any field in order to win grudging recognition from the whites. This produced a pathological motivation in the blacks to equal or surpass the whites, and a pathological motivation in the whites to maintain a distance from the blacks. This is the rack on which black and white Americans receive their delicious torture! At first there was the color bar, flatly denying the blacks entrance to certain spheres of activity. When this no longer worked, and blacks invaded sector after sector of American life and economy, the whites evolved other methods of keeping their distance. The illusion of the Negro's inferior nature had to be maintained.

One device evolved by the whites was to tab whatever the blacks did with the prefix "Negro." We had *Negro* literature, *Negro* athletes, *Negro* music, *Negro* doctors, *Negro* politicians, *Negro* workers. The malignant ingeniousness of this device is that although it accurately describes an objective biological fact—or, at least, a sociological fact in America—it concealed the paramount psychological fact: that to the white mind, prefixing anything with "Negro" automatically consigned it to an inferior category. A well-known example of the white necessity to deny due credit to blacks is in the realm of music. White musicians were famous for going to Harlem and other Negro cultural centers literally to steal the black man's music, carrying it back across the color line into the Great White World and passing off the watered-down loot as their own original creations. Blacks, meanwhile, were ridiculed as *Negro* musicians playing inferior coon music.

The Negro revolution at home and national liberation movements abroad have unceremoniously shattered the world of fantasy in which the whites have been living. It is painful that many do not yet see that their fantasy world has been rendered uninhabitable in the last half of the twentieth century. But it is away from this world that the white youth of today are turning. The "paper tiger" hero, James Bond, offering the whites a triumphant image of themselves, is saying that many whites want desperately to hear reaffirmed: *I am still the White Man, lord of the land, licensed to kill, and the world is still an empire at my feet.* James Bond feeds on that secret little anxiety, the psychological white backlash, felt in some degree by most whites alive. It is exasperating to see little brown men and little yellow men from the mysterious Orient, and the opaque black men of Africa (to say nothing of these impudent

American Negroes!) who come to the UN and talk smart to us, who are scurrying all over *our* globe in their strange modes of dress—much as if they were new, unpleasant arrivals from another planet. Many whites believe in their ulcers that it is only a matter of time before the Marines get the signal to round up these truants and put them back securely in their cages. But it is away from this fantasy world that the white youth of today are turning.

In the world revolution now under way, the initiative rests with people of color. That growing numbers of white youth are repudiating their heritage of blood and taking people of color as their heroes and models is a tribute not only to their insight but to the resilience of the human spirit. For today the heroes of the initiative are people not usually thought of as white: Fidel Castro, Che Guevara, Kwame Nkrumah, Mao Tse-tung, Gamal Abdel Nasser, Robert F. Williams, Malcolm X, Ben Bella, John Lewis, Martin Luther King, Jr., Robert Parris Moses, Ho Chi Minh, Stokeley Carmichael, W. E. B. DuBois, James Forman, Chou En-lai.

The white youth of today have begun to react to the fact that the "American Way of Life" is a fossil of history. What do they care if their old baldheaded and crew-cut elders don't dig their caveman mops? They couldn't care less about the old, stiffassed honkies who don't like their new dances: Frug, Monkey, Jerk, Swim, Watusi. All they know is that it feels good to swing to way-out body-rhythms instead of dragassing across the dance floor like zombies to the dead beat of mind-smothered Mickey Mouse music. Is it any wonder that the youth have lost all respect for their elders, for law and order, when for as long as they can remember all they've witnessed is a monumental bickering over the Negro's place in American society and the right of people around the world to be left alone by outside powers? They have witnessed the law, both domestic and international, being spat upon by those who do not like its terms. Is it any wonder, then, that they feel justified, by sitting-in and freedom riding, in breaking laws made by lawless men? Old funny-styled, zipper-mouthed political night riders know nothing but to haul out an investigating committee *to look into the disturbance* to find the cause of the unrest among the youth. Look into a mirror! The cause is you, Mr. and Mrs. Yesterday, you with your forked tongues.

A young white today cannot help but recoil from the base deeds of his people. On every side, on every continent, he sees racial arrogance, savage brutality toward the conquered and subjugated people, genocide; he sees the human cargo of the slave trade; he sees the systematic extermination of American Indians; he sees the civilized nations of Europe fighting in imperial depravity over the lands of other people—and over possession of the very people themselves. There seems to be no end to the ghastly deeds of which his people are guilty. *GUILTY*. The slaughter of the Jews by the Germans, the dropping of atomic bombs on the Japanese people—these deeds weigh heavily upon the prostrate souls and tumultuous consciences of the white youth. The white heroes, their hands dripping with blood, are dead.

The young whites know that the colored people of the world, Afro-Americans included, do not seek revenge for their suffering. They seek the same things the white rebel wants: an end to war and exploitation. Black and white, the young rebels are free people, free in a way that Americans have never been before in the history of their country. And they are outraged.

There is in America today a generation of white youth that is truly worthy of a black man's respect, and this is a rare event in the foul annals of American history. From the beginning of the contact between blacks and whites, there has been very little reason for a black man to respect a white, with such exceptions as John Brown and others lesser known. But respect commands itself and it can neither be given nor withheld when it is due. If a man like Malcolm X could change and repudiate racism, if I myself and other former Muslims can change, if young whites can change, then there is hope for America. It was certainly strange to find myself, while steeped in the doctrine that all whites were devils by nature, commanded by the heart to applaud and acknowledge respect for these young whites—despite the fact that they are descendants of the masters and I the descendant of slave. The sins of the fathers are visited upon the heads of the children—but only if the children continue in the evil deeds of the fathers.

45. THE NEW LEFT
staughton lynd

Part of an international political development, the American New Left places strong emphasis on scholasticism, utopianism, and activism. Members of the New Left condemn existing American society as "corporate liberalism," and seek to replace it with "participatory democracy."

According to Professor Lynd, New Left theorists have made the mistake of assuming that success in unmaking such liberalism would result in drastic transformation of society rather than, as is likely, the imposition of even more repressive controls by the Establishment. He observes that the trend toward repression does not necessarily mean the end of the Left, though the prospects for its survival and success are small.

What is the New Left? It may provisionally be defined as that movement, largely of young people, associated with the Student Nonviolent Co-ordinating Committee (SNCC) and the Students for a Democratic Society (SDS). But even this common-sense definition has obvious limitations. It ignores the origins of the New Left in the period before the Southern student sit-ins of 1960. It does not deal adequately with the most recent phase of the black

From Staughton Lynd, "The New Left," *Annals of the American Academy of Political and Social Science,* CCCLXXXII, March 1969, pp. 64–72.

liberation movement, during which SNCC has declined. Above all, it is restricted to the New Left in one country, the United States.

This American New Left is actually part of an international political tendency. Differences in form notwithstanding, the student movements of the 1960's in the United States, West Europe, and Japan share certain common concerns: rejection both of capitalism and of the bureaucratic communism exemplified by the Soviet Union; anti-imperialism; and an orientation to decentralized "direct action," violent or nonviolent. And, clearly, such movements in the so-called free world are related to the heretical communisms of Tito, Mao Tse-tung, and Fidel Castro, to the libertarian currents in East Europe, and to various versions of "African socialism."

The year 1956 offers a convenient chronological peg for comprehension of the international New Left. That was the year of Khrushchev's condemnation of Stalin at the Twentieth Congress of the Soviet Communist party, and the year of the Soviet invasion of Hungary. These events put an end to the hegemony of Soviet communism in the world radical movement. Response was immediate. In France, Jean-Paul Sartre broke with the French Communist party. In England, former Communists and other radicals created the journals *Universities and Left Review* and *The New Reasoner,* later merged as *The New Left Review.* In China, Mao Tse-tung "suddenly changed course." According to a possibly apocryphal anecdote now current in Peking, "he made his decision after his journey to the USSR where he was appalled by the ideological level of foreign Communist leaders, and realized the ravages that bureaucratization had made in the Communist elite of the European socialist countries." [1] In the same year, 1956, contrasting New Left charismas were launched in the Western Hemisphere. Fidel Castro and his handful of followers landed from the *Granma* to conquer their Cuban homeland, and Martin Luther King led the successful bus boycott in Montgomery, Alabama.

The history of this revitalized Left in America is, in its general outline, well known. Its political philosophy is more controversial. [2]

[1] K. S. Karol, "Two Years of the Cultural Revolution," *The Socialist Register, 1968,* ed. Ralph Miliband and John Saville (New York, 1968), p. 60.

[2] The older histories of the movement are generally by sympathetic part-time or former participants, rather than by full-time activists. In his categoy are Howard Zinn, *SNCC: The New Abolitionists* (Boston: Beacon Press, 1964); Paul Jacobs and Saul Landau, *The New Radicals: A Report with Documents* (New York: Random House, New American Library, 1966); Jack Newfield, *A Prophetic Minority* (New York, 1966); and, in a more analytical genre, Richard Flacks, "The Liberated Generation: An Exploration of the Roots of Social Protest," *Journal of Social Issues* (July 1967), pp. 52–75. More recently, the activists have begun to write their own history. See, for example, C. Clark Kissinger, with the assistance of Bob Ross, "Starting in '60 or From Slid to Resistance," *New Left Notes,* June 10–July 8, 1968; and Richard Rothstein, "ERAP: Evolution of the Organizers," *Radical America* (March–April 1968), pp. 1–18. An excellent bibliography is available in three articles by James P. O'Brien, *ibid.* (May–June 1968), pp. 1–25; (September–October 1968), pp. 1–22; (November–December 1968), pp. 28–43.

INTELLECTUAL EMPHASES: ANTI-SCHOLASTICISM, UTOPIANISM, AND ACTIVISM

In 1960, the year of the Southern sit-ins, C. Wright Mills wrote a "Letter to the New Left," first published in England in *The New Left Review* and then reprinted in America by *Studies on the Left* and SDS. In 1967, the year of massive demonstrations against the Vietnam war in New York City and Washington, and of bloody black "riots" in Newark and Detroit, Howard Zinn spoke on "Marxism and the New Left" in a forum series sponsored by the Boston SDS. Mills was the theorist who most influenced early SDS. Zinn was the only white person to be elected an adviser by the early SNCC (later Zinn wrote a history of that organization, entitled *SNCC: The New Abolitionists*, and also the widely circulated *Vietnam: The Case for Immediate Withdrawal*). Together, the two presentations suggest some generalizations about the characteristic intellectual emphases of the New Left.[3]

First, then, the New Left opposes what Mills terms "a fetishism of empiricism." By this, Mills means "the disclosure of facts" which "are neither connected with one another nor related to any general view." Similarly, Zinn condemns intellectual activity which amounts to "the aimless dredging up of what is and what was, rather than a creative recollection of experience, pointed at the betterment of human life." Zinn's condemnation of such "scholasticism" continues:

> We are surrounded by solemn, pretentious argument about what Marx or Machiavelli or Rousseau really meant, about who was right and who was wrong—all of which is another way the pedant has of saying: "I am right and you are wrong." Too much of what passes for theoretical discussion of public issues is really a personal duel for honor or privilege—with each discussant like the character in *Catch-22* who saw every event in the world as either a feather in his cap or a black eye—and this while men were dying all around him.[4]

According to Zinn and Mills, the allegedly nonideological enumeration of unconnected facts (as in "academic journals which would be horrified at being called either Left or Right") is itself ideological. One can be content with uninterpreted minutiae only if the fundamental pattern of things-as-they-are is satisfactory. As Mills says:

> Underneath this style of observation and comment there is the assumption that in the West there are no more real issues or even problems of great seriousness. The mixed economy plus the welfare state plus prosperity—that

---

[3] All quotations in this section of the essay are taken from C. Wright Mills, *Letter to the New Left* (New York: SDS, 1961); and Howard Zinn, "Marxism and the New Left," in Alfred L. Young (ed.), *Dissent: Explorations in the History of American Radicalism* (DeKalb: Northern Illinois University Press, 1968), pp. 357–371.

[4] Zinn, *op. cit.,* p. 361. Here and elsewhere, I quote from the manuscript version of Zinn's talk, which differs slightly from the edited published version.

is the formula. U.S. capitalism will continue to be workable; the welfare state will continue along the road to ever greater justice. In the meantime, things everywhere are very complex; let us not be careless; there are great risks.[5]

"Empiricism," or "positivism," represents the self-image of intellectuals in the affluent West. "The end-of-ideology is a slogan of complacency, circulating among the prematurely middle-aged, centered in the present, and in the rich Western societies. . . . It is a consensus of a few provincials about their own immediate and provincial position." Mills adds that Western empiricism performs exactly the same function of blunting critical discourse about basic things which dogmatic Marxism accomplishes in the Soviet Union.

As the New Left views the intellectual situation, Western empiricism and "socialist realism," liberal academics and Old Left theorists, share an exaggerated interest in methodology at the expense of content. In the Soviet Union, essentially stylistic matters, such as the citation of correct authorities, and repetition of a limited basic vocabulary, complement the fact that "pessimism is permitted, but only episodically," that in place of "any systematic or structural criticism" there are "criticisms, first of this and then of that." In the West, "a pretentious methodology used to state trivialities about unimportant social areas" accompanies "a naïve journalistic empiricism" and "a cultural gossip in which 'answers' to the vital and pivotal issues are merely assumed." Complexity of manner and paucity of substance characterize official thought in both West and East for the very good reason that, in Mills' words, "the end-of-ideology is very largely a mechanical reaction . . . to the ideology of Stalinism. As such it takes from its opponent something of its inner quality."

Empiricism, however, is rejected not so much in the name of theory and analysis, as in the name of values. Thus, Zinn warns: "Because the New Left is a successor of the Old Left in American history, and because it comes, to a large extent, out of the academic world (whether the Negro colleges of the South or the Berkeleys of the North), it is always being tempted by theoretical irrelevancies." Zinn thinks that many of Marx's detailed economic propositions represent such irrelevancies.[6] Zinn would keep in focus the broad outlines of Marxist theory: "Instead of discussing the falling rate of profit, or the organic composition of capital, I would concentrate on what is readily observable—that this country has enormous resources which it wastes shamefully and distributes unjustly." In Zinn's view, the kind of theory which the Left most needs is "a vision of what it is working toward—one based on

[5] Mills, *op. cit.*, p. 2.
[6] Zinn adds: "The Marxian economic categories have long provided material for academic controversy—and I doubt that Marx intended this. But he was only human—and perhaps he fell prey to the kind of temptations that intellectuals often succumb to—his research, his curiosity, his passion for scheme-building and for scientific constructions ran away with him."—Zinn, *op. cit.*, p. 368.

transcendental human needs and not limited by the reality we are so far stuck with."

In the same spirit, Mills, too, defends being "utopian." To be Right means "celebrating society as it is," Mills says. To be Left "means, or ought to mean, just the opposite": structural criticism of what exists, at some point focusing "politically as demands and programs." Mills insists:

> What now is really meant by *utopian?* And is not our utopianism a major source of our strength? *Utopian* nowadays, I think, refers to any criticism or proposal that transcends the up-close milieux of a scatter of individuals, the milieux which men and women can understand directly and which they can reasonably hope directly to change.[7]

Both Mills and Zinn are content to define the moral criteria in terms of which change is demanded as "humanist." Mills speaks of "the humanist and secular ideals of Western civilization—above all, the ideals of reason, freedom, and justice." And Zinn refers to a "consensus of humanistic values that has developed in the modern world" which "Marxists and liberals, at their best (and they have not usually been at their best), share."

In summary, New Left intellectuality looks beyond existing empirical reality to what Zinn terms "a vision of the future." But this orientation still does not sufficiently delineate the New Left mind. A certain kind of liberal, for example, a Lewis Mumford or an Eric Fromm, shares the orientation just described. What decisively distinguishes New Left radicalism from all varieties of liberalism is its insistence on action.

Mills ends *A Letter to the New Left* with a hymn of praise to young radicals the world over who, in the face of the pessimism of theorists, nevertheless act.

> "But it is just some kind of moral upsurge, isn't it?" Correct. But under it: no apathy. Much of it is direct non-violent action, and it seems to be working, here and there. Now we must learn from the practice of these young intellectuals and with them work out new forms of action. . . .
> "But it is utopian, after all, isn't it?" No, not in the sense you mean. Whatever else it may be, it's not that. Tell it to the students of Japan. Tell it to the Negro sit-ins. Tell it to the Cuban Revolutionaries. Tell it to the people of the Hungry-nation bloc.[8]

Zinn develops a rationale for action-oriented radicalism at greater length. For instance:

> The contributions of the Old Left—and they were considerable—came not out of its ideological fetishism but out of its action. What gave it dynamism was not the classes on surplus value but the organization of the CIO, not the analysis of Stalin's views on the National and Colonial Question, but the fight for the Scottsboro boys, not the labored rationale for dictatorship of the proletariat, but the sacrifices of the Abraham Lincoln Battalion.[9]

[7] Mills, *op. cit.,* p. 6.
[8] *Ibid.,* p. 10.
[9] Zinn, *op. cit.,* p. 361.

And again:

> There has been much talk about a Christian-Marxist dialogue, but if such a
> dialogue is to be useful perhaps it should begin with the idea that God is dead
> and Marx is dead, but Yossarian lives—which is only a way of saying: let's
> not spend our time arguing whether God exists or what Marx really meant,
> because while we argue, the world moves, while we publish, others perish,
> and the best use of our energy is to resist those who would send us—after so
> many missions of murder—on still one more.[10]

Zinn finds the New Left's concern for action similar to Marxism in some
ways, different in others. He approvingly quotes Marx's eleventh thesis on
Feuerbach ("The philosophers have only interpreted the world in various
ways; the point, however, is to change it.") He notes the resemblance between
the Marxist vision of the withering away of the state, and the attempt of the
New Left "to create constellations of power outside the state, to pressure
it into human actions, to resist its inhumane actions, and to replace it in the
carrying on of voluntary activities by people who want to maintain, in small
groups, both individuality and co-operation."

At the same time, Zinn criticizes the Marxist claim that the vision of a
society in which men could be free and unalienated "springs not from a wish
but from an observation—from a scientific plotting of an historical curve."
Zinn observes that "we don't have such confidence in inevitability these days"
because "we've had too many surprises in this century." Because a desirable
future is not inevitable, commitment to action is all the more important. Zinn
concludes:

> It is very easy to feel helpless in our era. We need, I think, the Existentialist
> emphasis on our freedom. . . . To stress our freedom . . . is not the result
> of ignorance that we do have a history, and we do have a present environ-
> ment. . . . Existentialism, knowing of these pressures on us, is also aware
> that there is a huge element of indeterminacy in the combat between us and
> the obstacles around us. We never know exactly the depth or the shallowness
> of the resistance to our actions. We never know exactly what effect our
> actions will have.[11]

The existential commitment to action, in the knowledge that the consequences of action can never be fully predicted, is the single most characteristic
element in the thought-world of the New Left. It has survived all changes in
political fashion. Thus, in 1968, Daniel Cohn-Bendit defined the role of a
political *avant-garde* as setting an example, "to light the first fuse and make
the first breakthrough." [12] And Huey Newton of the Black Panther party
declared:

[10] *Ibid.*, pp. 362–363.

[11] *Ibid.*, p. 371.

[12] An interview between Jean-Paul Sartre and Daniel Cohn-Bendit, quoted from *Le
Nouvel Observateur,* May 20, 1968, by Liberation News Service, May 30, 1968.

The large majority of black people are either illiterate or semi-literate. They don't read. They need activity to follow. . . . The same thing happened in Cuba where it was necessary for twelve men with a leadership of Ché and Fidel to take to the hills and then attack the corrupt administration. . . . They could have leafleted the community and they could have written books, but the people would not respond. They had to act and the people could see· and hear about it and therefore become educated on how to respond to oppression.

In this country black revolutionaries have to set an example.[13]

"PARTICIPATORY DEMOCRACY" VERSUS "CORPORATE LIBERALISM"

So much for the New Left's general intellectual orientation. More concretely, the New Left condemns existing American society as "corporate liberalism" and seeks to replace it with "participatory democracy."

Participatory democracy is a phrase coined by Tom Hayden in drafting the 1962 Port Huron Statement. It is an easy concept for Americans to understand, because the vision of a society administered by direct town-meeting-style democracy is widespread on both Right and Left. (For this very reason, most New Leftists would now add that the good society which they have in mind would be socialist, too).

Corporate liberalism is a more complex idea, which became current among the New Left only when early hopes of quick advance toward racial equality and international peace began to fade. Carl Oglesby explained it in this way to an antiwar demonstration in Washington in 1965:

We are here to protest against a growing war. Since it is a very bad war, we acquire the habit of thinking that it must be caused by very bad men. But we only conceal reality, I think, to denounce on such grounds the menacing coalition of industrial and military power, or the brutality of the blitzkrieg we are waging against Vietnam, or the ominous signs around us that heresy may soon no longer be permitted. We must simply observe, and quite plainly say, that this coalition, this blitzkrieg, and this demand for acquiescence are creatures, all of them, of a government that since 1932 has considered itself to be fundamentally *liberal*. [Italics in original.][14]

Corporate liberalism, Oglesby went on, justified corporate exploitation with liberal rhetoric. "It performs for the corporate state a function quite like what the Church once performed for the feudal state. It seeks to justify its burdens and protect it from change." [15]

Other young radicals discerned the same phenomenon in other areas of social life, such as education. The Berkeley Free Speech Movement (FSM)

[13] An interview with Huey Newton, *The Movement,* August 1968.
[14] Carl Oglesby, Speech on November 27, 1965, published in Jacobs and Landau (eds.), *The New Radicals,* p. 258.
[15] *Ibid.,* p. 265.

of 1964–1965 discovered that behind the liberal rhetoric of Berkeley president
Clark Kerr stood the corporate power of Senator William Knowland and the
California Board of Regents. Students were free, FSM insisted, only so long
as they did not attack that power. As Mario Savio stated in a speech on the
steps of the university administration building during a sit-in there: "Students
are permitted to talk all they want so long as their speech has no consequences." [16]

Corporate liberalism, then, is understood by the New Left as an ideology
which makes reactionary power appear to be liberal. It is an instrument of
mystification, which solicits the oppressed to accept their oppression willingly
because oppression describes itself as freedom. This aspect of power in
modern America was partially perceived by the New Left as early as the Port
Huron Statement of 1962. "The dominant institutions," SDS then declared,
"are complex enough to blunt the minds of their potential critics. . . . The
American political system is not the democratic model of which its glorifiers
speak. In actuality it frustrates democracy by confusing the individual citizen,
paralyzing policy discussion, and consolidating the irresponsible power of
military and business interests." [17]

Accordingly, the celebrated New Left revolt against authority is especially a revolt against paternalistic, indirect authority which hides the
iron hand of power in the velvet glove of rhetorical idealism. A notorious
instance is the so-called channeling policy of the Selective Service System
(SSS). According to an official SSS memorandum, withdrawn only after it
had been discovered and publicized by the New Left, a major purpose of the
conscription system is to guide young men into occupations "considered to
be most important" by using "the club of induction." The memorandum itself
makes the explicit point that "pressurized guidance" is an alternative means
for accomplishing what outright coercion achieves in other societies.

> The psychology of granting wide choice under pressure to take action is the
> American or indirect way of achieving what is done by direction in foreign
> countries where choice is not permitted. . . . Selective Service processes
> do not compel people by edict as in foreign systems to enter pursuits having
> to do with essentiality and progress. They go because they know that by
> going they will be deferred. [18]

The New Left's perception of corporate liberalism as a pattern evident
in the exercise of authority by universities and draft boards has been but-
tressed by the work of sympathtic social scientists of an older generation. The

[16] *Ibid.*, p. 232. Sometimes the demystifiers are themselves bemused. Witness the fact
that the Foreword to the only collection of New Left writing edited by student radicals
themselves, published in 1966, illustrates the mood of radical youth with a long quotation
from a commencement address by—President Grayson Kirk of Columbia University!—
Mitchell Cohen and Dennis Hale (eds.), *The New Student Left: An Anthology* (Boston:
Beacon Press, 1966), pp. viii–ix.
[17] Jacobs and Landau (eds.), *The New Radicals*, pp. 152, 160.
[18] "Channeling," *Ramparts* (December 1967).

historian William Appelman Williams and his students, at the University of Wisconsin, document the use of liberal rhetoric to mask expansionism throughout American history. Educators such as Paul Goodman, John Holt, and A. S. Neill argue that the mistake of "progressive education" was to abandon overt coercion only to substitute for it, in Holt's words, "the idea of painless, non-threatening coercion." [19] Introducing Neill's *Summerhill,* Erich Fromm stresses the similarity in the exercise of authority within the classroom and in society at large.

> The change from the overt authority of the nineteenth century to the anonymous authority of the twentieth was determined by the organizational needs of our modern industrial society. The concentration of capital led to the formation of giant enterprises managed by hierarchically organized bureaucracies. . . . The individual worker becomes merely a cog in this machine. In such a production organization, the individual is managed and manipulated.
>
> And in the sphere of consumption (in which the individual allegedly expresses his free choice) he is likewise managed and manipulated.
>
> Our economic system must create men who fit its needs; men who co-operate smoothly; men who *want* to consume more and more. Our system must create men whose tastes are standardized, men who can be easily influenced, men whose needs can be anticipated. Our system needs men who *feel* free and independent but who are nevertheless willing to do what is expected of them. . . . It is not that authority has disappeared, nor even that it has lost in strength, but that it has been transformed from the overt authority of force to the anonymous authority of persuasion and suggestion. . . . Modern man is obliged to nourish the illusion that everything is done with his consent, even though such consent be extracted from him by subtle manipulation. His consent is obtained, as it were, behind his back, or behind his consciousness.
>
> The same artifices are employed in progressive education. The child is forced to swallow the pill, but the pill is given a sugar coating. Parents and teachers have confused true nonauthoritarian education with *education by means of persuasion and hidden coercion.* [Italics in original.][20]

The single, most comprehensive, scholarly statement supporting the New Left analysis of corporate liberalism is undoubtedly Herbert Marcuse's *One-Dimensional Man.* Marcuse's pessimistic thesis in this influential work is that contemporary industrial society "seems to be capable of containing social change," indeed, that traditional forms of protest are "perhaps even dangerous because they preserve the illusion of popular sovereignty." [21]

The New Left counterposes to the subtle coercion of corporate liberalism

[19] John Holt, *How Children Fail* (New York: Dell, 1964), p. 179.

[20] Erich Fromm, Introduction to A. S. Neill, *Summerhill: A Radical Approach to Child-Rearing* (2nd ed.; New York: Hart, 1964), pp. x–xi.

[21] Herbert Marcuse, *One-Dimensional Man: Studies in the Ideology of Advanced Industrial Society* (Boston: Beacon Press, 1966), pp. xii, 256.

a participatory democracy in which individuals "control the decisions that affect their lives." However, at this writing (August 1968), the sentiment is growing in the movement that participatory democracy, like nonviolence, may have been the product of a naïve early stage of protest, before the magnitude of the movement's task was fully recognized. Nonviolence and participatory democracy will exist in the good society created after the revolution, it is increasingly said. But the work of transformation requires tools suited to this age of blood and iron: insurrectionary violence and a Marxist-Leninist party.

This new tendency to return to a dogmatic Marxism and to Bolshevik forms of organization reflects a weakness in the New Left's central concept of corporate liberalism. The theorists of corporate liberalism believed their main enemy to be, not the reactionary Right, but the liberal Center. Their attitude may be compared to that of the German Communist party in the early 1930's, which directed more hostility toward its Social Democratic competitor than toward the Nazis. American New Left theory made the implicit assumption that capitalism in the United States would not turn to overt authoritarianism. It overlooked the possibility that the very success of the New Left in unmasking corporate liberalism, the very growth of a serious internal opposition, would change the character of the situation and force upon the governing class a felt need for more rigorous controls. The young radicals' assessment of the American reality has been, in this sense, not too negative but too hopeful.

THE FUTURE

The prospect is not bright. But some hope is justified when it is recognized that repression, far from being alien to the new radicalism, is the medium in which the New Left first emerged. Not only is it the case that the first major action of the white New Left in America was the May 1960 demonstration against the House Un-American Activities Committee, and that in Europe the New Left began as a response to repression in the Soviet Union, but it is also true that the origins of the New Left go back beyond the mid-1950's to the thought and action of the resistance against fascism in the 1930's and 1940's: to men like Sartre, Camus, Silone, Buber, Bonhoeffer, and, in America, A. J. Muste. Therefore, the trend toward repression does not necessarily signify the end of the New Left. The spirit of resistance, even, possibly, of nonviolent resistance, may yet rise to the occasion.

46. PRESCRIPTION FOR REBELLION

robert lindner

Earlier selections have referred to society as a mold. The good person, we are told, is well adjusted. He conforms to the rules of society and strives to meet the expectations of his parents and peers. It is urged that the well adjusted person is also the most happy one and makes the greatest contribution to society.

The author of the ensuing article does not agree. To the contrary, he argues that adjustment corrupts, is a fraud, and that the myth of adjustment is a scourge upon humanity. Which view is correct?

As we proceed through the following chapters I intend to reveal the truth about adjustment, to show it for what it is—a mendacious idea, biologically false, philosophically untenable, and psychologically harmful. Together with a gradually increasing group of psychologists and scientists from other fields, I regard it as perhaps the single great myth of our time, and one to be exposed to its roots lest it continue to sap human vitality and exhaust the energies which men require to build the better society they seek.

Those of us who reject adjustment as a prescription for living, who believe that it is a concept that disregards many if not all of the pertinent facts of human nature, who feel that it is an untruth that is rendering man impotent at a time when he needs the fullest possible mastery over his creative abilities, are in a sad minority. Ranged against us is an entire world, committed to the concept despite the fact that it is founded on fallacy. For there is perhaps no idea so ubiquitous as the idea of adjustment. Latterly, to adjust— or to be adjusted, or to make an adjustment—has come to be deemed the highest good and the goal of every effort. At every turning the Commandment —"You must adjust"—confronts us. Monotonous and persistent, the phrase is repeated over and over at all levels of our society and for every conceivable purpose. It is offered to us as medicine when we are sick, as hope when we are unhappy, as faith when we are perplexed. There is no escaping from it. Woe to him who does not adjust! Upon him will fall every imaginable kind of ill and, what is more, he will deserve what he gets, for there is no crime so great as the crime of unadjustment. To violate this Eleventh Commandment is to court social ostracism and to invite a pariah's destiny. Nor is there any acceptable compromise. You adjust—or else! . . .

. . . Remarkably, there actually exists today neither creed, organization, nor ideology not devoted to the myth of adjustment. If our institutions and philosophies differ in all else—and they obviously do—here is the point of their unity: that the only acceptable way of life is the way of conformity. On this diverse philosophies agree; on this political Left and Right unite; here Churches meet and Schisms join; at this place even Religion and Science embrace. All— regardless of their differences—find in the concept of adjustment a meeting ground. Commonly, all of them—although each does so in its own interest— regard protest as unforgivable and believe—covertly if not openly—that the flame of rebellion that burns in every human breast must be gutted. . . .

Now, partisans of causes, criers of ideologies, makers of philosophies, and servitors of religion will, of course, deny the thesis here stated: that all of them aim, by exploiting the adjustment fallacy, to enslave man. Each proclaims its heartfelt desire only to free man, to ensure for him a permissive and expansive existence, to unchain him—providing, naturally, that he first makes his surrender and adjusts. Significantly, those who more loudly proclaim such good intentions are the most insistent on reducing him initially to the status of an obedient and unprotesting automaton. Their denials to the contrary, the fact remains that, without exception, they endorse the adjustment idea. With fervor and persistence they spread the concept abroad. With enthusiasm they lend their influence to the propagation and enforcement of the Eleventh Commandment. And in the doing of these things they disclose themselves; for the no longer inescapable truth about adjustment is that it has an aim: the reduction of the variability of man to an undistinguished formlessness, a sameness, an amorphous homogeneity so that dominion over him can more easily and more completely be established. . . .

With all the weight of this history behind it, entrapped and stultified by the collusive efforts—as we have seen—of science, religion, and philosophy, it is not to be wondered at that ordinary men uncritically accept the myth of adjustment as truth. The notion is, in a sense, bred into them. In any case, from the cradle forward they are schooled in renunciation. From babyhood they are rewarded only when they conform, made comfortable only when they surrender, given love only when they relinquish what gives them satisfaction. By the time of their presumed maturity—or at least their physical adulthood—their lessons have been learned well. Their senses inform them continuously that protest and rebellion are fruitless and, if expressed, are met with immediate and severe reprisals. Their minds are pinioned by an imperative from which there is no escape. The things they crave must be bought with the coin of resignation. Forced thusly to suppress the most vagrant protestant urge, they are ever tormented by disquiet and unease. This, then, must be the real source of that anxiety which has been the outstanding characteristic in the psychology of mankind, and the wellspring of that abiding guilt all men feel particularly in our time. For the best that an individual can do in a world dominated by such a fallacy is to turn inward his revolt, either upon himself as illness or as vague and restless longing from which he fabricates his dreams and fantasies, sometimes his hallucinations and delusions. And to his children he passes on the heritage of suppression and its techniques. In this way the denial of instinct proceeds apace, meeting nowhere more than the shade of resistance. In its wake lie human wreckage, tumbled civilizations, countless generations of potentialities unrealized, the whole sorry gamut of disease, frustration, and despair. . . .

The propagation of adjustment as a way of life is leading inexorably to the breeding of a weak race of men who will live and die in slavery, the meek and unprotesting tools of their self-appointed masters. This, so it seems, is the goal of almost every ideology, creed, and philosophy to which we have been asked or forced to subscribe not only today but for ages past. This is why we are literally commanded to adjust and, as I shall show, are threatened with disbarment from the human race if we do not. The unspoken aim, it appears, is to make of all of us Mass Men, beings who will be alike to each other in every aspect of form and feature; in thought, desire, feeling, and expression. In such a condition we can be ruled. To realize this aim the injunction to adjust has been laid upon the planet.

. . . From almost the moment of a child's birth forward, the single aim of most parents is to discourage its innate rebelliousness and to find techniques to bury deep within that child its every protestant urge. Supported by the authority of all institutions, parenthood has come to amount to little more than a campaign against individuality. Every father and every mother trembles lest an offspring, in act or thought, should be different from his fellows; and the smallest display of uniqueness in a child becomes the signal for the application of drastic measures aimed at stamping out that small fire of noncompliance by which personal distinctness is expressed. In an atmosphere of anxiety, in a climate of apprehension, the parental conspiracy against children is planned. By the light of day the strategies and tactics that have taken form in whispered conclaves during the dark are put into operation. Few children can survive the barrage: most develop that soft rottenness within, that corruption which forms the embryo of their coming Mass Manhood. And like some hereditary disease of the body, generation after generation proliferates a sickness which can be fatal to our culture. . . .

Beneath the verbiage of description and classification of human types there remains a simple but significant dichotomy. Mankind largely divides itself, on the one hand, into a great mass of pawns, prisoners of conformity, and those who are untroubled in mind and spirit having signed a treaty with tractability; and, on the other, into the nonconforming, the protesting, and the rebellious. The fashion this day—a fashion dictated by the increasing preoccupation with regimentation evident on all sides—is to praise and encourage the former. The neurotic is scorned, on the maladjusted we heap abuse, and the different we vilify. But when the dominant illusion of our era is subjected to a closer scrutiny than that usually accorded it, a surprising truth emerges. This truth is that those who don a coat of many colors to set themselves apart from the uniform drabness that clothes the rest of us are the objects of our envy and the victims of our own frustrations. For there is no escaping the recognition that those whom we are wont to deride with the derogation of the label "sick" may well be the really healthy among us and the potential instruments for the salvation of the species.

47. THE CRIME OF PUNISHMENT
karl menninger

It is commonplace to assume that punishment of crime is "natural" and therefore ensures social harmony and the protection of "proper" values against "deviant" behavior. In the selection below, a noted psychiatrist takes a different—and revealing—view of punishment. He asserts that "society secretly *wants* crime, *needs* crime, and gains definite satisfactions from the present mishandling of it!" The implication intended is indeed disturbing, namely, that punishment reflects ignorance and malice, and actually breeds the very thing—crime—it seeks so piously to eliminate.

Few words in our language arrest our attention as do "crime," "violence," "revenge," and "injustice." We abhor crime; we adore justice; we boast that we live by the rule of law. Violence and vengefulness we repudiate as unworthy of our civilization, and we assume this sentiment to be unanimous among all human beings.

Yet crime continues to be a national disgrace and a world-wide problem. It is threatening, alarming, wasteful, expensive, abundant, and apparently increasing! In actuality it is decreasing in frequency of occurrence, but it is certainly increasing in visibility and the reactions of the public to it.

Our system for controlling crime is ineffective, unjust, expensive. Prisons seem to operate with revolving doors—the same people going in and out and in and out. *Who cares?*

Our city jails and inhuman reformatories and wretched prisons are jammed. They are known to be unhealthy, dangerous, immoral, indecent, crime-breeding dens of iniquity. Not everyone has smelled them, as some of us have. Not many have heard the groans and the curses. Not everyone has seen the hate and despair in a thousand blank, hollow faces. But, in a way, we we all know how miserable prisons are. *We want them to be that way.* And they are. *Who cares?*

Professional and big-time criminals prosper as never before. Gambling syndicates flourish. White-collar crime may even exceed all others, but goes undetected in the majority of cases. We are all being robbed and we know who the robbers are. They live nearby. *Who cares?*

The public filches millions of dollars worth of food and clothing from stores, towels and sheets from hotels, jewelry and knick-knacks from shops. The public steals, and the same public pays it back in higher prices. *Who cares?*

Time and time again somebody shouts about this state of affairs, just as I am shouting now. The magazines shout. The newspapers shout. The television and radio commentators shout (or at least they "deplore"). Psychologists, sociologists, leading jurists, wardens, and intelligent police chiefs join the chorus. Governors and mayors and Congressmen are sometimes heard. They shout that the situation is bad, bad, bad, and getting worse. Some suggest that we immediately replace obsolete procedures with scientific methods. A few short contrary sentiments. Do the clear indications derived from scientific discovery for appropriate changes continue to fall on deaf ears? Why is the public so long-suffering, so apathetic and thereby so continuingly self-destructive? How many Presidents (and other citizens) do we have to lose before we do something?

The public behaves as a sick patient does when a dreaded treatment is proposed for his ailment. We all know how the aching tooth may suddenly quiet down in the dentist's office, or the abdominal pain disappear in the surgeon's examining room. Why should a sufferer seek relief and shun it? Is it merely the fear of pain of the treatment? Is it the fear of unknown complications? Is it distrust of the doctor's ability? All of these, no doubt.

But, as Freud made so incontestably clear, the sufferer is always somewhat deterred by a kind of subversive, internal opposition to the work of cure. He suffers on the one hand from the pains of his affliction and yearns to get well. But he suffers at the same time from traitorous impulses that fight against the accomplishment of any change in himself, even recovery! Like Hamlet, he wonders whether it may be better after all to suffer the familiar pains and aches associated with the old method than to face the complications of a new and strange, even though possibly better way of handling things.

The inescapable conclusion is that society secretly *wants* crime, *needs* crime, and gains definite satisfactions from the present mishandling of it! We condemn crime; we punish offenders for it; but we need it. The crime and punishment ritual is a part of our lives. We need crimes to wonder at, to enjoy vicariously, to discuss and speculate about, and to publicly deplore. We need criminals to identify ourselves with, to envy secretly, and to punish stoutly. They do for us the forbidden, illegal things we *wish* to do and, like scapegoats of old, they bear the burdens of our displaced guilt and punishment—"the iniquities of us all." . . .

Although most of us *say* we deplore cruelty and destructiveness, we are partially deceiving ourselves. We disown violence, ascribing the love of it to other people. But the facts speak for themselves. We do love violence, all of us, and we all feel secretly guilty for it, which is another clue to public resistance to crime-control reform.

The great sin by which we all are tempted is the wish to hurt others, and this sin must be avoided if we are to live and let live. If our destructive energies can be mastered, directed, and sublimated, we can survive. If we can love, we can live. Our destructive energies, if they cannot be controlled, may destroy our best friends, as in the case of Alexander the Great, or they may destroy supposed "enemies" or innocent strangers. Worst of all—from the standpoint of the individual—they may destroy us. . . .

Violence and crime are often attempts to escape from madness; and there can be no doubt that some mental illness is a flight from the wish to do the violence or commit the act. Is it hard for the reader to believe that suicides are sometimes committed to forestall the committing of murder? There is no doubt of it. Nor is there any doubt that murder is sometimes committed to avert suicide.

Strange as it may sound, many murderers do not realize whom they are killing, or, to put it another way, that they are killing the wrong people. To be sure, killing anybody is reprehensible enough, but the worst of it is that the person who the killer thinks should die (and he has reasons) is not the person he attacks. Sometimes the victim himself is partly responsible for the crime that is committed against him. It is this unconscious (perhaps sometimes conscious) participation in the crime by the victim that has long held up the very humanitarian and progressive-sounding program of giving compensation to victims. The public often judges the victim as well as the attacker. . . .

Do I believe there is effective treatment for offenders, and that they *can* be changed? *Most certainly and definitely I do.* Not all cases, to be sure; there are also some physical afflictions which we cannot cure at the moment. Some provision has to be made for incurables—pending new knowledge—and these will include some offenders. But I believe the majority of them would prove to be curable. The willfulness and the viciousness of offenders are part of the thing for which they have to be treated. These must not thwart the therapeutic attitude.

It is simply not true that most of them are "fully aware" of what they are doing, nor is it true that they want no help from anyone, although some of them say so. Prisoners are individuals: some want treatment, some do not. Some don't know what treatment is. Many are utterly despairing and hopeless. Where treatment is made available in institutions, many prisoners seek it even with the full knowledge that doing so will not lessen their sentences. In some prisons, seeking treatment by prisoners is frowned upon by the officials.

Various forms of treatment are even now being tried in some progressive courts and prisons over the country—educational, social, industrial, religious, recreational, and psychological treatments. Socially acceptable behavior, new work-play opportunities, new identity and companion patterns all help toward community reacceptance. Some parole officers and some wardens have been extremely ingenious in developing these modalities of rehabilitation and recon-struction—more than I could list here even if I knew them all. But some are trying. The secret of succss in all programs, however, is the replacement of the punitive attitude with a therapeutic attitude.

Offenders with propensities for impulsive and predatory aggression should not be permitted to live among us unrestrained by some kind of social control. *But the great majority of offenders, even "criminals," should never become prisoners if we want to "cure" them.*

48. MASS MOVEMENTS
AND PERSONAL SALVATION
eric hoffer

Mass movements such as communism and fascism appeal primarily to persons who "crave to be rid of an unwanted self," who have a "passion for self-renunciation," says the next author.

Protest and deviant behavior through commitment to radical move-ments may have their origins in loss of confidence in oneself, leading eventually to inordinate concern with other people's business, to great interest in such subjects as nationalism, race, and religion, and above all to a passionate conviction that one has a holy duty to save others from imminent disaster. In short, faith in such a movement may become a substitute for faith in oneself. Does the evidence bear this theory out? If true, does it apply to non-radical groups as well?

There is a fundamental difference between the appeal of a mass movement and the appeal of a practical organization. The practical organization offers opportunities for self-advancement, and its appeal is mainly to self-interest. On the other hand, a mass movement, particularly in its active, revivalist phase, appeals not to those intent on bolstering and advancing a cherished self, but to those who crave to be rid of an unwanted self. A mass movement attracts and holds a following not because it can satisfy the desire for self-advancement, but because it can satisfy the passion for self-renunciation.

People who see their lives as irremediably spoiled cannot find a worthwhile purpose in self-advancement. The prospect of an individual career cannot stir them to a mighty effort, nor can it evoke in them faith and a single-minded dedication. They look on self-interest as on something tainted and evil; something unclean and unlucky. Anything undertaken under the auspices of the self seems to them foredoomed. Nothing that has its roots and reasons in the self can be good and noble. Their innermost craving is for a new life—a rebirth—or, failing this, a chance to acquire new elements of pride, confidence, hope, a sense of purpose and worth by an identification with a holy cause. An active mass movement offers them opportunities for both. If they join the movement as full converts they are reborn to a new life in its close-knit collective body, or if attracted as sympathizers they find elements of pride, confidence and purpose by identifying themselves with the efforts, achievements and prospects of the movement.

To the frustrated a mass movement offers substitutes either for the whole self or for the elements which make life bearable and which they cannot evoke out of their individual resources.

It is true that among the early adherents of a mass movement there are also adventurers who join in the hope that the movement will give a spin to their wheel of fortune and whirl them to fame and power. On the other hand, a degree of selfless dedication is sometimes displayed by those who join corporations, orthodox political parties and other practical organizations. Still, the fact remains that a practical concern cannot endure unless it can appeal to and satisfy self-interest, while the vigor and growth of a rising mass movement depend on its capacity to evoke and satisfy the passion for self-renunciation. When a mass movement begins to attract people who are interested in their individual careers, it is a sign that it has passed its vigorous stage; that it is no longer engaged in molding a new world but in possessing and preserving the present. It ceases then to be a movement and becomes an enterprise. According to Hitler, the more "posts and offices a movement has to hand out, the more inferior stuff it will attract, and in the end these political hangers-on overwhelm a successful party in such number that the honest fighter of former days no longer recognizes the old movement. . . . When this happens, the 'mission' of such a movement is done for."

Faith in a holy cause is to a considerable extent a substitute for the lost faith in ourselves.

The less justified a man is in claiming excellence for his own self, the more ready is he to claim all excellence for his nation, his religion, his race or his holy cause.

A man is likely to mind his own business when it is worth minding. When it is not, he takes his mind off his own meaningless affairs by minding other people's business.

This minding of other people's business expresses itself in gossip, snooping and meddling, and also in feverish interest in communal, national and racial affairs. In running away from ourselves we either fall on our neighbor's shoulder or fly at his throat.

The burning conviction that we have a holy duty toward others is often a way of attaching our drowning selves to a passing raft. What looks like giving a hand is often a holding on for dear life. Take away our holy duties and you leave our lives puny and meaningless. There is no doubt that in exchanging a self-centered for a selfless life we gain enormously in self-esteem. The vanity of the selfless, even those who practice utmost humility, is boundless.

One of the most potent attractions of a mass movement is its offering of a substitute for individual hope. This attraction is particularly effective in a society imbued with the idea of progress. For in the conception of progress, "tomorrow" looms large, and the frustration resulting from having nothing to look forward to is the more poignant. Hermann Rauschning says of pre-Hitlerian Germany that "The feeling of having come to the end of all things was one of the worst troubles we endured after that lost war." In a modern society people can live without hope only when kept dazed and out of breath by incessant hustling. The despair brought by unemployment comes not only from the threat of destitution, but from the sudden view of a vast nothingness ahead. The unemployed are more likely to follow the peddlers of hope than the handers-out of relief.

Mass movements are usually accused of doping their followers with hope of the future while cheating them of the enjoyment of the present. Yet to the frustrated the present is irremediably spoiled. Comforts and pleasures cannot make it whole. No real content or comfort can ever arise in their minds but from hope.

When our individual interests and prospects do not seem worth living for, we are in desperate need of something apart from us to live for. All forms of dedication, devotion, loyalty and self-surrender are in essence a desperate clinging to something which might give worth and meaning to our futile, spoiled lives. Hence the embracing of a substitute will necessarily be passionate and extreme. We can have qualified confidence in ourselves, but the faith we have in our nation, religion, race or holy cause has to be extravagant and uncompromising. A substitute embraced in moderation cannot supplant and efface the self we want to forget. We cannot be sure that we have something worth living for unless we are ready to die for it. This readiness to die is evidence to ourselves and others that what we had to take as a substitute for an irrevocably missed or spoiled first choice is indeed the best there ever was.

part

five

CONFLICT RESOLUTION AND SOCIAL REINTEGRATION

In Part Four, attention was drawn to some fundamental dimensions of social conflict, to man's probable inability to master the forces that threaten him unless he develops a social technology that assures a stable and cooperative life for all.

The readings in Part Five are of two kinds. Those in Section I concern measures that must be taken if man is to extricate himself from the crises that now engulf him. The first selection by Russian nuclear physicist Andrei D. Sakharov contains an urgent appeal that the United States and the Soviet Union control their powerful nuclear capabilities lest ideological conflict lead to devastation of the human race. In the second selection, John G. Mitchell outlines measures which must be taken if the ecological balance of our planet is to be preserved.

The selections in Section II stand in sharp contrast to those in the preceding section. Rather than illustrate what must be done to save man from himself, these selections indicate how man haphazardly goes about the task of muddling through his problems. The first reading, from Arthur M. Schlesinger's *A Thousand Days,* describes in detail the confusion and agony that characterized American efforts to forestall a Russian missile buildup in Cuba. The Cuban missile crisis is probably the closest the two superpowers have yet come to nuclear war. The second selection, taken from the *Congressional Record,* is a verbatim account of debate in the House of Representatives over legislation designed to curb the infestation of rats in New York City housing ghettos. These selections illustrate the art of muddling through, of coping with crisis on a makeshift, "pragmatic" basis. Such responses ought to be contrasted with the kinds of effective, long-range solutions to urgent issues that are a special responsibility of all the social sciences.

▌ CREATING BETTER SOCIETIES

49. MANKIND IS IN JEOPARDY
andrei d. sakharov

Beginning as an underground and private expression of viewpoints circulated among friends, the following selection was written by an eminent Soviet scientist deeply concerned about the state of the world in
general and the human costs of United States-Soviet rivalry in particular.
The author expresses two theses, first, that "the division of mankind
threatens it with destruction," second, that "intellectual freedom is
essential to human society" because such freedom "is the only guarantee of the feasibility of a scientific democratic approach to politics,
economy, and culture," He views the pacification and transformation of
a troubled world as the prime task of all intellectuals and political
leaders. Do his views surprise you? Are they constructive?

The international policies of the world's two leading superpowers (the United
States and the Soviet Union) must be based on a universal acceptance of unified and general principles, which we initially would formulate as follows:

All peoples have the right to decide their own fate with a free expression
of will. This right is guaranteed by international control over observance by
all governments of the "Declaration of the Rights of Man." International control presupposes the use of economic sanctions as well as the use of military
forces of the United Nations in defense of "the rights of man."

All military and military-economic forms of export of revolution and
counterrevolution are illegal and are tantamount to aggression.

All countries strive toward mutual help in economic, cultural, and gen-
eral-organizational problems with the aim of eliminating painlessly all domes-

tic and international difficulties and preventing a sharpening of international tensions and a strengthening of the forces of reaction.

International policy does not aim at exploiting local, specific conditions to widen zones of influence and create difficulties for another country. The goal of international policy is to insure universal fulfillment of the "Declaration of the Rights of Man" and to prevent a sharpening of international tensions and a strengthening of militarist and nationalist tendencies.

Such a set of principles would in no way be a betrayal of the revolutionary and national liberation struggle, the struggle against reaction and counterrevolution. On the contrary, with the elimination of all doubtful cases, it would be easier to take decisive action in those extreme cases of reaction, racism, and militarism that allow no course other than armed struggle. A strengthening of peaceful coexistence would create an oportunity to avert such tragic events as those in Greece and Indonesia.

Such a set of principles would present the Soviet armed forces with a precisely defined defensive mission, a mission of defending our country and our allies from aggression. As history has shown, our people and their armed forces are unconquerable when they are defending their homeland and its great social and cultural achievements.

Having examined in the first part of this essay the development of mankind according to the worse alternative, leading to annihilation, we must now attempt, even schematically, to suggest the better alternative. (The author concedes the primitiveness of his attempts at prognostication, which requires the joint efforts of many specialists, and here, even more than elsewhere, invites positive criticism.)

In the first stage, a growing ideological`struggle in the socialist countries between Stalinist and Maoist forces, on the one hand, and the realistic forces of leftist Leninist Communists (and leftist Westerners), on the other, will lead to a deep ideological split on an international, national, and intraparty scale.

In the Soviet Union and other socialist countries, this process will lead first to a multiparty system (here and there) and to acute ideological struggle and discussions, and then to the ideological victory of the realists, affirming the policy of increasing peaceful coexistence, strengthening democracy, and expanding economic reforms (1960–80). The dates reflect the most optimistic unrolling of events.

The author, incidentally, is not one of those who consider the multiparty system to be an essential stage in the development of the socialist system or, even less, a panacea for all ills, but he assumes that in some cases a multiparty system may be an inevitable consequence of the course of events when a ruling Communist party refuses for one reason or another to rule by the scientific democratic method required by history.

In the second stage, persistent demands for social progress and peaceful coexistence in the United States and other capitalist countries, and pressure exerted by the example of the socialist countries and by internal progressive forces (the working class and the intelligentsia) will lead to the victory of the leftist reformist wing of the bourgeoisie, which will begin to implement a program of rapprochement (convergence) with socialism, i.e., social progress, peaceful coexistence, and collaboration with socialism on a world scale and changes in the structure of ownership.This phase includes an expanded role for the intelligentsia and an attack on the forces of racism and militarism (1972–85). (The various stages overlap.)

In the third stage, the Soviet Union and the United States, having overcome their alienation, solve the problem of saving the poorer half of the world. The aforementioned 20 per cent tax on the national income of developed countries is applied. Gigantic fertilizer factories and irrigation systems using atomic power will be built [in the developing countries], the resources of the sea will be used to a vastly greater extent, indigenous personnel will be trained, and industrialization will be carried out. Gigantic factories will produce synthetic amino acids and synthesize proteins, fats, and carbohydrates. At the same time disarmament will proceed (1972–90).

In the fourth stage, the socialist convergence will reduce differences in social structure, promote intellectual freedom, science, and economic progress and lead to creation of a world government and the smoothing of national contradictions (1980–2000). During this period decisive progress can be expected in the field of nuclear power, both on the basis of uranium and thorium and, probably, deuterium and lithium.

Some authors consider it likely that explosive breeding (the reproduction of active materials such as plutonium, uranium 233 and tritium) may be used in subterranean or other enclosed explosions.

During this period the expansion of space exploration will require thousands of people to work and live continuously on other planets and on the moon, on artificial satellites and on asteroids whose orbits will have been changed by nuclear explosions.

The synthesis of materials that are superconductors at room temperature may completely revolutionize electrical technology, cybernetics, transportation, and communications. Progress in biology (in this and subsequent periods) will make possible effective control and direction of all life processes at the levels of the cell, organism, ecology, and society, from fertility and aging to psychic processes and heredity.

If such an all-encompassing scientific and technological revolution, promising uncounted benefits for mankind, is to be possible and safe, it will require the greatest possible scientific foresight and care and concern for human values of a moral, ethical, and personal character. (I touched briefly on the danger of a thoughtless bureaucratic use of the scientific and technological revolution in a divided world in the section on "Dangers," but could add a great deal more.) Such a revolution will be possible and safe only under highly intelligent worldwide guidance.

The foregoing program presumes:

a.   worldwide interest in overcoming the present diversions;
b.   the expectation that modifications in both the socialist and capitalist countries will tend to reduce contradictions and differences;
c.   worldwide interest of the intelligentsia, the working class, and other progressive forces in a scientific democratic approach to politics, economics, and culture;
d.   the absence of insurmountable obstacles to economic development in both world economic systems that might otherwise lead inevitably into a blind alley, despair, and adventurism.

Every honorable and thinking person who has not been poisoned by narrow-minded indifference will seek to insure that future development will be along the lines of the better alternative. However only broad, open discussion, without the pressure of fear and prejudice, will help the majority to adopt the correct and best course of action.

50. GOOD EARTH
john g. mitchell

Man has struggled for centuries to survive the vicissitudes of nature. That struggle has now been reversed. Can nature survive man?
    The following selection suggests that nature may not survive "civilization." Perhaps the failure of conservation and anti-pollution efforts lies in the fact that both have been treated as technological rather than social problems.

Viewed from space, the earth appears benign, blue and beautiful. Astronaut Frank Borman, from his vantage point aboard Apollo 8, called the planet "that good earth." Up close, the perspective is less pleasing. The same technological impulse that is carrying Apollo 11 outward to the moon is also threatening the home environment. In a report last week to the United Nations, Secretary-General U Thant warned that a worldwide "crisis of the human environment" could lead the planet toward global suicide. Unless action is taken against the pollution of air, water and land, U Thant said, "the future of life on earth could be endangered."
    To be sure, ecologists and conservationists have been predicting the apocalypse for so long now—it is seven years since Rachel Carson summoned

up an image of a "Silent Spring" when all the birds are cut down by DDT—
that most listeners have tended to discount warnings about the deteriorating
quality of life, or else have assumed that something at last was being done.
After all, didn't Pittsburgh muffle its belching smokestacks? And didn't Lady
Bird Johnson's beautify-America campaign hide some roadside junk heaps
behind fences?

The depressing answer appears to be that these measures are piecemeal,
inadequate and essentially defensive—like a doctor treating symptoms rather
than the disease. What was once visible—and repugnant—like the black
plumes of industrial smoke, is now being made invisible, but more deadly.
Pollution-control technology has turned smoke into toxic gases which penetrate even further into the lungs. Sewage-treatment plants now purify human
wastes, but their phosphate and nitrate effluents still flow into rivers and lakes
—and help feed algal blooms that eventually choke and "kill" the water, as in
the case of Lake Erie. Thus, the esthetic victories are not necessarily healthy
ones. Some scientists, despairing of an imminent victory, search instead for a
civil-defense-style checkmate. One laboratory is developing pollution shelters
for the home and astronaut life-support helmets for the man-on-the-smoggy-
street.

In every area, it seems, man is a victim of his own technological virtu-
osity and of his own habits and shortsightedness. Though birth-control and
family-planning techniques are beginning to make slight inroads on population
growth in the developed countries, the individual's "right to breed" still remains
enshrined around the world. The "good earth" is crowded with 3.5 billion
people, and more than 7 billion are expected by the end of the century. And
as the people increase, so do the pressures they exert on the earth's balance of
air, water and soil.

A WORLD WITHOUT SUNSHINE?

Neo-Malthusians, like Cornell ecologist Lamont Cole, foresee the disaster of global famine as one likely result of overpopulation. The threat of famine
may also accelerate other catastrophes. In the rush to produce more food,
more nitrate and phosphate fertilizers will be broadcast upon the croplands
of the world, only to run off into more waterways and contribute to new
blooms of lake-destroying algae. And the persistent pesticides, which already
threaten some species of birds, would be sprayed over still more of the world's
acreage.

The automobile is now held accountable for 60 percent of all air pollution
generated in the U.S. and for an increasing amount in other Western nations.
Now scientists are also worrying about the proliferation of jet aircraft and
their contribution to the contamination of the upper atmosphere. At very high
altitudes, there is no washing effect, so that effluents from planes may circle
the earth many times before settling by gravitation. "If transportation con-

tinues to grow in the direction it's going," says Alfred Hulstrunck, assistant director of the Atmospheric Sciences Research Center at the State University of New York in Albany, "it's possible the next generation will never see the sun."

Yet while some scientists foresee an age of global gloom, others fear the planet may become a giant hothouse. Transparent to sunlight but opaque to the earth's radiation, a blanket of moisture and carbon dioxide conceivably could raise the surface temperatures of the earth enough to melt the polar icepacks and raise sea levels 300 feet. Even 200 feet would inundate New York, Boston and most of Florida.

Farfetched? Perhaps. A more imminent threat is the vast accumulation of garbage that is stifling the developed world. Nearly 5 pounds are generated daily by every American: burning it fouls the air and burying it often destroys valuable wetlands. As for noxious-waste disposal, instead of dumping acids, poison gases, pharmaceutical and petrochemical by-products into some convenient waterway, the new alternative is to drop the fluids down wells. Many of the nation's 130 disposal wells, however, are less than 2,000 feet deep; most are in relatively permeable sandstone or limestone strata, aquifers that feed eventually into surface waters. "This stuff they're dumping," says geologist David M. Evans of the Colorado School of Mines, "won't stay put. Once it gets into the drinking water, there's no way in the world you can clean it up. It may take 50 years to discover that it is on the march, and by that time the whole countryside has become poisoned."

Oceans are being poisoned for miles around, too. In fact, the sea is the final repository of just about everything man wants to get rid of. According to Code, we are putting some 500,000 different chemicals into our environment. Most find their way to the sea. Air borne lead from anti-knock gasoline falls into the ocean at the rate of about a quarter million tons a year—an amount equal to that introduced through natural processes. Pesticides are washed into the sea and reappear thousands of miles away, tankers spill oil and the military dumps chemical-warfare gases.

Environments gone awry are by no means found only in the industrial nations of the world. Egypt and its Aswan Dam provide an example of what happens when a predominantly agricultural nation moves rapidly into the twentieth century. As one of the world's largest structures of its kind, Aswan Dam was designed to reap a multitude of socioeconomic benefits: doubled electrical output, a 25 per cent increase in cultivated land. But already the balance sheet shows a different kind of account. Aswan's giant Lake Nasser, many experts foresee, will retain most of the silt on which the rich Nile delta farmland depends. The dam is also impounding natural minerals essential to the web of marine life in the delta; since Aswan began regulating the river's flow five years ago, Egypt has suffered a $7 million-a-year loss in its native sardine industry, and now there are reports that the delta shrimp fishery is also on the decline.

The damming of the Zambezi River in southern Africa brought similar results. According to one report by Caltech's Thayer Scudder, the Zambezi dam builders had predicted that an increase in the fisheries resources would offset the loss of flooded farmland. As it turned out, the fish catch fell off after an initial flourish, and the lakeshore soon enough bred hordes of tsetse flies that infected native livestock. Nevertheless, engineers now are designing massive dams for two of the world's longest rivers—the Mekong and the Amazon. One Amazonian proposal would call for creation of an inland sea almost as large as both East and West Germany.

Such examples of misguided and perhaps overambitious technology disturb economist Kenneth Boulding, now a professor of social dynamics and international systems at the University of Colorado, "We're going around heavy-footed," Boulding complains. "You can muck around with Ohio; it has resilience. But there's a precariousness about the tropics . . ."

Why this disdain for the environment? Man no longer has the excuse of innocence—presumably he has now advanced beyond the Mayan farmers who overtilled the soil with little thought for any harvests beyond the immediate ones. Ecologist Raymond F. Dasmann of Washington's Conservation Foundation says, only half-jokingly, that man's difficulties in living with his environment date to Eden—"the first place someone decided he wanted something he didn't need." Others attribute man's profligate ways to a deep emotional commitment to the idea—grounded mainly in Western Christian thought—that nothing exists in the universe apart from man. "The Copernican revolution," says historian Lynn White Jr. of Cornell, "should have taught us that man is part of nature. Yet curiously, even after Darwin, neither our scientists nor technicians absorbed this truth. We are still anthropocentric and ruthless toward our environment."

White's indictment of Western man is particularly applicable to the U.S., where the frontier and free enterprise still exert strong influence. If it can be done, the saying goes, do it—and then move on to the next virgin territory. C. C. Johnson, HEW's administrator for consumer protection and environmental health service, suggested recently that the "problems that plague us today are largely the result of our narrow pursuit of limited objectives—economic efficiency, fast transportation, agricultural abundance—and our tendency to endow these activities with a life and purpose of their own."

The narrow pursuit of limited objectives is still evident in Washington. In fact, according to one insider, many bureaus are manned by civil servants who believe that Rachel Carson made no valid case against DDT. At the Federal Water Pollution Control Administration, Commissioner David D. Dominick admits that the U.S. pure-waters program is still muddied and stagnant. Unable to get Congress to appropriate sufficient matching funds (some $3.4 billion) for municipalities to complete construction of waste treatment facilities by 1972 (a deadline set by U.S. law), the FWPCA is considering an alternative: financing the sewage plants through local bond issues which the Federal government would help retire over the next 30 years. The trouble with this scheme, however, is that Washington has scant assurance U.S. voters will approve the issues at the polls. Though a recent public-opinion survey found that three out of four Americans would be willing to pay higher taxes to clean up the environment, the fact remains that in general Americans are apathetic about their environment—short of a catastrophe—and are reluctant to pay for its upkeep.

Everyone in Washington is for cleanliness right next to godliness: clean air, clean water, clean cities, clean recreation areas—as long as too many sacred cows are not disturbed. It took a lot of pressure to get action against auto-exhaust pollution. For example, even though the Justice Department has brought suit against Detroit manufacturers for conspiring to suppress anti-pollution technology, it is going to take a great deal more vigorous action on the part of the Administration, the courts and Congress to clean up the auto-exhaust and other man-made environmental problems.

As an effort in that direction, no fewer than four bills were introduced in Congress this session to create a national technology-assessment board or an environmental-advisory council that would function in the ecological arena as the President's Council of Economic Advisers presides over fiscal affairs. President Nixon recently created his own Cabinet-level environment council which will be meeting from time to time to consider such problems as the debate over a jetport at the edge of the Everglades National Park in Florida.

Testifying at a recent hearing on one environmental bill, W. H. Ferry, for ten years a vice president of the Center for the Study of Democratic Institutions in Santa Barbara, noted somewhat dourly that while councils and committees can do no harm diagnosing "the warts" on technology's "chin," drastic surgery is needed. Ferry proposes a two-year moratorium on technological innovation to "compel a searching revision of our national aims"; amendment of the U.S. Constitution to permit, for example, limitations on the number of autos one family might own, and finally, establishment of a national ecological authority, with sweeping regulatory powers over all major technological undertakings that might pose ecological hazards.

Social scientist Richard A. Falk of Princeton University goes further than Ferry and proposes a limited world government and an international, "macro-functional" approach to such global undertakings as climate control and cleaning up of the oceans. Economist Hans H. Landsberg of the Washington-based Conservation Foundation is more specific. "We've passed the point where water and air can be free and therefore squandered," says Landsberg. "We've got to have incentives to behave less wastefully." One suggested incentive: water metering that would make the consumer pay for what he uses. Boulding advocates taxes on pollution—on cars, for example, whose emissions exceed permissible limits.

One good sign is the universal restlessness of the young and their unwillingness to accept shoddiness or further deterioration in the name of progress or property rights. It is not simply a matter of a hip generation worshiping Thoreau and doing battle over a "people's park." Few of the youthful dissidents are truly tuned into nature—yet. But they do insist that beauty and quality should be a part of man's legitimate inheritance on earth, and that technology must be led by man instead of leading him. This was certainly the prevailing mood among students gathered in Berkeley's Sproul Plaza one day this spring for an environment teach-in. "The politics of ecology," shouted one rebel with a cause, "is going to replace both capitalism and Marxism."

Technology, of course, need not alienate man from anything. If used wisely, it might well allow him to restore some measure of harmony to the biosphere. The sophisticated technology required to create the Apollo space-ship, for example, has done much to demonstrate the ecological principles of "interrelatedness" in a closed system. NASA has spent billions to provide the moonbound astronauts with the ecology of the "good earth"—pure air, pure water and careful disposal of waste. Each spaceship, in effect, is a model and a reminder of what earth should be like.

More specifically, space technology is now capable of providing new understanding and control of the earth environment itself. Remote sensing devices, like infra-red scanners and radar, and high-resolution cameras aboard satellites far above the earth's surface will be able to pick out blighted trees from healthy forest areas and determine the amount of pollution an industrial plant contributes to rivers or harbors. Already, Gemini and Apollo photos have revealed remote—and possibly mineral-rich—volcanic areas, noted urban air pollution and charted deep ocean currents. U.S. and Russian weather satellites now follow hurricanes and icebergs, issuing warnings to countries and ships in their path. In the 1970s, NASA will orbit a series of unmanned Earth Resources Technology Satellites, which may discover new mineral resources beneath the sea, spot likely fishing areas and record evidence of coastal erosion.

"This is no longer pie-in-the-sky," says J. Lynn Helms of the Bendix Aerospace Electronics Co. Satellite sensors, he explains, will be able to judge when the right temperature and moisture combine to produce the best moment for planting crops. They will tell a farmer not only when to plant, but on which acreage and how much fertilizer to use. Such information, Helms predicts on the basis of recent tests, could increase American farm production by 300 per cent.

The question that remains is whether man, forearmed with this kind of reconnaissance, will in the future choose to use it wisely and avoid some of the blunders of the past.

Now man is going to the moon. He will undoubtedly go beyond the moon to Mars, and, some day, beyond that. A few pioneers may even decide to live there—inside plastic bubbles, dining on algae cultures and recycling their fluid wastes. Anything is possible. It is even possible that technological man will begin to apply what he has learned about keeping astronauts func-tioning efficiently in space to the task of keeping Homo sapiens alive and well on planet earth.

II

POLITICAL REALITIES
AND THE ART OF
MUDDLING THROUGH

51. THE CUBAN MISSILE CRISIS

arthur m. schlesinger, jr.

The United States is frequently criticized for employing a "crisis" approach to decision making, for allowing problems to build, relatively unheeded, until they reach the breaking-point. Then, on the brink of disaster, Americans launch a crash program designed to extricate themselves from the latest crisis.

In the following selection, one of President Kennedy's advisors recounts the crash approach to the Cuban missile crisis.

Do the problems outlined in earlier sections of this book—war, riots, and poverty in particular—lend themselves to solutions by way of crash programs? Why is it that the American system of government experiences difficulty in planning for the future?

. . . on the fourteenth the U-2 plane returned from its mission. The negatives went swiftly to the processing laboratories, then to the interpretation center, where specialists pored over the blown-up photographs frame by frame. Late Monday afternoon, reading the obscure and intricate markings, they identified a launching pad, a series of buildings for ballistic missiles and even one missile on the ground in San Cristóbal.

About 8:30 that evening the CIA informed Bundy of the incredible discovery. Bundy reflected on whether to inform the President immediately, but he knew that Kennedy would demand the photographs and supporting interpretation in order to be sure the report was right and knew also it would take all night to prepare the evidence in proper form. Furthermore, an immediate meeting would collect officials from dinner parties all over town, signal Washington that something was up and end any hope of secrecy. It was better,

From Arthur M. Schlesinger, Jr., *A Thousand Days*. Boston: Houghton Mifflin Company, 1965, pp. 801–819. By permission of Houghton Mifflin Company and Andre Deutsch Ltd.

Bundy thought, to let the President have a night's sleep in preparation for the ordeal ahead.

The President was having breakfast in his dressing gown at eight forty-five on Tuesday morning when Bundy brought the news. Kennedy asked at once about the nature of the evidence. As soon as he was convinced that it was conclusive, he said that the United States must bring the threat to an end: one way or another the missiles would have to be removed. He then directed Bundy to institute low-level photographic flights and to set up a meeting of top officials. Privately he was furious: if Khrushchev could pull this after all his protestations and denials, how could he ever be trusted on anything?

The meeting, beginning at eleven forty-five that morning, went on with intermissions for the rest of the week. The group soon became known as the Executive Committee, presumably of the National Security Council; the press later dubbed it familiarly ExCom, though one never heard that phrase at the time. It carried on its work with the most exacting secrecy: nothing could be worse than to alert the Russians before the United States had decided on its own course. For this reason its members—the President, the Vice-President, Rusk, McNamara, Robert Kennedy, General Taylor, McCone, Dillon, Adlai Stevenson, Bundy, Sorensen, Ball, Gilpatrick, Llewellyn Thompson, Alexis Johnson, Edwin Martin, with others brought in on occasion, among them Dean Acheson and Robert Lovett—had to attend their regular meetings, keep as many appointments as possible and preserve the normalities of life. Fortunately the press corps, absorbed in the congressional campaign, was hardly disposed or situated to notice odd comings and goings. And so the President himself went off that night to dinner at Joseph Alsop's as if nothing had happened. After dinner the talk turned to the contingencies of history, the odds for or against any particular event taking place. The President was silent for a time. Then he said, "Of course, if you simply consider mathematical chances, the odds are even on an H-bomb war within ten years." Perhaps he added to himself, "or within ten days."

In the Executive Committee consideration was free, intent and continuous. Discussion ranged widely, as it had to in a situation of such exceptional urgency, novelty and difficulty. When the presence of the President seemed by virtue of the solemnity of his office to have a constraining effect, preliminary meetings were held without him. Every alternative was laid on the table for examination, from living with the missiles to taking them out by surprise attack, from making the issue with Castro to making it with Khrushchev. In effect, the members walked around the problem, inspecting it first from this angle, then from that, viewing it in a variety of perspectives. In the course of the long hours of thinking aloud, hearing new arguments entertaining new considerations, they almost all found themselves moving from one position to another. "If we had had to act on Wednesday in the first twenty-four hours," the President said later, "I don't think probably we would have chosen as prudently as we finally did." They had, it was estimated, about ten days before the missiles would be on pads ready for firing. The deadline defined the strategy. It meant that the response could not, for example, be confided to the United Nations, where the Soviet delegate would have ample opportunity to stall action until the nuclear weapons were in place and on target. It meant that we could not even risk the delay involved in consulting our allies. It meant that the total responsibility had to fall on the United States and its President.

On the first Tuesday morning the choice for a moment seemed to lie between an air strike or acquiescence—and the President had made clear that acquiescence was impossible. Listening to the discussion, the Attorney General scribbled a wry note: "I now know how Tojo felt when he was planning Pearl Harbor." Then he said aloud that the group needed more alternatives: surely there was some course in between bombing and doing nothing; suppose, for example, we were to bring countervailing pressure by placing nuclear missiles in Berlin? The talk continued, and finally the group dispersed for further reflection.

The next step was military preparation for Caribbean contingencies. A Navy-Marine amphibious exercise in the area, long scheduled for this week, provided a convenient cover for the buildup of an amphibious task force, soon including 40,000 Marines; there were 5000 more in Guantanamo. The Army's 82nd and 101st Airborne Divisions were made ready for immediate deployment; altogether the Army soon gathered more than 100,000 troops in Florida. SAC bombers left Florida airfields to make room for tactical fighter aircraft flown in from bases all over the country. Air defense facilities were stripped from places outside the range of the Cuban missiles and re-installed in the Southeast. As the days went by, 14,000 reservists were recalled to fly transport planes in the eventuality of airborne operations.

In the meantime, the Pentagon undertook a technical analysis of the requirements for a successful strike. The conclusion, as it evolved during the week, was that a 'surgical' strike confined to the nuclear missile bases alone would leave the airports and IL-28 untouched; moreover, we could not be sure in advance that we had identified or could destroy all the missile sites. A limited strike therefore might expose the United States to nuclear retaliation. Military prudence called for a much larger strike to eliminate all sources of danger; this would require perhaps 500 sorties. Anything less, the military urged, would destroy our credibility before the world and leave our own nation in intolerable peril. Moreover, this was a heaven-sent opportunity to get rid of the Castro regime forever and re-establish the security of the hemisphere.

It was a strong argument, urged by strong men. But there were arguments on the other side. The Soviet experts pointed out that even a limited strike would kill the Russians manning the missile sites and might well provoke the Soviet Union into drastic and unpredictable response, perhaps nuclear war. The Latin American experts added that a massive strike would kill thousands of innocent Cubans and damage the United States permanently in the hemisphere. The Europeanists said the world would regard a surprise strike as an excessive response. Even if it did not produce Soviet retaliation against the United States, it would invite the Russians to move against Berlin in circumstances where the blame would fall, not on them, but on us. It would thereby give Moscow a chance to shift the venue to a place where the stake was greater than Cuba and our position weaker. In the Caribbean, we had overwhelming superiority in conventional military force; the only recourse for the Soviet Union there would be to threaten the world with nuclear war. But in Berlin, where the Russians had overwhelming conventional superiority, it was the United States which would have to flourish nuclear bombs.

All these considerations encouraged the search for alternatives. When the Executive Committee met on Wednesday, Secretary McNamara advanced an idea which had been briefly mentioned the day before and from which he did not thereafter deviate—the conception of a naval blockade designed to stop the further entry of offensive weapons into Cuba and hopefully to force the removal of the missiles already there. Here was a middle course between inaction and battle, a course which exploited our superiority in local conventional power and would permit subsequent movement either toward war or toward peace.

As the discussion proceeded through Thursday, the supporters of the air strike marshaled their arguments against the blockade. They said that it would not neutralize the weapons already within Cuba, that it could not possibly bring enough pressure on Khrushchev to remove those weapons, that it would permit work to go ahead on the bases and that it would mean another Munich. The act of stopping and searching ships would engage us with Russians instead of Cubans. The obvious retort to our blockade of Cuba would be a Soviet blockade of Berlin. Despite such arguments, however, the majority of the Executive Committee by the end of the day was tending toward a blockade.

That afternoon, in the interests of normality, the President received the Soviet Foreign Minister Andrei Gromyko .It was one of the more extraordinary moments of an extraordinary week. Kennedy knew that there were Soviet nuclear missiles in Cuba. Gromyko unquestionably knew this too, but did not know that Kennedy knew it. His emphasis was rather grimly on Berlin, almost as if to prepare the ground for demands later in the autumn. When the talk turned to Cuba, Gromyko heavily stressed the Cuban fears of an American invasion and said with due solemnity that the Soviet aid had "solely the purpose of contributing to the defense capabilities of Cuba"; "if it were otherwise," the Russian continued, "the Soviet Government would never become involved in rendering such assistance." To dispel any illusion about possible American reactions, the President read the Foreign Minister the key sentences from his statement of September 13. He went no further because he did not wish to indicate his knowledge until he had decided on his course.

In the evening the President met with the Executive Committee. Listening again to the alternatives over which he had been brooding all week, he said crisply, "Whatever you fellows are recommending today you will be sorry about a week from now." He was evidently attracted by the idea of the blockade. It avoided war, preserved flexibility and offered Khrushchev time to reconsider his actions. It could be carried out within the framework of the Organization of American States and the Rio Treaty. Since it could be extended to non-military items as occasion required, it could become an instrument of steadily intensifying pressure. It would avoid the shock effect of a surprise attack, which would hurt us politically through the world and might provoke Moscow to an insensate response against Berlin or the United States itself. If it worked, the Russians could retreat with dignity. If it did not work, the Americans retained the option of military action. In short, the blockade, by enabling us to proceed one step at a time, gave us control over the future. Kennedy accordingly directed that preparations be made to put the weapons blockade into effect on Monday morning.

The next day the President, keeping to his schedule, left Washington for a weekend of political barnstorming in Ohio and Illinois. In Springfield, Illinois, after a speech at the State Fairgrounds, he paused to lay flowers on Lincoln's tomb.

Kennedy left behind a curiously restless group of advisers. This became evident when they met at the State Department at eleven on Friday morning. Over Ted Sorensen's protest that a decision had been reached the night before and should not be reopened now, several began to re-argue the inadequacy of the blockade. Someone said: Why not confront the world with a *fait accompli* by taking out the bases in a clean and swift operation? It was a test of wills, another said, and the sooner there was a showdown, the better. Someone else said that it was now or never; we must hit the bases before they become operational. If we took a decision that morning, the planes could strike on Sunday. But, if we committed ourselves to a blockade, it would be hard, if not impossible, to move on thereafter to military action.

Secretary McNamara, however, firmly reaffirmed his opposition to a strike and his support for the blockade. Then Robert Kennedy, speaking with quiet intensity, said that he did not believe that, with all the memory of Pearl Harbor and all the responsibility we would have to bear in the world afterward, the President of the United States could possibly order such an operation. For 175 years we had not been that kind of country. Sunday-morning surprise blows on small nations were not in our tradition. Thousands of Cubans would be killed without warning, and hundreds of Russians too. We were fighting for something more than survival, and a sneak attack would constitute a betrayal of our heritage and our ideals. The blockade, the Attorney General concluded, would demonstrate the seriousness of our determination to get the missiles out of Cuba and at the same time allow Moscow time and room to pull back from its position of peril. It was now proposed that the committee break up into working groups to write up the alternative courses for the

President—one to analyze the quarantine policy, the other to analyze the strike. Then everyone dispersed to meet again at four o'clock for a discussion of the competing scenarios.[1]

At the second meeting the balance of opinion clearly swung back to the blockade (though, since a blockade was technically an act of war, it was thought better to refer to it as a quarantine). In retrospect most participants regarded Robert Kennedy's speech as the turning point. The case was strengthened too when the military representatives conceded that a quarantine now would not exclude a strike later. There was brief discussion of a *démarche* to Castro, but it was decided to concentrate on Khrushchev. Then they turned to the problem of the missiles already in Cuba. Someone observed that the United States would have to pay a price to get them out; perhaps we should throw in our now obsolescent and vulnerable Jupiter missile bases in Italy and Turkey, whose removal the Joint Congressional Committee on Atomic Energy as well as the Secretary of Defense had recommended in 1961. After a couple of hours, Adlai Stevenson, who had had to miss the day's meetings because of UN commitments, arrived from New York. He expressed his preference for the quarantine over the strike but wondered whether it might not be better to try the diplomatic route also. We must, he said, start thinking about our negotiating position; for example, a settlement might include the neutralization of Cuba under international guarantees and UN inspection; demilitarization would, of course, include our own base at Guantanamo as well as the Soviet installations. The integrity of Cuba should be guaranteed. He also echoed the suggestion that we might want to consider giving up the Italian and Turkish bases now, since we were planning to do so eventually.

The President, still campaigning, received reports from his brother in Washington. The schedule now called for a speech to the nation on Sunday night. By Saturday morning, however, it was evident that preparations would not be complete in time, so it was decided to hold things for another twenty-four hours. Meanwhile, the President, pleading a cold, canceled the rest of his political trip and returned to Washington. Before leaving Chicago, he called Jacqueline and suggested that she and the children come back from Glen Ora, where they had gone for the weekend.

That afternoon he presided over the Executive Committee and its final debate. McNamara impressively presented the case for the blockade. The military, with some civilian support, argued for the strike. Stevenson spoke

[1] The Secretary of State took little part in these discussions. John M. Hightower, who covers the State Department for the Associated Press, wrote on August 22, 1965: "Criticism over his role in the missile crisis angered Rusk to the point that he heatedly defended it in talks with newsmen on one or two occasions. He said that the responsibility of the Secretary of State was to advise the President and he did not think he should commit himself before all the facts were in. Therefore he withdrew himself from the argument for several days though Under Secretary of State George Ball, instructed by Rusk to take a free hand, presented the State Department viewpoint."

with force about the importance of a political program, the President agreeing in principle but disagreeing with his specific proposals. A straw vote indicated eleven for the quarantine, six for the strike. The President observed that everyone should hope his plan was not adopted; there just was no clear-cut answer. When someone proposed that each participant write down his recommendation, Kennedy said he did not want people, if things went wrong, claiming that their plans would have worked. Then he issued orders to get everything ready for the quarantine. On Sunday morning a final conference with the military leaders satisfied him that the strike would be a mistake. His course was now firmly set.

I knew nothing about any of this until late Friday, October 19, when Adlai Stevenson phoned me, saying casually that he was in Washington and wondered when we could get together. He was staying at the house of his friend Dr. Paul Magnuson across the street from my own house in Georgetown, and we agreed to ride down to the State Department together the next day. When we met after breakfast on Saturday morning, he beckoned me into the Magnuson house. "I don't want to talk in front of the chauffeur," he said; and then in a moment, "Do you know what the secret discussions this week have been about?" I said I knew of no discussions; the President was out campaigning; I had presumed that everything was fine. Adlai, observing gravely that there was trouble and he had the President's permission to tell me about it, described the seesaw during the week between the diplomatic and military solutions. The quarantine, he now felt, was sure to win. He would have to make a speech early in the week at the Security Council, and he wanted me to help on it. He outlined the argument and, with due discretion, I set to work.

The secret had been superbly kept. But later in the day, when the President returned from the campaign and Rusk canceled a speech that night, a sense of premonitory excitement began to engulf Washington. Already those whose business it was to sniff things out were on the track. In the British Embassy, where a delegation of intelligence officers had come to Washington for a long-scheduled conference with the CIA, suspicions had been aroused early in the week when the meetings drew a diminishing American representation or were called off altogether. By process of elimination the 007s decided on Friday that it must be Cuba. The *New York Times,* noting the troop movements and other unusual activities, also deduced Cuba by the weekend and even speculated about nuclear missiles. James Reston wrote the story and checked it with the White House. The President himself called Orville Dryfoos, the publisher of the *Times,* to say that publication might confront him with a Moscow ultimatum before he had the chance to put his own plans into effect; once again, the *Times* killed a story about Cuba. By Saturday night the town was alive with speculation and anticipation. A good deal of the government found itself late that evening at a dance given by the James Rowes. Here the gap between the witting and the unwitting could almost be detected by facial expressions—on the one hand, anxiety tinged with self-satisfaction; on the other, irritation and frustration. Henry Brandon, the Washington correspondent of the London *Sunday Times,* who had just returned from a trip to Cuba, began to wonder when a succession of top officials asked him elaborately off-hand questions about the mood in Havana.

On Sunday Stevenson, contemplating the problems of gathering UN backing for the quarantine, wrote down his thoughts about our UN strategy. He saw no hope of mustering enough votes in the UN to authorize action against Cuba in advance; but the OAS offered an opportunity for multilateral support, and OAS approval could provide some protection in law and a great deal in public opinion. As for the UN, he said, we must seize the initiative, bringing our case to the Security Council at the same time we imposed the quarantine. In order to avert resolutions against the quarantine, he continued, we should be ready to propose a political path out of the military crisis. His negotiating program, following his remarks to the Executive Committee, centered on the removal of Soviet military equipment and personnel—i.e., missiles, installations and the several thousand Russian specialists—under UN observation and the introduction of UN influence into Cuba in the hope of ending communist domination of the Cuban government. He would throw a non-invasion guarantee and Guantanamo into the bargain to evidence our restraint and good faith. Exercising the prerogative freely employed that week by nearly all his colleagues, he now wrote that Turkey and Italy should not be included; this would only divert attention from the Cuban threat to the general issue of foreign bases. That problem might later be considered apart from Cuba in the context of general disarmament.

The President, however, rightly regarded any political program as premature. He wanted to concentrate on a single issue—the enormity of the introduction of the missiles and the absolute necessity for their removal. Stevenson's negotiating program was accordingly rejected. Stevenson, when I saw him that week-end, took this realistically; he felt he had done his job as the custodian of our UN interests in making the recommendation, and the decision was the President's. However, some of his colleagues on the Executive Committee felt strongly that the thought of negotiations at this point would be taken as an admission of the moral weakness of our case and the military weakness of our posture. They worried considerably over the weekend (and some of them vocally thereafter) whether, denied his political program, Stevenson would make the American argument with sufficient force in the UN debate.

I spent all day Sunday till well after midnight working at the State Department with Harlan Cleveland, Joseph Sisco and Thomas Wilson on the UN speech. At ten o'clock on Monday morning the President called me in to instruct me to go to New York and assist Stevenson on the UN presentation. He was in a calm and reflective mood. It was strange, he said, how no one in the intelligence community had anticipated the Soviet attempt to transform Cuba into a nuclear base; everyone had assumed that the Russians would not be so stupid as to offer us this pretext for intervention. I asked why he thought Khrushchev had done such an amazing thing. He said that, first, it might draw Russia and China closer together, or at least strengthen the Soviet position in the communist world, by showing that Moscow was capable of bold action in support of a communist revolution; second, that it would radically redefine the setting in which the Berlin problem could be reopened after the election; third, that it would deal the United States a tremendous political blow. When I remarked that the Russians must have supposed we would not respond, Kennedy said, "They thought they had us either way. If we did nothing, we would be dead. If we reacted, they hoped to put us in an exposed position, whether with regard to Berlin or Turkey or the UN."

I met with him again at eleven to go over the draft of the UN speech with Rusk, Robert Kennedy and others. The President suggested a few omissions, including a passage threatening an American strike if the Soviet buildup in Cuba continued; he preferred to leave that to Moscow's imagination. The Attorney General drew me aside to say, "We're counting on you to watch things in New York. . . . We will have to make a deal at the end, but we must stand absolutely firm now. Concessions must come at the end of negotiation, not at the beginning." Then, clutching the speech, I caught the first plane to New York.

In Washington everything awaited the President's television broadcast that night to the nation. Sorensen had been laboring over the draft since Friday. Kennedy himself was never more composed. At four o'clock he had an appointment with Prime Minister Milton Obote of Uganda. Wholly at ease, he talked for forty-five minutes about the problems of Africa and Uganda as if he had nothing on his mind and all the time in the world. Angier Biddle Duke of the State Department remarked to Obote on their way back to Blair House that a crisis of some sort was imminent; the Ugandan was incredulous and, when he heard Kennedy's speech that evening, forever impressed.

At five o'clock Kennedy saw the congressional leaders, many of whom had flown in from their home states in Air Force planes. He showed them the U-2 photographs and told them what he proposed to do. Senator Russell of Georgia disagreed; the quarantine, he said, would be too slow and too risky—the only solution was invasion. To the President's surprise, Fulbright, who had opposed invasion so eloquently eighteen months before, now supported Russell. The President listened courteously but was in no way shaken in his decision. (Kennedy told me later, "The trouble is that, when you get a group of senators together, they are always dominated by the man who takes the boldest and strongest line. That is what happened the other day. After Russell spoke, no one wanted to take issue with him. When you can talk to them individually, they are reasonable.")

Then at seven o'clock the speech: his expression grave, his voice firm and calm, the evidence set forth without emotion, the conclusion unequivocal— "The purpose of these bases can be none other than to provide a nuclear strike capability against the Western Hemisphere." He recited the Soviet assurances, now revealed as "deliberate deception," and called the Soviet action "a deliberately provocative and unjustified change in the status quo which cannot be accepted by this country, if our courage and our commitments are ever to be trusted again by either friend or foe." Our "unswerving objective," he continued, was to end this nuclear threat to the Americans. He then laid out what he called with emphasis his *initial* steps: a quarantine on all offensive military equipment under shipment to Cuba; an intensified surveillance of Cuba itself; a declaration that any missile launched from Cuba would be regarded as an attack by the Soviet Union on the United States, requiring full retaliatory response upon the Soviet Union; an immediate convening of the Organization of American States to consider the threat to hemisphere security; an emergency meeting of the UN Security Council to consider the threat to world peace; and an appeal to Chairman Khrushchev "to abandon this course of world domination, and to join in an historic effort to end the perilous arms race and to transform the history of man."

He concluded with quiet solemnity. "My fellow citizens: let no one doubt that this is a difficult and dangerous effort. . . . No one can foresee precisely what course it will take or what costs or casualties will be incurred. . . . But the greatest danger of all would be to do nothing. . . . Our goal is not the victory of might, but the vindication of right—not peace at the expense of freedom, but both peace *and* freedom, here in this hemisphere, and, we hope, around the world. God willing, that goal will be achieved."

After the broadcast the President returned to the Mansion, sought out Caroline and told her stories until it was time for dinner. He dined alone with Jacqueline.

We listened to the speech clustered around a television set in Stevenson's office in New York. I had found Adlai unperturbed in the midst of pandemonium. The Mission was a frenzy of activity in preparation for the Security Council. The UN had never seemed so much like a permanent political convention: so many people to be considered and cajoled, so many issues going at once, such an inherent unpredictability about the parliamentary sequence. From the moment of the President's statement, Stevenson had to talk so much to UN delegates from other nations that he had little time left for his own speeches and strategy. Through Monday evening and Tuesday morning he snatched moments to revise and edit his remarks for the Security Council. It was reminiscent of his presidential campaigns: the last part of his address was still in the typewriter at the Mission on Tuesday afternoon when he had already begun to speak across the street at the UN.

The speech began at four o'clock. The OAS had been meeting since nine that morning. Edwin Martin had done a splendid job briefing the OAS ambassadors the night before, and Secretary Rusk, invoking the security resolution of Punta del Este, was now offering a resolution authorizing the use of force, individually or collectively, to carry out the quarantine. No one could doubt the OAS sentiment, but a number of ambassadors had not yet received instructions from their governments. As a result, the resolution establishing the legal basis for United States action was not passed until Stevenson was well into his speech.[2]

Martin, by prior arrangement, notified Harlan Cleveland the moment the OAS acted, and Cleveland instantly called Sisco in New York. Watching Stevenson on television, Cleveland could see Sisco leave the chamber to take the call, then in a moment return and place the text of the resolution on the desk in front of Stevenson. Stevenson, absorbed in his speech, talked on, apparently unaware of the sheet of paper before him. At this moment Kennedy, with characteristic attention to detail, called Cleveland and asked whether Stevenson knew about the OAS action. Cleveland replied that he had sent a message but feared that Adlai had not seen it. Just then on the screen Stevenson reached for the paper. Kennedy, who was also watching television, said, "I guess he has it now."

In New York Stevenson, who had been speaking with extraordinary eloquence to a hushed chamber, now read the OAS resolution. In another moment he concluded: "Since the end of the Second World War, there has been no threat to the vision of peace so profound, no challenge to the world of the Charter so fateful. The hopes of mankind are concentrated in this room. . . . Let [this day] be remembered, not as the day when the world came to the edge of nuclear war, but as the day when men resolved to let nothing thereafter stop them in their quest for peace." The President immediatley dictated a telegram:

DEAR ADLAI: I WATCHED YOUR SPEECH THIS AFTERNOON WITH GREAT SATIS-FACTION. IT HAS GIVEN OUR CAUSE A GREAT START. . . . THE UNITED STATES IS FORTUNATE TO HAVE YOUR ADVOCACY. YOU HAVE MY WARM AND PERSONAL THANKS.

And now the tension was rising. In Cuba workmen were laboring day and night to complete the bases. Forty-two medium-range nuclear missiles were being unpacked and prepared for launching pads with desperate speed. IL-28 aircraft were being assembled. On the Atlantic at least twenty-five Soviet merchant ships, some no doubt loaded with intermediate-range missiles, were steaming toward Cuba, their courses thus far unaltered after the President's speech. Ninety ships of the American fleet, backed up by sixty-eight aircraft squadrons and eight aircraft carriers, were moving into position to intercept and search the onrushing ships. In Florida and neighboring states the largest United States invasion force since the Second World War was gathering. In Moscow, the Soviet government in a long and angry statement insisted that the

[2] It was passed unanimously. Uruguay, still awaiting instructions, abstained on Tuesday but changed its vote to affirmative on Wednesday.

weapons in Cuba were defensive, ignored the charges of nuclear missiles and savagely denounced the American quarantine.

The United Nations was only the first step in gaining world understanding of the American position. Africa now assumed vital strategic importance because Soviet flights to Cuba would have to refuel at African airports. Both Sékou Touré in Guinea and Ben Bella in Algeria sent Kennedy their assurances that they would deny Russian aircraft transit rights. (Touré later added that the problem must be kept in a Soviet-American context; if it became a Cuban-American problem, we would lose support in the uncommitted world.) Most African states, moved no doubt by their faith in the American President, indicated private sympathy.

In Western Europe support was general, though there were waverings in Britain and Italy. In Paris General de Gaulle received Dean Acheson, the President's special emissary, and, without waiting to see the aerial photographs Acheson had brought along, said, "If there is a war, I will be with you. But there will be no war." De Gaulle went on to wonder whether the quarantine would be enough, and so did Adenauer, but both strongly backed the American position.

The British had received their first notification on Saturday, October 20. At Sunday noon Kennedy called David Ormsby Gore to the White House and outlined the alternatives. Ormsby Gore expressed strong support for the quarantine and, with his knowledge of Macmillan, assured the President of a sympathetic British reaction. Later the same day Kennedy explained directly to Macmillan that he had found it essential in the interests of security and speed to make his first decision on his own responsibility, but that from now on he expected to keep in the closest touch. He added that, if Khrushchev tried anything in Berlin, the United States would be ready to take a full role there as well as in the Caribbean.

Macmillan responded on Monday that Britain would give all the support it could in the Security Council, though he did not then or later offer to take part in specific action on the Atlantic. He added that two aspects of the problem particularly troubled him. European opinion, he said, would need attention, because Europeans had grown so accustomed to living under the nuclear gun that they might wonder what all the fuss was about. The other and more worrying point was that, if it came to a negotiation, Khrushchev might try to trade Cuba for Berlin. The President, no doubt detecting an element of reserve in Macmillan's tone, tried to reassure him that the Cuban decision was not simply a response to aroused public opinion or to private passion against Cuba; he had no interest in a squabble with Castro. This was something very different: a major showdown with Khrushchev, whose action had so contradicted all the Kremlinologists had prophesied that it was necessary to revise our whole estimate of his desperation or ambition or both. Thereafter Macmillan did not falter, and his counsel and support proved constant through the week.

Macmillan's initial caution reflected a peculiar reaction throughout his country. The British had greeted Kennedy's Monday night speech with surprising skepticism. Some questioned whether nuclear missiles really were in Cuba; maybe CIA was up to its old tricks again, or maybe this was a pretext to justify an American invasion. Even Hugh Gaitskell doubted the legality of the quarantine and wondered why Kennedy had not gone first to the United Nations; and the *Economist* as late as Friday warned against "forcing a showdown over the shipment of Russian arms to Cuba." The *Manchester Guardian* said on Tuesday that, if Khrushchev had really brought in nuclear missiles, "he has done so primarily to demonstrate to the U.S. and the world the meaning of American bases close to the Soviet frontier." The *Guardian* added two days later, "In the end the United States may find that it has done its cause, its friends, and its own true interests little good." By Saturday it was suggesting that Britain vote against the United States in the UN. A group of intellectuals—A. J. Ayer, A. J. P. Taylor, Richard Titmuss and others—attacked the quarantine and advocated British neutrality. The *Tribune* wrote, "It may well be that Kennedy is risking blowing the world to hell in order to sweep a few Democrats into office." Among the pacifists, Bertrand Russell, who was already on record calling Kennedy "much more wicked than Hitler," sent messages to Khrushchev:

> MAY I HUMBLY APPEAL FOR YOUR FURTHER HELP IN LOWERING THE TEMPERATURE. . . . YOUR CONTINUED [*sic*] FORBEARANCE IS OUR GREAT HOPE.

and to Kennedy:

> YOUR ACTION DESPERATE. . . . NO CONCEIVABLE JUSTIFICATION. WE WILL NOT HAVE MASS MURDER. . . . END THIS MADNESS.

There was some of the same in the United States. The followers of Stuart Hughes's peace party denounced the quarantine, sought excuses for Khrushchev and prayed for American acceptance of the missiles.

On Tuesday night Kennedy dined quietly at the White House with English friends. Cuba was hardly mentioned at the table; but after dinner he beckoned David Ormsby Gore out into the long central hall, where they quietly talked while the gaiety continued in the dining room. The British Ambassador, mentioning the dubious reaction in his own country, suggested the need for evidence: could not the aerial photographs be released? The President sent for a file, and together they went through them picking out the ones that might have the greatest impact on skeptics. In a while Robert Kennedy walked in, bleak, tired and disheveled. He had just been to see Ambassador Dobrynin in an effort to find out whether the Soviet ships had instructions to turn back if challenged on the high seas. The Soviet Ambassador, the Attorney General said, seemed very shaken, out of the picture and unaware of any instructions. This meant that the imposition of the quarantine the next day might well bring a clash.

The three old friends talked on. Ormsby Gore recalled a conversation with Defense Department officials who had declared it important to stop the Soviet ships as far out of the reach of the jets in Cuba as possible. The British Ambassador now suggested that Khrushchev had hard decisions to make and that every additional hour might make it easier for him to climb down gracefully; why not, therefore, make the interceptions much closer to Cuba and thereby give the Russians a little more time? If Cuban aircraft tried to interfere, they could be shot down. Kennedy, agreeing immediately, called McNamara and, over emotional Navy protests, issued the appropriate instruction. This decision was of vital importance in postponing the moment of irreversible action. They soon parted, looking forward with concern to the crisis of the morrow.

And so around the world emotions rose—fear, doubt, incertitude, apprehension. In the White House the President went coolly about his affairs, watching the charts with the Soviet ships steadily advancing toward Cuba, scrutinizing every item of intelligence for indications of Soviet purpose, reviewing the deployment of American forces. At one point the Air Force produced a photograph of planes lined wingtip to wingtip on a Cuban airfield, arguing that only a few bombs could wipe out the enemy air power. The President asked the Air Force to run similar reconnaissance over our own airfields; to the Pentagon's chagrin, the photographs showed American planes also lined up row by row. In this manner he preserved a taut personal control over every aspect of the situation; the Bay of Pigs had not been in vain. He said to someone, "I guess this is the week I earn my salary."

He never had a more sober sense of his responsibility. It was a strange week; the flow of decision was continuous; there was no day and no night. In the intervals between meetings he sought out his wife and children as if the imminence of catastrophe had turned his mind more than ever to his family and, through them, to children everywhere in the world. This was the cruel question—the young people who, if things went wrong, would never have the chance to learn, to love, to fulfill themselves and serve their countries. One noon, swimming in the pool, he said to David Powers, "If it weren't for these people that haven't lived yet, it would be easy to make decisions of this sort."

In Buenos Aires Billy Graham preached to 10,000 people on "The End of the World."

52. RIOTS, RIGHTS, AND RATS: THE RAT CONTROL BILL OF 1967

In 1967, the United States House of Representatives debated a bill calling for Federal expenditures in order to "develop and carry out extensive local programs of rat control and extermination." While the subject

From *Congressional Record*, July 20, 1967, pp. 19548–19555.

of both concern and occasional humor, the House debate reported below is significant in that it reveals a wide and sometimes conflicting variety of Congressional political values and social perspectives. Apprehension and humor are interlaced in a discussion that touches on profound issues of poverty, violence, resource allocation, and the satisfaction of basic human needs.

Mr. MATSUNAGA. Mr. Speaker, by direction of the Committee on Rules, I call up House Resolution 749, and ask for its immediate consideration. . . .

The SPEAKER. The gentleman from Hawaii is recognized for 1 hour.

Mr. MATSUNAGA. Mr. Speaker, I yield to the gentleman from Ohio, 30 minutes, pending which I yield myself such time as I may consume.

Mr. Speaker, House Resolution 749 provides an open rule with 1 hour of general debate for consideration of H.R. 11000 to provide Federal financial assistance to help cities and communities of the Nation develop and carry out intensive local programs of rat control and extermination.

Mr. Speaker, I believe we can have a lot of fun with this bill. I am sure there will be humor injected into the matter throughout the debate. Some may call it the second "antiriot" bill. Others may call it the civil rats bill. Still others may insist that we should make this applicable to two-legged rats as well as four-legged ones. And there may be those who claim that this is throwing money down a rathole. But, Mr. Speaker, in the final analysis there is a serious side to this proposed legislation.

The need for this legislation is clearly evident in the fact that last year, in seven cities alone in the United States there were approximately 1,000 reported cases of ratbite. There is reason to believe that the actual statistics are much higher because many persons are reluctant to report ratbite incidents, and many units of local and State government do not require such reports. Only 2 days ago, it was reported by the news media that an 8-month-old boy was bitten to death by rats right here in our Nation's Capital. What a shame that we should allow such a thing to happen in any of our cities or towns in the world's most affluent nation.

In addition to the disease-carrying threat which these pesky animals pose, they, in fact, cause enormous damage to both food and property. It has been estimated that there are at least 90 million rats in the United States and that each causes an average of $10 damage per year. This means a national loss of $900 million to the rats every year, unless we do something about it.

The conditions which breed rats, as well as the techniques for removing these conditions, are now well known. However, there remains a critical need to allocate sufficient public financial and technical resources to these problems and to undertake remedial measures on an intensive and continuing basis. Because no present Federal program or combination of Federal programs can assist a locality to undertake, separately, the whole needed combination of rat control activities, it is believed that the proper Federal role in this problem is the provision of Federal grant assistance, limited in time but comprehensive in scope.

H.R. 11000 would authorize Federal assistance to cover two-thirds of the cost of 3-year local programs for rat extermination and control. The grants would be made to local governments, and the bill requires that the community have an approved workable program in order to be eligible for such aid. The Secretary of Housing and Urban Development, who would make the grants, would be required to cooperate and consult with other departments which have responsibilities related to the problem of rat control. Appropriations of $20 million would be authorized for each of the fiscal years 1968 and 1969 to make these grants. In view of the savings in property damages and the relief in human misery, which are sure to result, this legislation may be properly considered as a worthwhile investment.

Mr. Speaker, I urge the adoption of House Resolution 749 in order that H.R. 11000 may be considered.

Mr. GROSS. Mr. Speaker, will the gentleman yield?

Mr. MATSUNAGA. I yield to the gentleman from Iowa.

Mr. GROSS. I thank the gentleman for yielding. I believe the gentleman said that there are some 90 million rats in the United States of the four-legged variety. I do not know how many others there may be.

Is that correct; 90 million rats?

Mr. MATSUNAGA. It has been estimated by three experts in the area of rat control that there are approximately 90 million rats, or a minimum of that many. The Department of the Interior estimated it to be about 100 million, and the World Health Organization has estimated that there is a rat for every person in the world. The gentleman can take his choice.

Mr. GROSS. Does the gentleman imply that with the passage of this $40 million bill we are then going to embark upon rat killing around the world?

Mr. MATSUNAGA. Not around the world. This bill would be confined to the United States, to cities, townships, and communities within our own country.

Mr. GROSS. I have read the hearings fairly carefully. I do not know whether the gentleman has or not. Nowhere do I find any evidence as to who took the rat census in the United States, much less in the world.

Mr. MATSUNAGA. The experts in this area did.

Mr. GROSS. Who are the experts?

Mr. MATSUNAGA. There are three of them.

I cannot think of the names of them right now. I can give them to the gentleman later, if the gentleman will permit. But the report will show too— perhaps the chairman of the subcommittee might be able to help me in this instance.

Mr. BARRETT. Mr. Speaker, will the gentleman yield to me?

Mr. MATSUNAGA. I yield to the distinguished gentleman from Pennsylvania.

Mr. BARRETT. Mr. Speaker, in answer to the gentleman's question—and I think it is a very good question—this census, more or less, was taken by D. E. Davis, of the Department of Zoology of Pennsylvania State University, at the seminar on rodents which was held in Geneva, Switzerland, on October 24–28, 1966, and sponsored by the World Health Organization.

They indicated at that time, as the gentleman has pointed out, that there were over 100 million rats in the United States alone.

Mr. GROSS. Mr. Speaker, will the gentleman yield further?

Mr. MATSUNAGA. I yield further to the gentleman from Iowa.

Mr. GROSS. The gentleman spoke of city rats. What about country rats?

Mr. MATSUNAGA. The country rats are being taken care of under existing programs.

Mr. BARRETT. Mr. Speaker, will the gentleman yield at that point?

Mr. MATSUNAGA. I yield to the gentleman from Pennsylvania.

Mr. BARRETT. I would like to tell the gentleman from Iowa, because he is so very enthusiastic about this type of program, they do have an agricultural program directed toward rat extermination, and there is also a program in the Department of the Interior. They are doing a fairly good job on this problem, but are not doing a consistent job.

Mr. Speaker, what we are after here is a continuity of rat control in the cities in order to exterminate the rats.

Mr. REUSS. Mr. Speaker, will the gentleman yield?

Mr. MATSUNAGA. I yield to the gentleman from Wisconsin.

Mr. REUSS. Mr. Speaker, in response to the query of the gentleman from Iowa as to what kind of expert it was who estimated that there were 90 million rats in the United States, I would refer the gentleman from Iowa to page 2 of the report where it is said that it has been conservatively estimated there are at least 90 million rats in the United States. This was a conservative expert.

Mr. GROSS. I am glad to hear that the gentleman has suddenly turned conservative, if he has.

Mr. HALEY. Mr. Speaker, will the gentleman yield?

Mr. MATSUNAGA. I yield to the gentleman from Florida.

Mr. HALEY. Mr. Speaker, I wonder sometimes if some of our distinguished committees that bring before us a monstrosity such as this, would just take into consideration the fact that we have a lot of cat lovers in the Nation, and why not just buy some cats and turn them loose on the rats and thereby we could take care of this situation, without any $25 million from the Treasury of the United States.

Mr. MATSUNAGA. I would support such a program, if the gentleman from Florida will introduce such a bill.

Mr. KYL. Mr. Speaker, will the gentleman yield further?

Mr. MATSUNAGA. I yield to the gentleman from Iowa [Mr. KYL].

Mr. KYL. Mr. Speaker, on page 11 of the report there is a figure specified for expenditures for rat control which is currently contained in the OEO in the amount of $2,373,671, which was a pilot program in the city of Chicago.

Now, has that program succeeded in doing away with the rat population in the city of Chicago?

Mr. MATSUNAGA. I would appreciate it if the gentleman would withhold that question until general debate so that members of the committee may answer it for the gentleman.

Mr. KYL. I thank the gentleman from Hawaii, but I would hope we never get to general debate. However, I withhold the question for the time being.

Mr. MATSUNAGA. Mr. Speaker, I reserve the balance of my time.

Mr. LATTA. Mr. Speaker, I yield myself such time as I may consume.

Mr. Speaker, I agree with my colleague, the gentleman from Hawaii [Mr. MATSUNAGA], that this matter does have a serious side, and I hasten to point out that the serious side of this piece of legislation is the sum of $20 million for fiscal year 1968 and for fiscal year 1969, another $20 million, and Lord knows how much thereafter, because this program does not terminate after 2 years. This is the beginning of an all-new program.

Mr. Speaker, every person with experience in this Congress well knows that when these programs start, future years bring greater and greater appropriations. This will be only the beginning.

I say to my colleagues, in view of the fiscal situation facing this country today, this is one program we can do without. This Congress has already raised the debt ceiling during this session in order to be able to meet its financial responsibilities. We are now to face the possibility of a surtax ranging from six percent to 10 percent. The President of the United States is going to send a surtax message to the Congress. He has been talking about it since the first of the year, and I wager that before the end of this Congress, it will be up here, and you and I will be faced with the question of saddling our constituents, the taxpayers of this country, if you please, with a new tax.

Mr. Speaker, it seems to me that here is a request for $20 million for 1968 and $20 million for 1969, that we can refuse.

Mr. Speaker, there is still some local responsibility remaining in this country and the killing of rats is one of them. This is not a national matter.

There is also some responsibility on the part of individual citizens. Certainly the Federal Government cannot, and should not, fulfill every need or wish of every one of its citizens. Our tax structure cannot stand it. The matter of putting out a little bit of rat poison should not be requested of the Federal Government.

We already have rodent control programs for specific purposes. We have a rodent control program in the Department of the Interior, a rodent control program in the Department of Agriculture, there is a pilot program in HEW, even though they do not want to admit it, out in San Francisco. They have not been known for their success.

Here is what they have been doing in the Department of Agriculture for the farmer—whom this administration seems to have completely forgotten —and the farmer is losing millions and millions of dollars each year to rodents. Here is what they have been doing for the farmers in the State of Illinois. In 1966 the Department of Agriculture spent through the ASCS office the grand total of $700. In the State of Iowa, in 1966, they expended the grand sum of $300.

In Nebraska, in 1966, the Department of Agriculture expended the grand total of $665 through the ASCS program on rodent control, if you please. Anyone familiar with the farmers' plight knows full well they are suffering a loss figured in the millions of dollars every year, but not one single dime—not one single dime of this $20 million is going to be spent to reduce this loss of the American farmers.

Now, who is getting short-changed? Who is getting short-changed by this administration?

The rat bill before us came to this Congress in a Presidential recommendation, if you please.

It seems to me, my colleagues, that here is a matter that could be laid aside until the fiscal situation in this country has brightened. Certainly when we are expending the billions of dollars that we are in Vietnam, we can lay this proposal aside. If there is any local responsibility on the part of local government remaining, this proposal can be laid aside. If the individual has any responsibility remaining, we can lay this matter aside. The individual does not want to pay for a new rat control program at this time with all of the costly new Federal employees to be employed to put out rat poison that the individual citizen could put out for himself.

Mr. Speaker, this bill is extremely broad and the sky is the limit. I call your attention to the bill itself.

On page 2, line 10, it says:

> (2) the elimination or modification of physical surroundings and conditions (including rat harborages and food supplies) which encourage or tend to encourage persistent rat habitation and increases in their numbers; and

It reads, "the elimination or modification of physical surroundings." This, if you please, can mean a building. They could move in and tear down a building under this legislation.

Oh, it might be denied that they have that intent and purpose, but I have been around here long enough to know that if you give the bureaucrats the general language, they are going to interpret it and use it any way they see fit.

I say to you, that here is a piece of legislation that this country can do without. When the time comes when you and I are asked to vote for a surtax ranging from 6 to 10 percent, we will be asking ourselves whether it was wise for this Congress today to be taking its time considering legislation local in nature and not as pressing as some of the national problems facing this Congress.

Mr. BROYHILL of Virginia. Mr. Speaker, will the gentleman yield?

Mr. LATTA. I yield to the gentleman from Virginia.

Mr. BROYHILL of Virginia. Mr. Speaker, the gentleman made a very clear statement on how this rat bill discriminates against a lot of rats in this country. The committee report also shows that the bill discriminates against 97½ percent of the rats.

But I think the most profound statement the gentleman made is the fact that it does set up a new bureau and sets up possibly a commissioner on rats or an administrator of rats and a bunch of new bureaucrats on rats. There is no question but that there will be a great demand for a lot of rat patronage. I think by the time we get through taking care of all of the bureaucrats in this new rat bureau along with the waste and empire building, none of the $40 million will be left to take care of the 2½ percent of the rats who were supposed to be covered in the bill.

Mr. Speaker, I think the "rat smart thing" for us to do is to vote down this rat bill "rat now."

Mr. LATTA. I may say to the gentleman that when he raises the question of discriminating between city and country rats, it also discriminates against persons suffering from bites from other animals.

Forgetting about the rodents for a moment, it was mentioned by the gentleman from Hawaii that we have over 1,000 rat bite cases in the United States in a year's time.

How about the snake bite cases?

If we are going to start eradicating all the rats—how about snakes in the West? How about bugs? You can go into homes and apartment buildings here in the city of Washington and find bugs galore. What are you going to do about the bugs? Are we to forget about the people bitten by bugs? Should we start a bug corps?

Mr. JOELSON. Mr. Speaker, will the gentleman yield?

Mr. LATTA. I am pleased to yield to the gentleman.

Mr. JOELSON. Do I remember correctly that the gentleman now in the well appeared before the Subcommittee in Interior Appropriations of the Committee on Appropriations complaining about the fact that not enough money was being spent on blackbird control and urging and begging for very sizable sums of money for blackbird control, and making no mention of the fiscal problem or local initiative.

Mr. LATTA. The gentleman is absolutely correct but the figure requested was small compared to the amount in this bill. Blackbirds are migratory and create a national rather than a local problem. I pointed out, and the Department of Interior pointed out, that our American farmers are losing some $58 million a year in crops due to blackbird damage.

Mr. JOELSON. This report states it is estimated that a billion dollars a year is being lost through rat damage.

Mr. MULTER. Mr. Speaker, will the gentleman yield?

Mr. LATTA. I yield to the gentleman.

Mr. MULTER. I do not know too much about birds and snakes but I think I would support the gentleman in his attempt to control birds, particularly blackbirds, in this country, because I understand that blackbirds do a tremendous job in eradicating snakes.

Mr. GROSS. Mr. Speaker, will the gentleman yield?

Mr. LATTA. I yield to the gentleman from Iowa.

Mr. GROSS. On the matter of rat bites, it would be interesting to know how many children are bitten by squirrels that they feed and try to handle. On the basis of that does anyone suggest a program to exterminate squirrels?

Mr. LATTA. The gentleman raises a question which indicates that the bill has a lot of possibilities for amendment.

Mr. Speaker, I yield 5 minutes to the gentleman from Iowa [Mr. GROSS].

Mr. GROSS. Mr. Speaker, this bill is so ludicrous that we should not even entertain the rule. We should vote down the rule on this bill, and it is my hope the House will do just that.

As the gentleman from Ohio [Mr. LATTA] has so well said, Congress will soon be confronted with another Federal tax increase. Soon we will receive a tax bill requesting an increase of somewhere between 6 percent and 10 percent. It could be even higher. Today we are being asked to ladle out $40 million, unknown as to the future, but for the next 2 years $20 million a year for rat extermination, something the people of this country, the municipalities, and other subdivisions of government, ought to do themselves instead of passing it on to the busted Federal Treasury.

We are asked to raise the debt ceiling, to raise taxes, and yet embark upon another bureaucratic program that is a responsibility which ought to be discharged by the people themselves.

I have spent some time trying to find evidence to back up this request for $40 million. I do not know of a legislative committee in Congress that has a larger staff than the Committee on Banking and Currency, yet in the index of the hearings I can find only one reference to rat extermination, and that is to page 39 of the hearings, if I remember correctly.

Mr. BARRETT. Mr. Speaker, will the gentleman yield?

Mr. GROSS. I yield to the gentleman from Pennsylvania.

Mr. BARRETT. I refer the gentleman to the hearings that covered 2 weeks, and particularly the testimony we had around April 20. Many of those who testified in that 2-week period testified on the subject of rat extermination.

Mr. GROSS. I would think that with the staff that you have on this committee, one of the biggest in the House of Representatives, you would tell us where we could find that evidence instead of having to read every line and every word of wholly unrelated testimony in an attempt to find the pertinent material. The only reference, so far as I could find, in your index, is to page 39. Why did you not give us a little help so that we could find what we need to understand what you are trying to do?

Mr. BARRETT. Mr. Speaker, will the gentleman yield?

Mr. GROSS. Yes, I yield briefly.

Mr. BARRETT. Certainly it would never be my purpose to tell the distinguished gentleman what to do and what to read, because he is one of the most knowledgeable men in the House. But I do want to call your attention to this. We are asking $40 million to save the buying public $1 billion.

Mr. GROSS. You can make that speech on your own time. I thought you were going to tell me why you did not refer us to the rat extermination testimony in connection with this bill.

There is a so-called expert running around over the country by the name, I believe, of Leonard Czarniecki. I suppose he is going to be the high cockalorum of the rat corps extermination program, or whatever it is. I do not find in the hearing record a single reference to him. His name does not appear in the hearing index. Why did you not have this so-called expert, who is pushing out publicity over the country in behalf of this $40 million expenditure, to come before the committee? Or did you have him? The silence seems to indicate you did not.

Mr. BARRETT. Mr. Speaker, will the gentleman yield?

Mr. GROSS. Yes; I yield to the gentleman from Pennsylvania.

Mr. BARRETT. I can tell you that we had some very fine experts before the committee.

Mr. GROSS. Did you have this Czarniecki individual before your committee? He is apparently set up "to rule the roost" so far as rats are concerned?

Mr. BARRETT. We had the Secretary and Assistant Secretaries of HUD who testified and he is the HUD staff technician. You will find those figures, I am sure, in the testimony.

Mr. GROSS. I am constrained to believe the program is devised to take care of some more broken down political hacks.

Mr. ASHLEY. Mr. Speaker, will the gentleman yield?

Mr. GROSS. I will yield briefly to the gentleman from Ohio.

Mr. ASHLEY. Mr. Speaker, if the gentleman has read the bill, he has to know we are talking about local programs. That is the requirement under the legislation. We are not talking about the establishment of a high commissioner or anything of this kind.

Mr. GROSS. Who is going to run it, there is not going to be a high commissioner or administrator of the rat corps?

Mr. ASHLEY. Mr. Speaker, we are talking about a very modest program.

Mr. GROSS. I am sure the gentleman is—at $40 million. I have heard that before. Now let me use a little of my time, if the gentleman does not mind.

Mr. ASHLEY. Mr. Speaker, does the gentleman mean to suggest to the House that in the absence of any legislation to provide for the establishment of a new bureau, that there would in fact be a new bureau created?

Mr. GROSS. Mr. Speaker, I see three names on the bill. I wonder if I can assume that the rat problems of the country are in New Jersey, Texas, and Pennsylvania? Can it be that this is where the rat infestation is heaviest?

Mr. PATMAN. Mr. Speaker, will the gentleman yield?

Mr. GROSS. I yield very briefly to the gentleman from Texas.

Mr. PATMAN. Mr. Speaker, this is a bill to prevent infant mortality, unnecessary infant mortality, and for the health and protection of the people.

Mr. GROSS. The gentleman can make that speech if he wants to on his own time.

I am trying to get information as to who is responsible for this monstrosity. I noticed in the paper last night that there is a Peace Corps contingent from Argentina in this country. We are the underdeveloped, the underprivileged country now. The Argentines have invaded us with a Peace Corps, and they apparently are going to hold forth in two of the most underdeveloped and underprivileged areas of the country, in Los Angeles, Calif., and in Boston, Mass.

I would like to suggest that whoever is running the Argentine Peace Corps in the United States—and we are financing it in this country—should assign the members to clean out the rats in Boston and Los Angeles. I believe this would be an excellent undertaking for them and would save the taxpayers of this country some part of the $40 million that is proposed to be spent.

I will have amendments to offer to this bill if it gets past the rule. It ought to be defeated without further loss of time.

Mr. Speaker, if there is anything this country does not need to be plastered with at this time it is a rat killing deal at a cost of $40 million and no one knows how many more millions after the next 2 years.

It is time for fiscal sanity, not insanity.

Mr. MATSUNAGA. Mr. Speaker, I yield 5 minutes to the gentlewoman from Michigan [Mrs. GRIFFITHS].

Mrs. GRIFFITHS. Mr. Speaker, I thank the chairman.

Before this bill becomes too funny, I would like to say a few words for it. I am in support of this bill, Mr. Speaker. When I first came to this Congress I asked the Library of Congress how much money this Nation had spent on defense in its history. They put some Ph. D.'s to work on the subject, and after 3 months replied that at that time—13 years ago—we had spent more than $1 trillion on defense. I observed the other day, when we had the Defense appropriation bill—which as I recall was for more than $75 billion—there was only one person who voted "No."

I would like to point out to those who may not be aware of it or to those who may have forgotten it, that rats are Johnny-come-latelys to recorded history. They were unknown in the ancient cities of the world. They came in out of the Arabian deserts about the 12th century, and from that day to this they have killed more human beings than all of the generals in the world combined. They have made Genghis Khan, Hitler, and all the other men look like pikers. Man has attempted to kill them and he has won a few battles, but he has lost the war.

The only enemy that has ever really killed rats is other rats.

For the benefit of those who may not know it, the average rat lives 3 years. It has a rootless tooth that grows 29½ inches in those 3 years. They have been known to cut through 4 feet of reinforced concrete.

All of the methods that one could possibly use cannot conceivably kill off more than 98 percent of the rats in one block. If there are left two males and 10 females, there will be 3,000 rats in 1 year to replace those that have been killed.

Perhaps Members think it does not make any real difference, and perhaps they think this is really a local problem, that it is a family problem, and why not get some rat poison and kill the rats in the household?

I should like to remind the Members who sit here in this body that they eat in restaurants night after night after night, and that all that can be done in this Capitol cannot control the rat population.

Rats are a living cargo of death. Their tails swish through sewers and over that food we eat. Their stomachs are filled with tularemia, amebic dysentery. They carry the most deadly diseases, and some think it is funny. Some do not want to spend $40 million.

Mr. Speaker, if we are going to spend $79 billion to try to kill off a few Vietcong, believe me I would spend $40 million to kill off the most devastating enemy man has ever had.

Mr. LATTA. Mr. Speaker, I have no further requests for time.

Mr. MATSUNAGA. Mr. Speaker, I yield such time as he may consume to the gentleman from Ohio [Mr. FEIGHAN].

Mr. FEIGHAN. Mr. Speaker, H.R. 11000, a bill to provide $20 million of Federal financial assistance to help cities and communities develop and carry out rat control programs, represents a most significant legislative attempt to meet the challenge of an unbelievable problem in our modern industrial age. That rats infest our cities in almost overwhelming numbers in the year 1967, reminiscent of medieval civilization, should arouse the indignation of any citizen to such a point that he would act affirmatively to erase this very dark blot on our society.

As in other large cities, the rat problem in Cleveland is growing. It has progressed to a stage where Federal assistance is imperative. Rat infestation has spread throughout the core of Cleveland proper. Hough, Glenville, Central, and the near west side areas are all badly infested with rats. The fringe areas too have now been affected. The 1962 survey conducted by the Public Health Service revealed that 38 percent of the cities showed a sizable rat population; 1967 surveys, as recently as months ago, involving 132 blocks and 5,500 different properties located throughout Cleveland show that the percentage has increased to 60 percent.

Cleveland averages well over 50 rat bites a year. This figure is low because many persons are reluctant to report such incidents and also because many doctors, totally unfamiliar with the rat bite, do not recognize it. Obviously, rats pose an ominous disease-carrying threat. Were an epidemic to arise, it would quickly spread throughout the city. The great number of rats present also cause great property damage. In 1962, the damage in Cleveland was estimated to be approximately $2,000,000. This figure has risen to $3,000,000 annually. These destructive rodents chew up doors, walls, floors, woodwork, undermine foundations both interior and exterior, and undermine sidewalks and streets.

Finally, rat infestation has a tremendous demoralizing effect on the populace in these areas. They are reluctant to admit that rats exist and, thus, frequently do not cooperate with the Federal and State authorities in eliminating the menace. They are reluctant to repair or improve their property, for they know all too well that the rats soon will destroy it again. When the slightly above poverty level or average income neighborhoods become infested, the inhabitants move further out of the central city, thus accelerating the cancerous spread of deteriorated housing.

Under the auspices of Mr. Stephen Chorvat, chief of the bureau of neighborhood conservation, the public health service in Cleveland has been working diligently to contain and eliminate the rats. However, the present lack of manpower and facilities has made the task insurmountable. Cleveland has seven neighborhood sanitarians and 14 sanitarian aides fighting the city's millions of rats. They estimate a need for 25 sanitarians and 100 aides, as well as much additional equipment to exterminate these rodents.

The Federal Government must assist the States to help local governing bodies to undertake truly effective rat control programs. H.R. 11000 will do this. Therefore, I strongly urge the careful consideration and support for this essential legislation.

Mr. DEVINE. Mr. Speaker, I suppose this is another one of President Johnson's economy-in-Government schemes, although it is hard to try to label this as a reduction in domestic spending. In fact, it rings pretty hollow after the most recent gesture of L. B. J. when he "urges across the board cuts of 15 percent." How in the world does spending $40,000,000 chasing rats assist in trying to reduce the greatest deficit in history—now predicted at about $30 billion for fiscal 1968?

Some of us here in this body have been around long enough to remember when the American people were willing to exercise a little bit of initiative and personal resourcefulness and solve local problems on a local level. In fact they were frequently resolved on a personal basis, and Washington was not troubled with dotting every "i" and crossing every "t". The well-known television commercial, "Please, Mother, I would rather do it myself," was a source of pride and personal satisfaction. But, not if L. B. J. has his way.

The committee report claims "many children" are attacked, "maimed and even killed by rats, as an everyday occurrence." Come, now, let us have some supporting information. I am sure if rats were killing children every day, all of us would have heard something about it. The report goes on to say Philadelphia, St. Louis, and Cleveland have all recently averaged over 50 ratbites per year. Golly, almost one a week—so, spend $40 million.

The committee admits there are a number of Federal agencies already involved in programs for rat control, but, since many cities lack adequte refuse collection service, we better bribe the local officials to do their jobs, and create a new separate program. Of course, as usual, Federal control goes hand in hand with the Federal money and HUD established the program, an approved workable program required by the Secretary, and as an added incentive, to provide employment opportunities for residents in the rat-infested areas.

Honestly, Mr. Speaker, some have heard that the White House has a stable of "thinkers" whose job it is to dream up new schemes, and this one sure fits the pattern. Just to make sure, my home city and county figures were obtained in an effort to check the urgency of this legislation. We have a population in excess of 800,000 people. The health commissioner for Columbus, Ohio, reported a total of 75 ratbites during all of 1966 and 1967, including those sustained in experimental laboratories. It was estimated there could be 2½ or 3 million rats in the country, although nobody seems to know who counted them. In any event, another report indicates last year there were 406 bites from "warm mammals." I guess this includes dogs, cats, people, and so forth, in the country, and it appears to be eight or nine times greater than the rat bites. But, so far, nobody has suggested a multimillion program to exterminate these.

Inquiry through local dealers indicates rattraps—not mousetraps—sell for $3.30 per dozen or about 28 cents each. A pretty fair brand of cheese costs 49 cents per pound and would bait 35 traps. So, for an extremely small personal investment, nearly every citizen could cooperate and eliminate this problem, and at the same time, save their Government $40 million. Would not this seem to be a wise step, particularly when the President and his advisers are calling on all Americans for more taxes to pay for the costs of Government?

Finally, one of our respected colleagues tells me he has about 23 cats in and around his barns, all of which he will make available to HUD, without charge. These feline ratcatchers are most effective, particularly since they are led by a highly respected tomcat called Cotton that has earned a most enviable reputation in the ratcatching department.

Seriously, here is an excellent opportunity for the President, the administration, the Congress, to do more than pay lipservice to reducing Federal spending, and I urge my colleagues to vote against this bill known as H.R. 11000. . . .

Mr. BARRETT. Mr. Speaker, the bill before us today, H.R. 11000, the Rat Extermination Act of 1967, is one of the most humane and compassionate bills ever to be considered by this body. The rat menace which afflicts our urban areas is a shocking disgrace to our Nation, whose affluence is the wonder of the modern world.

This bill would provide the Federal aid our cities need to come to grips with this terrible problem. Frankly, it is incredible to me that any of our colleagues can oppose this bill. Even if they represent high-income suburban areas or areas where rats are not a serious menace to health and safety, they must know in their hearts that in every city in America, particularly in the slums and blighted sections, that talk about the rat problem is not an academic exercise but a grave matter which haunts day-to-day existence. The people in these areas face the threat of diseases borne by rats, they fear for their children's safety in the night, and they experience the disgust—and yes, the horror—of the constant presence of these noxious, vicious, disease-carrying animals.

We must act and act now to rid our cities of this ghastly threat to decent and safe living. And we must provide substantial Federal aid to get the job done because, as everyone knows, our cities do not have the financial resources and the tax sources to even carry on their present level of municipal activities.

Mr. Speaker, I have noticed an unfortunate tendency among a number of people when this bill is discussed to indulge in jesting remarks, puns, and supposedly comical cliches. Let me assure my colleagues, Mr. Speaker, that in many of the areas of our cities this is no laughing or joking matter. It is a matter of the utmost seriousness and gravity. Believe me, Mr. Speaker, there is nothing funny about rats and rat bites.

In the minority views of our committee report, the point is made that the funds authorized in this bill will be able to finance an intensified attack on rats in areas having a population of, and I quote, "only 5 million." I wish that the bill contained a larger authorization because the more money we authorize, the more rats we will exterminate. The $40 million authorized to cover 3-year programs was all we believed to be practically achievable. But let us not belittle a program that will offer the hope of ending the rat menace for 5 million human beings. Mr. Speaker, we should bear in mind that these 5 million people are the very millions who live in precisely the neighborhoods where the rat problem is most intense.

So, Mr. Speaker, I beseech and beg my colleagues from the bottom of my heart to vote overwhelmingly for this great, compassionate, and humane program for rat extermination which President Johnson recommended and which our committee endorsed.

Mr. GROVER. Mr. Speaker, I have requested information on annual bites from the health department in Nassau County, N.Y., a part of which county I represent.

The following bites are documented and I list them for the interest of the opponents and proponents of the legislation before us.

Bites by	Number
Dogs	5,779
Cats	323
Hamsters	123
Squirrels	73
Rabbits	51
Monkeys	19
Horses	18
Mice	39
Raccoon	7
Gerbils (desert rodent)	5
Possum	4
Chipmunk	4
Guinea pig	4
Bear	1
Mole	1
Chinchilla	1
Woodchuck	1

There were no wild rat bites and 16 bites by experiment-test rats.

In 1963 there was noted one llama bite.

Mr. BRAY. Mr. Speaker, the American people, of a certainty, are against rats; but this bill, which makes control of rats a Federal responsibility, reaches the height of absurdity. Rat control is certainly a local community responsibility. The immediate cost of this legislation if enacted would cost $20 million for the first year, and would only take care of one-half of 1 percent of our 18,000 communities. Needless to say, this would only be a foot in the door.

Every year the Federal Government would spend more and more money to control rats. Other branches of the Government are already involved in rat control. The Office of Economic Opportunity is spending over $2 million on merely a pilot project for rat control in Chicago; Health, Education, and Welfare, and General Services Administration also have rat control programs. If the Government expanded its rat program to give equal protection from rats to all communities in the country, it would come to over a billion dollars a year. Next, if the State planners have their way, will come pigeon, starling, English sparrow, roach, and flea control activities.

I am well aware that the liberal left, who would have the Government care for everyone and also have the Government dominate everyone's lives, will accuse those of us who do not want the Government in the rat control business of being for rats. I certainly want to eliminate rats but a Federal bureau certainly is not the answer. Now, I do not believe the Federal Government should pay for haircuts but this does not mean I am for beatniks. Neither do I believe the Government should buy soap for everyone, but this does not indicate I am against bathing.

This bill also contemplates that the Federal Government will become involved in the garbage control business to control rats. Garbage control certainly is important but placing the control of the garbage collection in a Federal bureaucracy would probably be a victory for the rats. We know dogs and cats turn over garbage cans, and we know that our own personal failures to put lids on garbage cans contributes to the rat menace. So, then, we know what we will have to do if under this, or similar legislation, the Government takes on garbage disposal as one of its activities, and your neighbor leaves his garbage cans in a mess: pick up the phone, call the Department of Housing and Urban Development—Code 202–393–4160.

When I was a boy, I did not realize it was the Federal Government's responsibility to eliminate rats. We did it ourselves.

I intend to vote against this bill and against the gradual encroachment of the Federal Government into the personal affairs of everyone, and, in turn, insisting upon the absolute control of the lives of all.

We who vote against this bill are well aware that we will be accused of being for rats, and against people. However, most of us were willing to face that baseless charge, in order to keep our Government from being financially ruined to the point where it cannot carry out its true responsibilities. I trust that the bureaucrats who are so eager to do everything for us will leave us a few pleasures and duties to perform for ourselves.

Mr. BERRY. Mr. Speaker, it surprises me somewhat that no one has rallied to the defense of the rat during the discussion of this bill before the House to spend $40 million over the next 2 years for local rat control programs. Certainly there must be someone who sees this as a threat to a species of wildlife.

In my State of South Dakota, the Interior Department has been conducting a program to control predatory animals which each year do millions of dollars of damage to the agricultural economy. To be sure, the program has been lukewarm and half-hearted from the start, but what little control has been mustered is continually shackled at every turn by those who see these controls as a threat to the predators.

I have just recently heard from several sheepmen in my district who have suffered great losses because of cutbacks in the Interior program. Many have had to take protective measures on their own. The opponents, of course, do not see the millions of dollars ruined each year. They do not see South Dakota's dwindling pheasant population which has been decimated by predators. This, in turn, has dried up a $25 million sport hunting economy in the State.

Where are these people now that we are trying to exterminate the rats? Certainly we cannot interfere with "nature's balance," or possible extinction of this species of animal. It would seem if we can spend $40 million on rat control, it is high time to beef up our predatory animal controls as well.

Mr. FINO. Mr. Speaker, I rise in support of this bill with some misgivings. This legislation, although a mere drop in the bucket, constitutes a real breakthrough for the Department of Housing and Urban Development.

Heretofore, the only bills HUD has sent to Congress have proposed all kinds of tricky housing schemes designed to subsidize the rents of a favored few or to break up existing residential patterns.

For example, only a few weeks ago, I noticed that the "demonstration cities" program is being used as a vehicle to move slumdwellers to the suburbs—at least according to the New York Times—because Congress did not take all the loopholes out of the bill.

Perhaps some of you noticed that Secretary Weaver told the Senate Housing Subcommittee that Newark's rioting means that we have to vote more money for rent subsidies and demonstration cities. Evidently, Dr. Weaver believes that the tranquillity of this Nation will be best served by moving the slums to the suburbs—putting a sniper in every subdivision. I seriously doubt that the people of this country agree.

However, I do want to praise HUD for recommending this bill because it is the first HUD bill which is not a payoff to the big builders or a gravy train for ivory tower social planners.

This rat bill is a bold step forward for HUD policy. Many of these rats HUD wants to exterminate have grown fat on liberal benevolence. Many of these same rats were born in slums financed by welfare handouts and perpetuated by pro-slumlord Democratic Federal tax policies.

I have introduced an antislumlord tax bill which would deny tax breaks to all slums not in compliance with local health and building ordinances. Although the idea has won approval from top architects and planners, I have not heard one word from Dr. Weaver in support of this measure.

For too many years, local city Democratic administrations have been giving tax breaks to slumlords. These same rats that HUD now wants to kill off spent their underprivileged childhoods nourishing themselves on garbage left uncollected by local city Democratic administrations. These same rats hid in darkness perpetuated by payola-ridden Democratic building departments.

For these reasons, I am sure America's rats are going to be bitterly resentful that this administration has turned on them after all these many years.

Perhaps HUD turned against these rats when they started biting rioters. If they had bitten policemen, nothing would have happened.

Frankly, after reading the newspapers and watching television during the past week, I do not think that the problem in the slums is four-legged rats —I think that the problem is the two-legged rats—the two-legged snipers and murderers who beat policemen to death with their own guns.

I will support this bill because it is a step in the right direction in our fight to improve the physical conditions in our slum areas.

Mr. LLOYD. Mr. Speaker, I believe this legislation suggests an inadequate and improper solution to a serious problem.

The problems of local government should not be attacked in this half-way, piecemeal fashion by the Federal Government.

In passing, may I point out that here again the tools of authority and responsibility of State government are totally ignored as the Central Government in Washington attempts to act as the sole mother hen of local government.

And again this legislation suggests a further proliferation of grant-in-aid programs, with Washington establishing priorities and criteria rather than local government officials, who know the most about it, establishing these local priorities and criteria as they were elected to do. Here indeed is a good illustration of the need to replace these grant-in-aid programs and Federal administration with the more workable concept of tax sharing, whereby local and State governments would receive not only funds, but a return of their local responsibility.

If this bill passes, we will have to borrow another $40 million at high rates just for the first 2 years, and for just 100 local areas. If the program were actually to be expanded in an attempt to destroy every rat in America, at least temporarily, the program would have to be expanded to 800 local areas at least, with the costs so astronomical as to be beyond the merely ridiculous.

I know we have to help eliminate the conditions which breed rats. I know that the filth of outside garbage facilities in many areas of this country are almost beyond comprehension. Perhaps closed paper bags are the answer, along with progress in garbage collection and useful application of garbage, accompanied by a better use of the police power. However, this is a local matter. This Federal program, piecemeal and inadequate, is wrong.

Mr. PETTIS. Mr. Speaker, the distinguished Member from Texas and other Members who are sponsoring and supporting H.R. 11000 have, in my opinion, done our Nation a great service. While our minds have been filled with such common problems as the war in Vietnam, the national debt, a deficit that may approach $30 billion, race riots, and the Middle East crisis, we are warned of an undetected and obviously neglected emergency, the war on rats.

I would not wish, Mr. Speaker, to go on record as a defender either of the four-legged rats whose future would be in clear jeopardy or of the two-legged tailless variety who, unfortunately, would escape the all-out effort called for in this bill.

I just believe that existing rat control programs can, with the cooperation of the American people, do the job that needs to be done. I do not believe that we need a Federal rat control program. If rats have become a growing problem or a national program, I suggest that our President call for increased vigilance on the part of those responsible for rat control and voluntary action on the part of individuals and groups across the Nation.

It is my opinion, Mr. Speaker, that one of our most serious urban problems is the growing tendency to do little or nothing about our environment. Millions sit and grow fat surrounded by ugliness and filth that could be eliminated by even a modest amount of personal pride and industry. Too many of our people are ready to let the Federal Government fight their battles. I am willing that this be the case in some matters, but I prefer to fight my own war on rats. Our Government's performance in some other wars suggests that this war on rats might not be won in 2 years. It is conceivable that a stalemate might develop with neither victory nor a negotiated peace. Since the war involves widespread destruction of habitats enjoyed by the rat population, it could also end up costing more than the bill calls for.

Promoters identify this rat crisis as a health problem. But this war would be directed by the Secretary of Housing and Urban Development. Would we be starting yet another war between this Department and various local health departments who are also fighting wars on rats?

When I was a boy, wars were fought against gophers, rats, and coyotes by placing a bounty on tails brought in. We did not make a lot of money, but we carried on the wars with relentless enthusiasm, developing all sorts of ingenious traps and, incidentally, keeping out of trouble.

The youth of many of our cities are bored nearly to death. Some are responding to the call of race wars and riots. Let us sound the alarm, calling on responsible local leaders and organizations to mount voluntary campaigns against this growing national hazard. Let us join forces and fight rats, not each other.

Mr. RYAN. Mr. Speaker, H.R. 11000, the Rat Extermination Act of 1967, is important. It is difficult to believe that anyone can be against the extermination of rats. What can be said in favor of rats? They have, directly and indirectly, killed more human beings than have been killed in all the wars since the beginning of time. Today, in New York City, over 700 rat bites are reported yearly. The rat depends on us for his food and shelter and, therefore, by a concentrated effort, can be eradicated at our will.

It is unfortunate that we have never made the concerted effort to change the physical surroundings and conditions which encourage persistent rat habitation and increase their numbers. It is indeed an unhappy fact that Congress has failed to take the steps necessary to eradicate the slums in our country. It is a tragedy that our greatest cities have ghetto areas in which some buildings, meant to be homes for human beings, have more rats living in them than people.

I hope that H.R. 11000 will be adopted and that Congress will begin to appropriate the funds needed for an effective rat control program.

However, rats are only one of the problems of our cities' slums. Rats and the diseases carried by them are inimical to health, but can one say they are any worse than the other evils characteristic of our urban slums. Is child malnutrition a lesser evil? Is juvenile delinquency of lower priority? Is the solving of drug addiction something we can afford to postpone? Can we wait until later to raise substandard housing conditions to an acceptable level; to eliminate widespread unemployment; to get high school dropouts to go back to school; to create adequate recreation facilities? Are we going to wait until riots flare up in each of our cities? Until the urban ghettos declare war on the rest of the country? It seems that it is the sense of the 90th Congress to indeed wait; to wait until our commitment in Southeast Asia has ended and then to wait some more. Mr. Speaker, I think the 90th Congress has a mandate to act now. A mandate coming from the elections of 1964 and again 1966. The summer riots are only proof of the urgency of this mandate.

Although the rat extermination bill will only be really adequate if it is enacted in conjunction with a massive legislative attack aimed at eliminating the slums, its purposes are nonetheless in the interest of all Americans to whom rats are a recurrent problem. The rat is not just a symbol of poverty. It is one of the cruelest manifestations of the urban slum. For the mother who has to leave her young children alone in her house, the rat is a danger that the mother thinks about in dread. For the family on welfare, the food which the rat seems to so readily devour cuts deeply into their small allowance. For the 14,000 people who were bitten by rats last year, the rat is a cause of great pain. For over 5,000 people who were inflicted with plague, typhus, leptospirosis, and other rat-associated diseases, the rat has caused incomparable hardships. For the Nation that suffers over a billion dollars worth of damages in a year directly because of rats, they are a great economic loss.

The fact, Mr. Speaker, is that we have the technical ability to control rats. We know how to exterminate rats and how to strike at the roots of their environment. Plans have been prepared for nationwide rat control programs, and various local communities have started to treat rat control as a serious problem. The emphasis on any rat control program should be at the community level, but the communities must be aided by the larger financial resources of the Federal Government.

Where community programs have gone into operation they have done a great deal to control rats. VISTA volunteers have taken an active part in mobilizing the community in the war against rats, putting out poison and traps for the rats, teaching families sanitary garbage disposal methods, and encouraging more sanitary neighborhood conditions. In New York City, the health department has carried on a rat extermination program in Harlem, and other areas of the city.

In Detroit an extensive effort to exterminate rats has had encouraging results. The four-point program to starve the rat, demolish his home, protect buildings from rat infestation, and kill the rat, involved improved garbage collection, home improvements, various means of rat extermination, and citizen participation. As a result the incidence of ratbites has decreased to under 20 reported cases per year.

It is a sad commentary that so few communities have even started to use the program that Detroit employed. In many communities the problem of rats has worsened. Not only have cities lacked the will to help their ghetto neighborhoods solve the problem of rats; they lack the money to launch a really effective campaign. The Detroit campaign which relied basically on community education programs cost money; other programs will also call for increased expenditures.

The President's Inter-Agency Task Force report on rat control estimated that an adequate nationwide program would require Federal grants of $125 million annually. It has also been estimated that the total cost of a nationwide program to exterminate rats would reach one and a half billion dollars. Only the Federal Government has the resources to fill such an order. The funds that are called for in H.R. 11000 are only $40 million over a 2-year period. This is clearly not enough to establish effective rat control programs throughout this country. Let us hope it is enough to make for an effective start.

The Rat Extermination Act of 1967 does have several significant provisions. It will finance and coordinate various community programs and help to initiate programs where there are now none. First, the Federal assistance is given directly to communities for local rat control and extermination programs to allow for a variety of methods especially suited to the needs and circumstances of each area. The communities which are most plagued with rats are those which are least able to pay for private exterminators or even for the metal trash cans which are basic to any eradication program. By giving matching grants on a two for one basis, it is hoped that local governments will be induced to allocate more of their resources to the community rat control programs. Furthermore, the program includes "the elimination or modification of physical surroundings and conditions—including rat harborages and food supplies—which encourage or tend to encourage persistant rat habitation and increases in their numbers; and any other actions which will reduce or eliminate, on more than a temporary basis disease, injury, and property damage caused by rats." It has too often been the case that the conditions which fostered the growth of the rat population in the area continue after the rats have been eradicated, and a new population quickly moves in to fill the ecological niche which has been created by extermination.

This bill does recognize that the problem of rat control is related to the conditions of the urban slums. It has a citizen education component which will train people in the community on basic standards of health and see that sanitary and healthful conditions are maintained after the rats are eradicated.

If the concern about riots expressed on the floor yesterday was genuine, then the House will approve this bill. However, it is not enough if the root causes of urban unrest are to be attacked.

Instead of the legislation now before us, we should be considering an adequate urban redevelopment bill attacking the slums on many fronts. If we use our resources to solve the problems of our slums, we will have solved a lot of related problems.

But because rat control, when we are unwilling to allocate the resources to solve the general problem of urban decay, does exist as a problem, and a very important one to many urban dwellers, I urge support for the rule and H.R. 11000.

Mr. MOORHEAD. Mr. Speaker, I rise in support of the Rat Extermination Act of 1967 because I think that it is urgent that national attention be called and national impetus given to a program to eliminate one of the main threats to disease and instigators of damage to property—the rat.

Since the rat is bred where there is poor housing and sanitation, in areas of urban and rural poverty, it is logical for the Department of Housing and Urban Development, which has the prime responsibility for improving the physical environment of our towns and cities, to work with the local governments in establishing a coordinated attack to combat the nasty and dangerous rodent.

It is not intended that the Federal Government get involved in the full-time rat extermination business; therefore, it is proposed that the Government cover the first two-thirds of the cost of 3-year local programs to provide communities with an initial boost.

It is also recognized that nothing will be gained by giving money to communities carte blanche. They are required to submit plans, tailored to meet their own particular needs and requirements in such areas as building and sanitation codes; adequate garbage and refuse collection; maintenance of public activities and services; extermination; community education and organization; and a system of evaluation, indicating their own intention to follow through.

In Pittsburgh this year so far, there have been over 1,200 complaints concerning rats. And not all of these stemmed from rat bites, for rats do not have to bite to be harmful or transmit disease—they also contaminate food. The annual report of the Allegheny County Health Department, where Pittsburgh is located, shows an appalling 50 percent increase over the last year in reinspections of dwellings to abate garbage, rodents, and other nuisances.

The No. 1 environmental health problem in Pittsburgh is reported to be slum housing, and we all know this to be the habitat of the rat.

Therefore, Mr. Speaker, I deem it urgent to adopt H.R. 11000 to provide a comprehensive, sophisticated approach toward eliminating this No. 1 public nuisance—who is certainly no laughing matter—Brother Rat.

Mr. MATSUNAGA. Mr. Speaker, I have no further requests for time. I move the previous question.

The previous question was ordered.

The SPEAKER pro tempore (Mr. ROONEY of New York). The question is on the resolution.

Mr. RHODES of Arizona. Mr. Speaker, on that I demand the yeas and nays.

The yeas and nays were ordered.

The question was taken; and there were—yeas 176, nays 207, not voting 49.

AFTERWORD

The editors admit to great curiosity about the student's general responses to the material found in this book and about the extent to which that material has facilitated intellectual growth as well as classroom objectives and dialogue.

It seems a safe assumption that there have been moments when many readers alternately have felt enlightened, confused, skeptical, and perhaps even outraged by the viewpoints expressed. If so, one need not be surprised, for these are common reactions to the relatively young and frequently contradictory literature of social and behavioral science. The readings hardly represent a unanimous perspective of the problems and crises of our time. Indeed, scientific analysis to some extent reflects the very conditions of conflict and ambiguity that are found in society itself. To illustrate, in Part Three, the reader will have encountered a wide range of interpretations of mechanisms of behavior that contribute to the expression of human liberty or that limit it through the impositions of certain forms of social control. In Part Four, similarly, we find considerable disagreement among such writers as Hobbes, Hoffer, Keniston, and Cleaver about the causes and consequences of disequilibrium and social conflict. The search for scientific answers to pressing problems proceeds very much like society's own quest for relief from tension and crisis—through definition, cooperation, conflict, clarity, and finally transformation. We trust that the reader has come to appreciate these qualities and has accordingly refined his understanding of and respect for the complexities of scientific inquiry.

Ultimately, the basic purpose of knowledge is action, the employment of human wisdom in the never-ending task of creating a better world for all persons of all societies. Hence a good part of the resources and impulses of science are directed at improvement of the human condition. Yet change is not

434

easily tolerated. Many years ago, Bertrand Russell spoke about the creative foundations of intelligent change in words that bear repeating now:

> It is a sad evidence of the weariness mankind has suffered from excessive toil that his heavens have usually been places where nothing else happened or changed. Fatigue produces the illusion that only rest is needed for happiness; but when men have rested for a time boredom drives them to renewed activity. For this reason, a happy life must be one in which there is activity. If it is also to be a useful life, the activity ought to be as far as possible creative, not merely predatory or defensive. But creative activity requires imagination and originality, which are apt to be subversive of the *status quo*. At present, those who have power dread a disturbance of the *status quo*, lest their unjust privileges should be taken away. In combination with the instinct for conventionality, which man shares with the other gregarious animals, those who profit by the existing order have established a system which punishes originality and starves imagination from the moment of first going to school down to the time of death and burial. The whole spirit in which education is conducted needs to be changed, in order that children may be encouraged to think and feel for themselves, not to acquiesce passively in the thoughts and feelings of others. It is not rewards after the event that will produce initiative, but a certain mental atmosphere. There have been times when such an atmosphere existed: the great days of Greece, and Elizabethan England, may serve as examples. But in our own day the tyranny of vast machinelike organizations, governed from above by men who know and care little for the lives of those whom they control, is killing individuality and freedom of mind, and forcing men more and more to conform to a uniform pattern. . . .
>
> Few men seem to realize how many of the evils from which we suffer are wholly unnecessary, and that they could be abolished by a united effort within a few years. If a majority in every civilized country so desired, we could, within twenty years, abolish all abject poverty, quite half the illness in the world, the whole economic slavery which binds down nine-tenths of our population; we could fill the world with beauty and joy, and secure the reign of universal peace. It is only because men are apathetic that this is not achieved, only because imagination is sluggish, and what always has been is regarded as what must be. With good-will, generosity, intelligence, these things could be brought about. [1]

Russell's appeal to good-will, generosity, and intelligence is not as romantic as it sounds. The crises that endanger modern man are so fundamental that perhaps nothing less than appeal to such universally needed qualities holds real promise of improving the human arena. Contemporary afflictions such as war, poverty, pollution, crime, and violence, to name a few, surely deserve that "romantic" effort.

It seems appropriate to close with some brief observations about the relevance of the readings for the development of a personal view of society

---

[1] Bertrand Russell, *Political Ideals.* London: Unwin Books, 1963, pp. 19–20, 25.

and the world. These may be put in the forms of several intellectual admonitions.

Cooperation, conflict, and reintegration are social processes that occur in a wide variety of places and circumstances. Almost every aspect of human life will contain "lessons" that, if heeded, can lead to an expanded awareness and understanding of the manner in which society and the individual experience integration and transformation. As man changes, so does his institutions. Perhaps less obvious but no less true is the fact that as institutions change, so does man. One should not be misled by rigid definitions of "human nature." In times of relative stability, there is a tendency to think of human nature in fixed, static terms. In revolutionary times of great change, such as ours, variability and flexibility seem to be the enduring characteristics of man.

Rigid adherence to general principles invariably turns out to be misleading. By illuminating the complexity of modern social life, contemporary science should lead one to considerable skepticism about fixed, dogmatic principles of social change. Most of these turn out to be oversimplifications, such as the persistent notion that all of life is a jungle in which the strong survive and the weak perish.

It is not stretching the analogy too far to observe that the change model is as useful in analyzing the life of the individual as that of society. Like society, the life of the individual is rich with important and interpenetrating aspects of cooperation, conflict, and reintegration. The analogy between the life of the individual and that of society is useful because it suggests that every individual has experiences which he may employ to help make sense of the complexities of social life. After all, social life is not something other-worldly or wholly alien to one's own encounters. Like this book, personal life contains a mixed bag of delights and disappointments, successes and failures, excitement and boredom. Change, then, is a fundamental key to the unfolding of both.

Science contributes simultaneously to social cooperation, conflict, and to reintegration. The social and behavioral sciences are helping to identify much-needed and newer forms of social interaction and problem solving. They are helping to clarify problems that many, unfortunately, would prefer to remain unpublicized, and to develop proposals for solving social problems based on bold and challenging perspectives. In this regard, such disciplines as anthropology, political science, sociology, psychology, and economics have a vital role to play, one that merits serious study and appreciation.

It is appropriate, finally, to make a plea on behalf of ambiguity. No one, including the best scientific minds among us, is capable of complete understanding of the fantastic complexities of modern social life. Science seeks to render more and more of that complexity intelligible to the average person. But in the end, none of us are immune from the sense of confusion in our attempt to "make sense" of the world that we see about us. The recognition that a good deal of what we see around us is ambiguous and may remain so is the beginning of wisdom and at least a partial assurance that we do not lapse into pure alienation and cynicism.

INDEX